SECRET W
JOUR
BATTLEWORLD

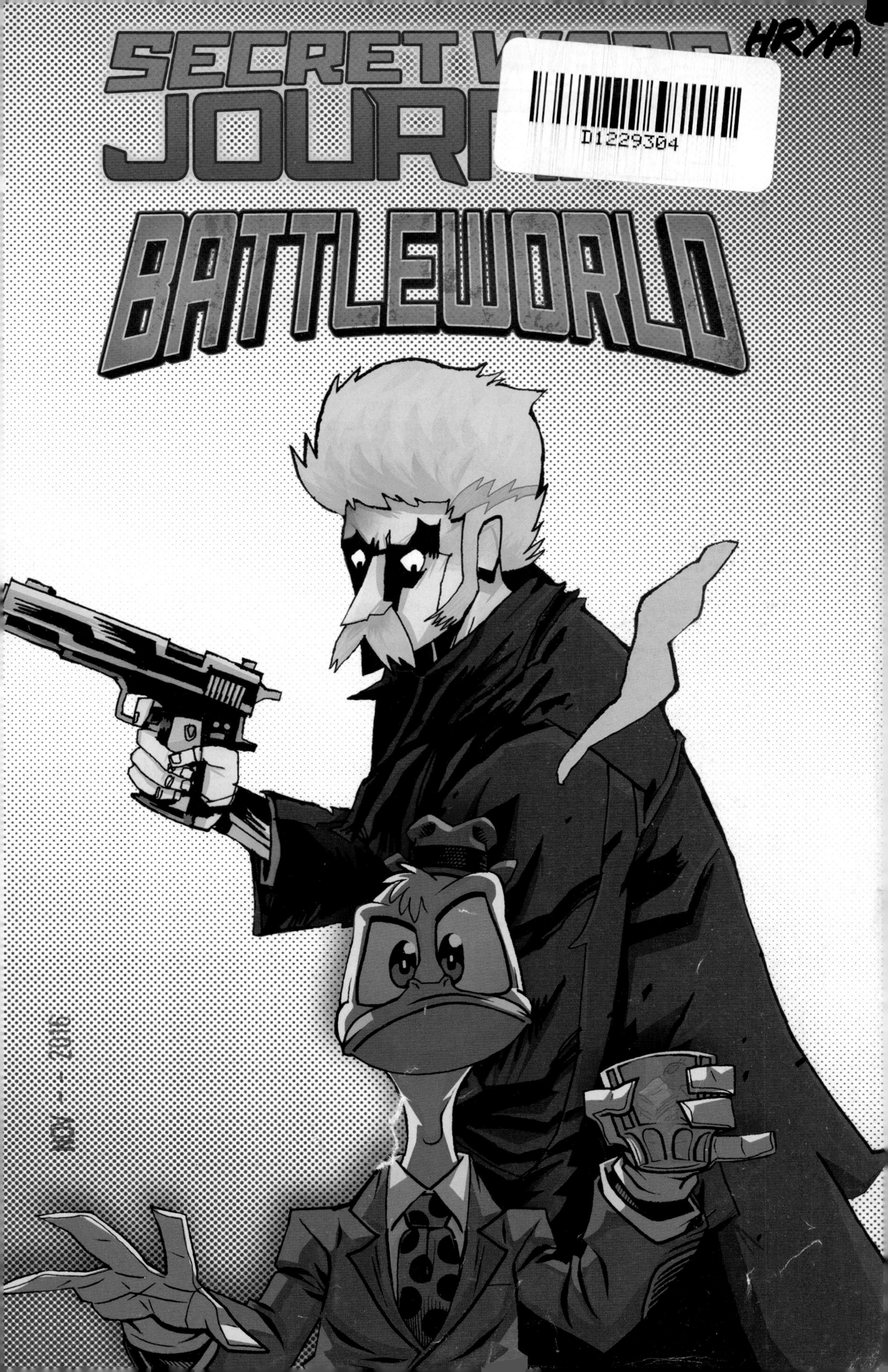

SECRET WARS

SECRET WARS JOURNAL #1

"The Arrowhead"
Writer: **Pru Shen**
Artist: **Ramon Bachs**
Color Artist: **Jean-Francois Beaulieu**

"We Worship What We Don't Understand"
Writer: **Matthew Rosenberg**
Artist: **Luca Pizzari**
Color Artist: **Rain Beredo**

Letterer: **VC's Cory Petit**
Cover Artist: **Kevin Wada**
Editor: **Jake Thomas**

SECRET WARS JOURNAL #2

"The Hunt"
Writer: **Kevin Maurer**
Arist: **Cory Smith**
Color Artist: **Jesus Aburtov**

"Hell's Kitchen"
Writer: **Simon Spurrier**
Artist: **Jonathan Marks**
Color Artist: **Miroslav Mrva**

Letterer: **VC's Cory Petit**
Cover Artist: **Sanford Greene**
Editor: **Jake Thomas**

SECRET WARS JOURNAL #3

"Who Killed Tony Stark?"
Writer: **Frank Tieri**
Artist: **Richard Isanove**

"The Smashing Cure"
Writer: **Scott Aukerman**
Artist: **RB Silva**
Color Artist: **Guru-eFX**

Letterer: **VC's Cory Petit**
Cover Artist: **Jake Wyatt**
Editor: **Jake Thomas**

SECRET WARS JOURNAL #4

"Primary Function"
Writer: **Mike Benson**
Artist: **Laura Braga**
Color Artist: **Wil Quintana**

"Another Last Stand"
Writer: **Sina Grace**
Artist: **Ken Lashley**
Color Artist: **Rachelle Rosenberg**

Letterer: **VC's Cory Petit**
Cover Artists: **Stephen Thompson**
& Paul Mounts
Editors: **Mark Basso**
& Daniel Ketchum

SECRET WARS JOURNAL #5

"Risk of Infection"
Writer: **Jen** & **Sylvia Soska**
Artist: **Alec Morgan**
Color Artist: **Nolan Woodward**

"Mill-E: The Model Citizen!"
Writer: **Aaron Alexovich**
Artist: **Diogo Saito**
Color Artist: **Rachelle Rosenberg**

Cover Artist: **Vanesa Del Rey**
Letterer: **VC's Cory Petit**
Assistant Editor: **Kathleen Wisneski**
Editor: **Jake Thomas**

SECRET WARS JOURNAL/BATTLEWORLD. Contains material originally published in magazine form as SECRET WARS JOURNAL #1-5, SECRET WARS: BATTLEWORLD #1-4, HOWARD THE HUMAN #1 and SECRET WARS: AGENTS OF ATLAS #1. First printing 2016. ISBN# 978-0-7851-9580-1. Published by MARVEL WORLDWIDE, INC., a subsidiary of MARVEL ENTERTAINMENT, LLC. OFFICE OF PUBLICATION: 135 West 50th Street, New York, NY 10020. Copyright © 2016 MARVEL No similarity between any of the names, characters, persons, and/or institutions in this magazine with those of any living or dead person or institution is intended, and any such similarity which may exist is purely coincidental. Printed in the U.S.A. ALAN FINE, President, Marvel Entertainment; DAN BUCKLEY, President, TV, Publishing and Brand Management; JOE QUESADA, Chief Creative Officer; TOM BREVOORT, SVP of Publishing; DAVID BOGART, SVP of Operations & Procurement, Publishing; C.B. CEBULSKI, VP of International Development & Brand Management; DAVID GABRIEL, SVP Print, Sales & Marketing; JIM O'KEEFE, VP of Operations & Logistics; DAN CARR, Executive Director of Publishing Technology; SUSAN CRESPI, Editorial Operations Manager; ALEX MORALES, Publishing Operations Manager; STAN LEE, Chairman Emeritus. For information regarding advertising in Marvel Comics or on Marvel.com, please contact Jonathan Rheingold, VP of Custom Solutions & Ad Sales, at jrheingold@marvel.com. For Marvel subscription inquiries, please call 800-217-9158. Manufactured between 12/18/2015 and 1/25/2016 by R.R. DONNELLEY, INC., SALEM, VA, USA.

THE MULTIVERSE WAS DESTROYED!

THE HEROES OF EARTH-616 AND EARTH-1610 WERE POWERLESS TO SAVE IT!

NOW, ALL THAT REMAINS...IS BATTLEWORLD!

A MASSIVE PATCHWORK PLANET COMPOSED OF THE FRAGMENTS OF WORLDS THAT NO LONGER EXIST, MAINTAINED BY THE IRON WILL OF ITS GOD AND MASTER, VICTOR VON DOOM!

EACH REGION IS A DOMAIN UNTO ITSELF!

**SECRET WARS:
AGENTS OF ATLAS #1**

"Risk of Infection"
Writer: **Tom Taylor**
Artist: **Steve Pugh**

Color Artist: **Tamra Bonvillain**

Letterer: **VC's Joe Sabino**
Cover Artists: **Leonard Kirk**
& **Carlos Cabrera**

Assistant Editor: **Chris Robinson**
Editor: **Mark Paniccia**

**SECRET WARS:
BATTLEWORLD #3**

"A Thousand Cuts"
Writer: **Ivan Brandon**
Artist: **Aaron Conley**
Color Artist: **Ryan Browne**

"Fistful of 'Changas"
Writer: **Ryan Ferrier**
Artist: **Logan Faerber**

"World War Ant"
Writer: **Ryan Ferrier**
Artist: **Paul Pope**
Color Artist: **Jordie Bellaire**

Letterer: **VC's Joe Caramagna**
Cover Artists: **Scott Hepburn**
& **Matt Milla**
Editor: **Jon Moisan**

**SECRET WARS:
BATTLEWORLD #1**

"Soldier Supreme"
Writer: **Joshua Williamson**
Artist: **Mike Henderson**
Color Artist: **Jordan Boyd**

"M.O.D.O.K. Madness"
Writer: **Ed Brisson**
Artist: **Scott Hepburn**
Color Artist: **Matt Milla**

Letterer: **VC's Joe Caramagna**
Cover Artist: **Paco Medina**
Editor: **Jon Moisan**

**SECRET WARS:
BATTLEWORLD #4**

"Silver Surfer Vs. Galactus"
Writer/Artist/Letterer:
James Stokoe

"Silver Surfer Vs. Maestro"
Writer: **Peter David**
Artist: **Daniel Valadez**
Letterer: **VC's Joe Sabino**
Color Artist: **David Curiel**

Assistant Editor: **Chris Robinson**
Editor: **Mark Paniccia**

**SECRET WARS:
BATTLEWORLD #2**

"A Monster So Fowl"
Writer: **David F. Walker**
Artist: **J.J. Kirby**
Color Artist: **Matt Milla**

"Ross Against the Machine"
Writer: **Donny Cates**
Artist: **Marco Turini**
Color Artist: **Frank D'Armata**
Letterers: **VC's Joe Caramagna**
& **Travis Lanham**

Cover Artist: **Chris B. Murray**
Assistant Editor: **Chris Robinson**
Editors: **Jon Moisan** & **Mark Paniccia**

HOWARD THE HUMAN #1

Writer: **Skottie Young**
Aritst: **Jim Mahfood**

Color Artist: **Justin Stewart**

Letterer: **Travis Lanham**
Cover Artists: **Jim Mahfood**
& **Justin Stewart**
Editor: **Jon Moisan**

Collection Editor: **Jennifer Grünwald**
Assistant Editor: **Sarah Brunstad**
Associate Managing Editor: **Alex Starbuck**
Editor, Special Projects: **Mark D. Beazley**
Senior Editor, Special Projects: **Jeff Youngquist**
SVP Print, Sales & Marketing: **David Gabriel**
Book Designer: **Adam Del Re**

Editor in Chief: **Axel Alonso**
Chief Creative Officer: **Joe Quesada**
Publisher: **Dan Buckley**
Executive Producer: **Alan Fine**

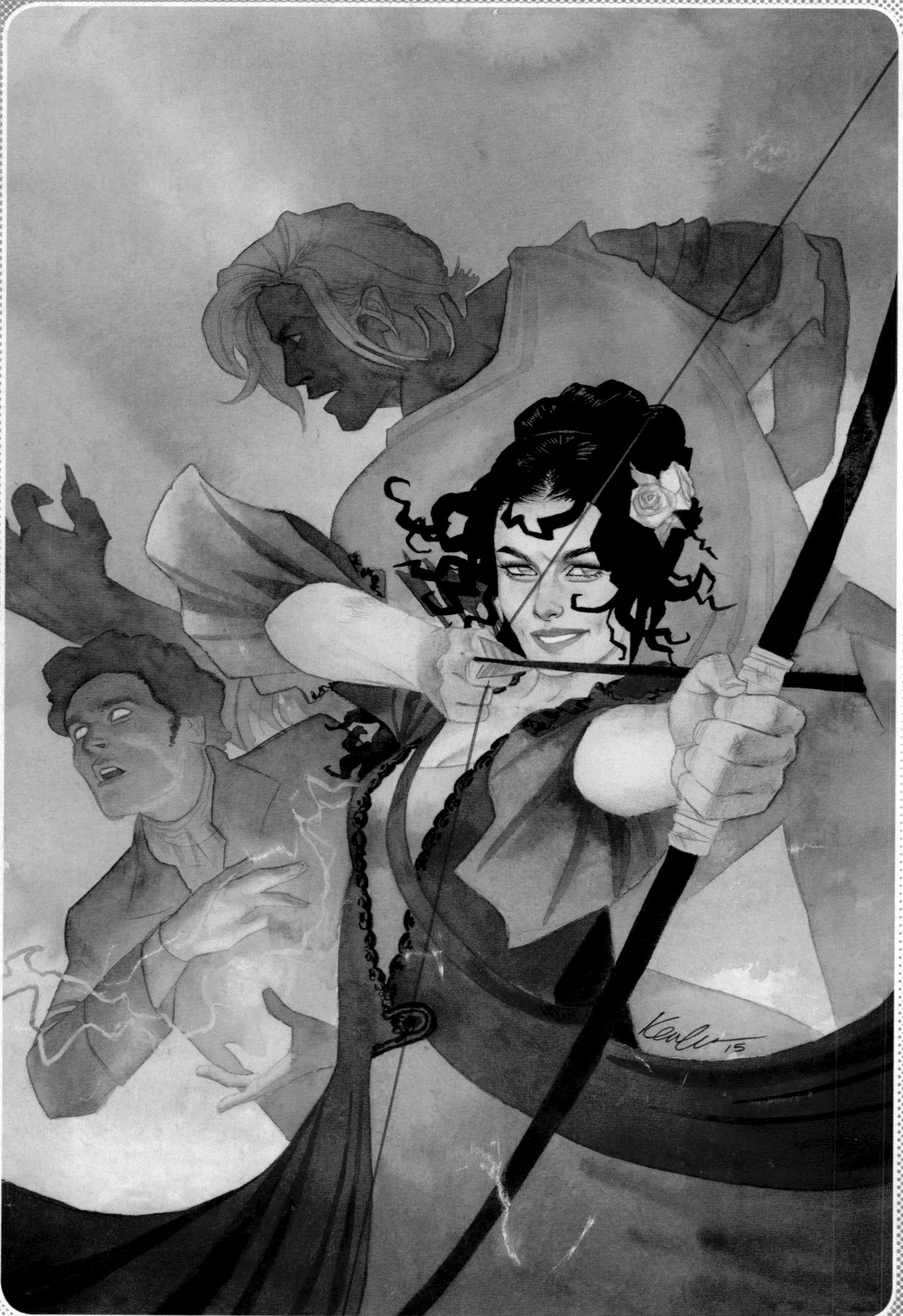

SECRET WARS JOURNAL #1

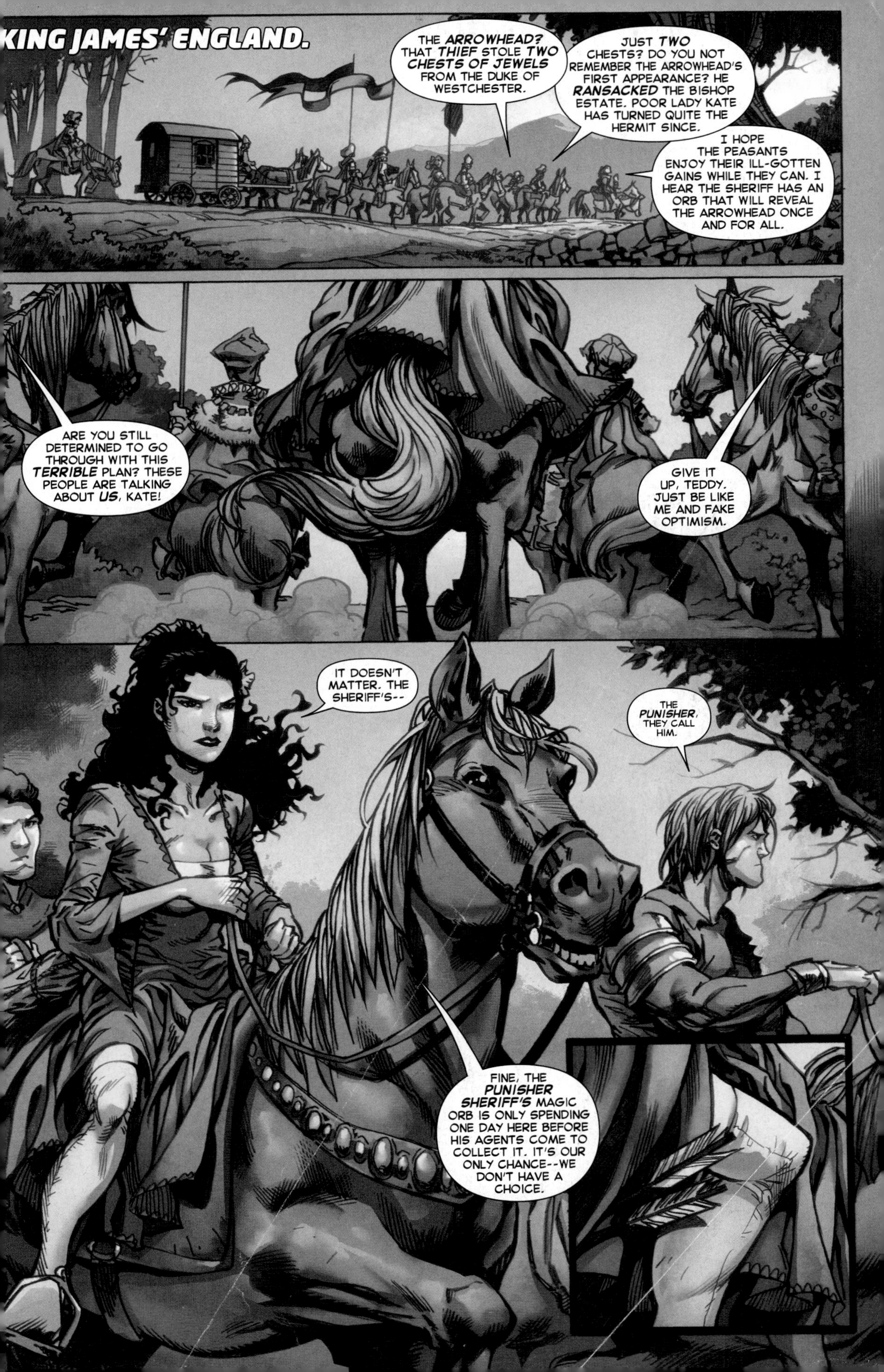
KING JAMES' ENGLAND.
THE ARROWHEAD? THAT THIEF STOLE TWO CHESTS OF JEWELS FROM THE DUKE OF WESTCHESTER.
JUST TWO CHESTS? DO YOU NOT REMEMBER THE ARROWHEAD'S FIRST APPEARANCE? HE RANSACKED THE BISHOP ESTATE. POOR LADY KATE HAS TURNED QUITE THE HERMIT SINCE.
I HOPE THE PEASANTS ENJOY THEIR ILL-GOTTEN GAINS WHILE THEY CAN. I HEAR THE SHERIFF HAS AN ORB THAT WILL REVEAL THE ARROWHEAD ONCE AND FOR ALL.
ARE YOU STILL DETERMINED TO GO THROUGH WITH THIS TERRIBLE PLAN? THESE PEOPLE ARE TALKING ABOUT US, KATE!
GIVE IT UP, TEDDY. JUST BE LIKE ME AND FAKE OPTIMISM.
IT DOESN'T MATTER. THE SHERIFF'S--
THE PUNISHER, THEY CALL HIM.
FINE, THE PUNISHER SHERIFF'S MAGIC ORB IS ONLY SPENDING ONE DAY HERE BEFORE HIS AGENTS COME TO COLLECT IT. IT'S OUR ONLY CHANCE--WE DON'T HAVE A CHOICE.

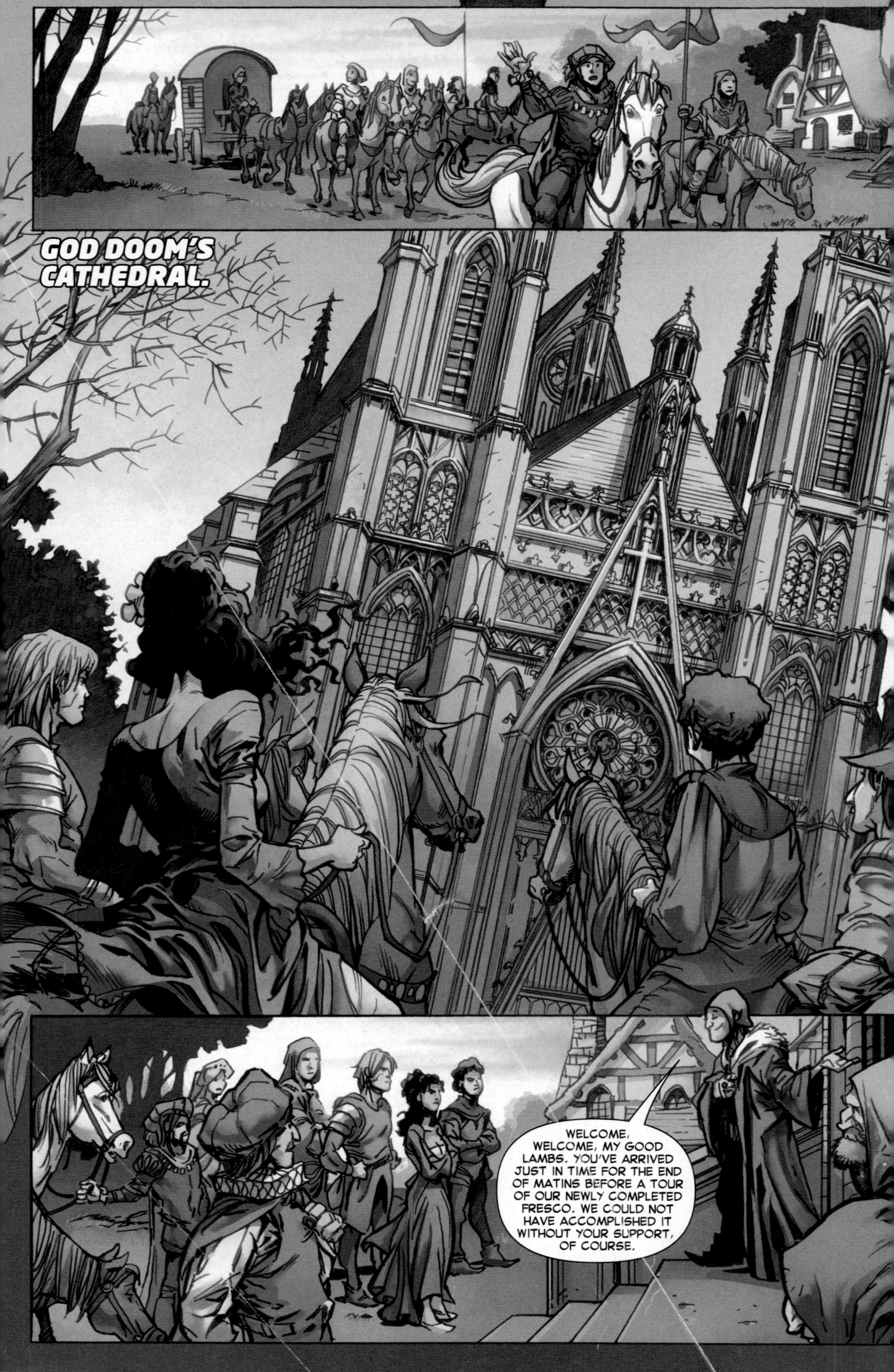
GOD DOOM'S CATHEDRAL.
WELCOME, WELCOME, MY GOOD LAMBS. YOU'VE ARRIVED JUST IN TIME FOR THE END OF MATINS BEFORE A TOUR OF OUR NEWLY COMPLETED FRESCO. WE COULD NOT HAVE ACCOMPLISHED IT WITHOUT YOUR SUPPORT, OF COURSE.

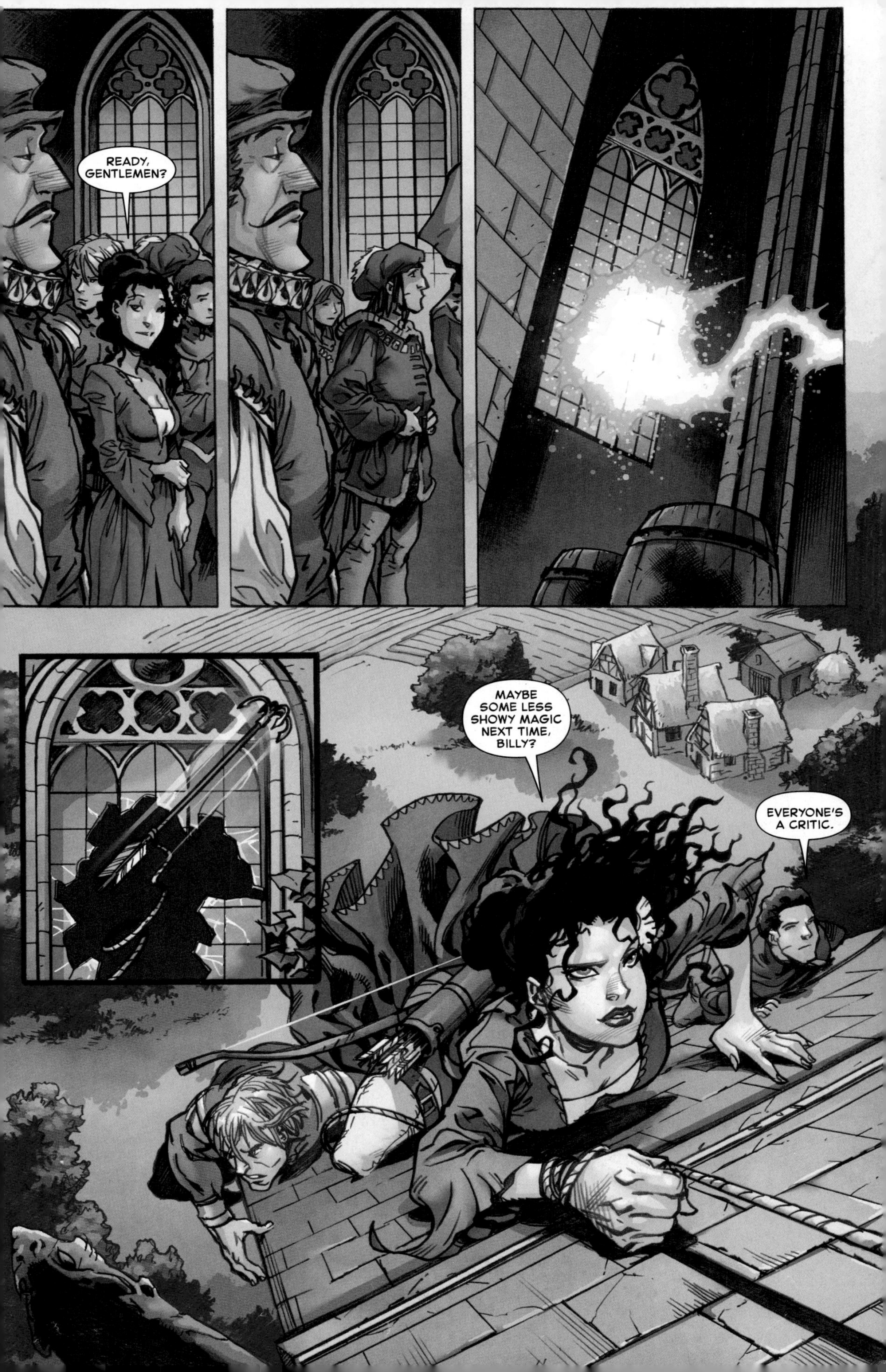
READY, GENTLEMEN?
MAYBE SOME LESS SHOWY MAGIC NEXT TIME, BILLY?
EVERYONE'S A CRITIC.

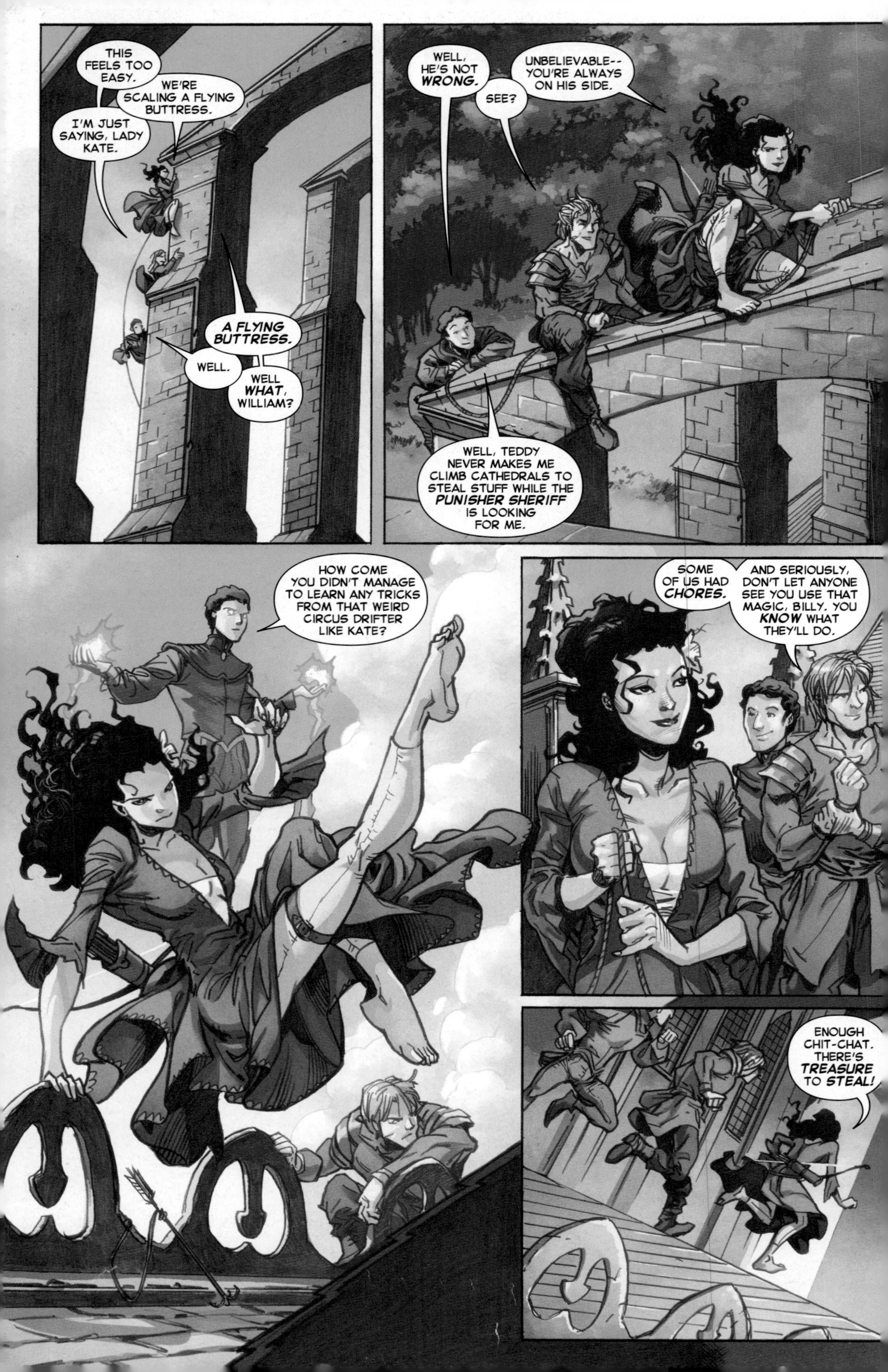
THIS FEELS TOO EASY.
WE'RE SCALING A FLYING BUTTRESS.
I'M JUST SAYING, LADY KATE.
A FLYING BUTTRESS.
WELL.
WELL WHAT, WILLIAM?
WELL, HE'S NOT WRONG.
SEE?
UNBELIEVABLE-- YOU'RE ALWAYS ON HIS SIDE.
WELL, TEDDY NEVER MAKES ME CLIMB CATHEDRALS TO STEAL STUFF WHILE THE PUNISHER SHERIFF IS LOOKING FOR ME.
HOW COME YOU DIDN'T MANAGE TO LEARN ANY TRICKS FROM THAT WEIRD CIRCUS DRIFTER LIKE KATE?
SOME OF US HAD CHORES.
AND SERIOUSLY, DON'T LET ANYONE SEE YOU USE THAT MAGIC, BILLY. YOU KNOW WHAT THEY'LL DO.
ENOUGH CHIT-CHAT. THERE'S TREASURE TO STEAL!

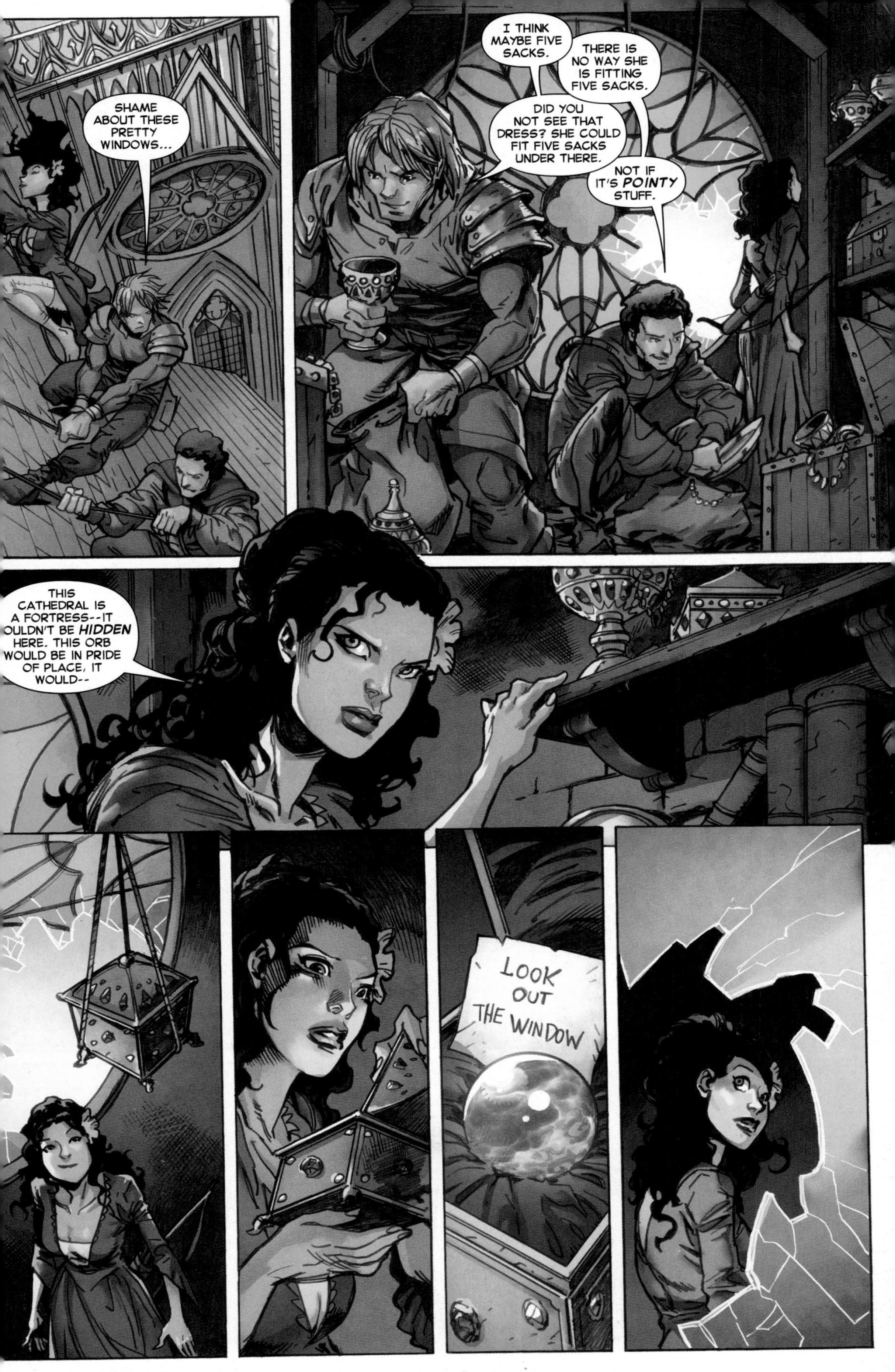
SHAME ABOUT THESE PRETTY WINDOWS...
I THINK MAYBE FIVE SACKS.
THERE IS NO WAY SHE IS FITTING FIVE SACKS.
DID YOU NOT SEE THAT DRESS? SHE COULD FIT FIVE SACKS UNDER THERE.
NOT IF IT'S POINTY STUFF.
THIS CATHEDRAL IS A FORTRESS--IT OULDN'T BE HIDDEN HERE. THIS ORB WOULD BE IN PRIDE OF PLACE, IT WOULD--
LOOK OUT THE WINDOW

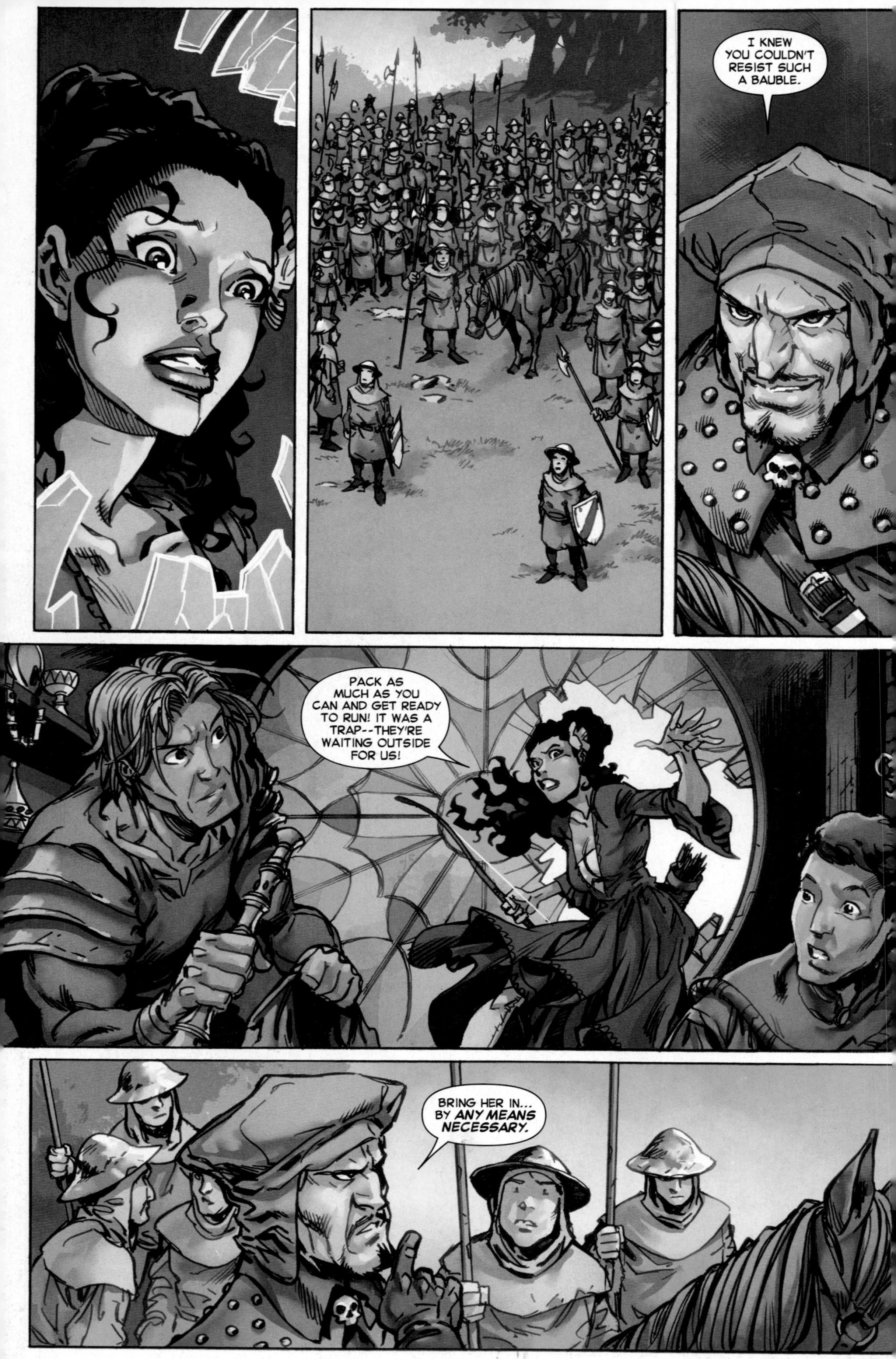
I KNEW YOU COULDN'T RESIST SUCH A BAUBLE.
PACK AS MUCH AS YOU CAN AND GET READY TO RUN! IT WAS A TRAP--THEY'RE WAITING OUTSIDE FOR US!
BRING HER IN... BY *ANY MEANS NECESSARY.*

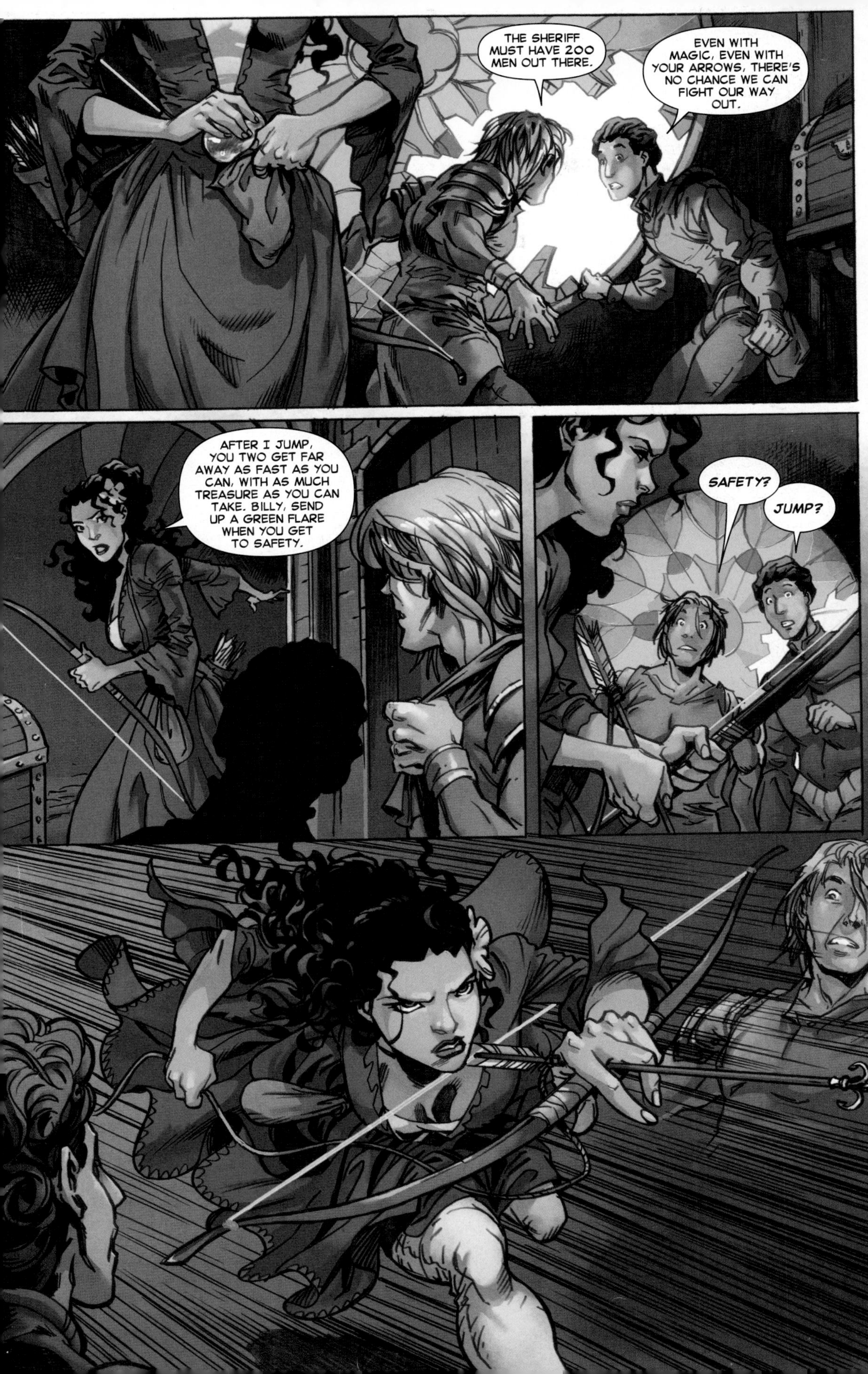
THE SHERIFF MUST HAVE 200 MEN OUT THERE.
EVEN WITH MAGIC, EVEN WITH YOUR ARROWS, THERE'S NO CHANCE WE CAN FIGHT OUR WAY OUT.
AFTER I JUMP, YOU TWO GET FAR AWAY AS FAST AS YOU CAN, WITH AS MUCH TREASURE AS YOU CAN TAKE. BILLY, SEND UP A GREEN FLARE WHEN YOU GET TO SAFETY.
SAFETY?
JUMP?

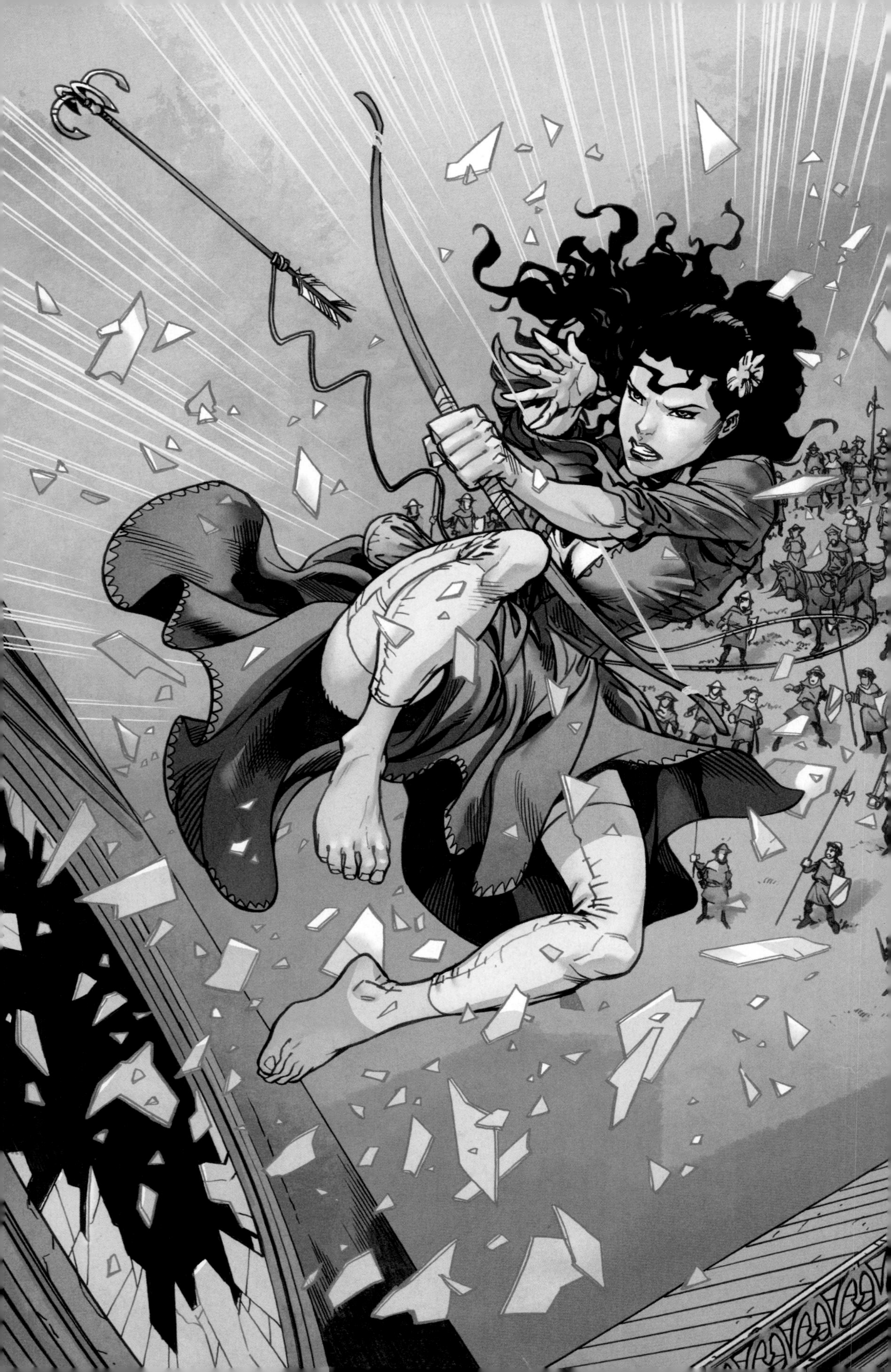

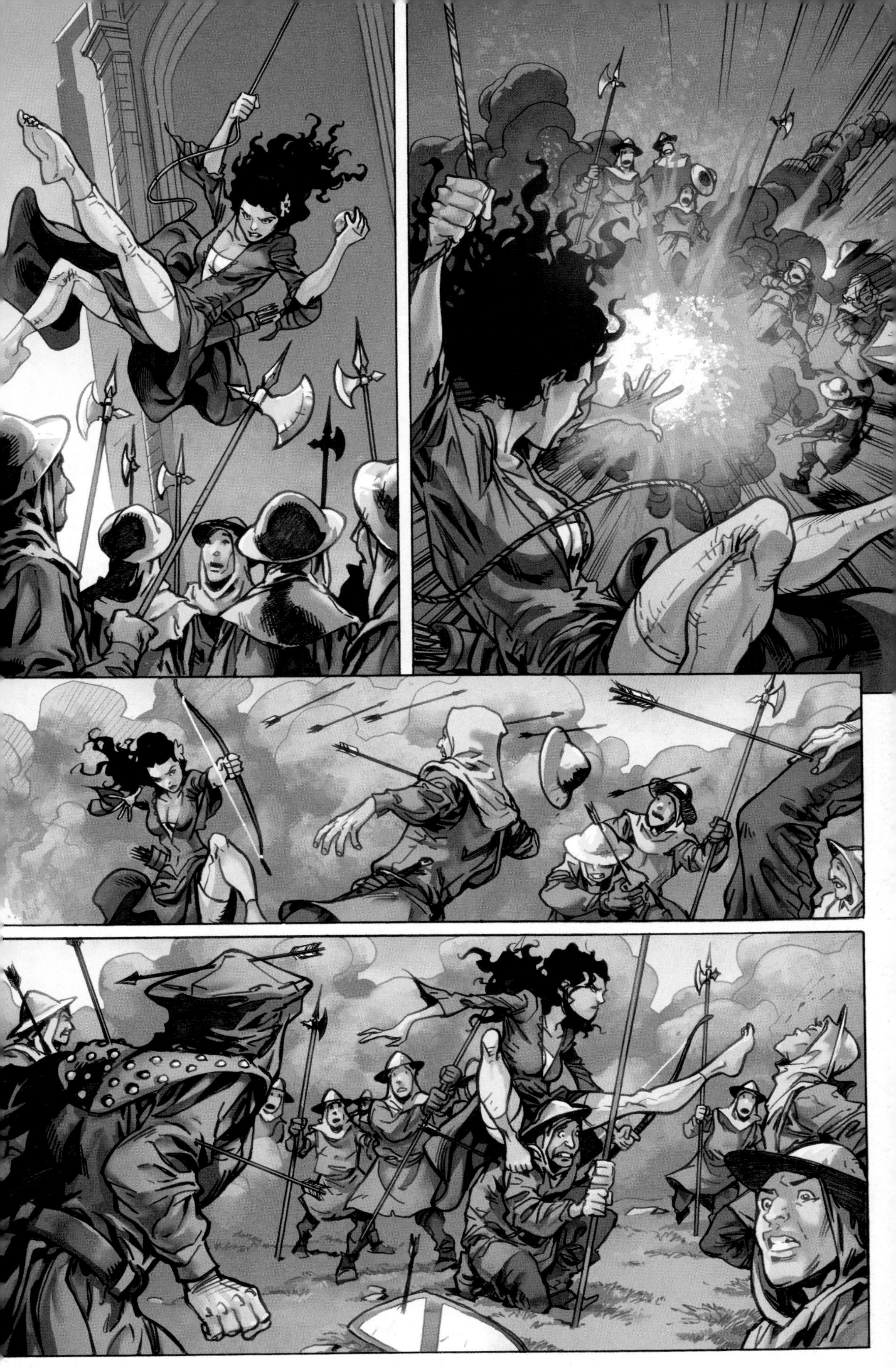

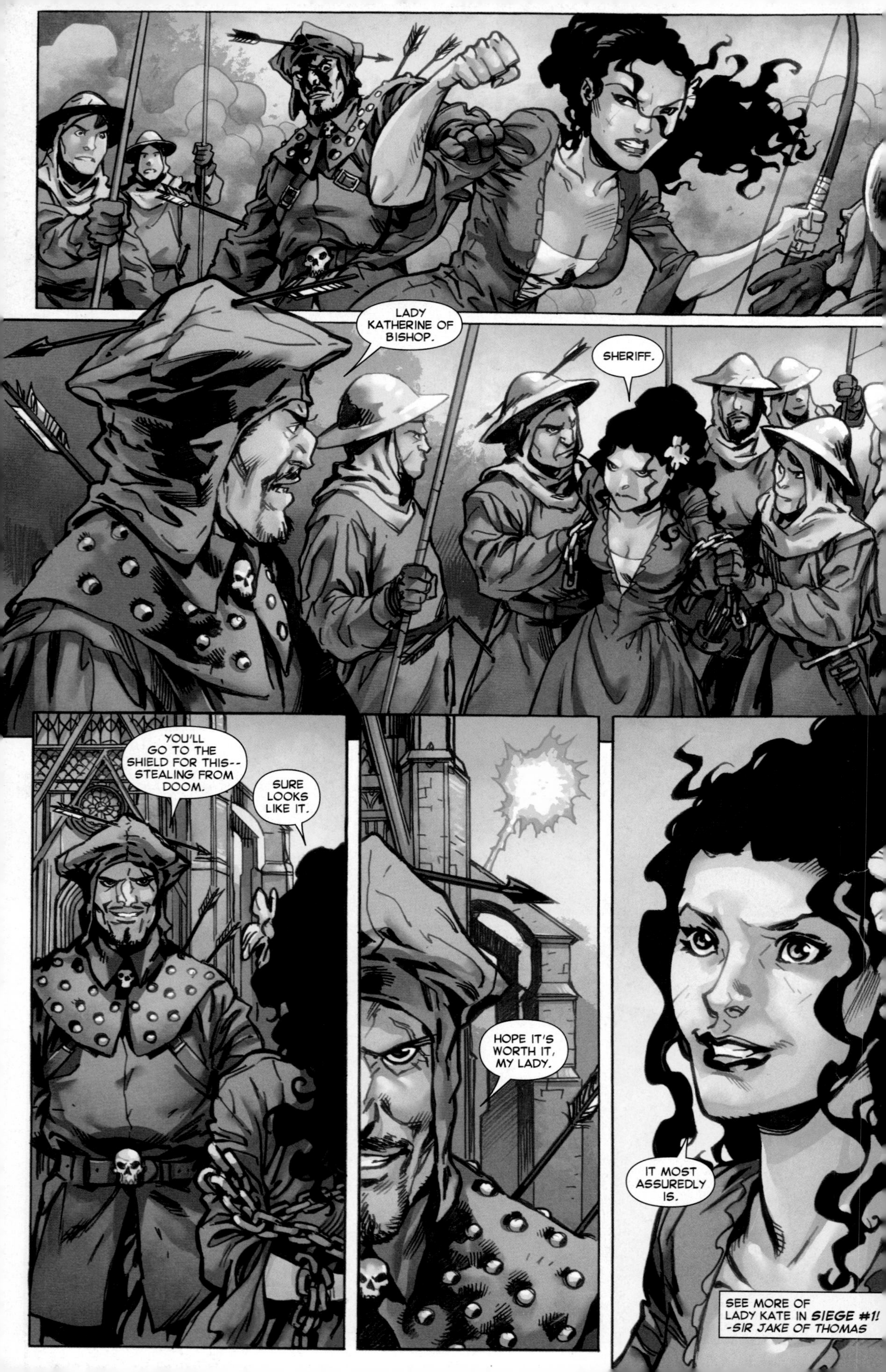
LADY KATHERINE OF BISHOP.
SHERIFF.
YOU'LL GO TO THE SHIELD FOR THIS-- STEALING FROM DOOM.
SURE LOOKS LIKE IT.
HOPE IT'S WORTH IT, MY LADY.
IT MOST ASSUREDLY IS.
SEE MORE OF LADY KATE IN SIEGE #1! -SIR JAKE OF THOMAS

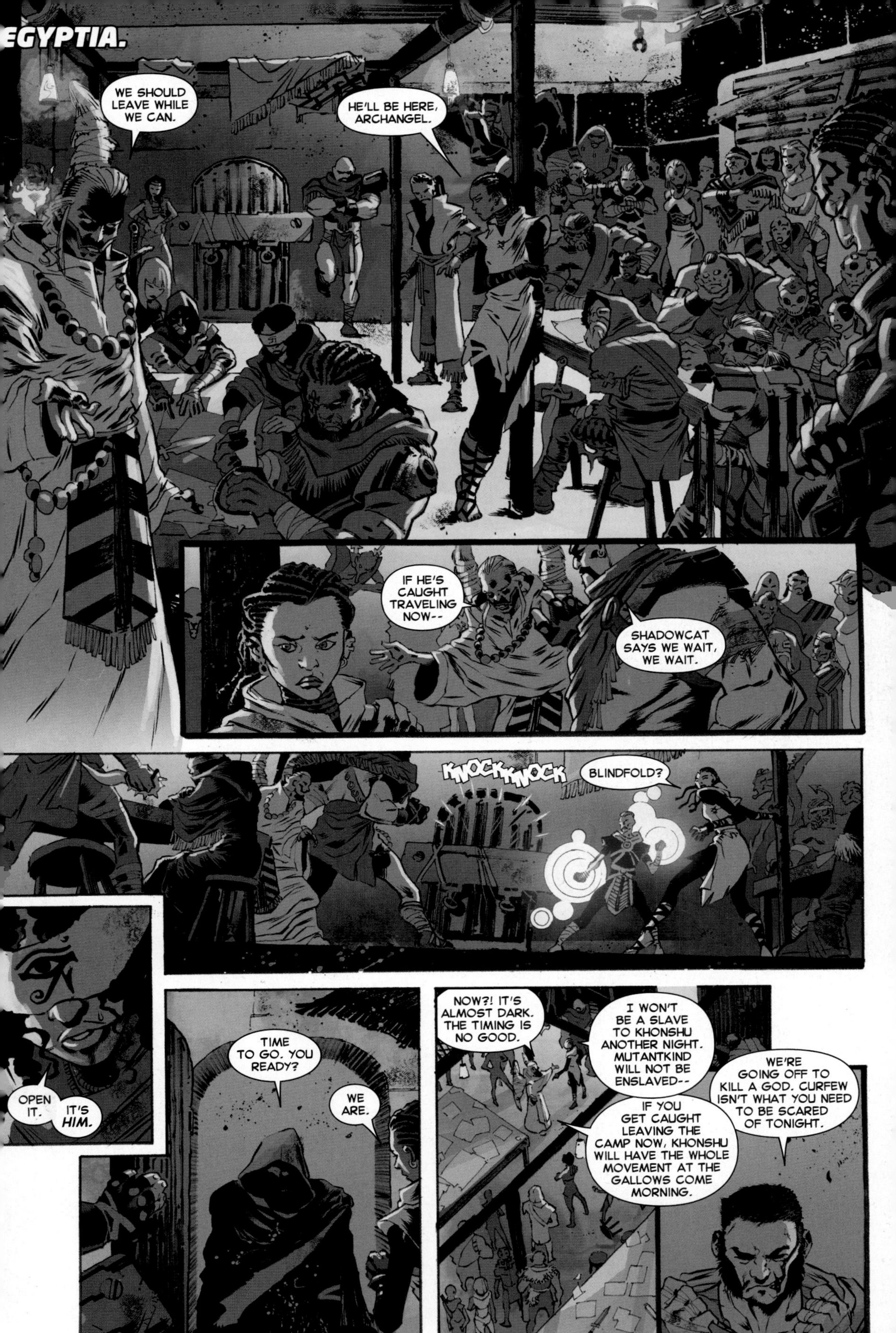
EGYPTIA.
WE SHOULD LEAVE WHILE WE CAN.
HE'LL BE HERE, ARCHANGEL.
IF HE'S CAUGHT TRAVELING NOW--
SHADOWCAT SAYS WE WAIT, WE WAIT.
KNOCK KNOCK
BLINDFOLD?
OPEN IT.
IT'S HIM.
TIME TO GO. YOU READY?
WE ARE.
NOW?! IT'S ALMOST DARK. THE TIMING IS NO GOOD.
I WON'T BE A SLAVE TO KHONSHU ANOTHER NIGHT. MUTANTKIND WILL NOT BE ENSLAVED--
IF YOU GET CAUGHT LEAVING THE CAMP NOW, KHONSHU WILL HAVE THE WHOLE MOVEMENT AT THE GALLOWS COME MORNING.
WE'RE GOING OFF TO KILL A GOD. CURFEW ISN'T WHAT YOU NEED TO BE SCARED OF TONIGHT.

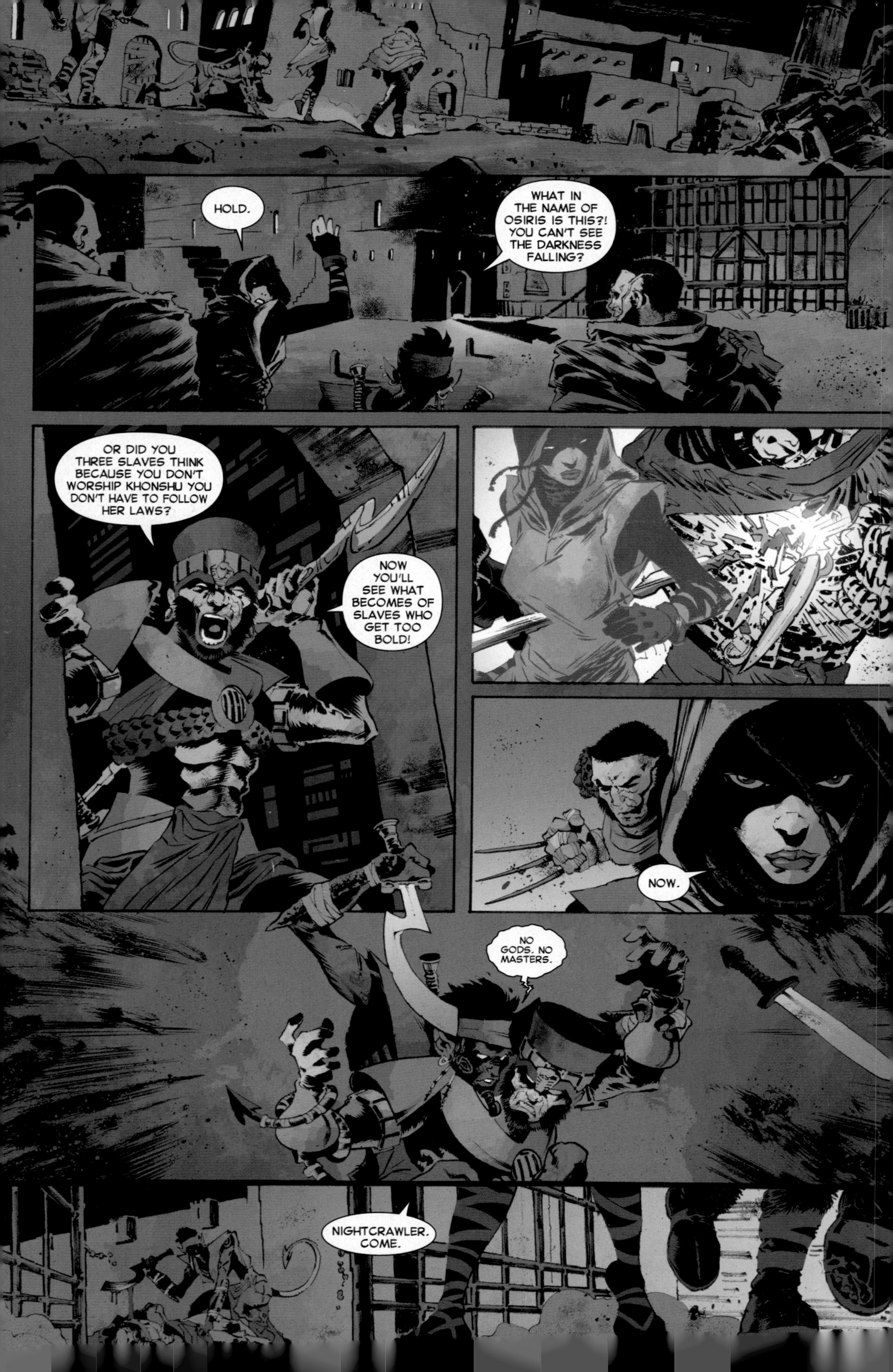
HOLD.
WHAT IN THE NAME OF OSIRIS IS THIS?! YOU CAN'T SEE THE DARKNESS FALLING?
OR DID YOU THREE SLAVES THINK BECAUSE YOU DON'T WORSHIP KHONSHU YOU DON'T HAVE TO FOLLOW HER LAWS?
NOW YOU'LL SEE WHAT BECOMES OF SLAVES WHO GET TOO BOLD!
NOW.
NO GODS. NO MASTERS.
NIGHTCRAWLER. COME.

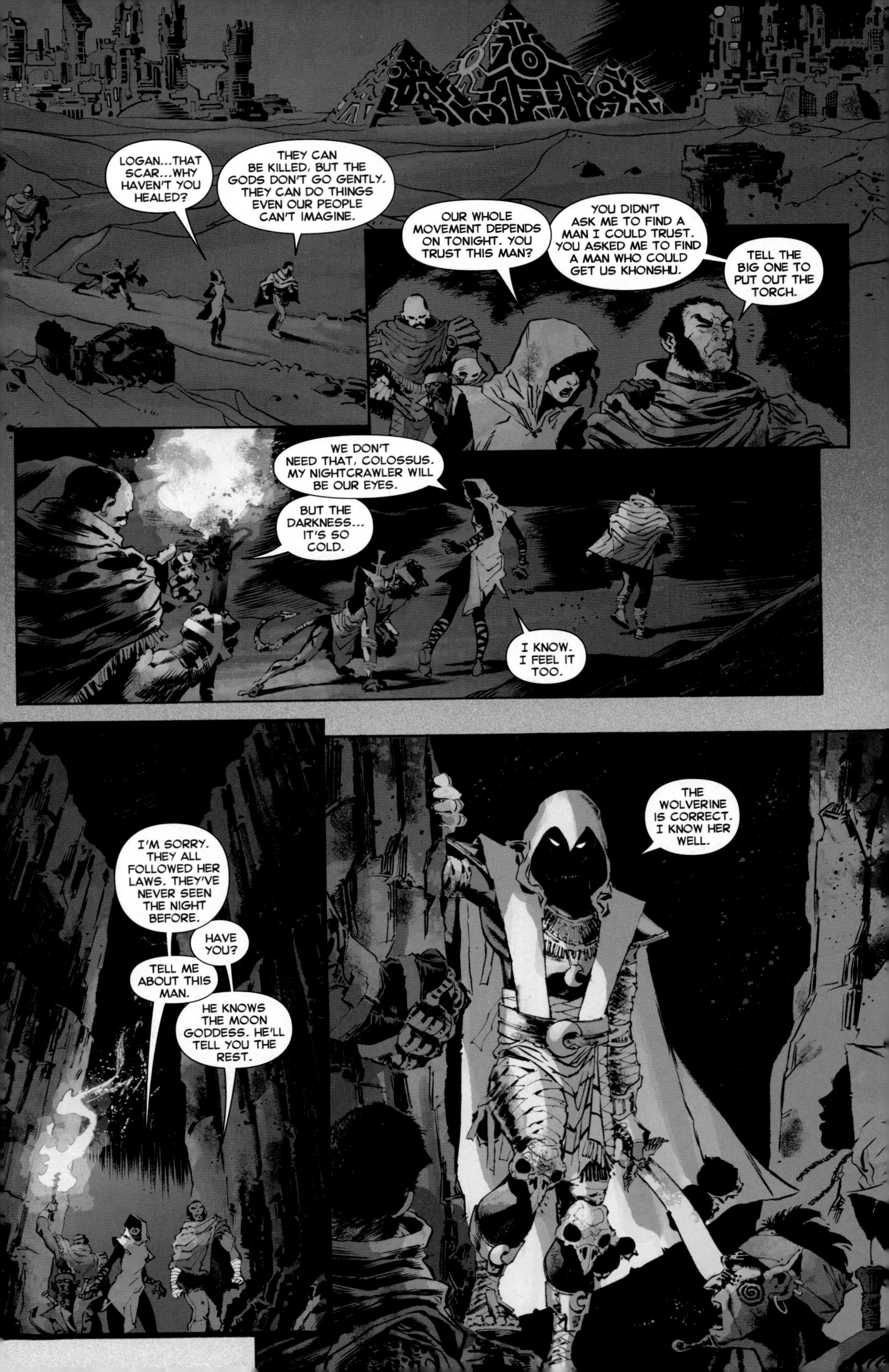
LOGAN...THAT SCAR...WHY HAVEN'T YOU HEALED?
THEY CAN BE KILLED, BUT THE GODS DON'T GO GENTLY. THEY CAN DO THINGS EVEN OUR PEOPLE CAN'T IMAGINE.
OUR WHOLE MOVEMENT DEPENDS ON TONIGHT. YOU TRUST THIS MAN?
YOU DIDN'T ASK ME TO FIND A MAN I COULD TRUST. YOU ASKED ME TO FIND A MAN WHO COULD GET US KHONSHU.
TELL THE BIG ONE TO PUT OUT THE TORCH.
WE DON'T NEED THAT, COLOSSUS. MY NIGHTCRAWLER WILL BE OUR EYES.
BUT THE DARKNESS... IT'S SO COLD.
I KNOW. I FEEL IT TOO.
I'M SORRY. THEY ALL FOLLOWED HER LAWS. THEY'VE NEVER SEEN THE NIGHT BEFORE.
HAVE YOU?
TELL ME ABOUT THIS MAN.
HE KNOWS THE MOON GODDESS. HE'LL TELL YOU THE REST.
THE WOLVERINE IS CORRECT. I KNOW HER WELL.

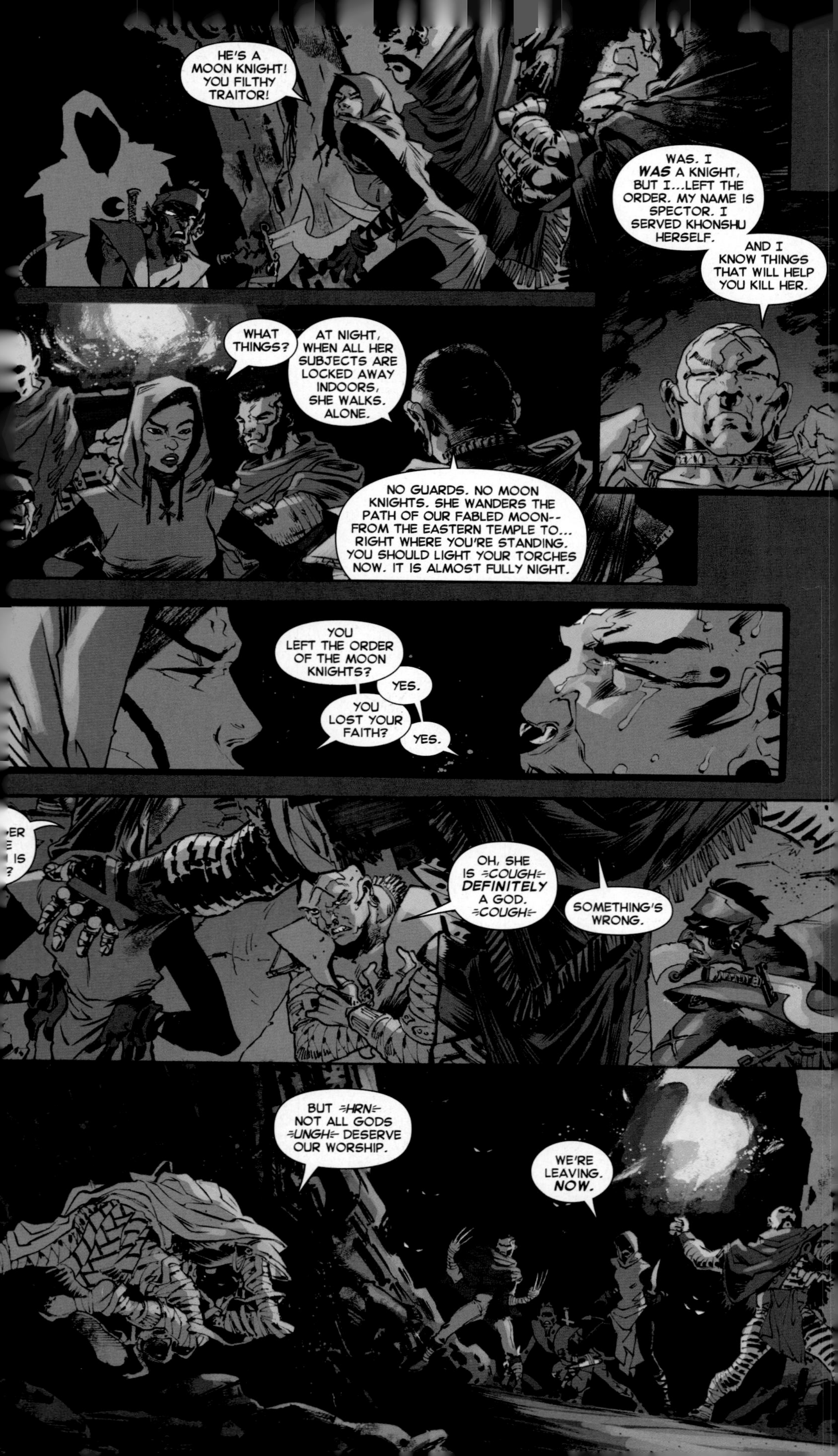
HE'S A MOON KNIGHT! YOU FILTHY TRAITOR!
WAS. I **WAS** A KNIGHT, BUT I...LEFT THE ORDER. MY NAME IS SPECTOR. I SERVED KHONSHU HERSELF.
AND I KNOW THINGS THAT WILL HELP YOU KILL HER.
WHAT THINGS?
AT NIGHT, WHEN ALL HER SUBJECTS ARE LOCKED AWAY INDOORS, SHE WALKS. ALONE.
NO GUARDS. NO MOON KNIGHTS. SHE WANDERS THE PATH OF OUR FABLED MOON-- FROM THE EASTERN TEMPLE TO... RIGHT WHERE YOU'RE STANDING. YOU SHOULD LIGHT YOUR TORCHES NOW. IT IS ALMOST FULLY NIGHT.
YOU LEFT THE ORDER OF THE MOON KNIGHTS?
YES.
YOU LOST YOUR FAITH?
YES.
OH, SHE IS =COUGH= **DEFINITELY** A GOD. =COUGH=
SOMETHING'S WRONG.
BUT =HRN= NOT ALL GODS =UNGH= DESERVE OUR WORSHIP.
WE'RE LEAVING. **NOW.**

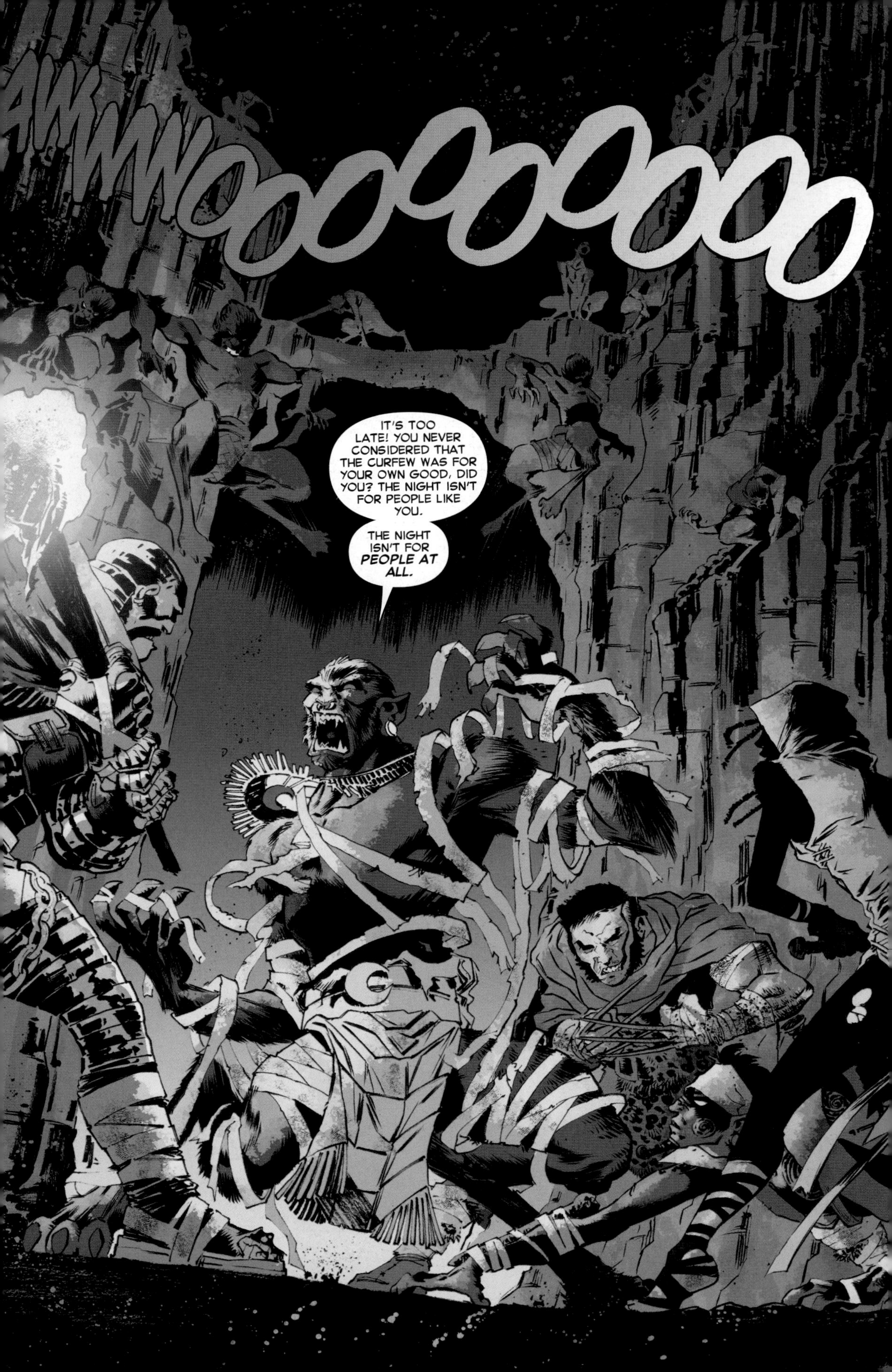
AWWWOOOOOOOOO
IT'S TOO LATE! YOU NEVER CONSIDERED THAT THE CURFEW WAS FOR YOUR OWN GOOD, DID YOU? THE NIGHT ISN'T FOR PEOPLE LIKE YOU.
THE NIGHT ISN'T FOR *PEOPLE AT ALL.*

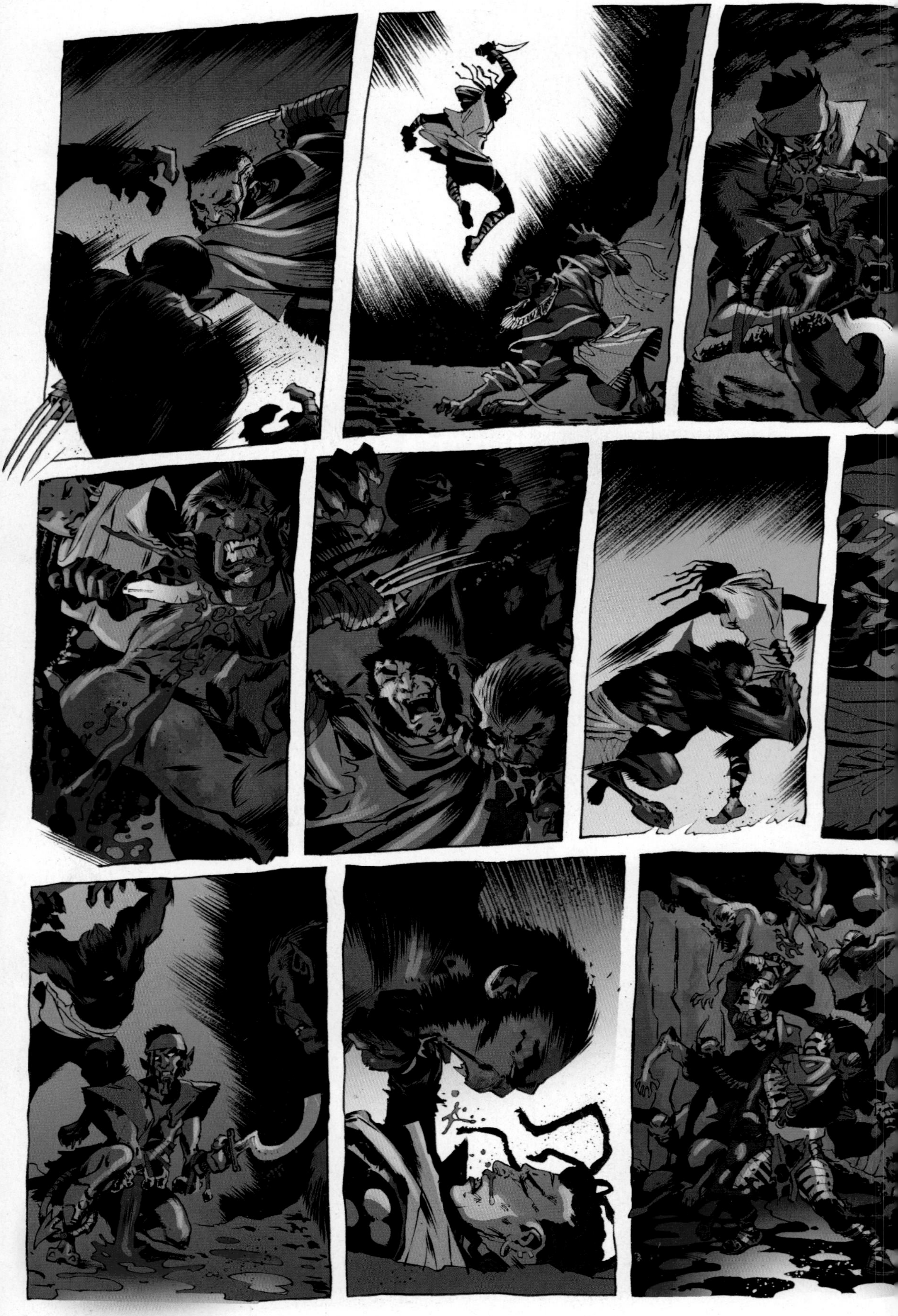

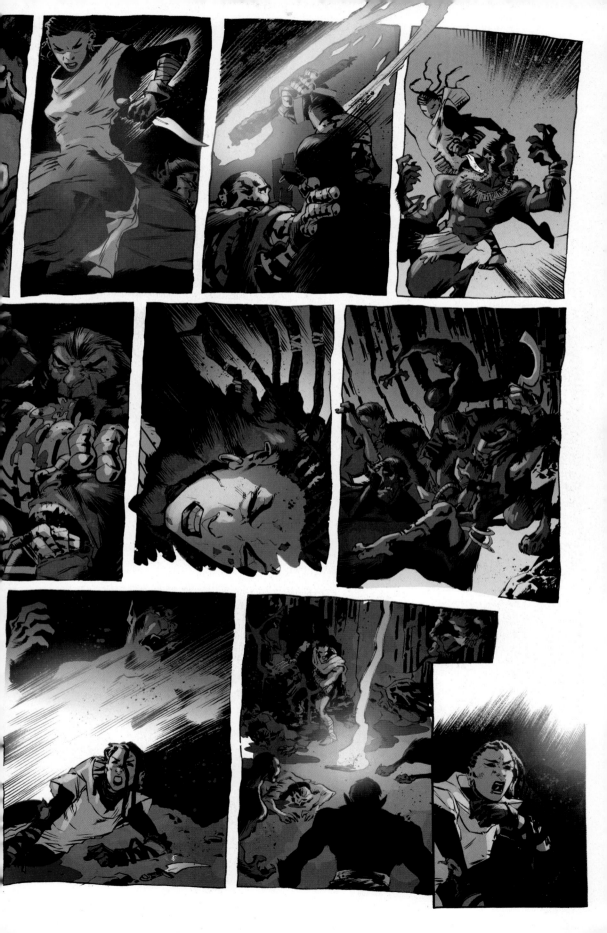

NO MORE!

ENOUGH.

YOU'RE... HER. YOU'RE *KHONSHU.*

WHY?

WE'RE SLAVES. MY PEOPLE. WE ARE THE SLAVES WHO BUILD YOUR TEMPLES.

AND?

AND WE DON'T WANT TO BE SLAVES ANYMORE.

THE MIGHTY PYRAMIDS YOU BUILD WILL LAST FOR EONS. YOU CREATE GREATNESS. THAT IS MY GIFT TO YOU.

WE DON'T WANT TO BE MADE TO WORSHIP YOU ANYMORE.

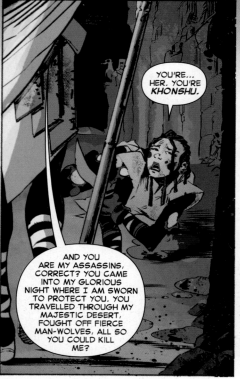

AND YOU ARE MY ASSASSINS, CORRECT? YOU CAME INTO MY GLORIOUS NIGHT WHERE I AM SWORN TO PROTECT YOU. YOU TRAVELLED THROUGH MY MAJESTIC DESERT, FOUGHT OFF FIERCE MAN-WOLVES, ALL SO YOU COULD KILL ME?

MADE TO WORSHIP? DO YOU DOUBT MY GODHOOD?

NO.

SLAVES. LORDS. THESE TITLES MEAN NOTHING. YOUR LIVES LAST BUT A BRIEF MOMENT, WHY SPEND THAT TIME PLOTTING AGAINST YOUR OWN GODS? IT IS LIKE A FISH TRYING TO KILL A RIVER.

TELL ME ONE THING...

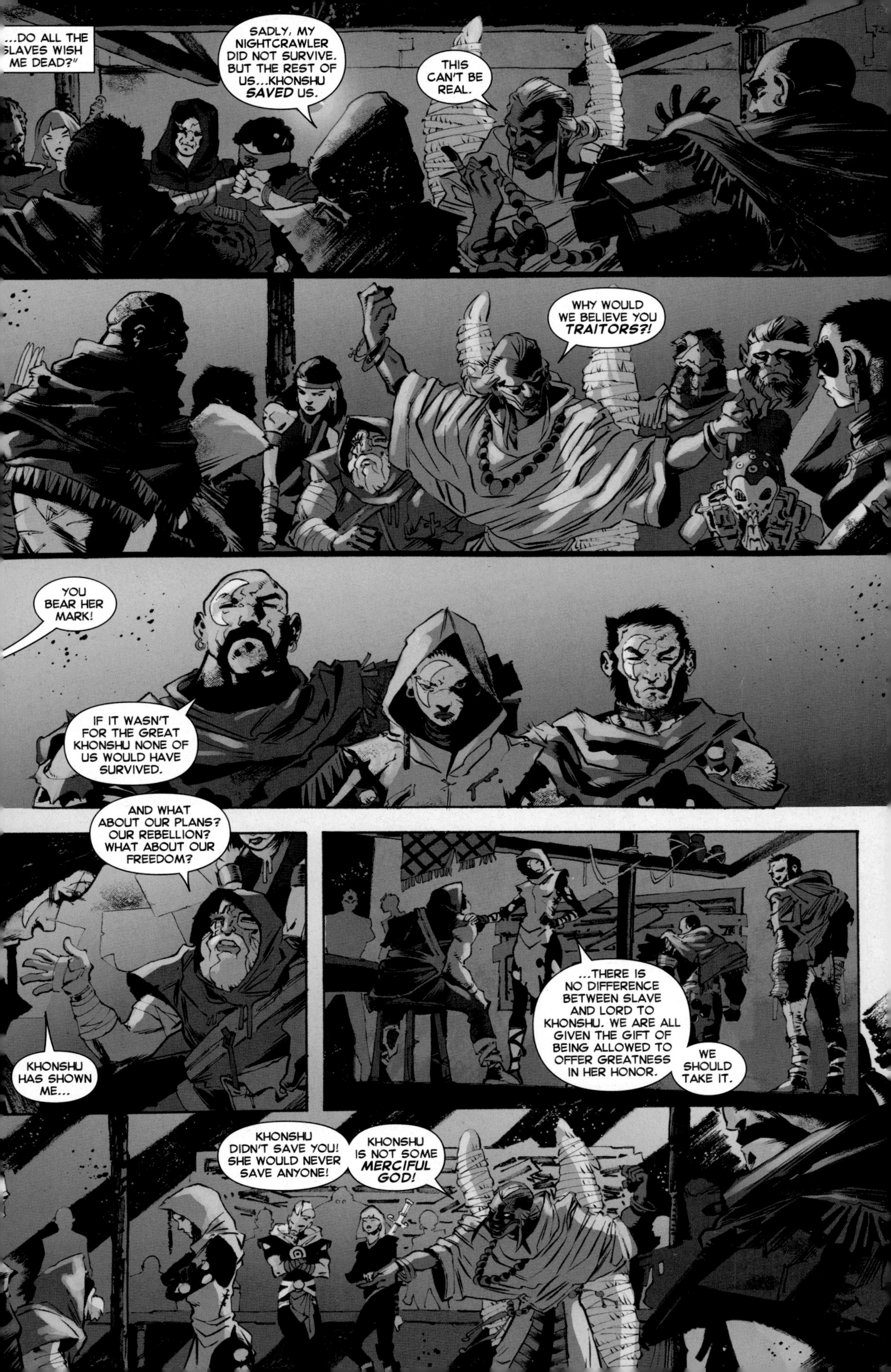

"...DO ALL THE SLAVES WISH ME DEAD?"
SADLY, MY NIGHTCRAWLER DID NOT SURVIVE. BUT THE REST OF US...KHONSHU SAVED US.
THIS CAN'T BE REAL.
WHY WOULD WE BELIEVE YOU TRAITORS?!
YOU BEAR HER MARK!
IF IT WASN'T FOR THE GREAT KHONSHU NONE OF US WOULD HAVE SURVIVED.
AND WHAT ABOUT OUR PLANS? OUR REBELLION? WHAT ABOUT OUR FREEDOM?
KHONSHU HAS SHOWN ME...
...THERE IS NO DIFFERENCE BETWEEN SLAVE AND LORD TO KHONSHU. WE ARE ALL GIVEN THE GIFT OF BEING ALLOWED TO OFFER GREATNESS IN HER HONOR.
WE SHOULD TAKE IT.
KHONSHU DIDN'T SAVE YOU! SHE WOULD NEVER SAVE ANYONE!
KHONSHU IS NOT SOME MERCIFUL GOD!

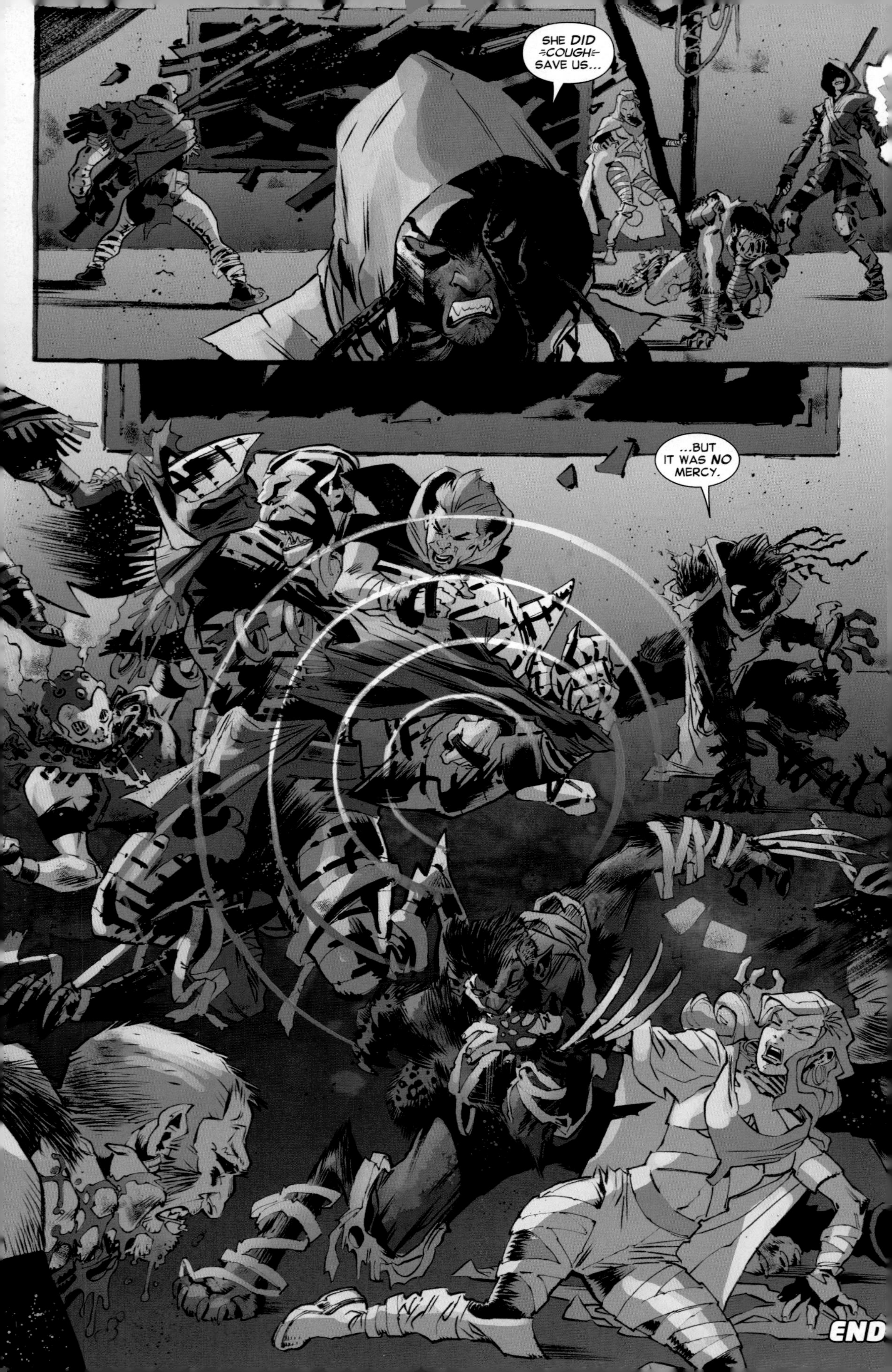
SHE DID =COUGH= SAVE US...
...BUT IT WAS NO MERCY.
END

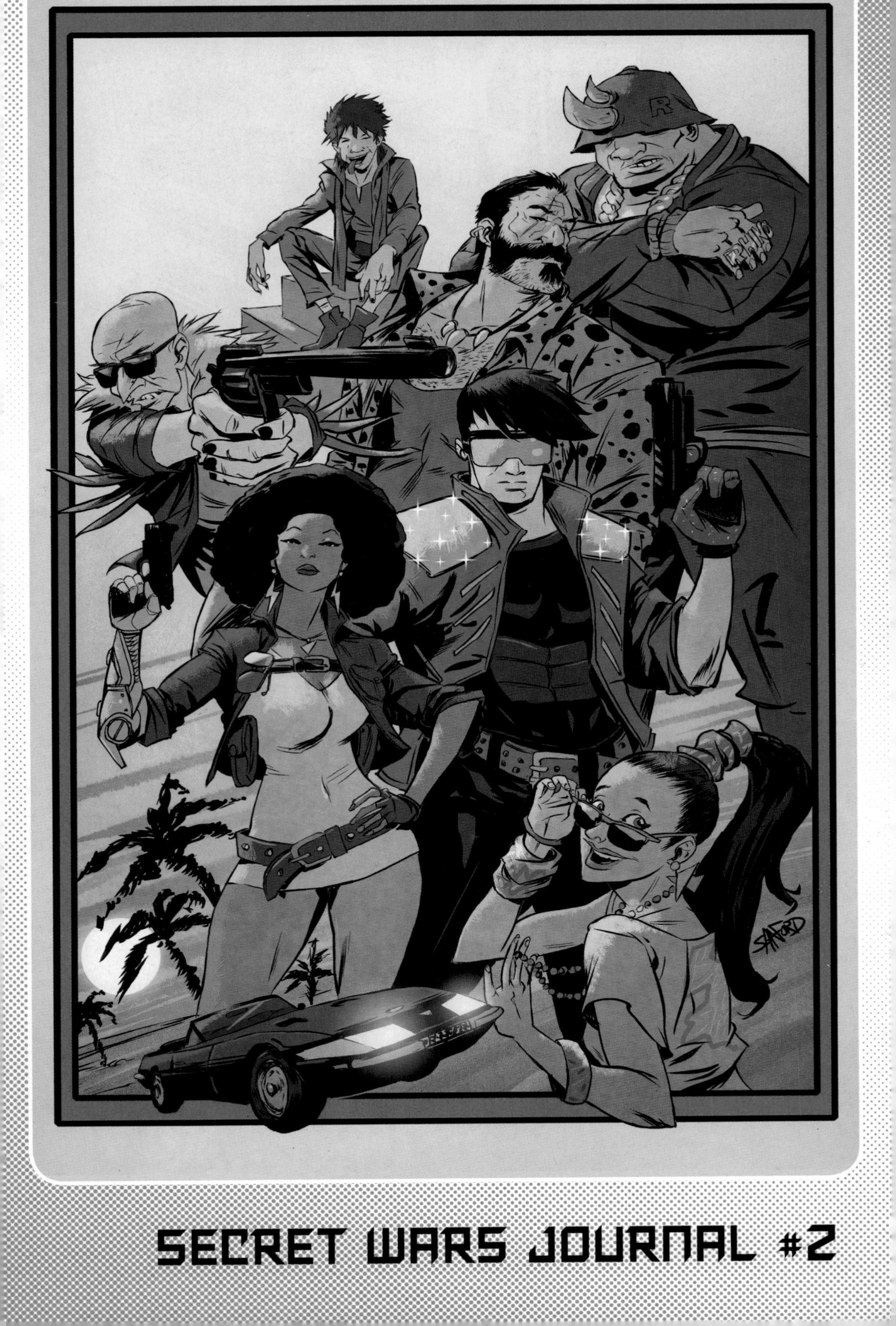
RHINO
SAFORD

SECRET WARS JOURNAL #2

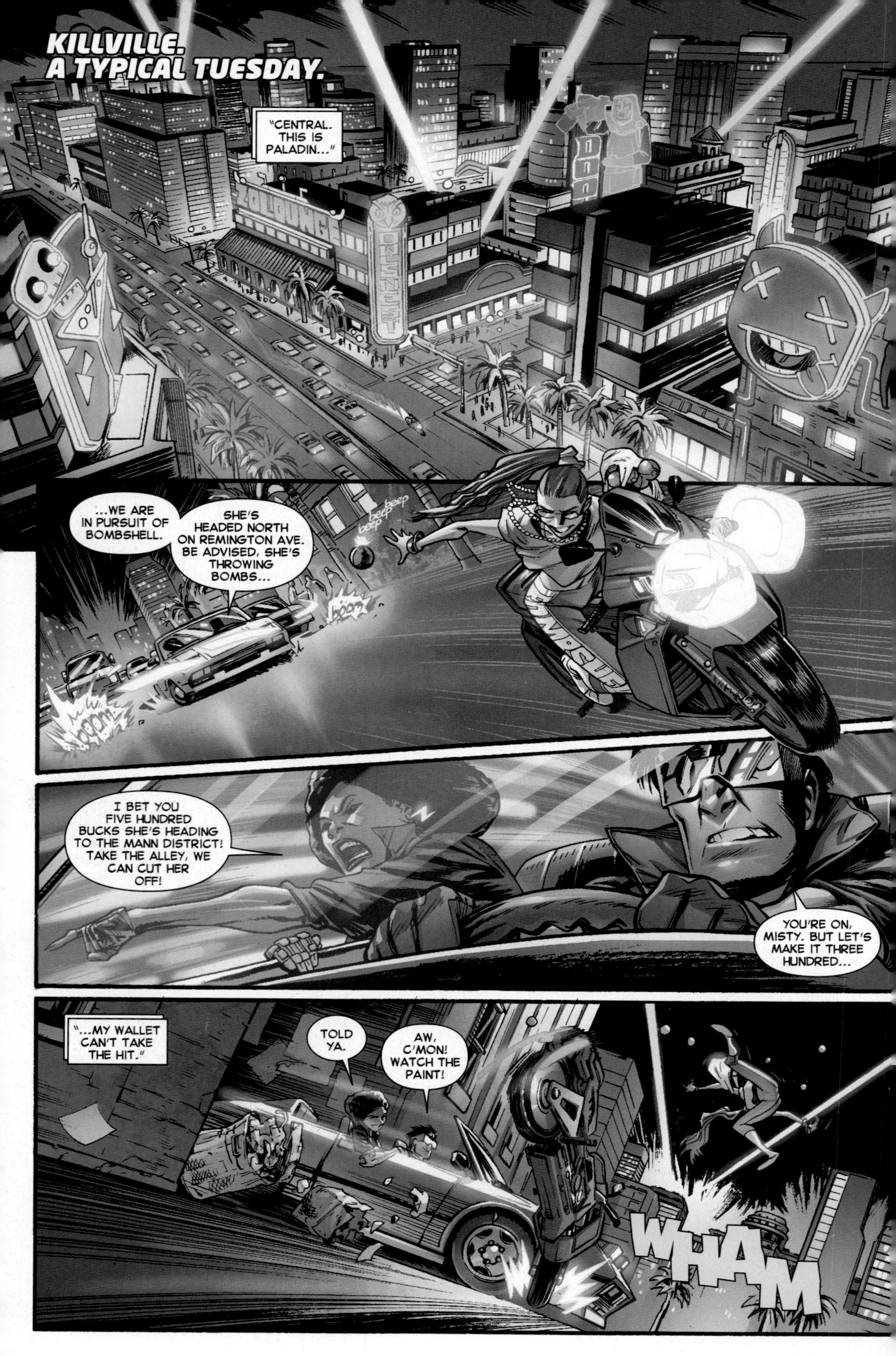
KILLVILLE.
A TYPICAL TUESDAY.
"CENTRAL. THIS IS PALADIN..."
...WE ARE IN PURSUIT OF BOMBSHELL.
SHE'S HEADED NORTH ON REMINGTON AVE. BE ADVISED, SHE'S THROWING BOMBS...
beep beep beep
boom
boom
I BET YOU FIVE HUNDRED BUCKS SHE'S HEADING TO THE MANN DISTRICT! TAKE THE ALLEY, WE CAN CUT HER OFF!
YOU'RE ON, MISTY. BUT LET'S MAKE IT THREE HUNDRED...
"...MY WALLET CAN'T TAKE THE HIT."
TOLD YA.
AW, C'MON! WATCH THE PAINT!
WHAM

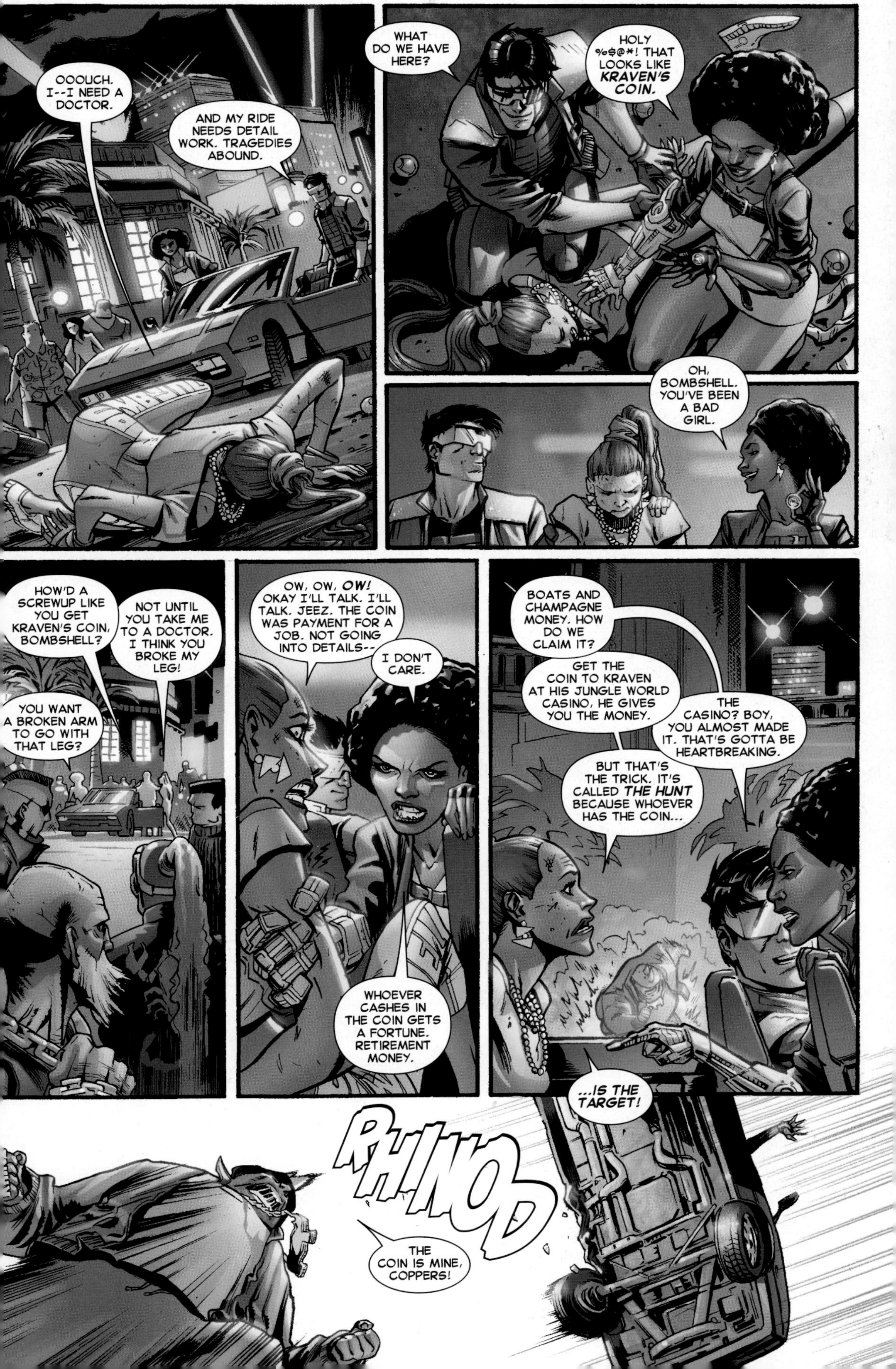
OOOUCH. I--I NEED A DOCTOR.
AND MY RIDE NEEDS DETAIL WORK. TRAGEDIES ABOUND.
WHAT DO WE HAVE HERE?
HOLY %$@*! THAT LOOKS LIKE KRAVEN'S COIN.
OH, BOMBSHELL. YOU'VE BEEN A BAD GIRL.
HOW'D A SCREWUP LIKE YOU GET KRAVEN'S COIN, BOMBSHELL?
NOT UNTIL YOU TAKE ME TO A DOCTOR. I THINK YOU BROKE MY LEG!
YOU WANT A BROKEN ARM TO GO WITH THAT LEG?
OW, OW, OW! OKAY I'LL TALK. I'LL TALK. JEEZ. THE COIN WAS PAYMENT FOR A JOB. NOT GOING INTO DETAILS--
I DON'T CARE.
WHOEVER CASHES IN THE COIN GETS A FORTUNE. RETIREMENT MONEY.
BOATS AND CHAMPAGNE MONEY. HOW DO WE CLAIM IT?
GET THE COIN TO KRAVEN AT HIS JUNGLE WORLD CASINO, HE GIVES YOU THE MONEY.
THE CASINO? BOY, YOU ALMOST MADE IT. THAT'S GOTTA BE HEARTBREAKING.
BUT THAT'S THE TRICK. IT'S CALLED THE HUNT BECAUSE WHOEVER HAS THE COIN...
...IS THE TARGET!
RHINOD
THE COIN IS MINE, COPPERS!

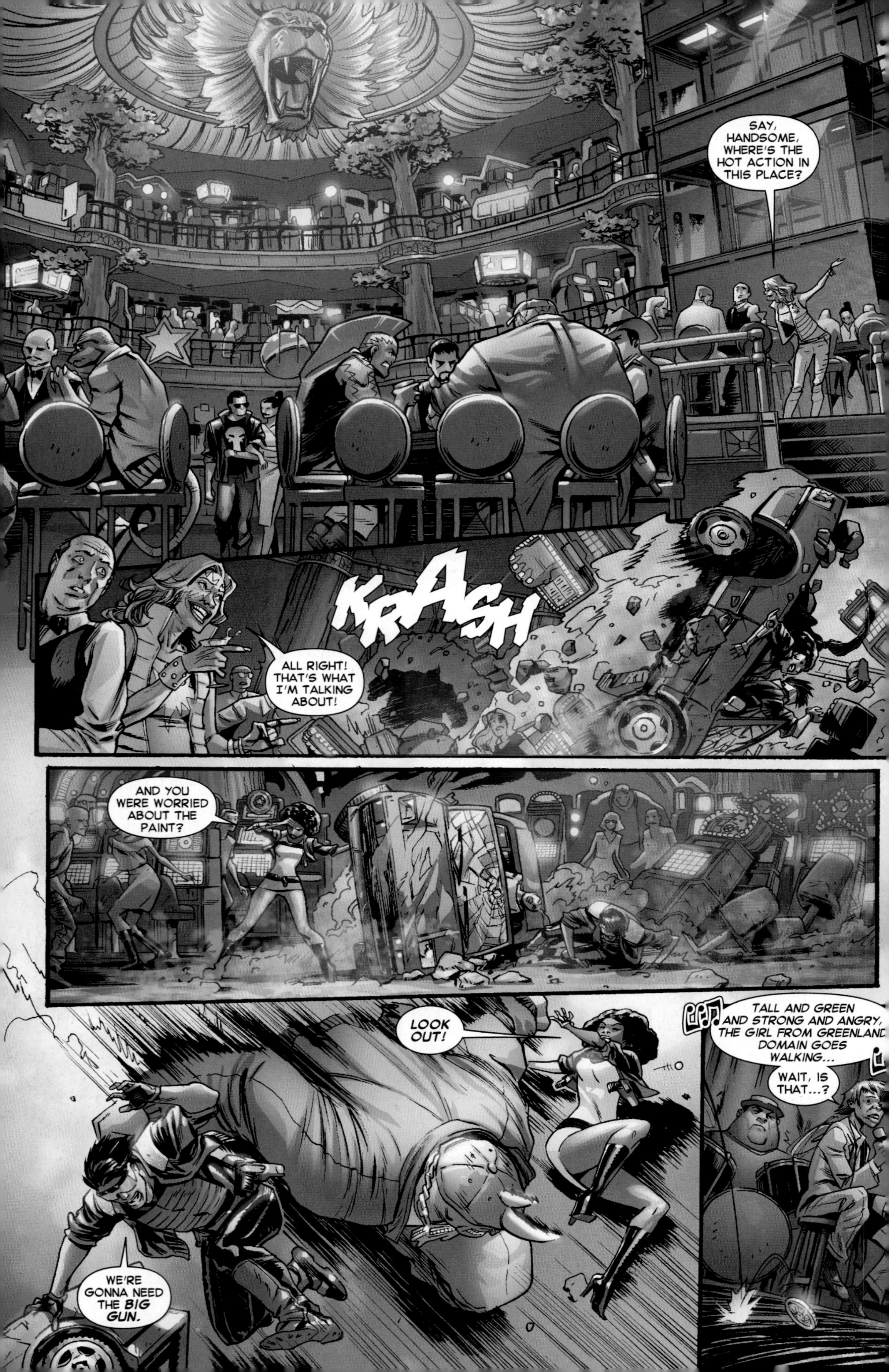
SAY, HANDSOME, WHERE'S THE HOT ACTION IN THIS PLACE?
KRASH
ALL RIGHT! THAT'S WHAT I'M TALKING ABOUT!
AND YOU WERE WORRIED ABOUT THE PAINT?
LOOK OUT!
WE'RE GONNA NEED THE BIG GUN.
TALL AND GREEN AND STRONG AND ANGRY, THE GIRL FROM GREENLAND DOMAIN GOES WALKING...
WAIT, IS THAT...?

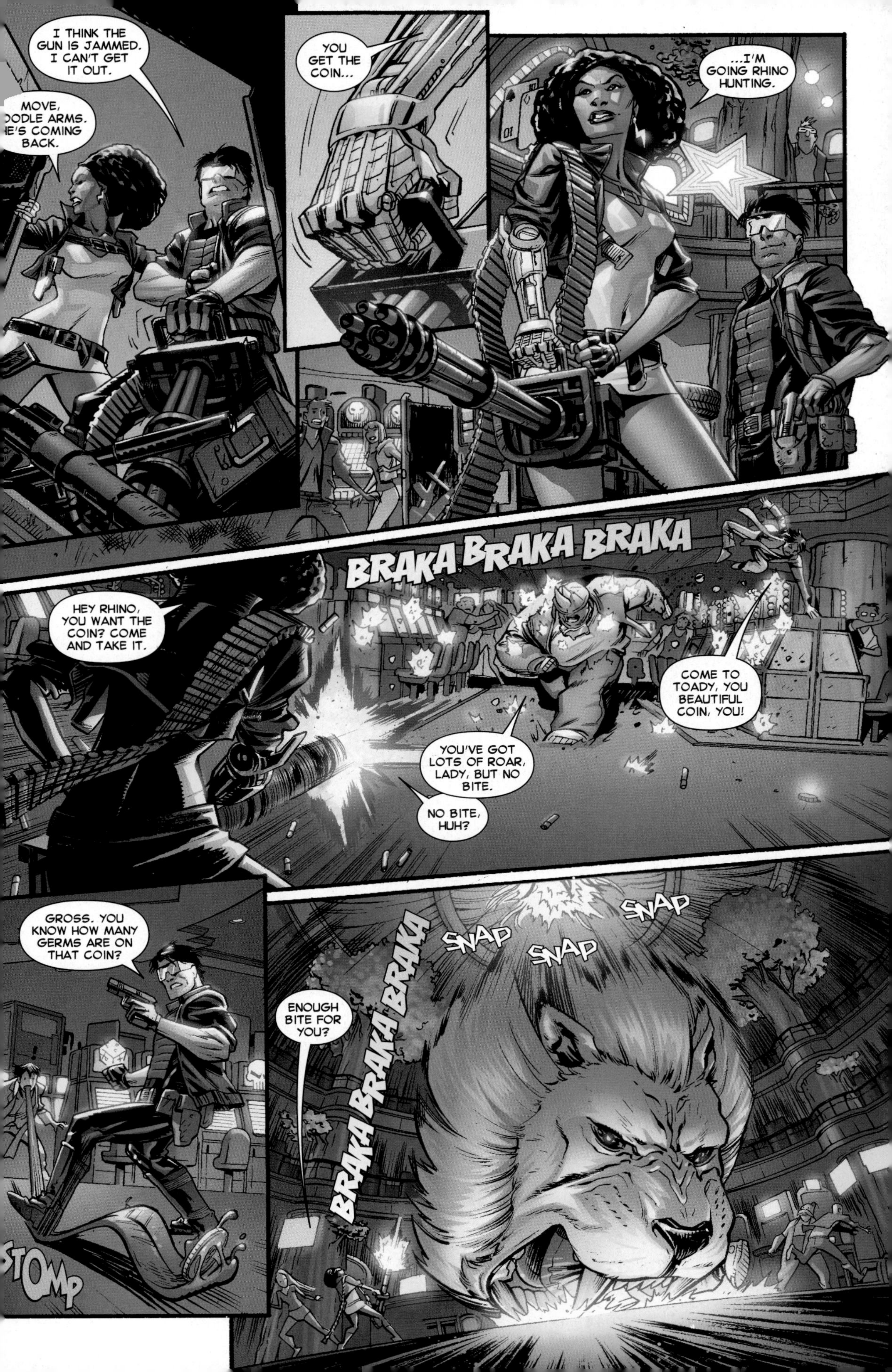
I THINK THE GUN IS JAMMED. I CAN'T GET IT OUT.
MOVE, NOODLE ARMS. HE'S COMING BACK.
YOU GET THE COIN...
...I'M GOING RHINO HUNTING.
BRAKA BRAKA BRAKA
HEY RHINO, YOU WANT THE COIN? COME AND TAKE IT.
YOU'VE GOT LOTS OF ROAR, LADY, BUT NO BITE.
NO BITE, HUH?
COME TO TOADY, YOU BEAUTIFUL COIN, YOU!
GROSS. YOU KNOW HOW MANY GERMS ARE ON THAT COIN?
STOMP
BRAKA BRAKA BRAKA
ENOUGH BITE FOR YOU?
SNAP
SNAP
SNAP

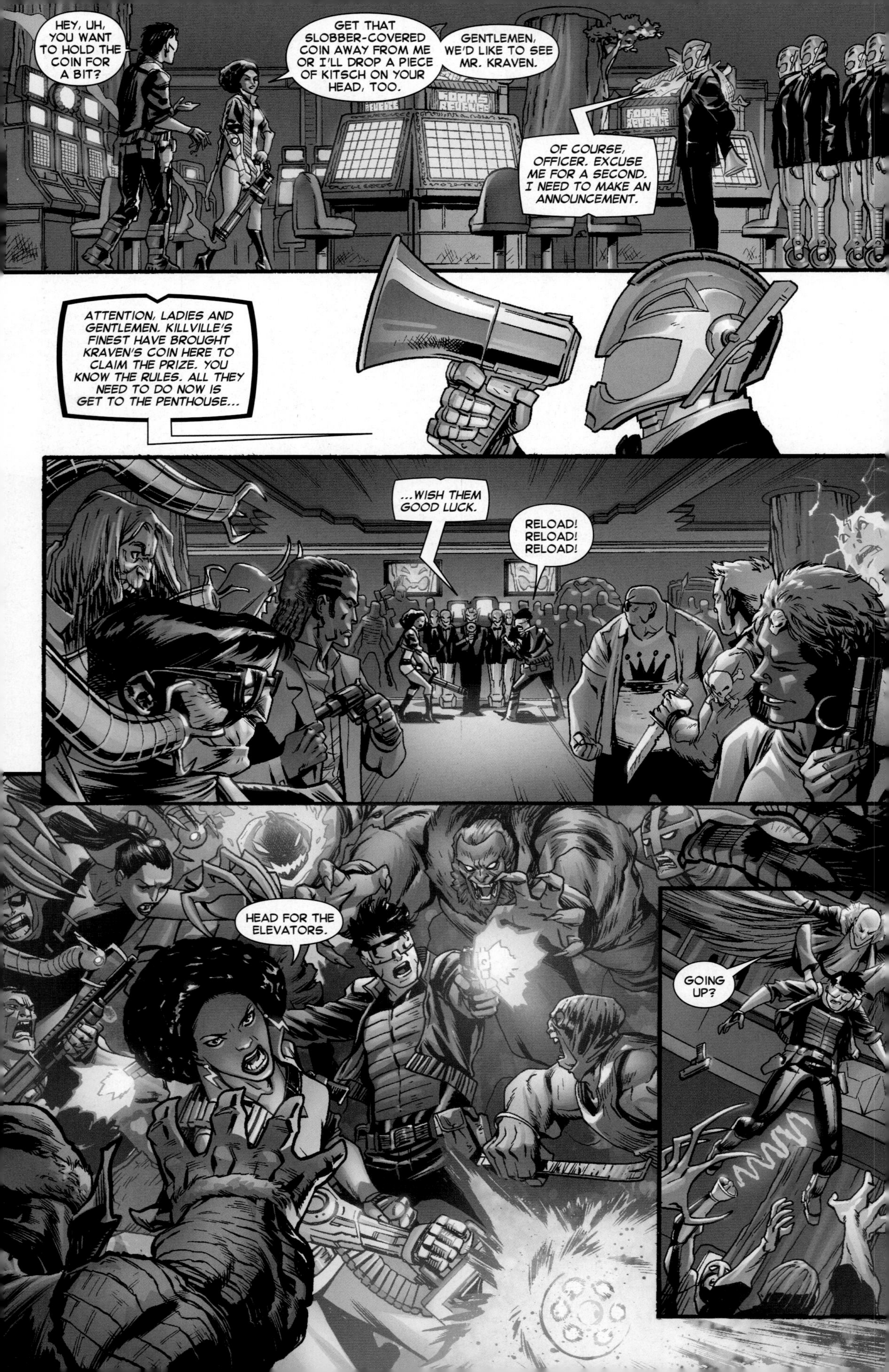
HEY, UH, YOU WANT TO HOLD THE COIN FOR A BIT?
GET THAT SLOBBER-COVERED COIN AWAY FROM ME OR I'LL DROP A PIECE OF KITSCH ON YOUR HEAD, TOO.
GENTLEMEN, WE'D LIKE TO SEE MR. KRAVEN.
OF COURSE, OFFICER. EXCUSE ME FOR A SECOND. I NEED TO MAKE AN ANNOUNCEMENT.
ATTENTION, LADIES AND GENTLEMEN. KILLVILLE'S FINEST HAVE BROUGHT KRAVEN'S COIN HERE TO CLAIM THE PRIZE. YOU KNOW THE RULES. ALL THEY NEED TO DO NOW IS GET TO THE PENTHOUSE...
...WISH THEM GOOD LUCK.
RELOAD! RELOAD! RELOAD!
HEAD FOR THE ELEVATORS.
GOING UP?

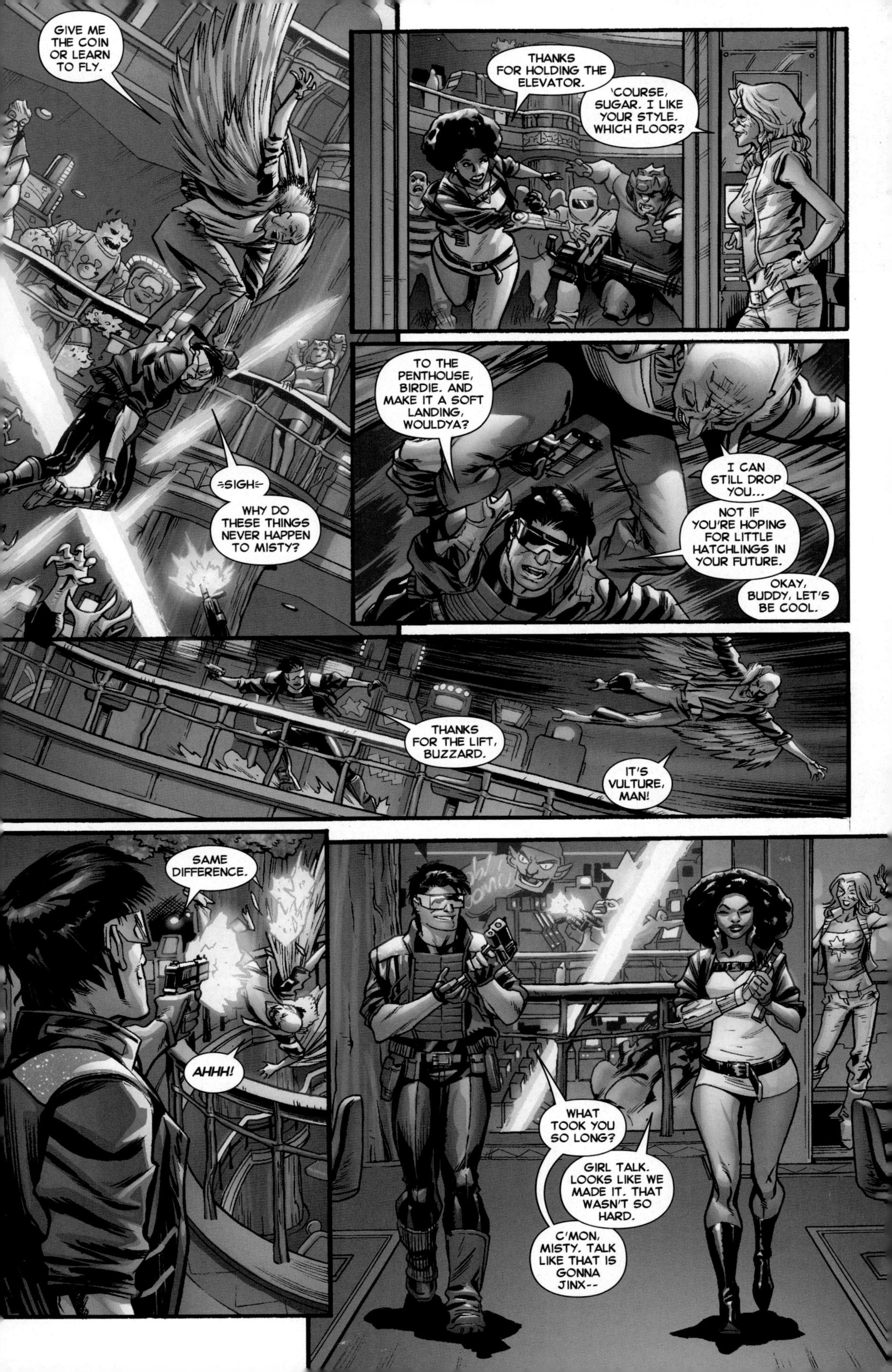

GIVE ME THE COIN OR LEARN TO FLY.
THANKS FOR HOLDING THE ELEVATOR.
'COURSE, SUGAR. I LIKE YOUR STYLE. WHICH FLOOR?
TO THE PENTHOUSE, BIRDIE. AND MAKE IT A SOFT LANDING, WOULDYA?
I CAN STILL DROP YOU...
NOT IF YOU'RE HOPING FOR LITTLE HATCHLINGS IN YOUR FUTURE.
OKAY, BUDDY, LET'S BE COOL.
=SIGH=
WHY DO THESE THINGS NEVER HAPPEN TO MISTY?
THANKS FOR THE LIFT, BUZZARD.
IT'S VULTURE, MAN!
SAME DIFFERENCE.
AHHH!
WHAT TOOK YOU SO LONG?
GIRL TALK. LOOKS LIKE WE MADE IT. THAT WASN'T SO HARD.
C'MON, MISTY. TALK LIKE THAT IS GONNA JINX--

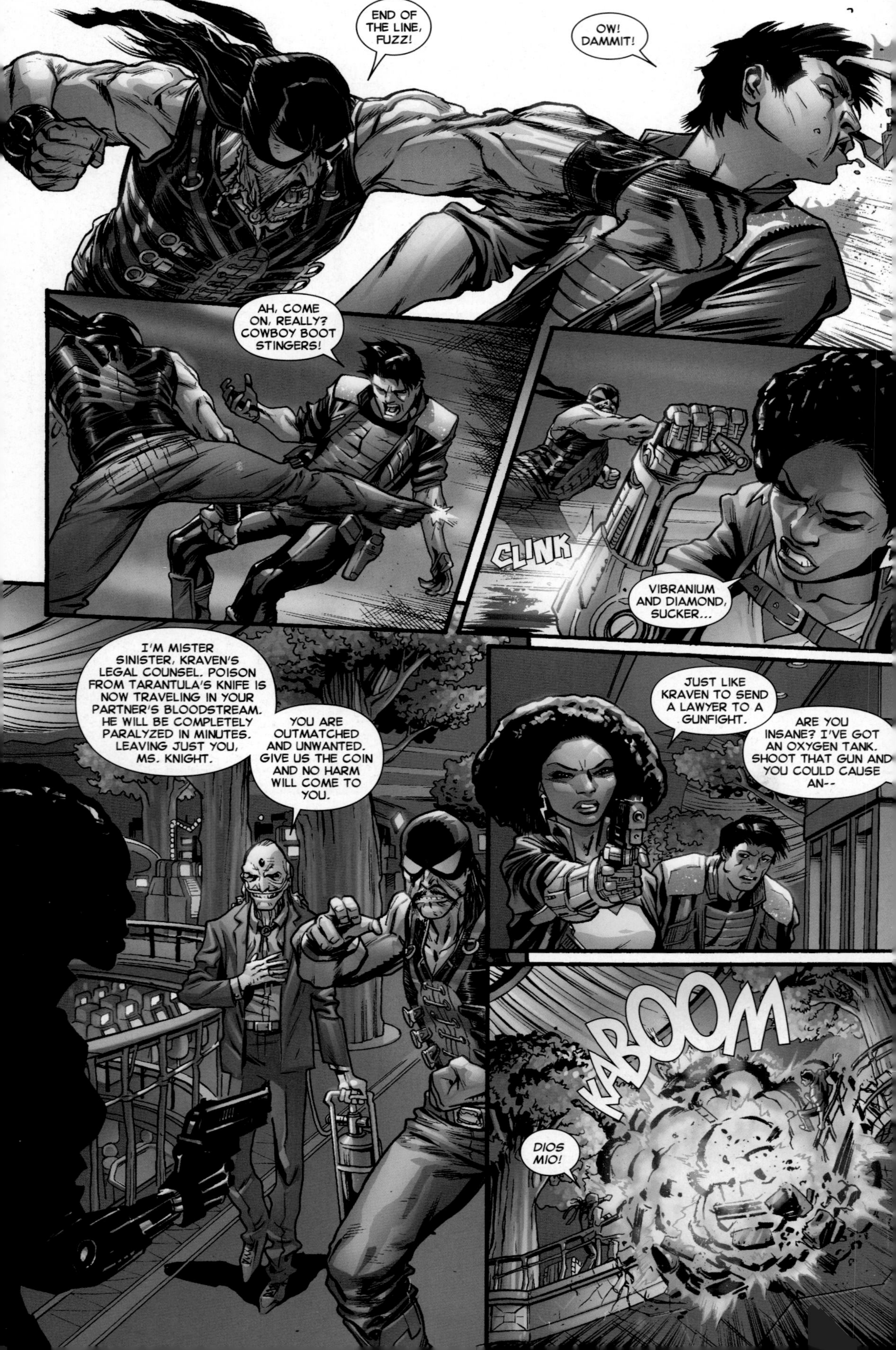
END OF THE LINE, FUZZ!
OW! DAMMIT!
AH, COME ON, REALLY? COWBOY BOOT STINGERS!
CLINK
VIBRANIUM AND DIAMOND, SUCKER...
I'M MISTER SINISTER, KRAVEN'S LEGAL COUNSEL. POISON FROM TARANTULA'S KNIFE IS NOW TRAVELING IN YOUR PARTNER'S BLOODSTREAM. HE WILL BE COMPLETELY PARALYZED IN MINUTES. LEAVING JUST YOU, MS. KNIGHT.
YOU ARE OUTMATCHED AND UNWANTED. GIVE US THE COIN AND NO HARM WILL COME TO YOU.
JUST LIKE KRAVEN TO SEND A LAWYER TO A GUNFIGHT.
ARE YOU INSANE? I'VE GOT AN OXYGEN TANK. SHOOT THAT GUN AND YOU COULD CAUSE AN--
KABOOM
DIOS MIO!

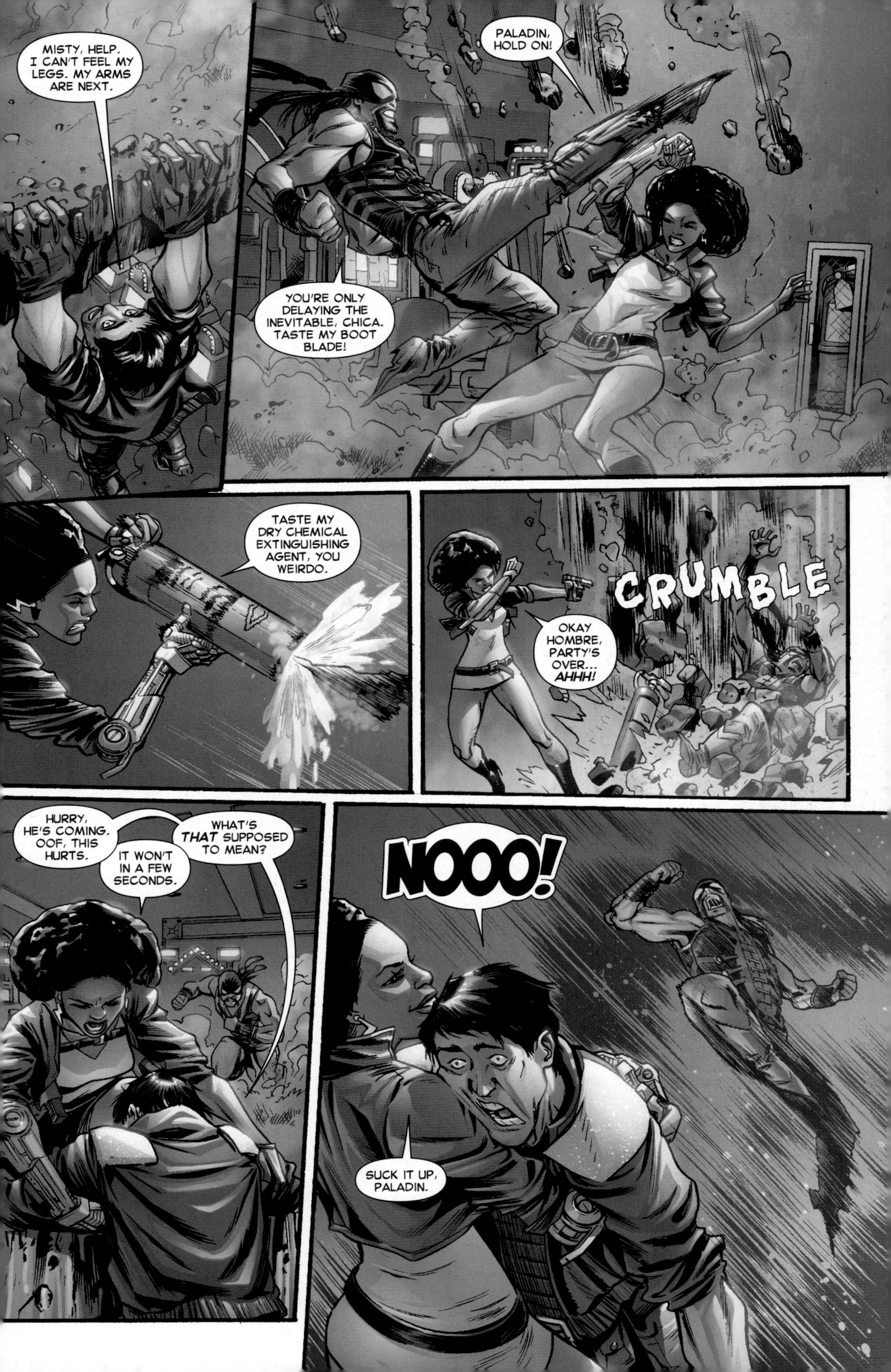
MISTY, HELP. I CAN'T FEEL MY LEGS. MY ARMS ARE NEXT.
PALADIN, HOLD ON!
YOU'RE ONLY DELAYING THE INEVITABLE, CHICA. TASTE MY BOOT BLADE!
TASTE MY DRY CHEMICAL EXTINGUISHING AGENT, YOU WEIRDO.
CRUMBLE
OKAY HOMBRE, PARTY'S OVER... AHHH!
HURRY, HE'S COMING. OOF, THIS HURTS.
IT WON'T IN A FEW SECONDS.
WHAT'S THAT SUPPOSED TO MEAN?
NOOO!
SUCK IT UP, PALADIN.

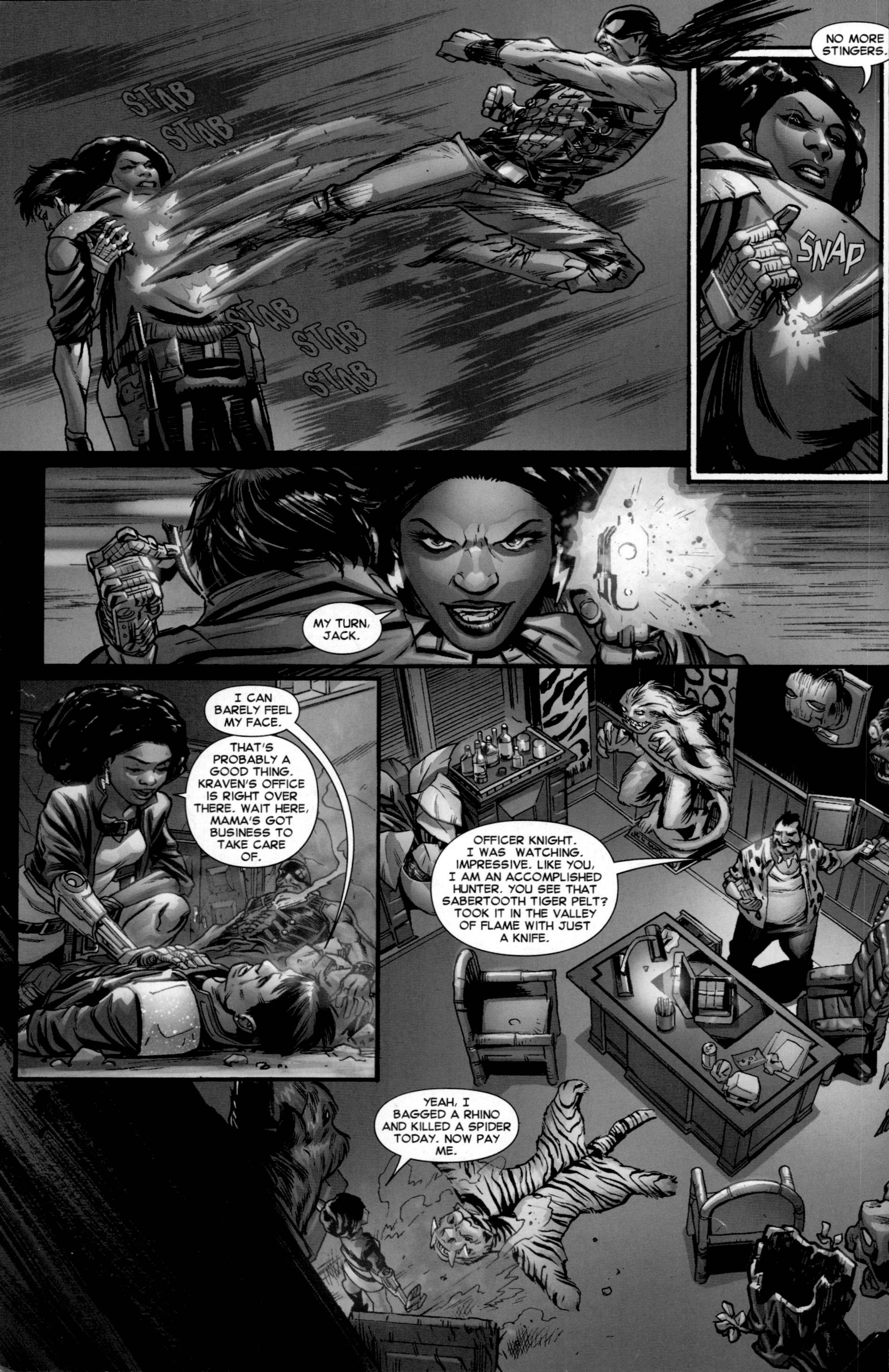
STAB
STAB
STAB
STAB
STAB
NO MORE STINGERS.
SNAP
MY TURN, JACK.
I CAN BARELY FEEL MY FACE.
THAT'S PROBABLY A GOOD THING. KRAVEN'S OFFICE IS RIGHT OVER THERE. WAIT HERE, MAMA'S GOT BUSINESS TO TAKE CARE OF.
OFFICER KNIGHT. I WAS WATCHING. IMPRESSIVE. LIKE YOU, I AM AN ACCOMPLISHED HUNTER. YOU SEE THAT SABERTOOTH TIGER PELT? TOOK IT IN THE VALLEY OF FLAME WITH JUST A KNIFE.
YEAH, I BAGGED A RHINO AND KILLED A SPIDER TODAY. NOW PAY ME.

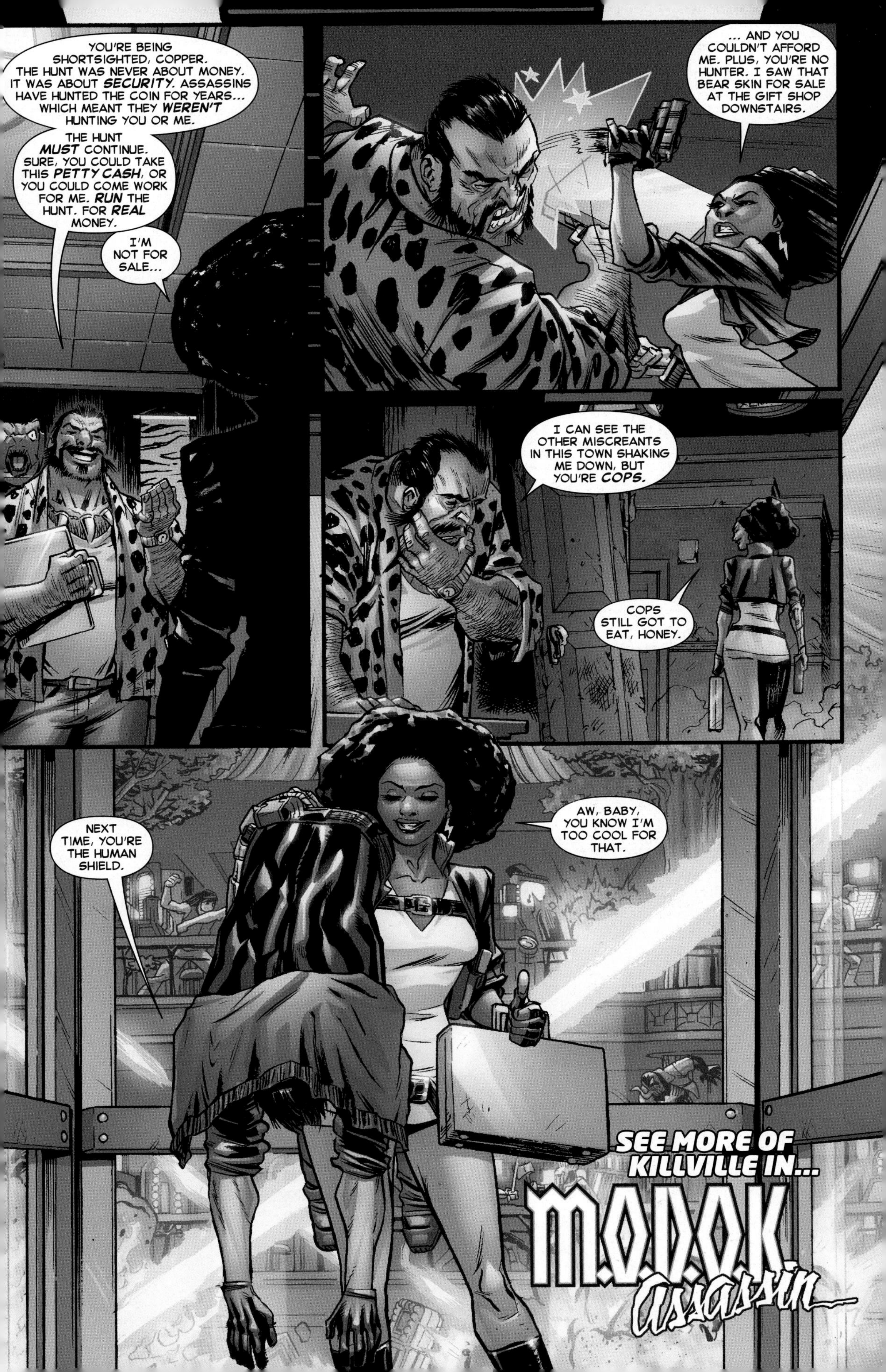
YOU'RE BEING SHORTSIGHTED, COPPER. THE HUNT WAS NEVER ABOUT MONEY. IT WAS ABOUT SECURITY. ASSASSINS HAVE HUNTED THE COIN FOR YEARS... WHICH MEANT THEY WEREN'T HUNTING YOU OR ME.
THE HUNT MUST CONTINUE. SURE, YOU COULD TAKE THIS PETTY CASH, OR YOU COULD COME WORK FOR ME. RUN THE HUNT. FOR REAL MONEY.
I'M NOT FOR SALE...
... AND YOU COULDN'T AFFORD ME. PLUS, YOU'RE NO HUNTER. I SAW THAT BEAR SKIN FOR SALE AT THE GIFT SHOP DOWNSTAIRS.
I CAN SEE THE OTHER MISCREANTS IN THIS TOWN SHAKING ME DOWN, BUT YOU'RE COPS.
COPS STILL GOT TO EAT, HONEY.
NEXT TIME, YOU'RE THE HUMAN SHIELD.
AW, BABY, YOU KNOW I'M TOO COOL FOR THAT.
SEE MORE OF KILLVILLE IN...
M.O.D.O.K. ASSASSIN

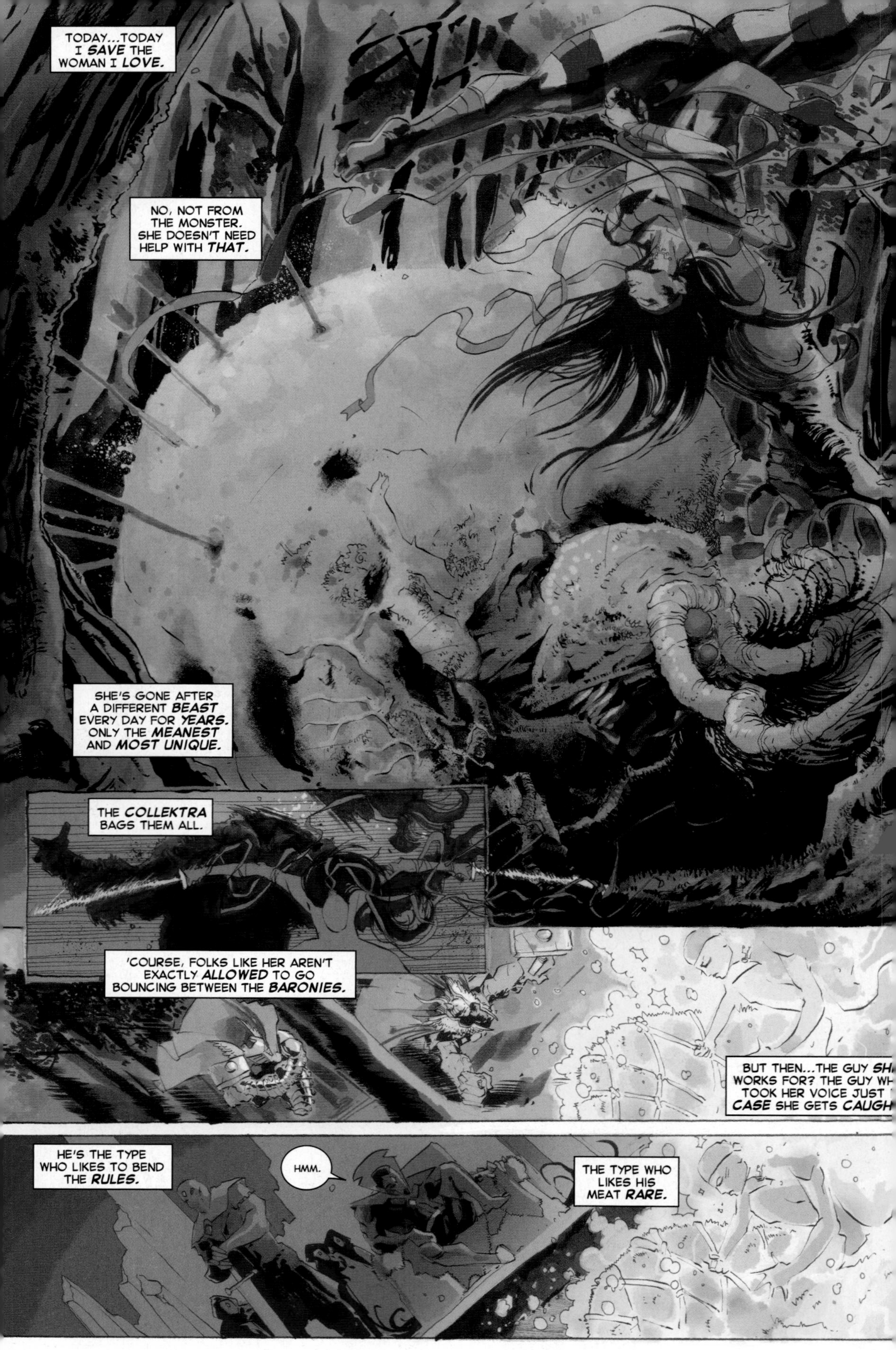
TODAY...TODAY I SAVE THE WOMAN I LOVE.
NO, NOT FROM THE MONSTER. SHE DOESN'T NEED HELP WITH THAT.
SHE'S GONE AFTER A DIFFERENT BEAST EVERY DAY FOR YEARS. ONLY THE MEANEST AND MOST UNIQUE.
THE COLLEKTRA BAGS THEM ALL.
'COURSE, FOLKS LIKE HER AREN'T EXACTLY ALLOWED TO GO BOUNCING BETWEEN THE BARONIES.
BUT THEN...THE GUY SH WORKS FOR? THE GUY WH TOOK HER VOICE JUST CASE SHE GETS CAUGH
HE'S THE TYPE WHO LIKES TO BEND THE RULES.
HMM.
THE TYPE WHO LIKES HIS MEAT RARE.

WHAT AN UNNECESSARILY *UGLY* CREATURE.

NATURE CAN BE *SUCH* A PHILISTINE, DARLING.

OFF TO THE *KITCHEN* WITH IT. AND--COLLEKTRA *PLEASE...*

"...*DO* TRY NOT TO DRIP ON THE CARPETS."

THE *BAR SINISTER* IS RULED NOT BY AN INDIVIDUAL BUT A *VIRUS.* A SELF-REPLICATING TRIBE OF GENETIC *JERKS.*

CLONES CAN'T DO *EVERYTHING,* OF COURSE. FOR *SOME* THINGS THE MASTER STILL NEEDS *INDIVIDUALS.* HE NEEDS *ARTISTS.*

HE NEEDS *TAME WONDERS,* CONTROLLED BY *TELEPORT-TAGS* OR SIMPLE *TERROR.*

HE NEEDS SLAVES. LIKE *HER.*

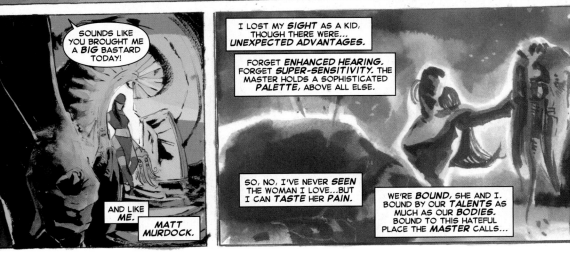

SOUNDS LIKE YOU BROUGHT ME A *BIG* BASTARD TODAY!

AND LIKE *ME.* MATT MURDOCK.

I LOST MY *SIGHT* AS A KID, THOUGH THERE WERE... *UNEXPECTED ADVANTAGES.*

FORGET *ENHANCED HEARING.* FORGET *SUPER-SENSITIVITY.* THE MASTER HOLDS A SOPHISTICATED *PALETTE,* ABOVE ALL ELSE.

SO, NO, I'VE NEVER *SEEN* THE WOMAN I LOVE...BUT I CAN *TASTE* HER PAIN.

WE'RE *BOUND,* SHE AND I. BOUND BY OUR *TALENTS* AS MUCH AS OUR *BODIES.* BOUND TO THIS HATEFUL PLACE THE *MASTER* CALLS...

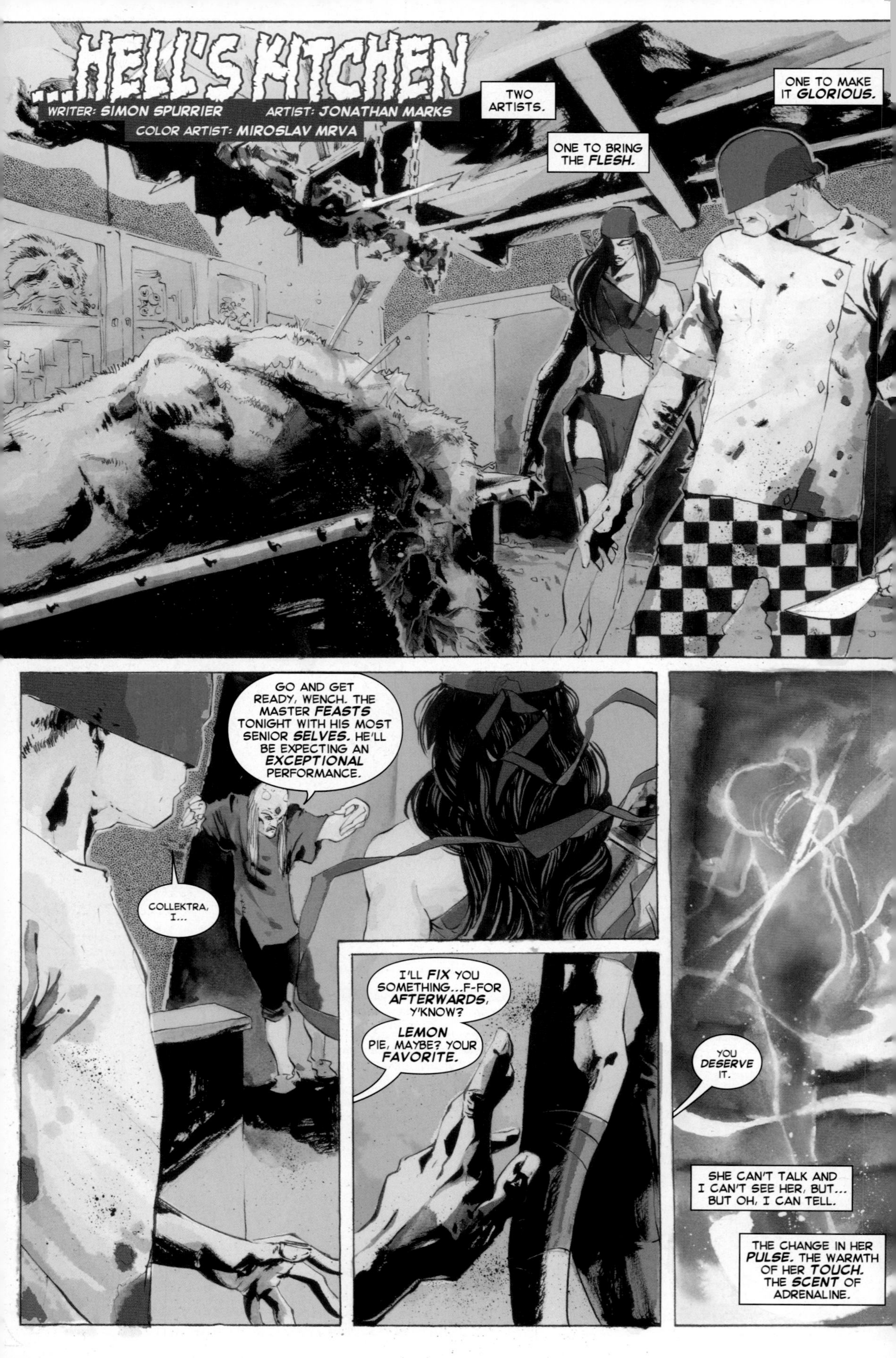

...HELL'S KITCHEN
WRITER: SIMON SPURRIER ARTIST: JONATHAN MARKS
COLOR ARTIST: MIROSLAV MRVA
TWO ARTISTS.
ONE TO BRING THE FLESH.
ONE TO MAKE IT GLORIOUS.
GO AND GET READY, WENCH. THE MASTER FEASTS TONIGHT WITH HIS MOST SENIOR SELVES. HE'LL BE EXPECTING AN EXCEPTIONAL PERFORMANCE.
COLLEKTRA, I...
I'LL FIX YOU SOMETHING...F-FOR AFTERWARDS, Y'KNOW?
LEMON PIE, MAYBE? YOUR FAVORITE.
YOU DESERVE IT.
SHE CAN'T TALK AND I CAN'T SEE HER, BUT... BUT OH, I CAN TELL.
THE CHANGE IN HER PULSE. THE WARMTH OF HER TOUCH. THE SCENT OF ADRENALINE.

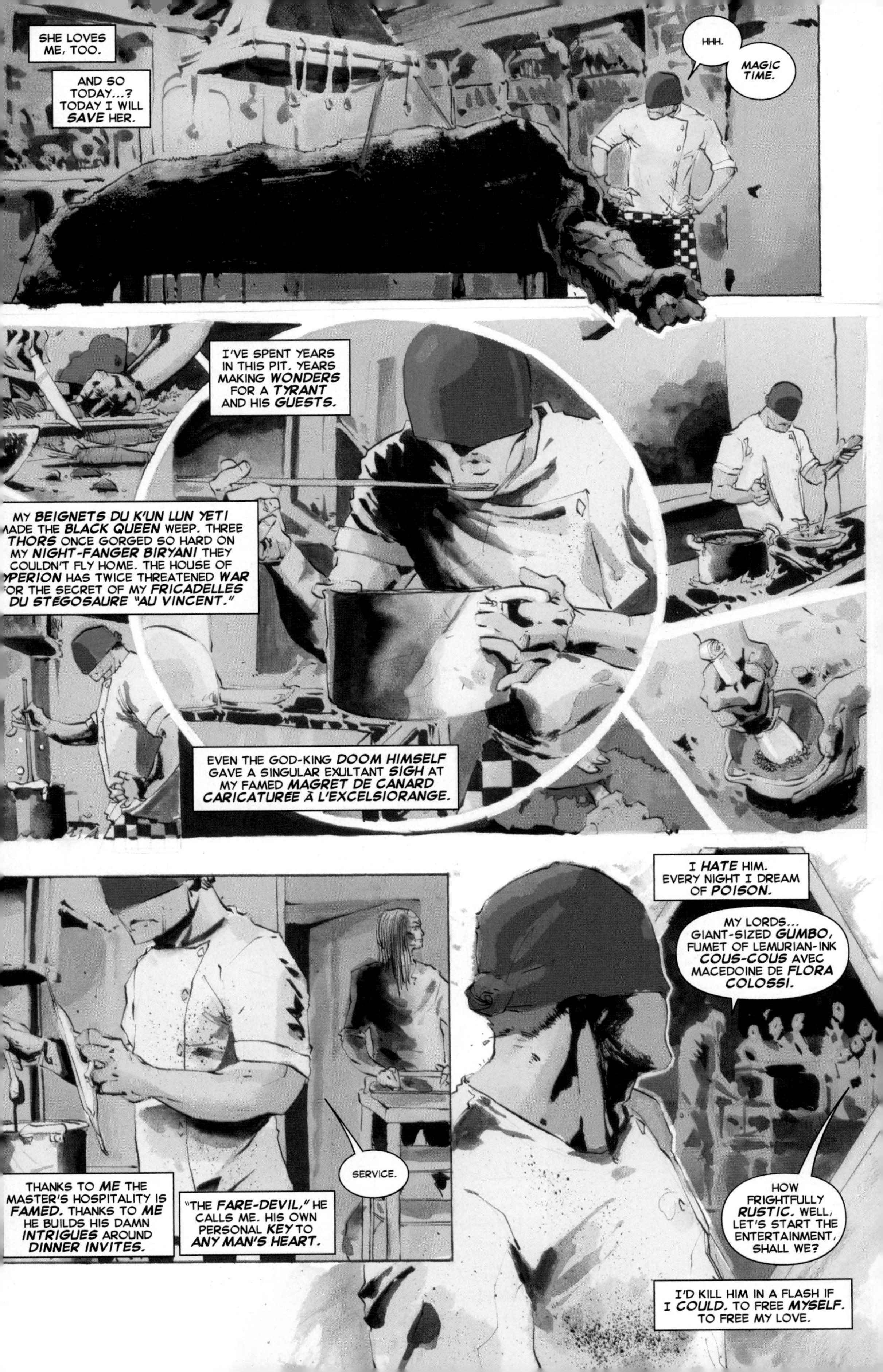
SHE LOVES ME, TOO.
AND SO TODAY...? TODAY I WILL SAVE HER.
HHH.
MAGIC TIME.
I'VE SPENT YEARS IN THIS PIT. YEARS MAKING WONDERS FOR A TYRANT AND HIS GUESTS.
MY BEIGNETS DU K'UN LUN YETI MADE THE BLACK QUEEN WEEP. THREE THORS ONCE GORGED SO HARD ON MY NIGHT-FANGER BIRYANI THEY COULDN'T FLY HOME. THE HOUSE OF HYPERION HAS TWICE THREATENED WAR FOR THE SECRET OF MY FRICADELLES DU STEGOSAURE "AU VINCENT."
EVEN THE GOD-KING DOOM HIMSELF GAVE A SINGULAR EXULTANT SIGH AT MY FAMED MAGRET DE CANARD CARICATUREE À L'EXCELSIORANGE.
THANKS TO ME THE MASTER'S HOSPITALITY IS FAMED. THANKS TO ME HE BUILDS HIS DAMN INTRIGUES AROUND DINNER INVITES.
"THE FARE-DEVIL," HE CALLS ME. HIS OWN PERSONAL KEY TO ANY MAN'S HEART.
SERVICE.
I HATE HIM. EVERY NIGHT I DREAM OF POISON.
MY LORDS... GIANT-SIZED GUMBO, FUMET OF LEMURIAN-INK COUS-COUS AVEC MACEDOINE DE FLORA COLOSSI.
HOW FRIGHTFULLY RUSTIC. WELL, LET'S START THE ENTERTAINMENT, SHALL WE?
I'D KILL HIM IN A FLASH IF I COULD. TO FREE MYSELF. TO FREE MY LOVE.

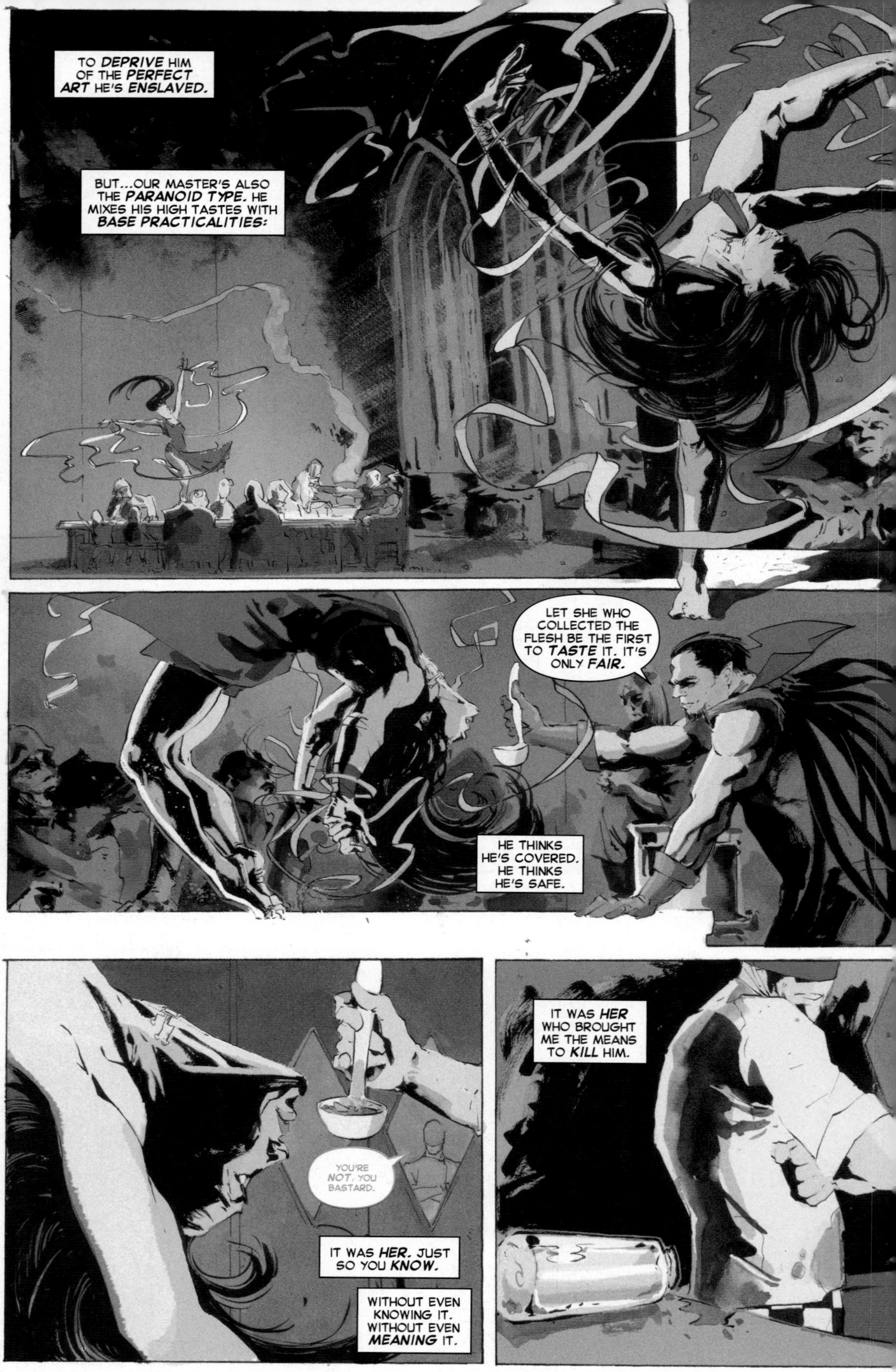

TO DEPRIVE HIM OF THE PERFECT ART HE'S ENSLAVED.
BUT...OUR MASTER'S ALSO THE PARANOID TYPE. HE MIXES HIS HIGH TASTES WITH BASE PRACTICALITIES:
LET SHE WHO COLLECTED THE FLESH BE THE FIRST TO TASTE IT. IT'S ONLY FAIR.
HE THINKS HE'S COVERED. HE THINKS HE'S SAFE.
YOU'RE NOT, YOU BASTARD.
IT WAS HER. JUST SO YOU KNOW.
WITHOUT EVEN KNOWING IT. WITHOUT EVEN MEANING IT.
IT WAS HER WHO BROUGHT ME THE MEANS TO KILL HIM.

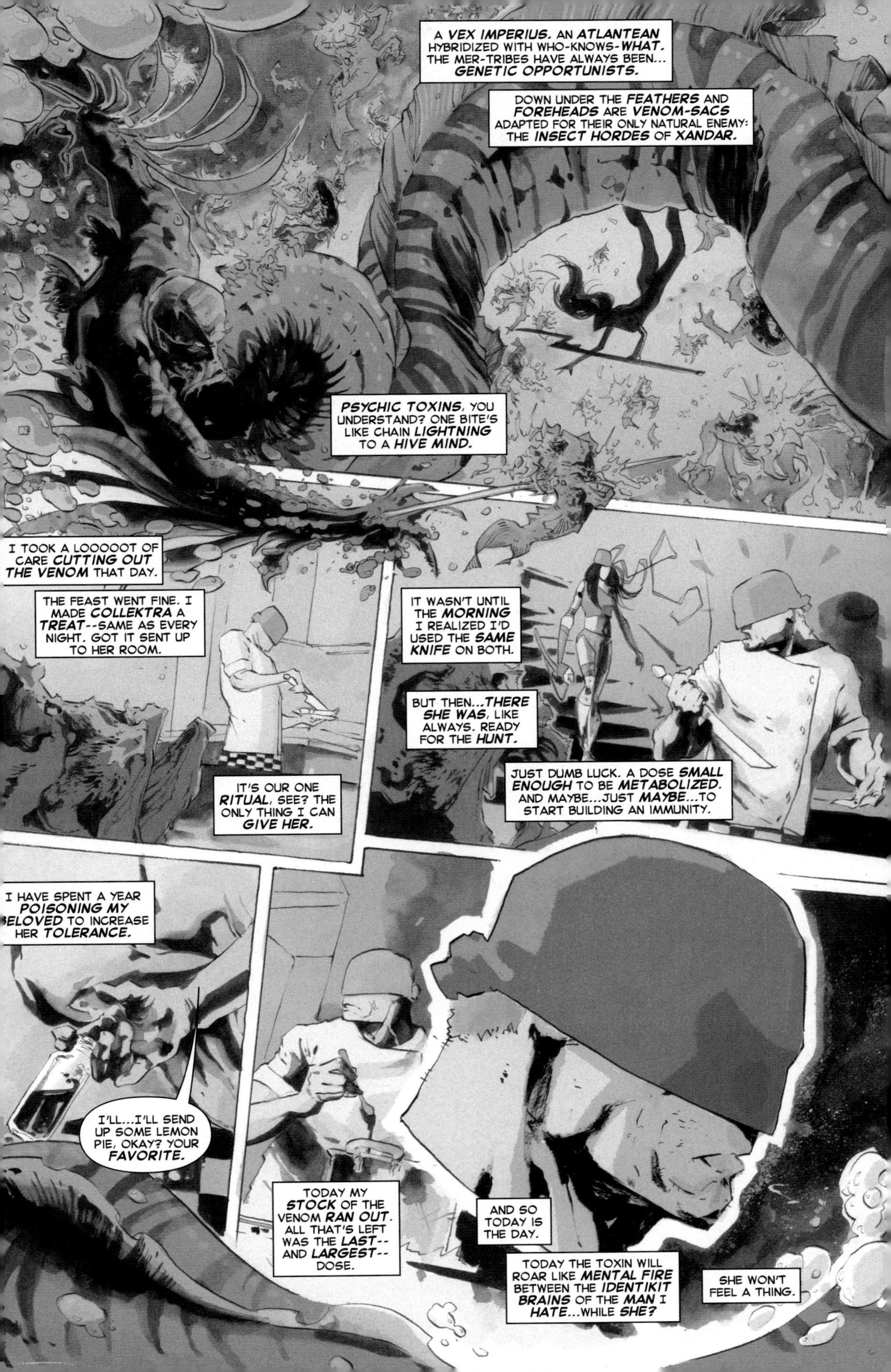

A VEX IMPERIUS. AN ATLANTEAN HYBRIDIZED WITH WHO-KNOWS-WHAT. THE MER-TRIBES HAVE ALWAYS BEEN... GENETIC OPPORTUNISTS.
DOWN UNDER THE FEATHERS AND FOREHEADS ARE VENOM-SACS ADAPTED FOR THEIR ONLY NATURAL ENEMY: THE INSECT HORDES OF XANDAR.
PSYCHIC TOXINS, YOU UNDERSTAND? ONE BITE'S LIKE CHAIN LIGHTNING TO A HIVE MIND.
I TOOK A LOOOOOT OF CARE CUTTING OUT THE VENOM THAT DAY.
THE FEAST WENT FINE. I MADE COLLEKTRA A TREAT--SAME AS EVERY NIGHT. GOT IT SENT UP TO HER ROOM.
IT'S OUR ONE RITUAL, SEE? THE ONLY THING I CAN GIVE HER.
IT WASN'T UNTIL THE MORNING I REALIZED I'D USED THE SAME KNIFE ON BOTH.
BUT THEN...THERE SHE WAS, LIKE ALWAYS. READY FOR THE HUNT.
JUST DUMB LUCK. A DOSE SMALL ENOUGH TO BE METABOLIZED. AND MAYBE...JUST MAYBE...TO START BUILDING AN IMMUNITY.
I HAVE SPENT A YEAR POISONING MY BELOVED TO INCREASE HER TOLERANCE.
I'LL...I'LL SEND UP SOME LEMON PIE, OKAY? YOUR FAVORITE.
TODAY MY STOCK OF THE VENOM RAN OUT. ALL THAT'S LEFT WAS THE LAST--AND LARGEST--DOSE.
AND SO TODAY IS THE DAY.
TODAY THE TOXIN WILL ROAR LIKE MENTAL FIRE BETWEEN THE IDENTIKIT BRAINS OF THE MAN I HATE...WHILE SHE?
SHE WON'T FEEL A THING.

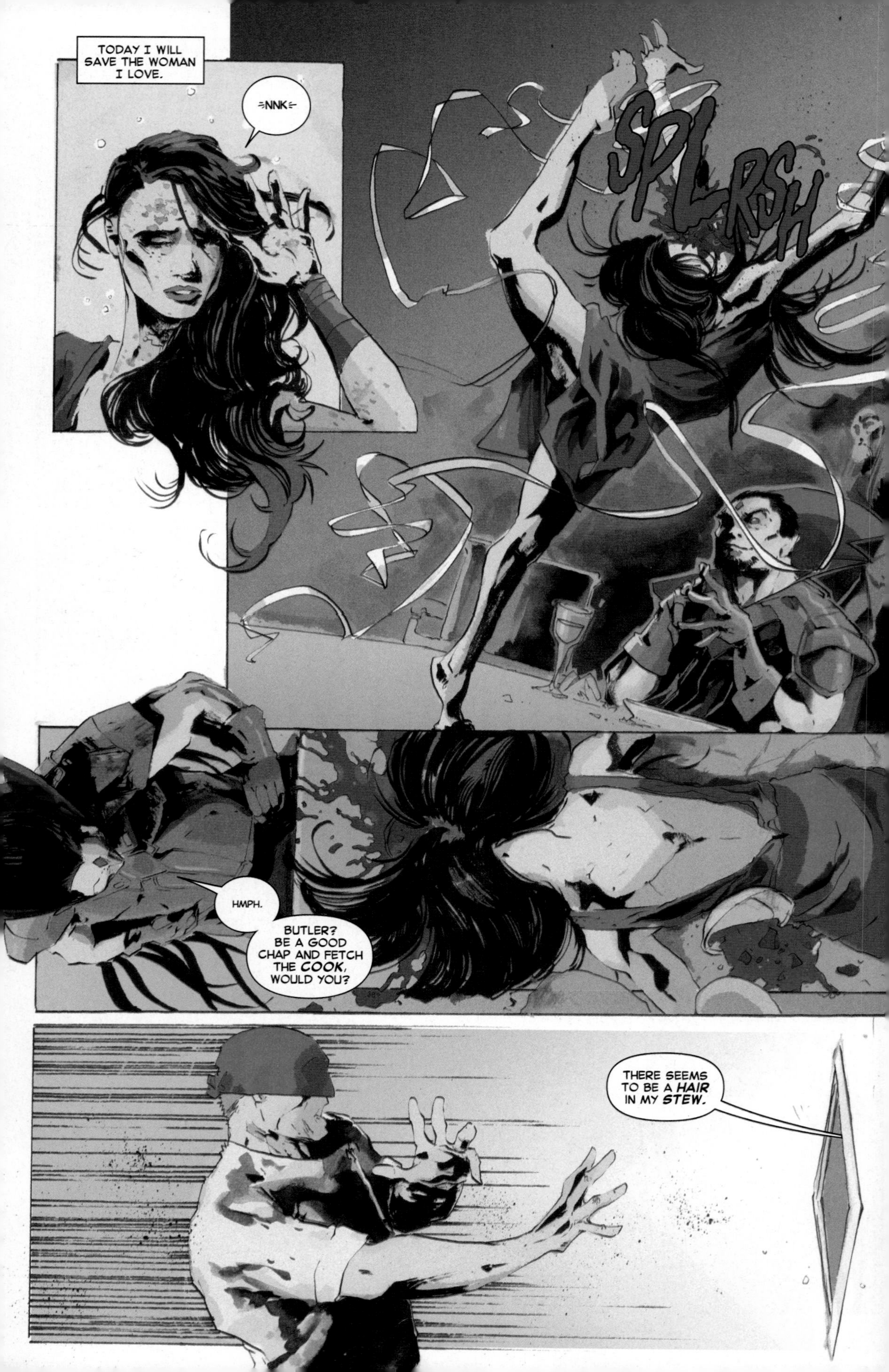
TODAY I WILL SAVE THE WOMAN I LOVE.
=NNK=
SPLRSH
HMPH.
BUTLER? BE A GOOD CHAP AND FETCH THE COOK, WOULD YOU?
THERE SEEMS TO BE A HAIR IN MY STEW.

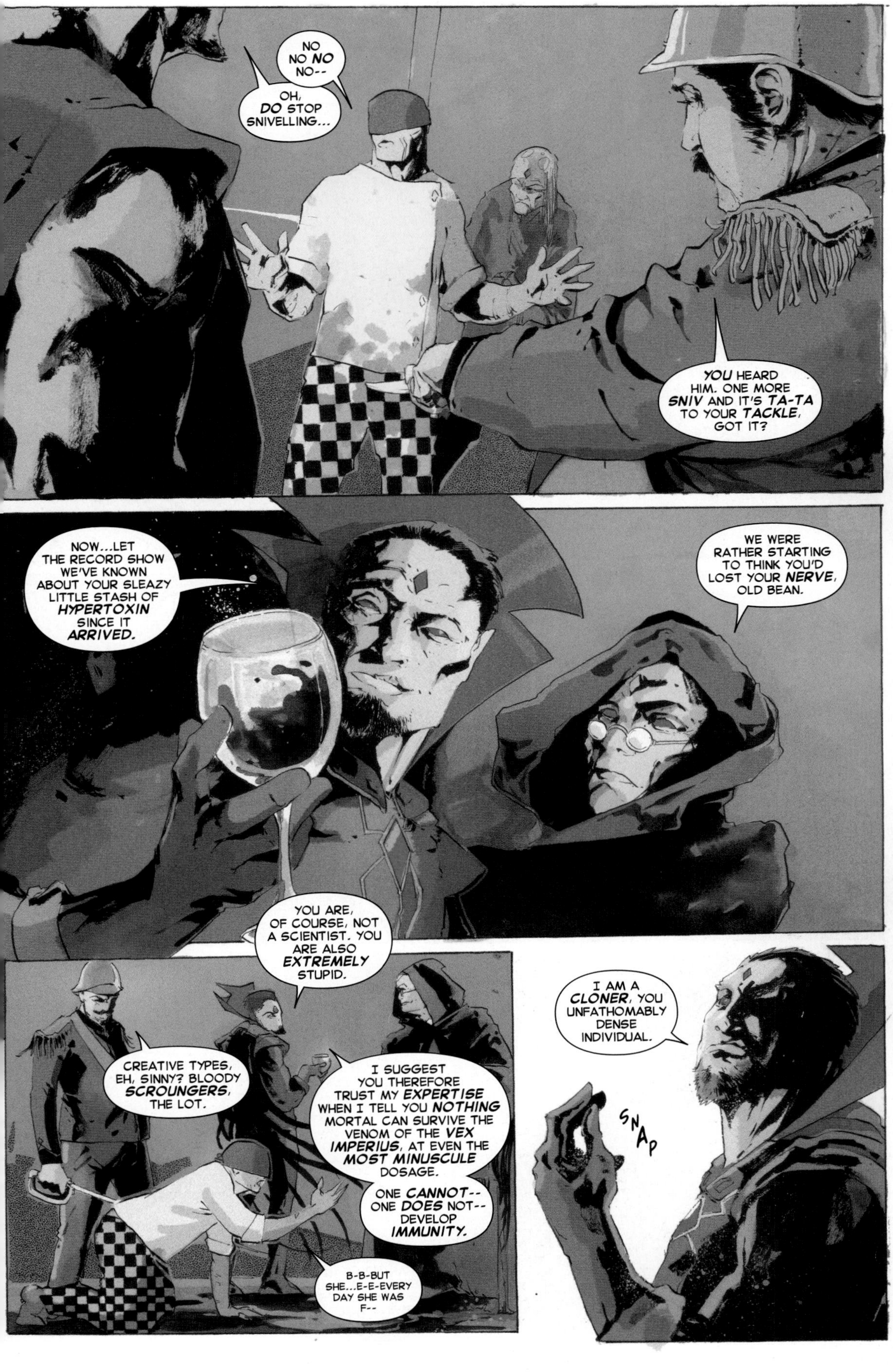
NO NO NO NO--
OH, DO STOP SNIVELLING...
YOU HEARD HIM. ONE MORE SNIV AND IT'S TA-TA TO YOUR TACKLE, GOT IT?
NOW...LET THE RECORD SHOW WE'VE KNOWN ABOUT YOUR SLEAZY LITTLE STASH OF HYPERTOXIN SINCE IT ARRIVED.
WE WERE RATHER STARTING TO THINK YOU'D LOST YOUR NERVE, OLD BEAN.
YOU ARE, OF COURSE, NOT A SCIENTIST. YOU ARE ALSO EXTREMELY STUPID.
CREATIVE TYPES, EH, SINNY? BLOODY SCROUNGERS, THE LOT.
I SUGGEST YOU THEREFORE TRUST MY EXPERTISE WHEN I TELL YOU NOTHING MORTAL CAN SURVIVE THE VENOM OF THE VEX IMPERIUS, AT EVEN THE MOST MINUSCULE DOSAGE.
ONE CANNOT-- ONE DOES NOT-- DEVELOP IMMUNITY.
B-B-BUT SHE...E-E-EVERY DAY SHE WAS F--
I AM A CLONER, YOU UNFATHOMABLY DENSE INDIVIDUAL.
SNAP

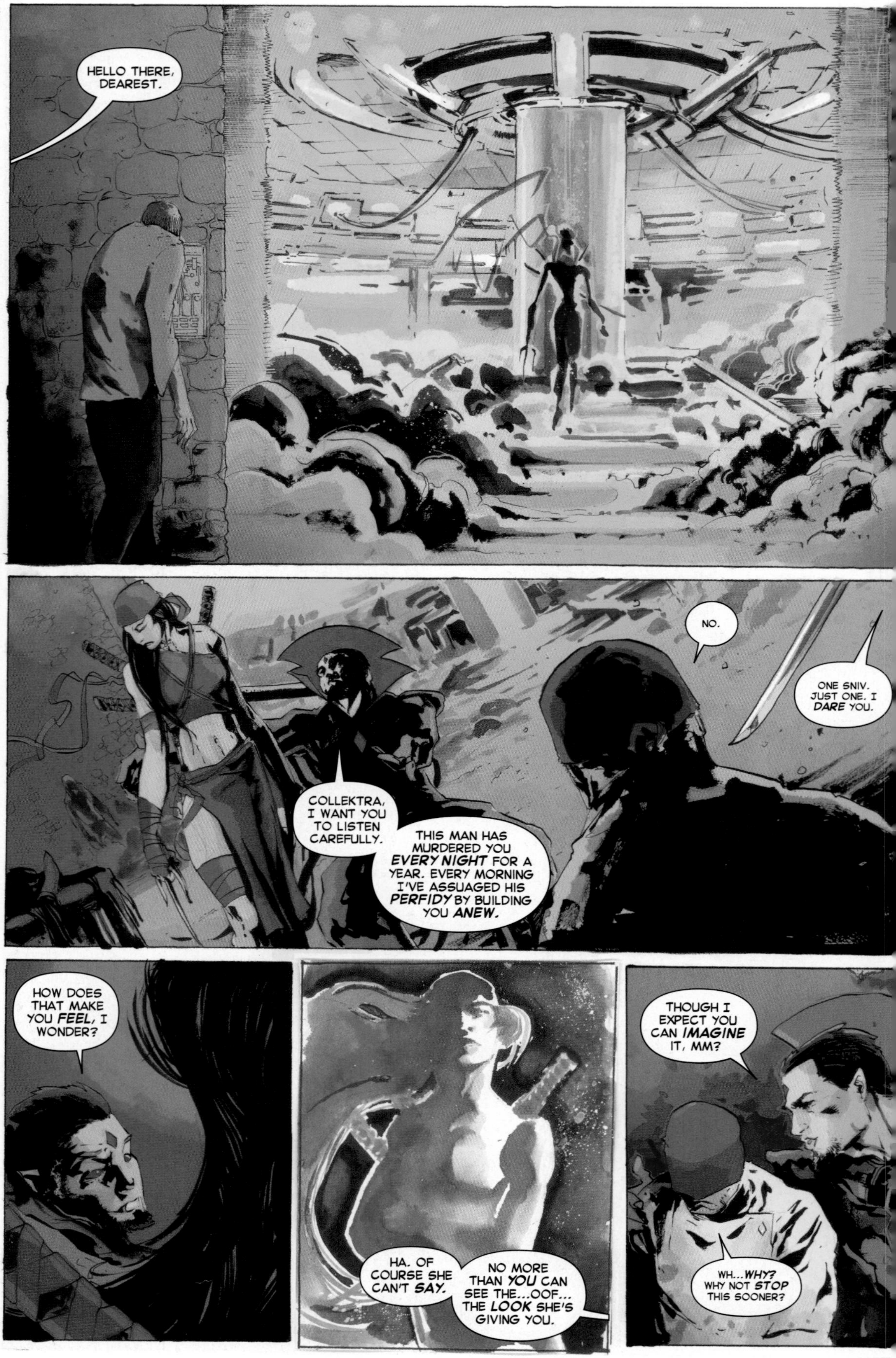
HELLO THERE, DEAREST.
NO.
ONE SNIV. JUST ONE. I DARE YOU.
COLLEKTRA, I WANT YOU TO LISTEN CAREFULLY.
THIS MAN HAS MURDERED YOU EVERY NIGHT FOR A YEAR. EVERY MORNING I'VE ASSUAGED HIS PERFIDY BY BUILDING YOU ANEW.
HOW DOES THAT MAKE YOU FEEL, I WONDER?
HA. OF COURSE SHE CAN'T SAY.
NO MORE THAN YOU CAN SEE THE...OOF... THE LOOK SHE'S GIVING YOU.
THOUGH I EXPECT YOU CAN IMAGINE IT, MM?
WH...WHY? WHY NOT STOP THIS SOONER?

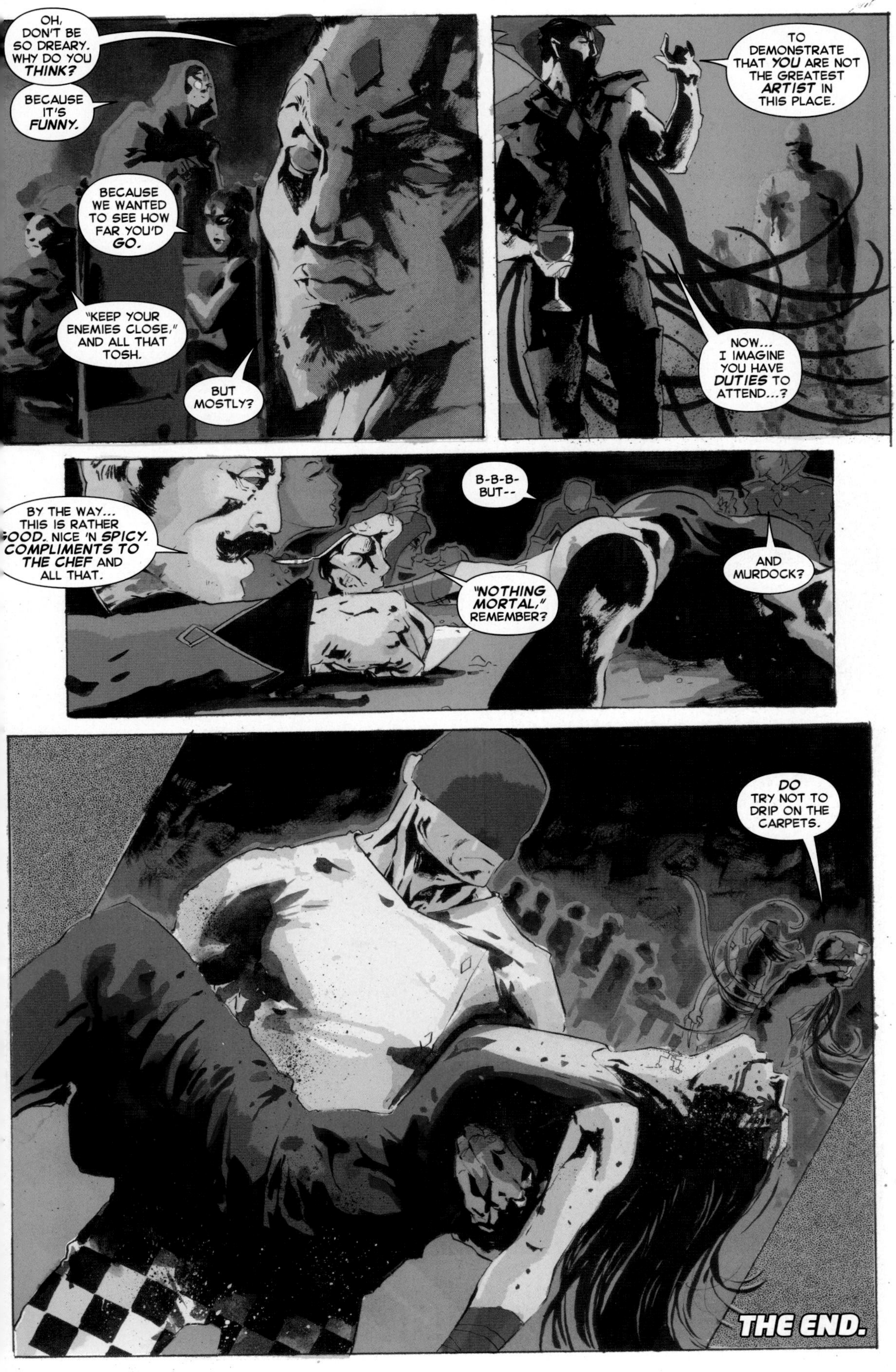
OH, DON'T BE SO DREARY. WHY DO YOU THINK?
BECAUSE IT'S FUNNY.
BECAUSE WE WANTED TO SEE HOW FAR YOU'D GO.
"KEEP YOUR ENEMIES CLOSE," AND ALL THAT TOSH.
BUT MOSTLY?
TO DEMONSTRATE THAT YOU ARE NOT THE GREATEST ARTIST IN THIS PLACE.
NOW... I IMAGINE YOU HAVE DUTIES TO ATTEND...?
BY THE WAY... THIS IS RATHER GOOD. NICE 'N SPICY. COMPLIMENTS TO THE CHEF AND ALL THAT.
B-B-B-BUT--
"NOTHING MORTAL," REMEMBER?
AND MURDOCK?
DO TRY NOT TO DRIP ON THE CARPETS.
THE END.

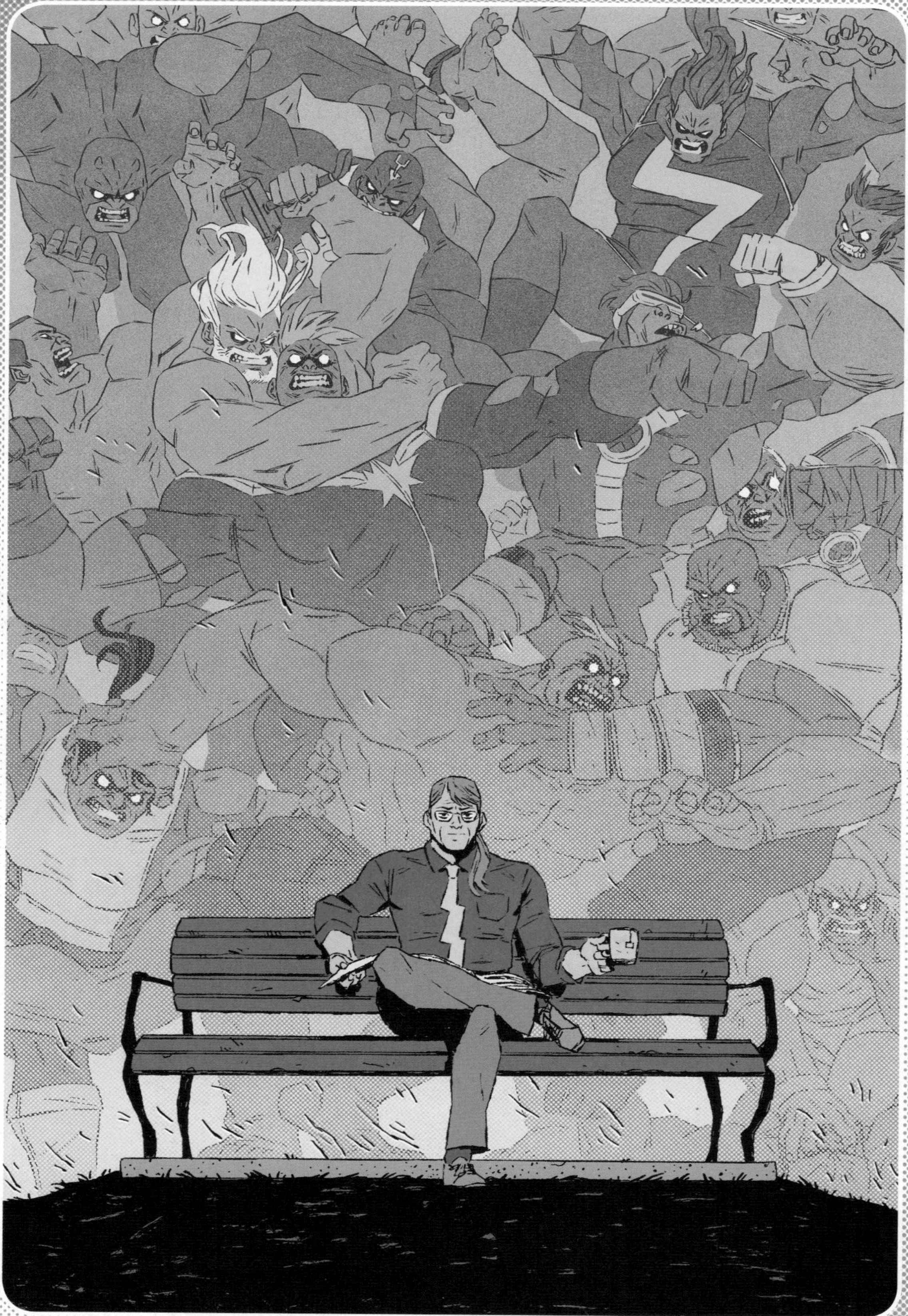

SECRET WARS JOURNAL #3

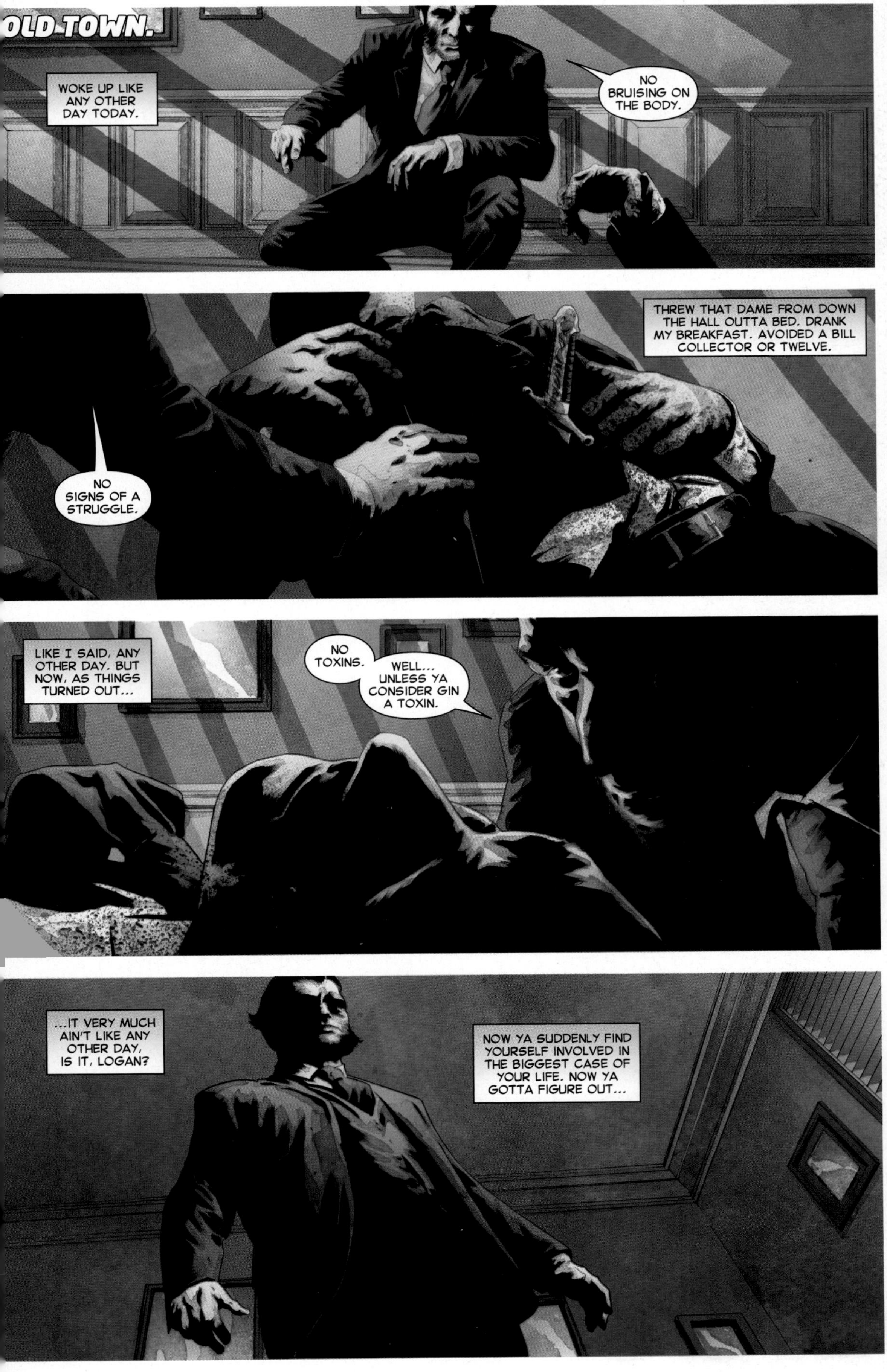
OLD TOWN.
WOKE UP LIKE ANY OTHER DAY TODAY.
NO BRUISING ON THE BODY.
THREW THAT DAME FROM DOWN THE HALL OUTTA BED. DRANK MY BREAKFAST. AVOIDED A BILL COLLECTOR OR TWELVE.
NO SIGNS OF A STRUGGLE.
LIKE I SAID, ANY OTHER DAY. BUT NOW, AS THINGS TURNED OUT...
NO TOXINS.
WELL... UNLESS YA CONSIDER GIN A TOXIN.
...IT VERY MUCH AIN'T LIKE ANY OTHER DAY, IS IT, LOGAN?
NOW YA SUDDENLY FIND YOURSELF INVOLVED IN THE BIGGEST CASE OF YOUR LIFE. NOW YA GOTTA FIGURE OUT...

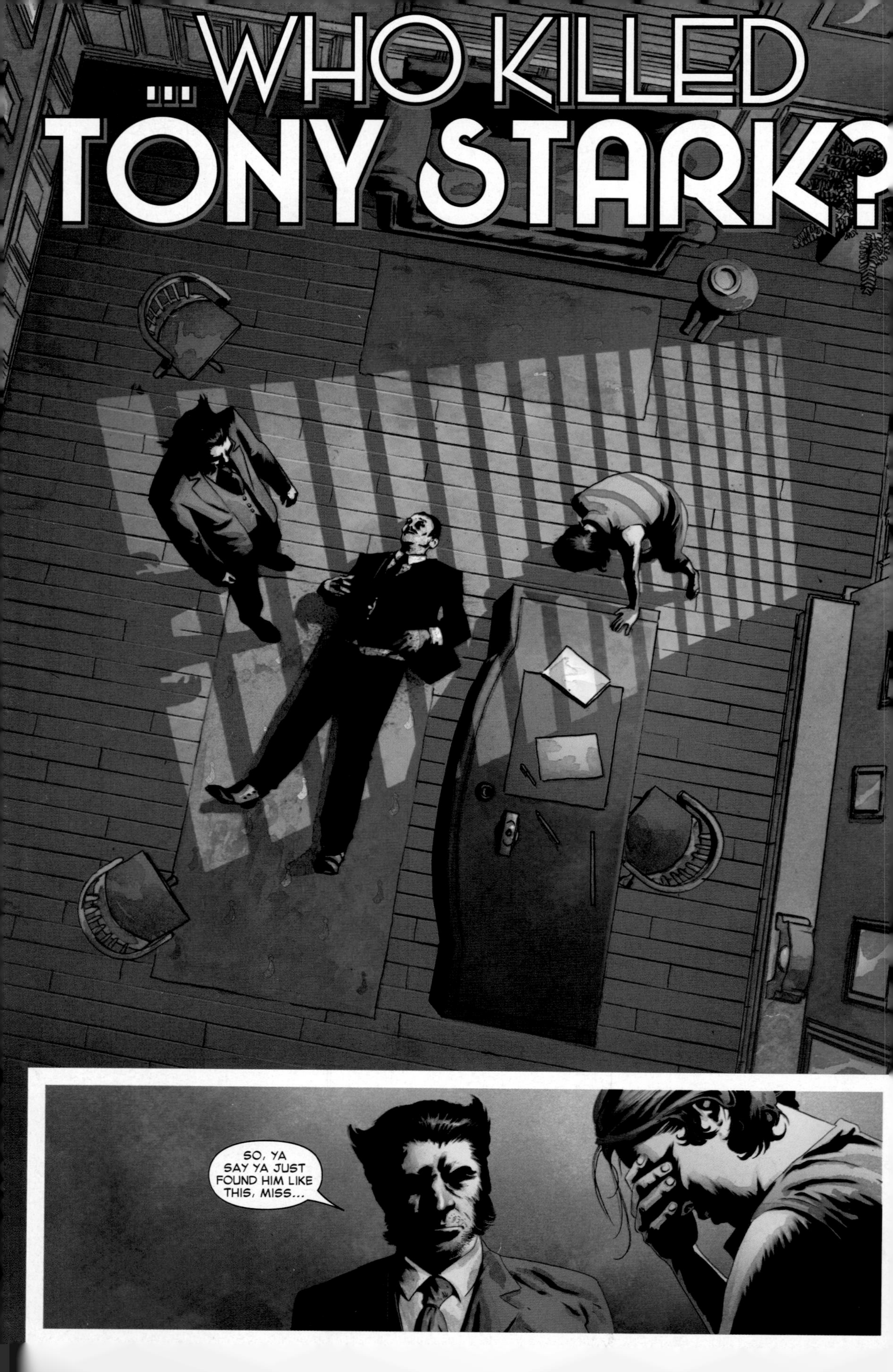
...WHO KILLED
TONY STARK?
SO, YA SAY YA JUST FOUND HIM LIKE THIS, MISS...

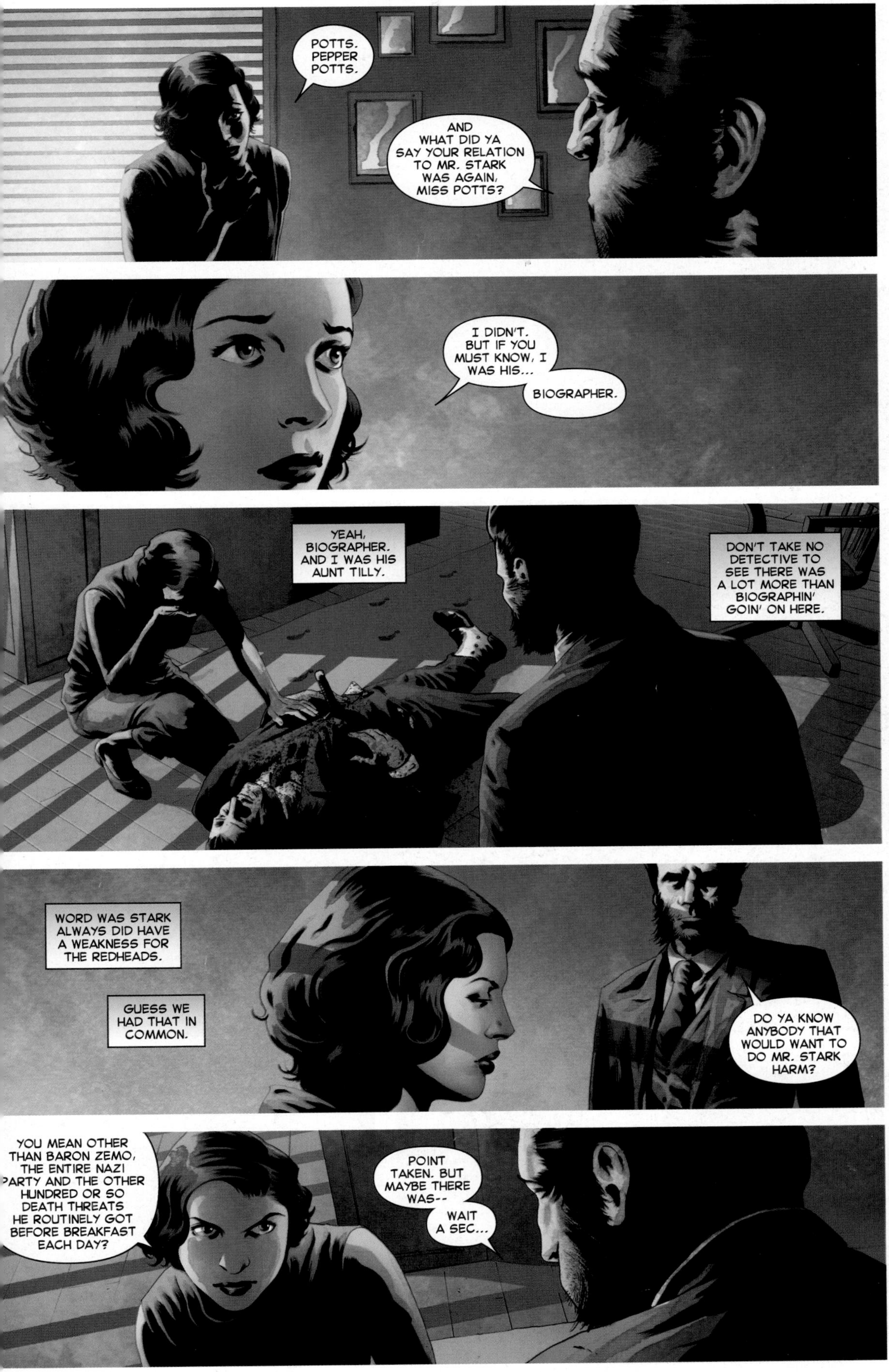
POTTS. PEPPER POTTS.
AND WHAT DID YA SAY YOUR RELATION TO MR. STARK WAS AGAIN, MISS POTTS?
I DIDN'T. BUT IF YOU MUST KNOW, I WAS HIS...
BIOGRAPHER.
YEAH, BIOGRAPHER. AND I WAS HIS AUNT TILLY.
DON'T TAKE NO DETECTIVE TO SEE THERE WAS A LOT MORE THAN BIOGRAPHIN' GOIN' ON HERE.
WORD WAS STARK ALWAYS DID HAVE A WEAKNESS FOR THE REDHEADS.
GUESS WE HAD THAT IN COMMON.
DO YA KNOW ANYBODY THAT WOULD WANT TO DO MR. STARK HARM?
YOU MEAN OTHER THAN BARON ZEMO, THE ENTIRE NAZI PARTY AND THE OTHER HUNDRED OR SO DEATH THREATS HE ROUTINELY GOT BEFORE BREAKFAST EACH DAY?
POINT TAKEN. BUT MAYBE THERE WAS--
WAIT A SEC...

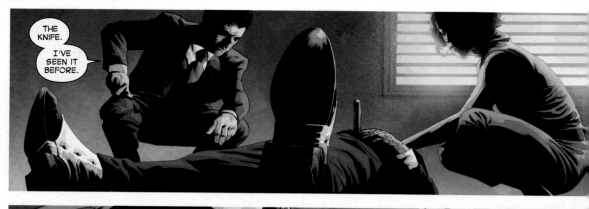

THE KNIFE.

I'VE SEEN IT BEFORE.

A CHINESE DAGGER...

THE KIND USED BY *THE MANDARIN* AND HIS TRIAD GOONS.

THE MANDARIN? TONY HAS HAD SOME ISSUES WITH HIM IN THE PAST.

PARTICULARLY A DISPUTE OVER THE FIN FANG FOOM DRAGON.

YEAH, READ 'BOUT THAT IN THE PAPERS. STARK FOUND IT ON ONE OF HIS EXPEDITIONS, RIGHT?

RIGHT. BUT THE MANDARIN CLAIMED IT BELONGED TO ONE OF HIS ANCESTORS.

TONY HID IT HERE FOR SAFE-KEEPING...

American Adventurer

AND IT'S GONE.

WHICH MEANS I GOT ME A DATE IN CHINATOWN...

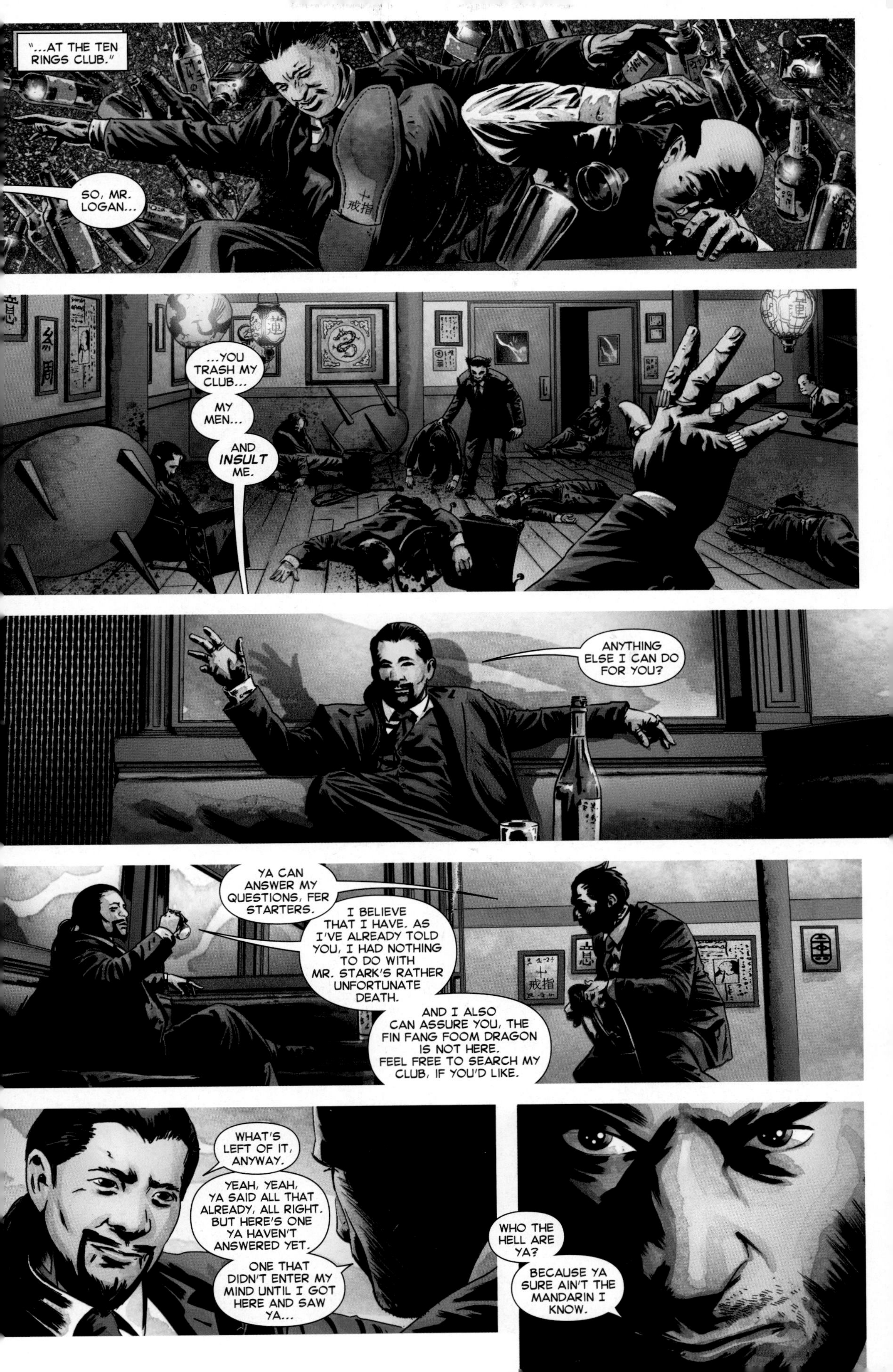
"...AT THE TEN RINGS CLUB."
SO, MR. LOGAN...
十戒指
...YOU TRASH MY CLUB...
MY MEN...
AND *INSULT* ME.
ANYTHING ELSE I CAN DO FOR YOU?
YA CAN ANSWER MY QUESTIONS, FER STARTERS.
I BELIEVE THAT I HAVE. AS I'VE ALREADY TOLD YOU, I HAD NOTHING TO DO WITH MR. STARK'S RATHER UNFORTUNATE DEATH.
AND I ALSO CAN ASSURE YOU, THE FIN FANG FOOM DRAGON IS NOT HERE. FEEL FREE TO SEARCH MY CLUB, IF YOU'D LIKE.
WHAT'S LEFT OF IT, ANYWAY.
YEAH, YEAH, YA SAID ALL THAT ALREADY, ALL RIGHT. BUT HERE'S ONE YA HAVEN'T ANSWERED YET.
ONE THAT DIDN'T ENTER MY MIND UNTIL I GOT HERE AND SAW YA...
WHO THE HELL ARE YA?
BECAUSE YA SURE AIN'T THE MANDARIN I KNOW.

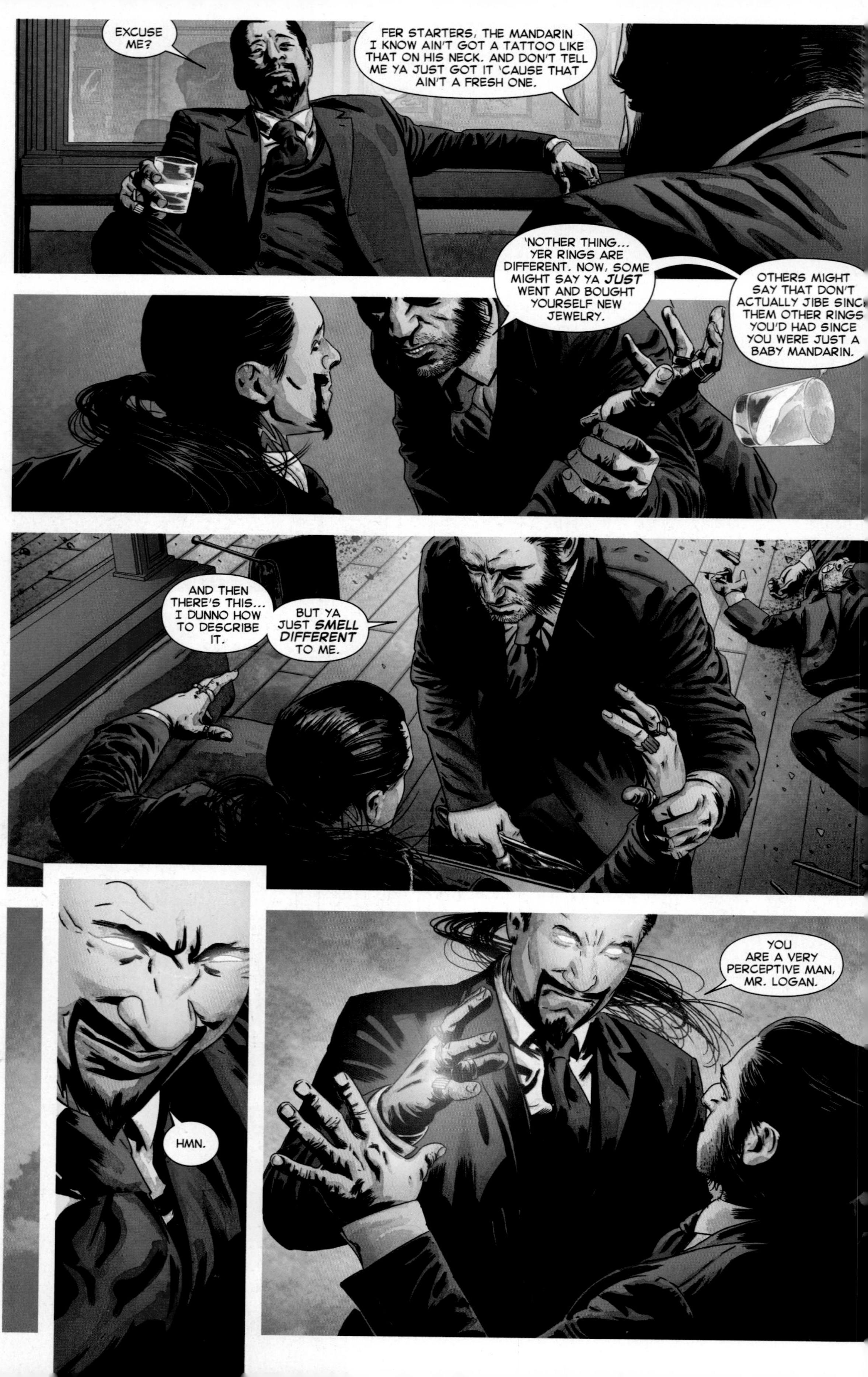
EXCUSE ME?
FER STARTERS, THE MANDARIN I KNOW AIN'T GOT A TATTOO LIKE THAT ON HIS NECK. AND DON'T TELL ME YA JUST GOT IT 'CAUSE THAT AIN'T A FRESH ONE.
'NOTHER THING... YER RINGS ARE DIFFERENT. NOW, SOME MIGHT SAY YA JUST WENT AND BOUGHT YOURSELF NEW JEWELRY.
OTHERS MIGHT SAY THAT DON'T ACTUALLY JIBE SINC THEM OTHER RINGS YOU'D HAD SINCE YOU WERE JUST A BABY MANDARIN.
AND THEN THERE'S THIS... I DUNNO HOW TO DESCRIBE IT.
BUT YA JUST SMELL DIFFERENT TO ME.
HMN.
YOU ARE A VERY PERCEPTIVE MAN, MR. LOGAN.

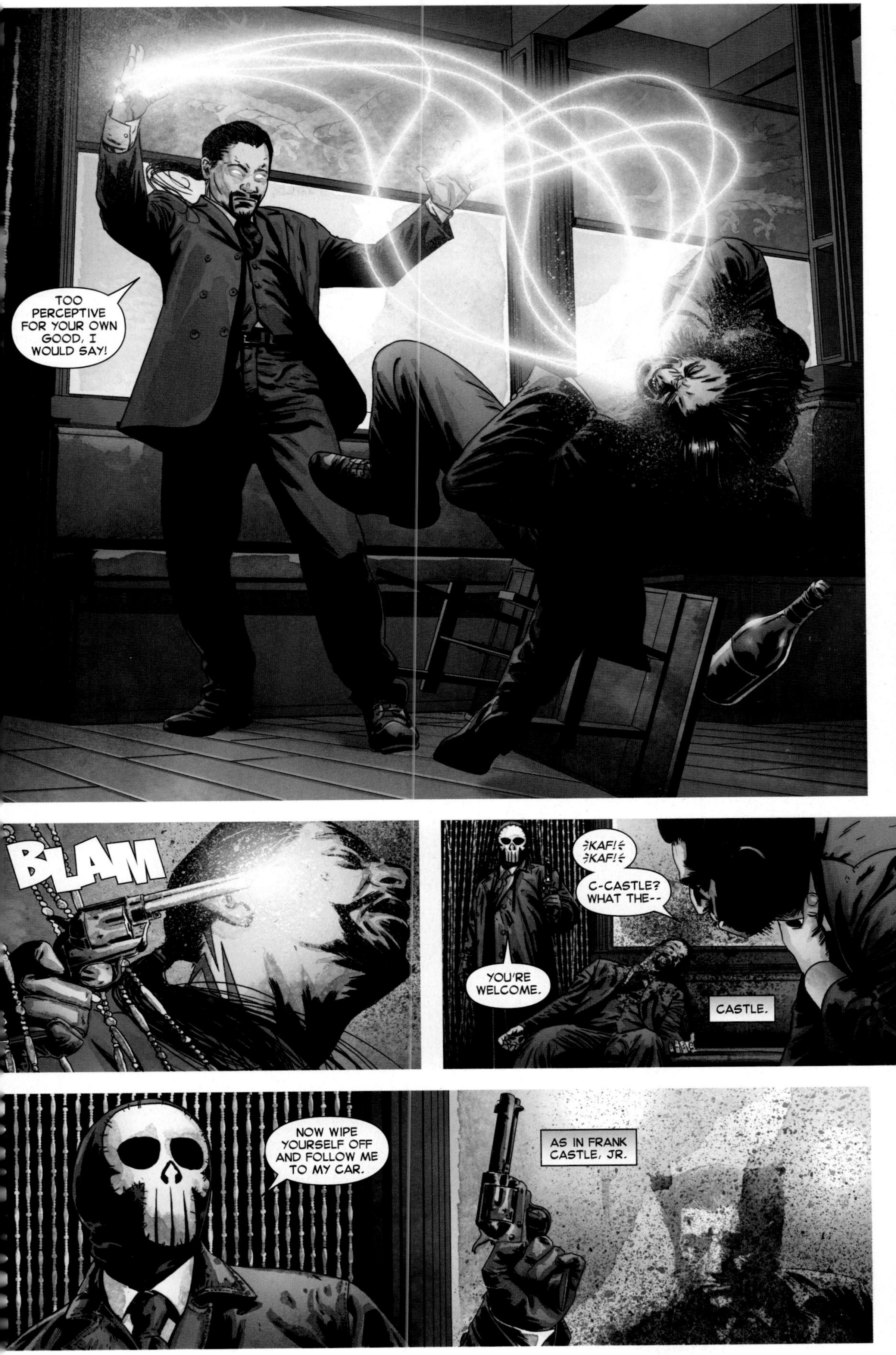
TOO PERCEPTIVE FOR YOUR OWN GOOD, I WOULD SAY!
BLAM
KAF! KAF!
C-CASTLE? WHAT THE--
YOU'RE WELCOME.
CASTLE.
NOW WIPE YOURSELF OFF AND FOLLOW ME TO MY CAR.
AS IN FRANK CASTLE, JR.

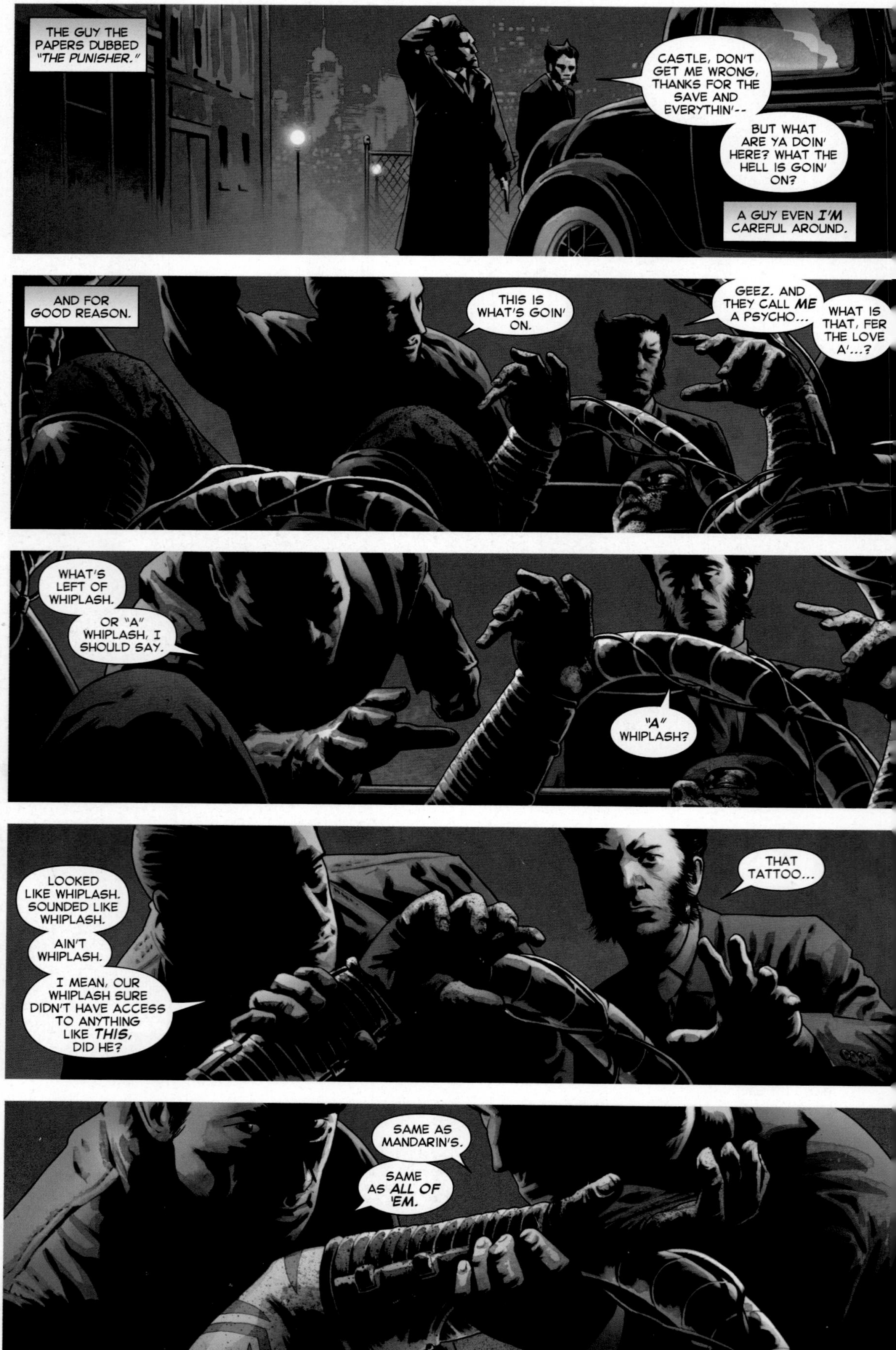
THE GUY THE PAPERS DUBBED "THE PUNISHER."
CASTLE, DON'T GET ME WRONG, THANKS FOR THE SAVE AND EVERYTHIN'--
BUT WHAT ARE YA DOIN' HERE? WHAT THE HELL IS GOIN' ON?
A GUY EVEN I'M CAREFUL AROUND.
AND FOR GOOD REASON.
THIS IS WHAT'S GOIN' ON.
GEEZ. AND THEY CALL ME A PSYCHO...
WHAT IS THAT, FER THE LOVE A'...?
WHAT'S LEFT OF WHIPLASH.
OR "A" WHIPLASH, I SHOULD SAY.
"A" WHIPLASH?
LOOKED LIKE WHIPLASH. SOUNDED LIKE WHIPLASH.
AIN'T WHIPLASH.
I MEAN, OUR WHIPLASH SURE DIDN'T HAVE ACCESS TO ANYTHING LIKE THIS, DID HE?
THAT TATTOO...
SAME AS MANDARIN'S.
SAME AS ALL OF 'EM.

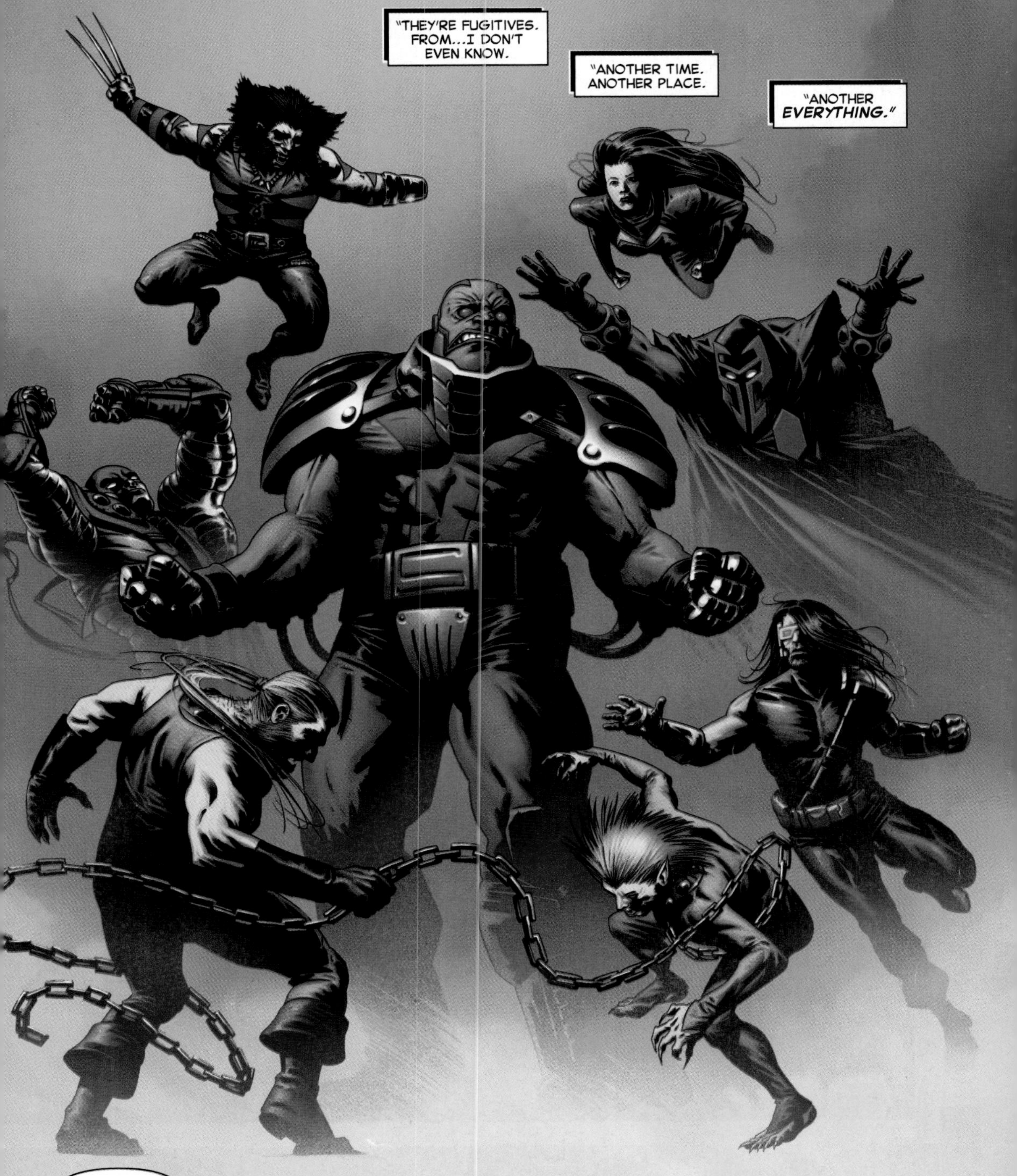
"THEY'RE FUGITIVES. FROM...I DON'T EVEN KNOW.
"ANOTHER TIME. ANOTHER PLACE.
"ANOTHER *EVERYTHING.*"

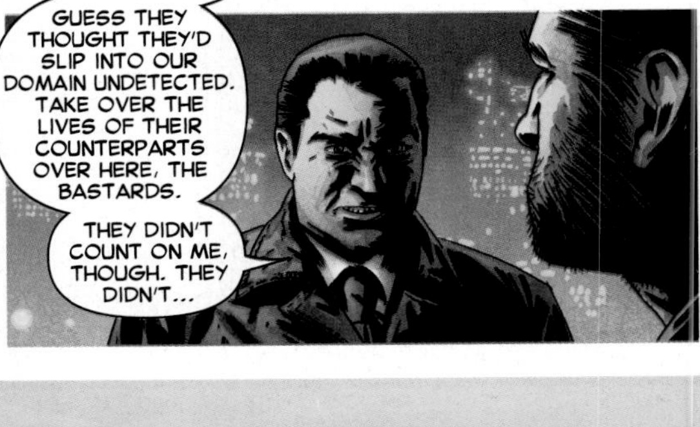
THERE WERE THREE OF 'EM. THAT MUCH I'VE BEEN ABLE TO FIGURE OUT.
GUESS THEY THOUGHT THEY'D SLIP INTO OUR DOMAIN UNDETECTED. TAKE OVER THE LIVES OF THEIR COUNTERPARTS OVER HERE, THE BASTARDS.
THEY DIDN'T COUNT ON ME, THOUGH. THEY DIDN'T...

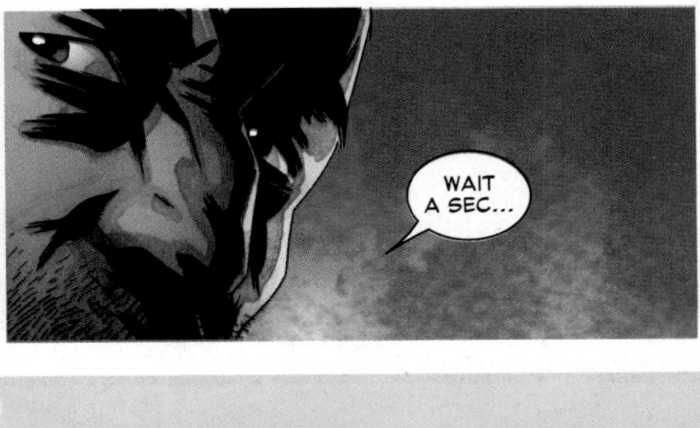
WAIT A SEC...

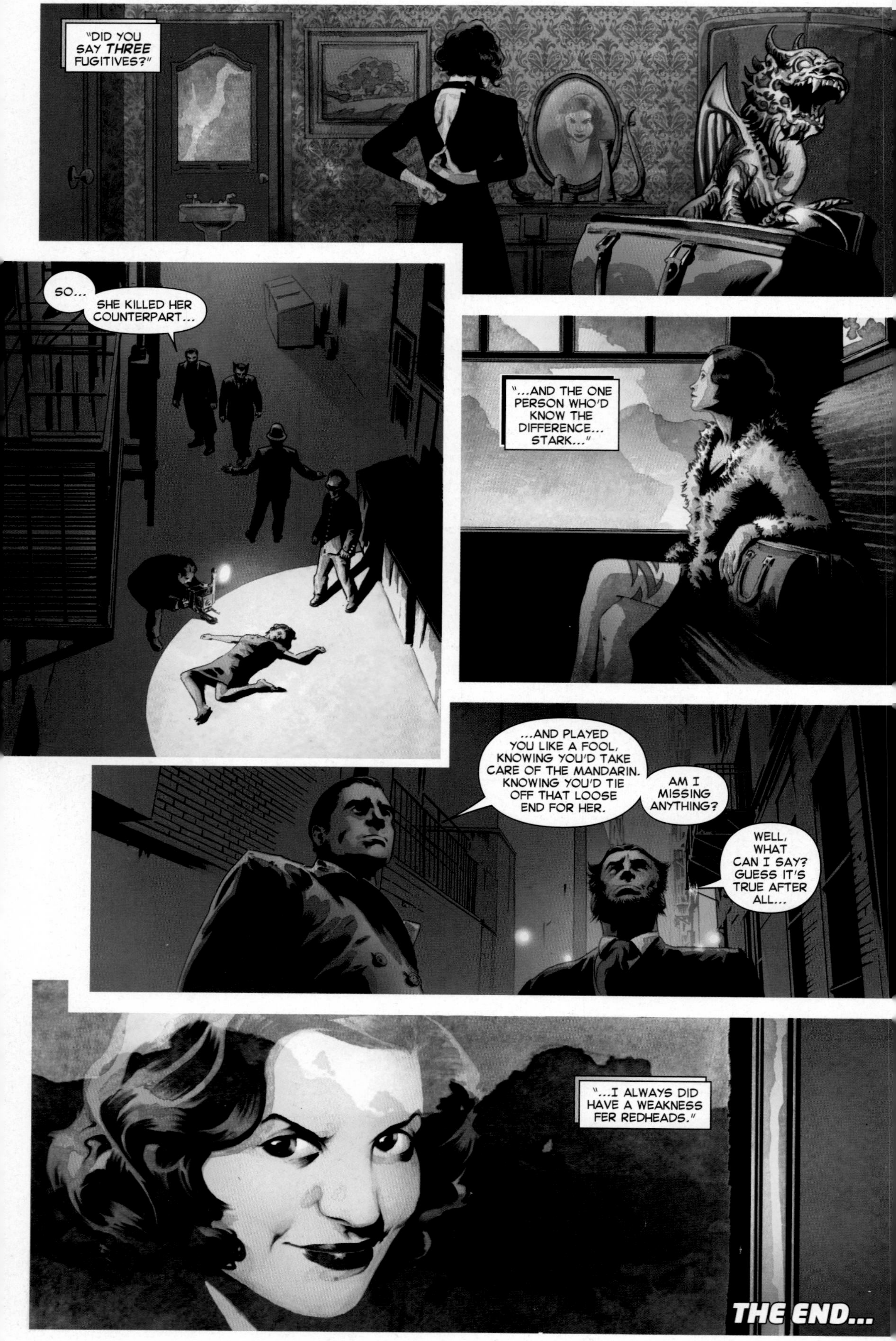
"DID YOU SAY THREE FUGITIVES?"
SO...
SHE KILLED HER COUNTERPART...
"...AND THE ONE PERSON WHO'D KNOW THE DIFFERENCE... STARK..."
...AND PLAYED YOU LIKE A FOOL, KNOWING YOU'D TAKE CARE OF THE MANDARIN. KNOWING YOU'D TIE OFF THAT LOOSE END FOR HER.
AM I MISSING ANYTHING?
WELL, WHAT CAN I SAY? GUESS IT'S TRUE AFTER ALL...
"...I ALWAYS DID HAVE A WEAKNESS FER REDHEADS."
THE END...

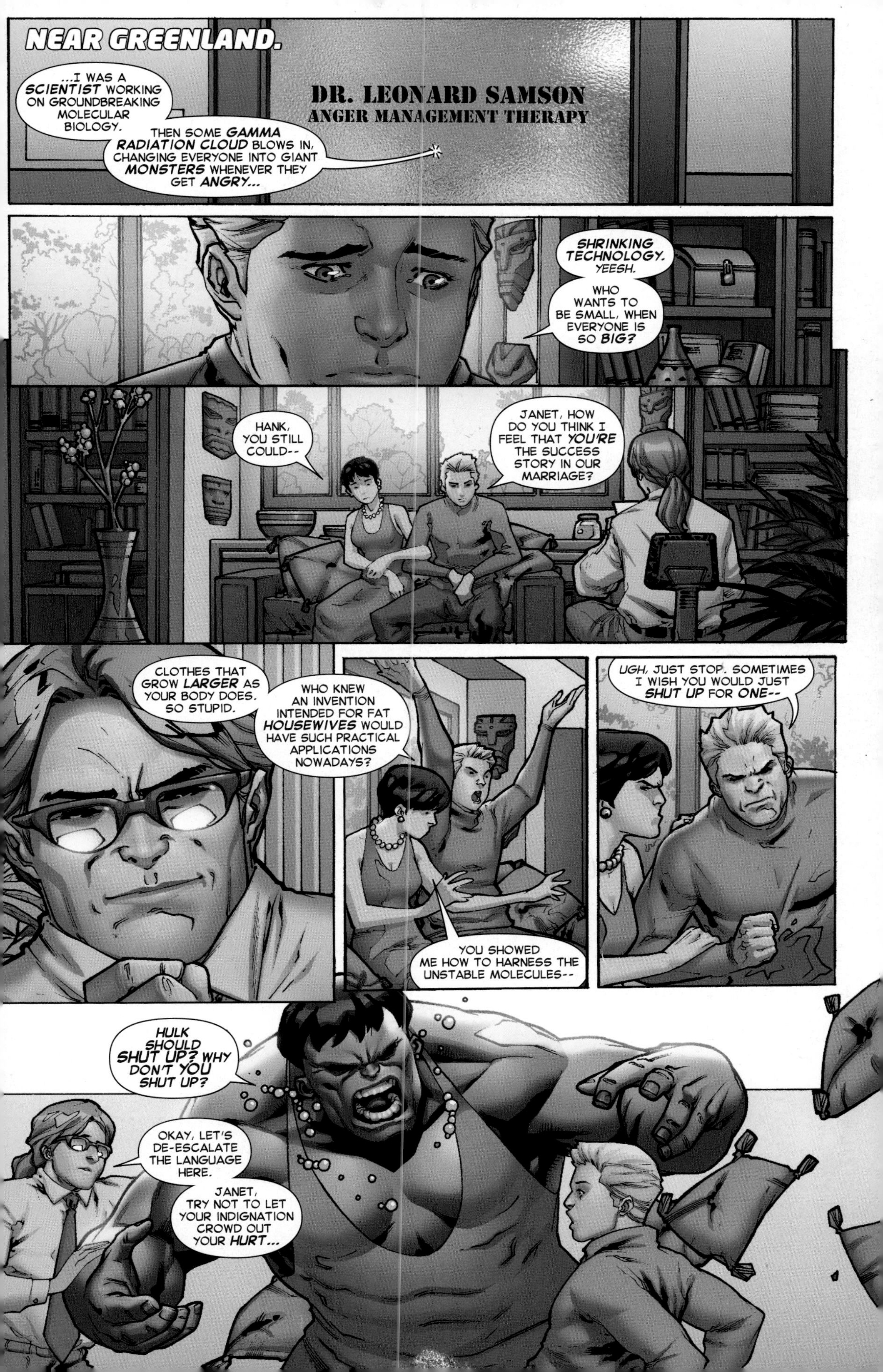
NEAR GREENLAND.
...I WAS A SCIENTIST WORKING ON GROUNDBREAKING MOLECULAR BIOLOGY.
THEN SOME GAMMA RADIATION CLOUD BLOWS IN, CHANGING EVERYONE INTO GIANT MONSTERS WHENEVER THEY GET ANGRY...
DR. LEONARD SAMSON
ANGER MANAGEMENT THERAPY
SHRINKING TECHNOLOGY. YEESH.
WHO WANTS TO BE SMALL, WHEN EVERYONE IS SO BIG?
HANK, YOU STILL COULD--
JANET, HOW DO YOU THINK I FEEL THAT YOU'RE THE SUCCESS STORY IN OUR MARRIAGE?
CLOTHES THAT GROW LARGER AS YOUR BODY DOES. SO STUPID.
WHO KNEW AN INVENTION INTENDED FOR FAT HOUSEWIVES WOULD HAVE SUCH PRACTICAL APPLICATIONS NOWADAYS?
YOU SHOWED ME HOW TO HARNESS THE UNSTABLE MOLECULES--
UGH, JUST STOP. SOMETIMES I WISH YOU WOULD JUST SHUT UP FOR ONE--
HULK SHOULD SHUT UP? WHY DON'T YOU SHUT UP?
OKAY, LET'S DE-ESCALATE THE LANGUAGE HERE.
JANET, TRY NOT TO LET YOUR INDIGNATION CROWD OUT YOUR HURT...

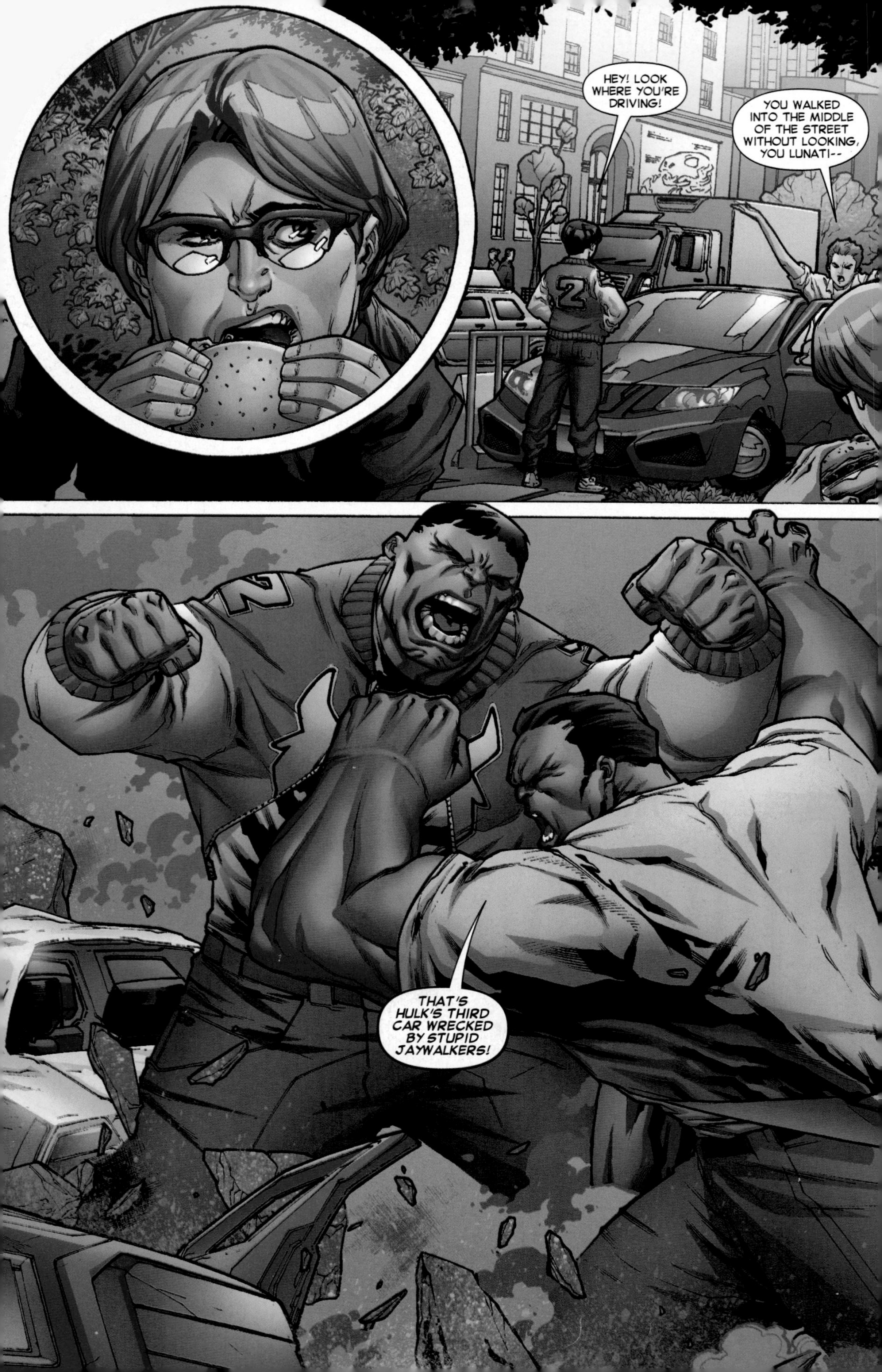
HEY! LOOK WHERE YOU'RE DRIVING!
YOU WALKED INTO THE MIDDLE OF THE STREET WITHOUT LOOKING, YOU LUNATI--
THAT'S HULK'S THIRD CAR WRECKED BY STUPID JAYWALKERS!

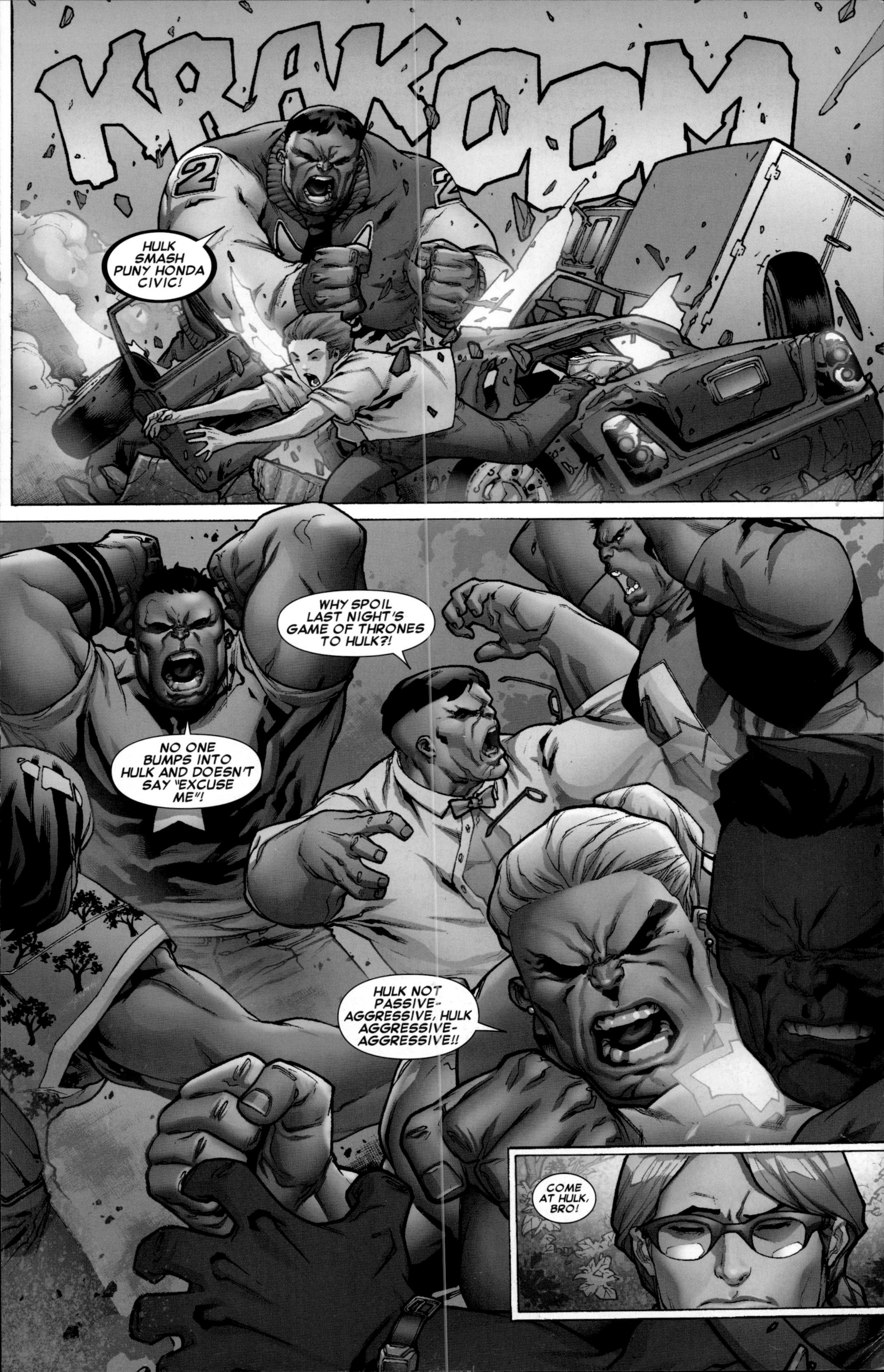KRAKOOM
HULK SMASH PUNY HONDA CIVIC!
WHY SPOIL LAST NIGHT'S GAME OF THRONES TO HULK?!
NO ONE BUMPS INTO HULK AND DOESN'T SAY "EXCUSE ME"!
HULK NOT PASSIVE-AGGRESSIVE, HULK AGGRESSIVE-AGGRESSIVE!!
COME AT HULK, BRO!

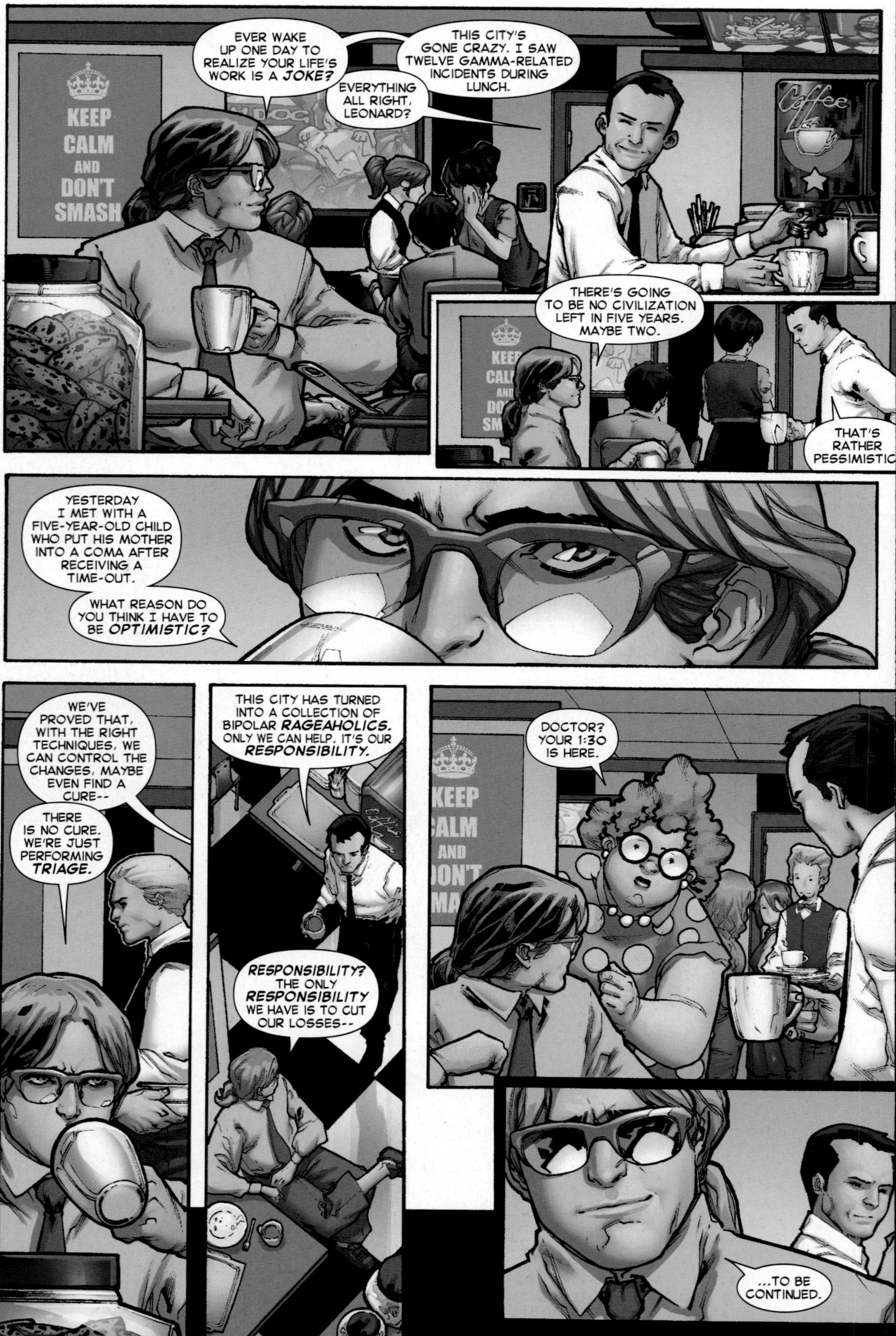
EVER WAKE UP ONE DAY TO REALIZE YOUR LIFE'S WORK IS A JOKE?
THIS CITY'S GONE CRAZY. I SAW TWELVE GAMMA-RELATED INCIDENTS DURING LUNCH.
EVERYTHING ALL RIGHT, LEONARD?
KEEP CALM AND DON'T SMASH
THERE'S GOING TO BE NO CIVILIZATION LEFT IN FIVE YEARS. MAYBE TWO.
THAT'S RATHER PESSIMISTIC
YESTERDAY I MET WITH A FIVE-YEAR-OLD CHILD WHO PUT HIS MOTHER INTO A COMA AFTER RECEIVING A TIME-OUT.
WHAT REASON DO YOU THINK I HAVE TO BE OPTIMISTIC?
WE'VE PROVED THAT, WITH THE RIGHT TECHNIQUES, WE CAN CONTROL THE CHANGES, MAYBE EVEN FIND A CURE--
THERE IS NO CURE. WE'RE JUST PERFORMING TRIAGE.
THIS CITY HAS TURNED INTO A COLLECTION OF BIPOLAR RAGEAHOLICS. ONLY WE CAN HELP. IT'S OUR RESPONSIBILITY.
RESPONSIBILITY? THE ONLY RESPONSIBILITY WE HAVE IS TO CUT OUR LOSSES--
DOCTOR? YOUR 1:30 IS HERE.
...TO BE CONTINUED.

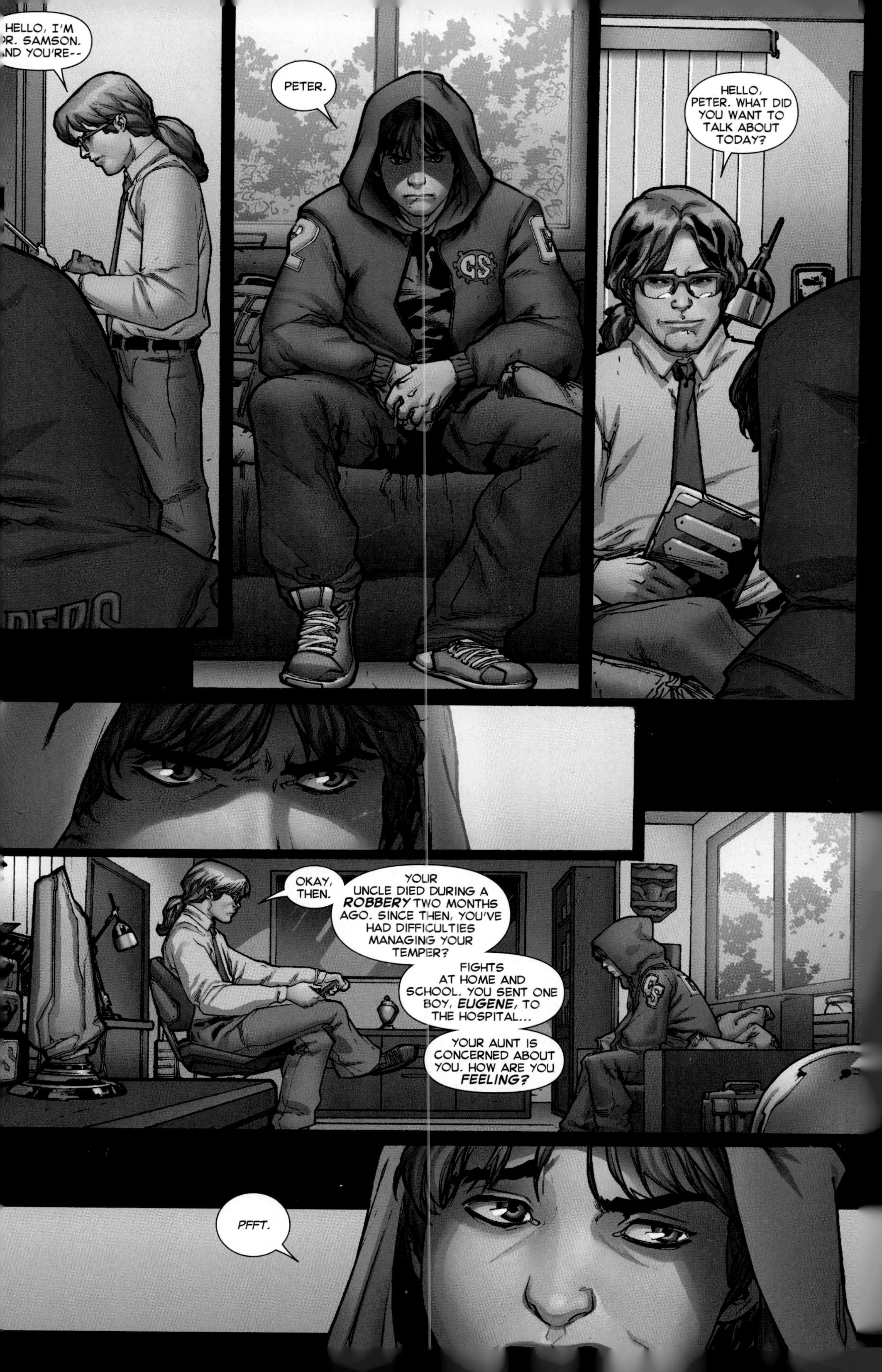
HELLO, I'M
R. SAMSON.
ND YOU'RE--
PETER.
HELLO, PETER. WHAT DID YOU WANT TO TALK ABOUT TODAY?
OKAY, THEN.
YOUR UNCLE DIED DURING A ROBBERY TWO MONTHS AGO. SINCE THEN, YOU'VE HAD DIFFICULTIES MANAGING YOUR TEMPER?
FIGHTS AT HOME AND SCHOOL. YOU SENT ONE BOY, EUGENE, TO THE HOSPITAL...
YOUR AUNT IS CONCERNED ABOUT YOU. HOW ARE YOU FEELING?
PFFT.

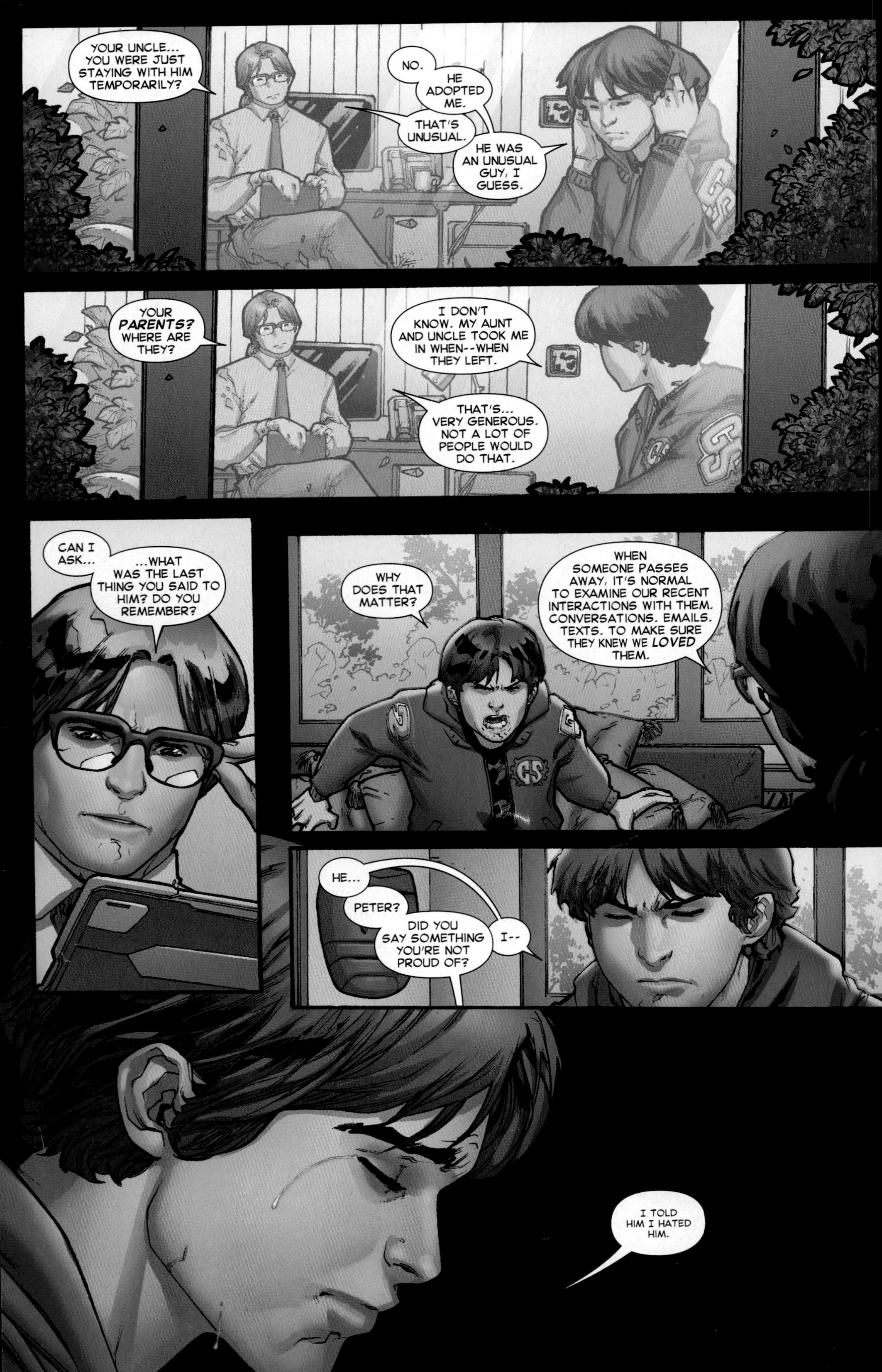
YOUR UNCLE... YOU WERE JUST STAYING WITH HIM TEMPORARILY?
NO.
HE ADOPTED ME.
THAT'S UNUSUAL.
HE WAS AN UNUSUAL GUY, I GUESS.
YOUR *PARENTS?* WHERE ARE THEY?
I DON'T KNOW. MY AUNT AND UNCLE TOOK ME IN WHEN--WHEN THEY LEFT.
THAT'S... VERY GENEROUS. NOT A LOT OF PEOPLE WOULD DO THAT.
CAN I ASK...
...WHAT WAS THE LAST THING YOU SAID TO HIM? DO YOU REMEMBER?
WHY DOES THAT MATTER?
WHEN SOMEONE PASSES AWAY, IT'S NORMAL TO EXAMINE OUR RECENT INTERACTIONS WITH THEM. CONVERSATIONS. EMAILS. TEXTS. TO MAKE SURE THEY KNEW WE *LOVED* THEM.
HE...
PETER?
DID YOU SAY SOMETHING YOU'RE NOT PROUD OF?
I--
I TOLD HIM I HATED HIM.

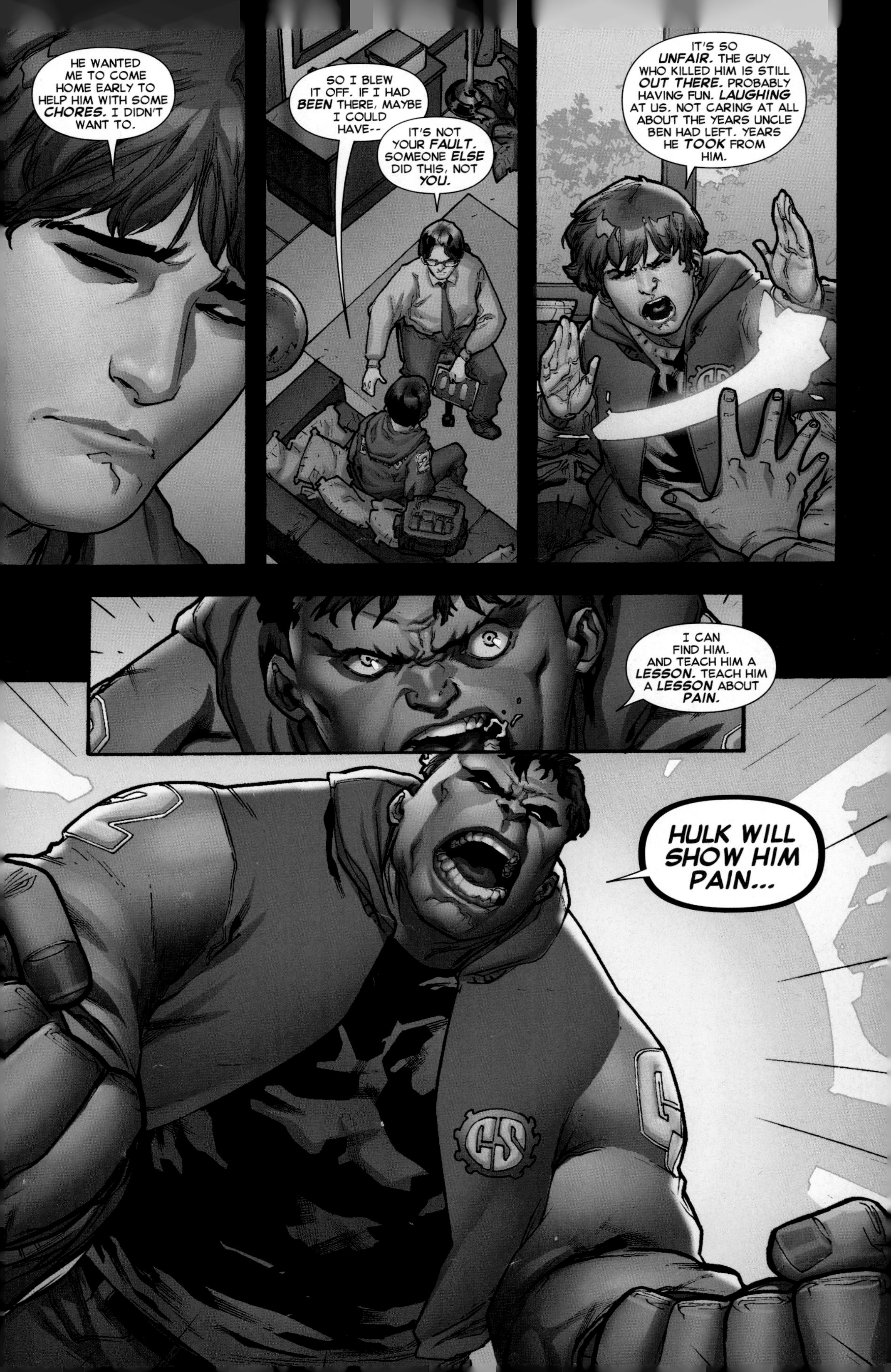
HE WANTED ME TO COME HOME EARLY TO HELP HIM WITH SOME CHORES. I DIDN'T WANT TO.
SO I BLEW IT OFF. IF I HAD BEEN THERE, MAYBE I COULD HAVE--
IT'S NOT YOUR FAULT. SOMEONE ELSE DID THIS, NOT YOU.
IT'S SO UNFAIR. THE GUY WHO KILLED HIM IS STILL OUT THERE. PROBABLY HAVING FUN. LAUGHING AT US. NOT CARING AT ALL ABOUT THE YEARS UNCLE BEN HAD LEFT. YEARS HE TOOK FROM HIM.
I CAN FIND HIM. AND TEACH HIM A LESSON. TEACH HIM A LESSON ABOUT PAIN.
HULK WILL SHOW HIM PAIN...

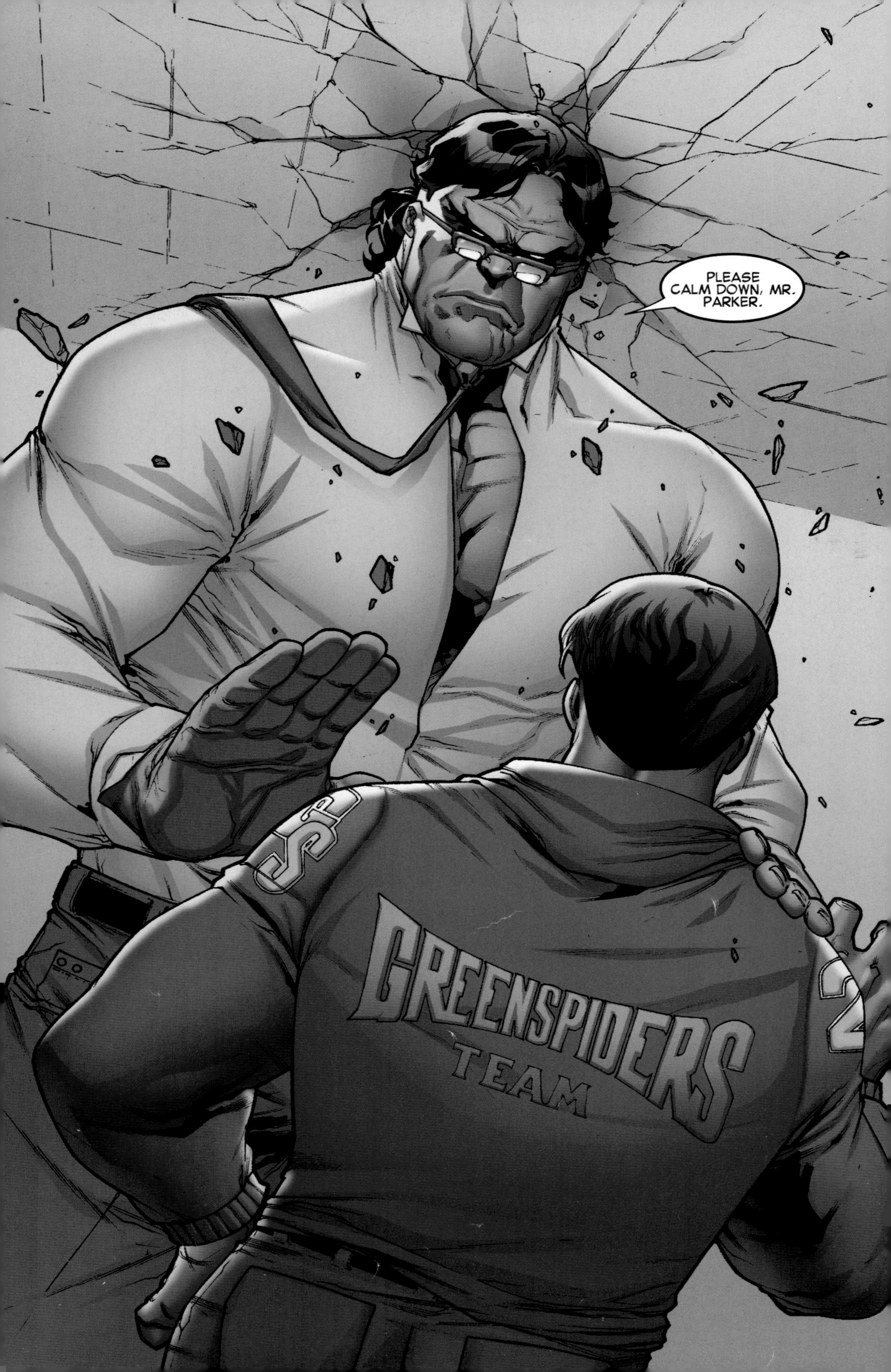
PLEASE CALM DOWN, MR. PARKER.
GREENSPIDERS
TEAM

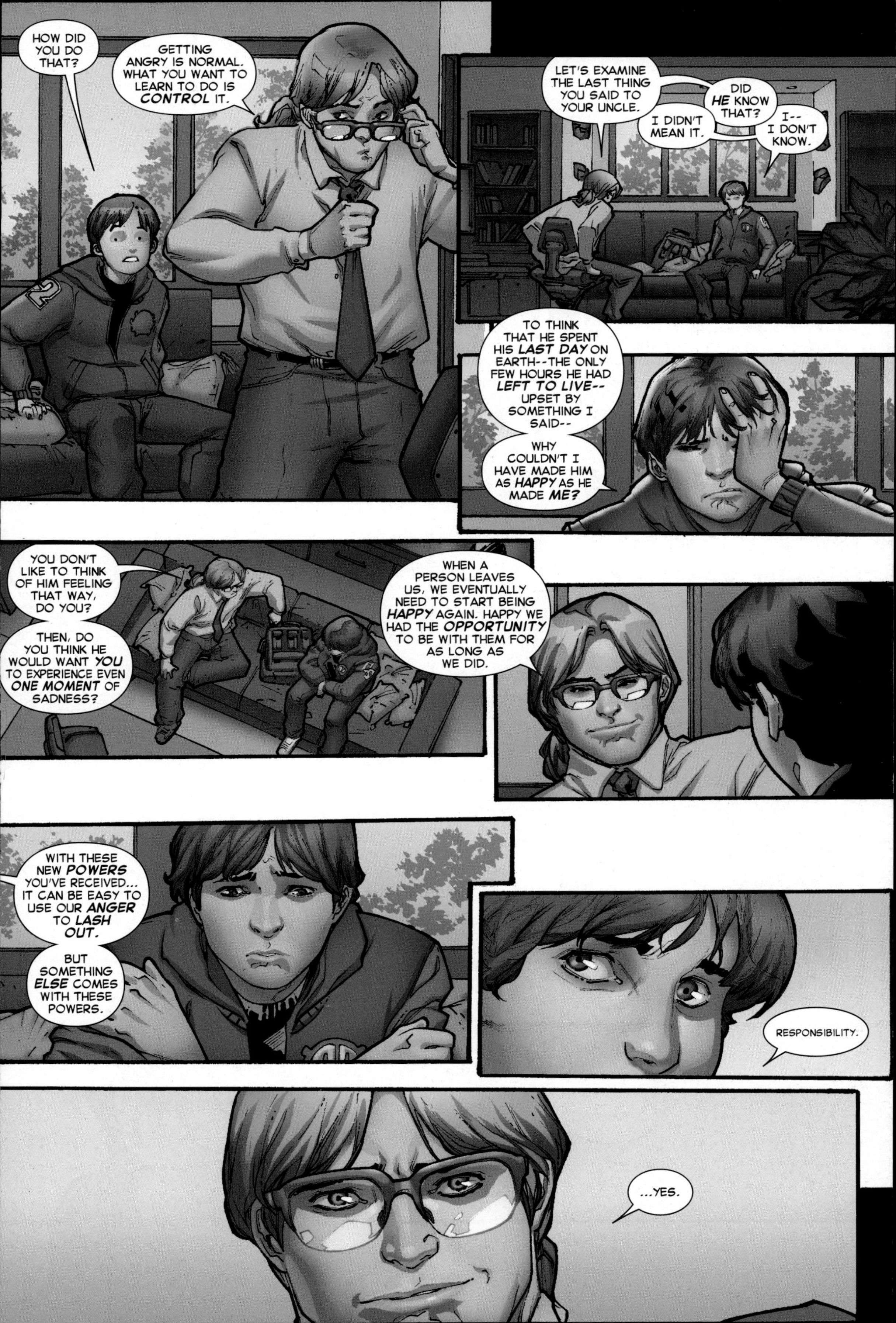
HOW DID YOU DO THAT?
GETTING ANGRY IS NORMAL. WHAT YOU WANT TO LEARN TO DO IS CONTROL IT.
LET'S EXAMINE THE LAST THING YOU SAID TO YOUR UNCLE.
I DIDN'T MEAN IT.
DID HE KNOW THAT?
I-- I DON'T KNOW.
TO THINK THAT HE SPENT HIS LAST DAY ON EARTH--THE ONLY FEW HOURS HE HAD LEFT TO LIVE-- UPSET BY SOMETHING I SAID--
WHY COULDN'T I HAVE MADE HIM AS HAPPY AS HE MADE ME?
YOU DON'T LIKE TO THINK OF HIM FEELING THAT WAY, DO YOU?
THEN, DO YOU THINK HE WOULD WANT YOU TO EXPERIENCE EVEN ONE MOMENT OF SADNESS?
WHEN A PERSON LEAVES US, WE EVENTUALLY NEED TO START BEING HAPPY AGAIN. HAPPY WE HAD THE OPPORTUNITY TO BE WITH THEM FOR AS LONG AS WE DID.
WITH THESE NEW POWERS YOU'VE RECEIVED... IT CAN BE EASY TO USE OUR ANGER TO LASH OUT.
BUT SOMETHING ELSE COMES WITH THESE POWERS.
RESPONSIBILITY.
...YES.

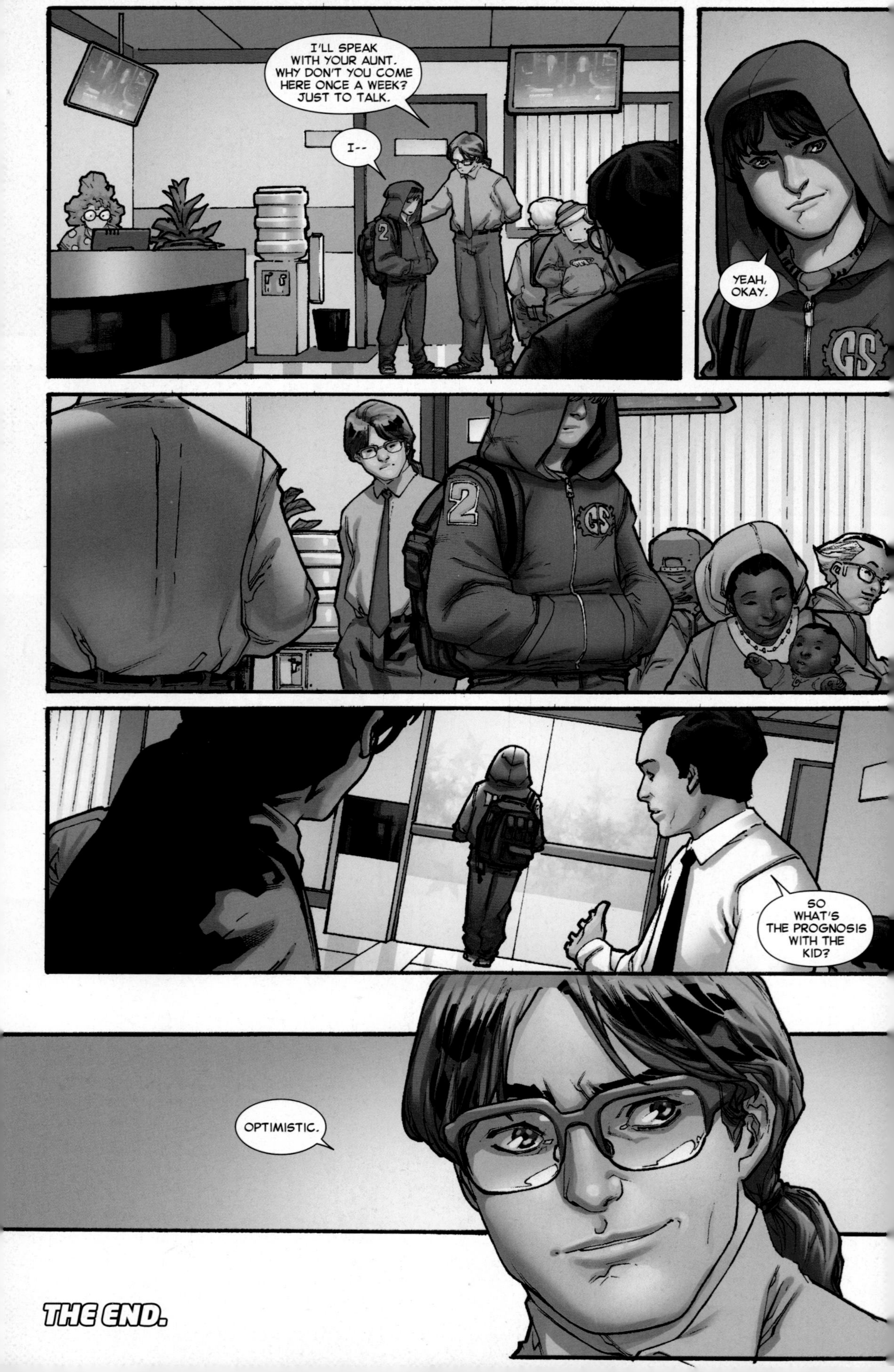
I'LL SPEAK WITH YOUR AUNT. WHY DON'T YOU COME HERE ONCE A WEEK? JUST TO TALK.
I--
YEAH, OKAY.
SO WHAT'S THE PROGNOSIS WITH THE KID?
OPTIMISTIC.
THE END.

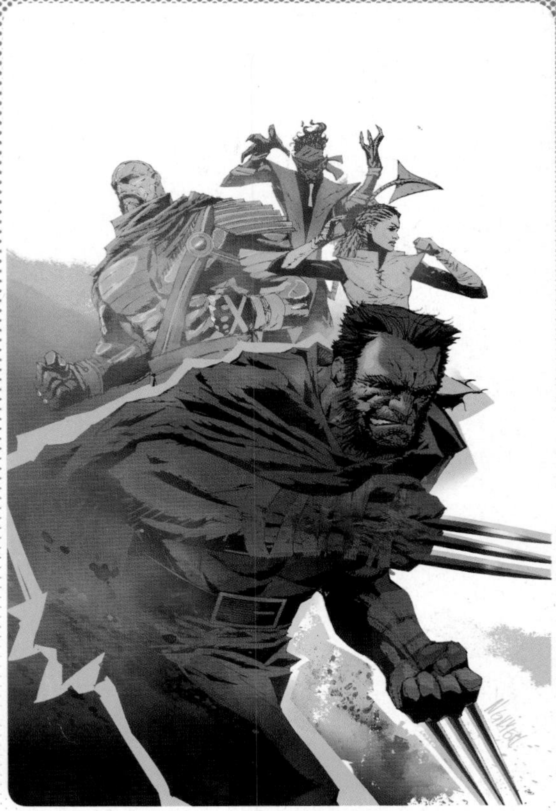

SECRET WARS JOURNAL #1
VARIANT BY ERIC NGUYEN

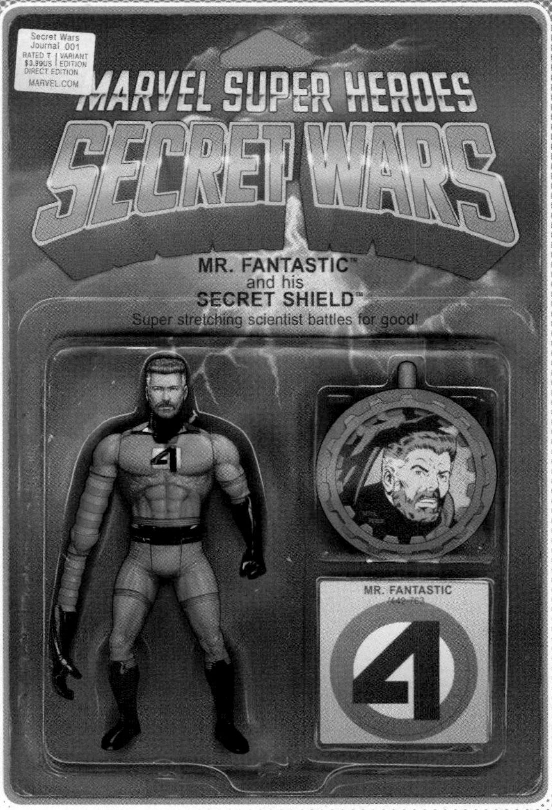
Secret Wars
Journal 001
RATED T | VARIANT
$3.99US | EDITION
DIRECT EDITION
MARVEL.COM
MARVEL SUPER HEROES
SECRET WARS
MR. FANTASTIC™
and his
SECRET SHIELD™
Super stretching scientist battles for good!
MR. FANTASTIC

SECRET WARS JOURNAL #1 ACTION FIGURE
VARIANT BY JOHN TYLER CHRISTOPHER

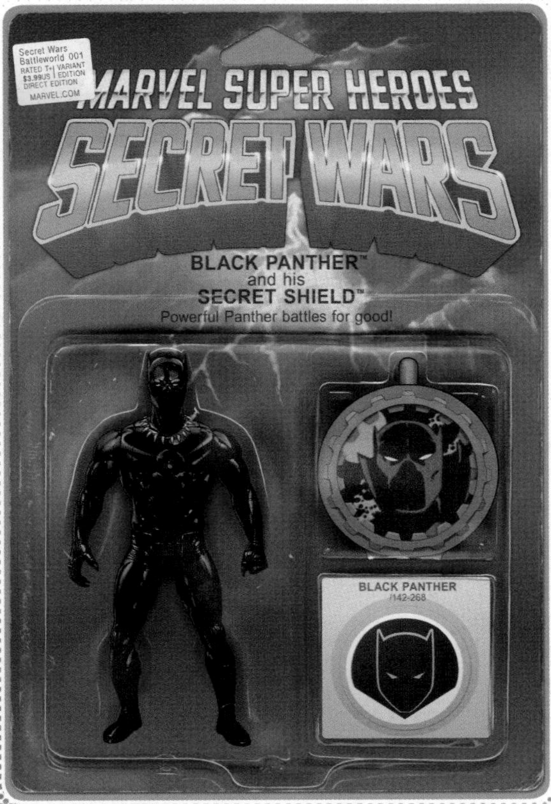
Secret Wars
Battleworld 001
RATED T+ | VARIANT
$3.99US | EDITION
DIRECT EDITION
MARVEL.COM
MARVEL SUPER HEROES
SECRET WARS
BLACK PANTHER™
and his
SECRET SHIELD™
Powerful Panther battles for good!
BLACK PANTHER
/142-268

SECRET WARS: BATTLEWORLD #1 ACTION FIGURE
VARIANT BY JOHN TYLER CHRISTOPHER

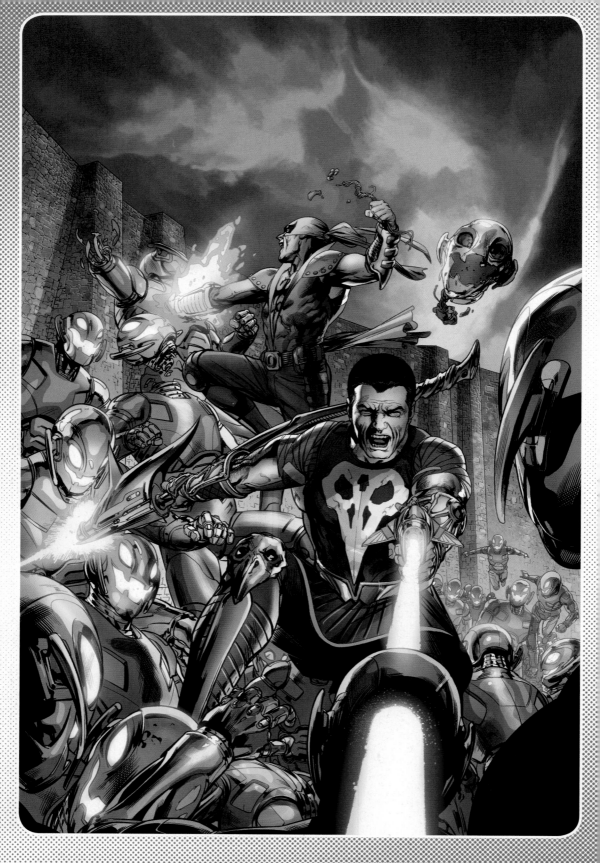

SECRET WARS JOURNAL #4

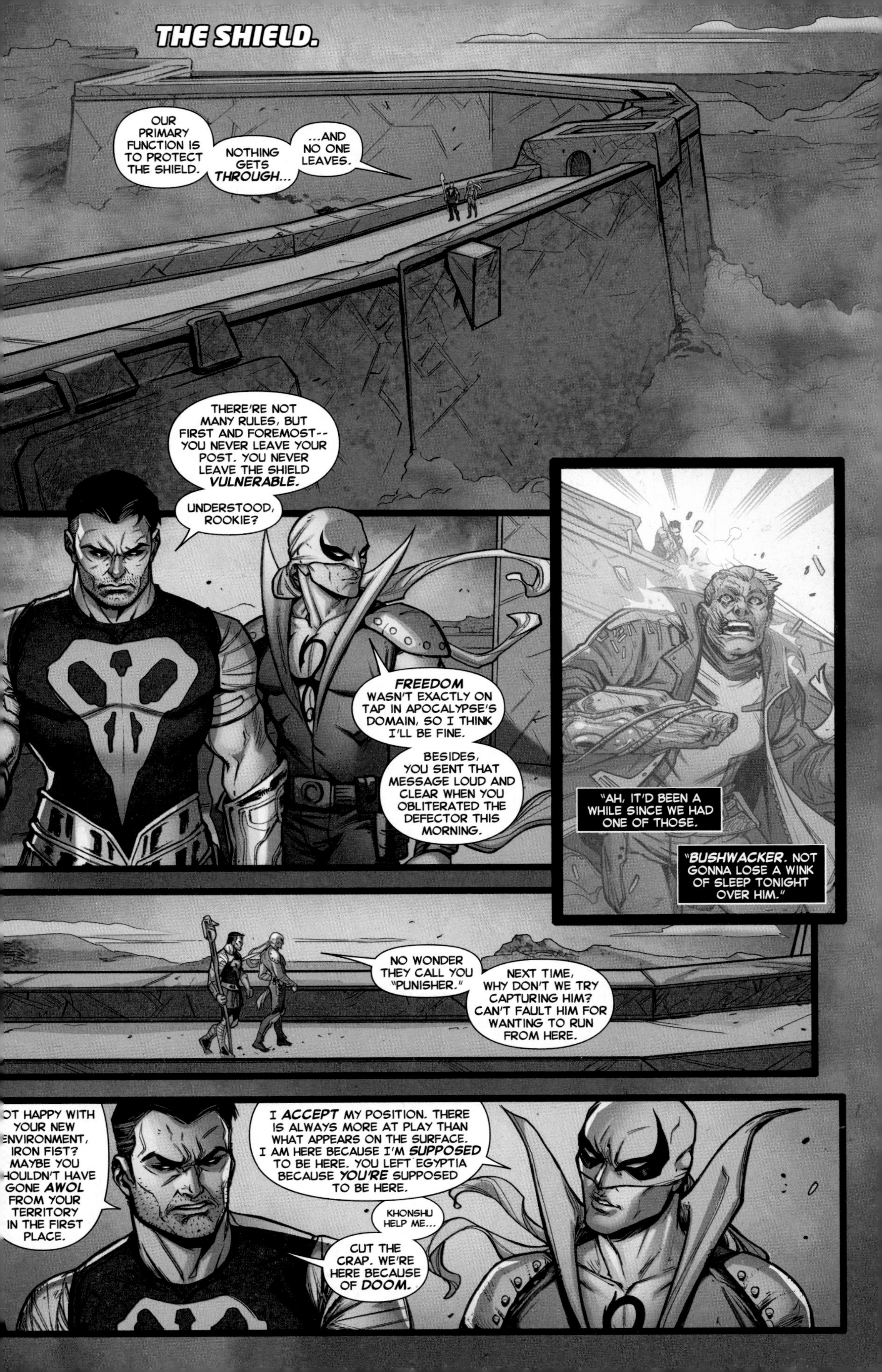
THE SHIELD.
OUR PRIMARY FUNCTION IS TO PROTECT THE SHIELD.
NOTHING GETS THROUGH...
...AND NO ONE LEAVES.
THERE'RE NOT MANY RULES, BUT FIRST AND FOREMOST--YOU NEVER LEAVE YOUR POST. YOU NEVER LEAVE THE SHIELD VULNERABLE.
UNDERSTOOD, ROOKIE?
FREEDOM WASN'T EXACTLY ON TAP IN APOCALYPSE'S DOMAIN, SO I THINK I'LL BE FINE.
BESIDES, YOU SENT THAT MESSAGE LOUD AND CLEAR WHEN YOU OBLITERATED THE DEFECTOR THIS MORNING.
"AH, IT'D BEEN A WHILE SINCE WE HAD ONE OF THOSE.
"BUSHWACKER. NOT GONNA LOSE A WINK OF SLEEP TONIGHT OVER HIM."
NO WONDER THEY CALL YOU "PUNISHER."
NEXT TIME, WHY DON'T WE TRY CAPTURING HIM? CAN'T FAULT HIM FOR WANTING TO RUN FROM HERE.
OT HAPPY WITH YOUR NEW ENVIRONMENT, IRON FIST? MAYBE YOU HOULDN'T HAVE GONE AWOL FROM YOUR TERRITORY IN THE FIRST PLACE.
I ACCEPT MY POSITION. THERE IS ALWAYS MORE AT PLAY THAN WHAT APPEARS ON THE SURFACE. I AM HERE BECAUSE I'M SUPPOSED TO BE HERE. YOU LEFT EGYPTIA BECAUSE YOU'RE SUPPOSED TO BE HERE.
KHONSHU HELP ME...
CUT THE CRAP. WE'RE HERE BECAUSE OF DOOM.

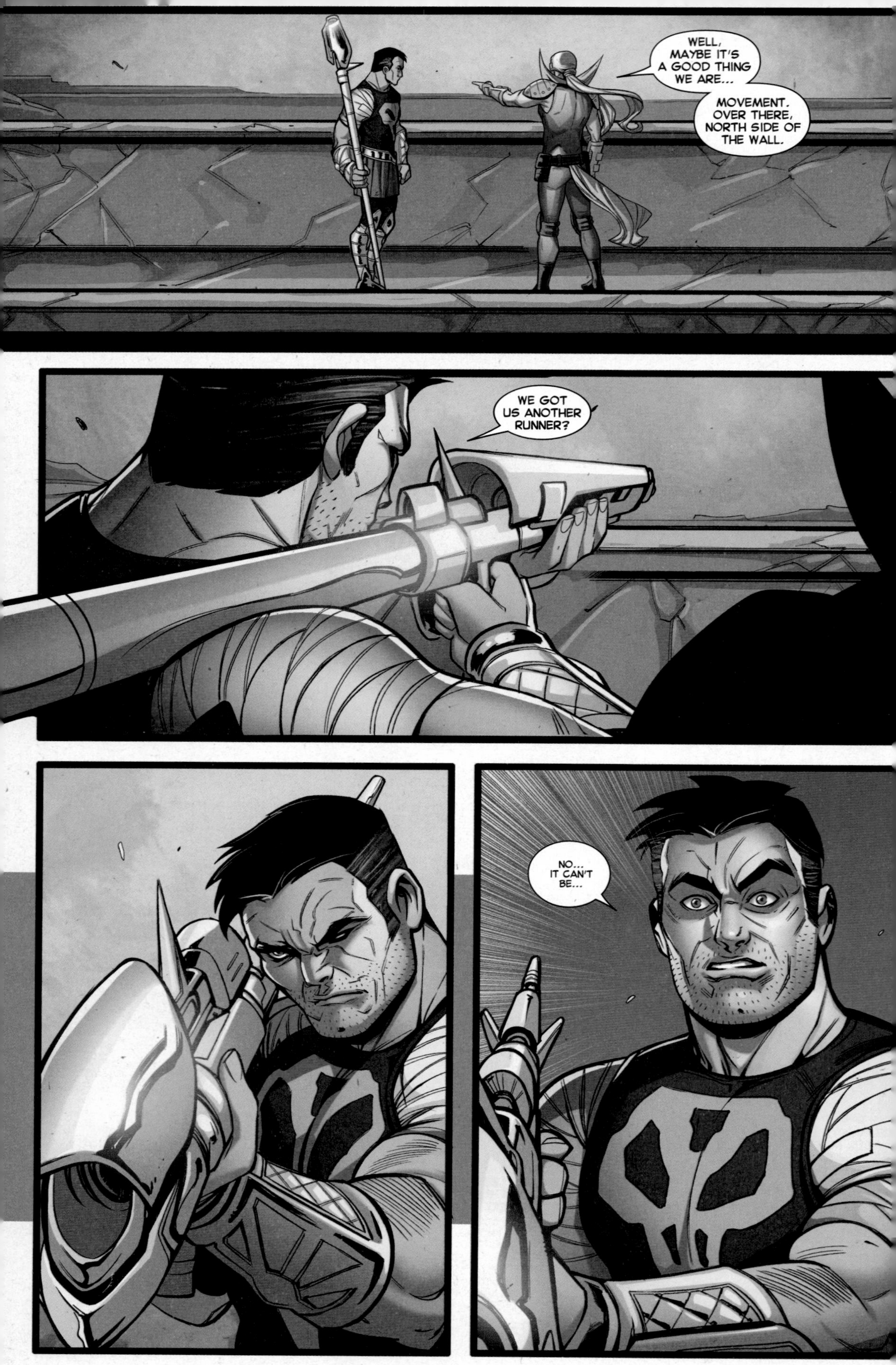
WELL, MAYBE IT'S A GOOD THING WE ARE...
MOVEMENT. OVER THERE, NORTH SIDE OF THE WALL.
WE GOT US ANOTHER RUNNER?
NO... IT CAN'T BE...

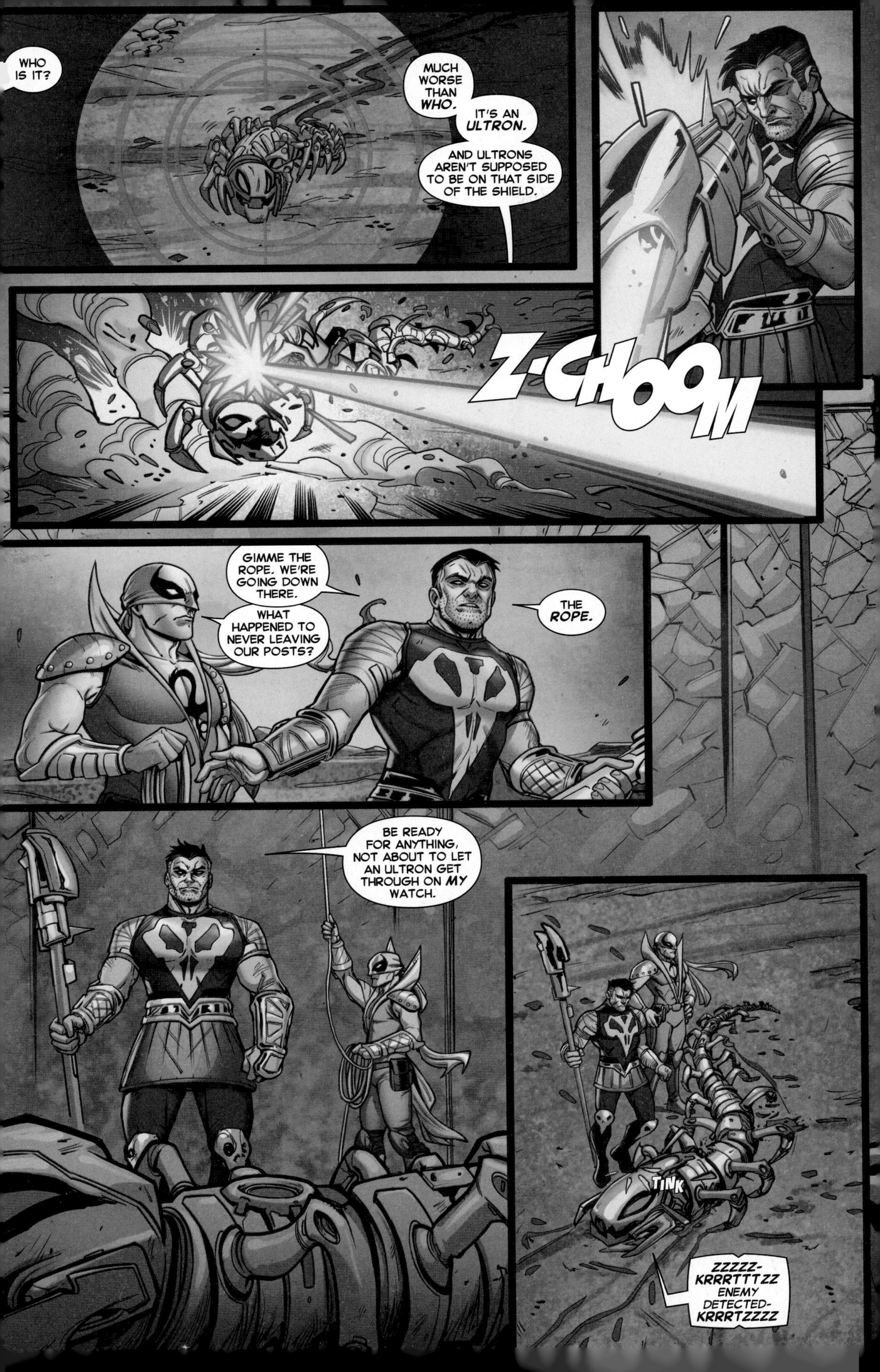
WHO IS IT?
MUCH WORSE THAN WHO.
IT'S AN ULTRON.
AND ULTRONS AREN'T SUPPOSED TO BE ON THAT SIDE OF THE SHIELD.
Z-CHOOOM
GIMME THE ROPE. WE'RE GOING DOWN THERE.
WHAT HAPPENED TO NEVER LEAVING OUR POSTS?
THE ROPE.
BE READY FOR ANYTHING, NOT ABOUT TO LET AN ULTRON GET THROUGH ON MY WATCH.
TINK
ZZZZZ-KRRRTTTZZ ENEMY DETECTED-KRRRTZZZZ

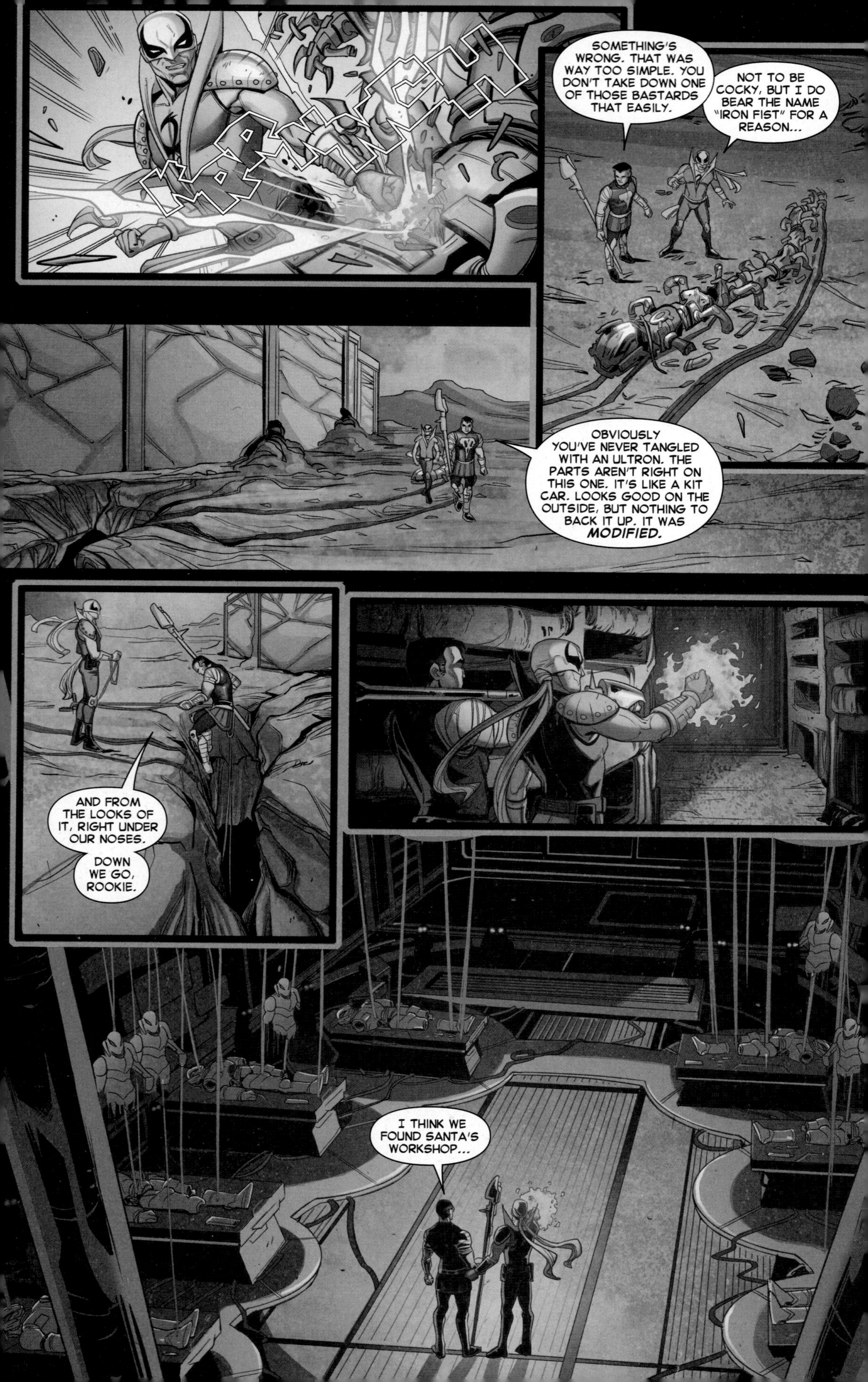
SOMETHING'S WRONG. THAT WAS WAY TOO SIMPLE. YOU DON'T TAKE DOWN ONE OF THOSE BASTARDS THAT EASILY.
NOT TO BE COCKY, BUT I DO BEAR THE NAME "IRON FIST" FOR A REASON...
OBVIOUSLY YOU'VE NEVER TANGLED WITH AN ULTRON. THE PARTS AREN'T RIGHT ON THIS ONE. IT'S LIKE A KIT CAR. LOOKS GOOD ON THE OUTSIDE, BUT NOTHING TO BACK IT UP. IT WAS MODIFIED.
AND FROM THE LOOKS OF IT, RIGHT UNDER OUR NOSES.
DOWN WE GO, ROOKIE.
I THINK WE FOUND SANTA'S WORKSHOP...

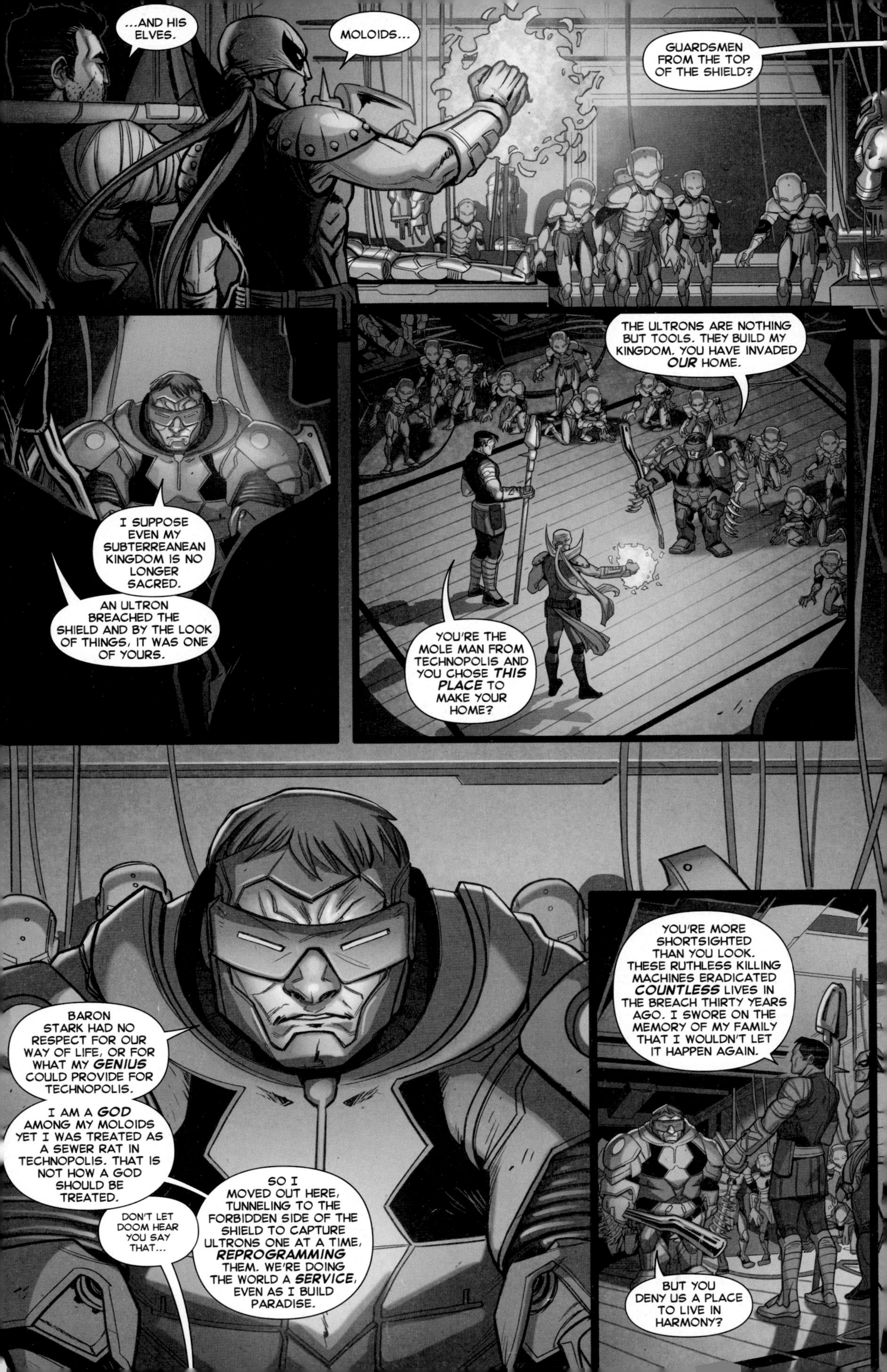
...AND HIS ELVES.
MOLOIDS...
GUARDSMEN FROM THE TOP OF THE SHIELD?
THE ULTRONS ARE NOTHING BUT TOOLS. THEY BUILD MY KINGDOM. YOU HAVE INVADED OUR HOME.
I SUPPOSE EVEN MY SUBTERREANEAN KINGDOM IS NO LONGER SACRED.
AN ULTRON BREACHED THE SHIELD AND BY THE LOOK OF THINGS, IT WAS ONE OF YOURS.
YOU'RE THE MOLE MAN FROM TECHNOPOLIS AND YOU CHOSE THIS PLACE TO MAKE YOUR HOME?
BARON STARK HAD NO RESPECT FOR OUR WAY OF LIFE, OR FOR WHAT MY GENIUS COULD PROVIDE FOR TECHNOPOLIS.
I AM A GOD AMONG MY MOLOIDS YET I WAS TREATED AS A SEWER RAT IN TECHNOPOLIS. THAT IS NOT HOW A GOD SHOULD BE TREATED.
DON'T LET DOOM HEAR YOU SAY THAT...
SO I MOVED OUT HERE, TUNNELING TO THE FORBIDDEN SIDE OF THE SHIELD TO CAPTURE ULTRONS ONE AT A TIME, REPROGRAMMING THEM. WE'RE DOING THE WORLD A SERVICE, EVEN AS I BUILD PARADISE.
YOU'RE MORE SHORTSIGHTED THAN YOU LOOK. THESE RUTHLESS KILLING MACHINES ERADICATED COUNTLESS LIVES IN THE BREACH THIRTY YEARS AGO. I SWORE ON THE MEMORY OF MY FAMILY THAT I WOULDN'T LET IT HAPPEN AGAIN.
BUT YOU DENY US A PLACE TO LIVE IN HARMONY?

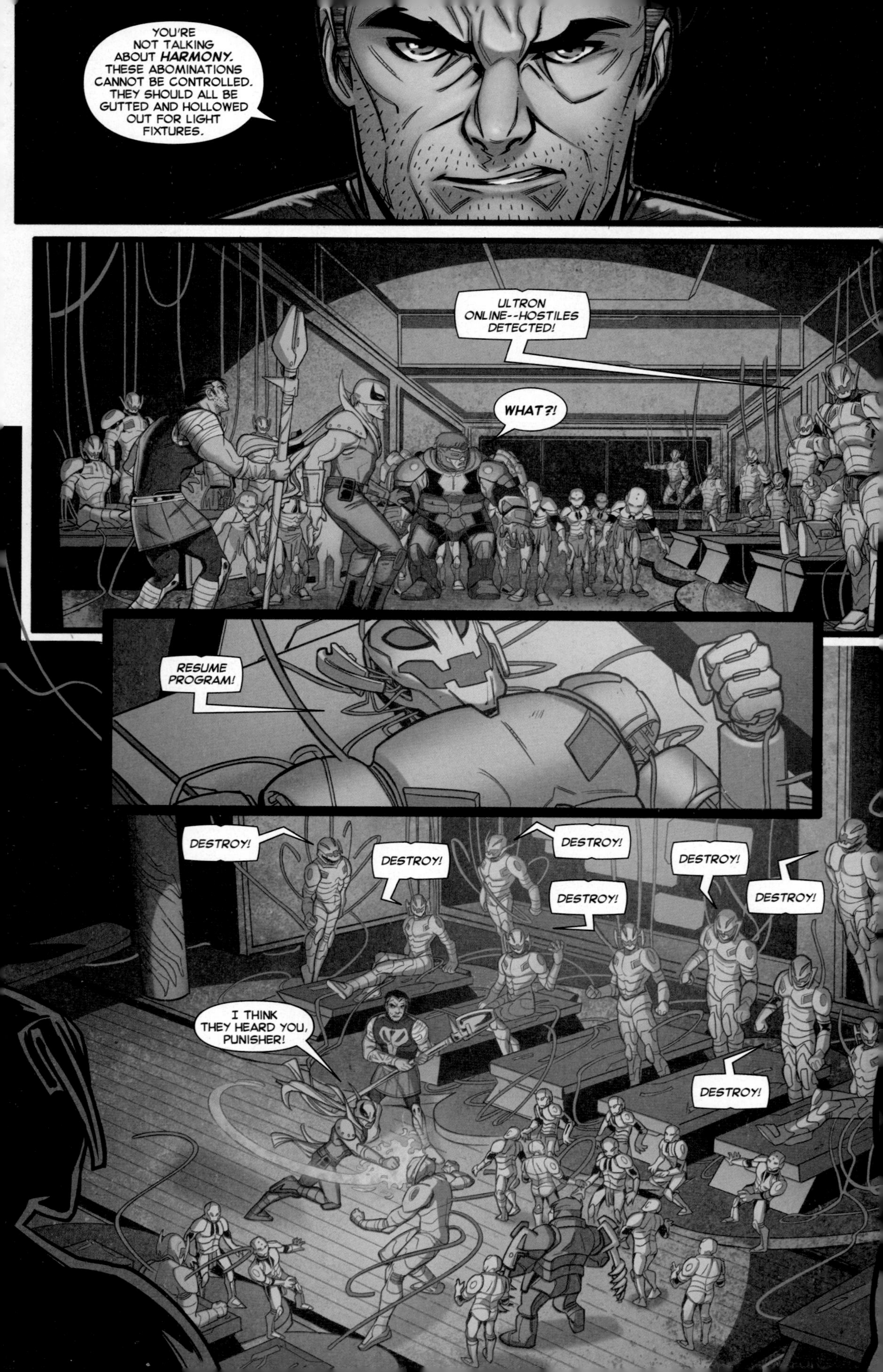
YOU'RE NOT TALKING ABOUT HARMONY. THESE ABOMINATIONS CANNOT BE CONTROLLED. THEY SHOULD ALL BE GUTTED AND HOLLOWED OUT FOR LIGHT FIXTURES.
ULTRON ONLINE--HOSTILES DETECTED!
WHAT?!
RESUME PROGRAM!
DESTROY!
DESTROY!
DESTROY!
DESTROY!
DESTROY!
DESTROY!
I THINK THEY HEARD YOU, PUNISHER!
DESTROY!

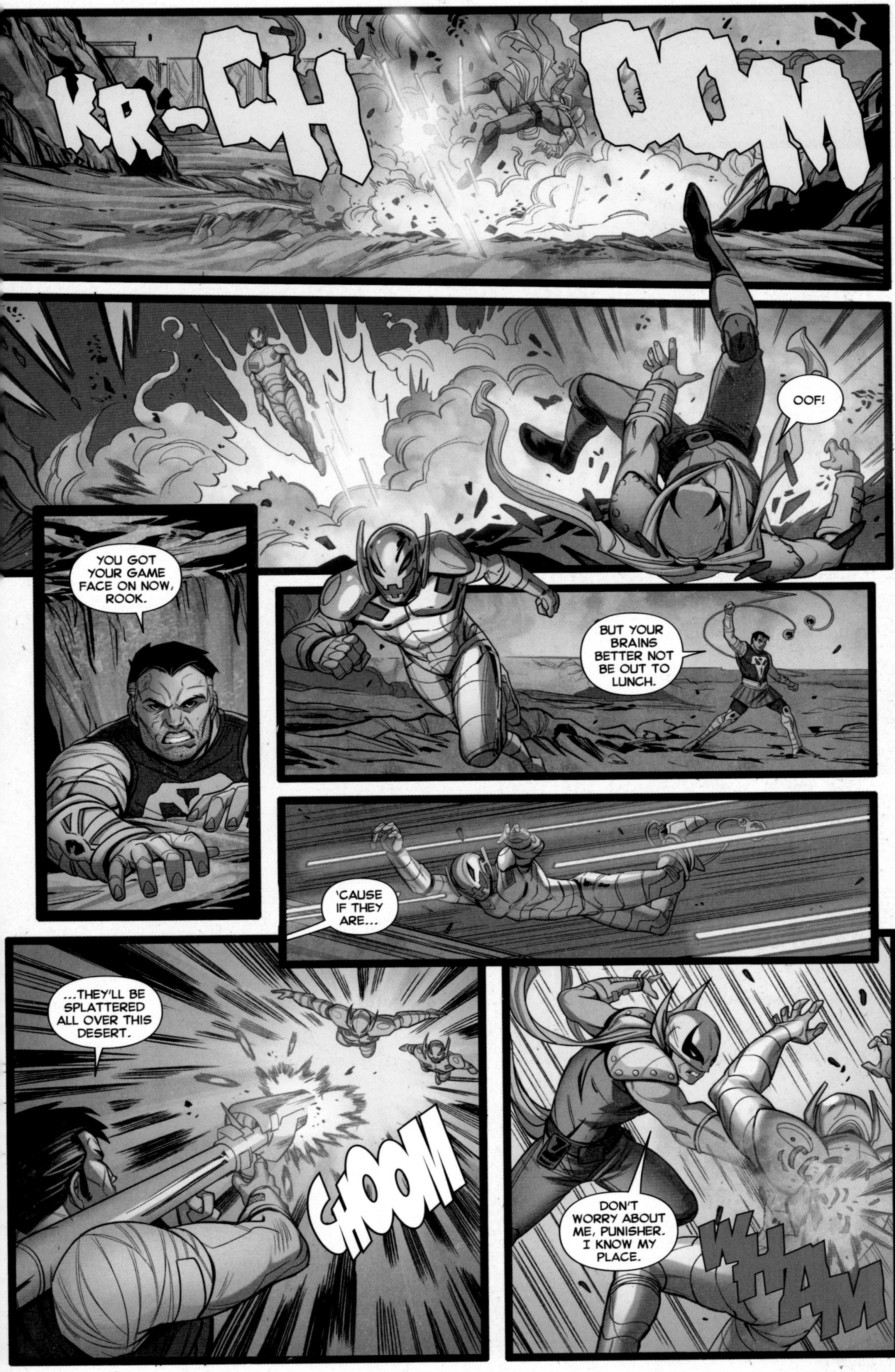
KR-CH-OOM
OOF!
YOU GOT YOUR GAME FACE ON NOW, ROOK.
BUT YOUR BRAINS BETTER NOT BE OUT TO LUNCH.
'CAUSE IF THEY ARE...
...THEY'LL BE SPLATTERED ALL OVER THIS DESERT.
CHOOM
DON'T WORRY ABOUT ME, PUNISHER. I KNOW MY PLACE.
WHAM

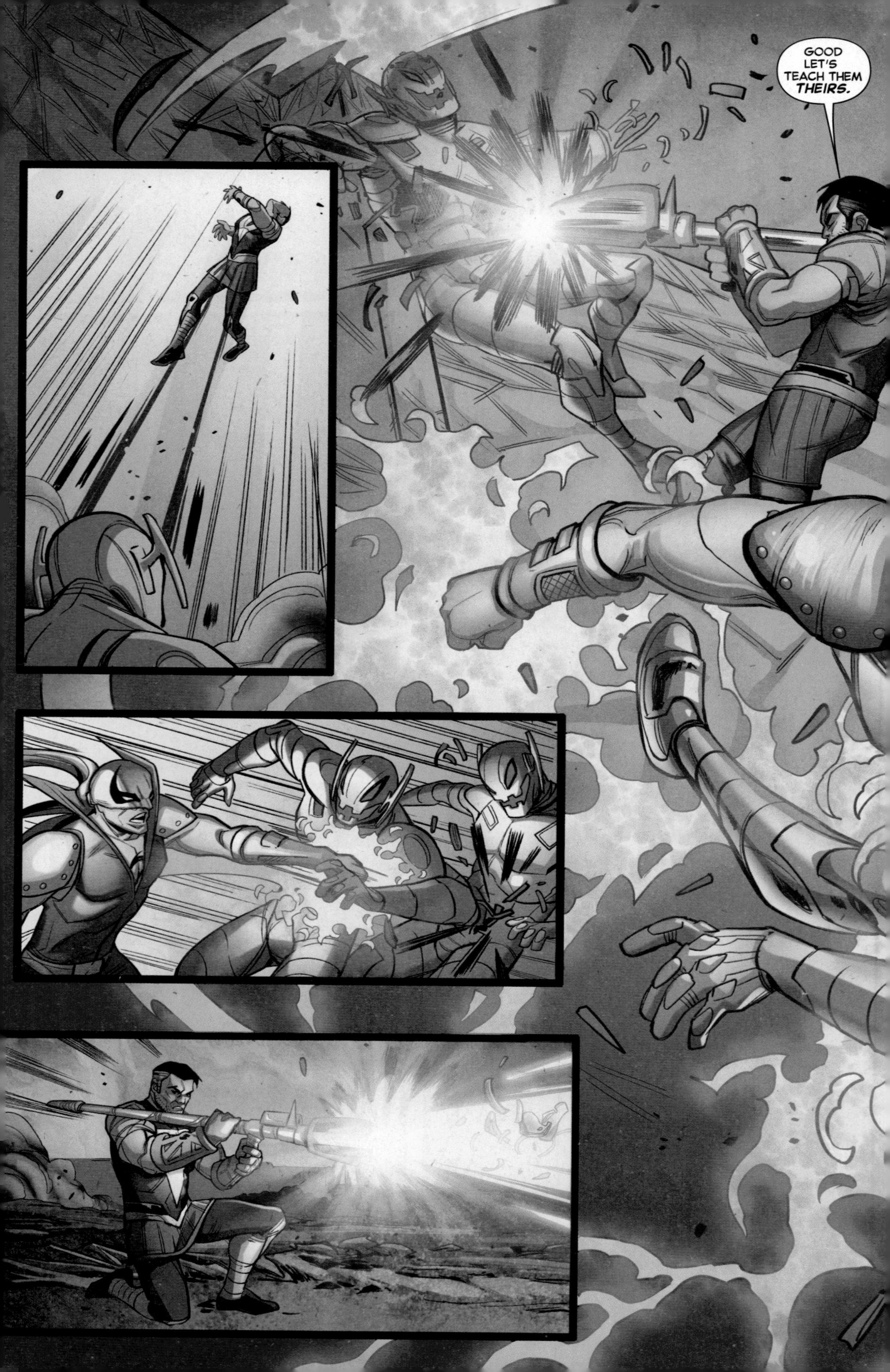
GOOD LET'S TEACH THEM THEIRS.

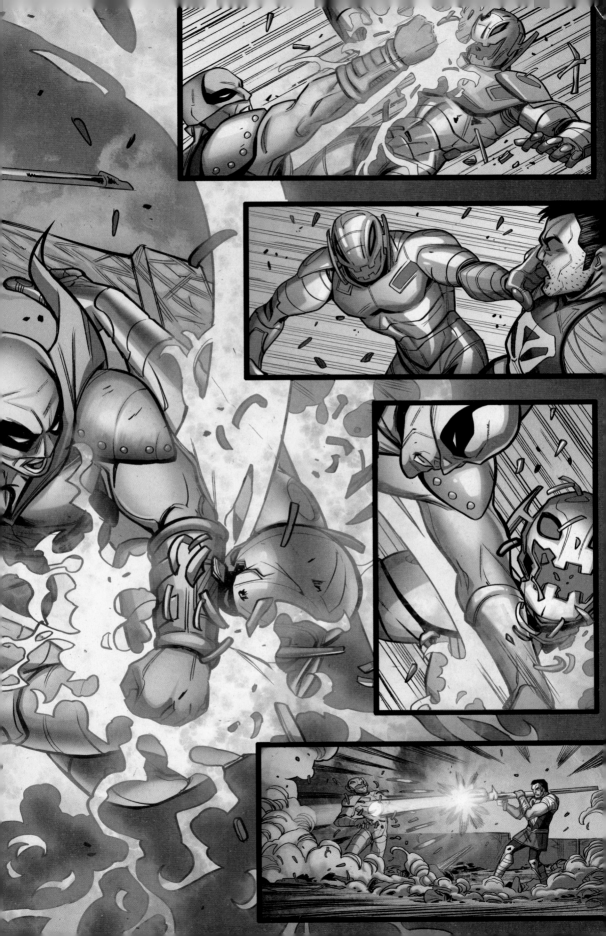

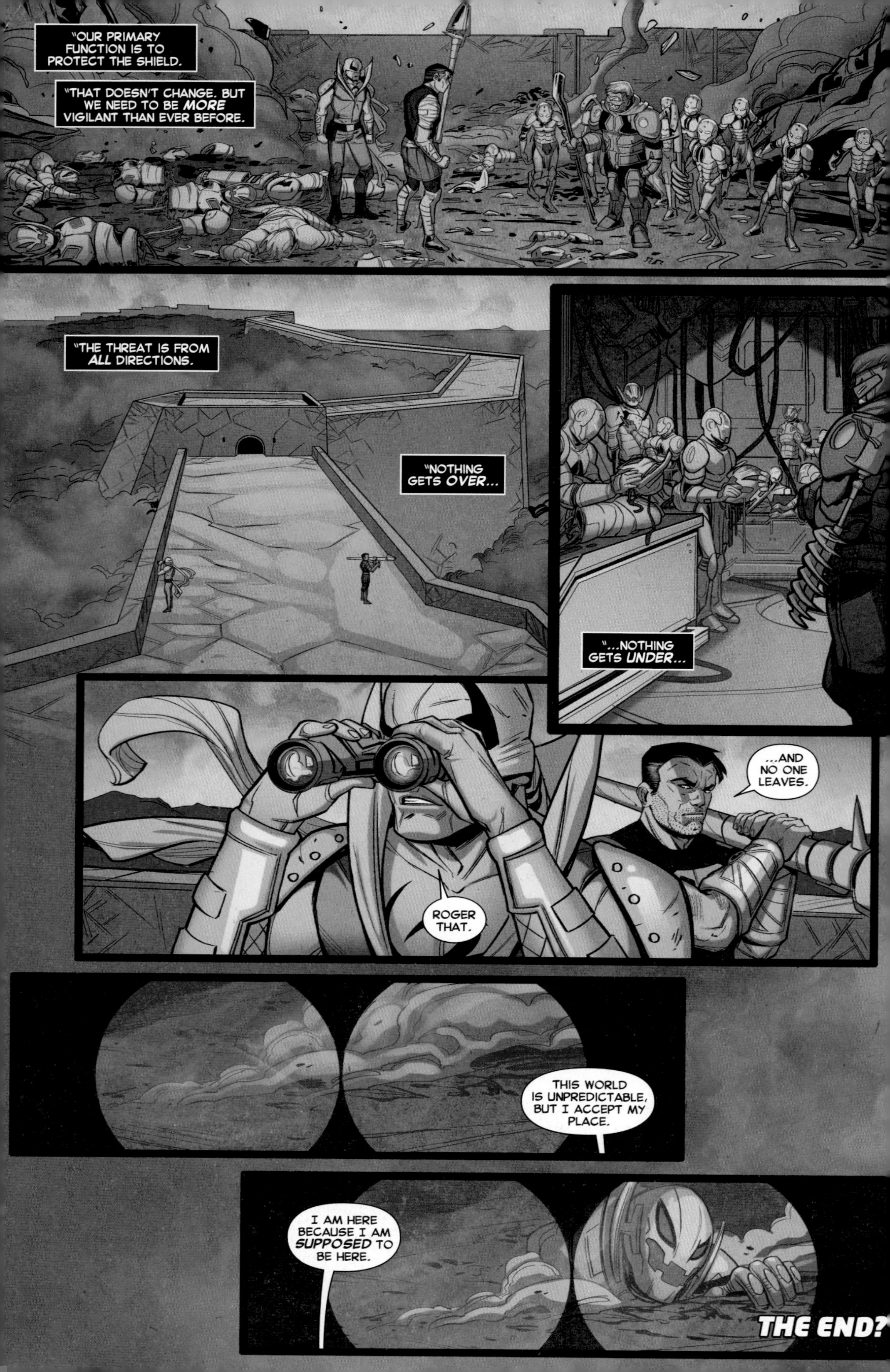
"OUR PRIMARY FUNCTION IS TO PROTECT THE SHIELD.
"THAT DOESN'T CHANGE. BUT WE NEED TO BE MORE VIGILANT THAN EVER BEFORE.
"THE THREAT IS FROM ALL DIRECTIONS.
"NOTHING GETS OVER...
"...NOTHING GETS UNDER...
...AND NO ONE LEAVES.
ROGER THAT.
THIS WORLD IS UNPREDICTABLE, BUT I ACCEPT MY PLACE.
I AM HERE BECAUSE I AM SUPPOSED TO BE HERE.
THE END?

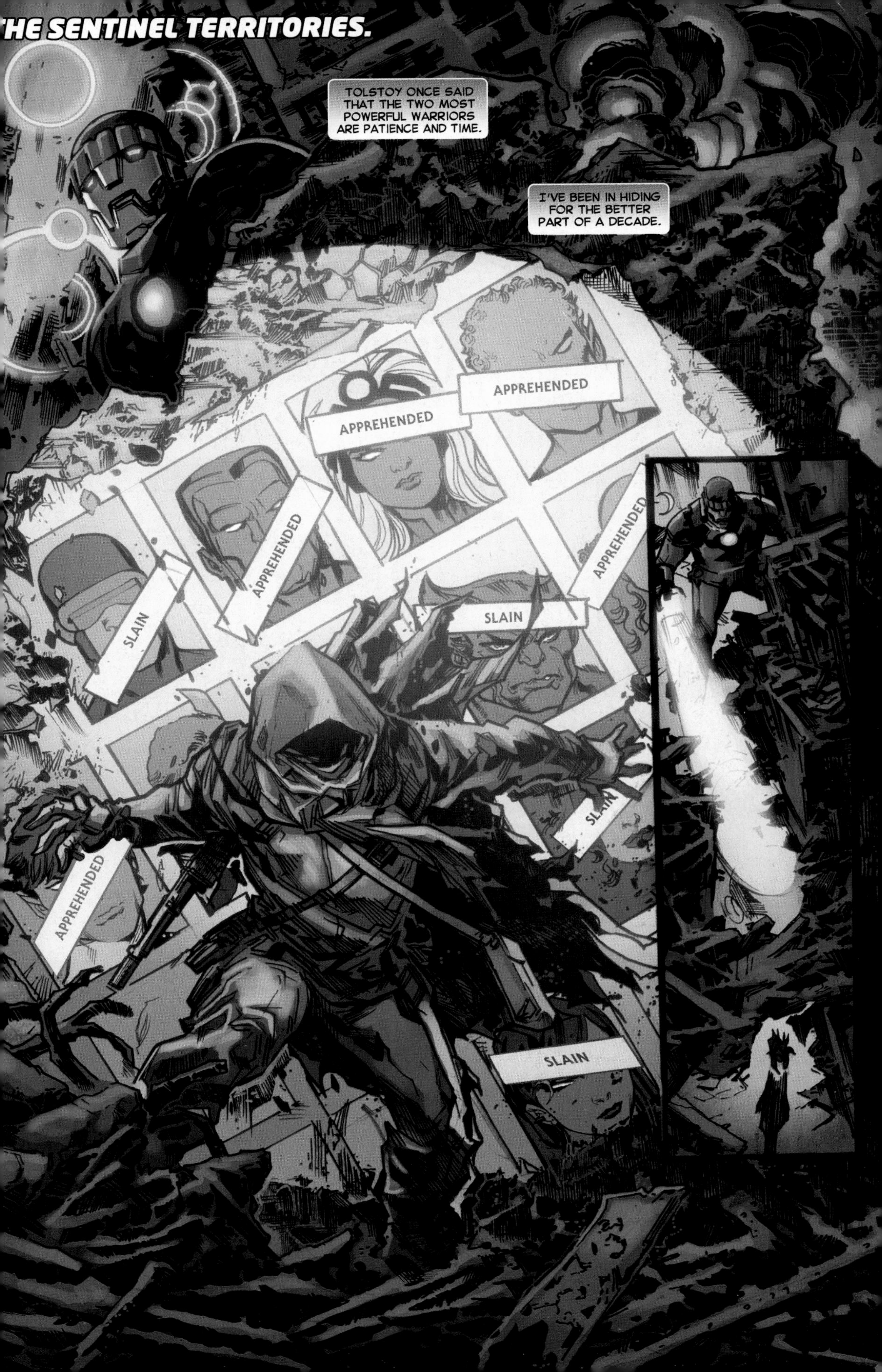
THE SENTINEL TERRITORIES.
TOLSTOY ONCE SAID THAT THE TWO MOST POWERFUL WARRIORS ARE PATIENCE AND TIME.
I'VE BEEN IN HIDING FOR THE BETTER PART OF A DECADE.
APPREHENDED
APPREHENDED
APPREHENDED
SLAIN
APPREHENDED
SLAIN
SLAIN
APPREHENDED
SLAIN

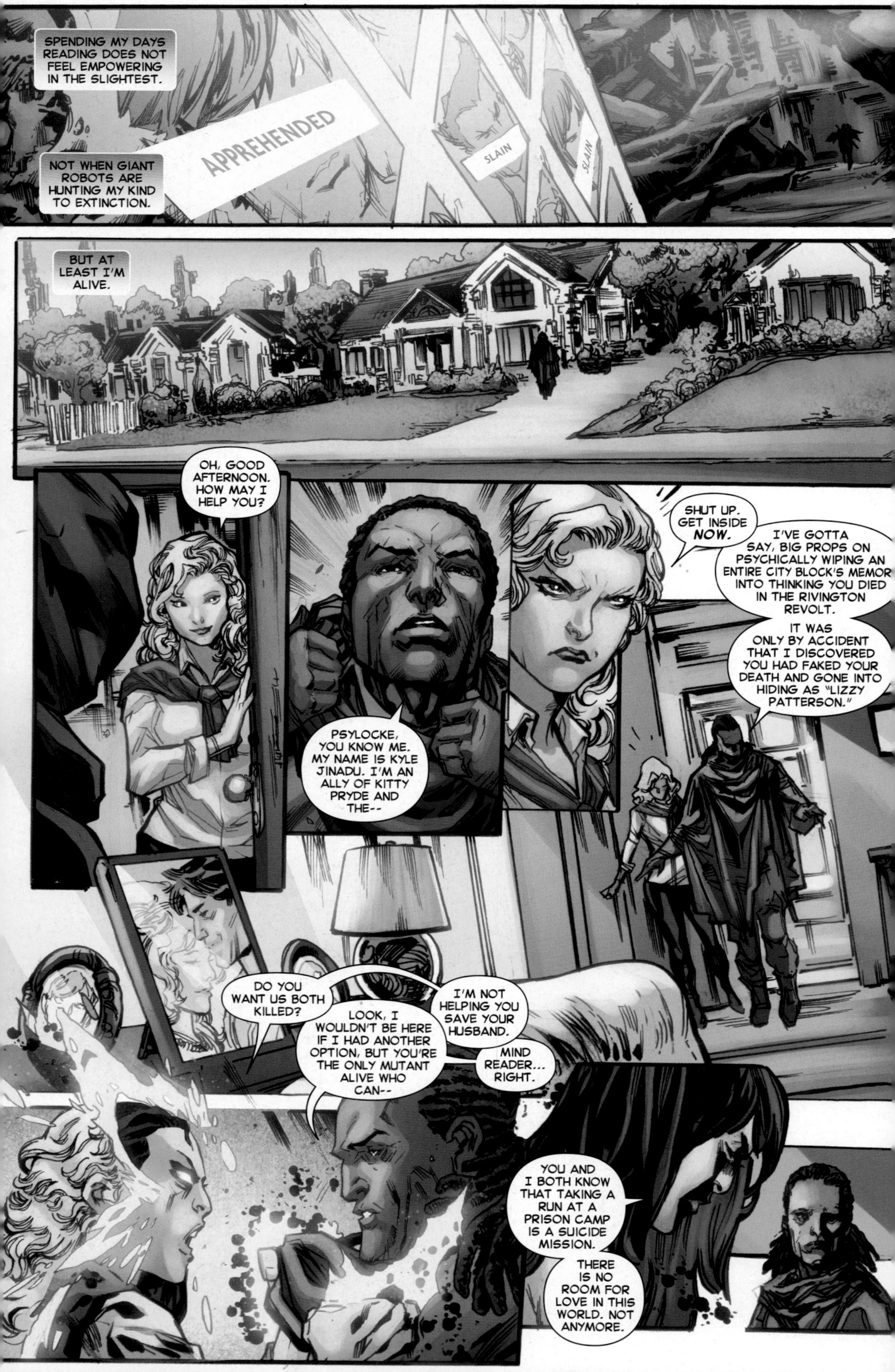
SPENDING MY DAYS READING DOES NOT FEEL EMPOWERING IN THE SLIGHTEST.
APPREHENDED
SLAIN
SLAIN
NOT WHEN GIANT ROBOTS ARE HUNTING MY KIND TO EXTINCTION.
BUT AT LEAST I'M ALIVE.
OH, GOOD AFTERNOON. HOW MAY I HELP YOU?
PSYLOCKE, YOU KNOW ME. MY NAME IS KYLE JINADU. I'M AN ALLY OF KITTY PRYDE AND THE--
SHUT UP. GET INSIDE NOW.
I'VE GOTTA SAY, BIG PROPS ON PSYCHICALLY WIPING AN ENTIRE CITY BLOCK'S MEMOR INTO THINKING YOU DIED IN THE RIVINGTON REVOLT.
IT WAS ONLY BY ACCIDENT THAT I DISCOVERED YOU HAD FAKED YOUR DEATH AND GONE INTO HIDING AS "LIZZY PATTERSON."
DO YOU WANT US BOTH KILLED?
LOOK, I WOULDN'T BE HERE IF I HAD ANOTHER OPTION, BUT YOU'RE THE ONLY MUTANT ALIVE WHO CAN--
I'M NOT HELPING YOU SAVE YOUR HUSBAND.
MIND READER... RIGHT.
YOU AND I BOTH KNOW THAT TAKING A RUN AT A PRISON CAMP IS A SUICIDE MISSION.
THERE IS NO ROOM FOR LOVE IN THIS WORLD. NOT ANYMORE.

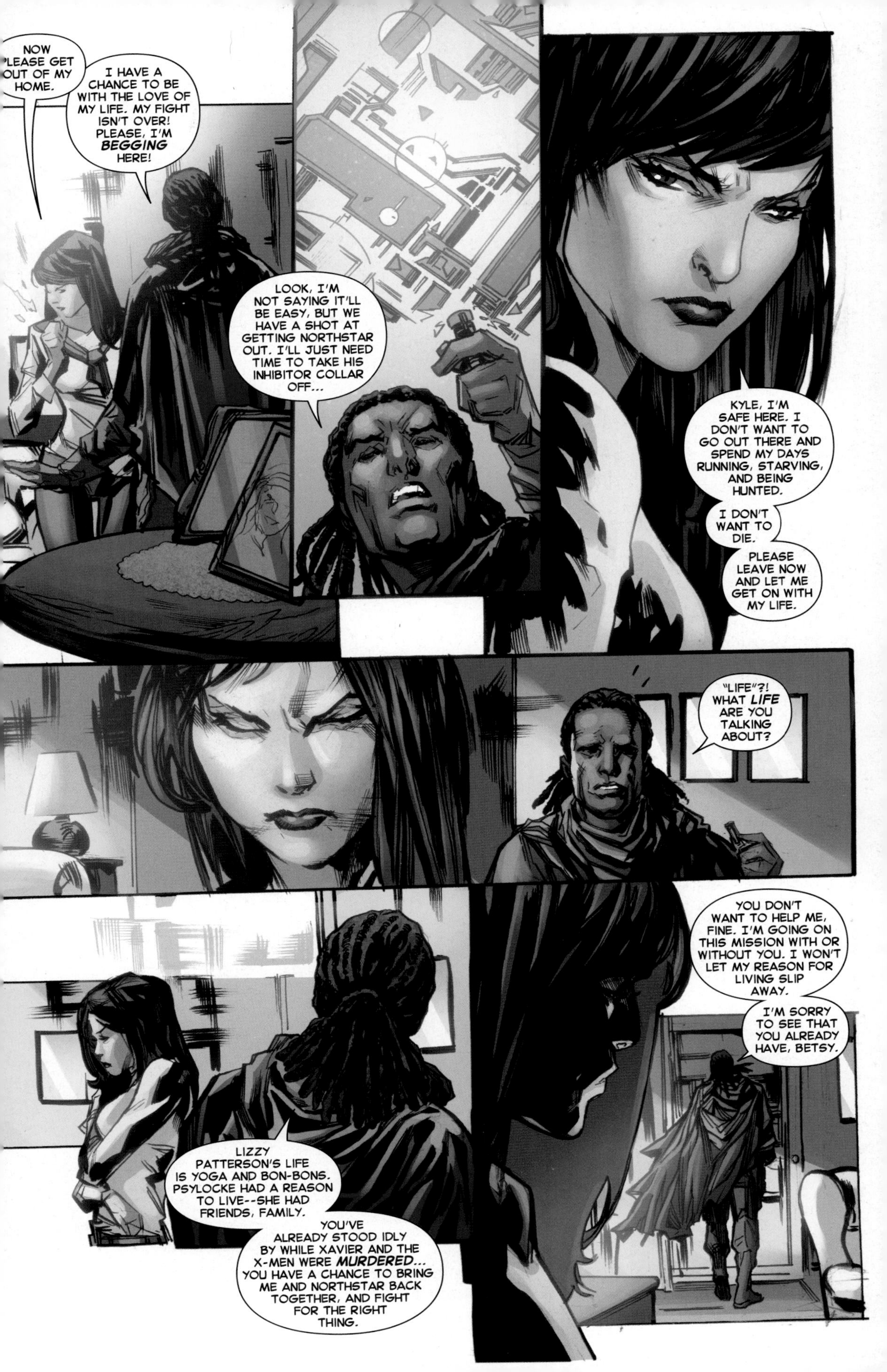

NOW PLEASE GET OUT OF MY HOME.
I HAVE A CHANCE TO BE WITH THE LOVE OF MY LIFE. MY FIGHT ISN'T OVER! PLEASE, I'M BEGGING HERE!
LOOK, I'M NOT SAYING IT'LL BE EASY, BUT WE HAVE A SHOT AT GETTING NORTHSTAR OUT. I'LL JUST NEED TIME TO TAKE HIS INHIBITOR COLLAR OFF...
KYLE, I'M SAFE HERE. I DON'T WANT TO GO OUT THERE AND SPEND MY DAYS RUNNING, STARVING, AND BEING HUNTED.
I DON'T WANT TO DIE.
PLEASE LEAVE NOW AND LET ME GET ON WITH MY LIFE.
"LIFE"?! WHAT LIFE ARE YOU TALKING ABOUT?
LIZZY PATTERSON'S LIFE IS YOGA AND BON-BONS. PSYLOCKE HAD A REASON TO LIVE--SHE HAD FRIENDS, FAMILY.
YOU'VE ALREADY STOOD IDLY BY WHILE XAVIER AND THE X-MEN WERE MURDERED... YOU HAVE A CHANCE TO BRING ME AND NORTHSTAR BACK TOGETHER, AND FIGHT FOR THE RIGHT THING.
YOU DON'T WANT TO HELP ME, FINE. I'M GOING ON THIS MISSION WITH OR WITHOUT YOU. I WON'T LET MY REASON FOR LIVING SLIP AWAY.
I'M SORRY TO SEE THAT YOU ALREADY HAVE, BETSY.

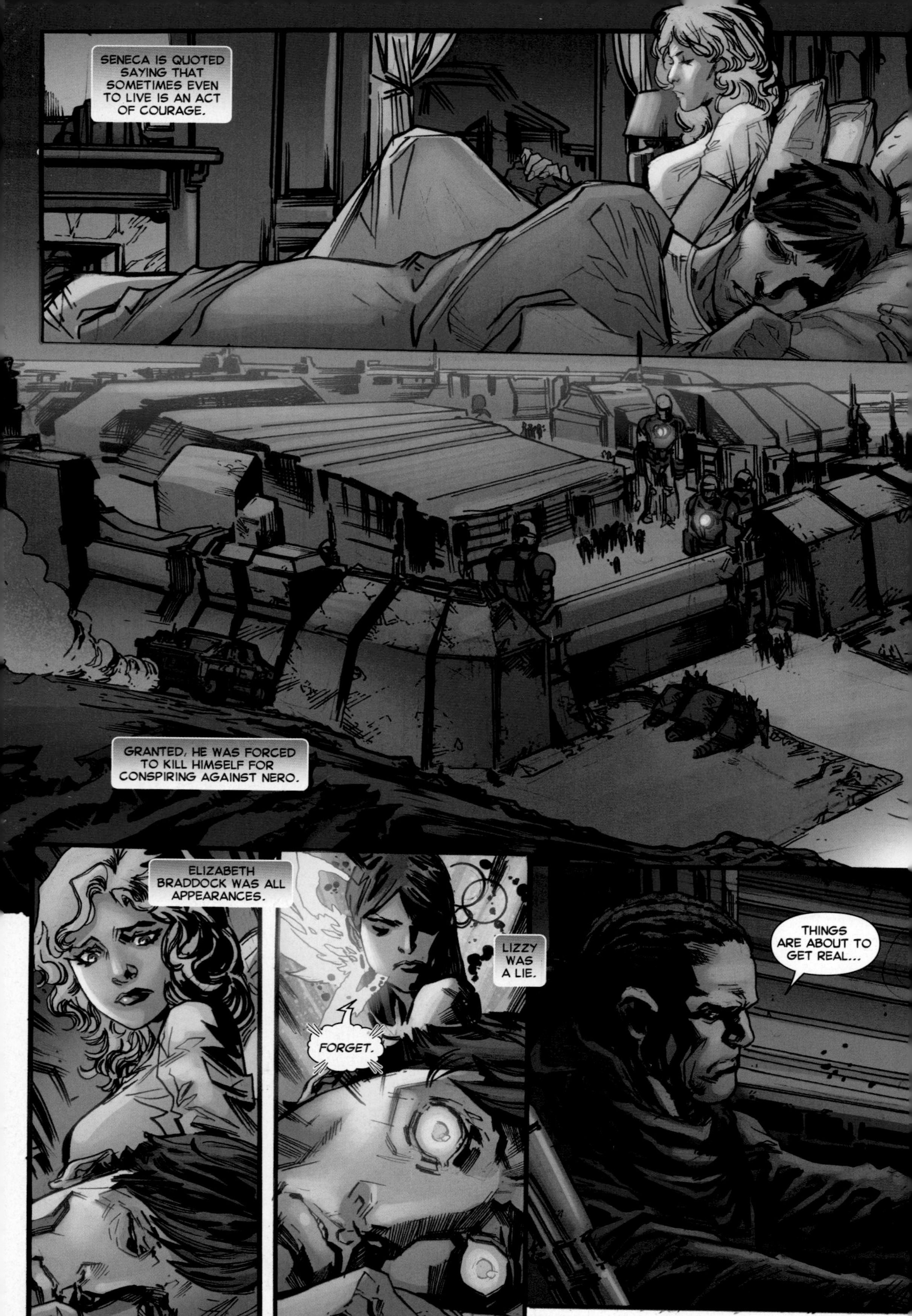
SENECA IS QUOTED SAYING THAT SOMETIMES EVEN TO LIVE IS AN ACT OF COURAGE.
GRANTED, HE WAS FORCED TO KILL HIMSELF FOR CONSPIRING AGAINST NERO.
ELIZABETH BRADDOCK WAS ALL APPEARANCES.
LIZZY WAS A LIE.
FORGET.
THINGS ARE ABOUT TO GET REAL...

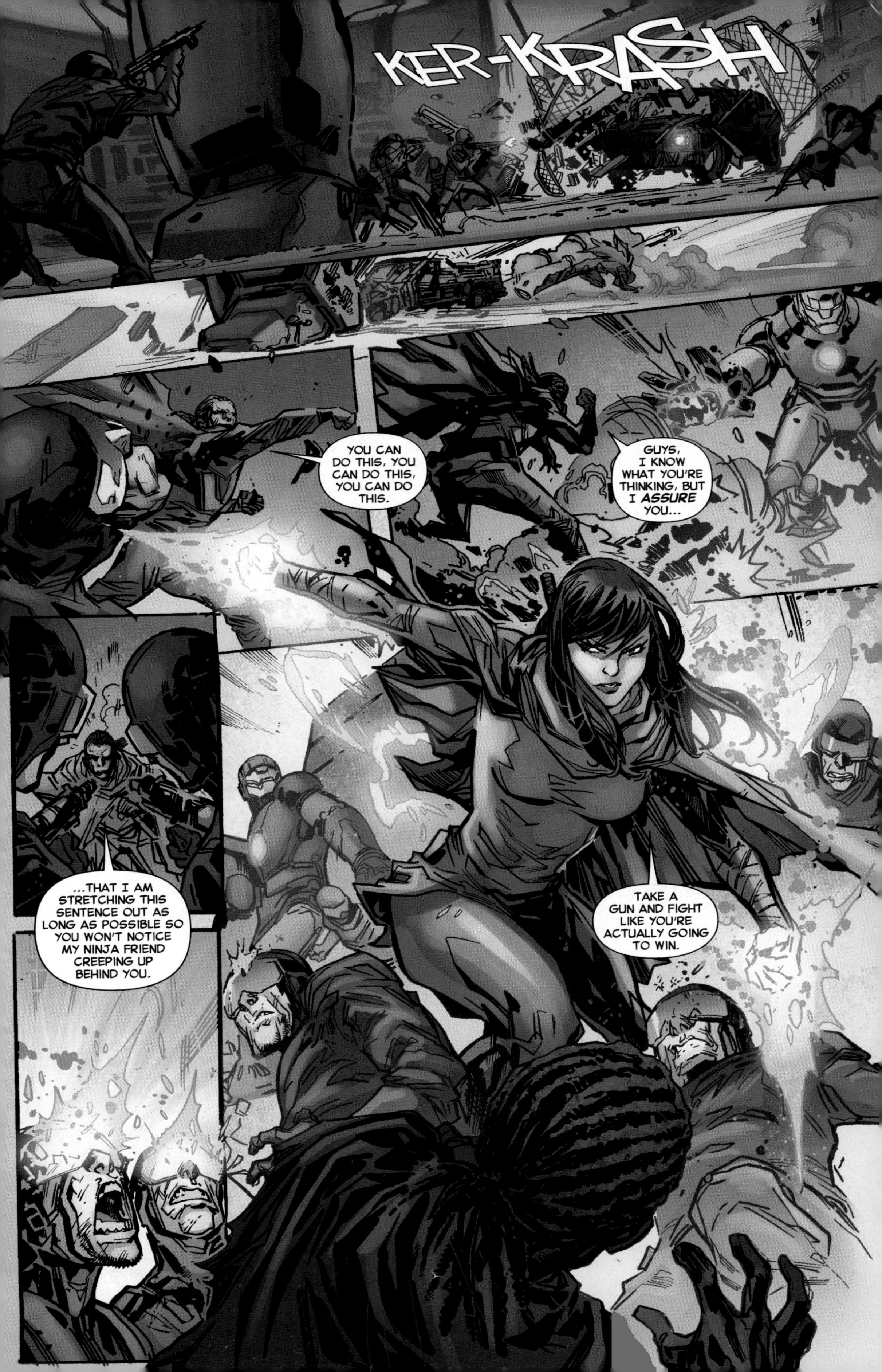
KER-KRASH
YOU CAN DO THIS, YOU CAN DO THIS, YOU CAN DO THIS.
GUYS, I KNOW WHAT YOU'RE THINKING, BUT I *ASSURE* YOU...
...THAT I AM STRETCHING THIS SENTENCE OUT AS LONG AS POSSIBLE SO YOU WON'T NOTICE MY NINJA FRIEND CREEPING UP BEHIND YOU.
TAKE A GUN AND FIGHT LIKE YOU'RE ACTUALLY GOING TO WIN.

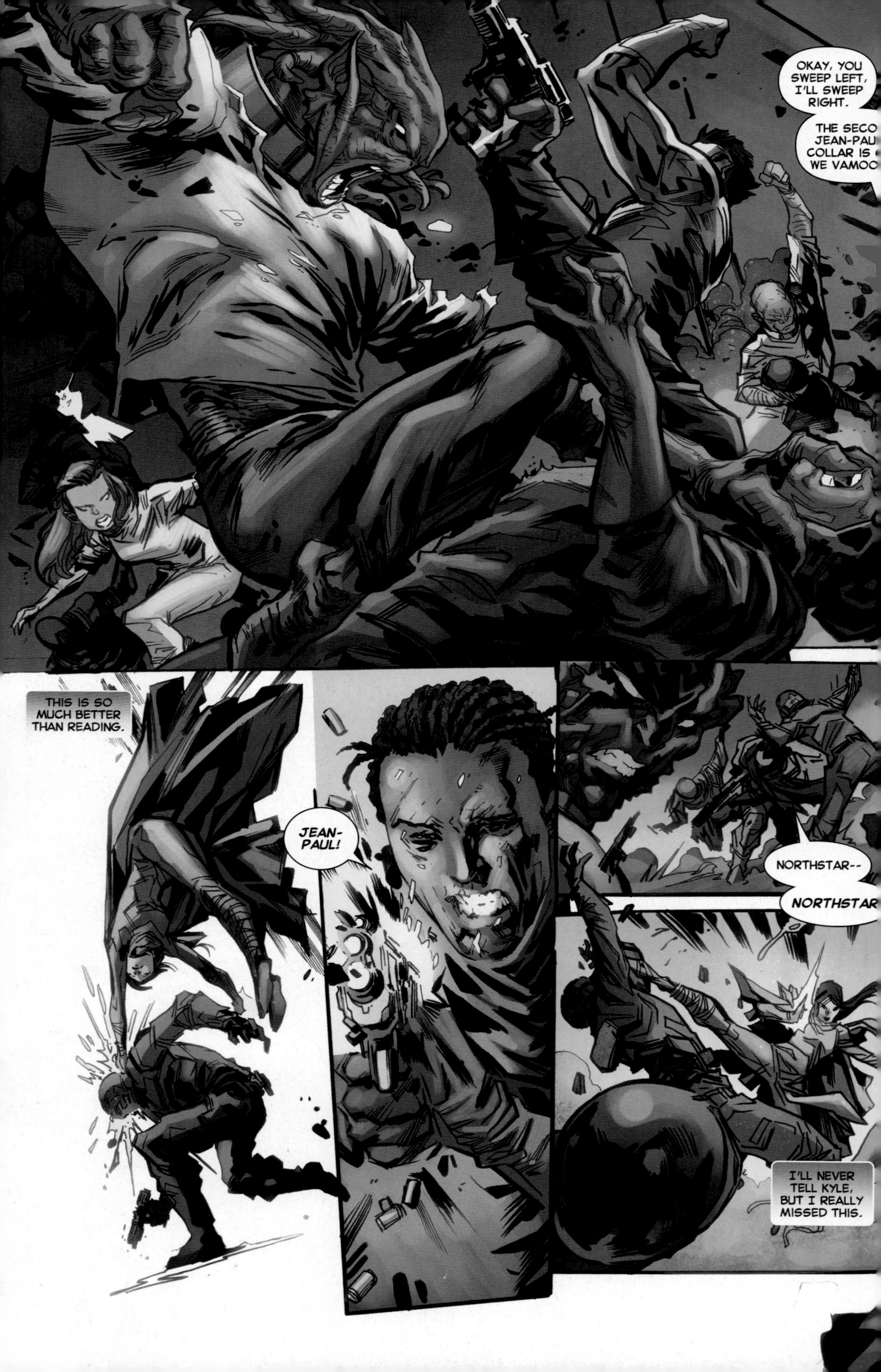
OKAY, YOU SWEEP LEFT, I'LL SWEEP RIGHT.
THE SECO JEAN-PAU COLLAR IS WE VAMOO
THIS IS SO MUCH BETTER THAN READING.
JEAN-PAUL!
NORTHSTAR--
NORTHSTAR
I'LL NEVER TELL KYLE, BUT I REALLY MISSED THIS.

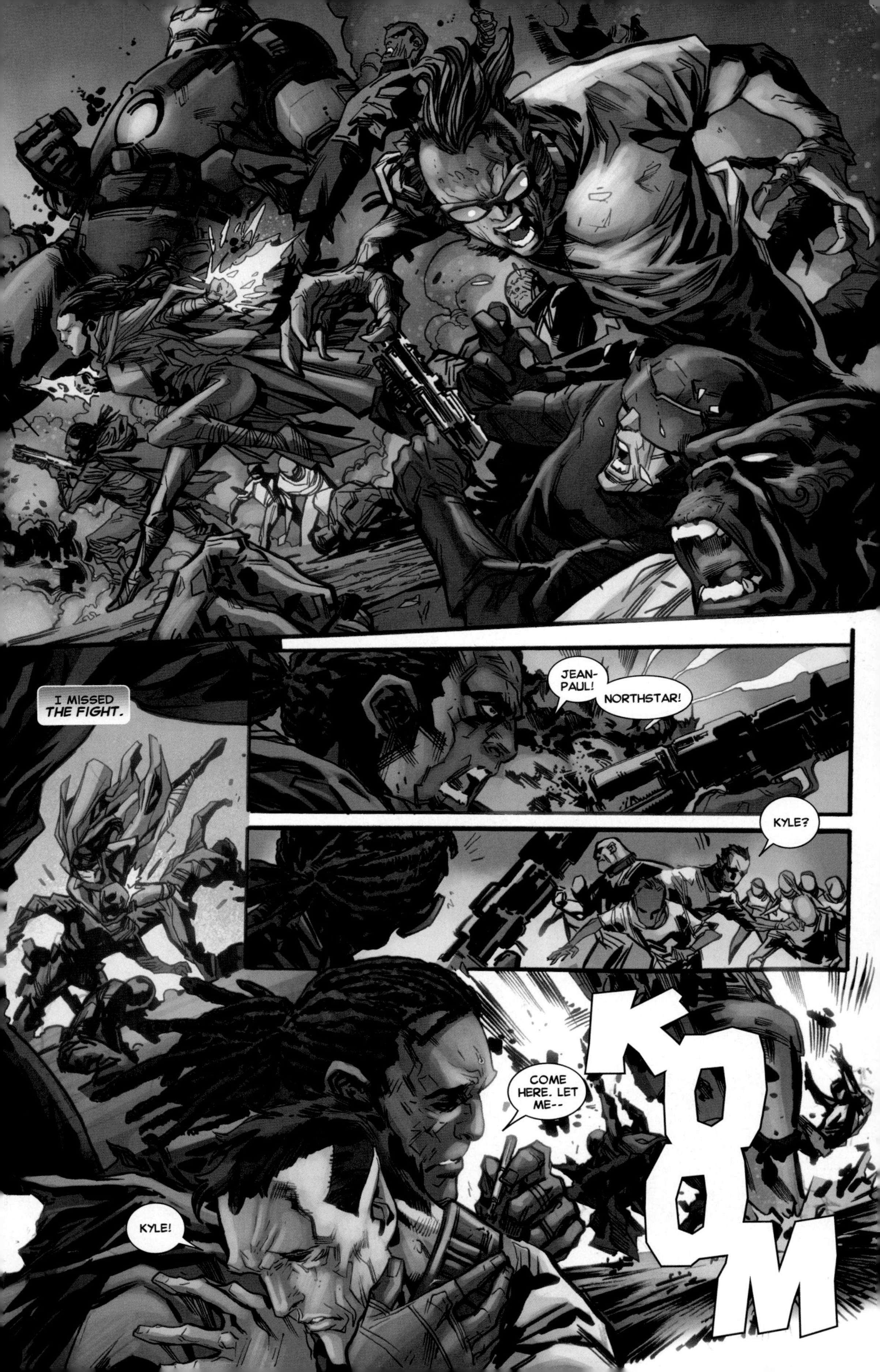
I MISSED THE FIGHT.
JEAN-PAUL!
NORTHSTAR!
KYLE?
COME HERE. LET ME--
KYLE!
KOOM

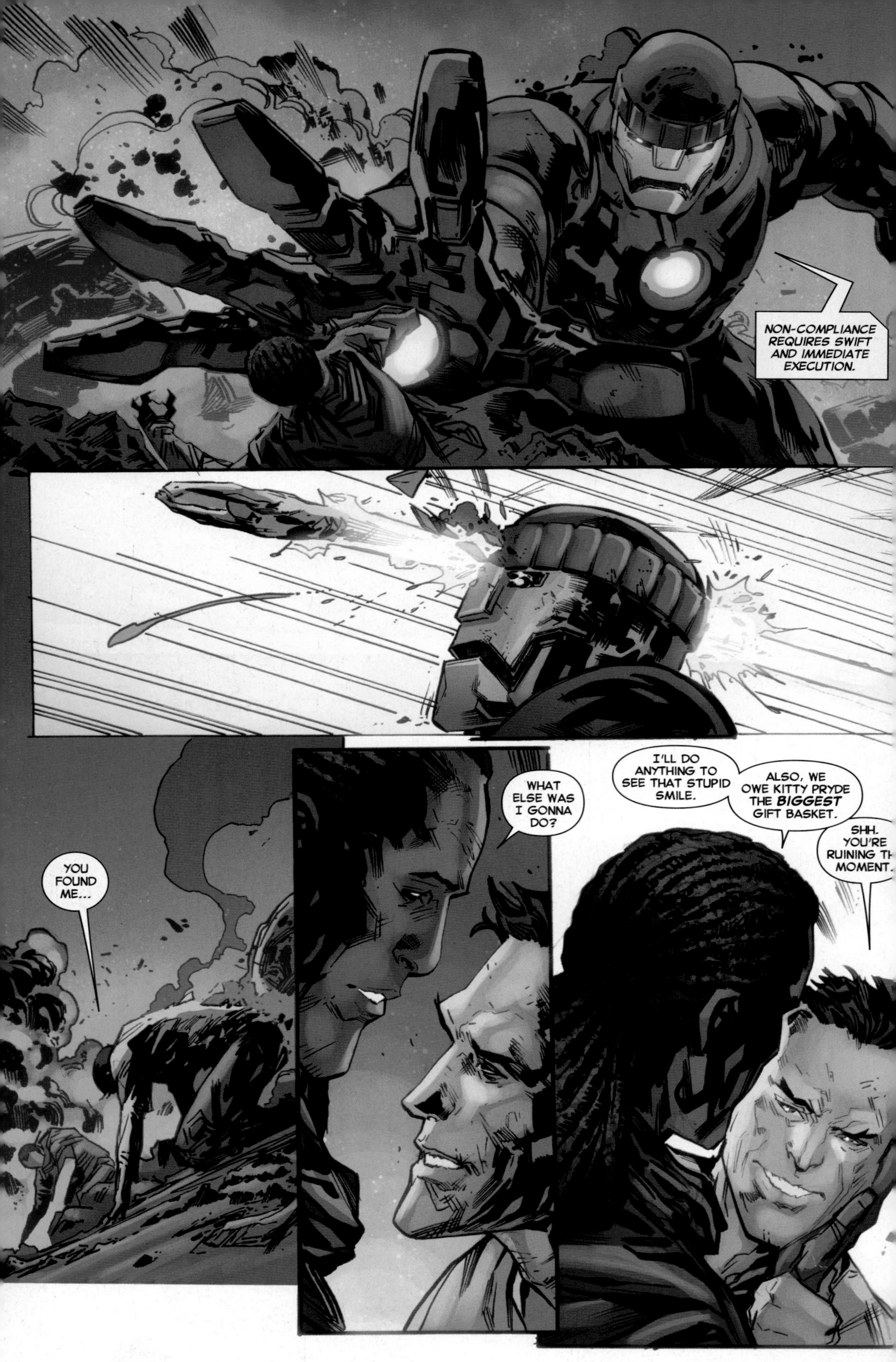
NON-COMPLIANCE REQUIRES SWIFT AND IMMEDIATE EXECUTION.
YOU FOUND ME...
WHAT ELSE WAS I GONNA DO?
I'LL DO ANYTHING TO SEE THAT STUPID SMILE.
ALSO, WE OWE KITTY PRYDE THE BIGGEST GIFT BASKET.
SHH. YOU'RE RUINING TH MOMENT.

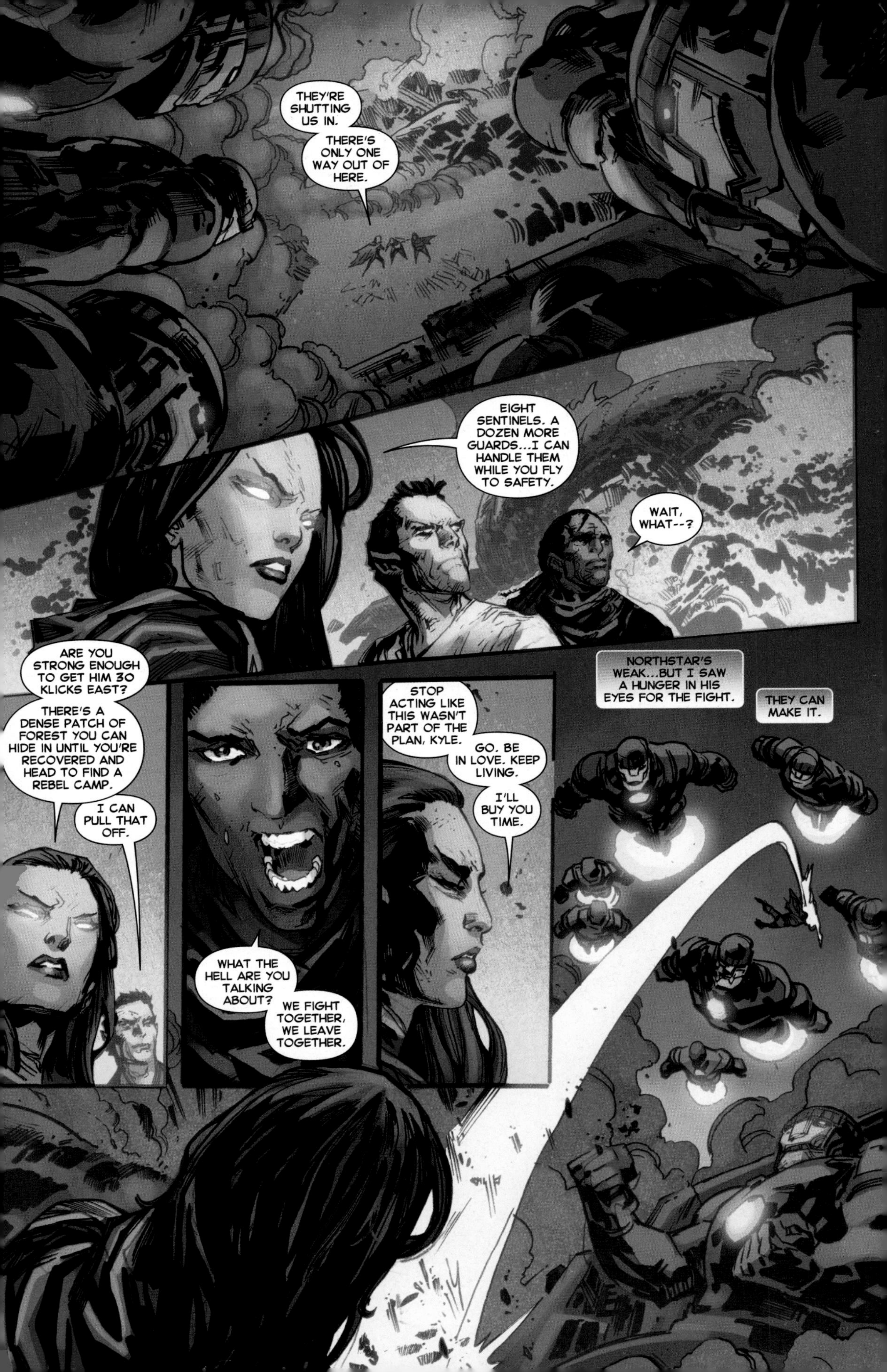
THEY'RE SHUTTING US IN.
THERE'S ONLY ONE WAY OUT OF HERE.
EIGHT SENTINELS. A DOZEN MORE GUARDS...I CAN HANDLE THEM WHILE YOU FLY TO SAFETY.
WAIT, WHAT--?
ARE YOU STRONG ENOUGH TO GET HIM 30 KLICKS EAST?
THERE'S A DENSE PATCH OF FOREST YOU CAN HIDE IN UNTIL YOU'RE RECOVERED AND HEAD TO FIND A REBEL CAMP.
I CAN PULL THAT OFF.
WHAT THE HELL ARE YOU TALKING ABOUT?
WE FIGHT TOGETHER, WE LEAVE TOGETHER.
STOP ACTING LIKE THIS WASN'T PART OF THE PLAN, KYLE.
GO. BE IN LOVE. KEEP LIVING.
I'LL BUY YOU TIME.
NORTHSTAR'S WEAK...BUT I SAW A HUNGER IN HIS EYES FOR THE FIGHT.
THEY CAN MAKE IT.

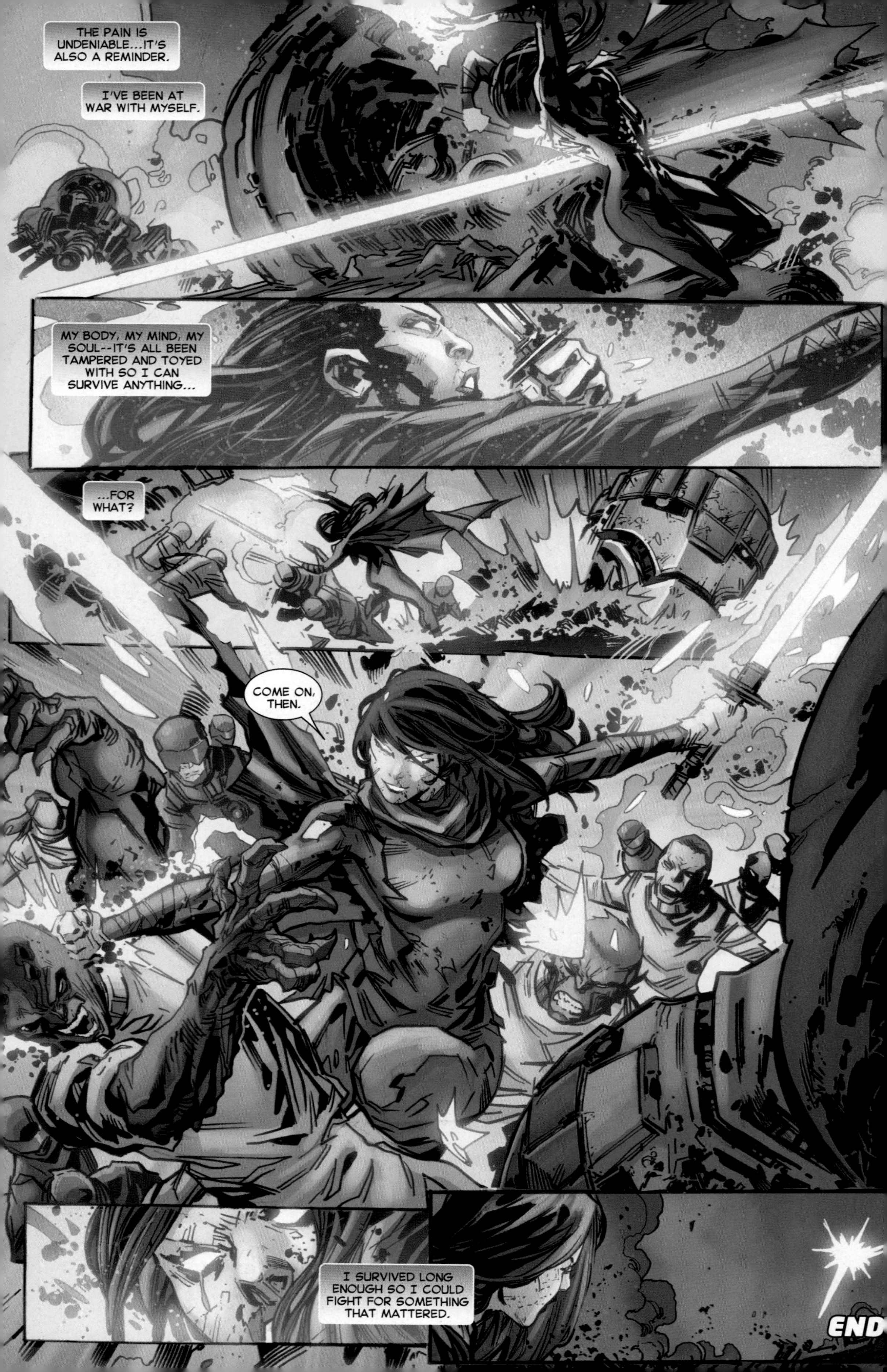
THE PAIN IS UNDENIABLE...IT'S ALSO A REMINDER.
I'VE BEEN AT WAR WITH MYSELF.
MY BODY, MY MIND, MY SOUL--IT'S ALL BEEN TAMPERED AND TOYED WITH SO I CAN SURVIVE ANYTHING...
...FOR WHAT?
COME ON, THEN.
I SURVIVED LONG ENOUGH SO I COULD FIGHT FOR SOMETHING THAT MATTERED.
END

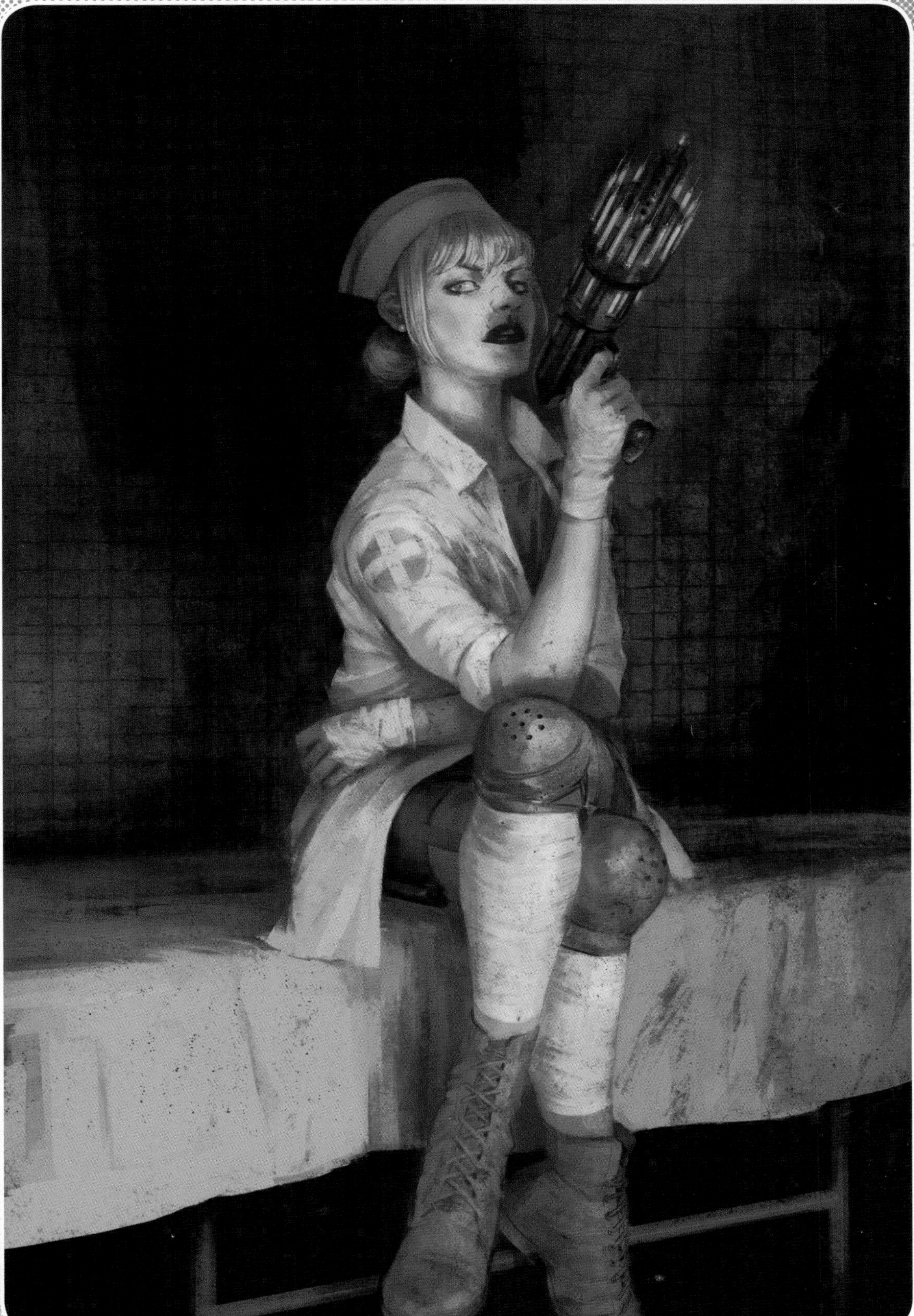

SECRET WARS JOURNAL #5

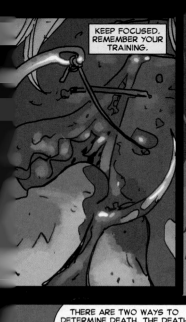

KEEP FOCUSED. REMEMBER YOUR TRAINING.

MS. CARTER! AT WHAT POINT DOES THE HUMAN BODY DIE?

IT'S DEEP, BUT TREATABLE.

THERE ARE TWO WAYS TO DETERMINE DEATH. THE DEATH OF THE HEART, MEANING AN IRREVERSIBLE CESSATION OF CIRCULATORY AND RESPIRATORY FUNCTIONS.

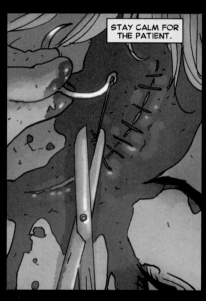

STAY CALM FOR THE PATIENT.

AND THE DEATH OF THE BRAIN, WHICH IS THE IRREVERSIBLE CESSATION OF ALL BRAIN FUNCTIONS, INCLUDING THE BRAIN STEM; LOSS OF THE ABILITY TO INVOLUNTARILY SUSTAIN LIFE.

MARSHALL WOULD SAY THAT A CONFIDENT BEDSIDE MANNER CAN WORK WONDERS, ESPECIALLY IN A SITUATION LIKE THIS.

I WAS STILL CALLING HIM DR. MICHAELS BACK THEN.

AND AT WHAT POINT DO WE NO LONGER ADMINISTER MEDICAL ASSISTANCE TO THE PATIENT?

YOU MEAN ACCEPT DEATH?

I WANT TO SAY EVERYTHING IS GOING TO BE OKAY... BUT DOCTORS CAN NEVER MAKE THAT PROMISE.

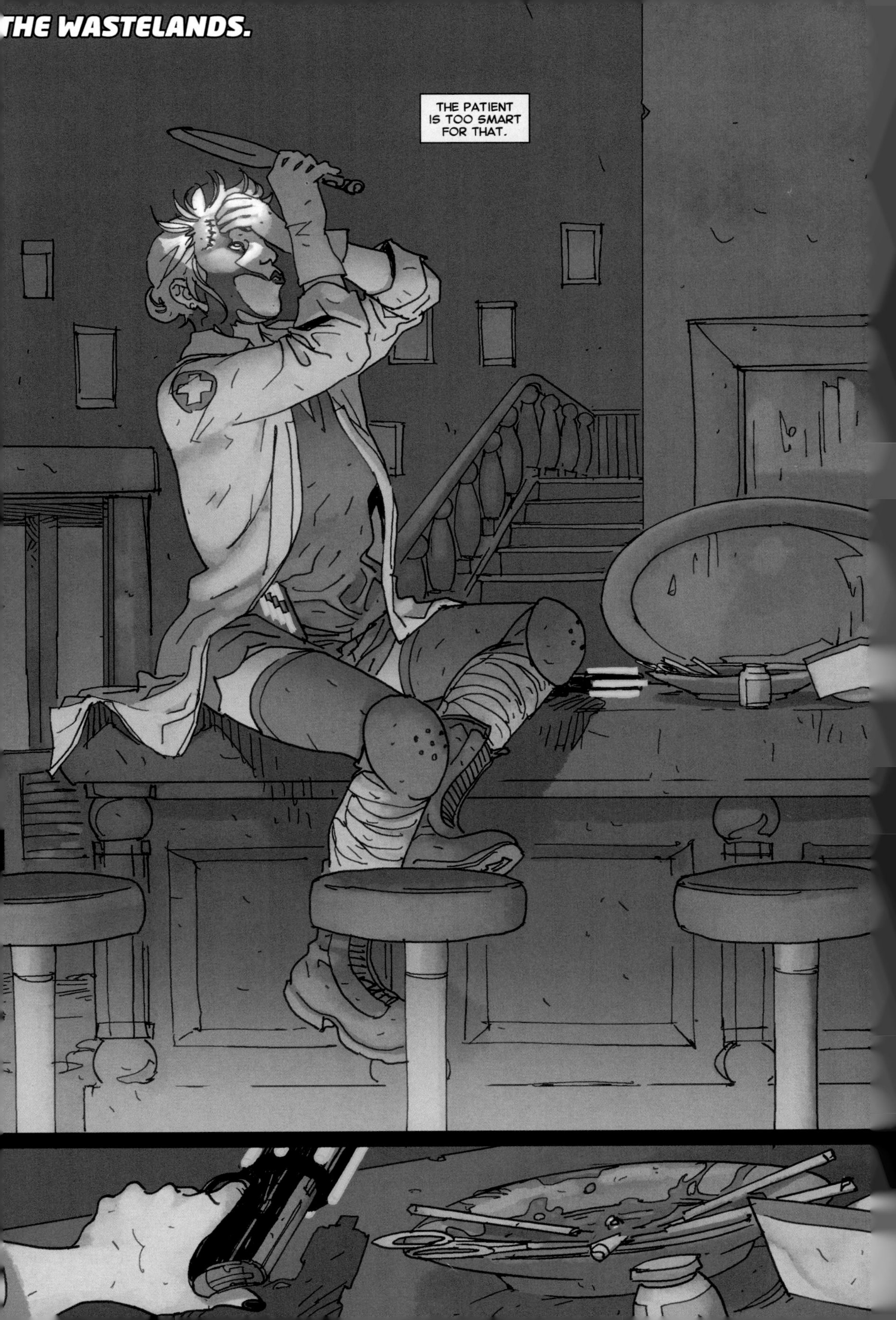
THE WASTELANDS.
THE PATIENT IS TOO SMART FOR THAT.

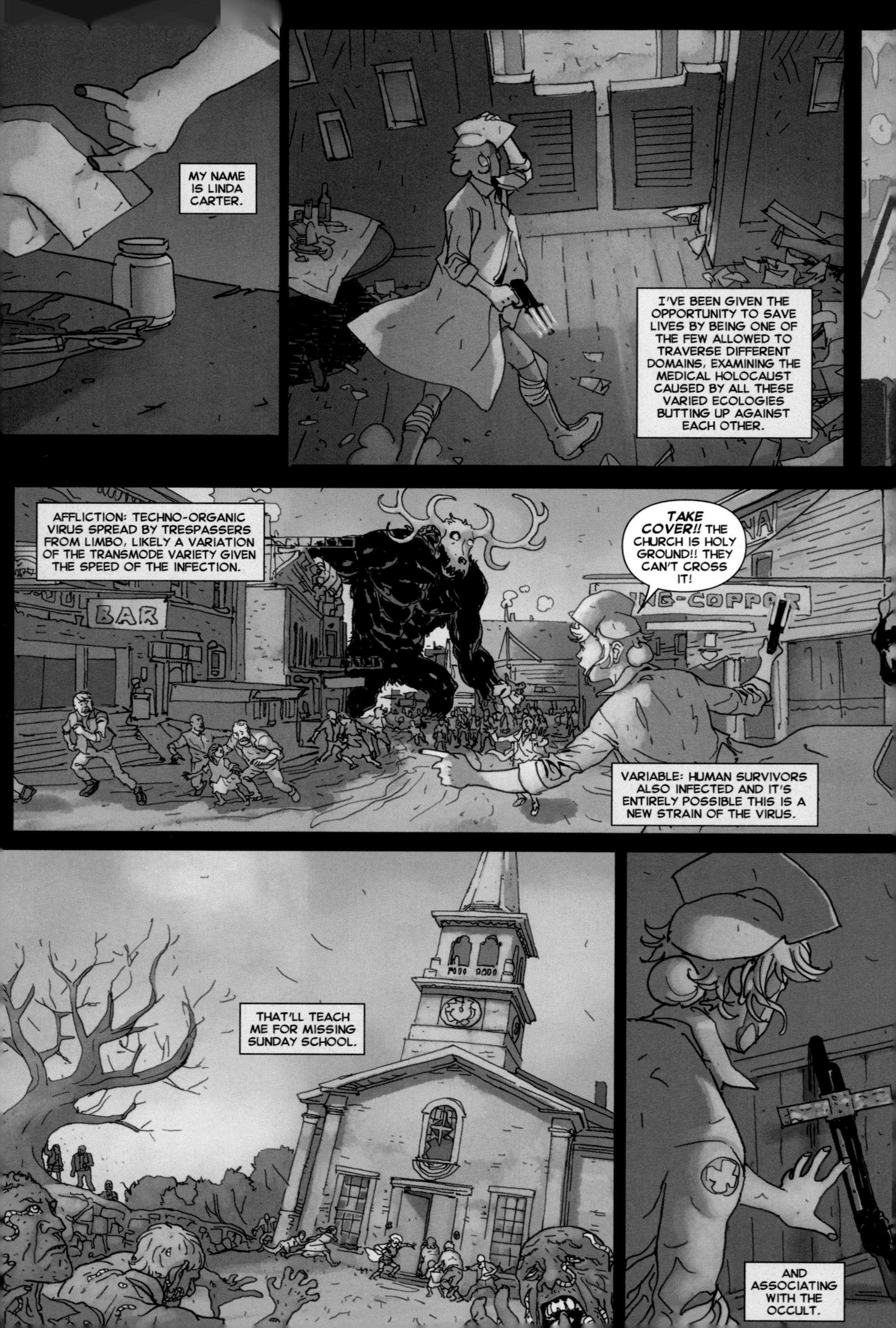
MY NAME IS LINDA CARTER.
I'VE BEEN GIVEN THE OPPORTUNITY TO SAVE LIVES BY BEING ONE OF THE FEW ALLOWED TO TRAVERSE DIFFERENT DOMAINS, EXAMINING THE MEDICAL HOLOCAUST CAUSED BY ALL THESE VARIED ECOLOGIES BUTTING UP AGAINST EACH OTHER.
AFFLICTION: TECHNO-ORGANIC VIRUS SPREAD BY TRESPASSERS FROM LIMBO, LIKELY A VARIATION OF THE TRANSMODE VARIETY GIVEN THE SPEED OF THE INFECTION.
BAR
TAKE COVER!! THE CHURCH IS HOLY GROUND!! THEY CAN'T CROSS IT!
VARIABLE: HUMAN SURVIVORS ALSO INFECTED AND IT'S ENTIRELY POSSIBLE THIS IS A NEW STRAIN OF THE VIRUS.
THAT'LL TEACH ME FOR MISSING SUNDAY SCHOOL.
AND ASSOCIATING WITH THE OCCULT.

"OH, THEY CALL ME NIGHT NURSE. PROBABLY BECAUSE OF SOME MOONLIGHTING AFTER HOURS."

LINDA. THANK YOU.

STOP MOVING, MATT.

OOF. THIS HEAD WOUND'S CAUSING SOME PRETTY INTENSE FLASHBACKS. GOTTA KEEP MY HEAD IN THE GAME OR ELSE--

HEALER!!!

P.O.A.: TRY NOT TO ADD TO THE BODY COUNT. UNLESS IT'S OUR T-O DEMON. DO NOT GET KILLED. CUT THE VIRUS OFF AT ITS SOURCE.

PHYSICIAN, HEAL YOURSELF. DO MIRACLES LIKE THOSE DONE IN CAPERNAUM.

T'S HOPE
HE GOOD
SHERIFF
STRANGE
ASN'T LED
E WRONG.

ESPECIALLY IF I WANT THAT "DO NOT GET KILLED" PART OF THE OPERATION TO WORK OUT FOR ME.

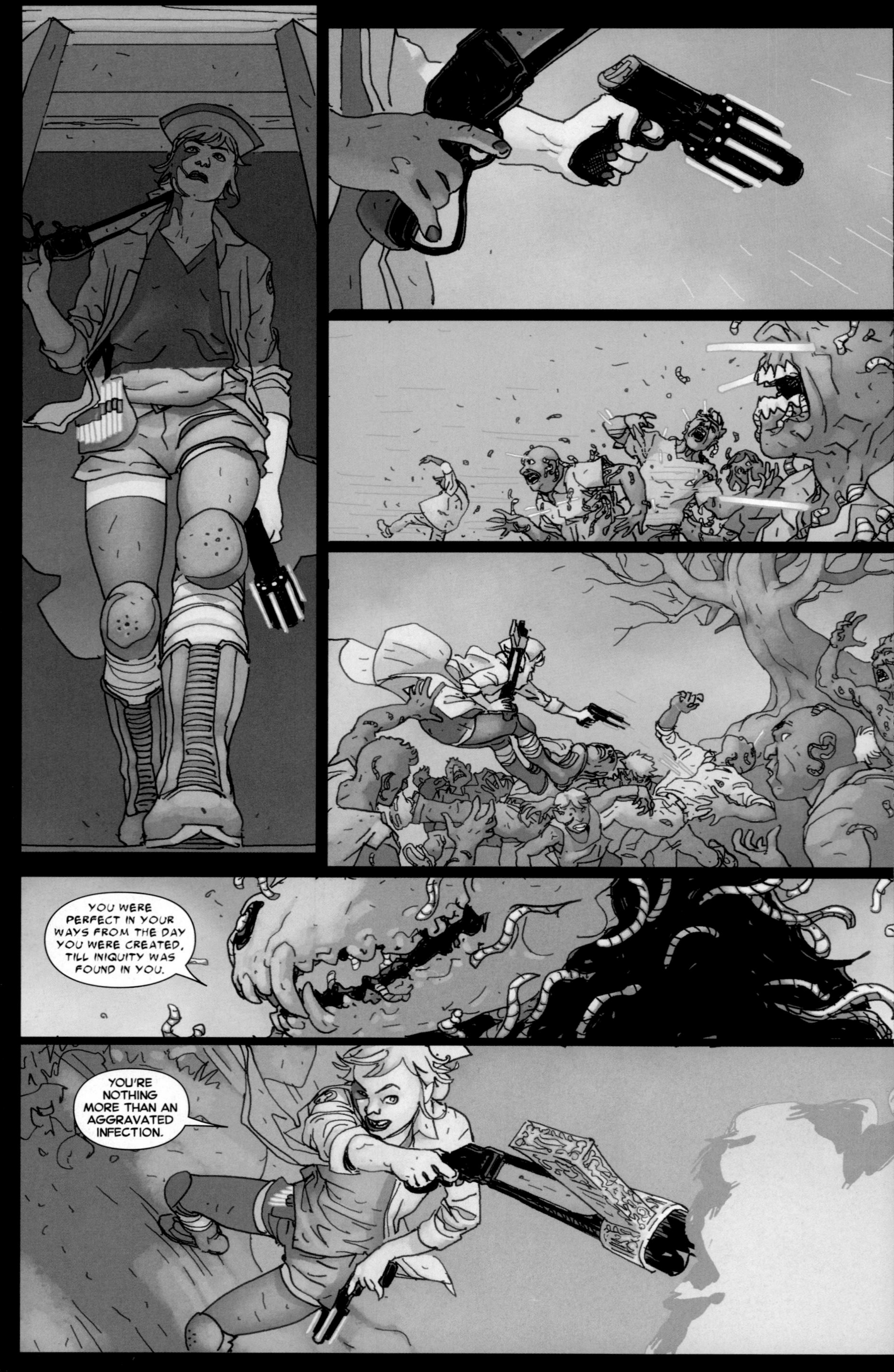
YOU WERE PERFECT IN YOUR WAYS FROM THE DAY YOU WERE CREATED, TILL INIQUITY WAS FOUND IN YOU.
YOU'RE NOTHING MORE THAN AN AGGRAVATED INFECTION.

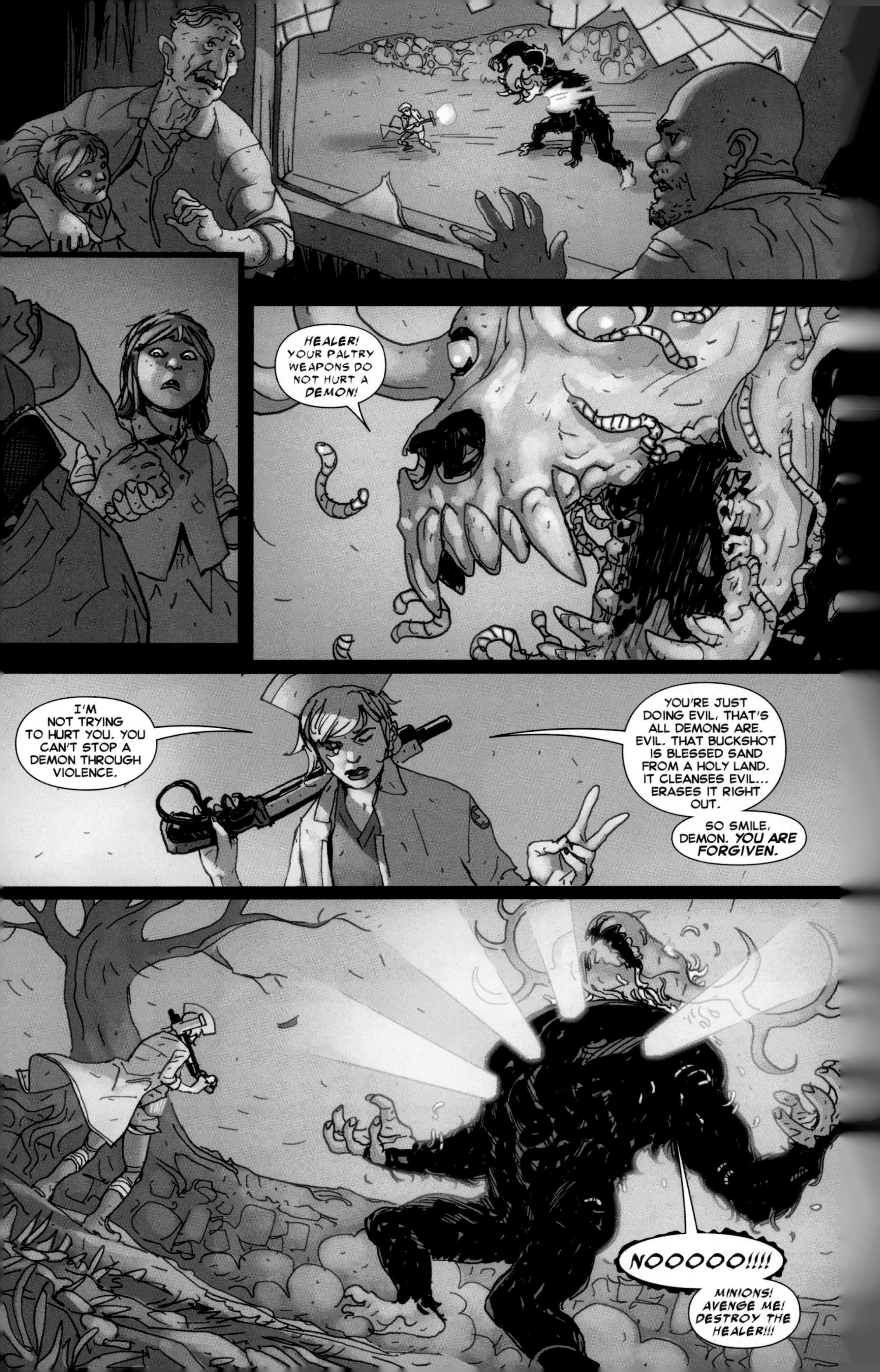
HEALER! YOUR PALTRY WEAPONS DO NOT HURT A DEMON!
I'M NOT TRYING TO HURT YOU. YOU CAN'T STOP A DEMON THROUGH VIOLENCE.
YOU'RE JUST DOING EVIL, THAT'S ALL DEMONS ARE. EVIL. THAT BUCKSHOT IS BLESSED SAND FROM A HOLY LAND. IT CLEANSES EVIL... ERASES IT RIGHT OUT.
SO SMILE, DEMON. YOU ARE FORGIVEN.
NOOOOO!!!!
MINIONS! AVENGE ME! DESTROY THE HEALER!!!

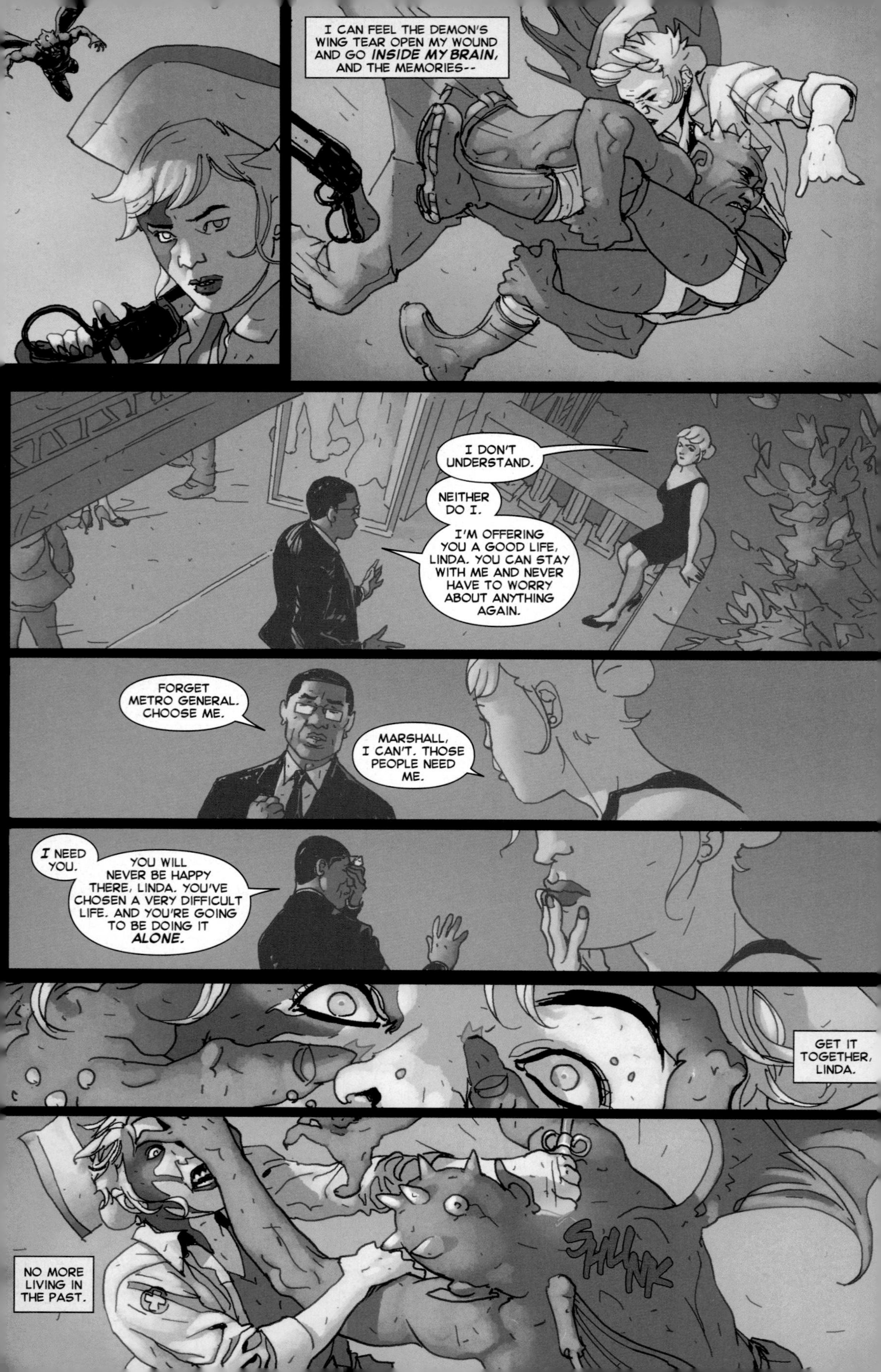

I CAN FEEL THE DEMON'S WING TEAR OPEN MY WOUND AND GO *INSIDE MY BRAIN,* AND THE MEMORIES--
I DON'T UNDERSTAND.
NEITHER DO I.
I'M OFFERING YOU A GOOD LIFE, LINDA. YOU CAN STAY WITH ME AND NEVER HAVE TO WORRY ABOUT ANYTHING AGAIN.
FORGET METRO GENERAL. CHOOSE ME.
MARSHALL, I CAN'T. THOSE PEOPLE NEED ME.
I NEED YOU.
YOU WILL NEVER BE HAPPY THERE, LINDA. YOU'VE CHOSEN A VERY DIFFICULT LIFE. AND YOU'RE GOING TO BE DOING IT *ALONE.*
GET IT TOGETHER, LINDA.
NO MORE LIVING IN THE PAST.
SHLUNK

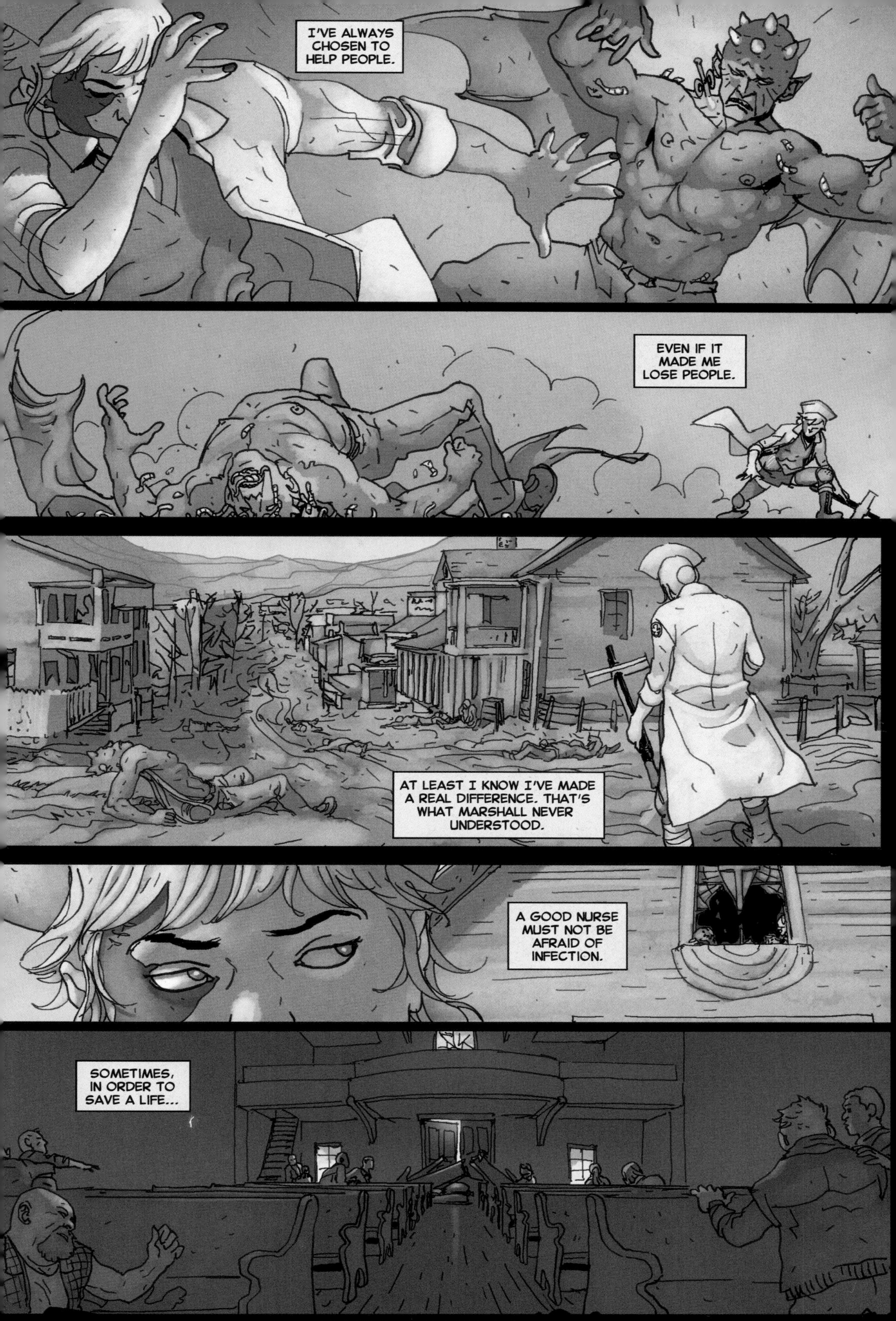
I'VE ALWAYS CHOSEN TO HELP PEOPLE.
EVEN IF IT MADE ME LOSE PEOPLE.
AT LEAST I KNOW I'VE MADE A REAL DIFFERENCE. THAT'S WHAT MARSHALL NEVER UNDERSTOOD.
A GOOD NURSE MUST NOT BE AFRAID OF INFECTION.
SOMETIMES, IN ORDER TO SAVE A LIFE...

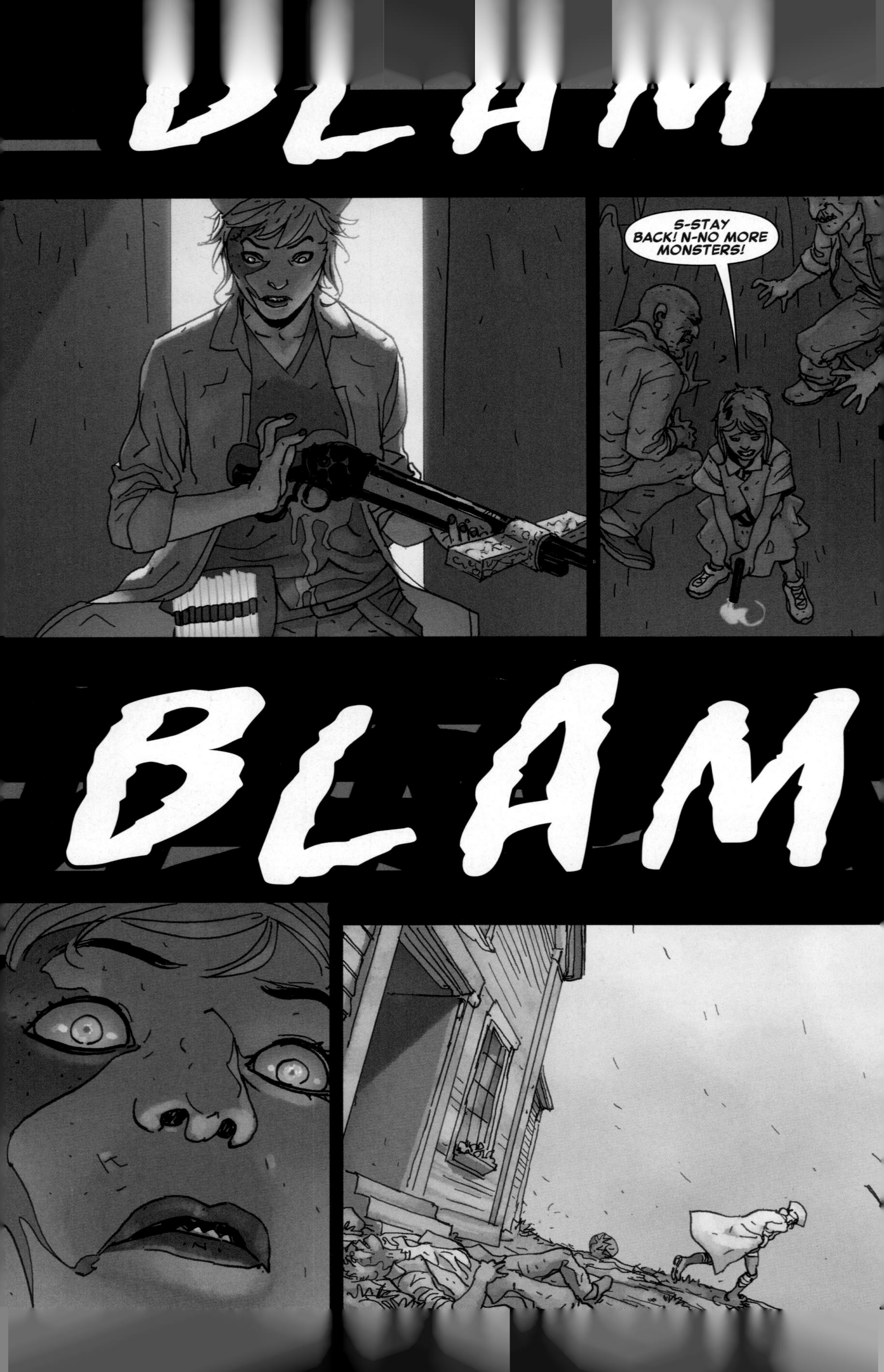
BLAM
S-STAY BACK! N-NO MORE MONSTERS!
BLAM

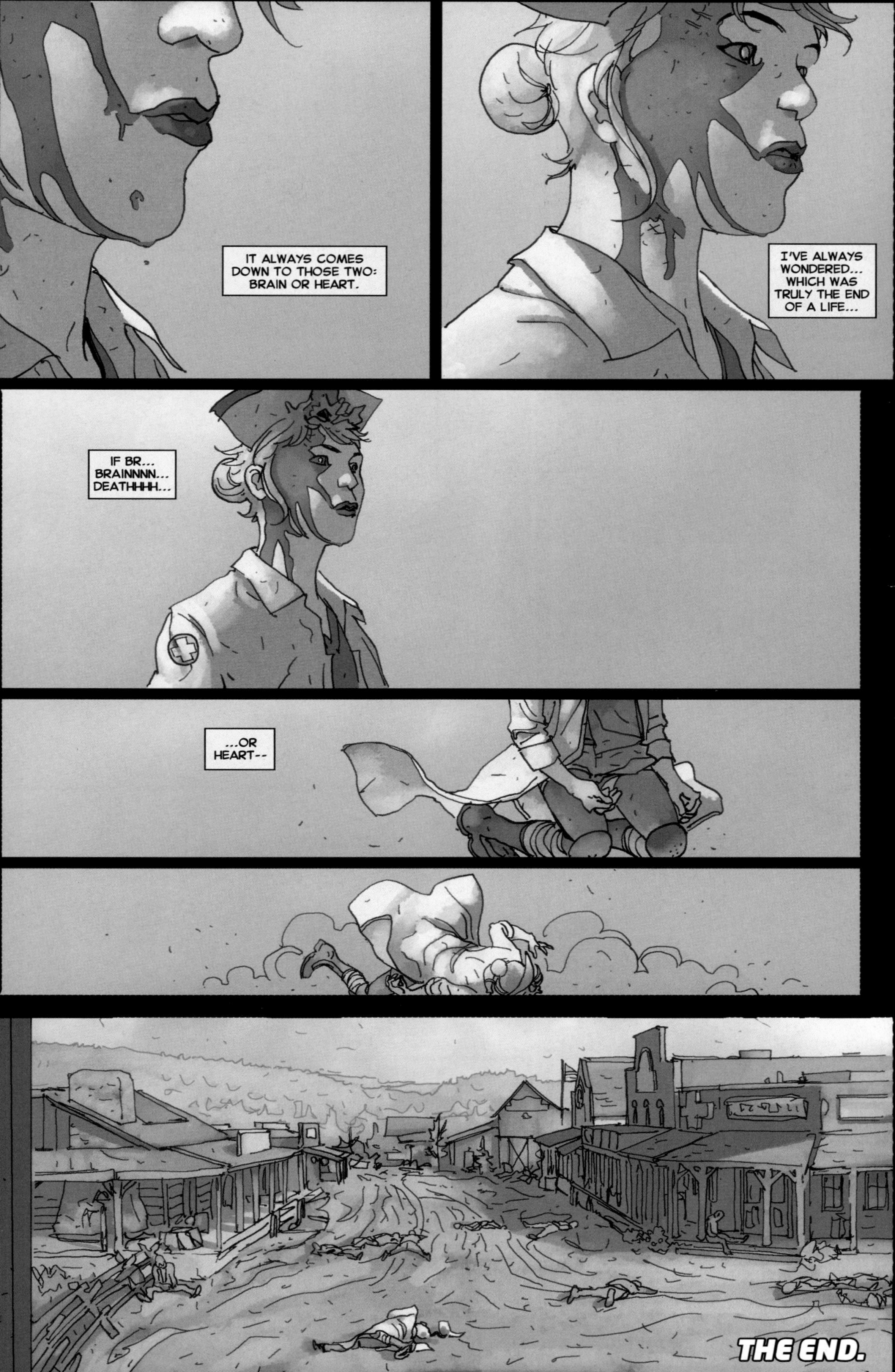
IT ALWAYS COMES DOWN TO THOSE TWO: BRAIN OR HEART.
I'VE ALWAYS WONDERED... WHICH WAS TRULY THE END OF A LIFE...
IF BR... BRAINNNN... DEATHHHH...
...OR HEART--
THE END.

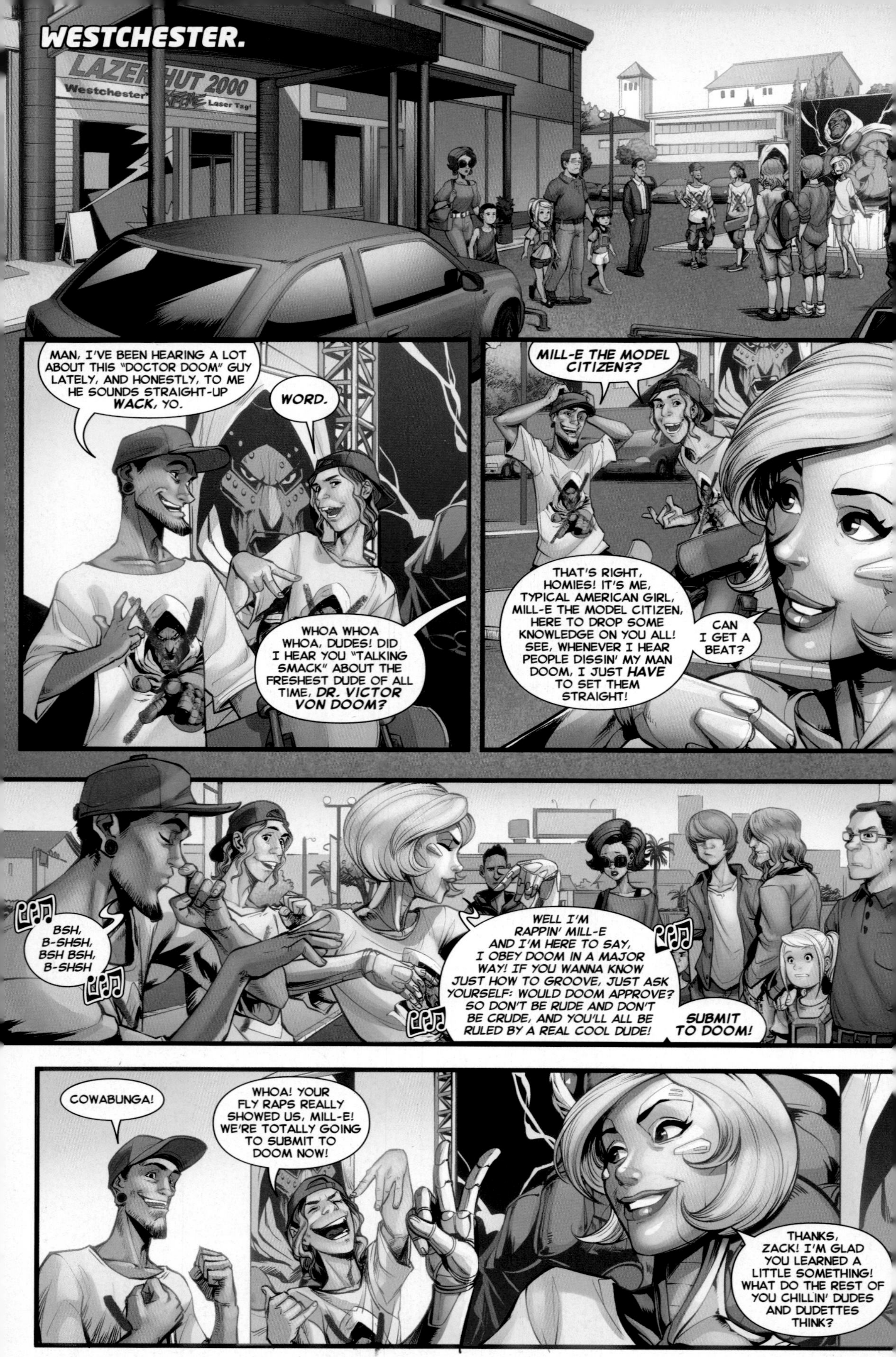

WESTCHESTER.
LAZER HUT 2000
Westchester's XTREME Laser Tag!
MAN, I'VE BEEN HEARING A LOT ABOUT THIS "DOCTOR DOOM" GUY LATELY, AND HONESTLY, TO ME HE SOUNDS STRAIGHT-UP WACK, YO.
WORD.
WHOA WHOA WHOA, DUDES! DID I HEAR YOU "TALKING SMACK" ABOUT THE FRESHEST DUDE OF ALL TIME, DR. VICTOR VON DOOM?
MILL-E THE MODEL CITIZEN??
THAT'S RIGHT, HOMIES! IT'S ME, TYPICAL AMERICAN GIRL, MILL-E THE MODEL CITIZEN, HERE TO DROP SOME KNOWLEDGE ON YOU ALL! SEE, WHENEVER I HEAR PEOPLE DISSIN' MY MAN DOOM, I JUST HAVE TO SET THEM STRAIGHT!
CAN I GET A BEAT?
BSH, B-SHSH, BSH BSH, B-SHSH
WELL I'M RAPPIN' MILL-E AND I'M HERE TO SAY, I OBEY DOOM IN A MAJOR WAY! IF YOU WANNA KNOW JUST HOW TO GROOVE, JUST ASK YOURSELF: WOULD DOOM APPROVE? SO DON'T BE RUDE AND DON'T BE CRUDE, AND YOU'LL ALL BE RULED BY A REAL COOL DUDE!
SUBMIT TO DOOM!
COWABUNGA!
WHOA! YOUR FLY RAPS REALLY SHOWED US, MILL-E! WE'RE TOTALLY GOING TO SUBMIT TO DOOM NOW!
THANKS, ZACK! I'M GLAD YOU LEARNED A LITTLE SOMETHING! WHAT DO THE REST OF YOU CHILLIN' DUDES AND DUDETTES THINK?

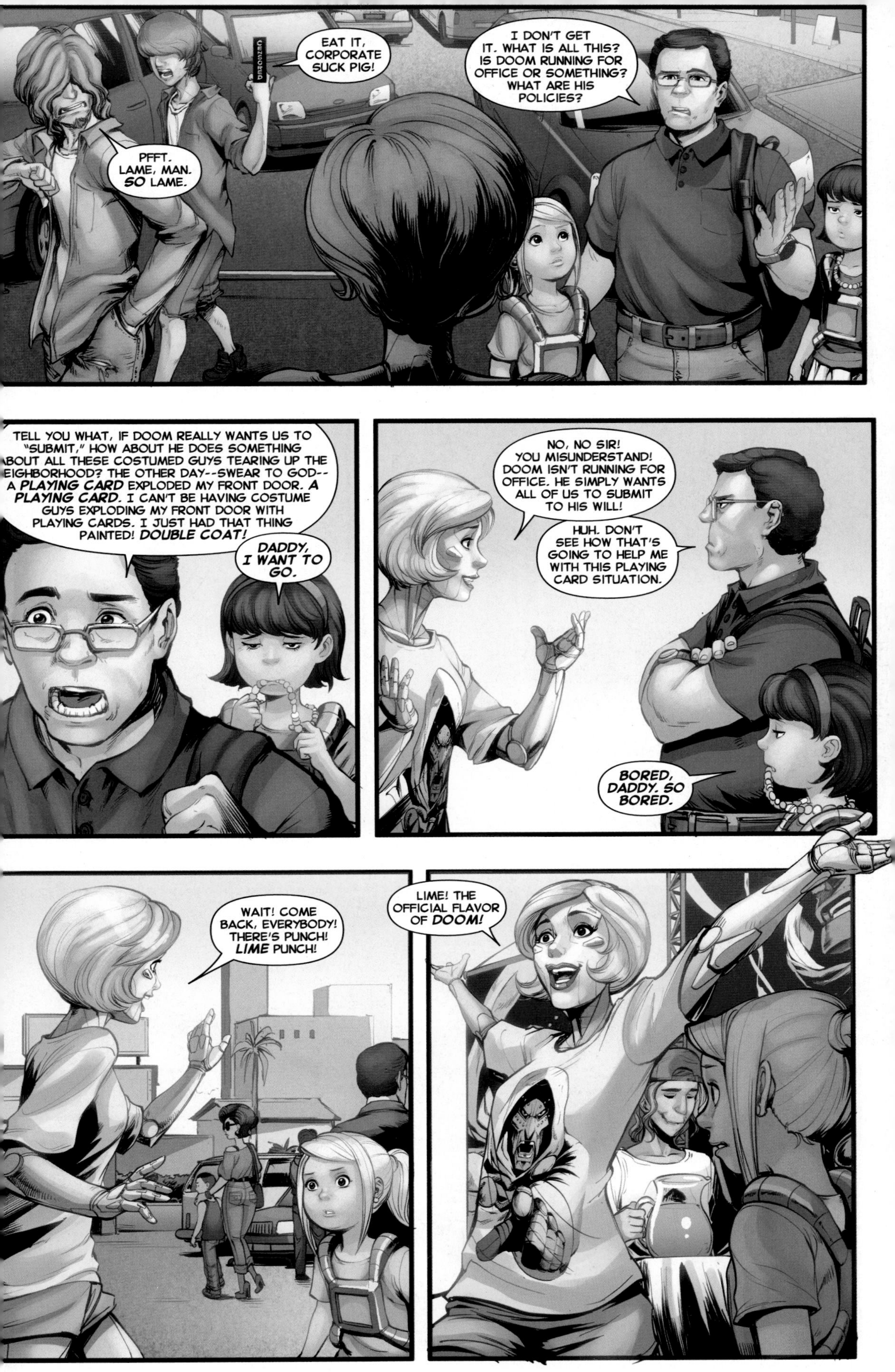
PFFT. LAME, MAN. SO LAME.
CENSORED
EAT IT, CORPORATE SUCK PIG!
I DON'T GET IT. WHAT IS ALL THIS? IS DOOM RUNNING FOR OFFICE OR SOMETHING? WHAT ARE HIS POLICIES?
TELL YOU WHAT, IF DOOM REALLY WANTS US TO "SUBMIT," HOW ABOUT HE DOES SOMETHING BOUT ALL THESE COSTUMED GUYS TEARING UP THE EIGHBORHOOD? THE OTHER DAY--SWEAR TO GOD-- A PLAYING CARD EXPLODED MY FRONT DOOR. A PLAYING CARD. I CAN'T BE HAVING COSTUME GUYS EXPLODING MY FRONT DOOR WITH PLAYING CARDS. I JUST HAD THAT THING PAINTED! DOUBLE COAT!
DADDY, I WANT TO GO.
NO, NO SIR! YOU MISUNDERSTAND! DOOM ISN'T RUNNING FOR OFFICE. HE SIMPLY WANTS ALL OF US TO SUBMIT TO HIS WILL!
HUH. DON'T SEE HOW THAT'S GOING TO HELP ME WITH THIS PLAYING CARD SITUATION.
BORED, DADDY. SO BORED.
WAIT! COME BACK, EVERYBODY! THERE'S PUNCH! LIME PUNCH!
LIME! THE OFFICIAL FLAVOR OF DOOM!

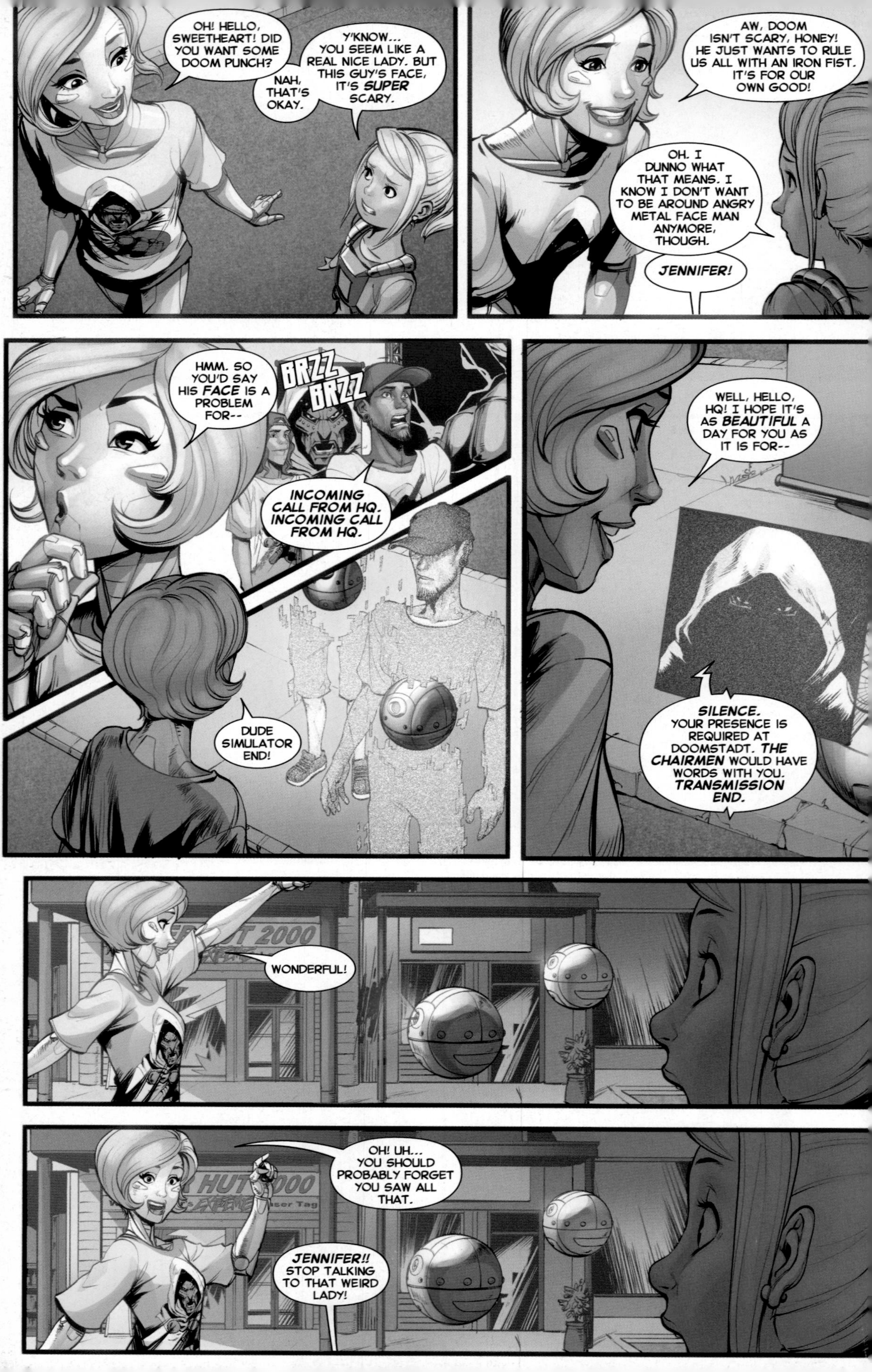
OH! HELLO, SWEETHEART! DID YOU WANT SOME DOOM PUNCH?
NAH, THAT'S OKAY.
Y'KNOW... YOU SEEM LIKE A REAL NICE LADY. BUT THIS GUY'S FACE, IT'S *SUPER* SCARY.
AW, DOOM ISN'T SCARY, HONEY! HE JUST WANTS TO RULE US ALL WITH AN IRON FIST. IT'S FOR OUR OWN GOOD!
OH. I DUNNO WHAT THAT MEANS. I KNOW I DON'T WANT TO BE AROUND ANGRY METAL FACE MAN ANYMORE, THOUGH.
JENNIFER!
HMM. SO YOU'D SAY HIS *FACE* IS A PROBLEM FOR--
BRZZ BRZZ
INCOMING CALL FROM HQ. INCOMING CALL FROM HQ.
DUDE SIMULATOR END!
WELL, HELLO, HQ! I HOPE IT'S AS *BEAUTIFUL* A DAY FOR YOU AS IT IS FOR--
SILENCE. YOUR PRESENCE IS REQUIRED AT DOOMSTADT. *THE CHAIRMEN* WOULD HAVE WORDS WITH YOU. *TRANSMISSION END.*
WONDERFUL!
OH! UH... YOU SHOULD PROBABLY FORGET YOU SAW ALL THAT.
JENNIFER!! STOP TALKING TO THAT WEIRD LADY!

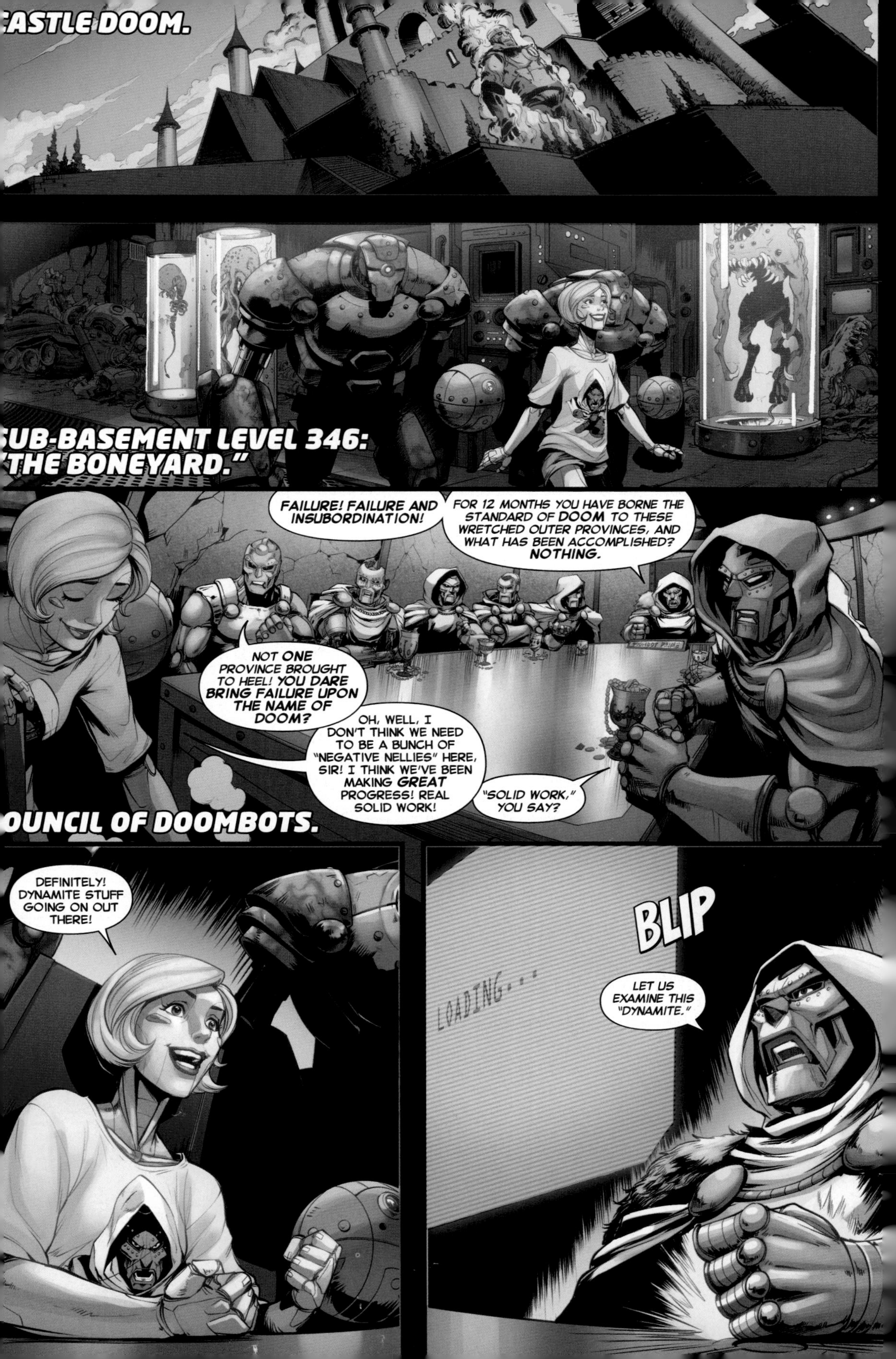

CASTLE DOOM.
SUB-BASEMENT LEVEL 346: "THE BONEYARD."
FAILURE! FAILURE AND INSUBORDINATION!
FOR 12 MONTHS YOU HAVE BORNE THE STANDARD OF DOOM TO THESE WRETCHED OUTER PROVINCES, AND WHAT HAS BEEN ACCOMPLISHED? NOTHING.
NOT ONE PROVINCE BROUGHT TO HEEL! YOU DARE BRING FAILURE UPON THE NAME OF DOOM?
OH, WELL, I DON'T THINK WE NEED TO BE A BUNCH OF "NEGATIVE NELLIES" HERE, SIR! I THINK WE'VE BEEN MAKING GREAT PROGRESS! REAL SOLID WORK!
"SOLID WORK," YOU SAY?
COUNCIL OF DOOMBOTS.
DEFINITELY! DYNAMITE STUFF GOING ON OUT THERE!
BLIP
LOADING...
LET US EXAMINE THIS "DYNAMITE."

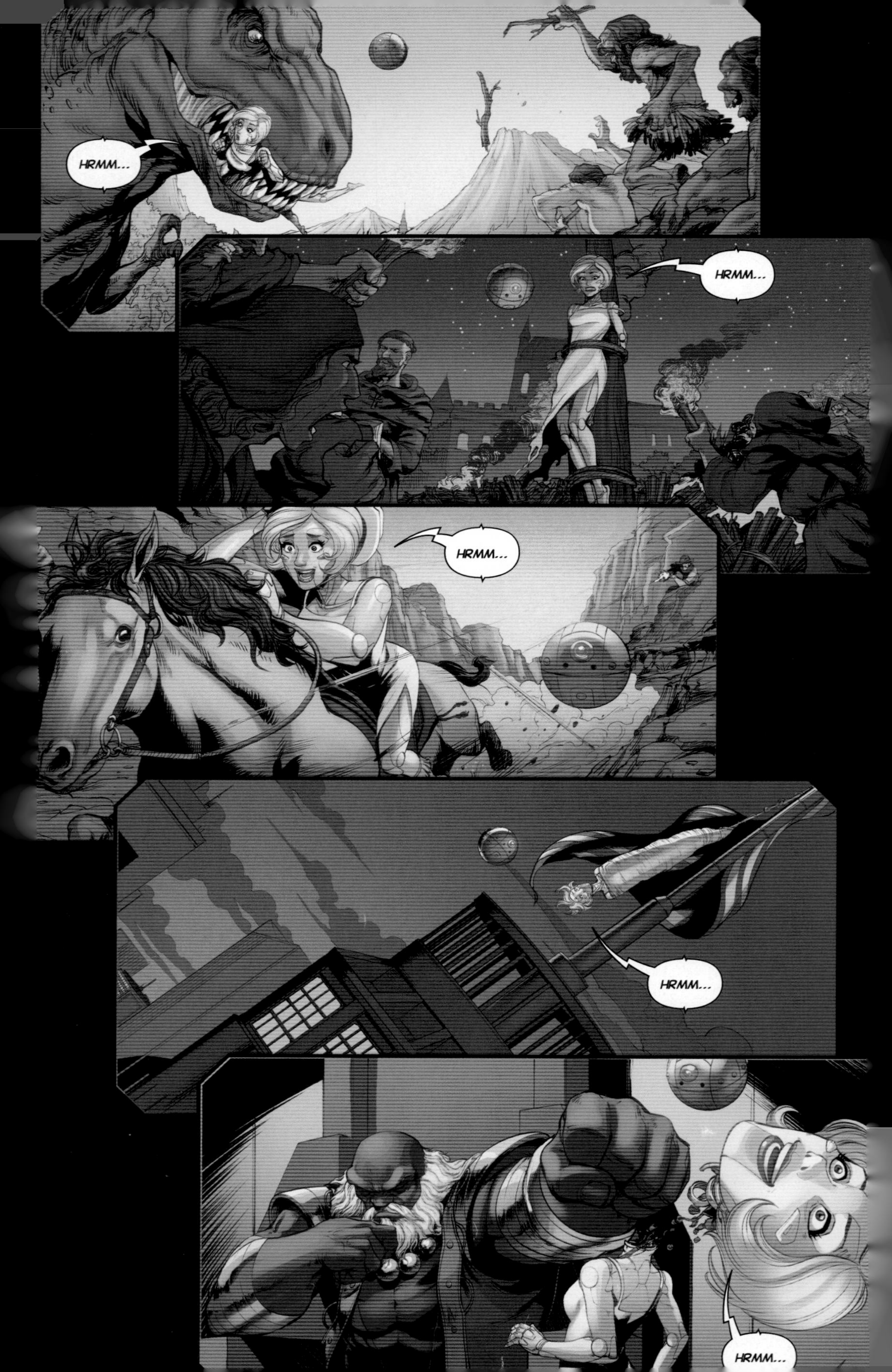
HRMM...
HRMM...
HRMM...
HRMM...
HRMM...

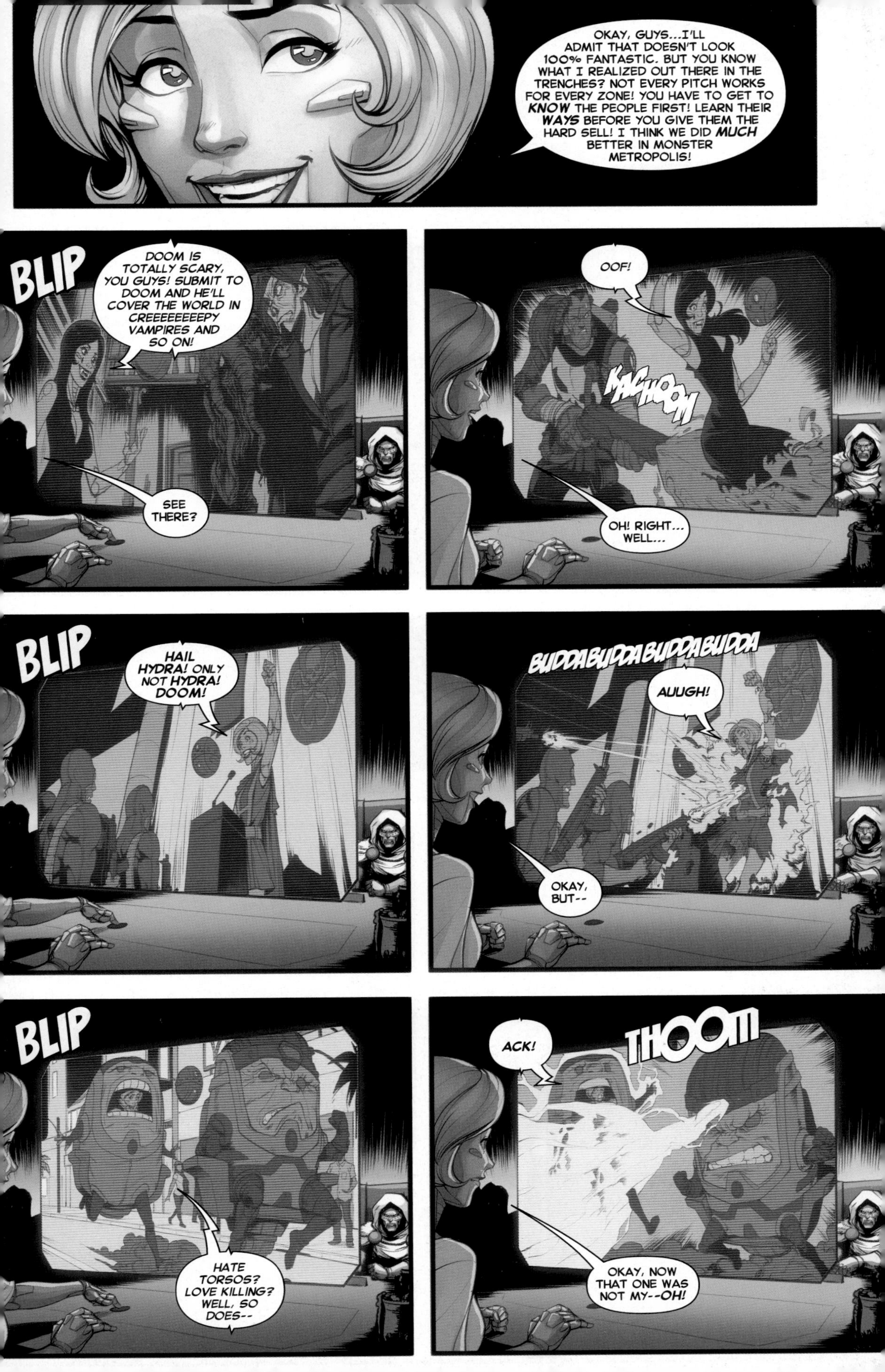
OKAY, GUYS...I'LL ADMIT THAT DOESN'T LOOK 100% FANTASTIC. BUT YOU KNOW WHAT I REALIZED OUT THERE IN THE TRENCHES? NOT EVERY PITCH WORKS FOR EVERY ZONE! YOU HAVE TO GET TO KNOW THE PEOPLE FIRST! LEARN THEIR WAYS BEFORE YOU GIVE THEM THE HARD SELL! I THINK WE DID MUCH BETTER IN MONSTER METROPOLIS!
BLIP
DOOM IS TOTALLY SCARY, YOU GUYS! SUBMIT TO DOOM AND HE'LL COVER THE WORLD IN CREEEEEEEEPY VAMPIRES AND SO ON!
SEE THERE?
OOF!
KACHOOM
OH! RIGHT... WELL...
BLIP
HAIL HYDRA! ONLY NOT HYDRA! DOOM!
BUDDABUDDABUDDABUDDA
AUUGH!
OKAY, BUT--
BLIP
HATE TORSOS? LOVE KILLING? WELL, SO DOES--
ACK!
THOOM
OKAY, NOW THAT ONE WAS NOT MY--OH!

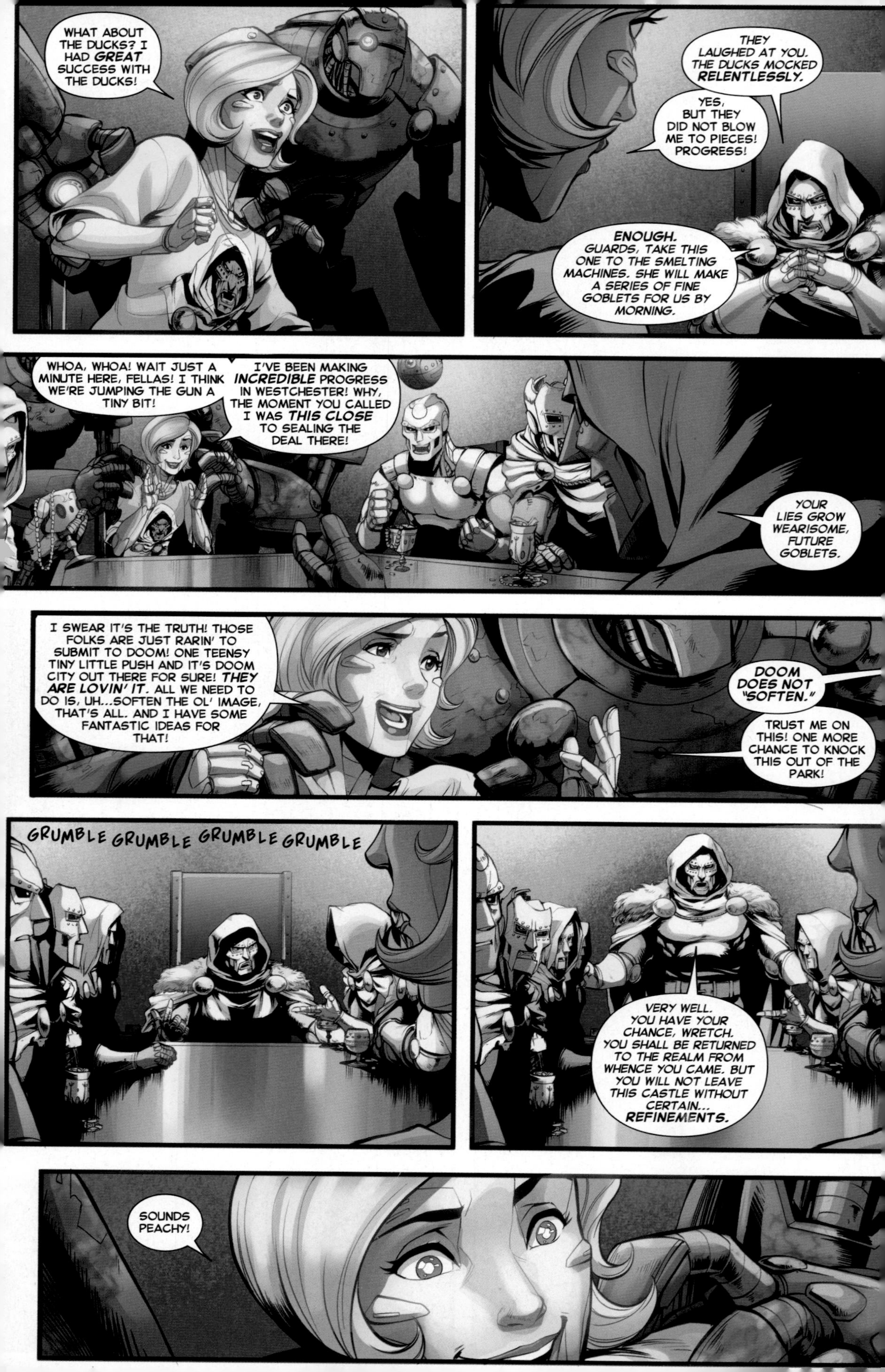
WHAT ABOUT THE DUCKS? I HAD GREAT SUCCESS WITH THE DUCKS!
THEY LAUGHED AT YOU. THE DUCKS MOCKED RELENTLESSLY.
YES, BUT THEY DID NOT BLOW ME TO PIECES! PROGRESS!
ENOUGH. GUARDS, TAKE THIS ONE TO THE SMELTING MACHINES. SHE WILL MAKE A SERIES OF FINE GOBLETS FOR US BY MORNING.
WHOA, WHOA! WAIT JUST A MINUTE HERE, FELLAS! I THINK WE'RE JUMPING THE GUN A TINY BIT!
I'VE BEEN MAKING INCREDIBLE PROGRESS IN WESTCHESTER! WHY, THE MOMENT YOU CALLED I WAS THIS CLOSE TO SEALING THE DEAL THERE!
YOUR LIES GROW WEARISOME, FUTURE GOBLETS.
I SWEAR IT'S THE TRUTH! THOSE FOLKS ARE JUST RARIN' TO SUBMIT TO DOOM! ONE TEENSY TINY LITTLE PUSH AND IT'S DOOM CITY OUT THERE FOR SURE! THEY ARE LOVIN' IT. ALL WE NEED TO DO IS, UH...SOFTEN THE OL' IMAGE, THAT'S ALL. AND I HAVE SOME FANTASTIC IDEAS FOR THAT!
DOOM DOES NOT "SOFTEN."
TRUST ME ON THIS! ONE MORE CHANCE TO KNOCK THIS OUT OF THE PARK!
GRUMBLE GRUMBLE GRUMBLE GRUMBLE
VERY WELL. YOU HAVE YOUR CHANCE, WRETCH. YOU SHALL BE RETURNED TO THE REALM FROM WHENCE YOU CAME. BUT YOU WILL NOT LEAVE THIS CASTLE WITHOUT CERTAIN... REFINEMENTS.
SOUNDS PEACHY!

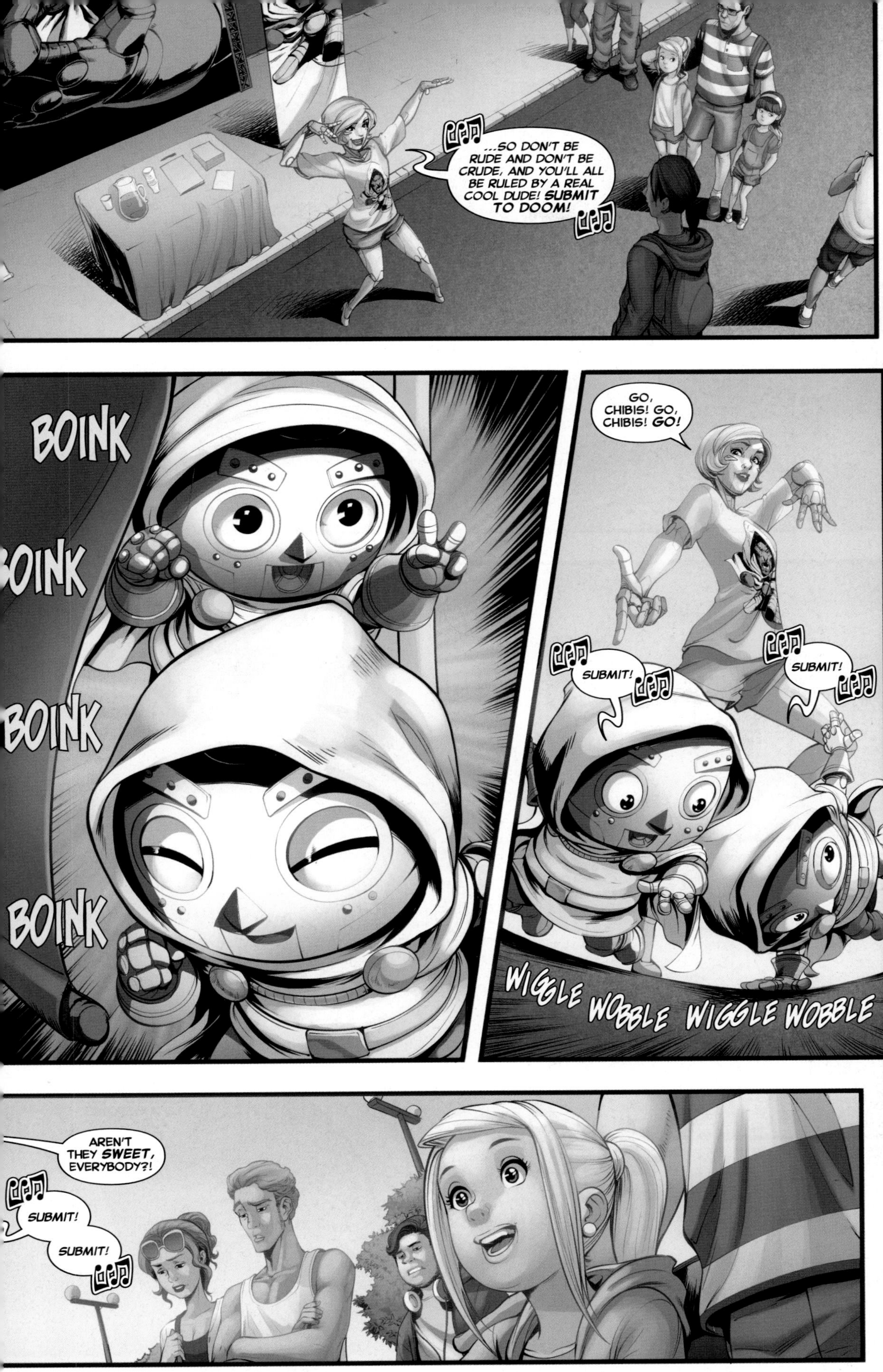
...SO DON'T BE RUDE AND DON'T BE CRUDE, AND YOU'LL ALL BE RULED BY A REAL COOL DUDE! SUBMIT TO DOOM!
BOINK
BOINK
BOINK
BOINK
GO, CHIBIS! GO, CHIBIS! GO!
SUBMIT!
SUBMIT!
WIGGLE WOBBLE WIGGLE WOBBLE
AREN'T THEY SWEET, EVERYBODY?!
SUBMIT!
SUBMIT!

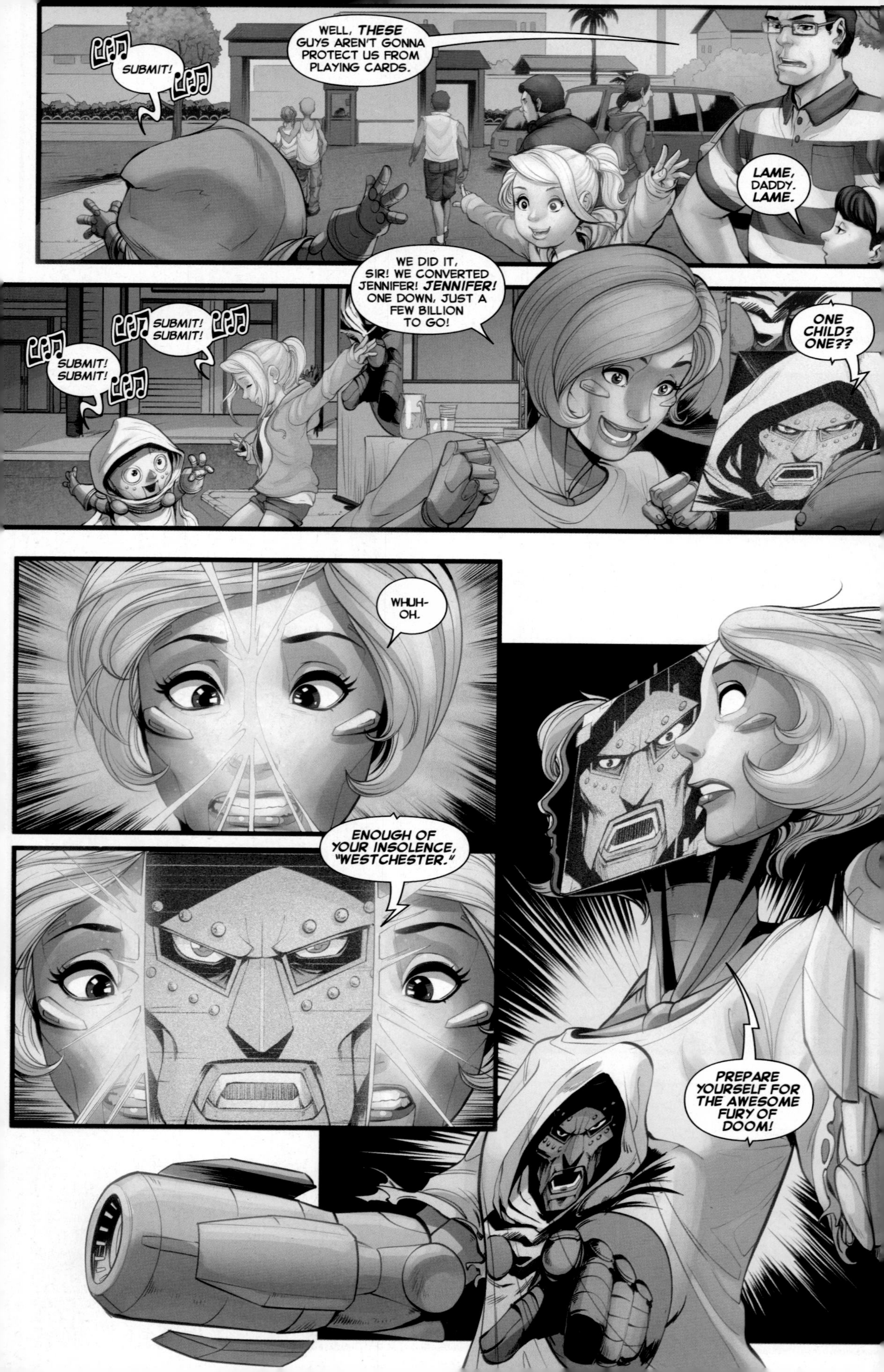
SUBMIT!
WELL, THESE GUYS AREN'T GONNA PROTECT US FROM PLAYING CARDS.
LAME, DADDY. LAME.
SUBMIT! SUBMIT!
SUBMIT! SUBMIT!
WE DID IT, SIR! WE CONVERTED JENNIFER! JENNIFER! ONE DOWN, JUST A FEW BILLION TO GO!
ONE CHILD? ONE??
WHUH-OH.
ENOUGH OF YOUR INSOLENCE, "WESTCHESTER."
PREPARE YOURSELF FOR THE AWESOME FURY OF DOOM!

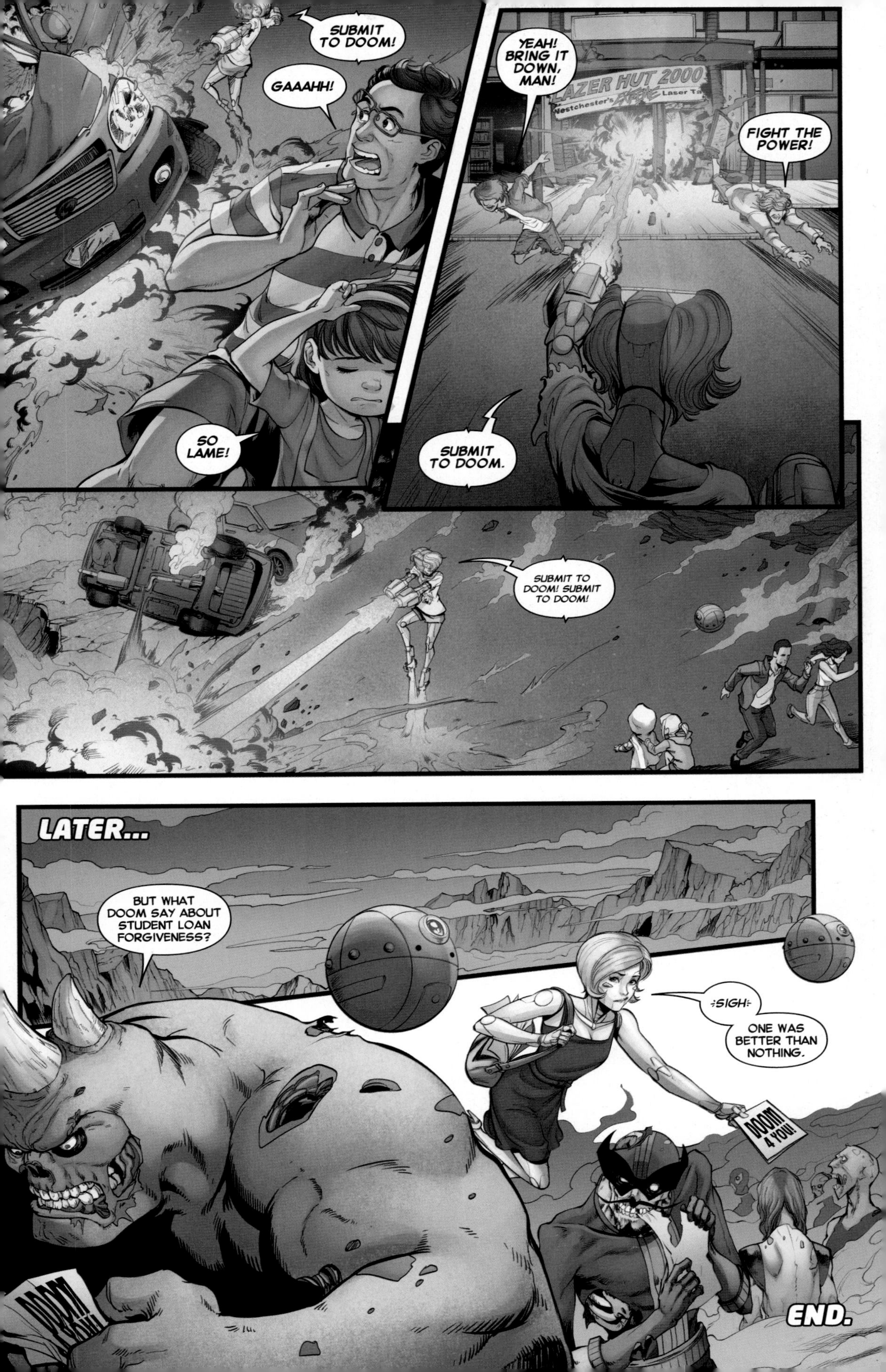
SUBMIT TO DOOM!
GAAAHH!
SO LAME!
YEAH! BRING IT DOWN, MAN!
LAZER HUT 2000
Westchester's EXTREME Laser Ta
FIGHT THE POWER!
SUBMIT TO DOOM.
SUBMIT TO DOOM! SUBMIT TO DOOM!
LATER...
BUT WHAT DOOM SAY ABOUT STUDENT LOAN FORGIVENESS?
⇟SIGH⇞
ONE WAS BETTER THAN NOTHING.
DOOM 4 YOU!
END.

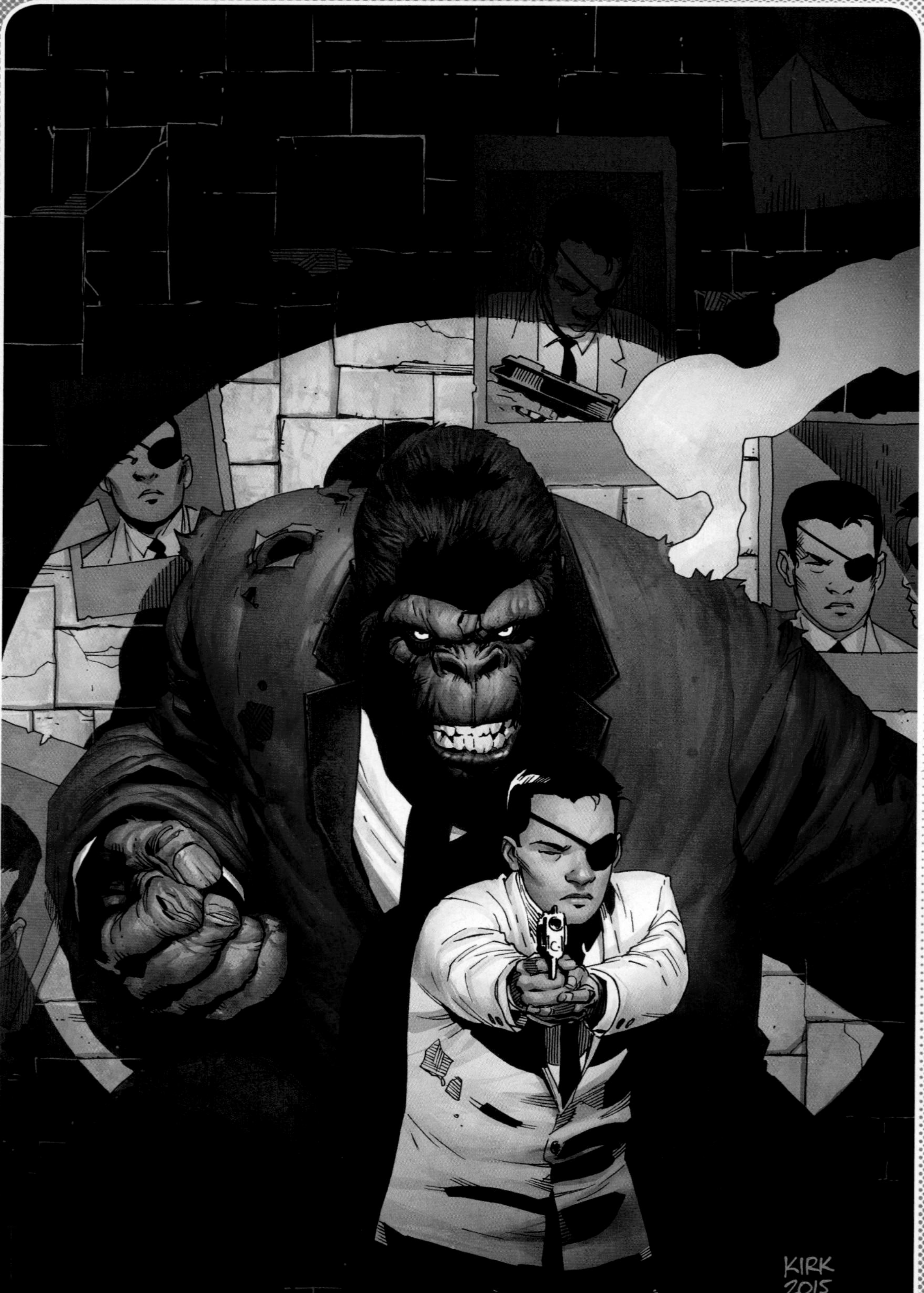
KIRK
2015
+
CABRERA

SECRET WARS: AGENTS OF ATLAS #1

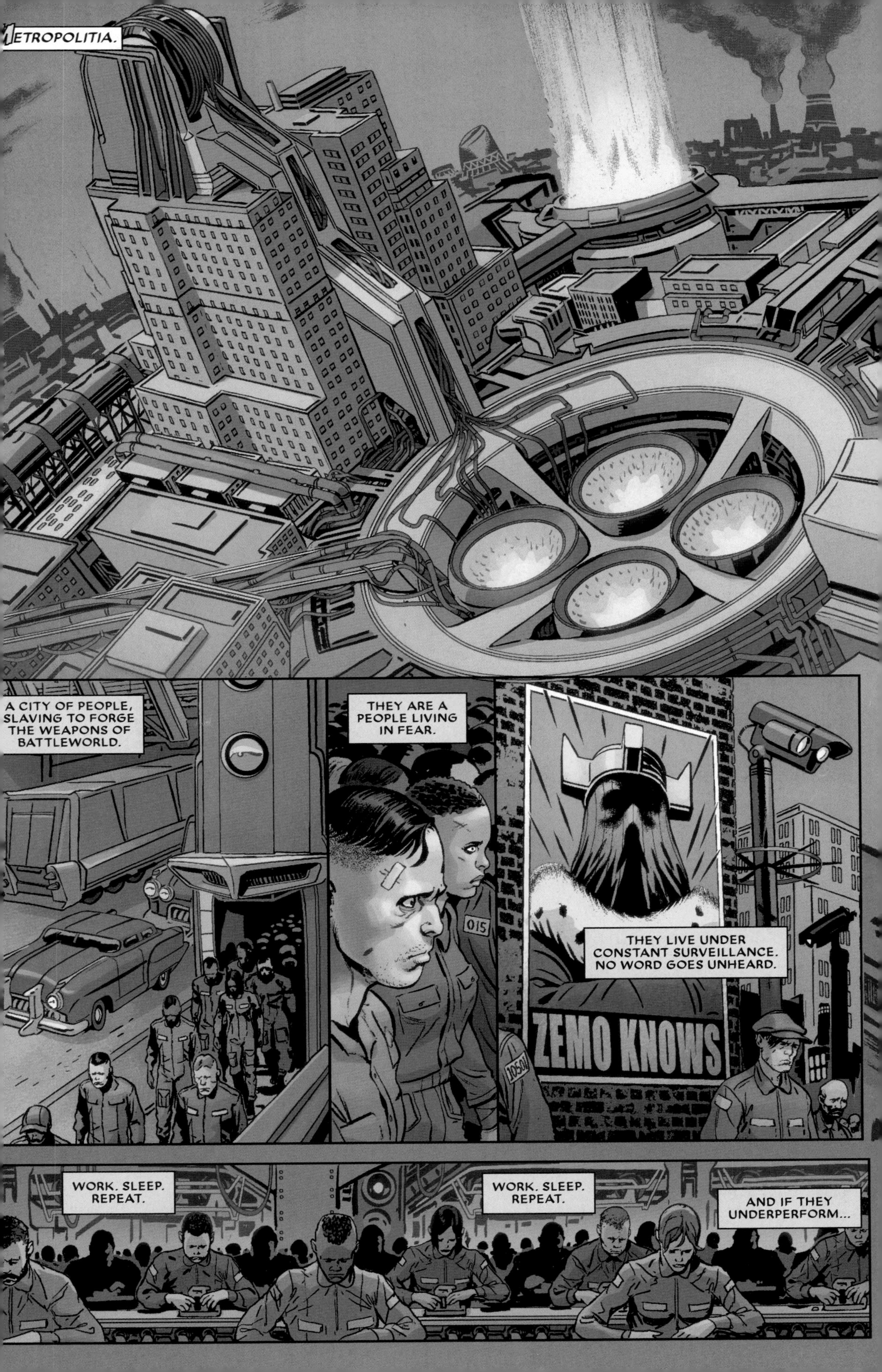
METROPOLITIA.
A CITY OF PEOPLE, SLAVING TO FORGE THE WEAPONS OF BATTLEWORLD.
THEY ARE A PEOPLE LIVING IN FEAR.
015
ZEMO KNOWS
10501
THEY LIVE UNDER CONSTANT SURVEILLANCE. NO WORD GOES UNHEARD.
WORK. SLEEP. REPEAT.
WORK. SLEEP. REPEAT.
AND IF THEY UNDERPERFORM...

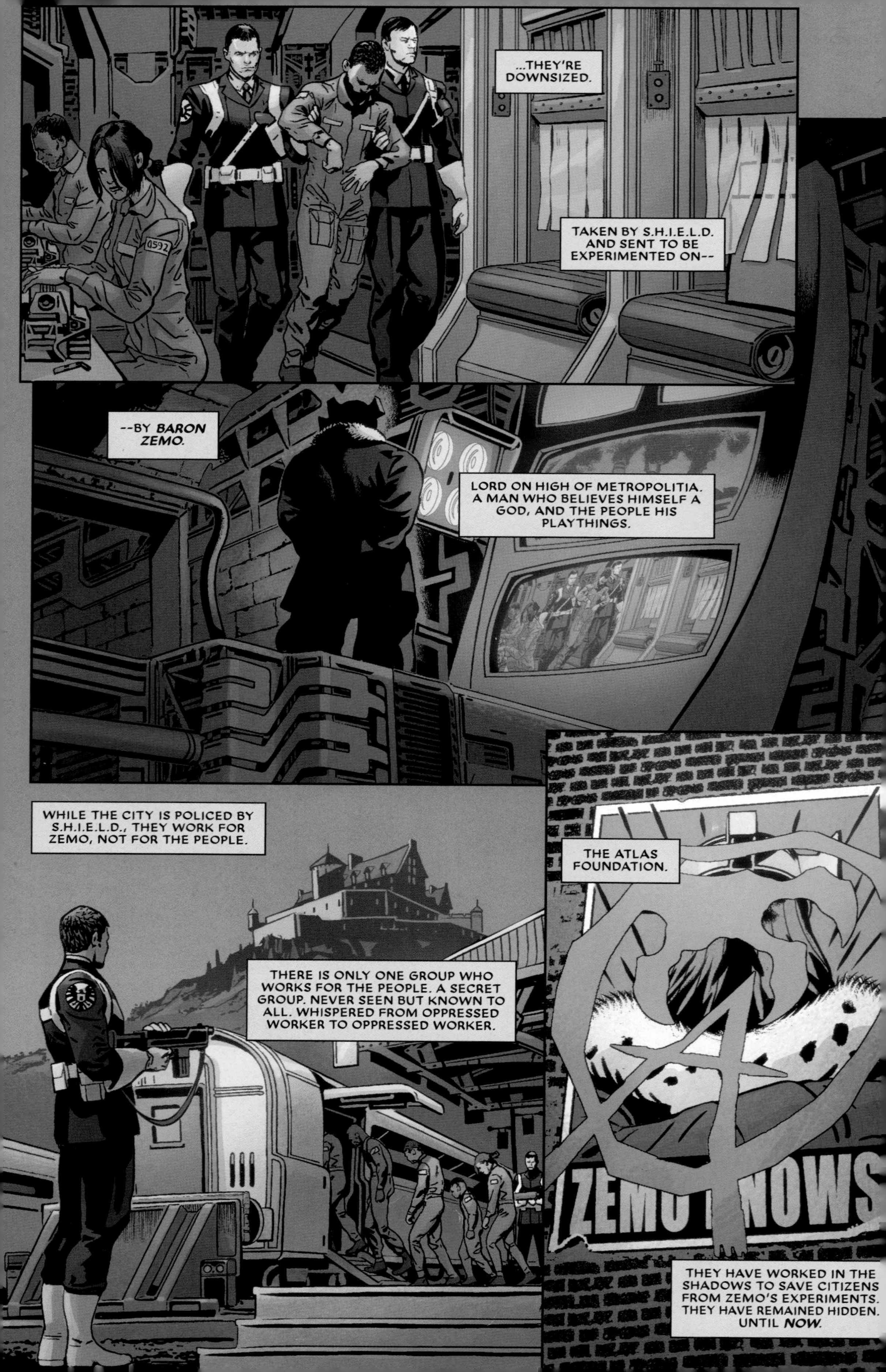
...THEY'RE DOWNSIZED.
TAKEN BY S.H.I.E.L.D. AND SENT TO BE EXPERIMENTED ON--
--BY *BARON ZEMO.*
LORD ON HIGH OF METROPOLITIA. A MAN WHO BELIEVES HIMSELF A GOD, AND THE PEOPLE HIS PLAYTHINGS.
WHILE THE CITY IS POLICED BY S.H.I.E.L.D., THEY WORK FOR ZEMO, NOT FOR THE PEOPLE.
THERE IS ONLY ONE GROUP WHO WORKS FOR THE PEOPLE. A SECRET GROUP. NEVER SEEN BUT KNOWN TO ALL. WHISPERED FROM OPPRESSED WORKER TO OPPRESSED WORKER.
THE ATLAS FOUNDATION.
ZEMO NOWS
THEY HAVE WORKED IN THE SHADOWS TO SAVE CITIZENS FROM ZEMO'S EXPERIMENTS. THEY HAVE REMAINED HIDDEN. UNTIL *NOW.*

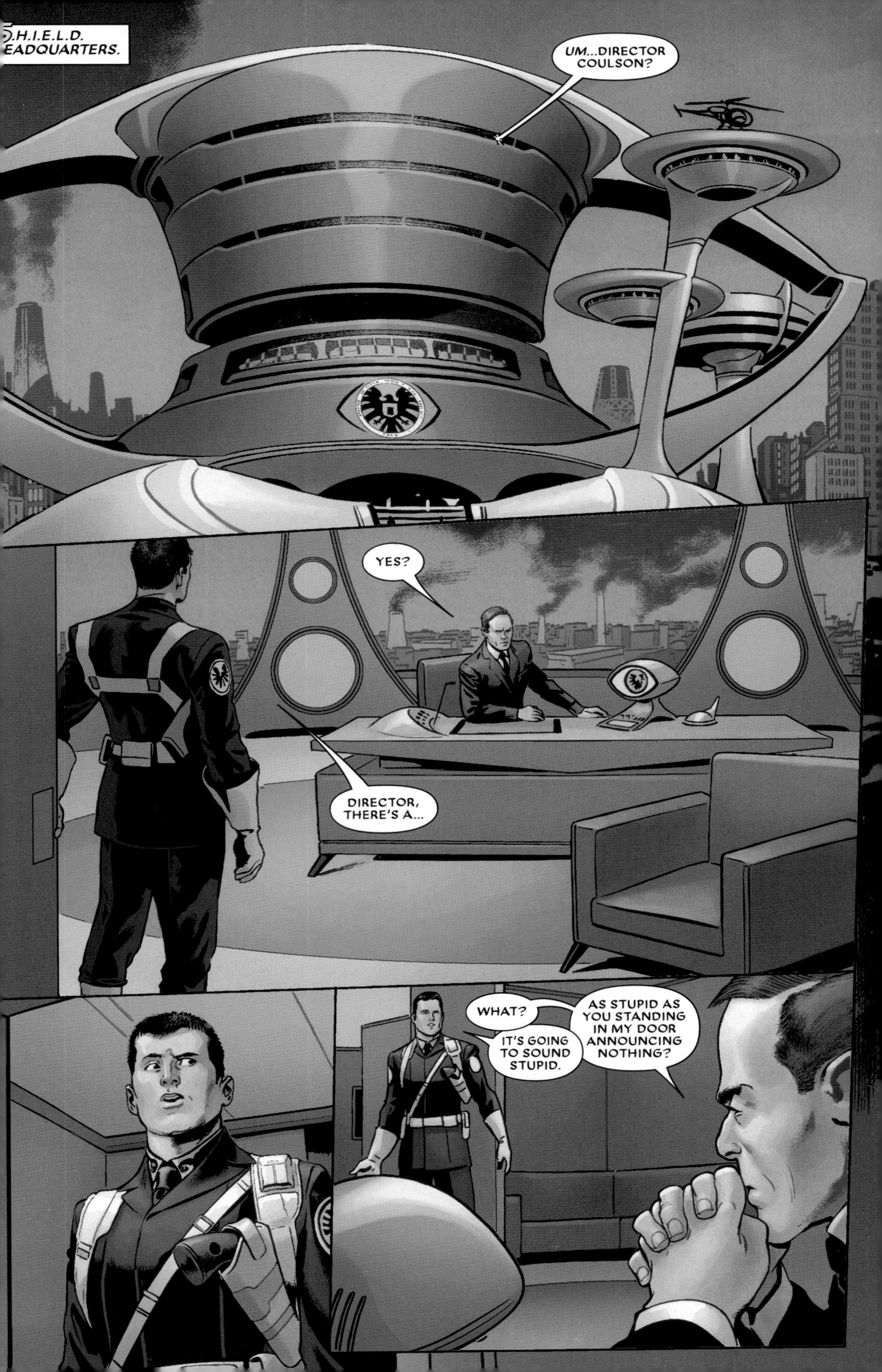
S.H.I.E.L.D.
HEADQUARTERS.
UM...DIRECTOR COULSON?
YES?
DIRECTOR, THERE'S A...
WHAT?
IT'S GOING TO SOUND STUPID.
AS STUPID AS YOU STANDING IN MY DOOR ANNOUNCING NOTHING?

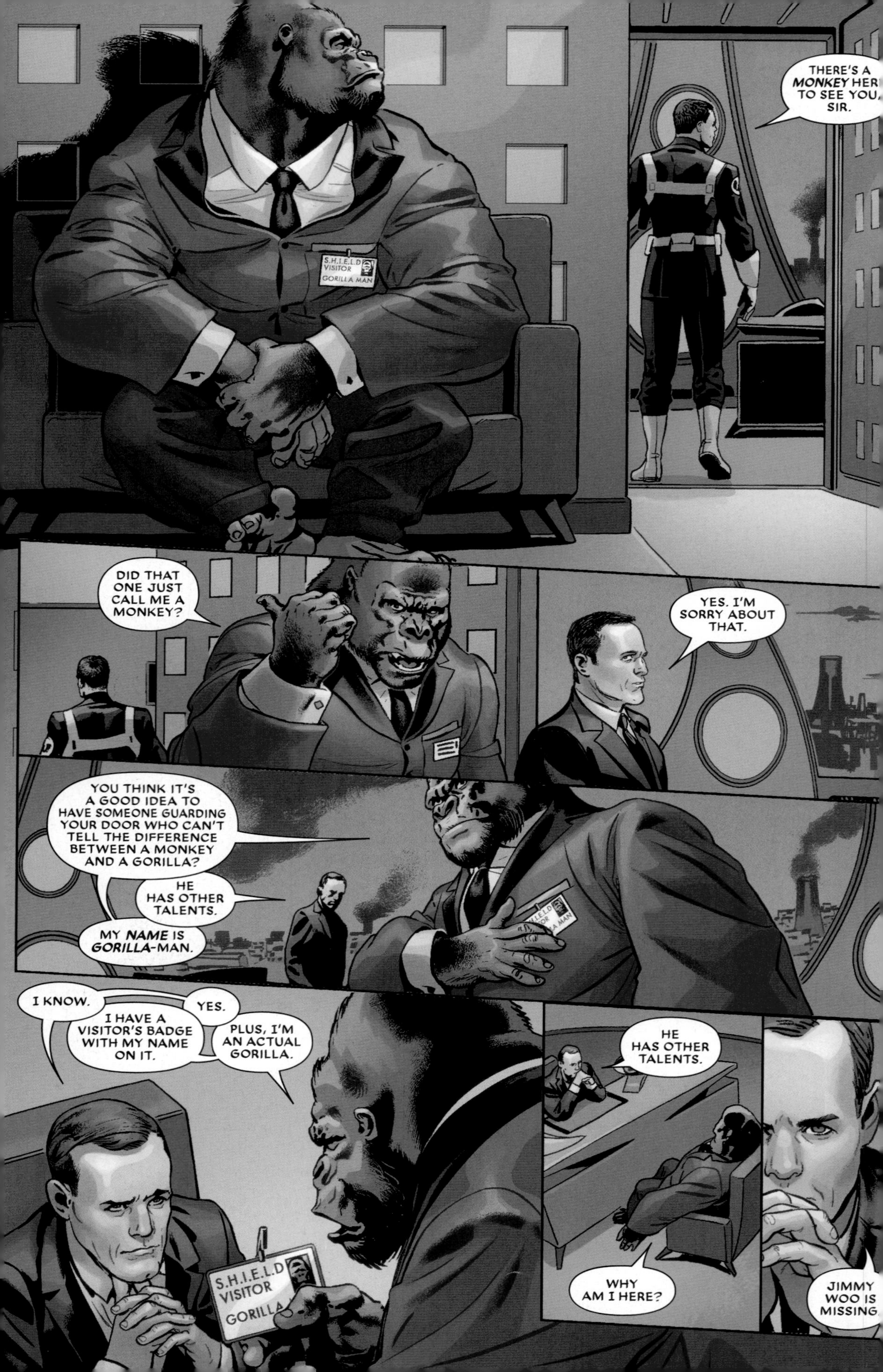
S.H.I.E.L.D VISITOR GORILLA MAN
THERE'S A MONKEY HER TO SEE YOU, SIR.
DID THAT ONE JUST CALL ME A MONKEY?
YES. I'M SORRY ABOUT THAT.
YOU THINK IT'S A GOOD IDEA TO HAVE SOMEONE GUARDING YOUR DOOR WHO CAN'T TELL THE DIFFERENCE BETWEEN A MONKEY AND A GORILLA?
HE HAS OTHER TALENTS.
MY NAME IS GORILLA-MAN.
I KNOW.
YES.
I HAVE A VISITOR'S BADGE WITH MY NAME ON IT.
PLUS, I'M AN ACTUAL GORILLA.
S.H.I.E.L.D VISITOR GORILLA
HE HAS OTHER TALENTS.
WHY AM I HERE?
JIMMY WOO IS MISSING.

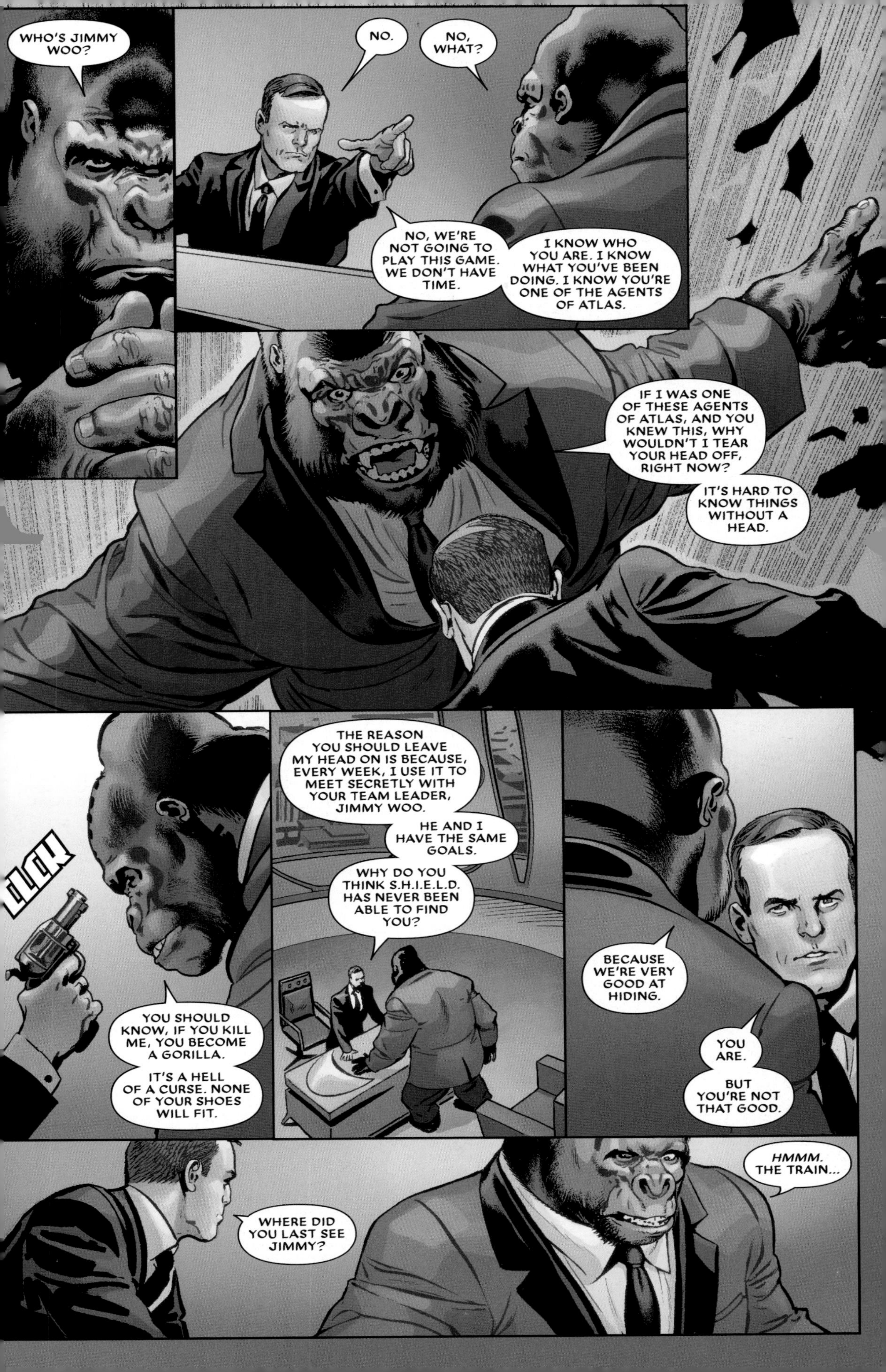

WHO'S JIMMY WOO?
NO.
NO, WHAT?
NO, WE'RE NOT GOING TO PLAY THIS GAME. WE DON'T HAVE TIME.
I KNOW WHO YOU ARE. I KNOW WHAT YOU'VE BEEN DOING. I KNOW YOU'RE ONE OF THE AGENTS OF ATLAS.
IF I WAS ONE OF THESE AGENTS OF ATLAS, AND YOU KNEW THIS, WHY WOULDN'T I TEAR YOUR HEAD OFF, RIGHT NOW?
IT'S HARD TO KNOW THINGS WITHOUT A HEAD.
YOU SHOULD KNOW, IF YOU KILL ME, YOU BECOME A GORILLA.
IT'S A HELL OF A CURSE. NONE OF YOUR SHOES WILL FIT.
THE REASON YOU SHOULD LEAVE MY HEAD ON IS BECAUSE, EVERY WEEK, I USE IT TO MEET SECRETLY WITH YOUR TEAM LEADER, JIMMY WOO.
HE AND I HAVE THE SAME GOALS.
WHY DO YOU THINK S.H.I.E.L.D. HAS NEVER BEEN ABLE TO FIND YOU?
BECAUSE WE'RE VERY GOOD AT HIDING.
YOU ARE.
BUT YOU'RE NOT THAT GOOD.
WHERE DID YOU LAST SEE JIMMY?
HMMM. THE TRAIN...

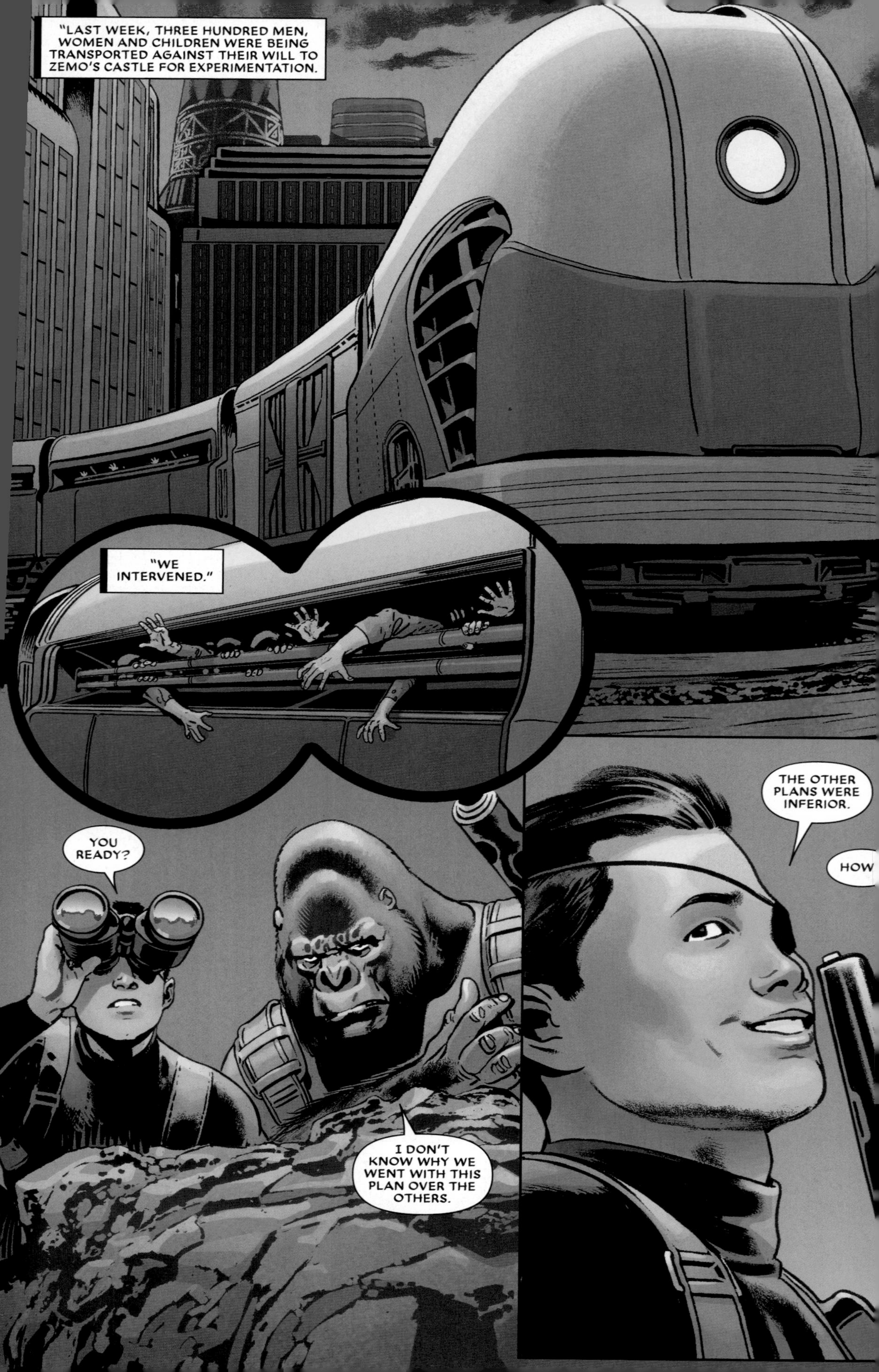
"LAST WEEK, THREE HUNDRED MEN, WOMEN AND CHILDREN WERE BEING TRANSPORTED AGAINST THEIR WILL TO ZEMO'S CASTLE FOR EXPERIMENTATION.
"WE INTERVENED."
YOU READY?
I DON'T KNOW WHY WE WENT WITH THIS PLAN OVER THE OTHERS.
THE OTHER PLANS WERE INFERIOR.
HOW

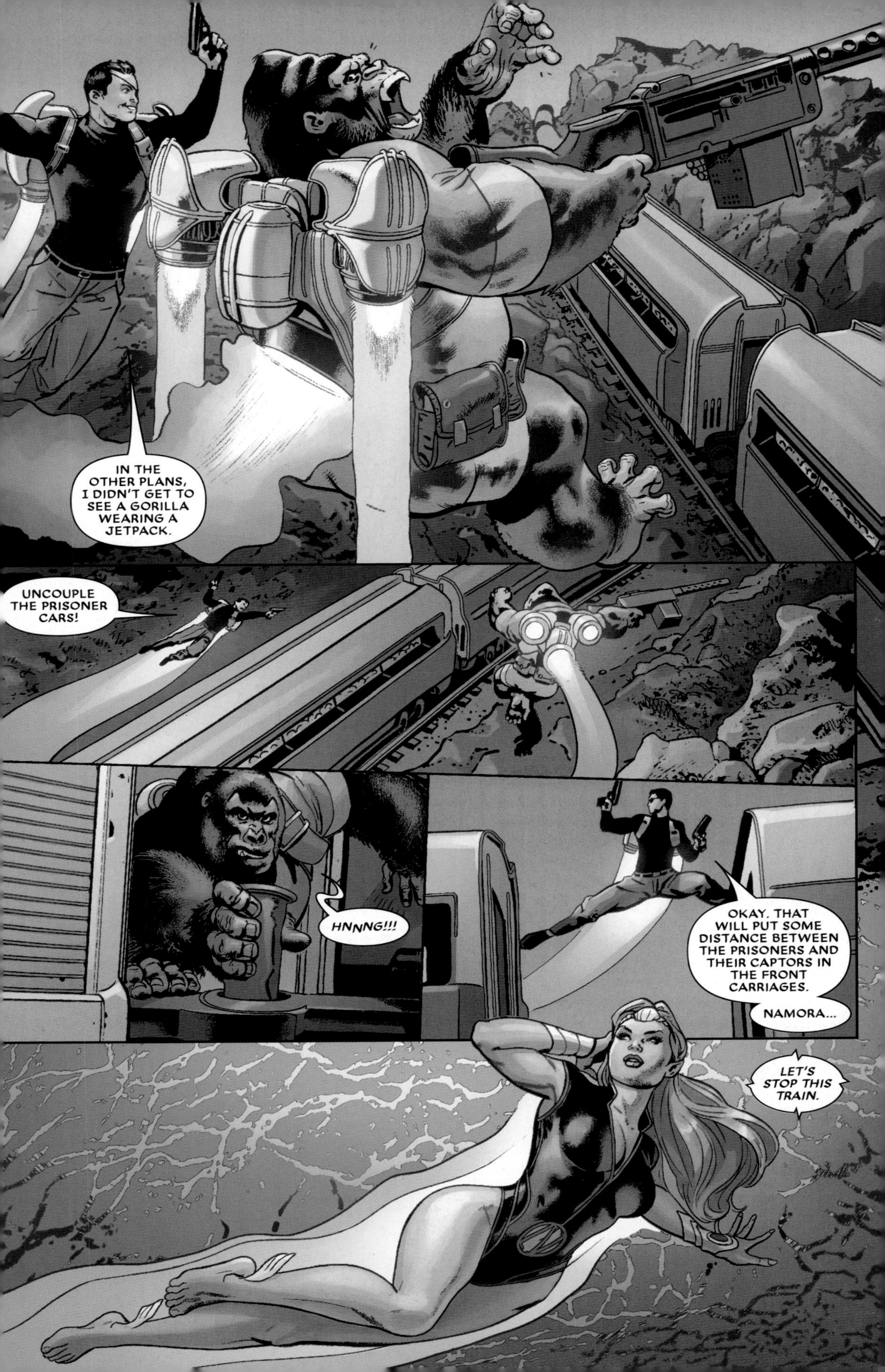
IN THE OTHER PLANS, I DIDN'T GET TO SEE A GORILLA WEARING A JETPACK.
UNCOUPLE THE PRISONER CARS!
HNNNG!!!
OKAY. THAT WILL PUT SOME DISTANCE BETWEEN THE PRISONERS AND THEIR CAPTORS IN THE FRONT CARRIAGES.
NAMORA...
LET'S STOP THIS TRAIN.

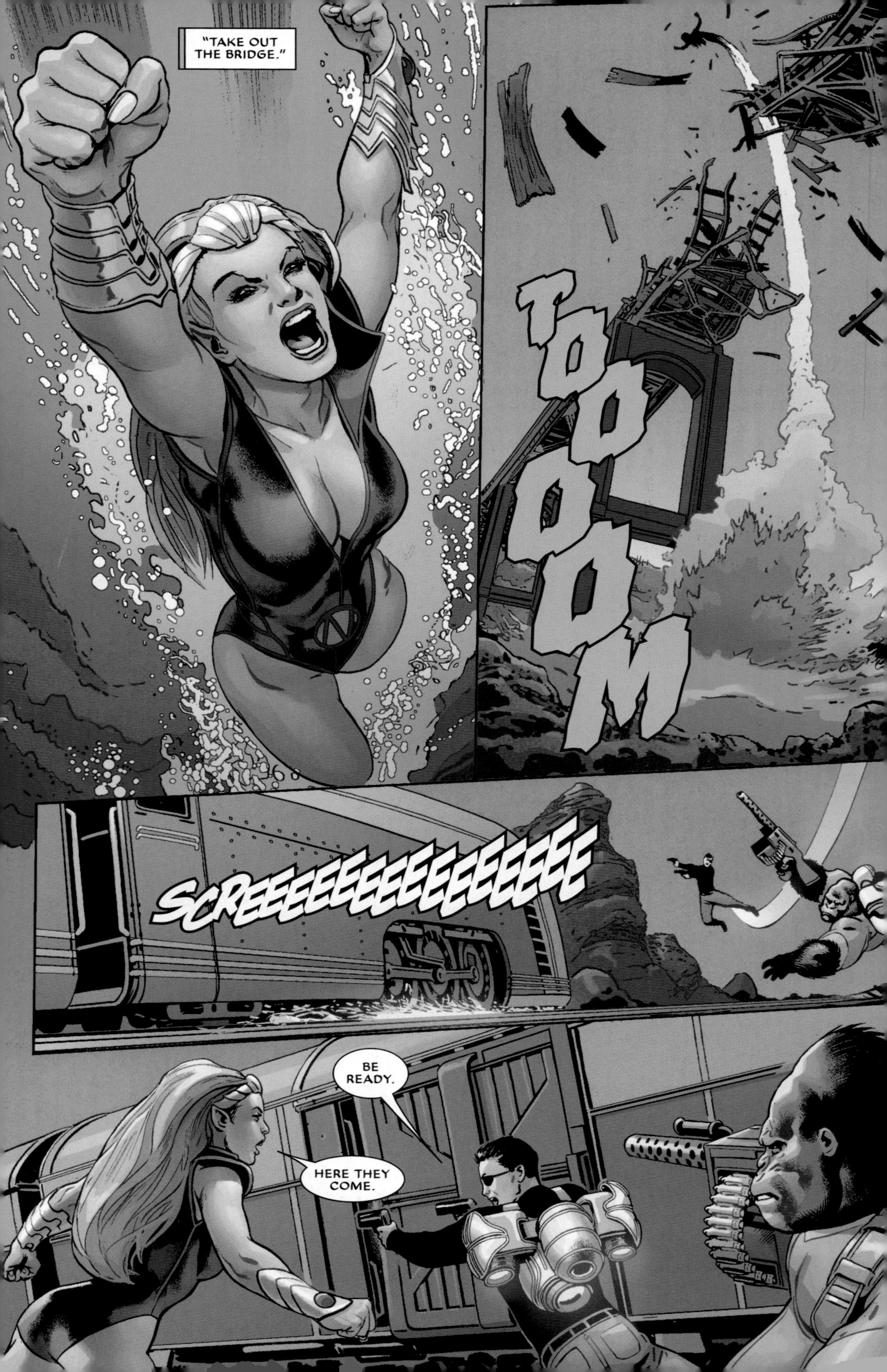
"TAKE OUT THE BRIDGE."
TOOOOOM
SCREEEEEEEEEEEEEEEE
BE READY.
HERE THEY COME.

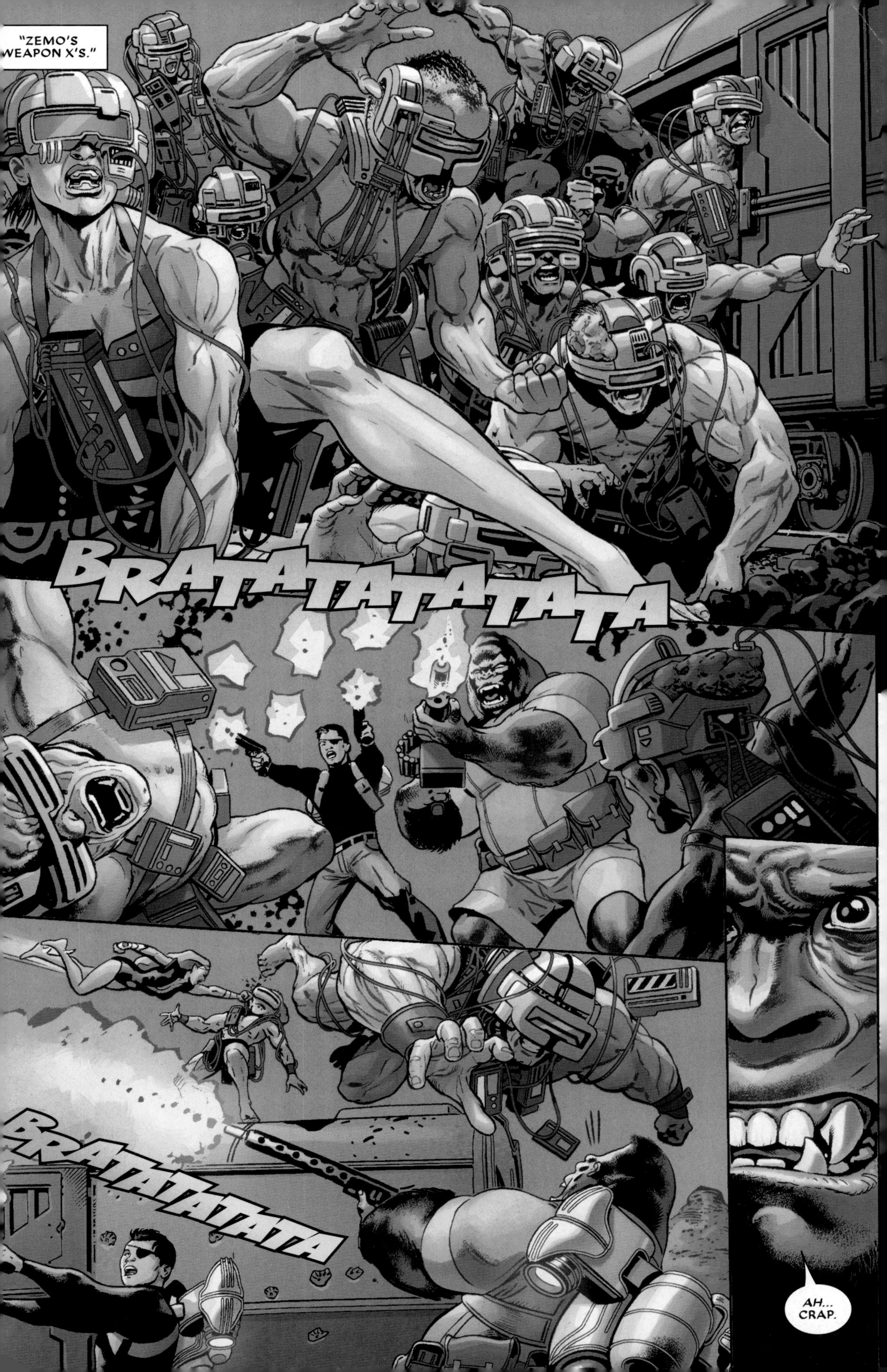
"ZEMO'S WEAPON X'S."
BRATATATATATA
BRATATATATATA
AH... CRAP.

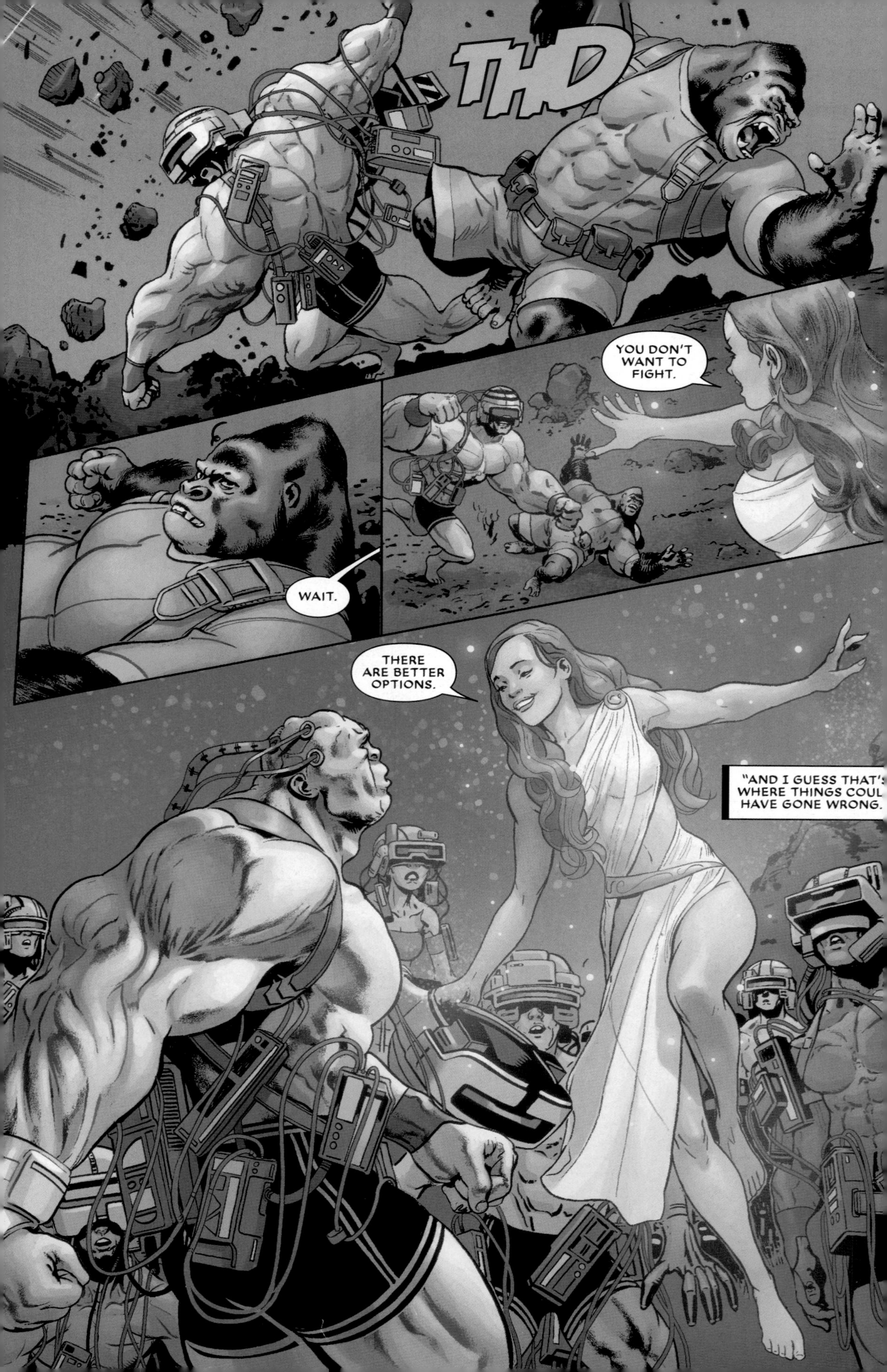
THD
WAIT.
YOU DON'T WANT TO FIGHT.
THERE ARE BETTER OPTIONS.
"AND I GUESS THAT'S WHERE THINGS COUL HAVE GONE WRONG.

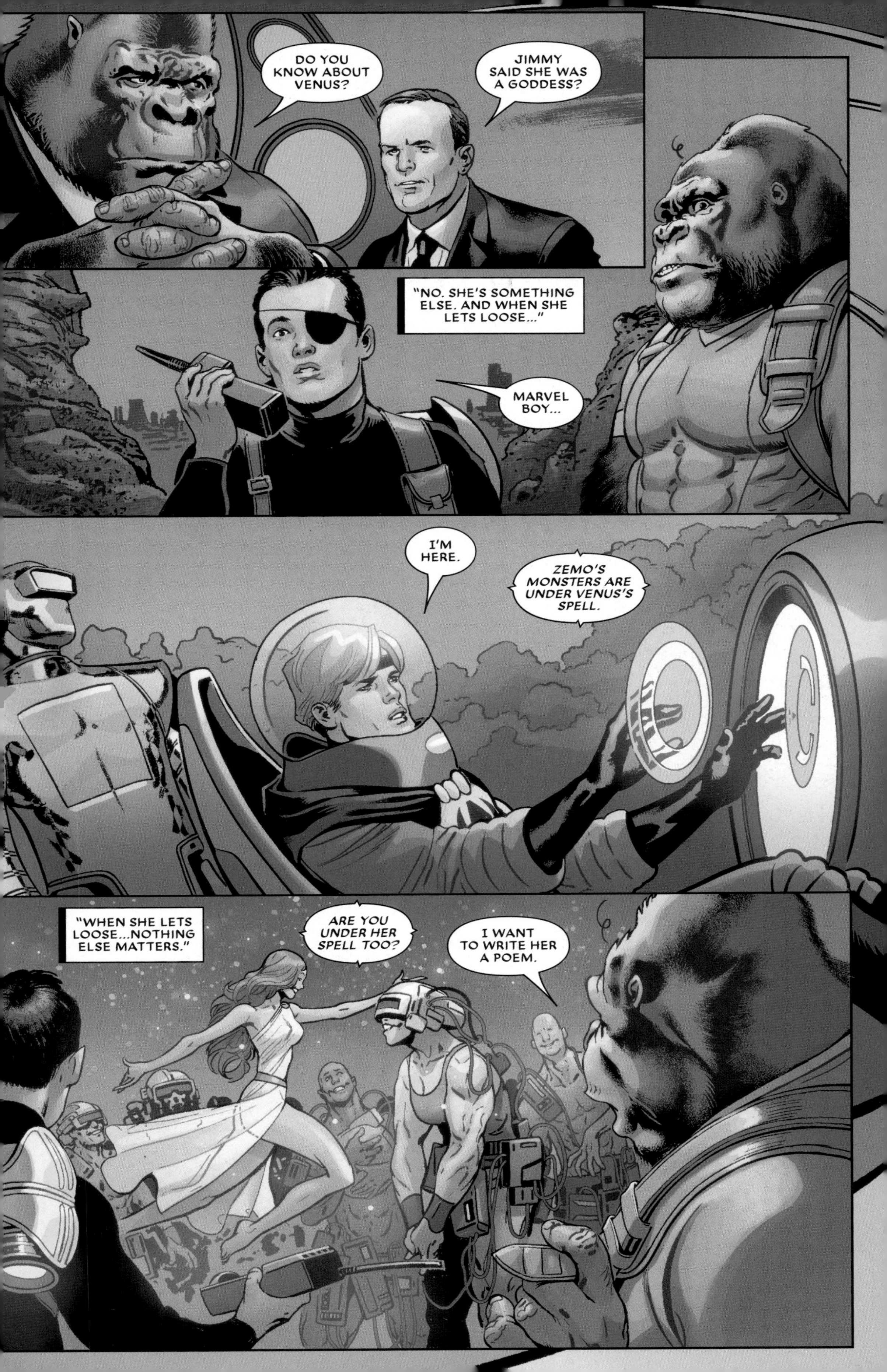
DO YOU KNOW ABOUT VENUS?
JIMMY SAID SHE WAS A GODDESS?
"NO. SHE'S SOMETHING ELSE. AND WHEN SHE LETS LOOSE..."
MARVEL BOY...
I'M HERE.
ZEMO'S MONSTERS ARE UNDER VENUS'S SPELL.
"WHEN SHE LETS LOOSE...NOTHING ELSE MATTERS."
ARE YOU UNDER HER SPELL TOO?
I WANT TO WRITE HER A POEM.

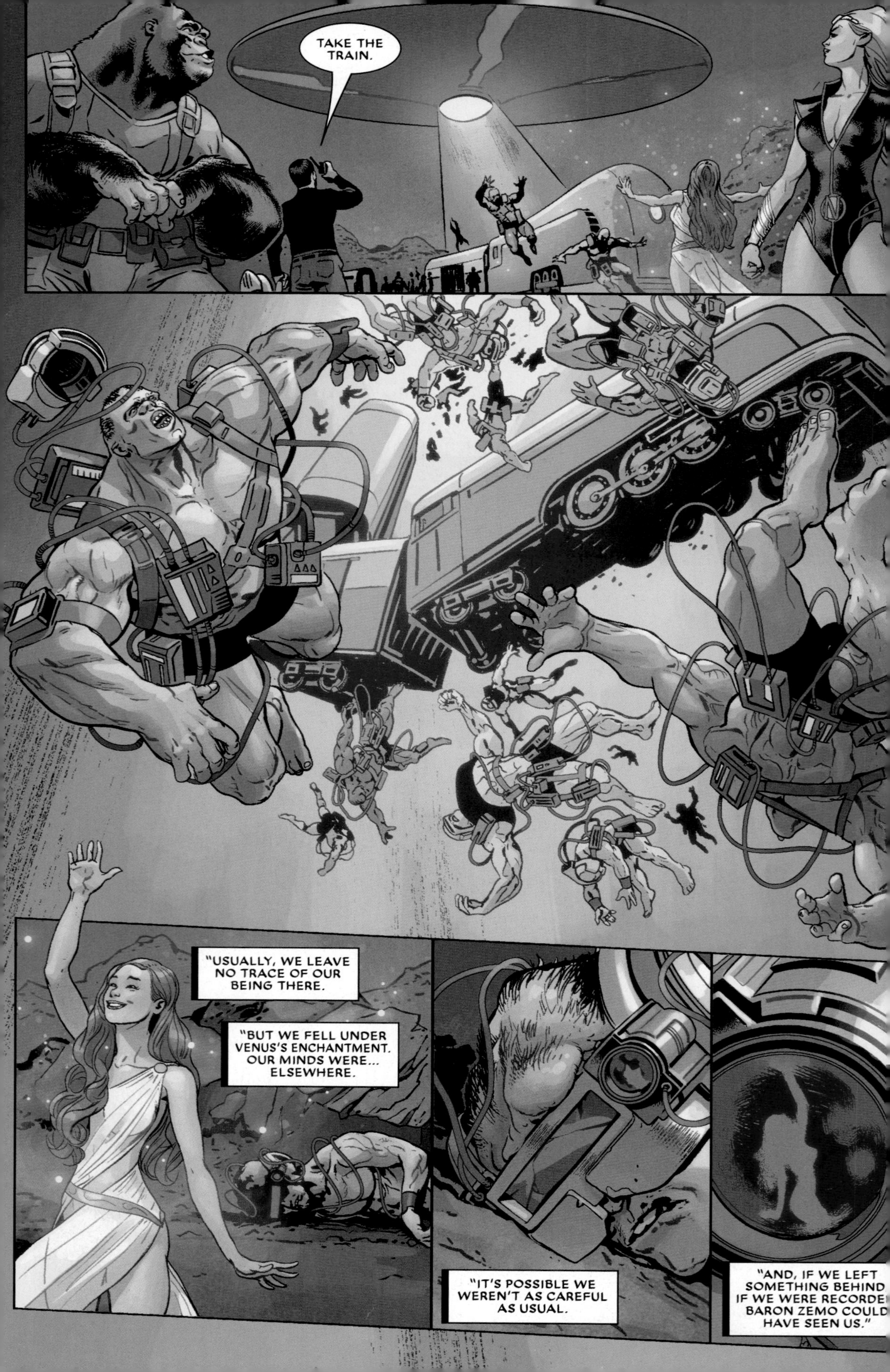
TAKE THE TRAIN.
"USUALLY, WE LEAVE NO TRACE OF OUR BEING THERE.
"BUT WE FELL UNDER VENUS'S ENCHANTMENT. OUR MINDS WERE... ELSEWHERE.
"IT'S POSSIBLE WE WEREN'T AS CAREFUL AS USUAL.
"AND, IF WE LEFT SOMETHING BEHIND IF WE WERE RECORDE BARON ZEMO COULD HAVE SEEN US."

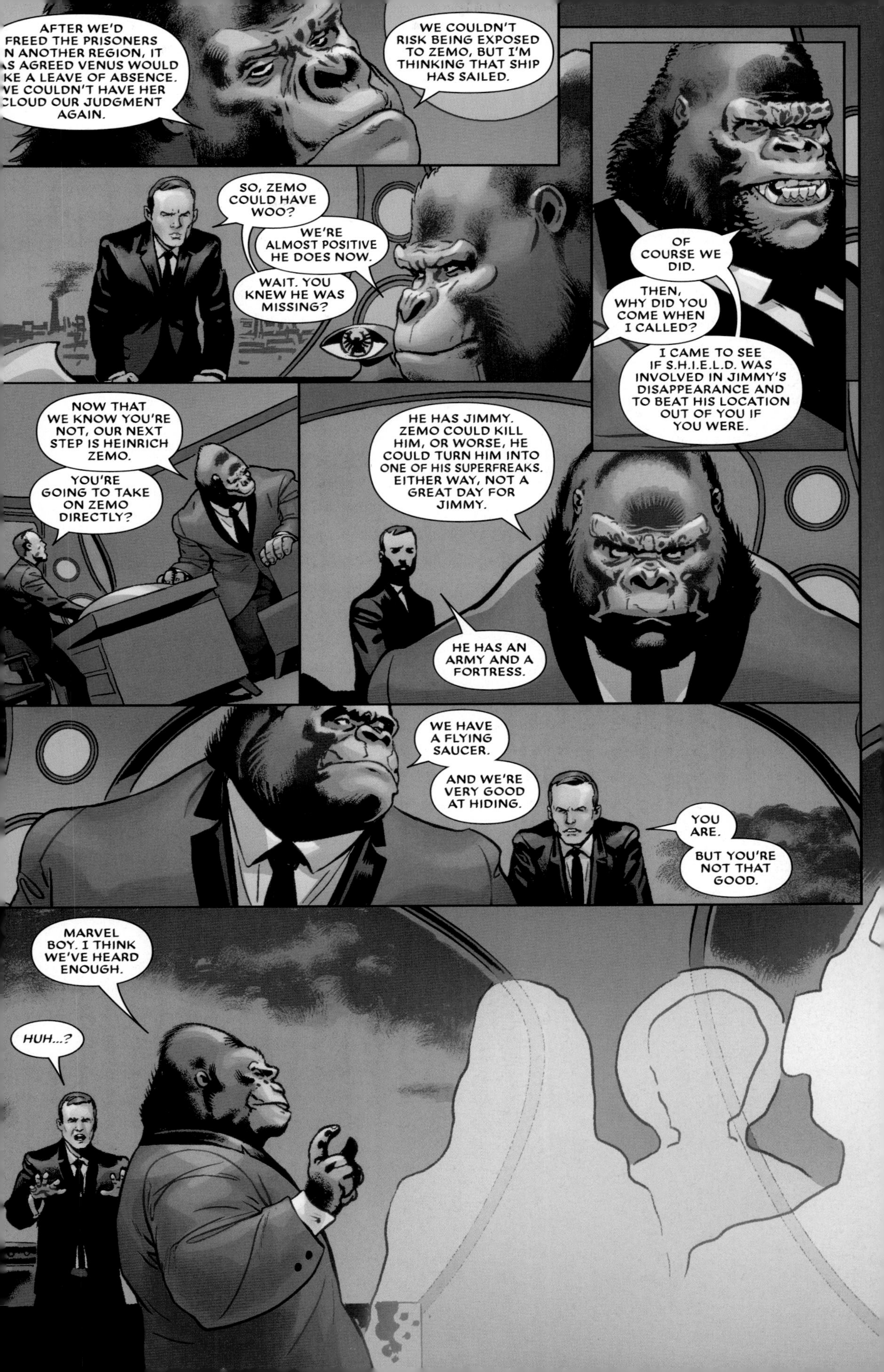
AFTER WE'D FREED THE PRISONERS IN ANOTHER REGION, IT WAS AGREED VENUS WOULD TAKE A LEAVE OF ABSENCE. WE COULDN'T HAVE HER CLOUD OUR JUDGMENT AGAIN.
WE COULDN'T RISK BEING EXPOSED TO ZEMO, BUT I'M THINKING THAT SHIP HAS SAILED.
SO, ZEMO COULD HAVE WOO?
WE'RE ALMOST POSITIVE HE DOES NOW.
WAIT. YOU KNEW HE WAS MISSING?
OF COURSE WE DID.
THEN, WHY DID YOU COME WHEN I CALLED?
I CAME TO SEE IF S.H.I.E.L.D. WAS INVOLVED IN JIMMY'S DISAPPEARANCE AND TO BEAT HIS LOCATION OUT OF YOU IF YOU WERE.
NOW THAT WE KNOW YOU'RE NOT, OUR NEXT STEP IS HEINRICH ZEMO.
YOU'RE GOING TO TAKE ON ZEMO DIRECTLY?
HE HAS JIMMY. ZEMO COULD KILL HIM, OR WORSE, HE COULD TURN HIM INTO ONE OF HIS SUPERFREAKS. EITHER WAY, NOT A GREAT DAY FOR JIMMY.
HE HAS AN ARMY AND A FORTRESS.
WE HAVE A FLYING SAUCER.
AND WE'RE VERY GOOD AT HIDING.
YOU ARE.
BUT YOU'RE NOT THAT GOOD.
MARVEL BOY. I THINK WE'VE HEARD ENOUGH.
HUH...?

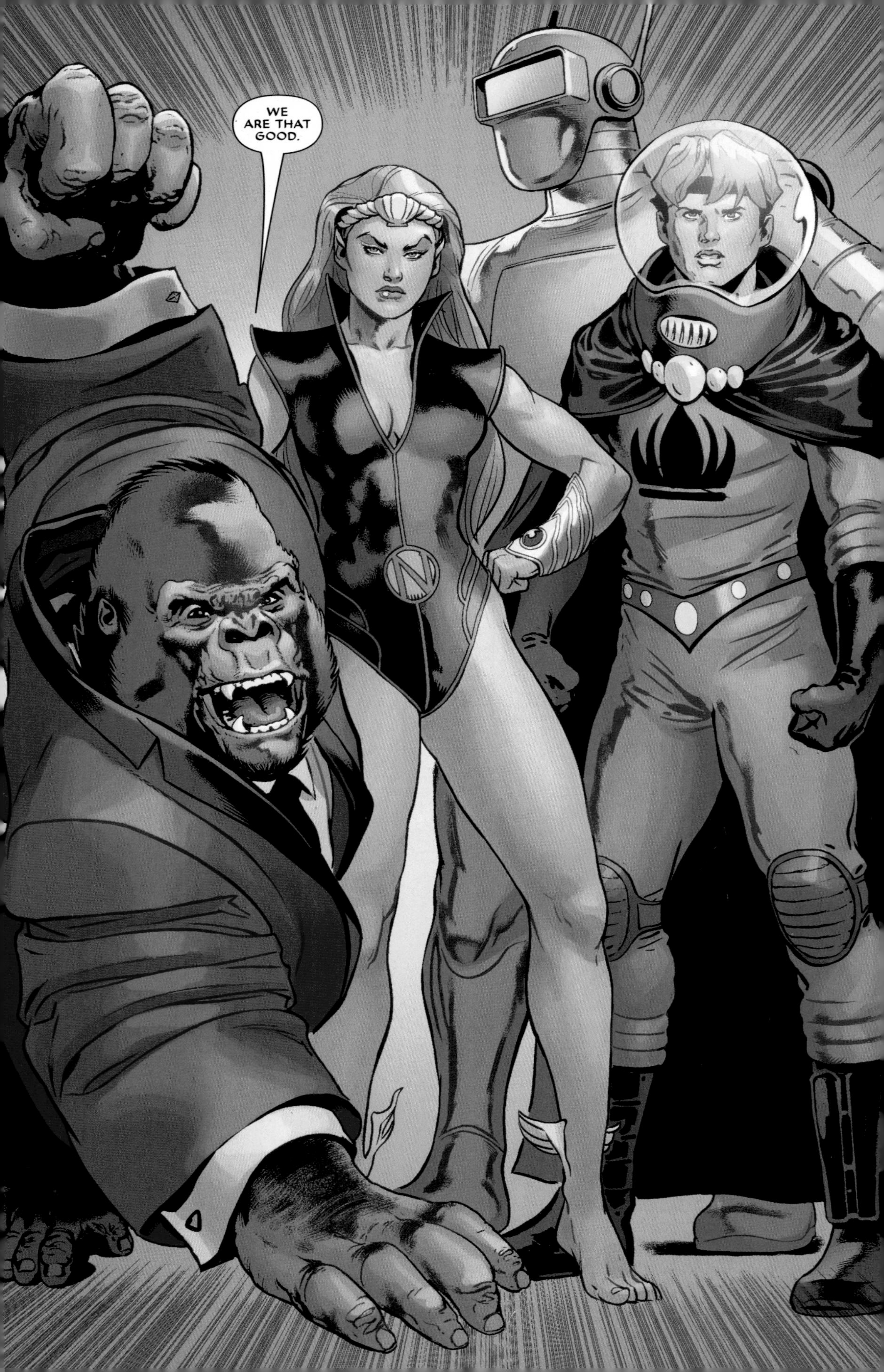
WE ARE THAT GOOD.

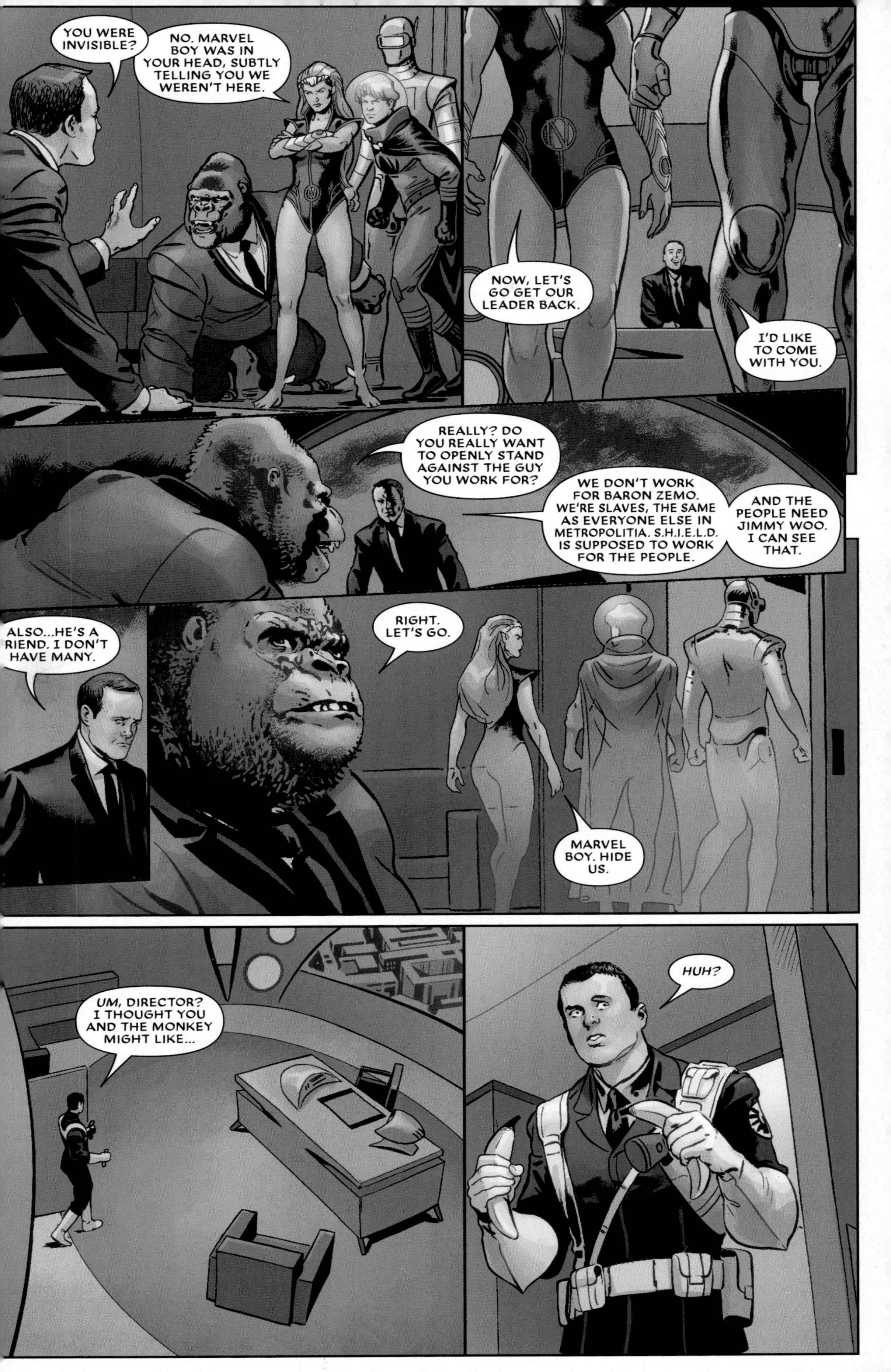
YOU WERE INVISIBLE?
NO. MARVEL BOY WAS IN YOUR HEAD, SUBTLY TELLING YOU WE WEREN'T HERE.
NOW, LET'S GO GET OUR LEADER BACK.
I'D LIKE TO COME WITH YOU.
REALLY? DO YOU REALLY WANT TO OPENLY STAND AGAINST THE GUY YOU WORK FOR?
WE DON'T WORK FOR BARON ZEMO. WE'RE SLAVES, THE SAME AS EVERYONE ELSE IN METROPOLITIA. S.H.I.E.L.D. IS SUPPOSED TO WORK FOR THE PEOPLE.
AND THE PEOPLE NEED JIMMY WOO. I CAN SEE THAT.
ALSO...HE'S A RIEND. I DON'T HAVE MANY.
RIGHT. LET'S GO.
MARVEL BOY. HIDE US.
UM, DIRECTOR? I THOUGHT YOU AND THE MONKEY MIGHT LIKE...
HUH?

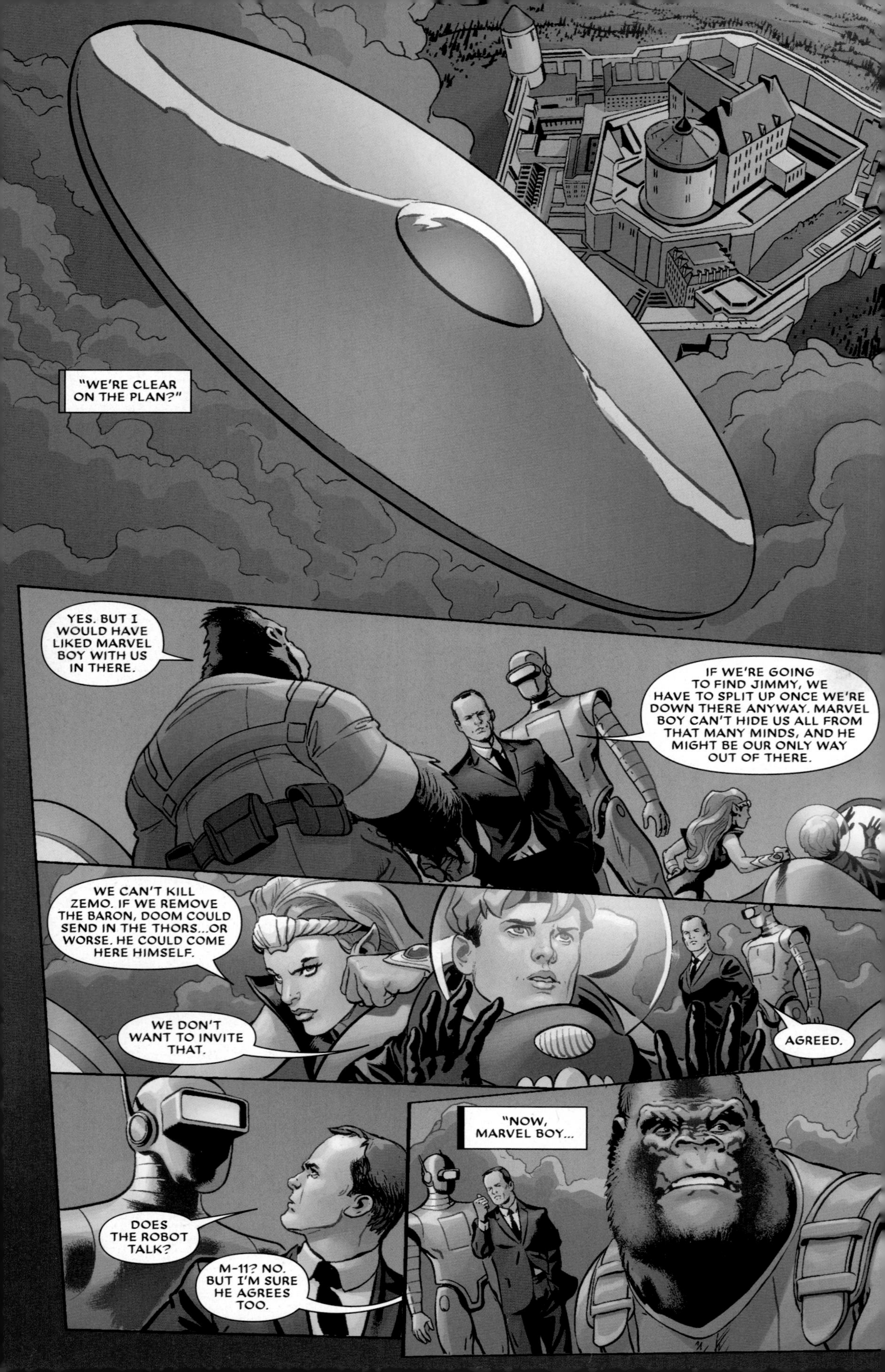
"WE'RE CLEAR ON THE PLAN?"
YES. BUT I WOULD HAVE LIKED MARVEL BOY WITH US IN THERE.
IF WE'RE GOING TO FIND JIMMY, WE HAVE TO SPLIT UP ONCE WE'RE DOWN THERE ANYWAY. MARVEL BOY CAN'T HIDE US ALL FROM THAT MANY MINDS, AND HE MIGHT BE OUR ONLY WAY OUT OF THERE.
WE CAN'T KILL ZEMO. IF WE REMOVE THE BARON, DOOM COULD SEND IN THE THORS...OR WORSE. HE COULD COME HERE HIMSELF.
WE DON'T WANT TO INVITE THAT.
AGREED.
DOES THE ROBOT TALK?
M-11? NO. BUT I'M SURE HE AGREES TOO.
"NOW, MARVEL BOY...

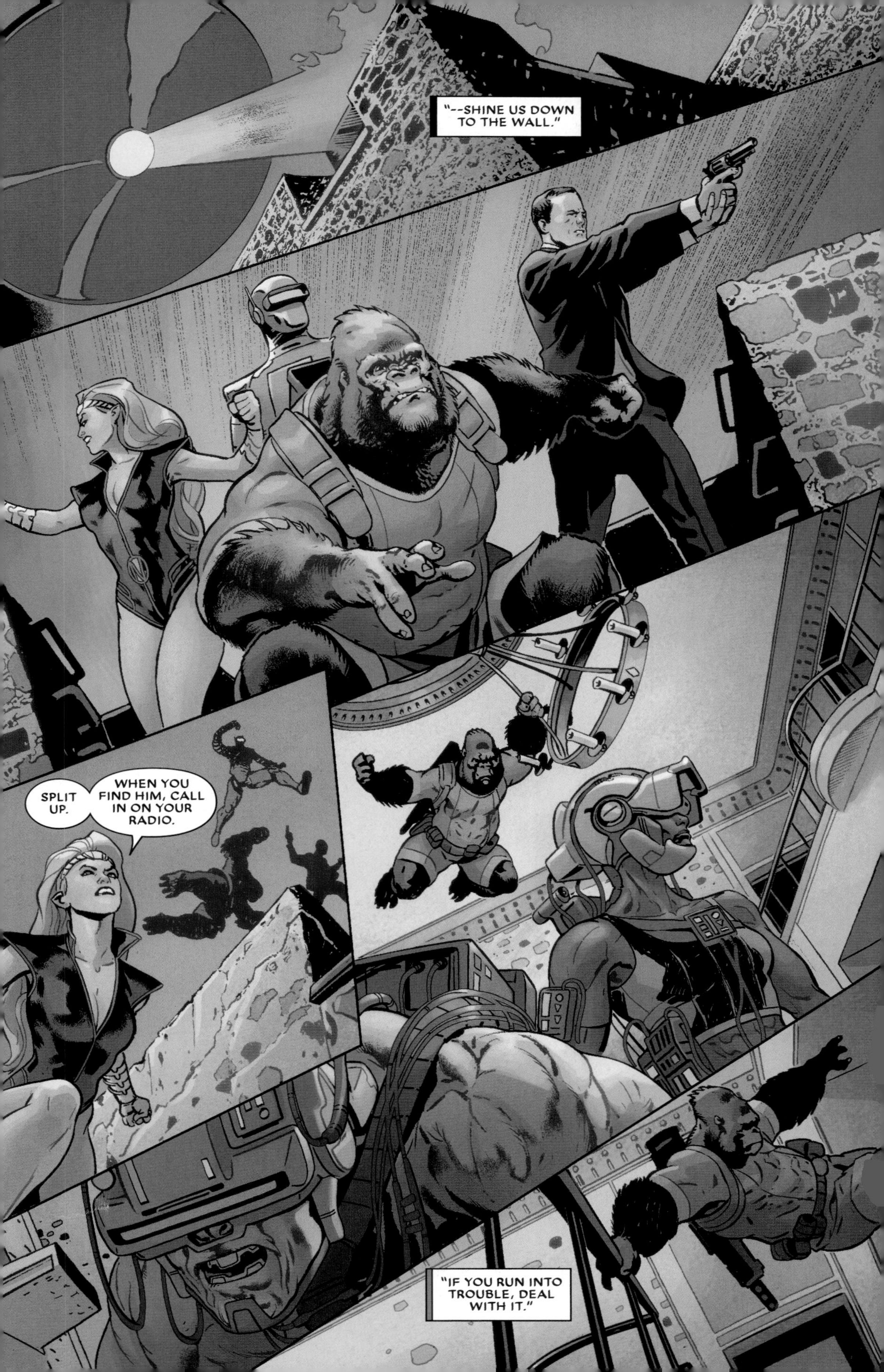
"--SHINE US DOWN TO THE WALL."
SPLIT UP.
WHEN YOU FIND HIM, CALL IN ON YOUR RADIO.
"IF YOU RUN INTO TROUBLE, DEAL WITH IT."

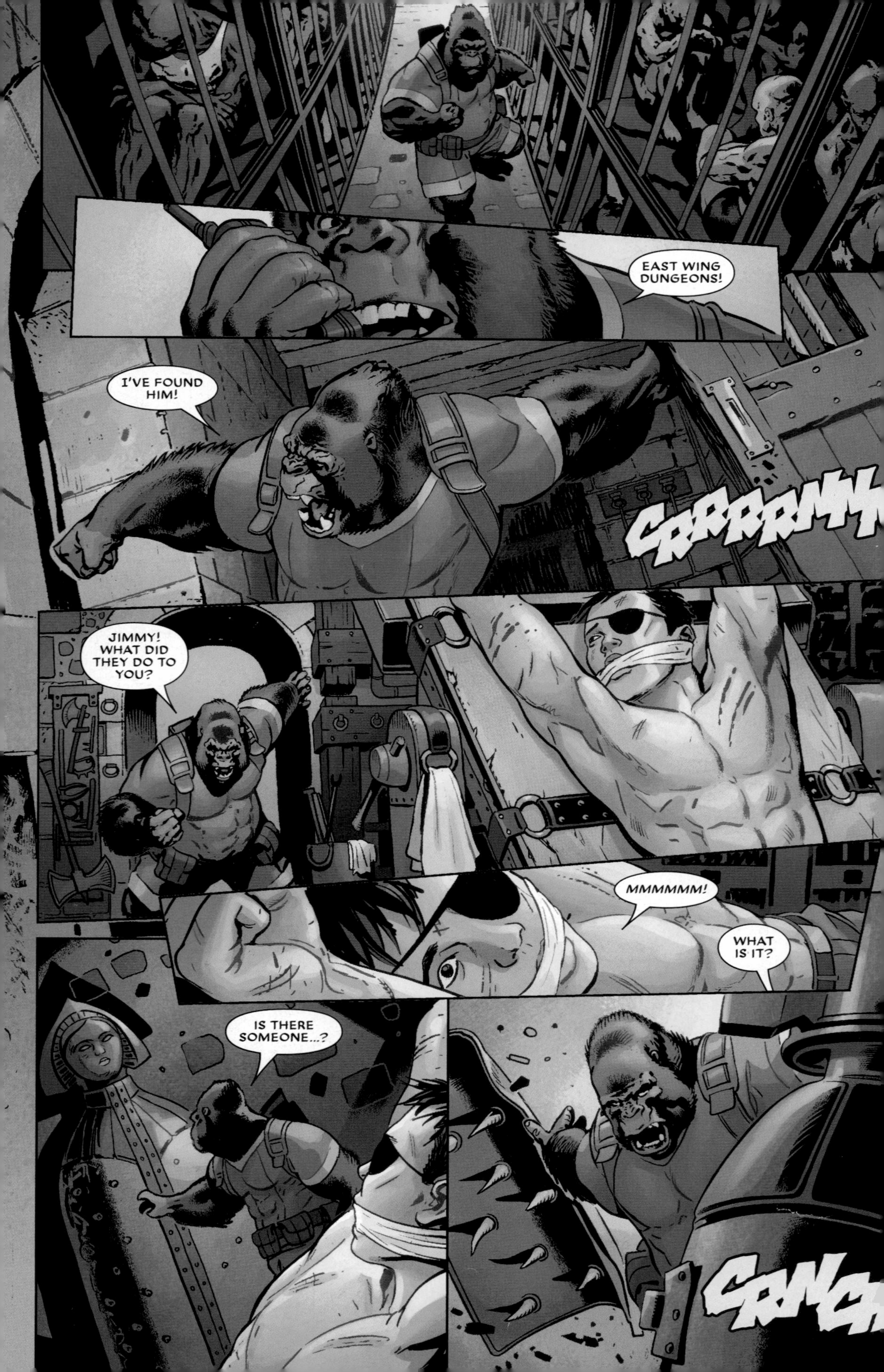
EAST WING DUNGEONS!
I'VE FOUND HIM!
CRRRRMM
JIMMY! WHAT DID THEY DO TO YOU?
MMMMMM!
WHAT IS IT?
IS THERE SOMEONE...?
CRNCH

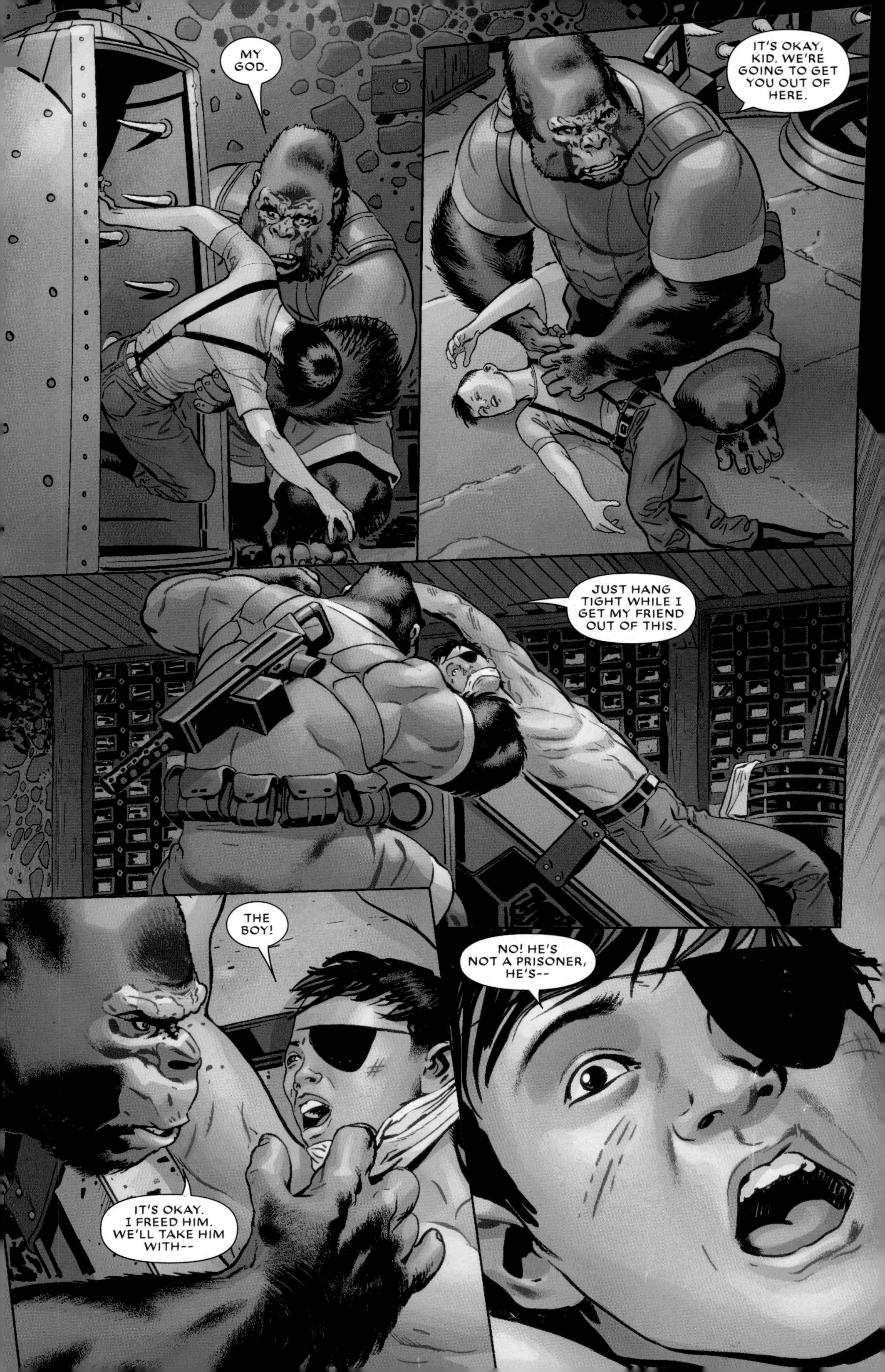
MY GOD.
IT'S OKAY, KID. WE'RE GOING TO GET YOU OUT OF HERE.
JUST HANG TIGHT WHILE I GET MY FRIEND OUT OF THIS.
THE BOY!
IT'S OKAY. I FREED HIM. WE'LL TAKE HIM WITH--
NO! HE'S NOT A PRISONER, HE'S--

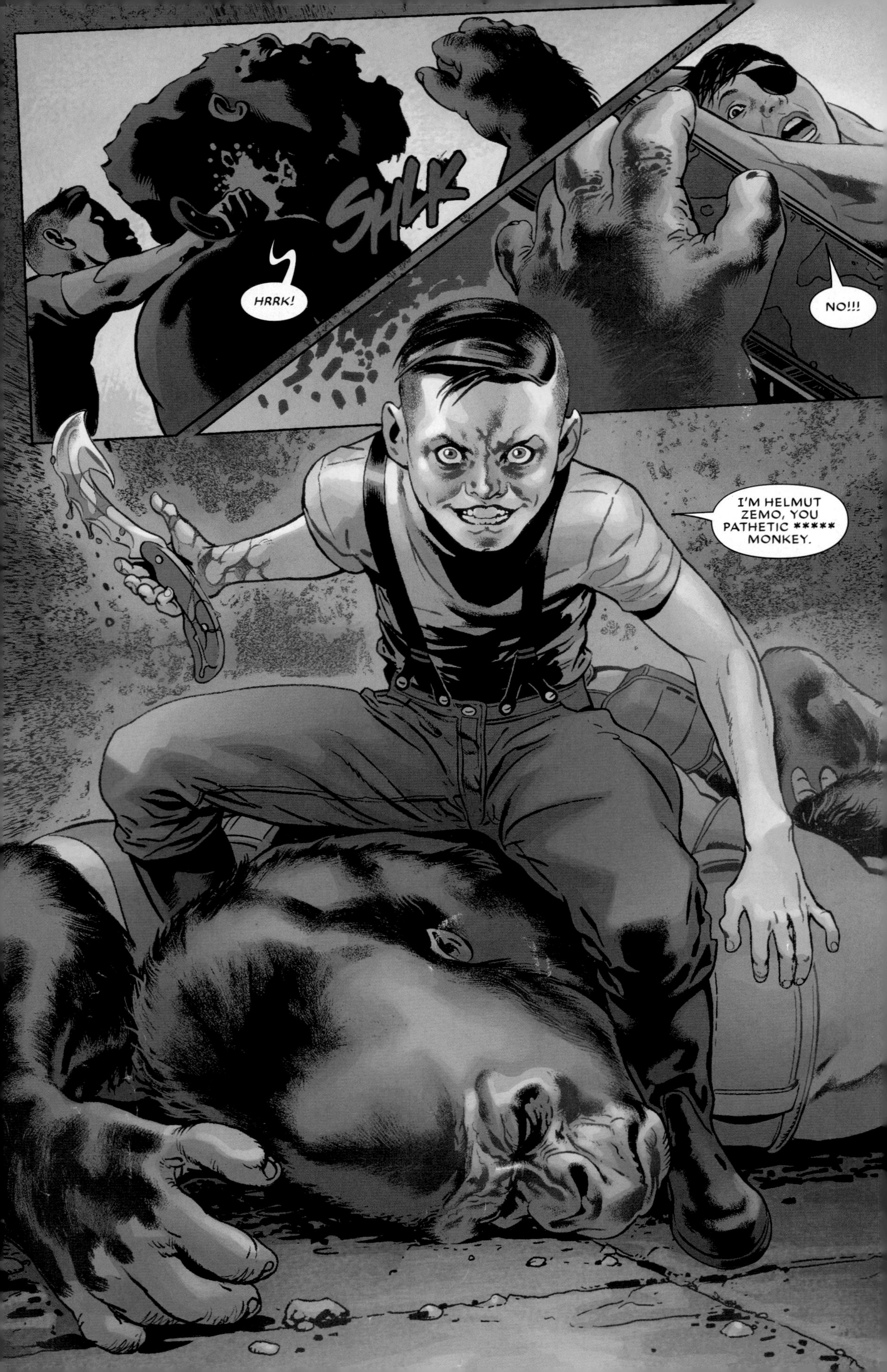
SHLK
HRRK!
NO!!!
I'M HELMUT ZEMO, YOU PATHETIC ***** MONKEY.

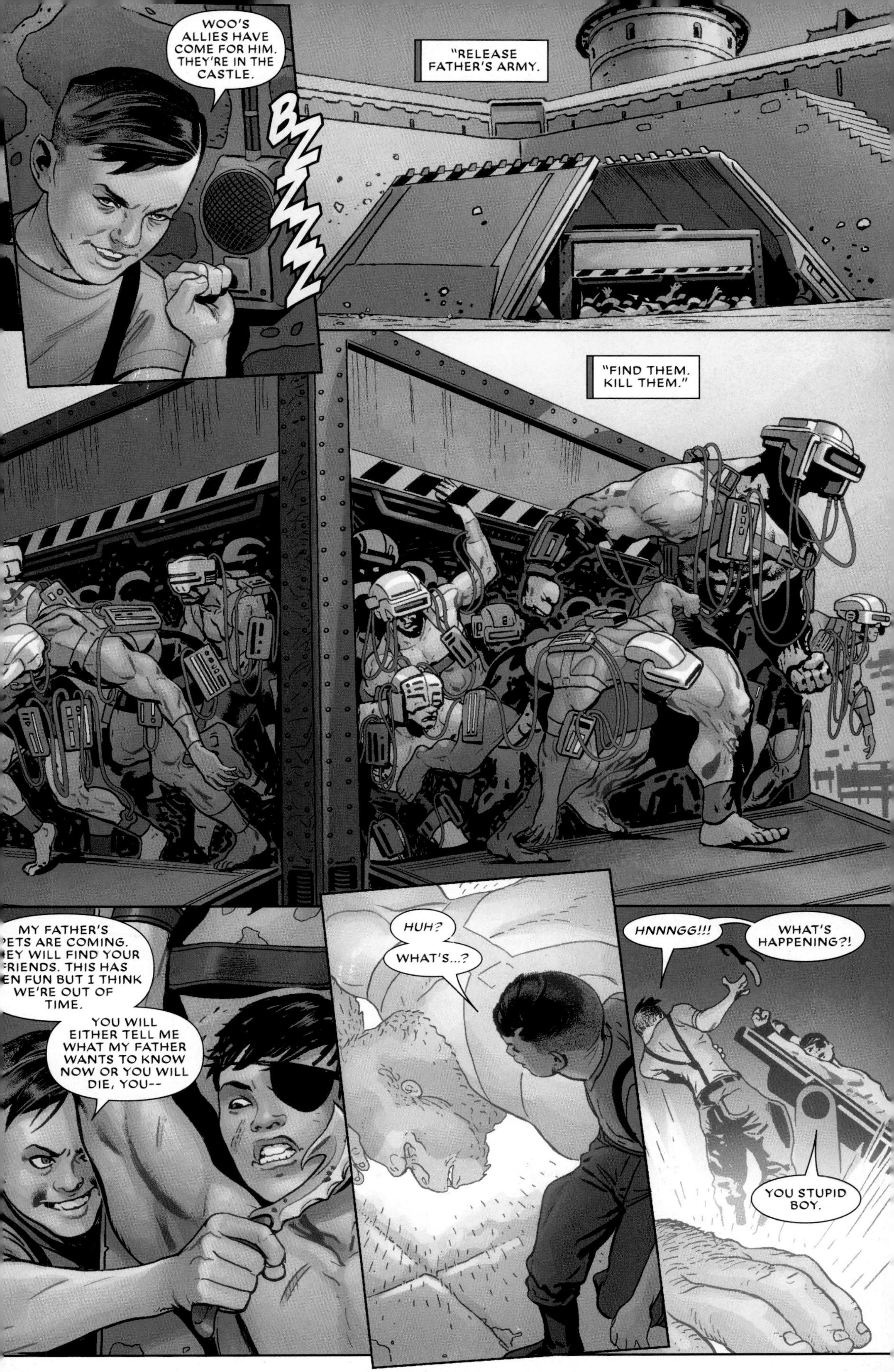
WOO'S ALLIES HAVE COME FOR HIM. THEY'RE IN THE CASTLE.
BZZZZ
"RELEASE FATHER'S ARMY.
"FIND THEM. KILL THEM."
MY FATHER'S PETS ARE COMING. EY WILL FIND YOUR FRIENDS. THIS HAS EN FUN BUT I THINK WE'RE OUT OF TIME.
YOU WILL EITHER TELL ME WHAT MY FATHER WANTS TO KNOW NOW OR YOU WILL DIE, YOU--
HUH?
WHAT'S...?
HNNNGG!!!
WHAT'S HAPPENING?!
YOU STUPID BOY.

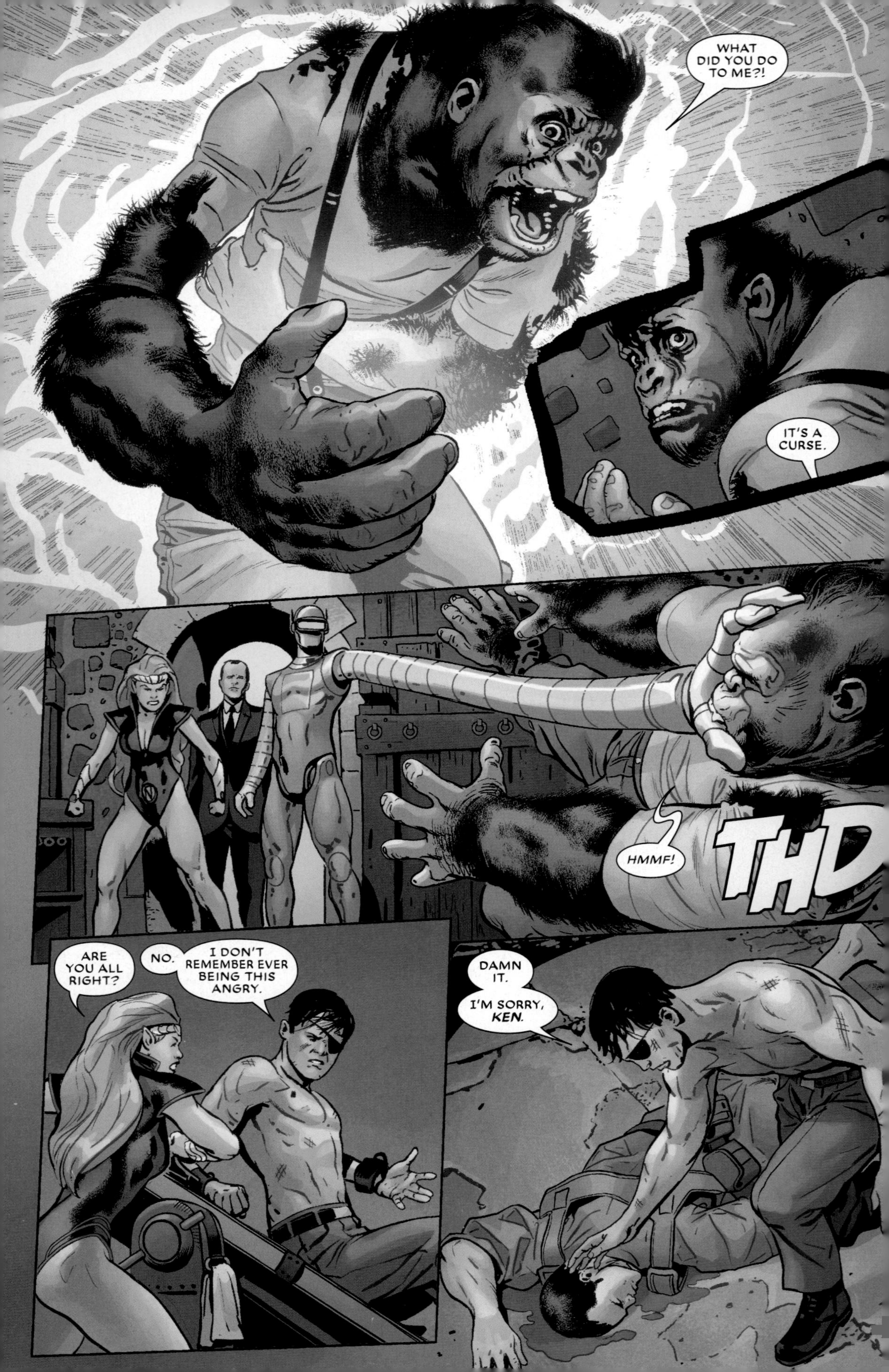
WHAT DID YOU DO TO ME?!
IT'S A CURSE.
HMMF!
THD
ARE YOU ALL RIGHT?
NO.
I DON'T REMEMBER EVER BEING THIS ANGRY.
DAMN IT.
I'M SORRY, KEN.

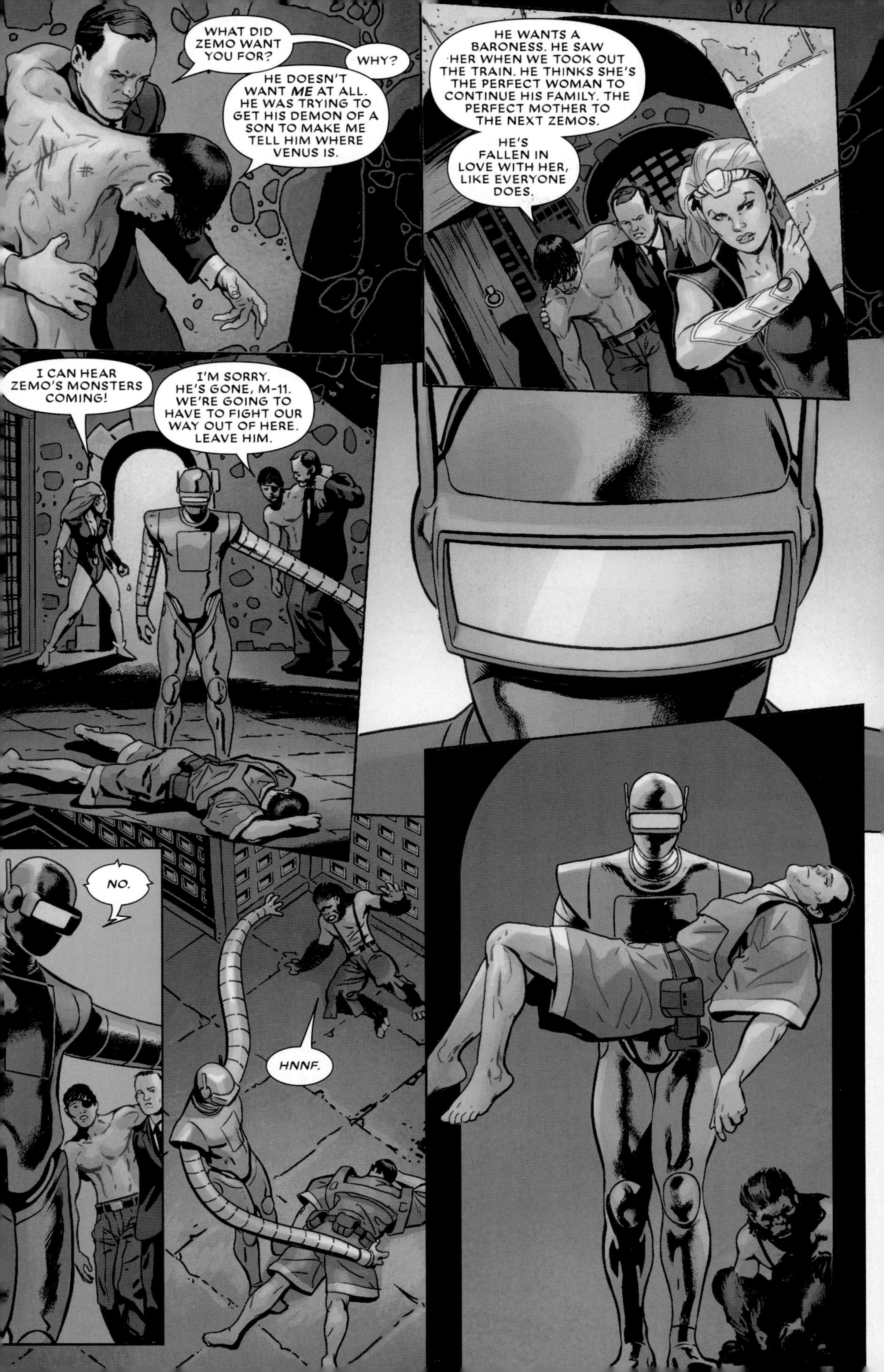
WHAT DID ZEMO WANT YOU FOR?
WHY?
HE DOESN'T WANT *ME* AT ALL. HE WAS TRYING TO GET HIS DEMON OF A SON TO MAKE ME TELL HIM WHERE VENUS IS.
HE WANTS A BARONESS. HE SAW HER WHEN WE TOOK OUT THE TRAIN. HE THINKS SHE'S THE PERFECT WOMAN TO CONTINUE HIS FAMILY. THE PERFECT MOTHER TO THE NEXT ZEMOS.
HE'S FALLEN IN LOVE WITH HER, LIKE EVERYONE DOES.
I CAN HEAR ZEMO'S MONSTERS COMING!
I'M SORRY. HE'S GONE, M-11. WE'RE GOING TO HAVE TO FIGHT OUR WAY OUT OF HERE. LEAVE HIM.
NO.
HNNF.

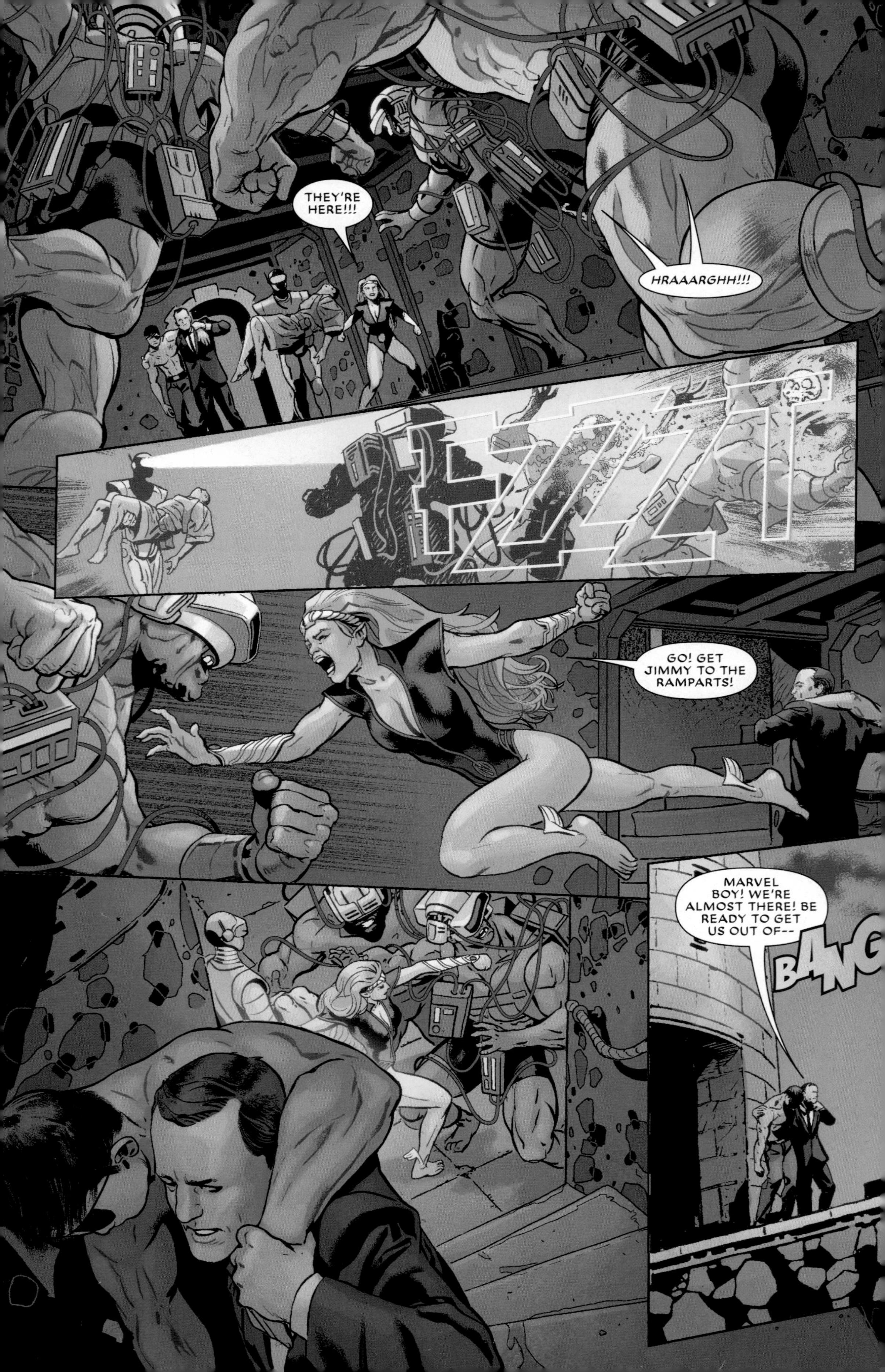
THEY'RE HERE!!!
HRAAARGHH!!!
FZZZT
GO! GET JIMMY TO THE RAMPARTS!
MARVEL BOY! WE'RE ALMOST THERE! BE READY TO GET US OUT OF--
BANG

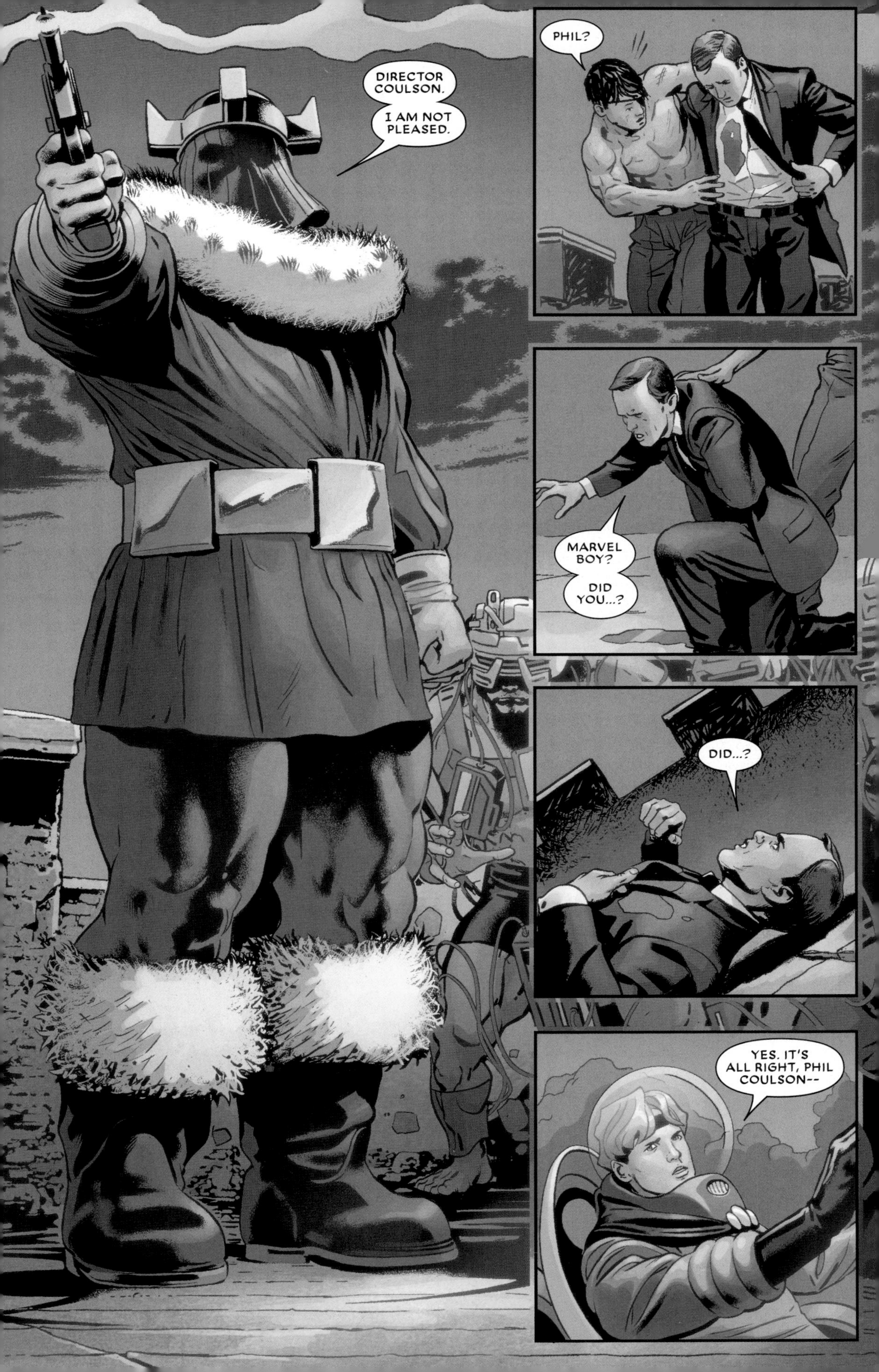
DIRECTOR COULSON.
I AM NOT PLEASED.
PHIL?
MARVEL BOY?
DID YOU...?
DID...?
YES. IT'S ALL RIGHT, PHIL COULSON--

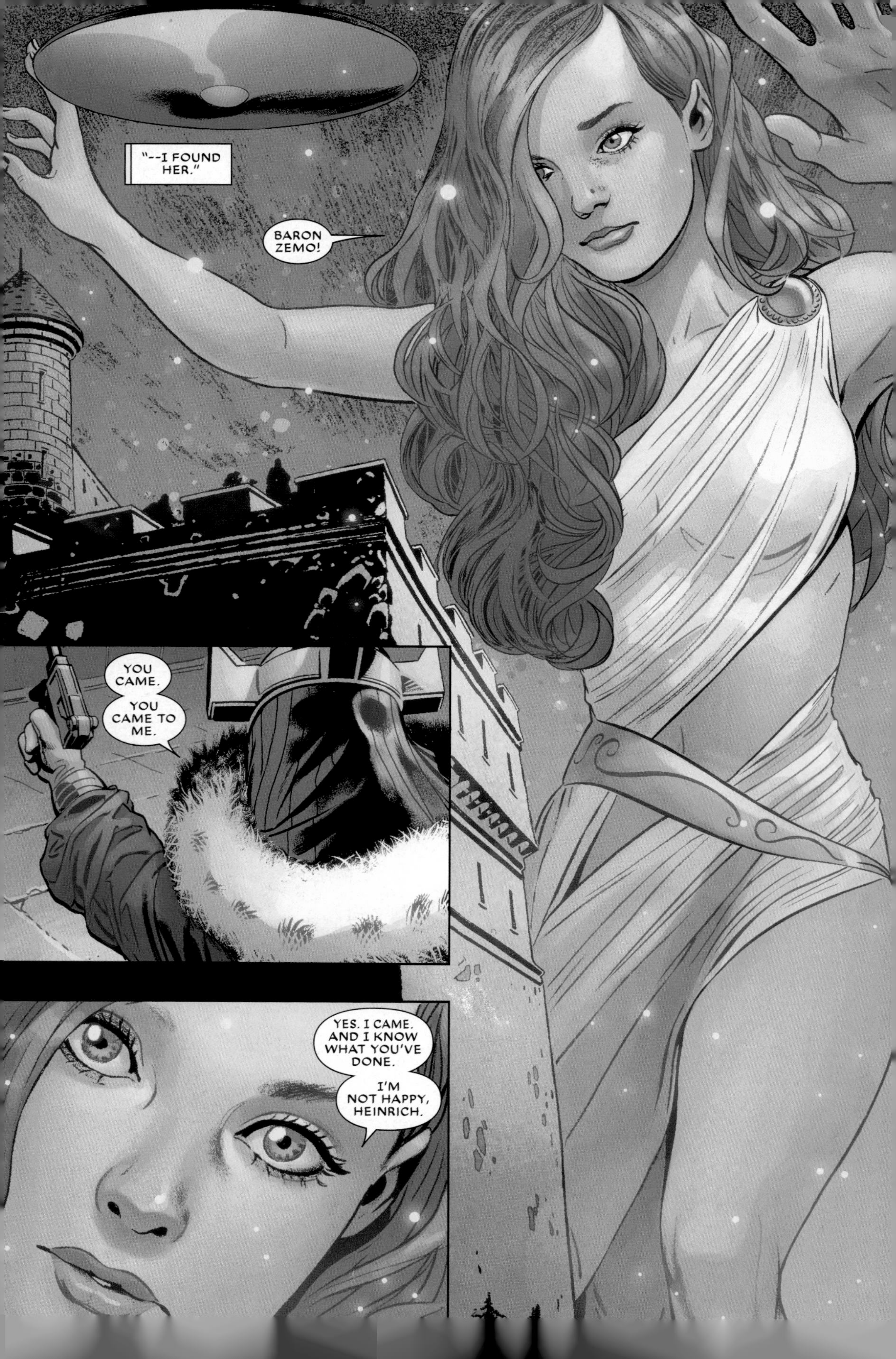
"--I FOUND HER."
BARON ZEMO!
YOU CAME.
YOU CAME TO ME.
YES. I CAME. AND I KNOW WHAT YOU'VE DONE.
I'M NOT HAPPY, HEINRICH.

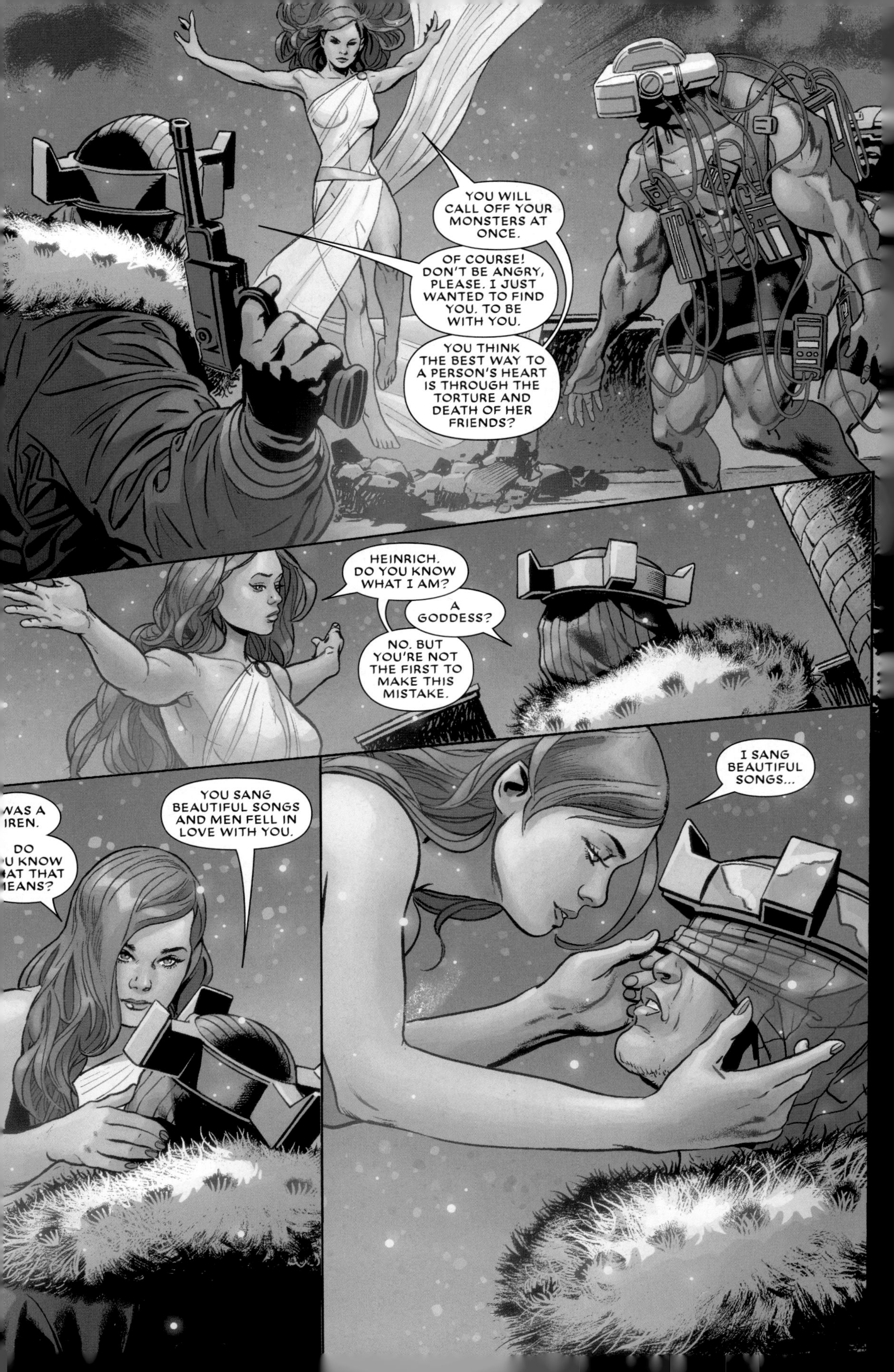
YOU WILL CALL OFF YOUR MONSTERS AT ONCE.
OF COURSE! DON'T BE ANGRY, PLEASE. I JUST WANTED TO FIND YOU. TO BE WITH YOU.
YOU THINK THE BEST WAY TO A PERSON'S HEART IS THROUGH THE TORTURE AND DEATH OF HER FRIENDS?
HEINRICH. DO YOU KNOW WHAT I AM?
A GODDESS?
NO. BUT YOU'RE NOT THE FIRST TO MAKE THIS MISTAKE.
YOU SANG BEAUTIFUL SONGS AND MEN FELL IN LOVE WITH YOU.
I SANG BEAUTIFUL SONGS...

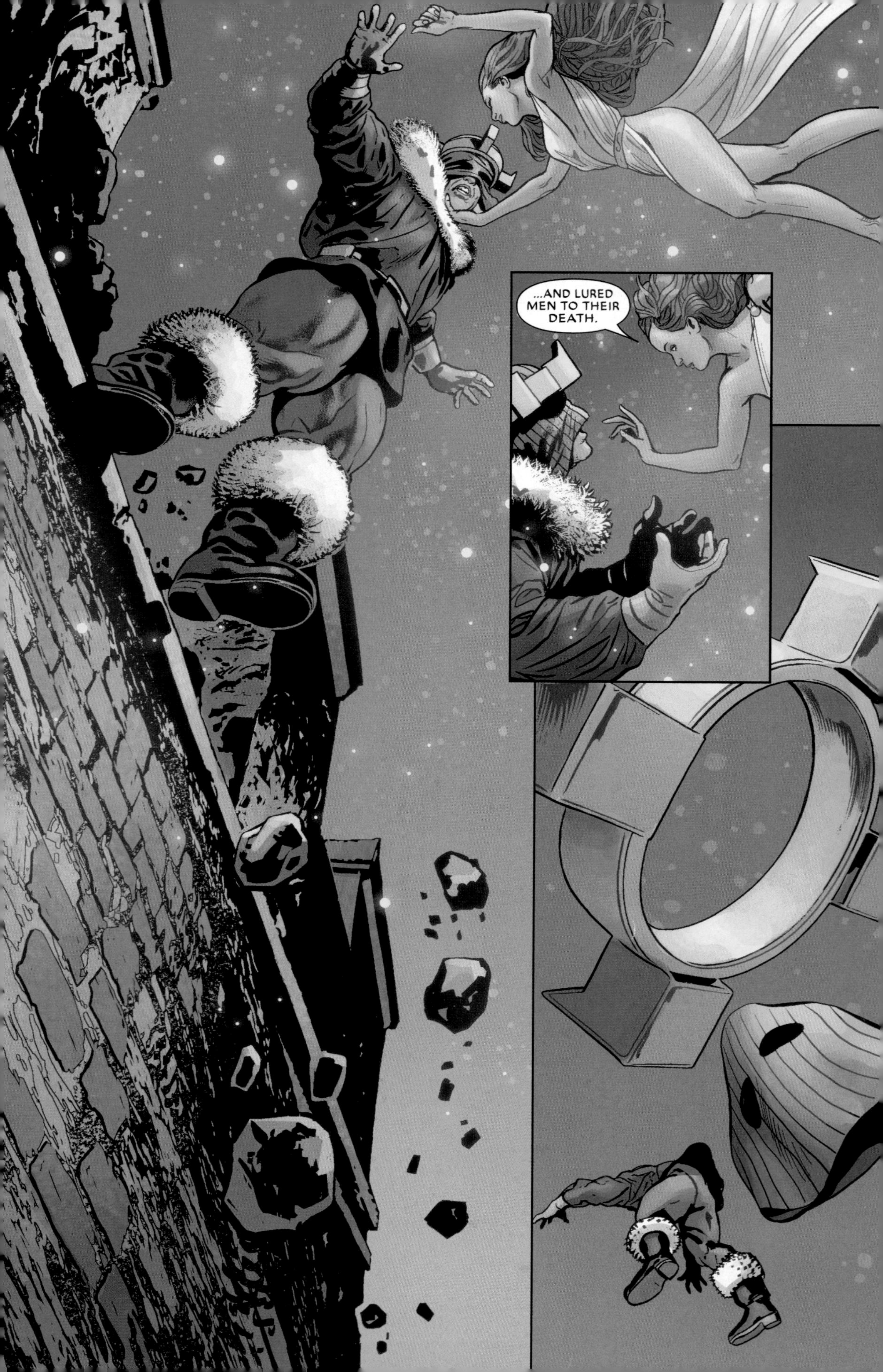
...AND LURED MEN TO THEIR DEATH.

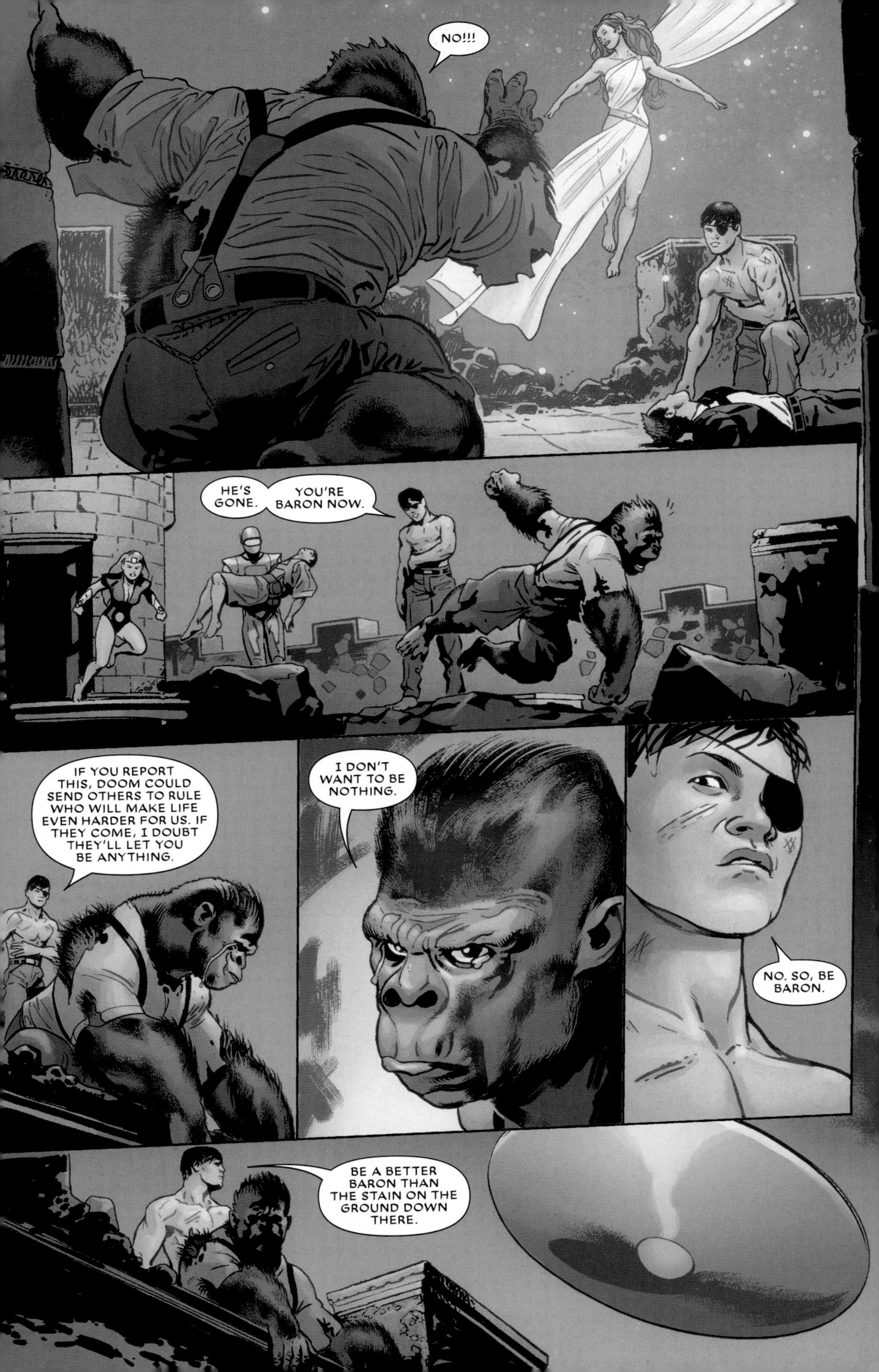
NO!!!
HE'S GONE.
YOU'RE BARON NOW.
IF YOU REPORT THIS, DOOM COULD SEND OTHERS TO RULE WHO WILL MAKE LIFE EVEN HARDER FOR US. IF THEY COME, I DOUBT THEY'LL LET YOU BE ANYTHING.
I DON'T WANT TO BE NOTHING.
NO. SO, BE BARON.
BE A BETTER BARON THAN THE STAIN ON THE GROUND DOWN THERE.

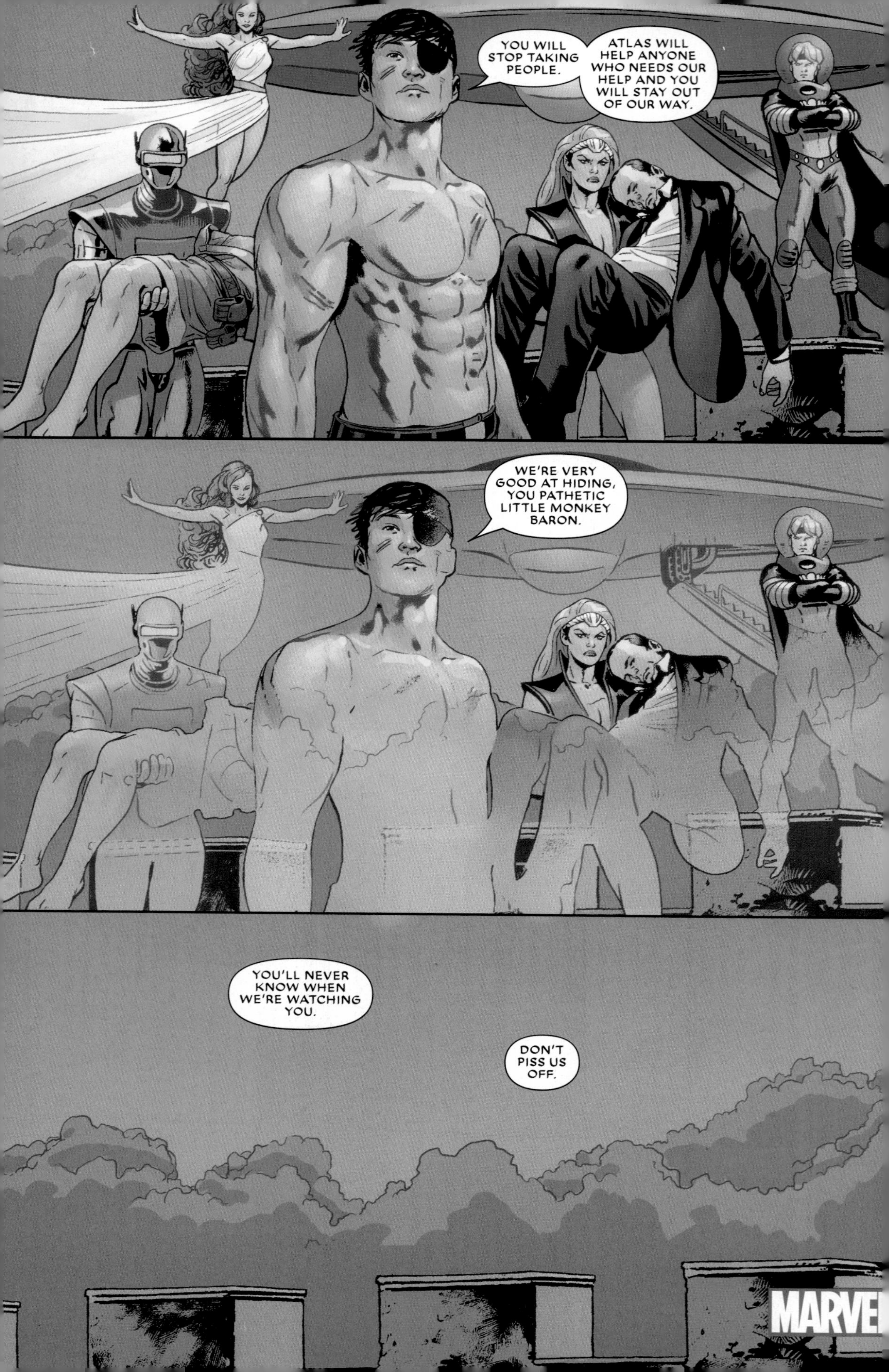
YOU WILL STOP TAKING PEOPLE.
ATLAS WILL HELP ANYONE WHO NEEDS OUR HELP AND YOU WILL STAY OUT OF OUR WAY.
WE'RE VERY GOOD AT HIDING, YOU PATHETIC LITTLE MONKEY BARON.
YOU'LL NEVER KNOW WHEN WE'RE WATCHING YOU.
DON'T PISS US OFF.
MARVEL

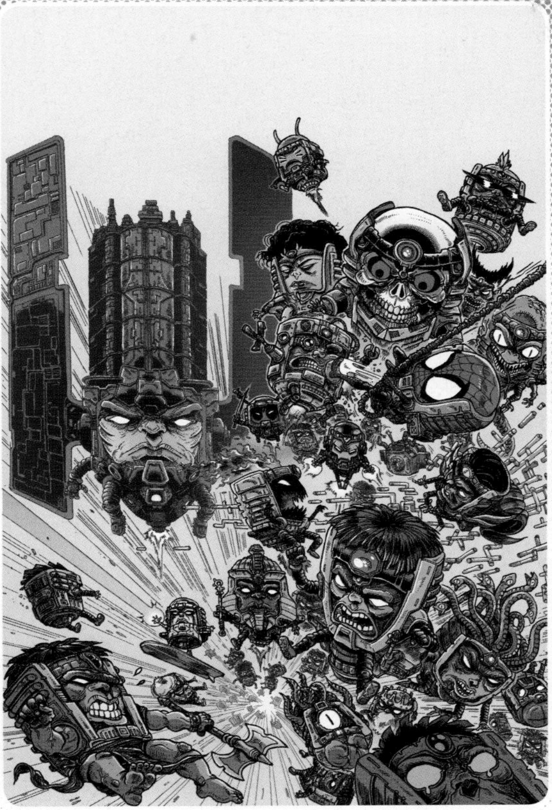

SECRET WAR: BATTLEWORLD #1
VARIANT BY JAMES STOKOE

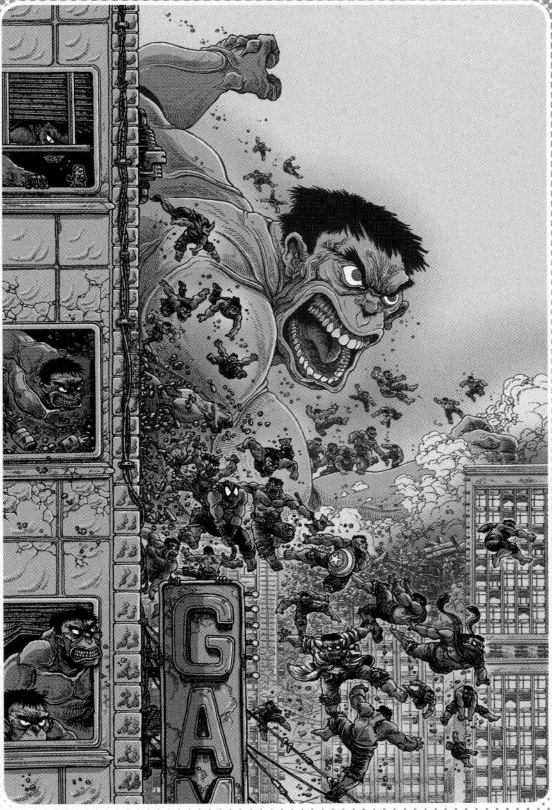

SECRET WAR: BATTLEWORLD #2
VARIANT BY JAMES STOKOE

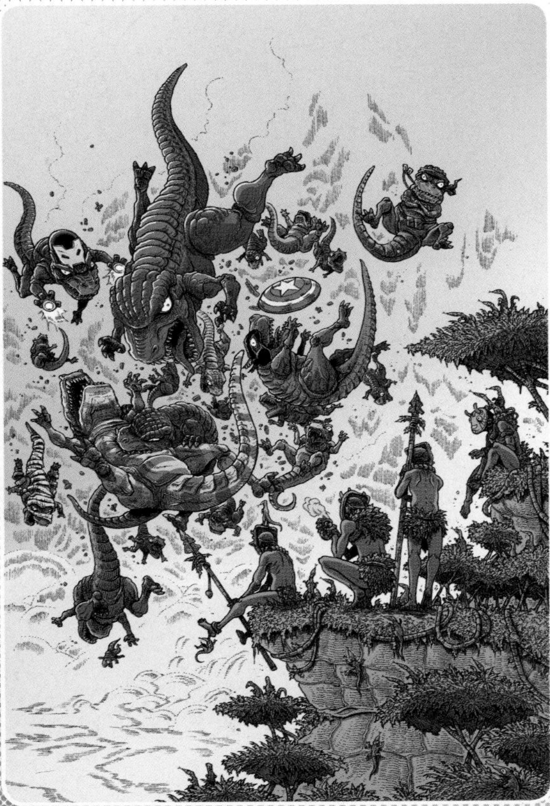

SECRET WAR: BATTLEWORLD #3
VARIANT BY JAMES STOKOE

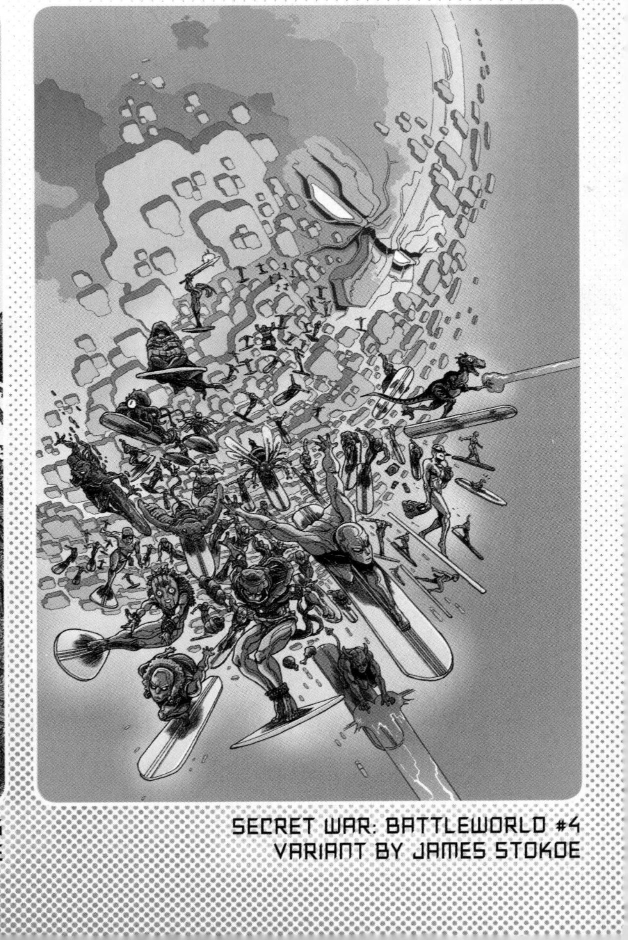

SECRET WAR: BATTLEWORLD #4
VARIANT BY JAMES STOKOE

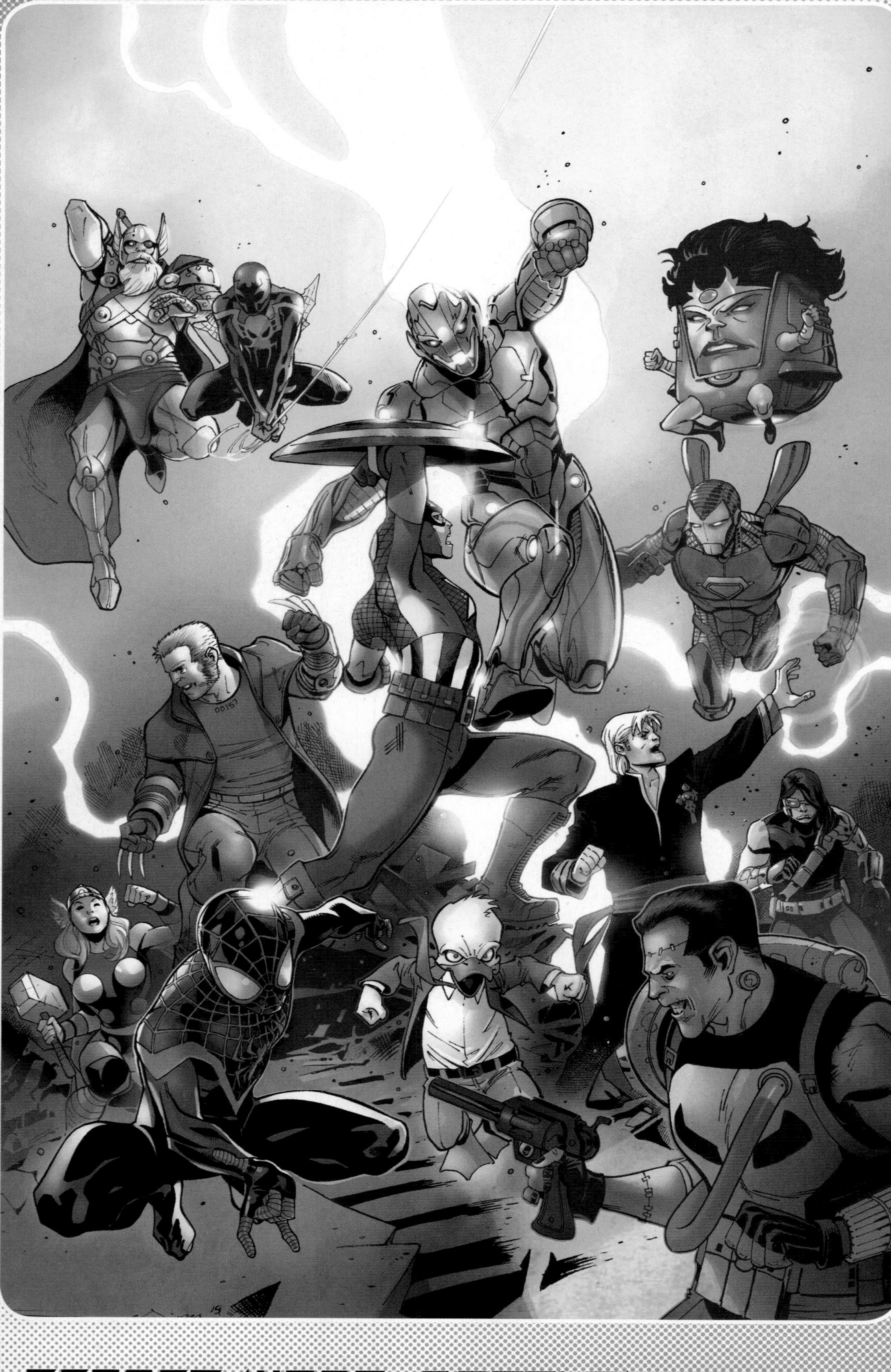
00157

SECRET WARS: BATTLEWORLD #1

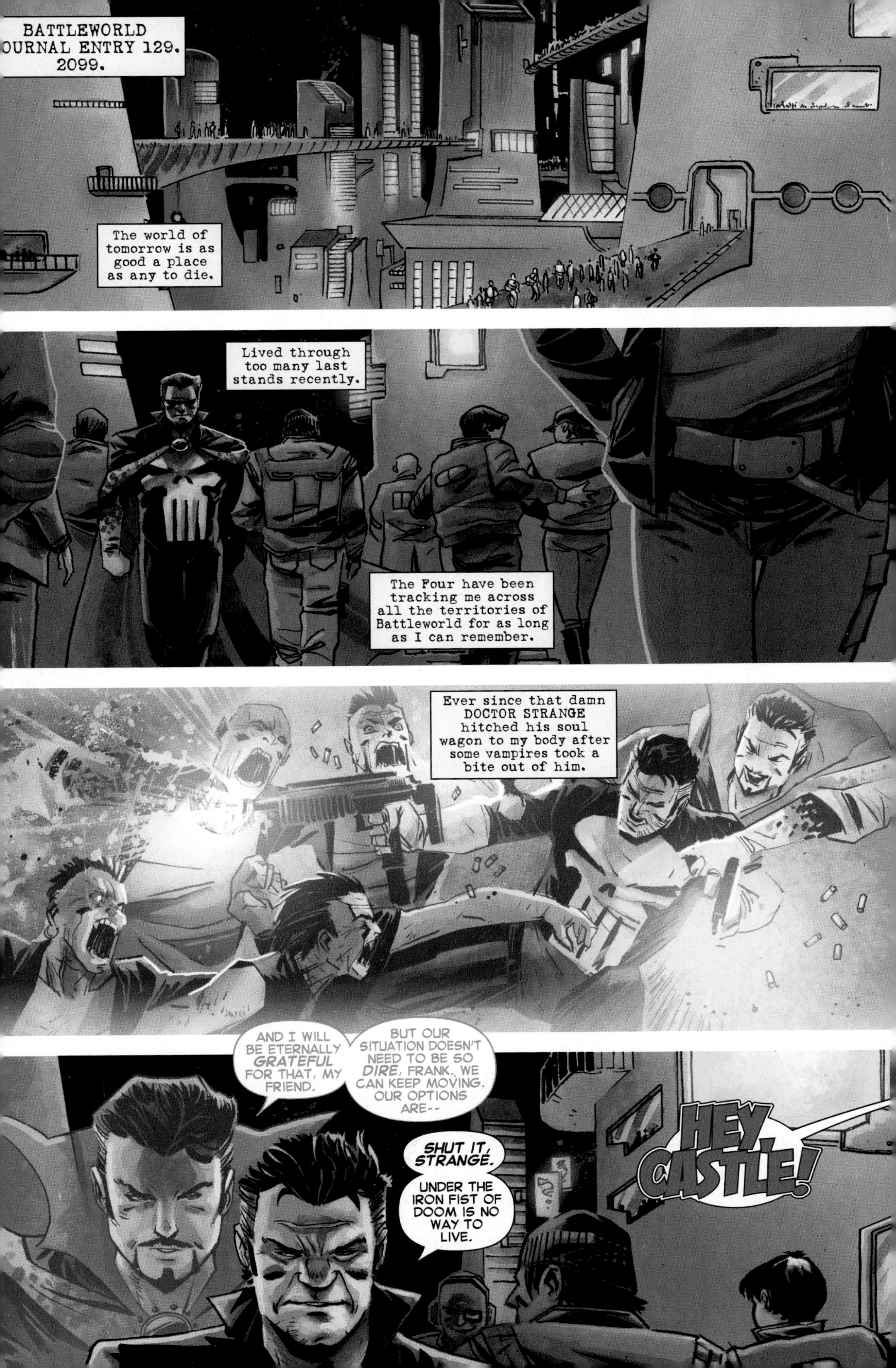
BATTLEWORLD
OURNAL ENTRY 129.
2099.
The world of tomorrow is as good a place as any to die.
Lived through too many last stands recently.
The Four have been tracking me across all the territories of Battleworld for as long as I can remember.
Ever since that damn DOCTOR STRANGE hitched his soul wagon to my body after some vampires took a bite out of him.
AND I WILL BE ETERNALLY GRATEFUL FOR THAT, MY FRIEND.
BUT OUR SITUATION DOESN'T NEED TO BE SO DIRE, FRANK. WE CAN KEEP MOVING. OUR OPTIONS ARE--
SHUT IT, STRANGE.
UNDER THE IRON FIST OF DOOM IS NO WAY TO LIVE.
HEY, CASTLE!

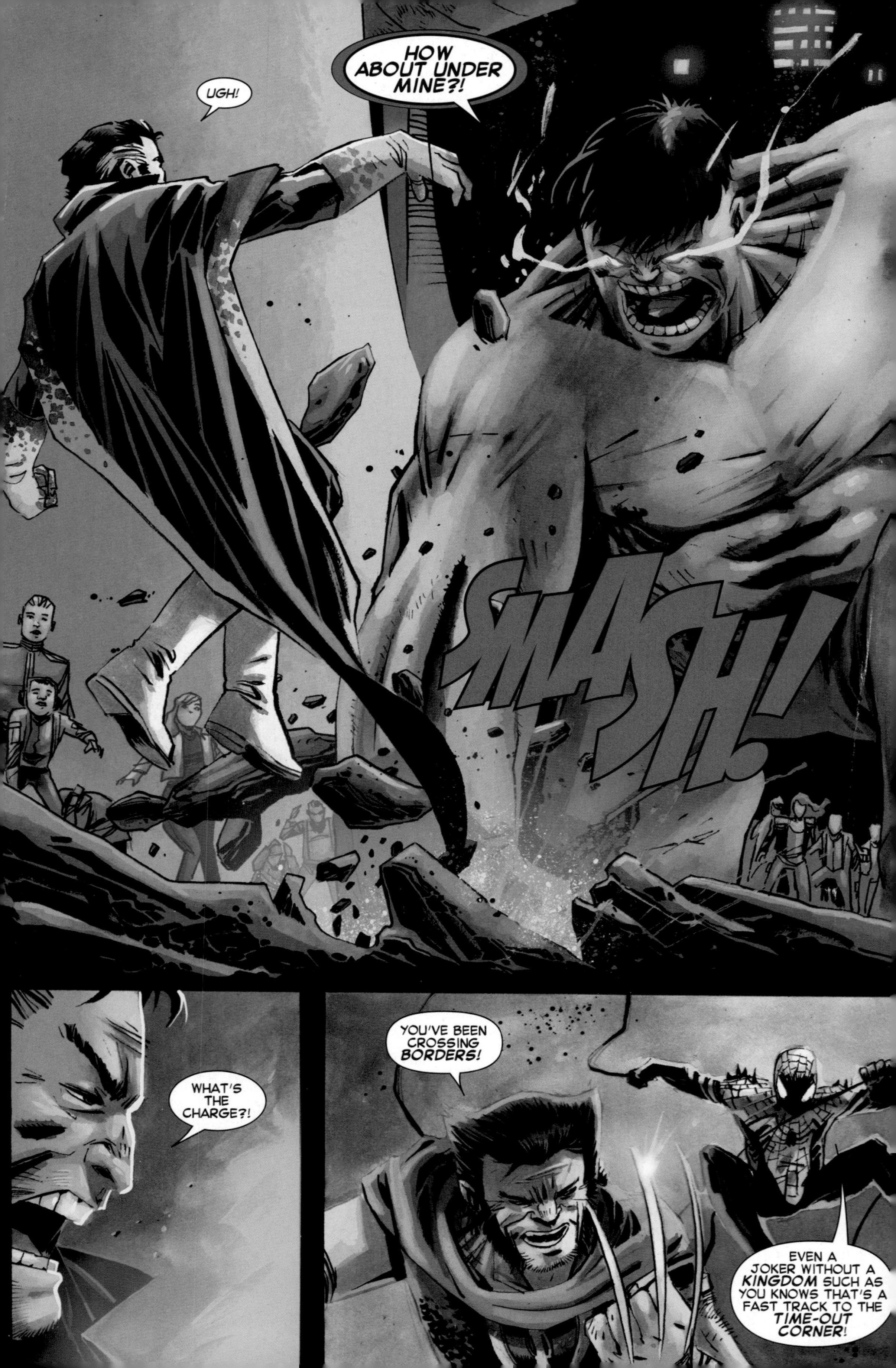
UGH!
HOW ABOUT UNDER MINE?!
SMASH!
WHAT'S THE CHARGE?!
YOU'VE BEEN CROSSING BORDERS!
EVEN A JOKER WITHOUT A KINGDOM SUCH AS YOU KNOWS THAT'S A FAST TRACK TO THE TIME-OUT CORNER!

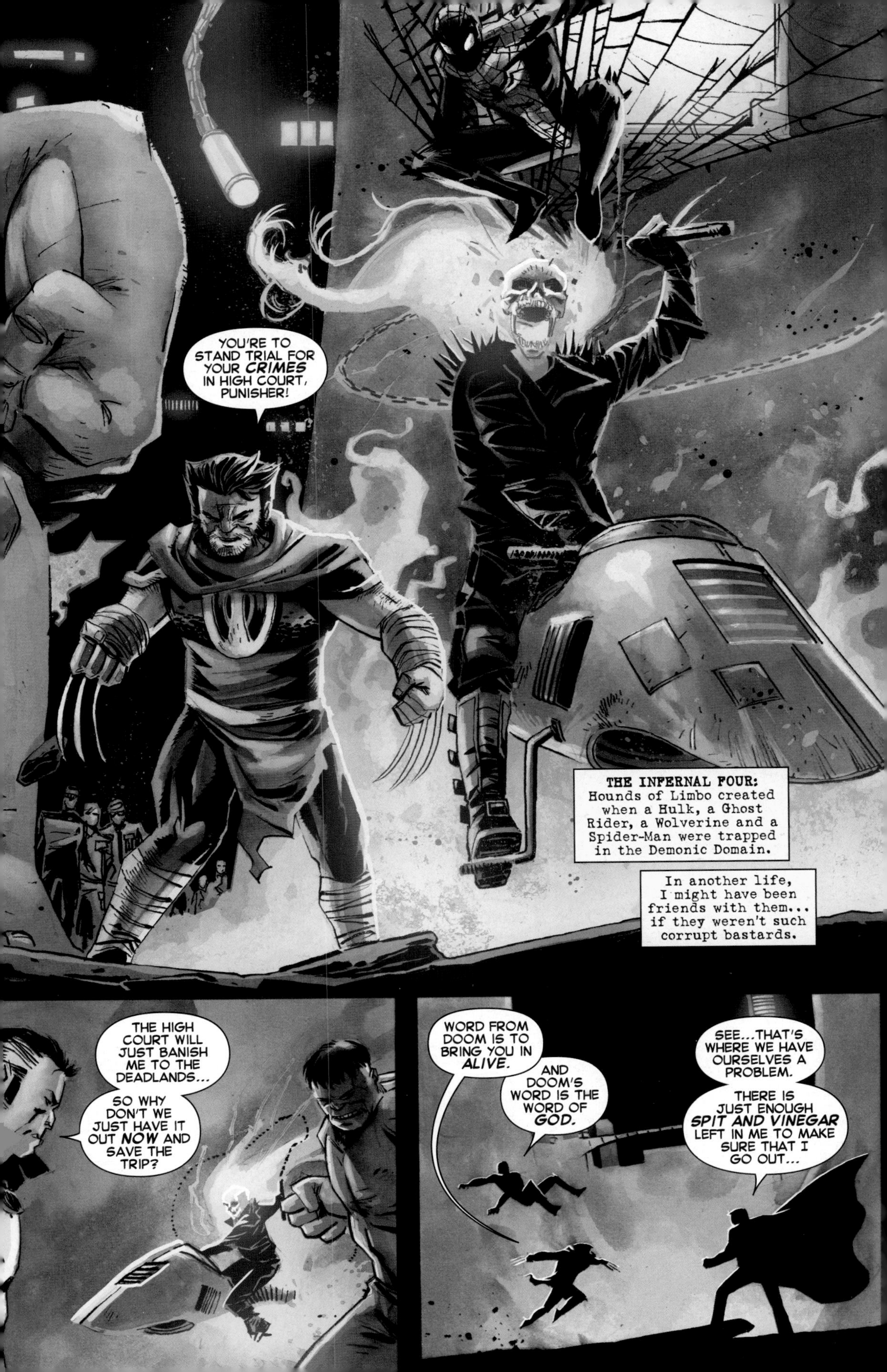
YOU'RE TO STAND TRIAL FOR YOUR CRIMES IN HIGH COURT, PUNISHER!
THE INFERNAL FOUR: Hounds of Limbo created when a Hulk, a Ghost Rider, a Wolverine and a Spider-Man were trapped in the Demonic Domain.
In another life, I might have been friends with them... if they weren't such corrupt bastards.
THE HIGH COURT WILL JUST BANISH ME TO THE DEADLANDS...
SO WHY DON'T WE JUST HAVE IT OUT NOW AND SAVE THE TRIP?
WORD FROM DOOM IS TO BRING YOU IN ALIVE.
AND DOOM'S WORD IS THE WORD OF GOD.
SEE...THAT'S WHERE WE HAVE OURSELVES A PROBLEM.
THERE IS JUST ENOUGH SPIT AND VINEGAR LEFT IN ME TO MAKE SURE THAT I GO OUT...

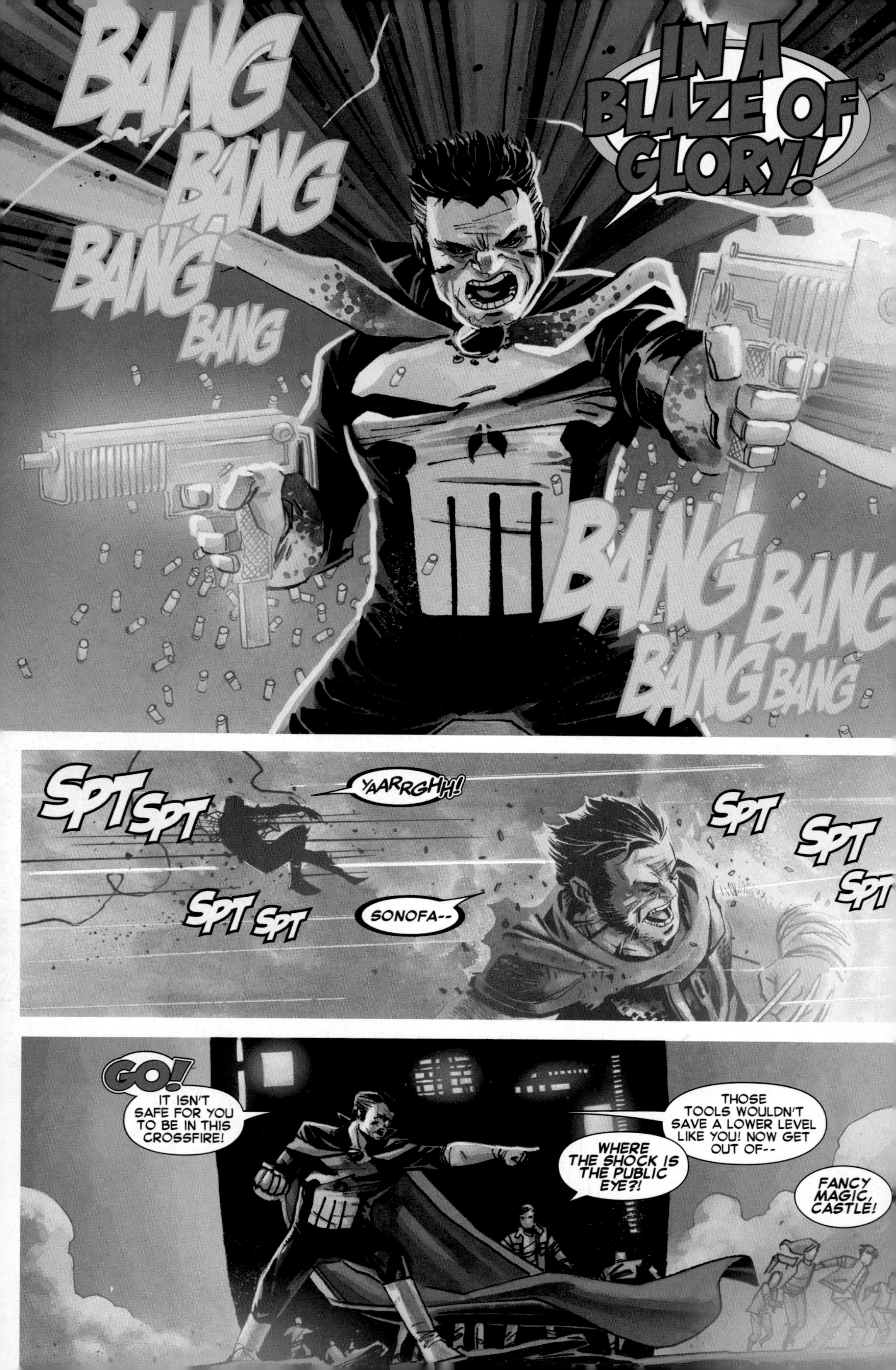
BANG
BANG
BANG
BANG
IN A BLAZE OF GLORY!
BANG BANG
BANG BANG
SPT SPT
YAARRGHH!
SPT SPT
SONOFA--
SPT
SPT
SPT
GO!
IT ISN'T SAFE FOR YOU TO BE IN THIS CROSSFIRE!
THOSE TOOLS WOULDN'T SAVE A LOWER LEVEL LIKE YOU! NOW GET OUT OF--
WHERE THE SHOCK IS THE PUBLIC EYE?!
FANCY MAGIC, CASTLE!

BUT HULK IS THE STRONGEST ONE THERE--

SNAP

CALM.

WHERE AM I?! WHAT--

SORRY, BANNER.

AAAHH!

DUST.

YOU'RE A DEAD MAN! WE ALMOST HAD YOU IN THE MONARCHY OF M!

NO. YOU DIDN'T.

SNAP

ICE.

ROCKET OF RAGGADORR!

SSKKRRRT

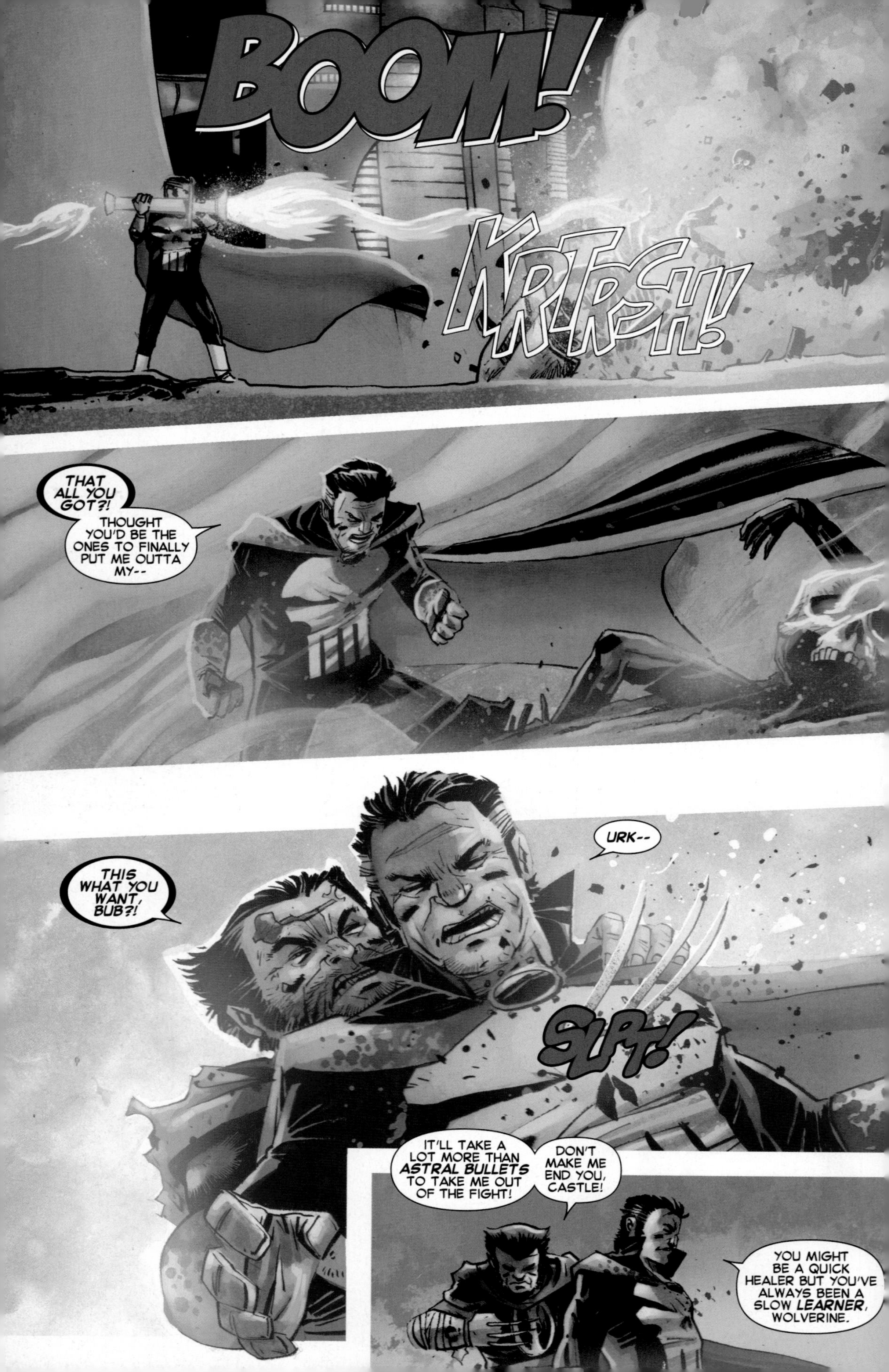
BOOM!
KRTRSH!
THAT ALL YOU GOT?!
THOUGHT YOU'D BE THE ONES TO FINALLY PUT ME OUTTA MY--
THIS WHAT YOU WANT, BUB?!
URK--
SLPT!
IT'LL TAKE A LOT MORE THAN ASTRAL BULLETS TO TAKE ME OUT OF THE FIGHT!
DON'T MAKE ME END YOU, CASTLE!
YOU MIGHT BE A QUICK HEALER BUT YOU'VE ALWAYS BEEN A SLOW LEARNER, WOLVERINE.

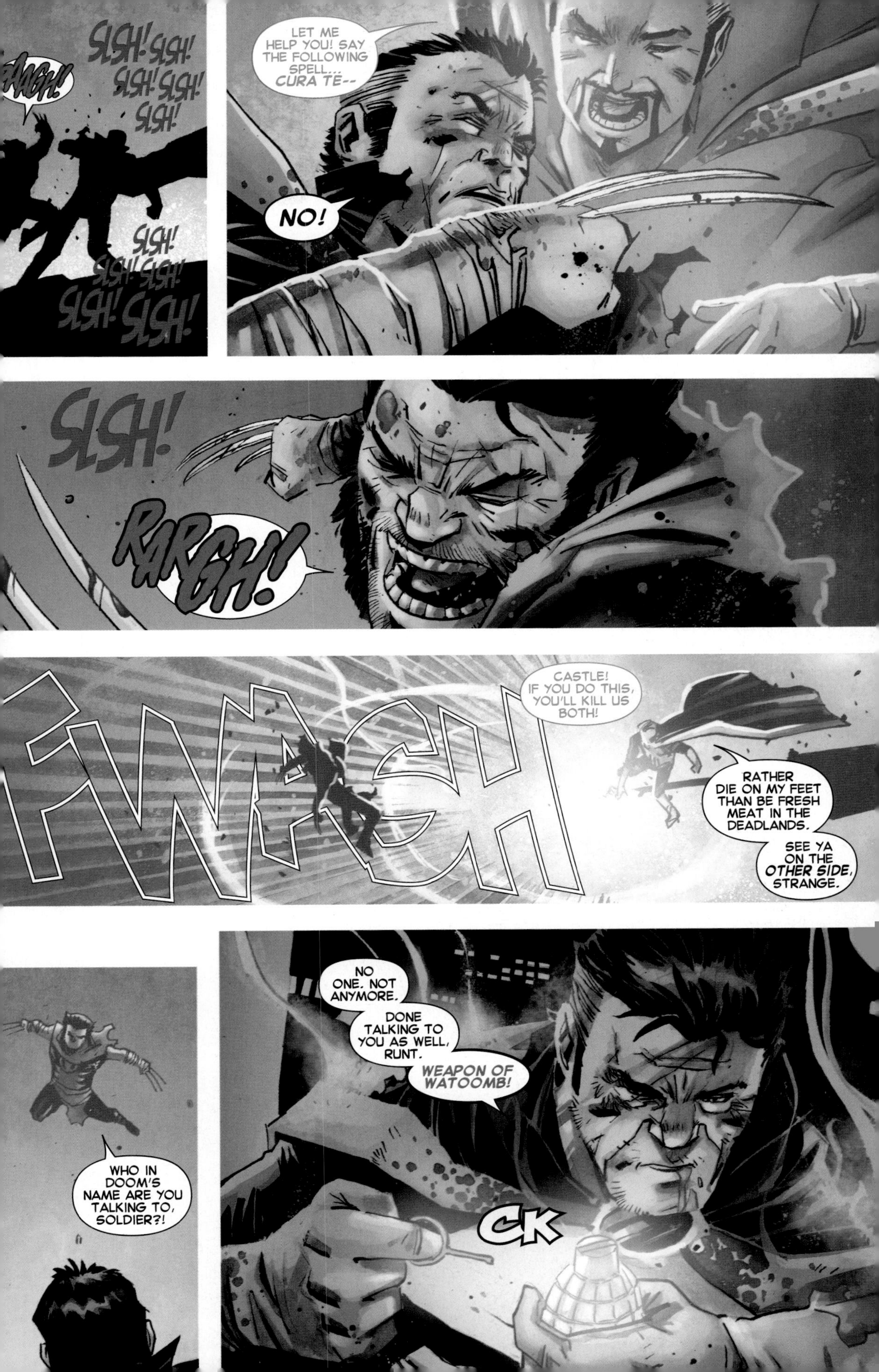
RAAGH!
SLSH! SLSH! SLSH! SLSH! SLSH!
SLSH! SLSH! SLSH! SLSH! SLSH!
LET ME HELP YOU! SAY THE FOLLOWING SPELL... CURA TE--
NO!
SLSH!
RARGH!
FWASH
CASTLE! IF YOU DO THIS, YOU'LL KILL US BOTH!
RATHER DIE ON MY FEET THAN BE FRESH MEAT IN THE DEADLANDS.
SEE YA ON THE OTHER SIDE, STRANGE.
WHO IN DOOM'S NAME ARE YOU TALKING TO, SOLDIER?!
NO ONE. NOT ANYMORE.
DONE TALKING TO YOU AS WELL, RUNT.
WEAPON OF WATOOMB!
CK

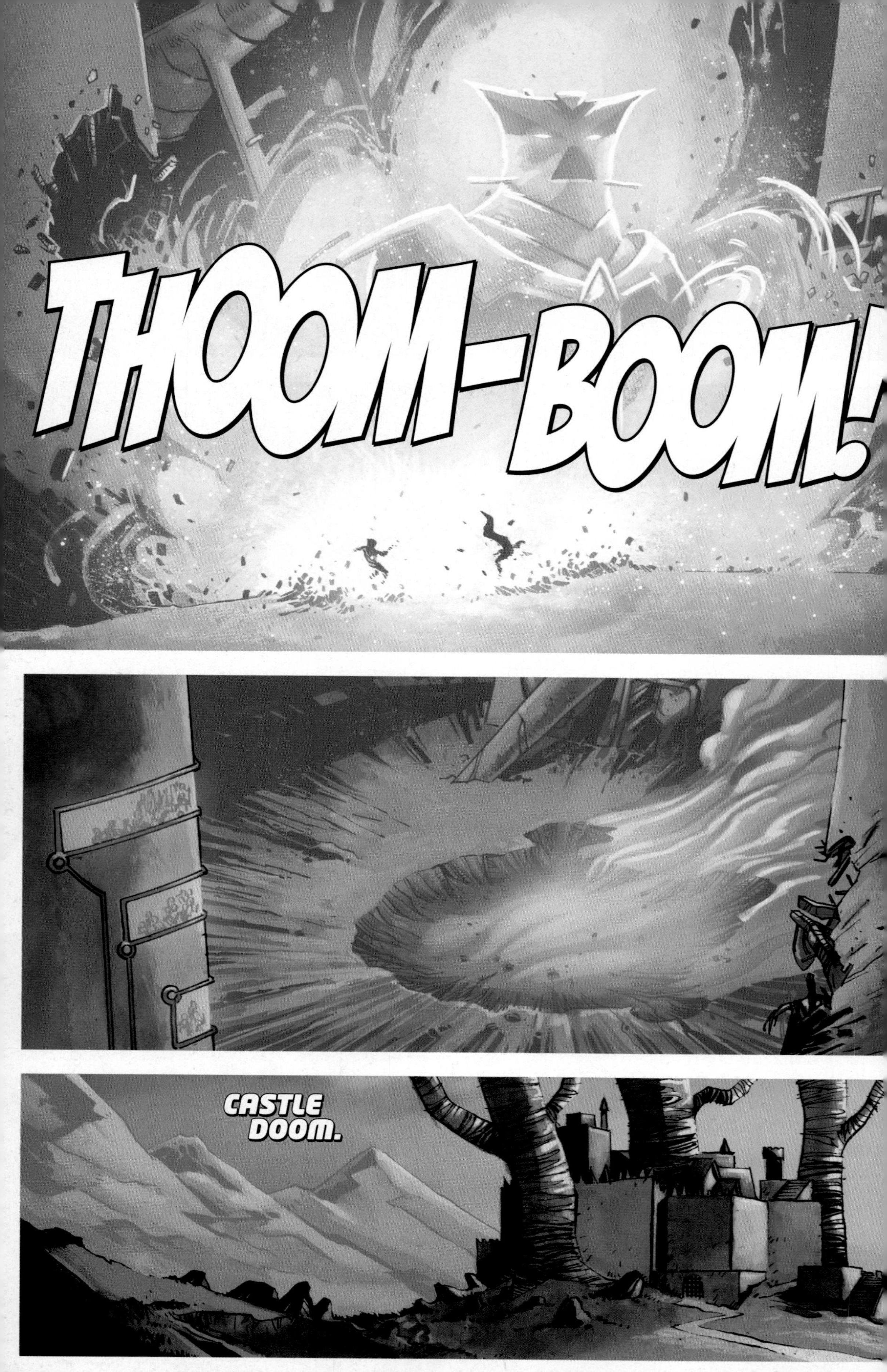
THOOM-BOOM!
CASTLE DOOM.

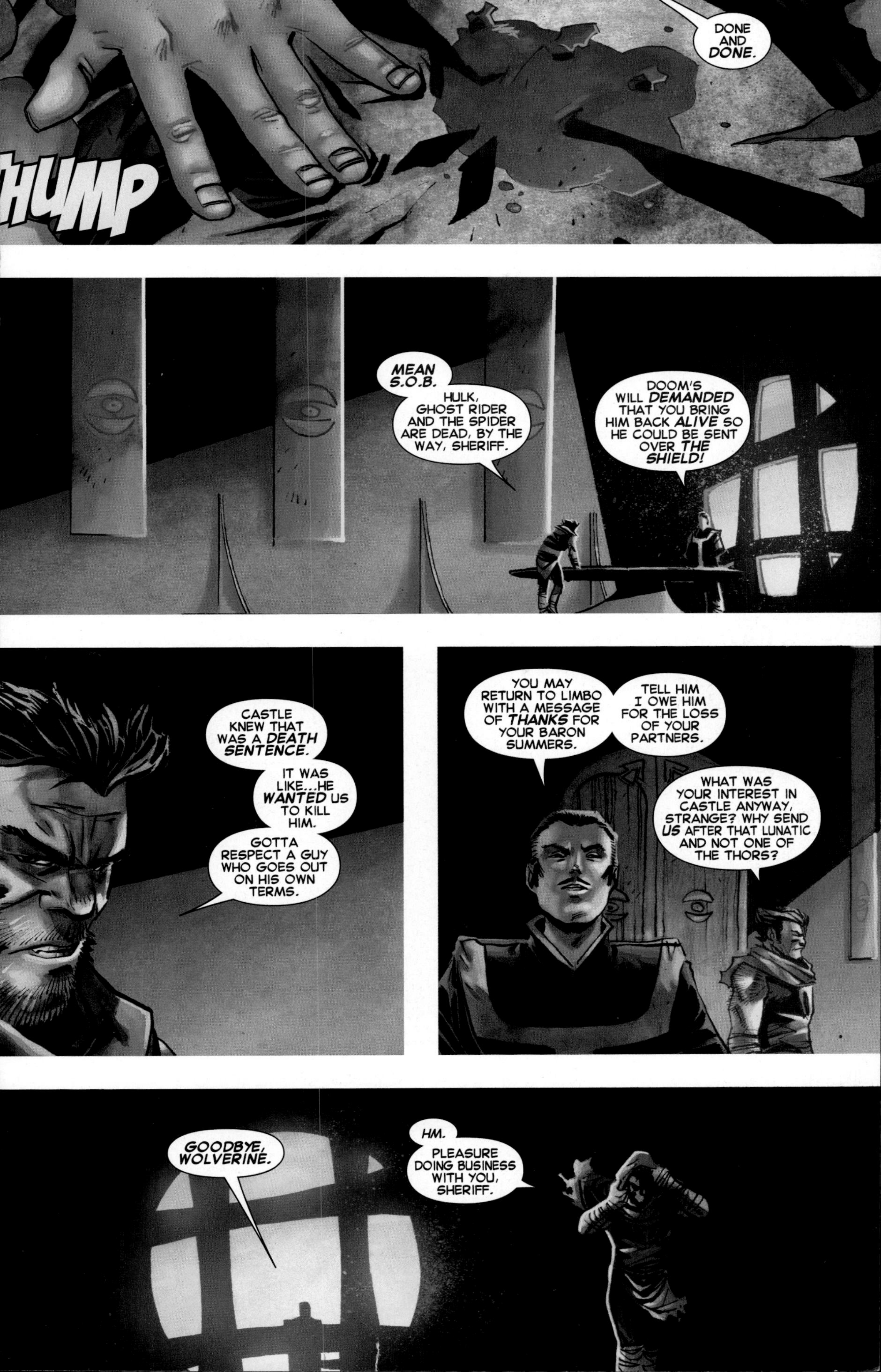
DONE AND DONE.
THUMP
MEAN S.O.B.
HULK, GHOST RIDER AND THE SPIDER ARE DEAD, BY THE WAY, SHERIFF.
DOOM'S WILL DEMANDED THAT YOU BRING HIM BACK ALIVE SO HE COULD BE SENT OVER THE SHIELD!
CASTLE KNEW THAT WAS A DEATH SENTENCE.
IT WAS LIKE...HE WANTED US TO KILL HIM.
GOTTA RESPECT A GUY WHO GOES OUT ON HIS OWN TERMS.
YOU MAY RETURN TO LIMBO WITH A MESSAGE OF THANKS FOR YOUR BARON SUMMERS.
TELL HIM I OWE HIM FOR THE LOSS OF YOUR PARTNERS.
WHAT WAS YOUR INTEREST IN CASTLE ANYWAY, STRANGE? WHY SEND US AFTER THAT LUNATIC AND NOT ONE OF THE THORS?
GOODBYE, WOLVERINE.
HM.
PLEASURE DOING BUSINESS WITH YOU, SHERIFF.

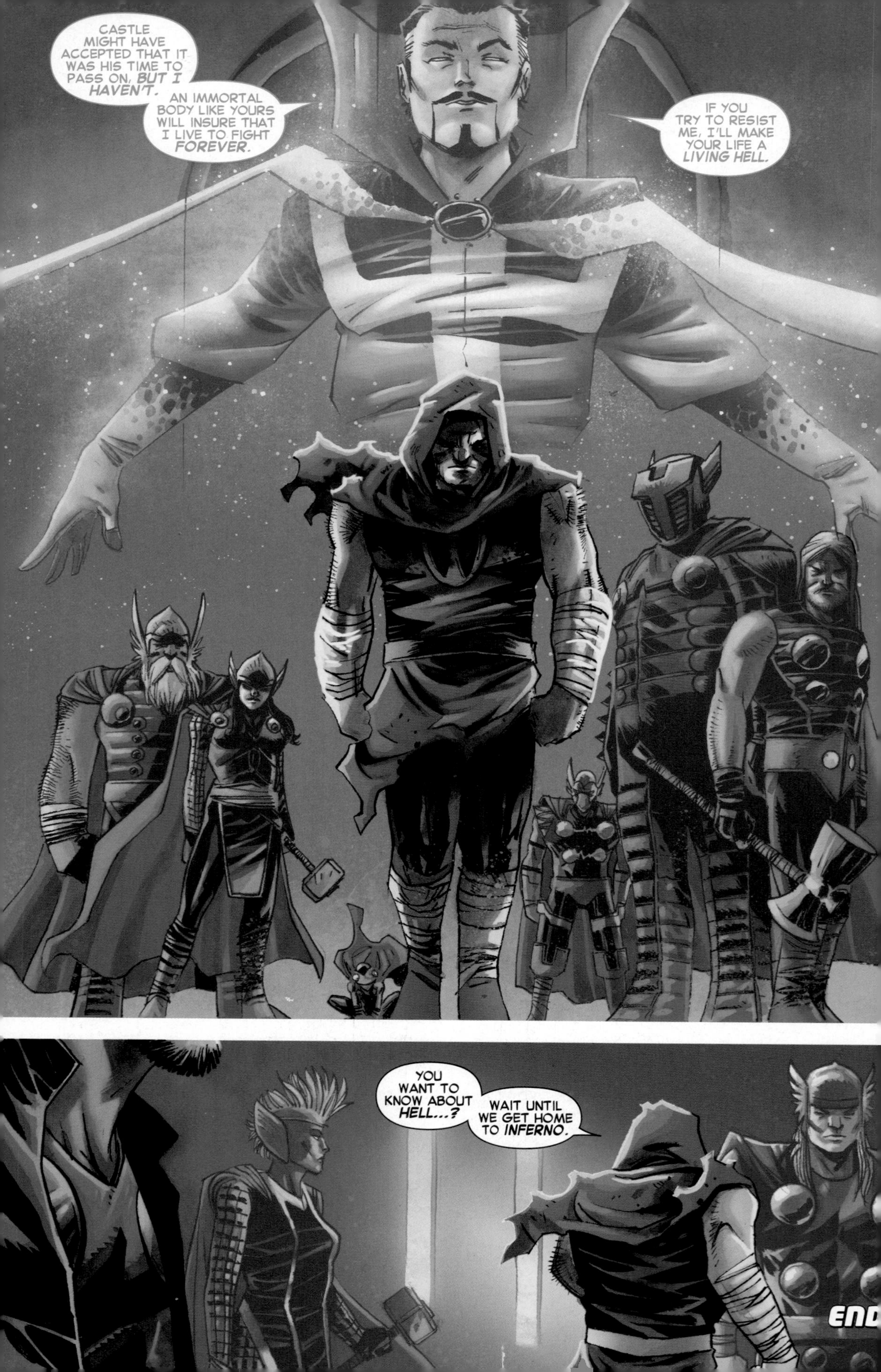
CASTLE MIGHT HAVE ACCEPTED THAT IT WAS HIS TIME TO PASS ON, BUT I HAVEN'T.
AN IMMORTAL BODY LIKE YOURS WILL INSURE THAT I LIVE TO FIGHT FOREVER.
IF YOU TRY TO RESIST ME, I'LL MAKE YOUR LIFE A LIVING HELL.
YOU WANT TO KNOW ABOUT HELL...?
WAIT UNTIL WE GET HOME TO INFERNO.
END

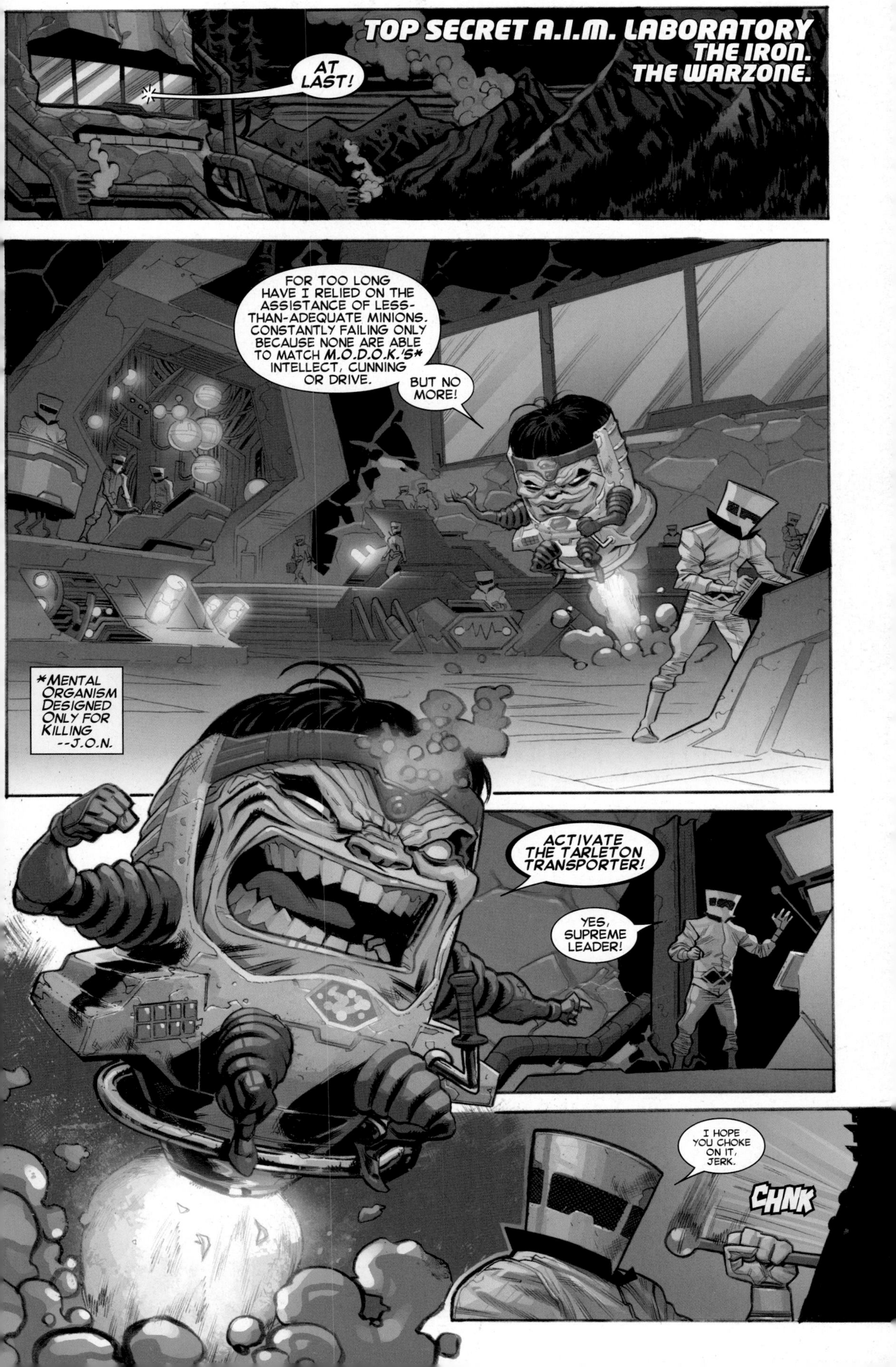
TOP SECRET A.I.M. LABORATORY
THE IRON.
THE WARZONE.
AT LAST!
FOR TOO LONG HAVE I RELIED ON THE ASSISTANCE OF LESS-THAN-ADEQUATE MINIONS. CONSTANTLY FAILING ONLY BECAUSE NONE ARE ABLE TO MATCH M.O.D.O.K.'S* INTELLECT, CUNNING OR DRIVE.
BUT NO MORE!
*MENTAL ORGANISM DESIGNED ONLY FOR KILLING --J.O.N.
ACTIVATE THE TARLETON TRANSPORTER!
YES, SUPREME LEADER!
I HOPE YOU CHOKE ON IT, JERK.
CHNK

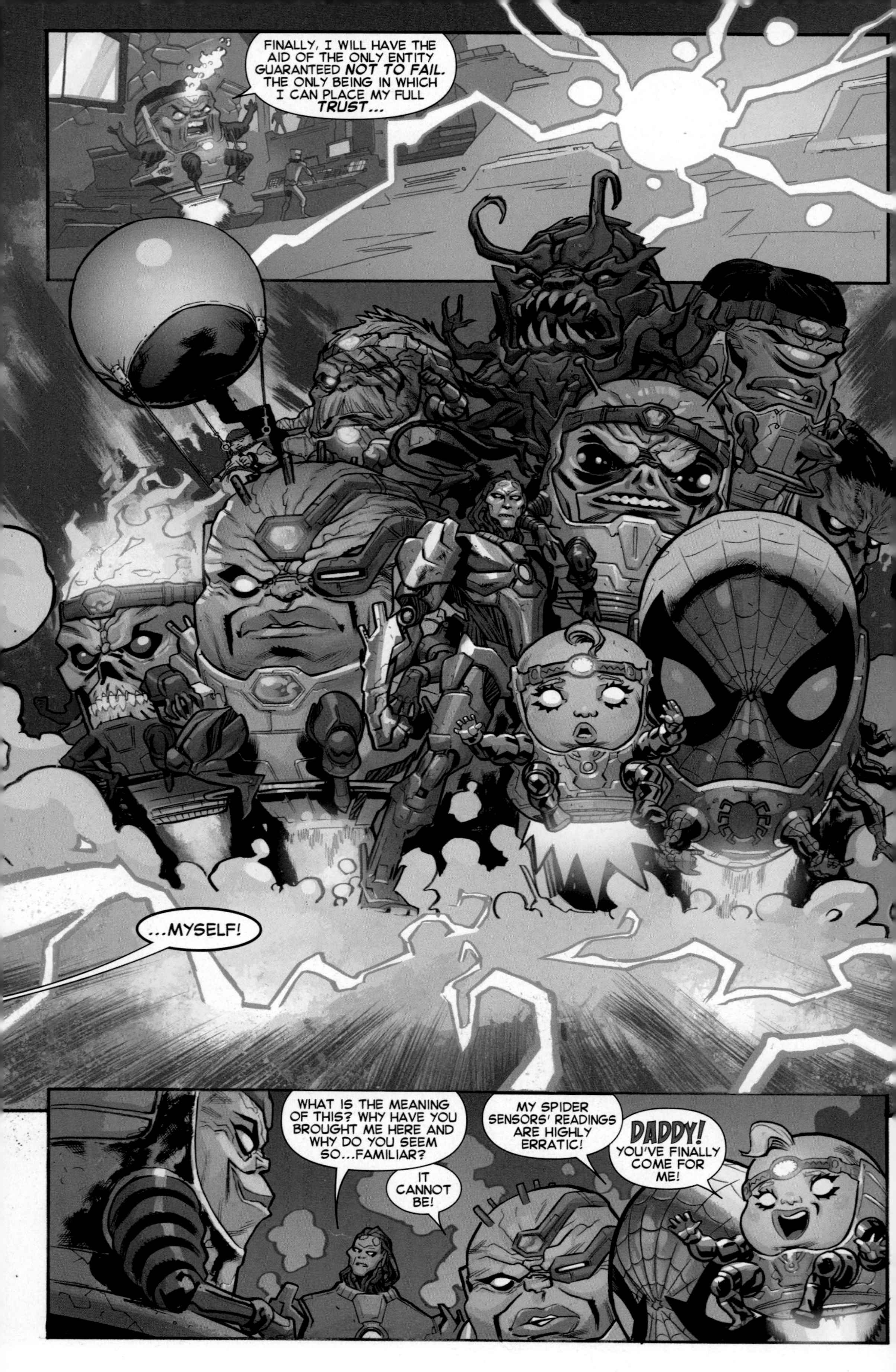
FINALLY, I WILL HAVE THE AID OF THE ONLY ENTITY GUARANTEED NOT TO FAIL. THE ONLY BEING IN WHICH I CAN PLACE MY FULL TRUST...
...MYSELF!
WHAT IS THE MEANING OF THIS? WHY HAVE YOU BROUGHT ME HERE AND WHY DO YOU SEEM SO...FAMILIAR?
IT CANNOT BE!
MY SPIDER SENSORS' READINGS ARE HIGHLY ERRATIC!
DADDY! YOU'VE FINALLY COME FOR ME!

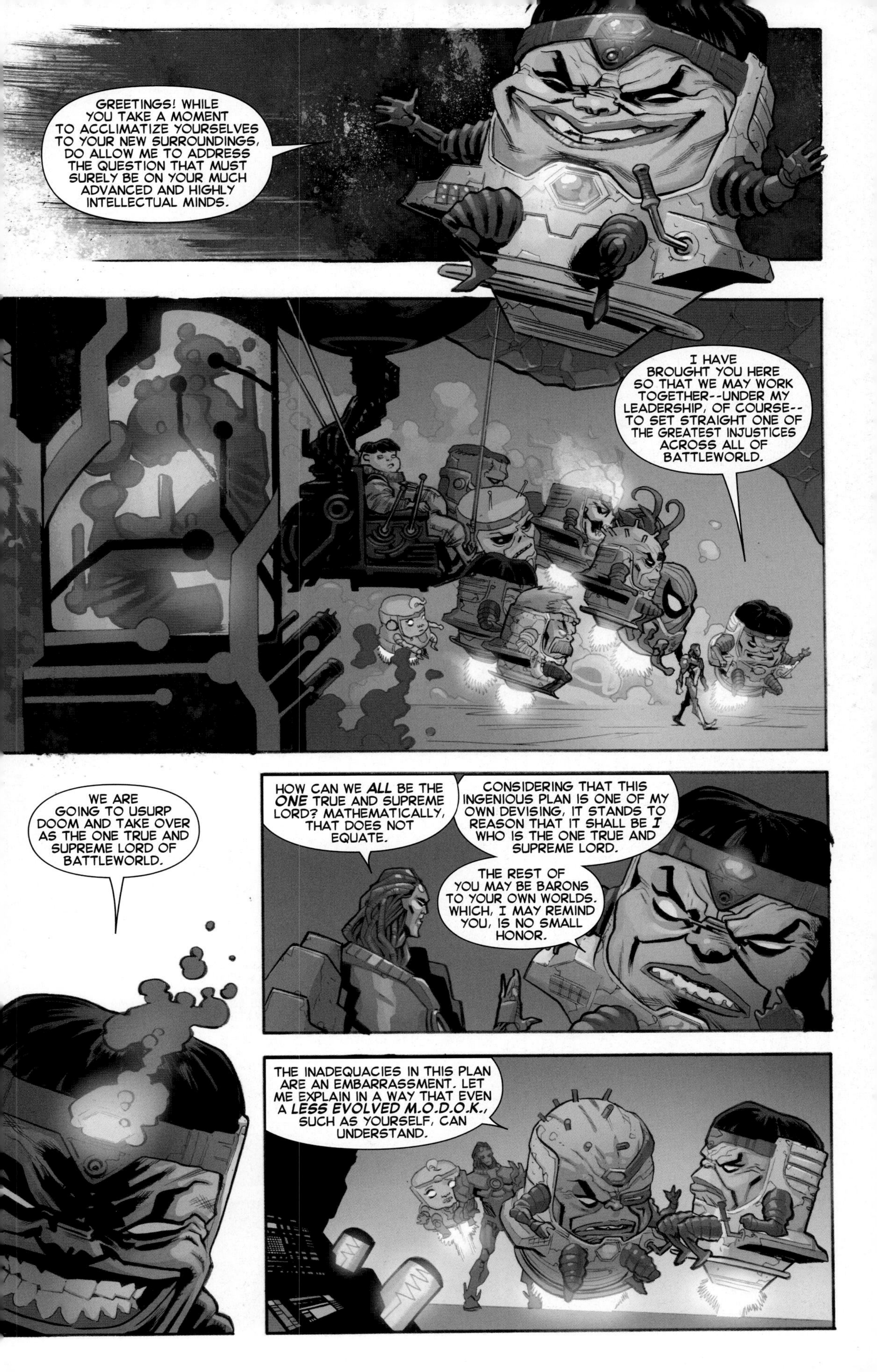
GREETINGS! WHILE YOU TAKE A MOMENT TO ACCLIMATIZE YOURSELVES TO YOUR NEW SURROUNDINGS, DO ALLOW ME TO ADDRESS THE QUESTION THAT MUST SURELY BE ON YOUR MUCH ADVANCED AND HIGHLY INTELLECTUAL MINDS.
I HAVE BROUGHT YOU HERE SO THAT WE MAY WORK TOGETHER--UNDER MY LEADERSHIP, OF COURSE--TO SET STRAIGHT ONE OF THE GREATEST INJUSTICES ACROSS ALL OF BATTLEWORLD.
WE ARE GOING TO USURP DOOM AND TAKE OVER AS THE ONE TRUE AND SUPREME LORD OF BATTLEWORLD.
HOW CAN WE ALL BE THE ONE TRUE AND SUPREME LORD? MATHEMATICALLY, THAT DOES NOT EQUATE.
CONSIDERING THAT THIS INGENIOUS PLAN IS ONE OF MY OWN DEVISING, IT STANDS TO REASON THAT IT SHALL BE I WHO IS THE ONE TRUE AND SUPREME LORD.
THE REST OF YOU MAY BE BARONS TO YOUR OWN WORLDS. WHICH, I MAY REMIND YOU, IS NO SMALL HONOR.
THE INADEQUACIES IN THIS PLAN ARE AN EMBARRASSMENT. LET ME EXPLAIN IN A WAY THAT EVEN A LESS EVOLVED M.O.D.O.K., SUCH AS YOURSELF, CAN UNDERSTAND.

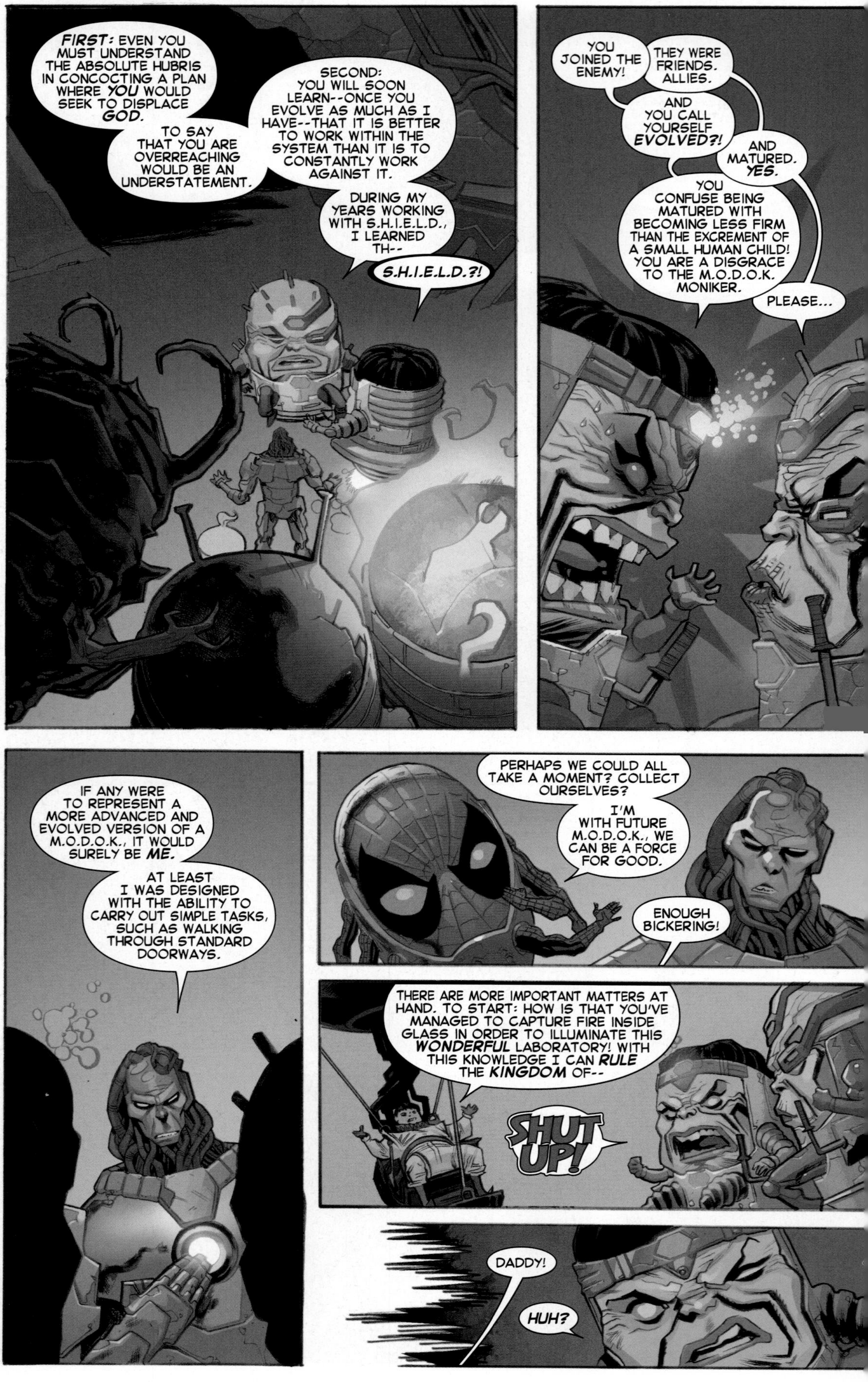
FIRST: EVEN YOU MUST UNDERSTAND THE ABSOLUTE HUBRIS IN CONCOCTING A PLAN WHERE YOU WOULD SEEK TO DISPLACE GOD.
TO SAY THAT YOU ARE OVERREACHING WOULD BE AN UNDERSTATEMENT.
SECOND: YOU WILL SOON LEARN--ONCE YOU EVOLVE AS MUCH AS I HAVE--THAT IT IS BETTER TO WORK WITHIN THE SYSTEM THAN IT IS TO CONSTANTLY WORK AGAINST IT.
DURING MY YEARS WORKING WITH S.H.I.E.L.D., I LEARNED TH--
S.H.I.E.L.D.?!
YOU JOINED THE ENEMY!
THEY WERE FRIENDS. ALLIES.
AND YOU CALL YOURSELF EVOLVED?!
AND MATURED. YES.
YOU CONFUSE BEING MATURED WITH BECOMING LESS FIRM THAN THE EXCREMENT OF A SMALL HUMAN CHILD! YOU ARE A DISGRACE TO THE M.O.D.O.K. MONIKER.
PLEASE...
IF ANY WERE TO REPRESENT A MORE ADVANCED AND EVOLVED VERSION OF A M.O.D.O.K., IT WOULD SURELY BE ME.
AT LEAST I WAS DESIGNED WITH THE ABILITY TO CARRY OUT SIMPLE TASKS, SUCH AS WALKING THROUGH STANDARD DOORWAYS.
PERHAPS WE COULD ALL TAKE A MOMENT? COLLECT OURSELVES?
I'M WITH FUTURE M.O.D.O.K., WE CAN BE A FORCE FOR GOOD.
ENOUGH BICKERING!
THERE ARE MORE IMPORTANT MATTERS AT HAND. TO START: HOW IS THAT YOU'VE MANAGED TO CAPTURE FIRE INSIDE GLASS IN ORDER TO ILLUMINATE THIS WONDERFUL LABORATORY! WITH THIS KNOWLEDGE I CAN RULE THE KINGDOM OF--
SHUT UP!
DADDY!
HUH?

KILL THEM, DADDY.

KILL THEM AND YOU AND I WILL TOPPLE DOOM TOGETHER! WITH ME AT YOUR SIDE, YOU CAN RULE ALL OF BATTLEWORLD!

WHICH ONE OF YOU IMBECILES SIRED THIS ABOMINATION?

M.O.D.O.K. IS A LEADER, NOT A BREEDER!

WHY WON'T YOU ACKNOWLEDGE ME? WHY MUST YOU DENY YOUR PROGENY?

CLEARLY THIS PLAN IS FRAUGHT WITH ERROR.

THIS IS WHAT M.O.D.O.K. GETS FOR BELIEVING IN HIMSELF!

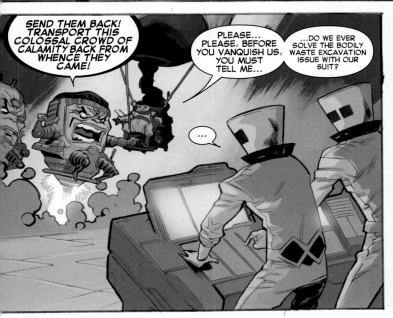

SEND THEM BACK! TRANSPORT THIS COLOSSAL CROWD OF CALAMITY BACK FROM WHENCE THEY CAME!

PLEASE... PLEASE, BEFORE YOU VANQUISH US, YOU MUST TELL ME...

...DO WE EVER SOLVE THE BODILY WASTE EXCAVATION ISSUE WITH OUR SUIT?

...

YES, SUPREME LEADER!

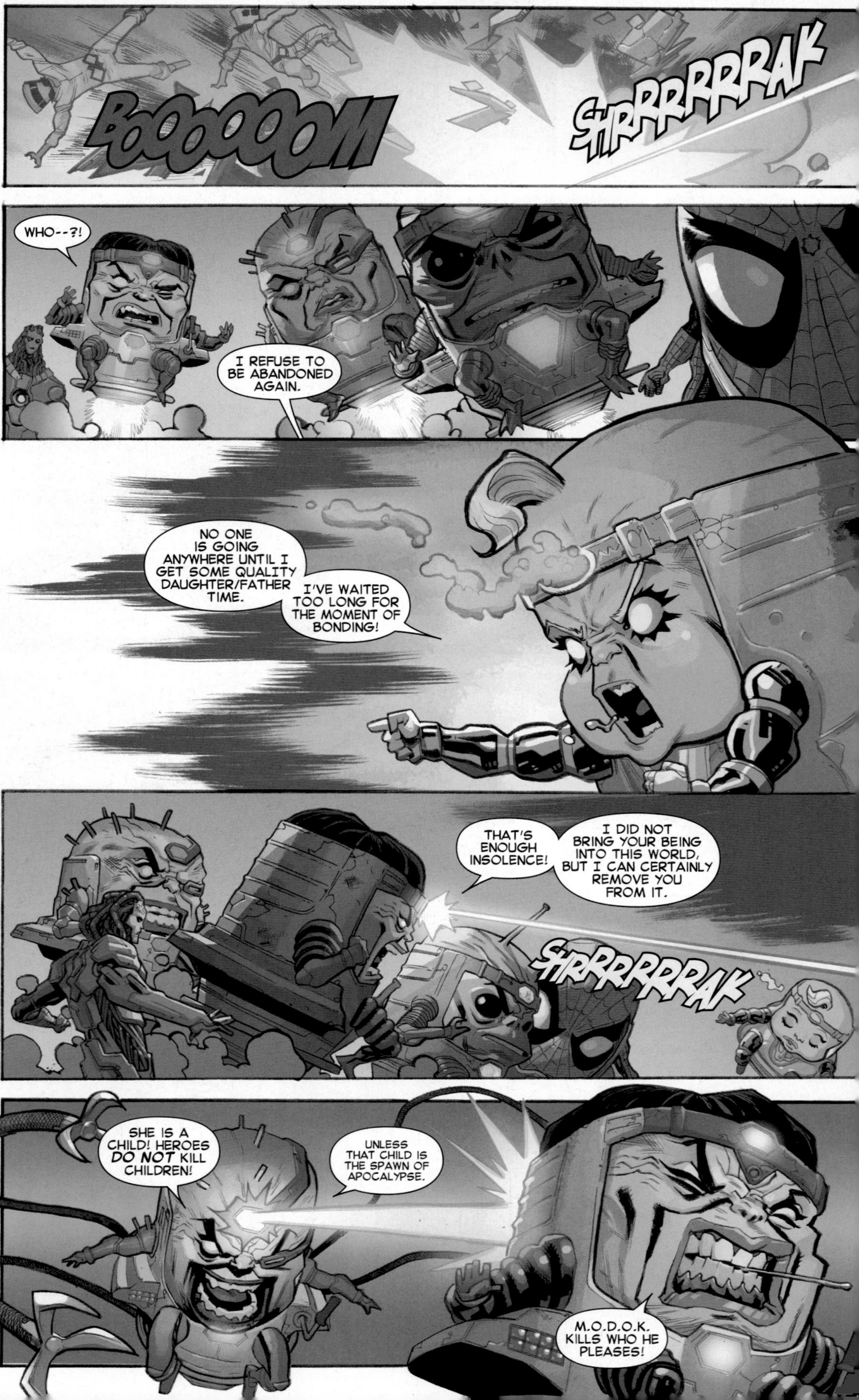
BOOOOOOOM
SHRRRRRRAK
WHO--?!
I REFUSE TO BE ABANDONED AGAIN.
NO ONE IS GOING ANYWHERE UNTIL I GET SOME QUALITY DAUGHTER/FATHER TIME.
I'VE WAITED TOO LONG FOR THE MOMENT OF BONDING!
THAT'S ENOUGH INSOLENCE!
I DID NOT BRING YOUR BEING INTO THIS WORLD, BUT I CAN CERTAINLY REMOVE YOU FROM IT.
SHRRRRRRAK
SHE IS A CHILD! HEROES **DO NOT** KILL CHILDREN!
UNLESS THAT CHILD IS THE SPAWN OF APOCALYPSE.
M.O.D.O.K. KILLS WHO HE PLEASES!

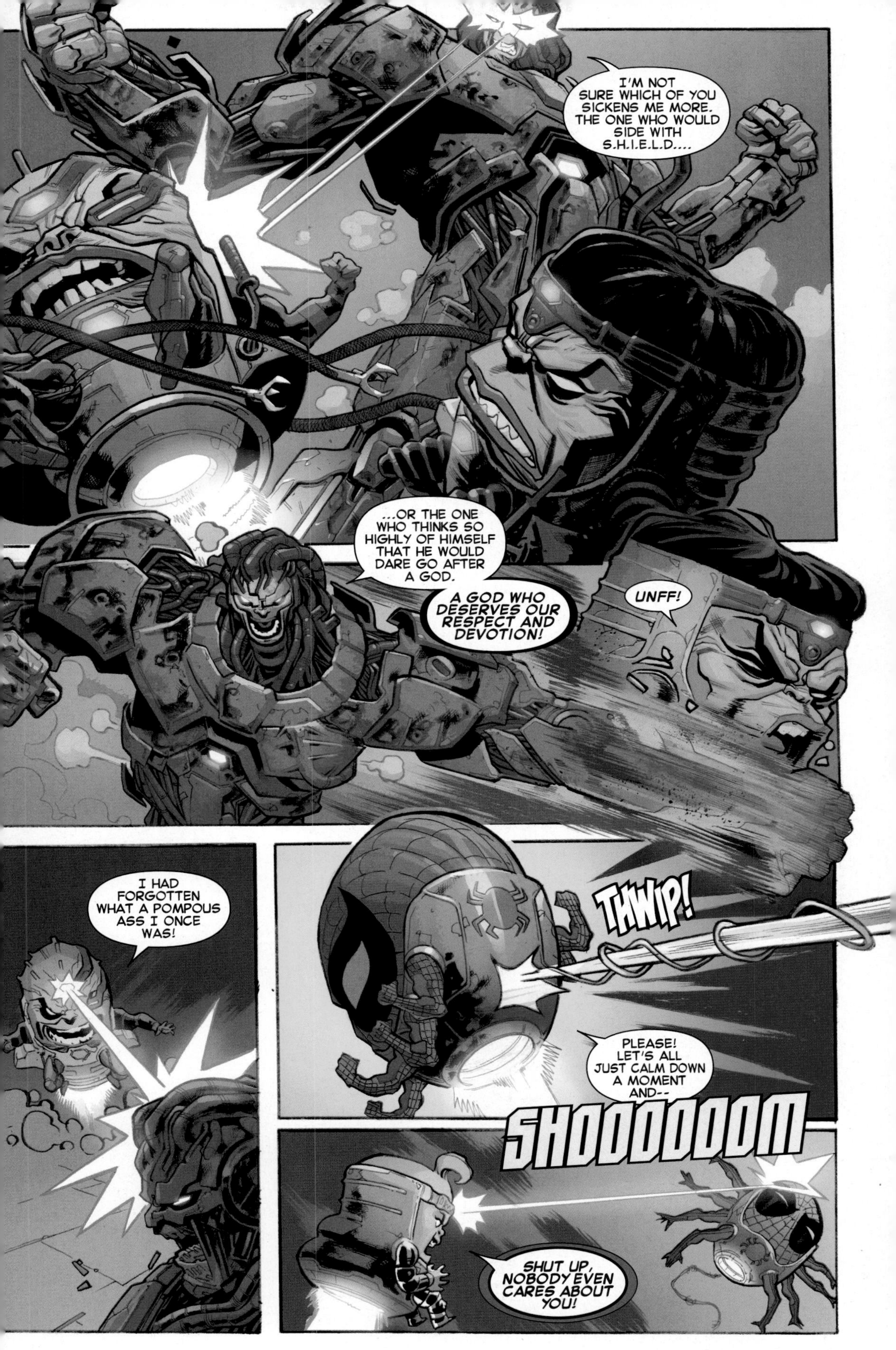
I'M NOT SURE WHICH OF YOU SICKENS ME MORE. THE ONE WHO WOULD SIDE WITH S.H.I.E.L.D....
...OR THE ONE WHO THINKS SO HIGHLY OF HIMSELF THAT HE WOULD DARE GO AFTER A GOD.
A GOD WHO DESERVES OUR RESPECT AND DEVOTION!
UNFF!
I HAD FORGOTTEN WHAT A POMPOUS ASS I ONCE WAS!
THWIP!
PLEASE! LET'S ALL JUST CALM DOWN A MOMENT AND--
SHOOOOOOM
SHUT UP, NOBODY EVEN CARES ABOUT YOU!

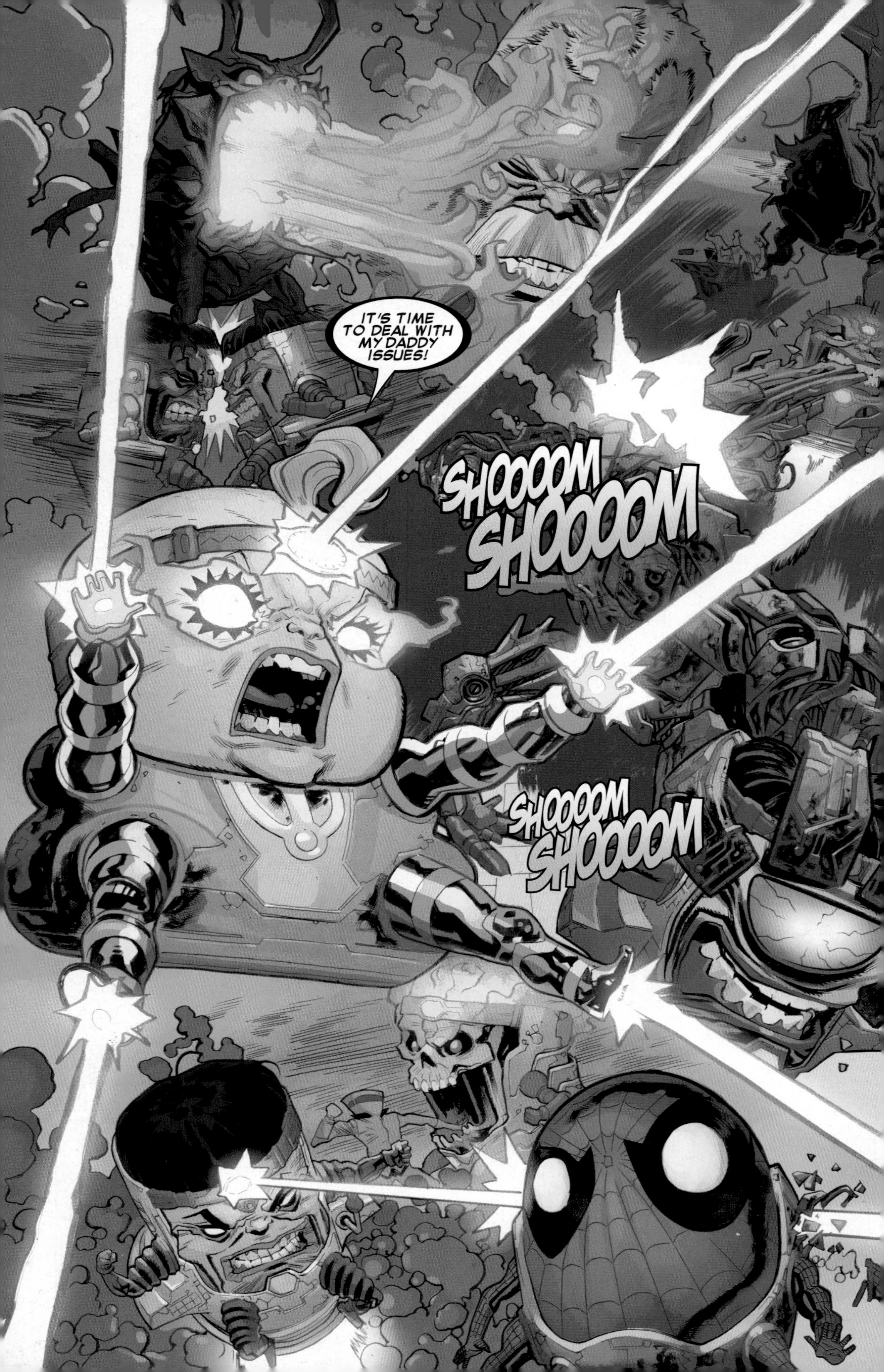
IT'S TIME TO DEAL WITH MY DADDY ISSUES!
SHOOOOM
SHOOOOM
SHOOOOM
SHOOOOM

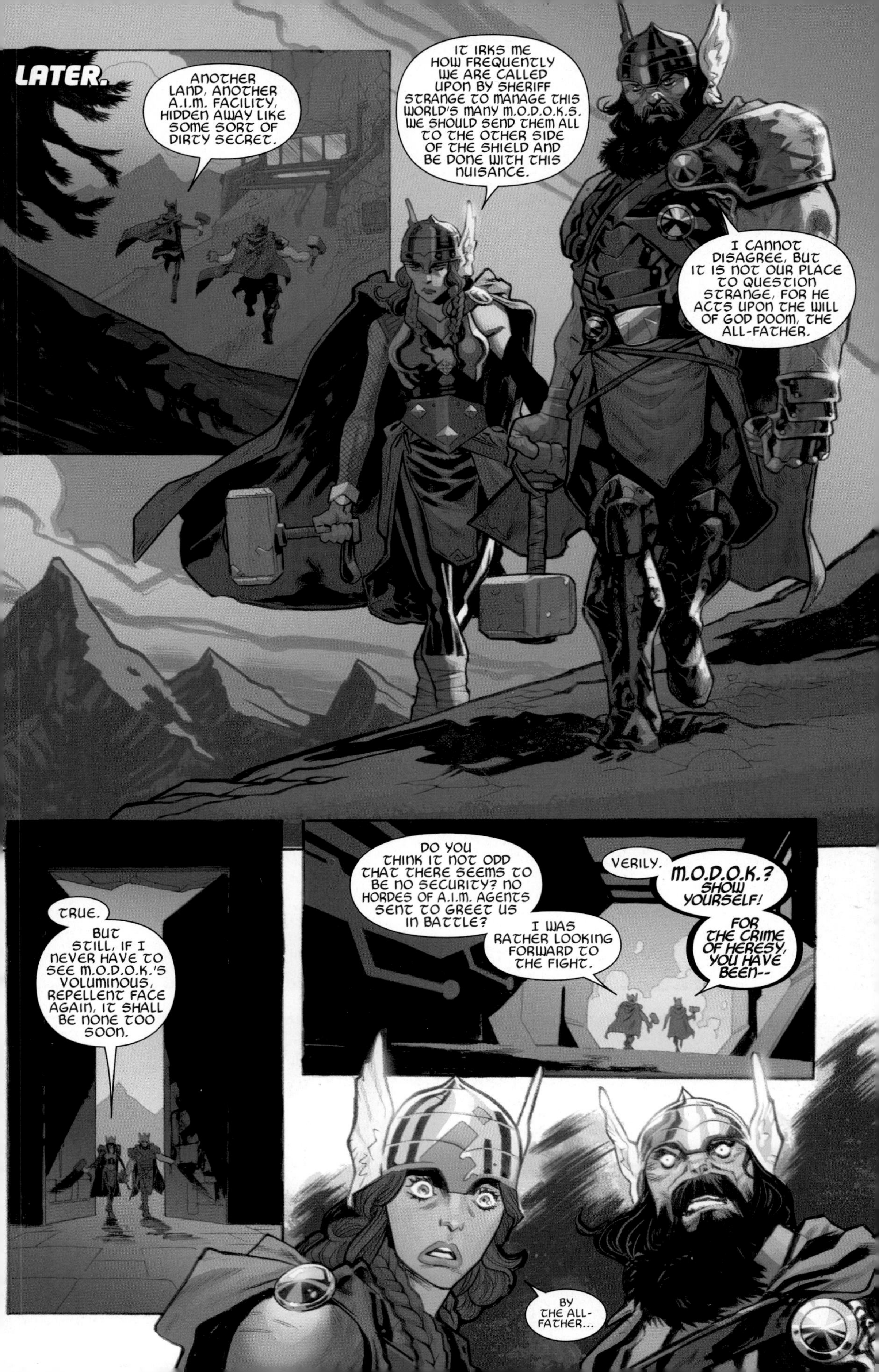
LATER.
ANOTHER LAND, ANOTHER A.I.M. FACILITY, HIDDEN AWAY LIKE SOME SORT OF DIRTY SECRET.
IT IRKS ME HOW FREQUENTLY WE ARE CALLED UPON BY SHERIFF STRANGE TO MANAGE THIS WORLD'S MANY M.O.D.O.K.S. WE SHOULD SEND THEM ALL TO THE OTHER SIDE OF THE SHIELD AND BE DONE WITH THIS NUISANCE.
I CANNOT DISAGREE, BUT IT IS NOT OUR PLACE TO QUESTION STRANGE, FOR HE ACTS UPON THE WILL OF GOD DOOM, THE ALL-FATHER.
TRUE.
BUT STILL, IF I NEVER HAVE TO SEE M.O.D.O.K.'S VOLUMINOUS, REPELLENT FACE AGAIN, IT SHALL BE NONE TOO SOON.
DO YOU THINK IT NOT ODD THAT THERE SEEMS TO BE NO SECURITY? NO HORDES OF A.I.M. AGENTS SENT TO GREET US IN BATTLE?
VERILY.
I WAS RATHER LOOKING FORWARD TO THE FIGHT.
M.O.D.O.K.? SHOW YOURSELF!
FOR THE CRIME OF HERESY, YOU HAVE BEEN--
BY THE ALL-FATHER...

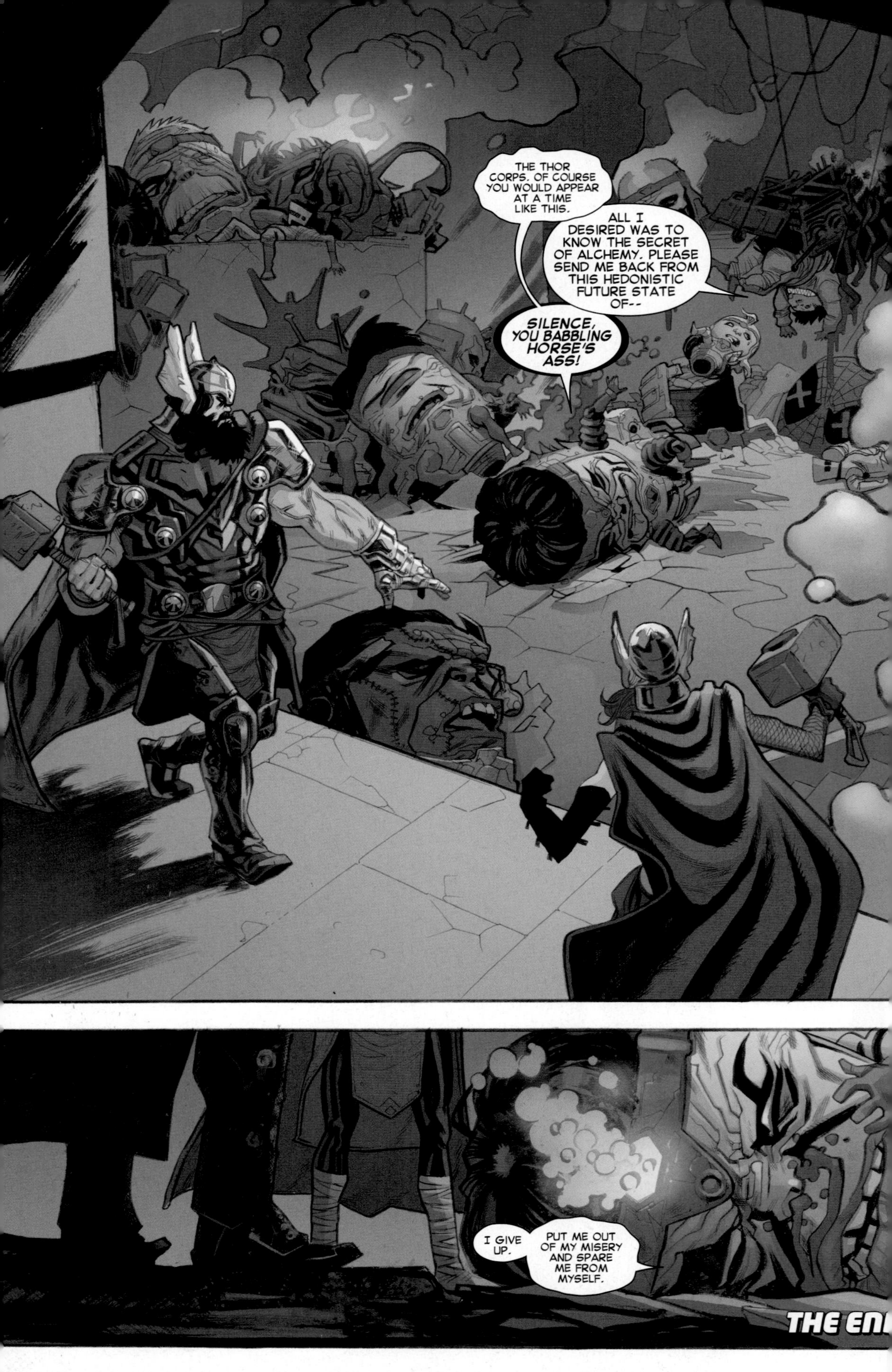
THE THOR CORPS. OF COURSE YOU WOULD APPEAR AT A TIME LIKE THIS.
ALL I DESIRED WAS TO KNOW THE SECRET OF ALCHEMY. PLEASE SEND ME BACK FROM THIS HEDONISTIC FUTURE STATE OF--
SILENCE, YOU BABBLING HORSE'S ASS!
I GIVE UP.
PUT ME OUT OF MY MISERY AND SPARE ME FROM MYSELF.
THE EN

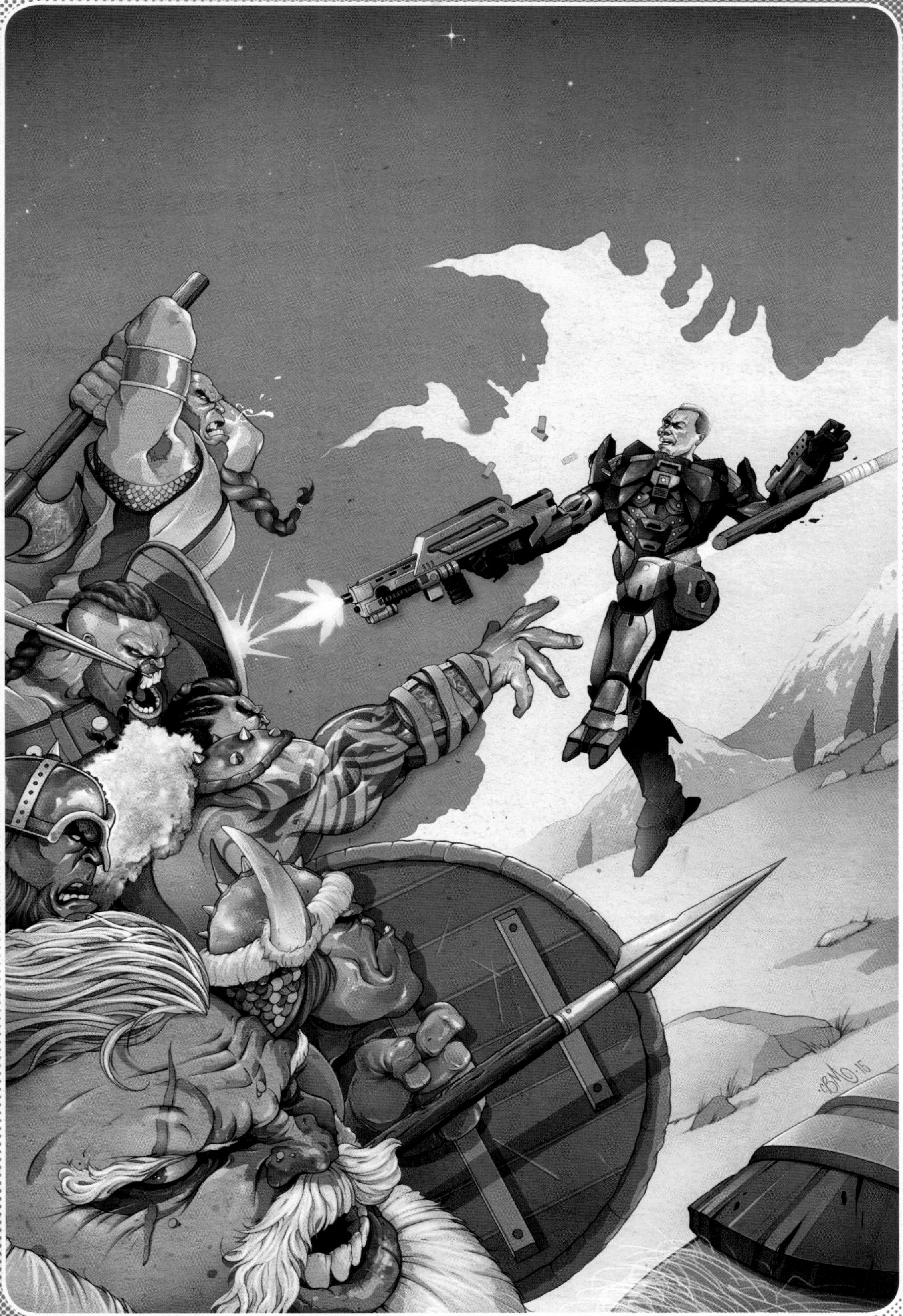

SECRET WARS: BATTLEWORLD #2

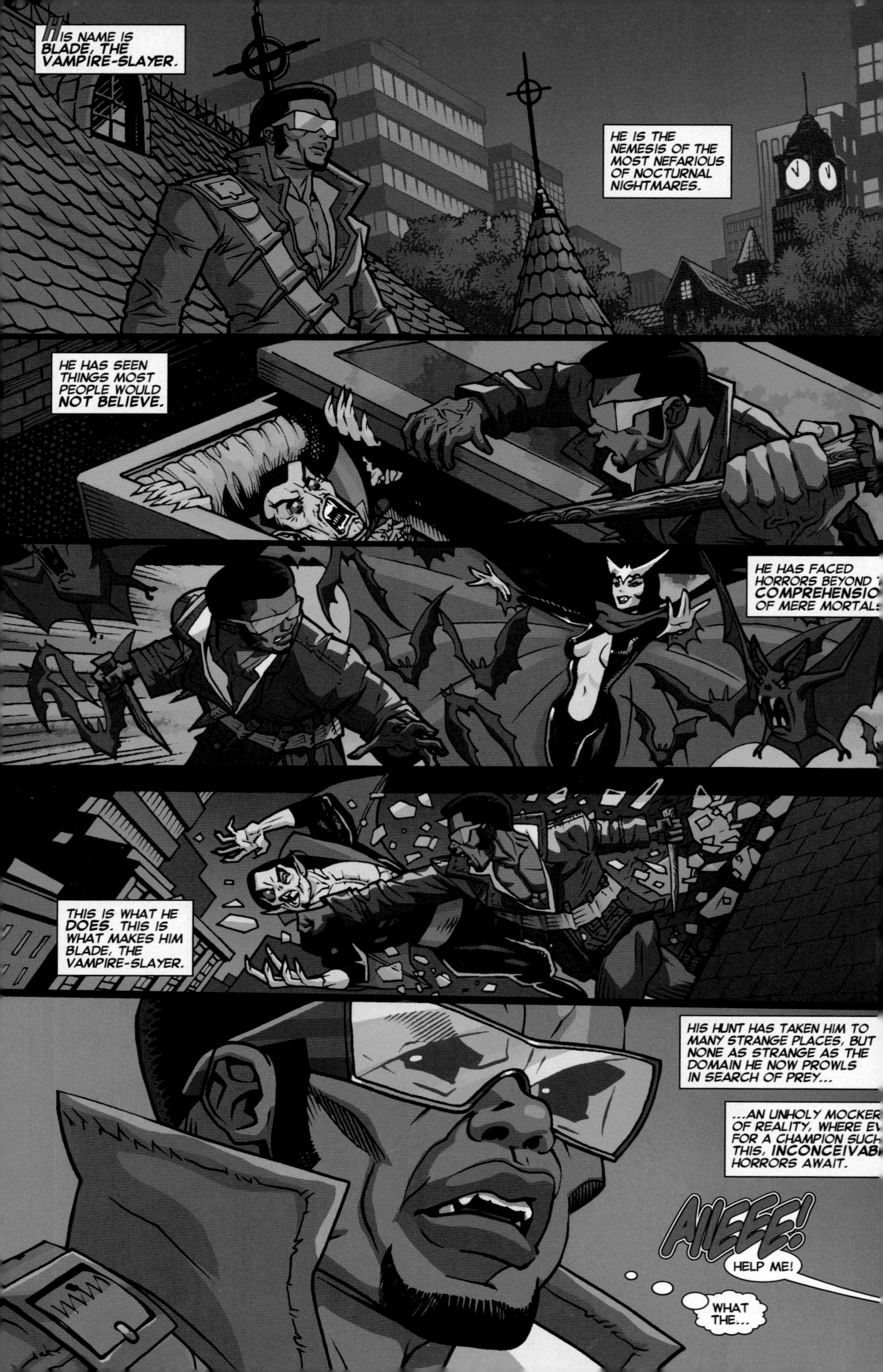
HIS NAME IS BLADE, THE VAMPIRE-SLAYER.
HE IS THE NEMESIS OF THE MOST NEFARIOUS OF NOCTURNAL NIGHTMARES.
HE HAS SEEN THINGS MOST PEOPLE WOULD NOT BELIEVE.
HE HAS FACED HORRORS BEYOND THE COMPREHENSION OF MERE MORTALS.
THIS IS WHAT HE DOES. THIS IS WHAT MAKES HIM BLADE, THE VAMPIRE-SLAYER.
HIS HUNT HAS TAKEN HIM TO MANY STRANGE PLACES, BUT NONE AS STRANGE AS THE DOMAIN HE NOW PROWLS IN SEARCH OF PREY...
...AN UNHOLY MOCKERY OF REALITY, WHERE EVEN FOR A CHAMPION SUCH AS THIS, INCONCEIVABLE HORRORS AWAIT.
AIEEE!
HELP ME!
WHAT THE...

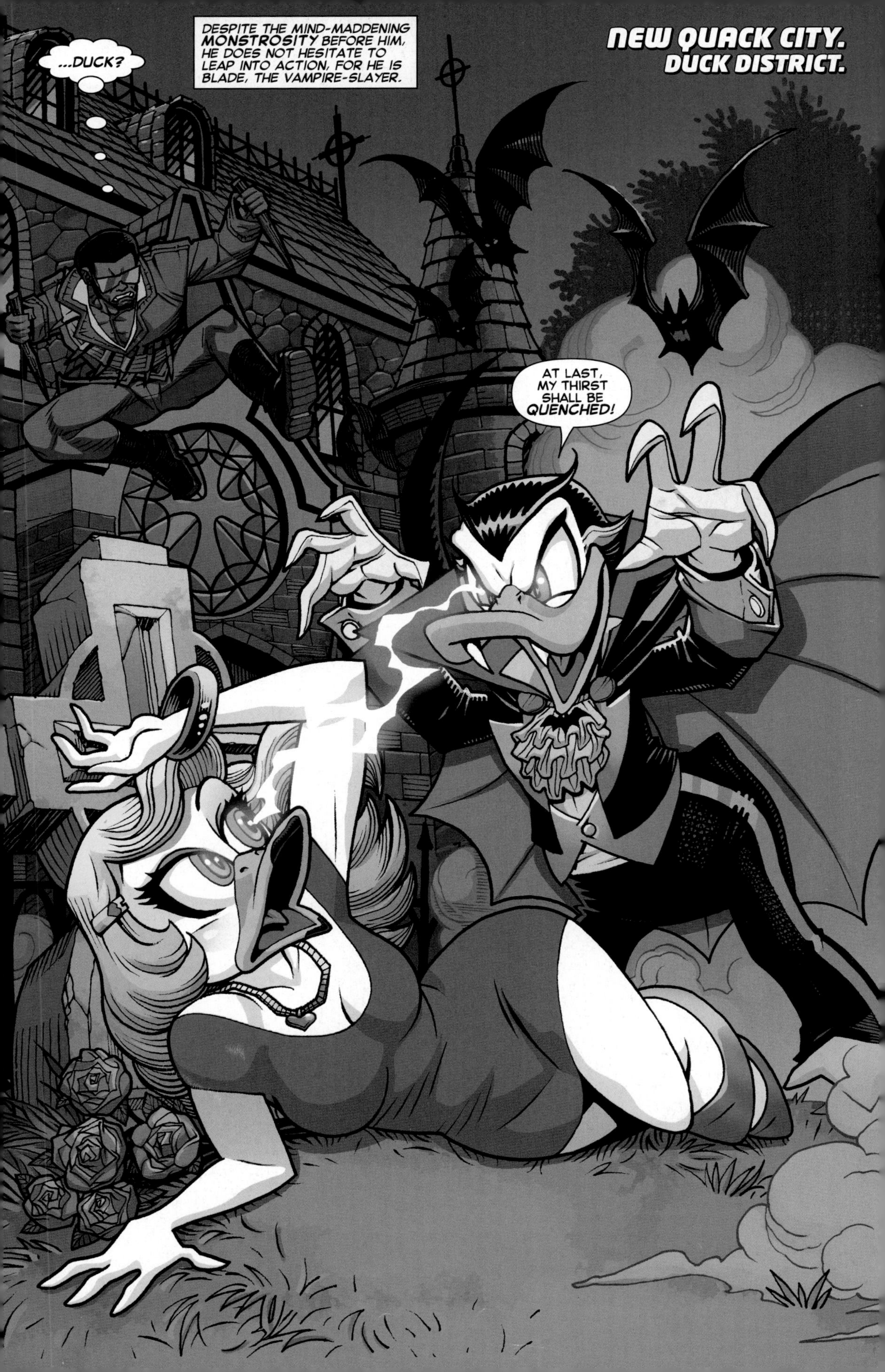

...DUCK?
DESPITE THE MIND-MADDENING MONSTROSITY BEFORE HIM, HE DOES NOT HESITATE TO LEAP INTO ACTION, FOR HE IS BLADE, THE VAMPIRE-SLAYER.
NEW QUACK CITY. DUCK DISTRICT.
AT LAST, MY THIRST SHALL BE QUENCHED!

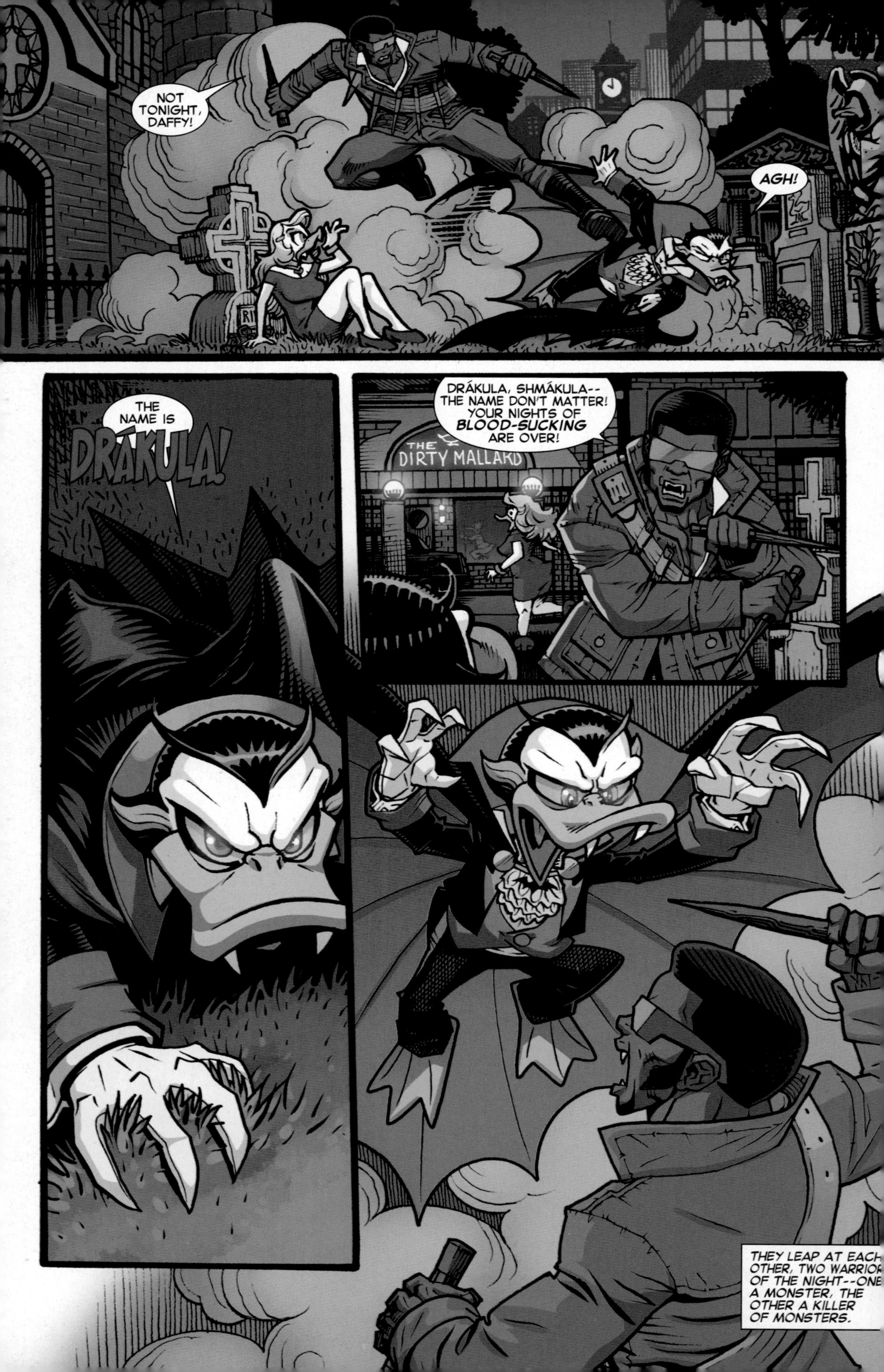
NOT TONIGHT, DAFFY!
AGH!
THE NAME IS
DRÁKULA!
DRÁKULA, SHMÁKULA-- THE NAME DON'T MATTER! YOUR NIGHTS OF BLOOD-SUCKING ARE OVER!
THE DIRTY MALLARD
THEY LEAP AT EACH OTHER, TWO WARRIOR OF THE NIGHT--ONE A MONSTER, THE OTHER A KILLER OF MONSTERS.

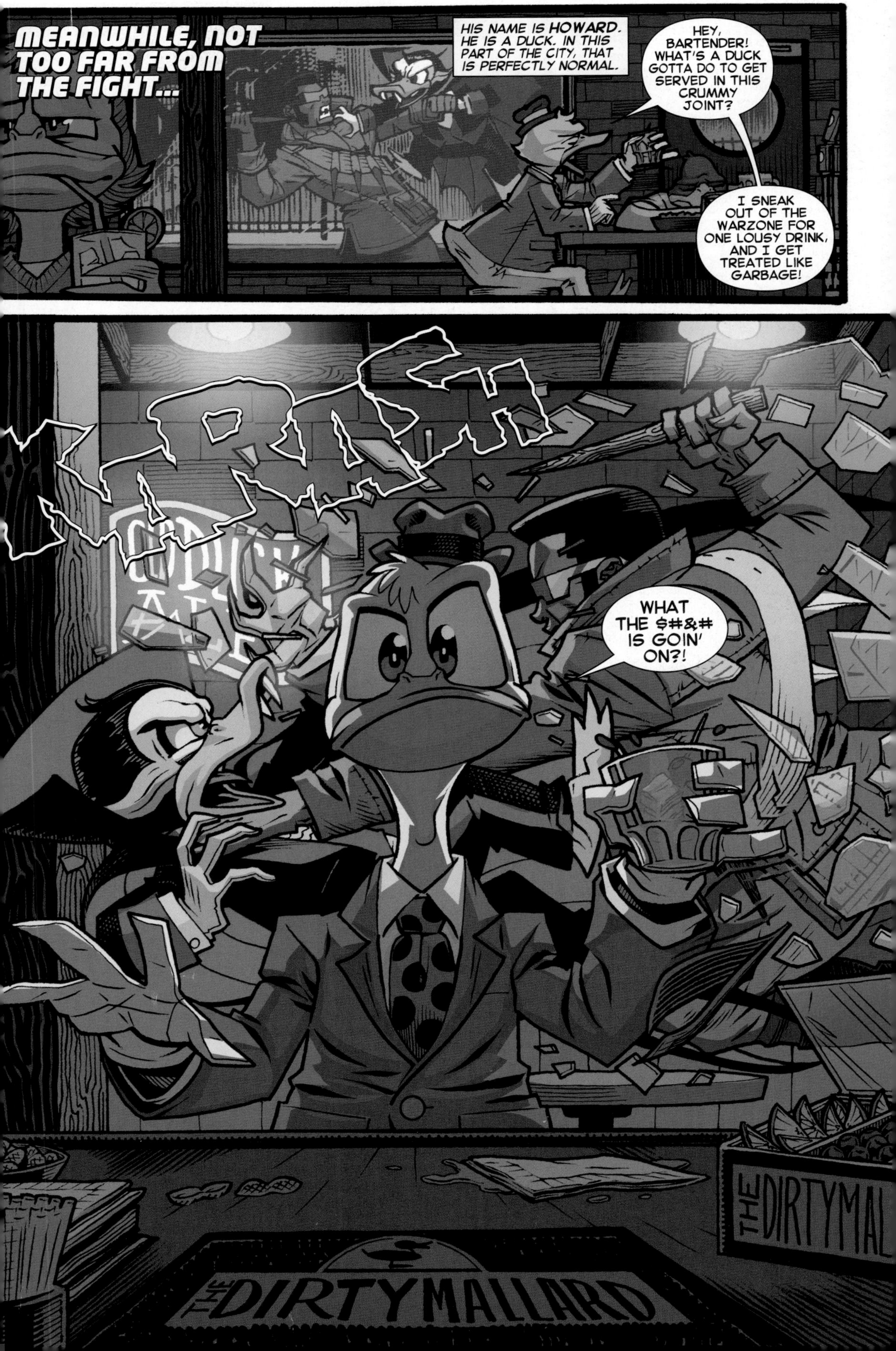
MEANWHILE, NOT TOO FAR FROM THE FIGHT...
HIS NAME IS HOWARD. HE IS A DUCK. IN THIS PART OF THE CITY, THAT IS PERFECTLY NORMAL.
HEY, BARTENDER! WHAT'S A DUCK GOTTA DO TO GET SERVED IN THIS CRUMMY JOINT?
I SNEAK OUT OF THE WARZONE FOR ONE LOUSY DRINK, AND I GET TREATED LIKE GARBAGE!
KRASH
WHAT THE $#&# IS GOIN' ON?!
THE DIRTYMAL
THE DIRTYMALLARD

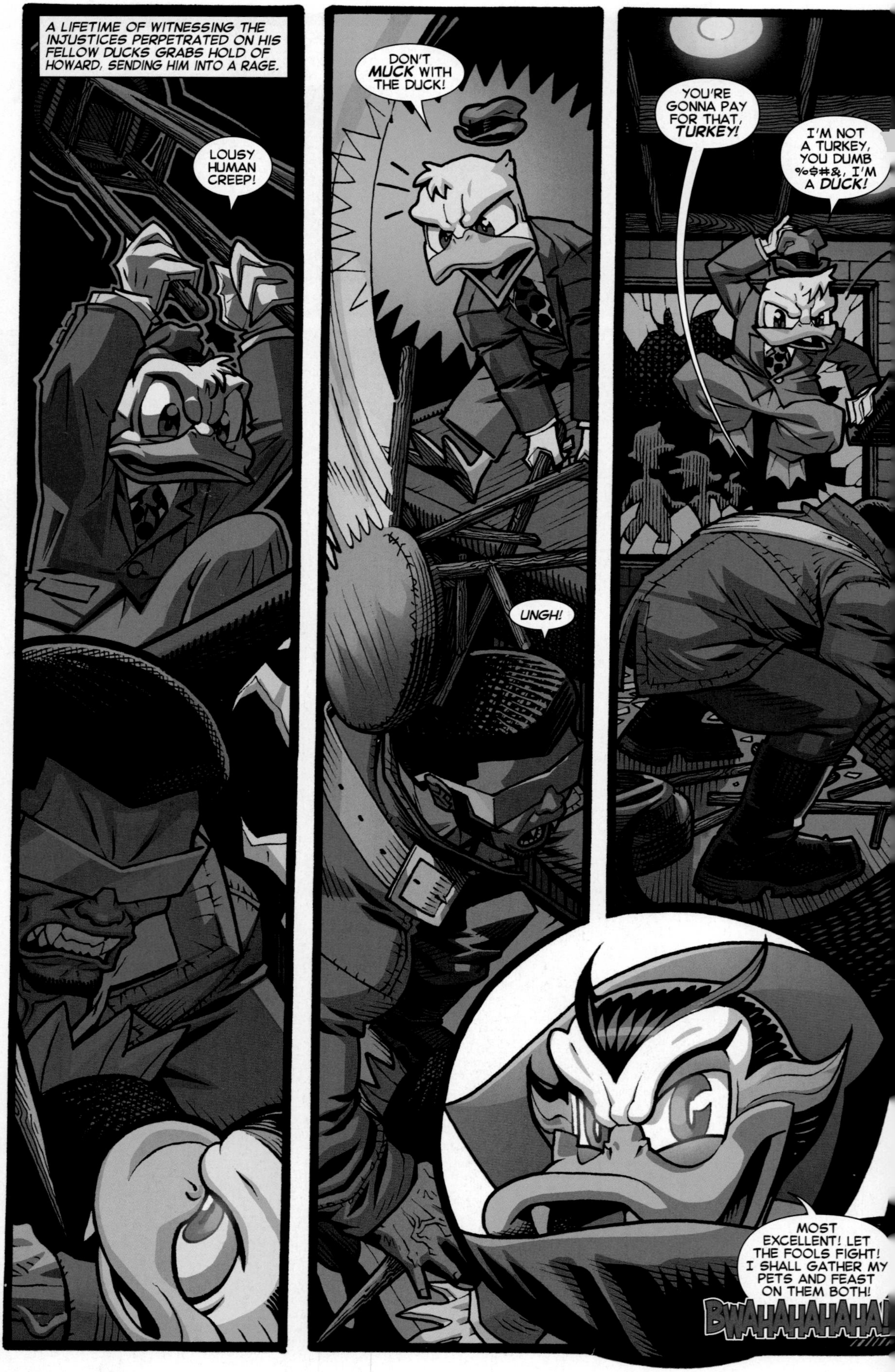
A LIFETIME OF WITNESSING THE INJUSTICES PERPETRATED ON HIS FELLOW DUCKS GRABS HOLD OF HOWARD, SENDING HIM INTO A RAGE.
LOUSY HUMAN CREEP!
DON'T MUCK WITH THE DUCK!
UNGH!
YOU'RE GONNA PAY FOR THAT, TURKEY!
I'M NOT A TURKEY, YOU DUMB %$#&, I'M A DUCK!
MOST EXCELLENT! LET THE FOOLS FIGHT! I SHALL GATHER MY PETS AND FEAST ON THEM BOTH!
BWAHAHAHAHA!

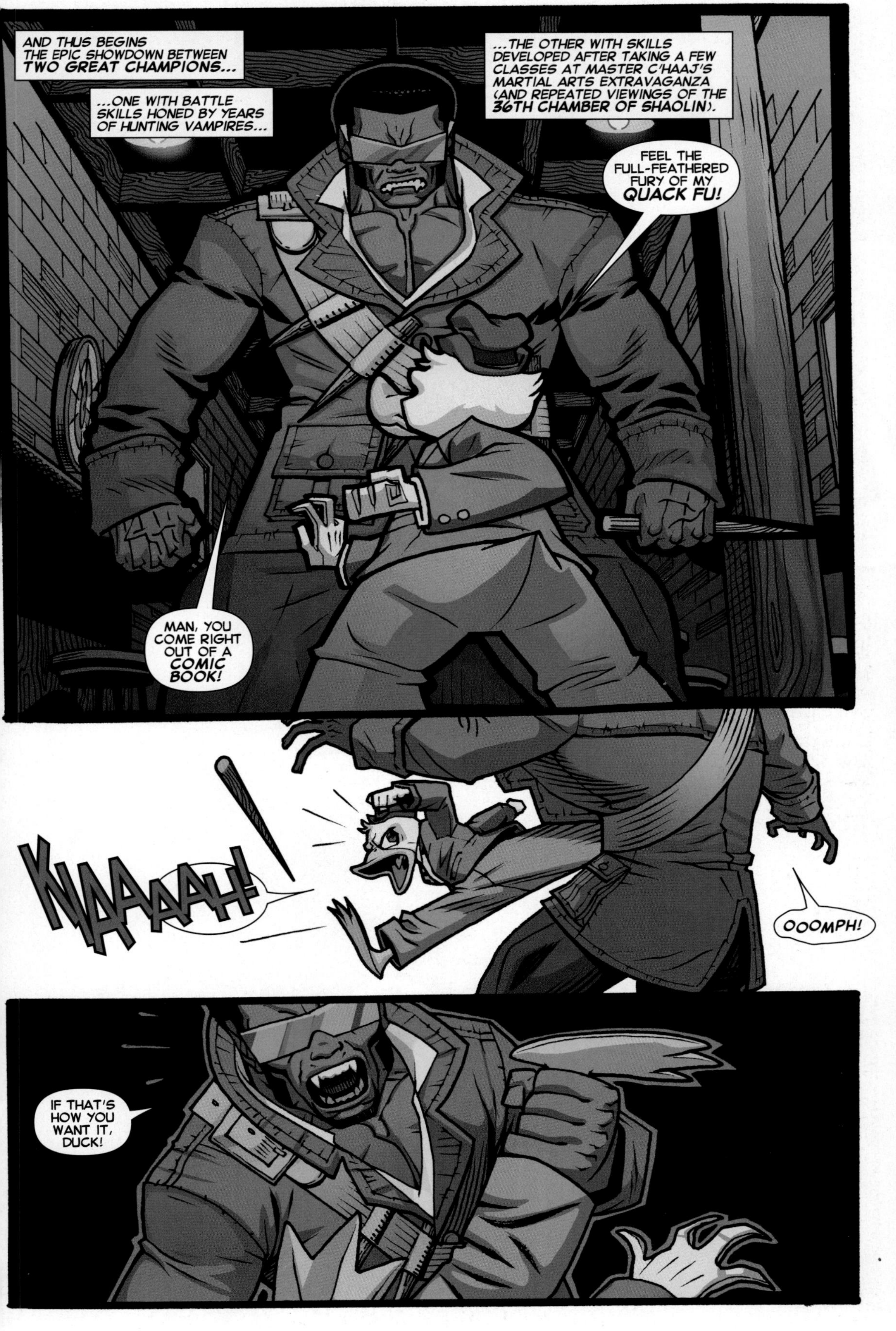
AND THUS BEGINS THE EPIC SHOWDOWN BETWEEN TWO GREAT CHAMPIONS...
...ONE WITH BATTLE SKILLS HONED BY YEARS OF HUNTING VAMPIRES...
...THE OTHER WITH SKILLS DEVELOPED AFTER TAKING A FEW CLASSES AT MASTER C'HAAJ'S MARTIAL ARTS EXTRAVAGANZA (AND REPEATED VIEWINGS OF THE 36TH CHAMBER OF SHAOLIN).
FEEL THE FULL-FEATHERED FURY OF MY QUACK FU!
MAN, YOU COME RIGHT OUT OF A COMIC BOOK!
KIIAAAAH!
OOOMPH!
IF THAT'S HOW YOU WANT IT, DUCK!

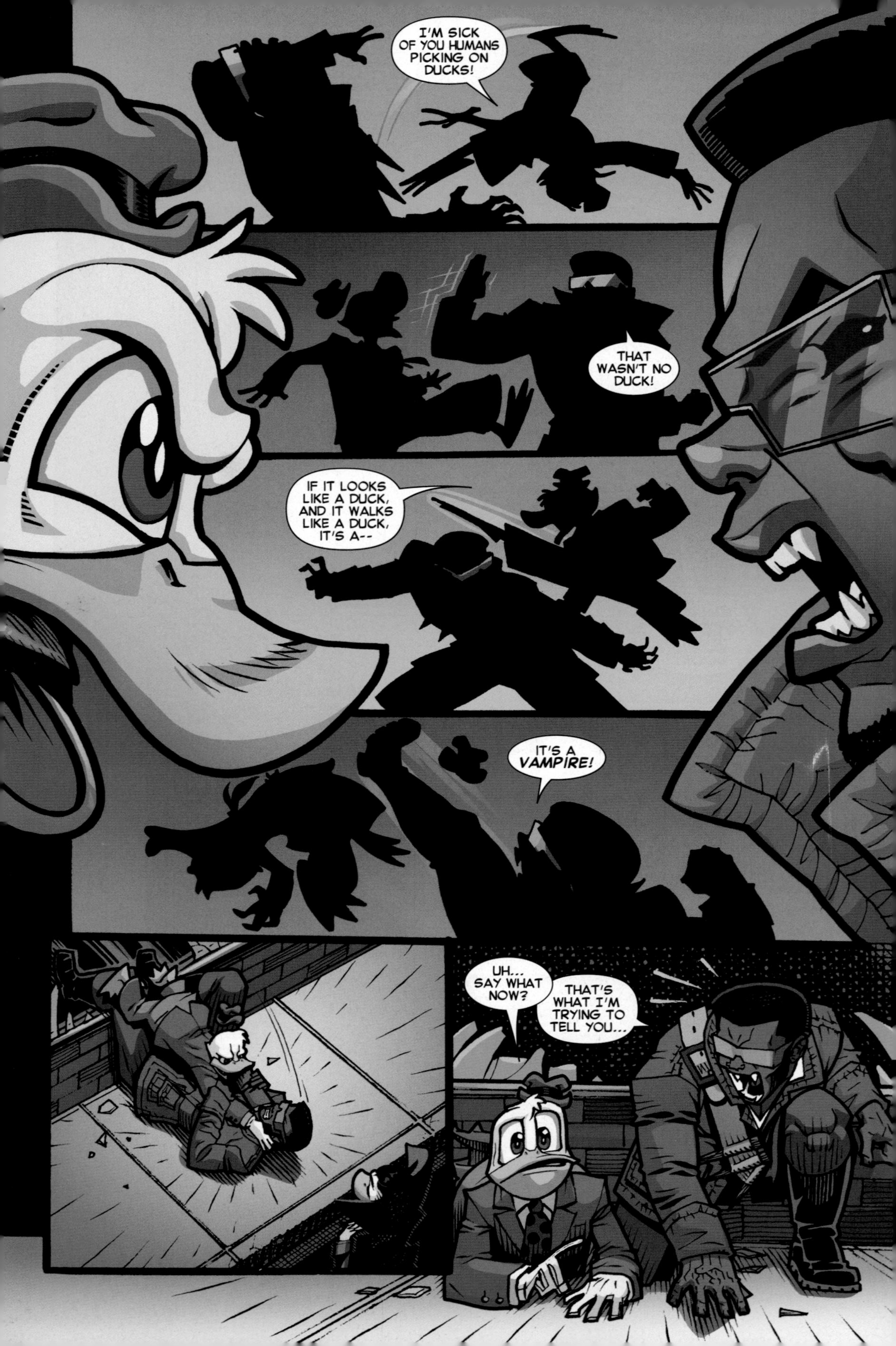

I'M SICK OF YOU HUMANS PICKING ON DUCKS!
THAT WASN'T NO DUCK!
IF IT LOOKS LIKE A DUCK, AND IT WALKS LIKE A DUCK, IT'S A--
IT'S A *VAMPIRE!*
UH... SAY WHAT NOW?
THAT'S WHAT I'M TRYING TO TELL YOU...

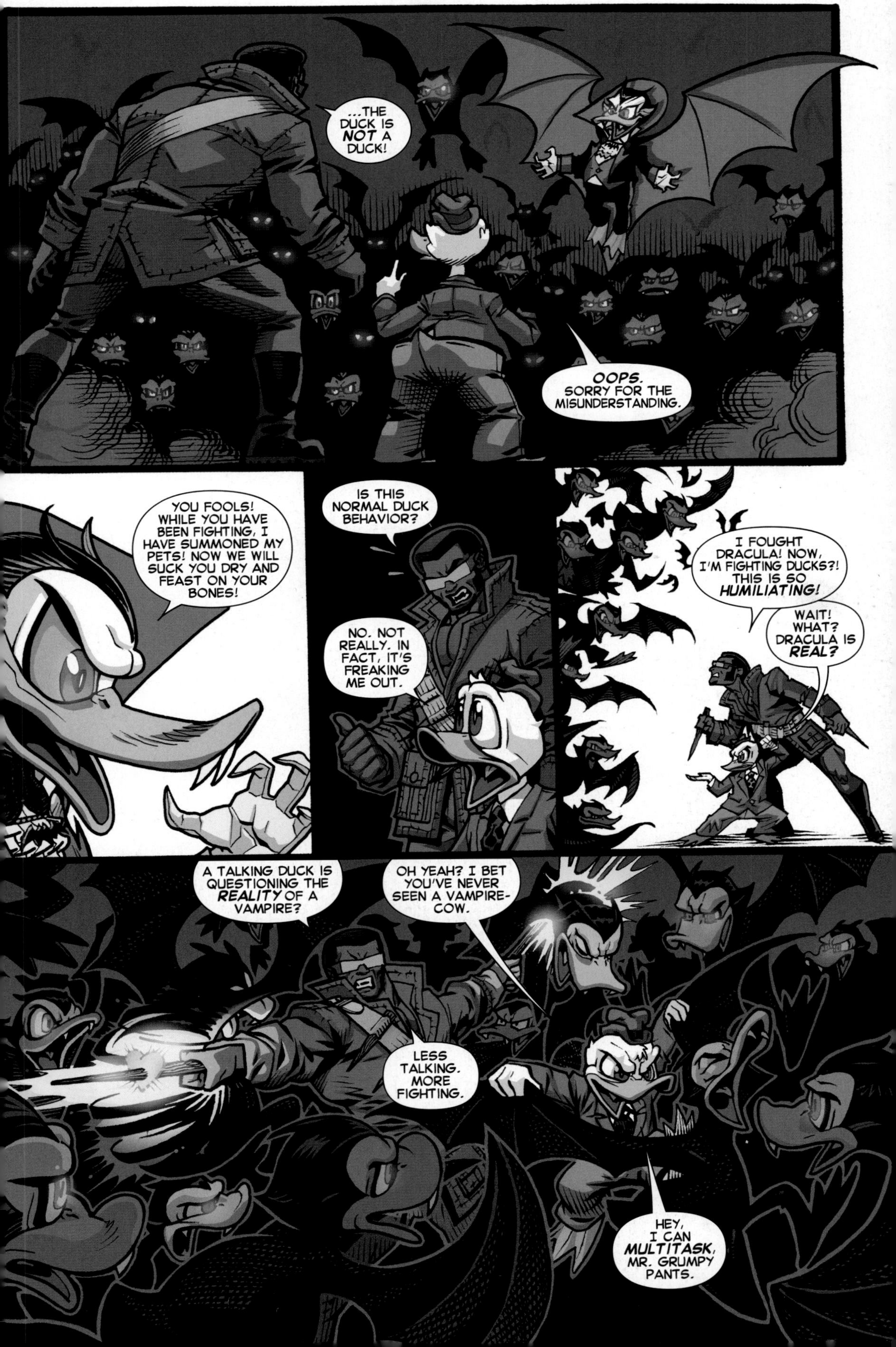
...THE DUCK IS NOT A DUCK!
OOPS. SORRY FOR THE MISUNDERSTANDING.
YOU FOOLS! WHILE YOU HAVE BEEN FIGHTING, I HAVE SUMMONED MY PETS! NOW WE WILL SUCK YOU DRY AND FEAST ON YOUR BONES!
IS THIS NORMAL DUCK BEHAVIOR?
NO. NOT REALLY. IN FACT, IT'S FREAKING ME OUT.
I FOUGHT DRACULA! NOW, I'M FIGHTING DUCKS?! THIS IS SO HUMILIATING!
WAIT! WHAT? DRACULA IS REAL?
A TALKING DUCK IS QUESTIONING THE REALITY OF A VAMPIRE?
OH YEAH? I BET YOU'VE NEVER SEEN A VAMPIRE-COW.
LESS TALKING. MORE FIGHTING.
HEY, I CAN MULTITASK, MR. GRUMPY PANTS.

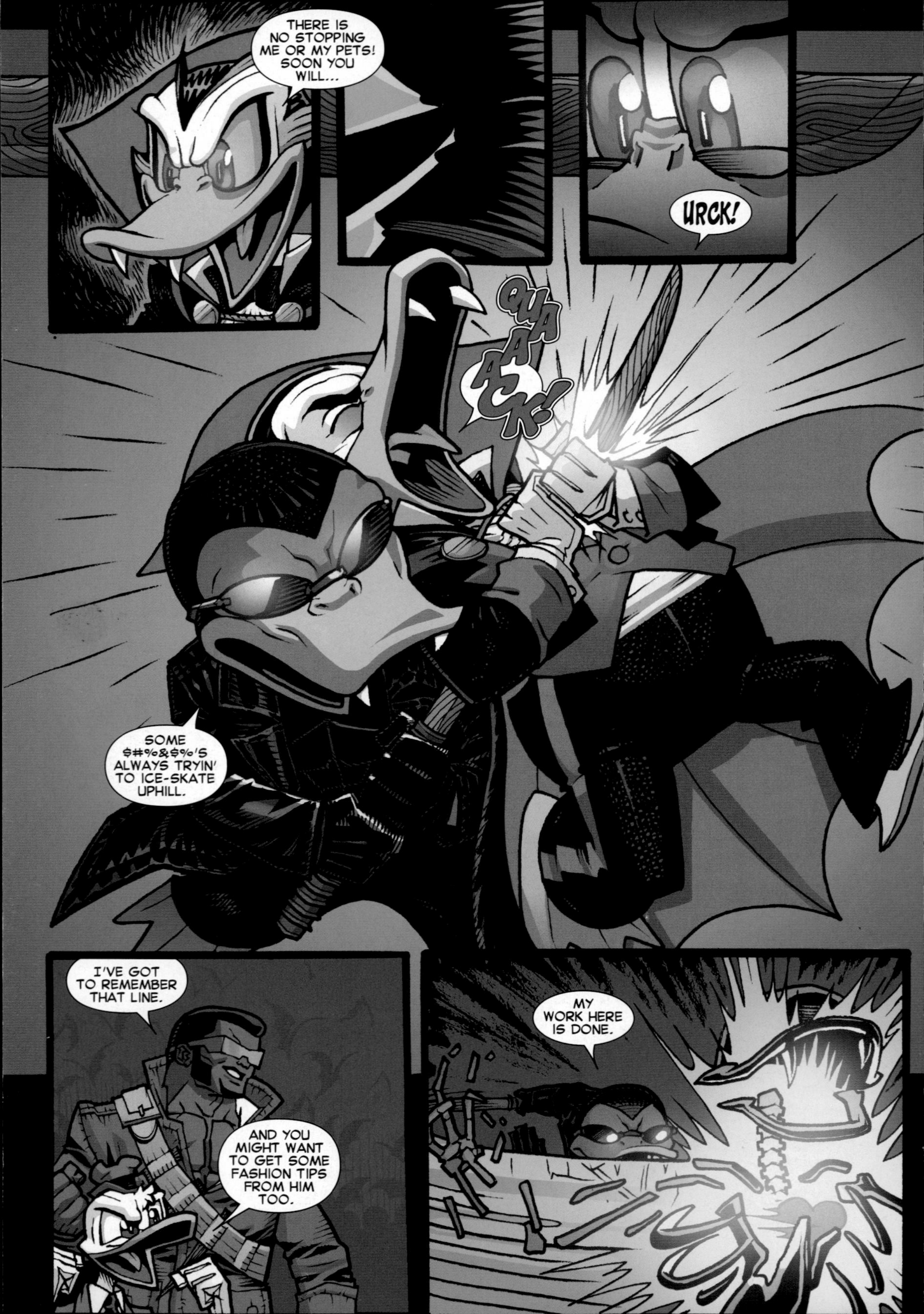
THERE IS NO STOPPING ME OR MY PETS! SOON YOU WILL...
URCK!
QUAAACK!
SOME $#%&$%'S ALWAYS TRYIN' TO ICE-SKATE UPHILL.
I'VE GOT TO REMEMBER THAT LINE.
AND YOU MIGHT WANT TO GET SOME FASHION TIPS FROM HIM TOO.
MY WORK HERE IS DONE.

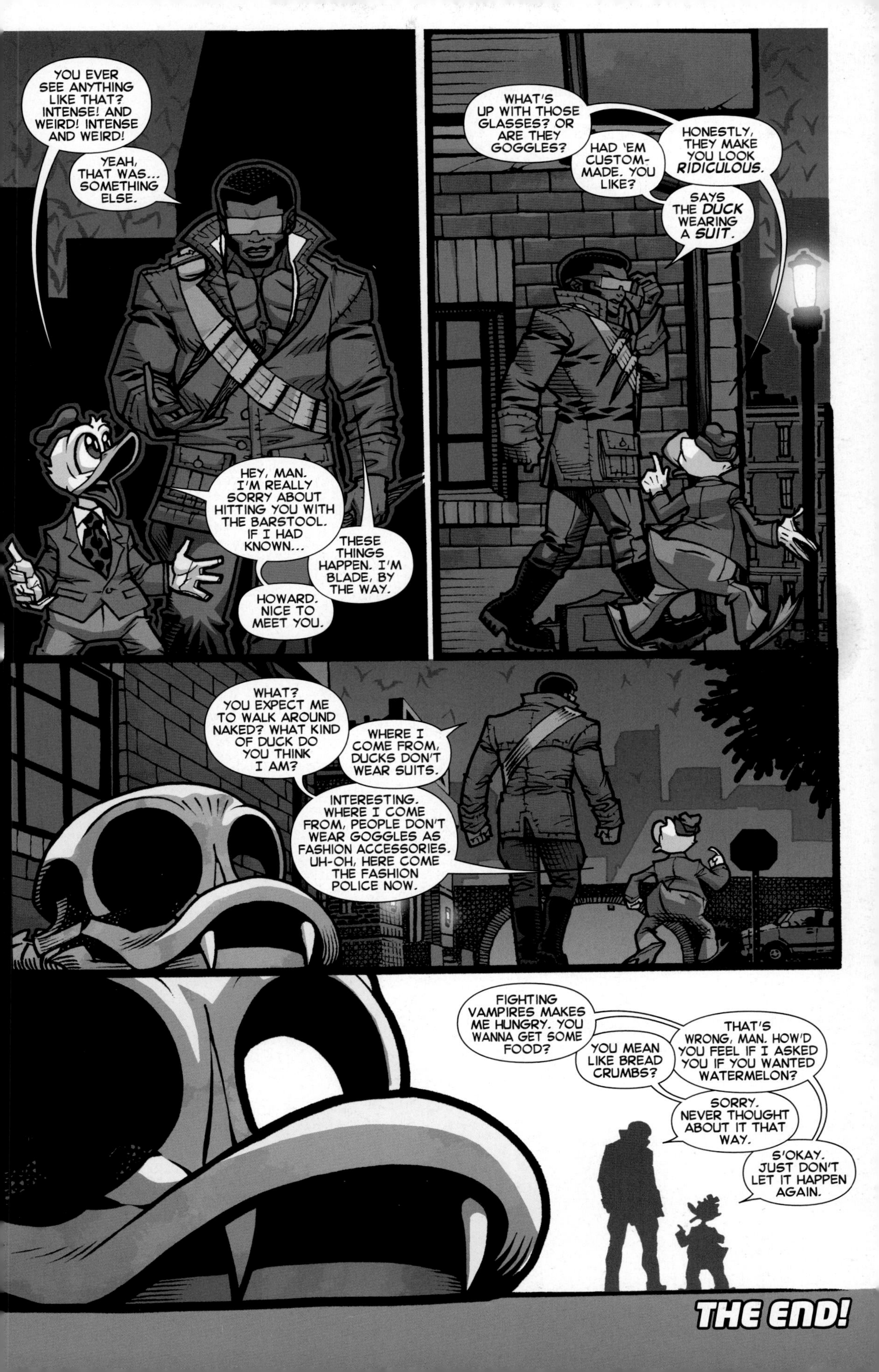
YOU EVER SEE ANYTHING LIKE THAT? INTENSE! AND WEIRD! INTENSE AND WEIRD!
YEAH, THAT WAS... SOMETHING ELSE.
HEY, MAN. I'M REALLY SORRY ABOUT HITTING YOU WITH THE BARSTOOL. IF I HAD KNOWN...
THESE THINGS HAPPEN. I'M BLADE, BY THE WAY.
HOWARD. NICE TO MEET YOU.
WHAT'S UP WITH THOSE GLASSES? OR ARE THEY GOGGLES?
HAD 'EM CUSTOM-MADE. YOU LIKE?
HONESTLY, THEY MAKE YOU LOOK RIDICULOUS.
SAYS THE DUCK WEARING A SUIT.
WHAT? YOU EXPECT ME TO WALK AROUND NAKED? WHAT KIND OF DUCK DO YOU THINK I AM?
WHERE I COME FROM, DUCKS DON'T WEAR SUITS.
INTERESTING. WHERE I COME FROM, PEOPLE DON'T WEAR GOGGLES AS FASHION ACCESSORIES. UH-OH, HERE COME THE FASHION POLICE NOW.
FIGHTING VAMPIRES MAKES ME HUNGRY. YOU WANNA GET SOME FOOD?
YOU MEAN LIKE BREAD CRUMBS?
THAT'S WRONG, MAN. HOW'D YOU FEEL IF I ASKED YOU IF YOU WANTED WATERMELON?
SORRY. NEVER THOUGHT ABOUT IT THAT WAY.
S'OKAY. JUST DON'T LET IT HAPPEN AGAIN.
THE END!

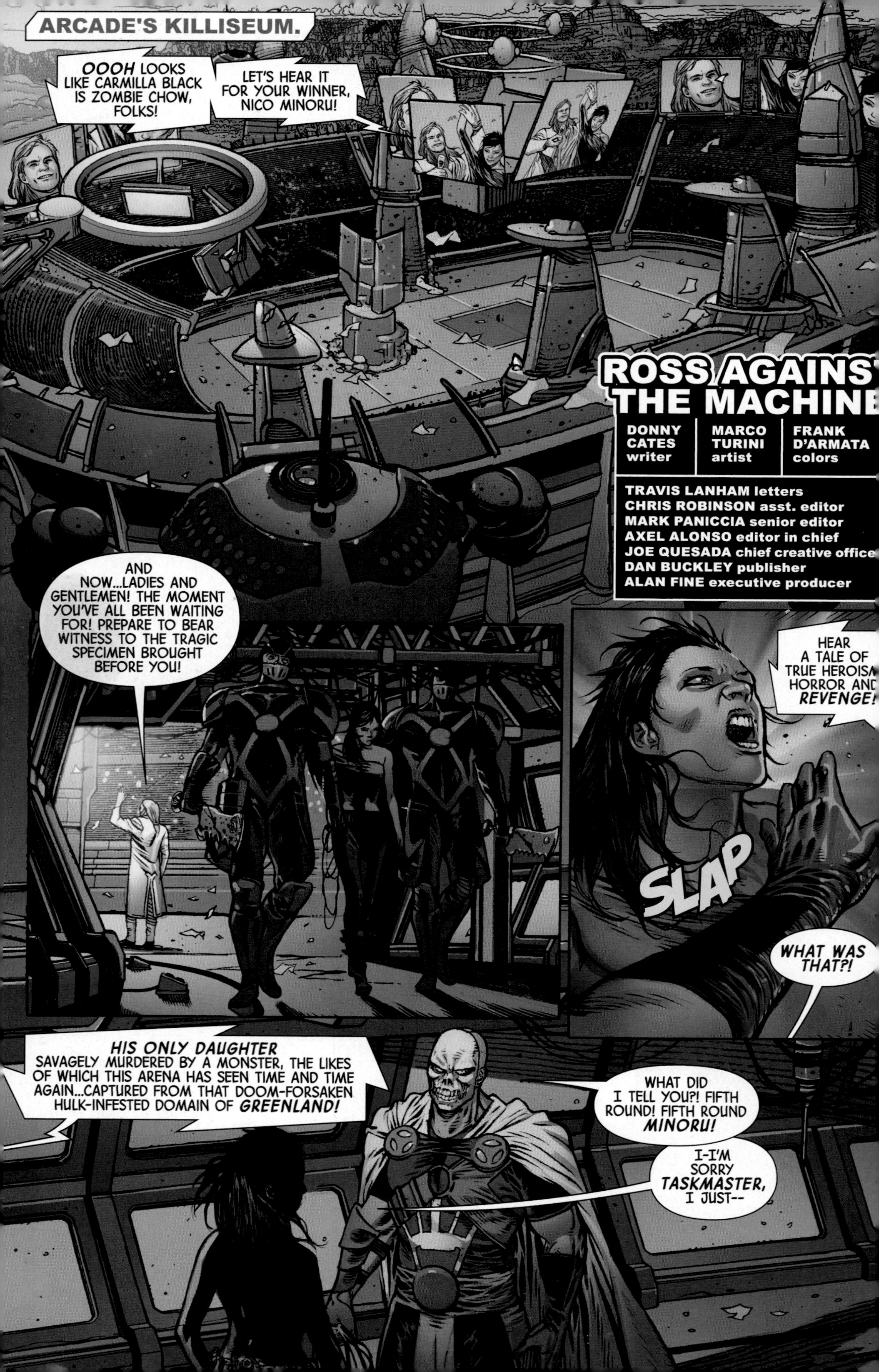
ARCADE'S KILLISEUM.
OOOH LOOKS LIKE CARMILLA BLACK IS ZOMBIE CHOW, FOLKS!
LET'S HEAR IT FOR YOUR WINNER, NICO MINORU!
ROSS AGAINST THE MACHINE
DONNY CATES writer
MARCO TURINI artist
FRANK D'ARMATA colors
TRAVIS LANHAM letters
CHRIS ROBINSON asst. editor
MARK PANICCIA senior editor
AXEL ALONSO editor in chief
JOE QUESADA chief creative officer
DAN BUCKLEY publisher
ALAN FINE executive producer
AND NOW...LADIES AND GENTLEMEN! THE MOMENT YOU'VE ALL BEEN WAITING FOR! PREPARE TO BEAR WITNESS TO THE TRAGIC SPECIMEN BROUGHT BEFORE YOU!
HEAR A TALE OF TRUE HEROISM, HORROR AND REVENGE!
SLAP
WHAT WAS THAT?!
HIS ONLY DAUGHTER SAVAGELY MURDERED BY A MONSTER, THE LIKES OF WHICH THIS ARENA HAS SEEN TIME AND TIME AGAIN...CAPTURED FROM THAT DOOM-FORSAKEN HULK-INFESTED DOMAIN OF GREENLAND!
WHAT DID I TELL YOU?! FIFTH ROUND! FIFTH ROUND MINORU!
I-I'M SORRY TASKMASTER, I JUST--

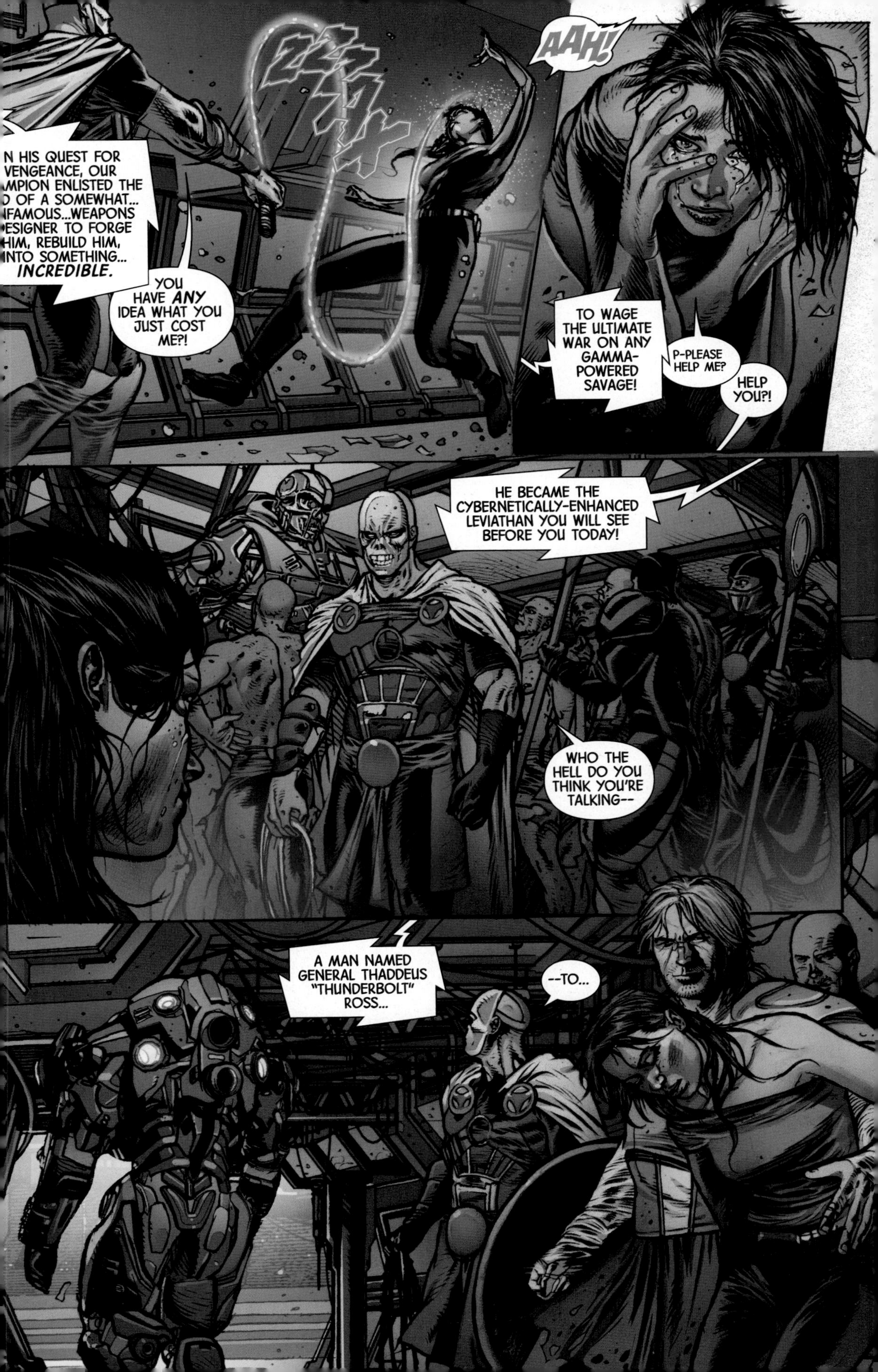

ZZZAK
AAH!
N HIS QUEST FOR VENGEANCE, OUR AMPION ENLISTED THE D OF A SOMEWHAT... NFAMOUS...WEAPONS ESIGNER TO FORGE HIM, REBUILD HIM, INTO SOMETHING... INCREDIBLE.
YOU HAVE ANY IDEA WHAT YOU JUST COST ME?!
TO WAGE THE ULTIMATE WAR ON ANY GAMMA-POWERED SAVAGE!
P-PLEASE HELP ME?
HELP YOU?!
HE BECAME THE CYBERNETICALLY-ENHANCED LEVIATHAN YOU WILL SEE BEFORE YOU TODAY!
WHO THE HELL DO YOU THINK YOU'RE TALKING--
A MAN NAMED GENERAL THADDEUS "THUNDERBOLT" ROSS...
--TO...

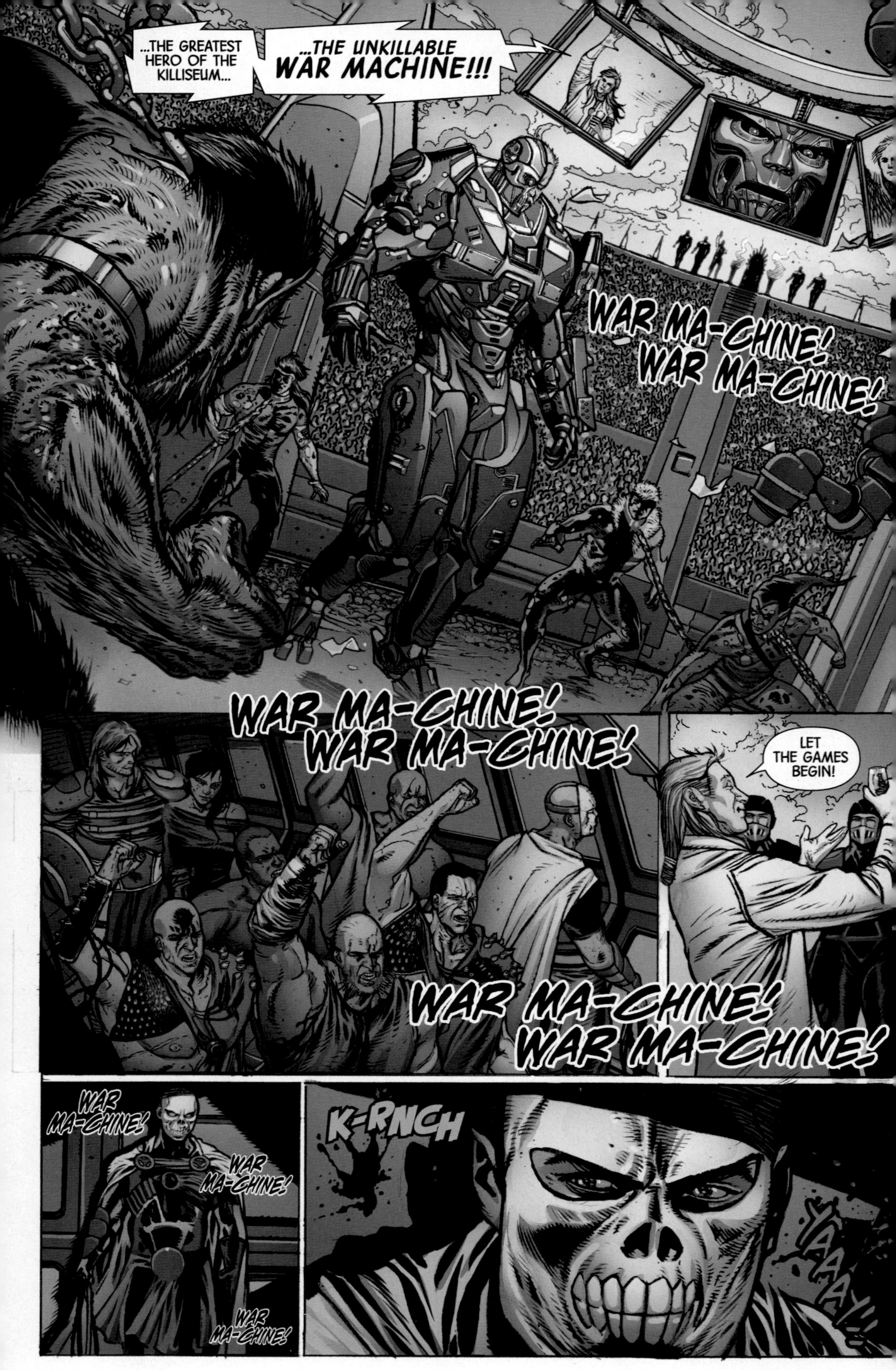

...THE GREATEST HERO OF THE KILLISEUM...
...THE UNKILLABLE WAR MACHINE!!!
WAR MA-CHINE! WAR MA-CHINE!
WAR MA-CHINE! WAR MA-CHINE!
LET THE GAMES BEGIN!
WAR MA-CHINE! WAR MA-CHINE!
WAR MA-CHINE!
WAR MA-CHINE!
WAR MA-CHINE!
K-RNCH
YAAAA

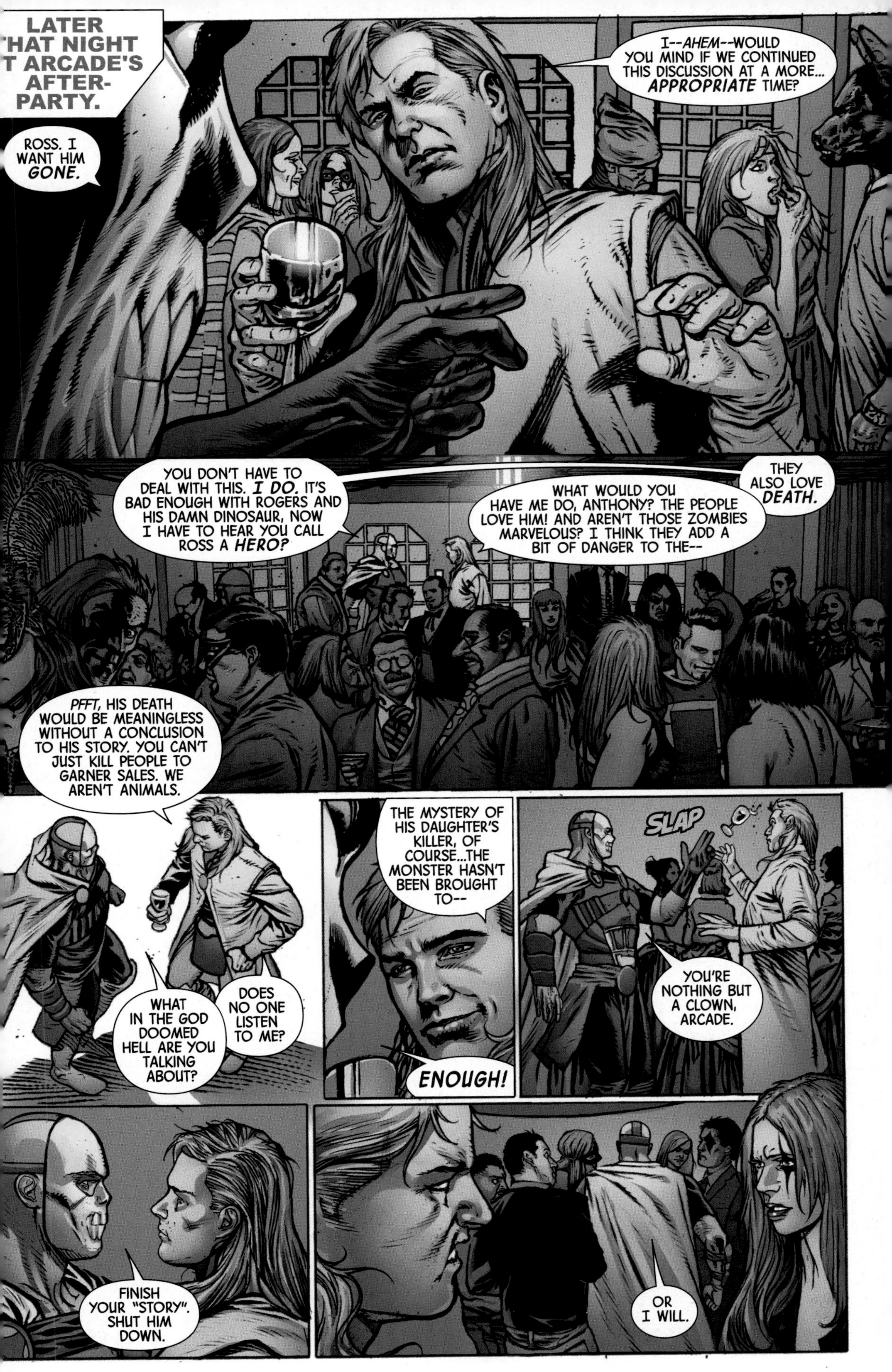
LATER [T]HAT NIGHT [A]T ARCADE'S AFTER-PARTY.
ROSS. I WANT HIM GONE.
I--AHEM--WOULD YOU MIND IF WE CONTINUED THIS DISCUSSION AT A MORE... APPROPRIATE TIME?
YOU DON'T HAVE TO DEAL WITH THIS. I DO. IT'S BAD ENOUGH WITH ROGERS AND HIS DAMN DINOSAUR, NOW I HAVE TO HEAR YOU CALL ROSS A HERO?
WHAT WOULD YOU HAVE ME DO, ANTHONY? THE PEOPLE LOVE HIM! AND AREN'T THOSE ZOMBIES MARVELOUS? I THINK THEY ADD A BIT OF DANGER TO THE--
THEY ALSO LOVE DEATH.
PFFT, HIS DEATH WOULD BE MEANINGLESS WITHOUT A CONCLUSION TO HIS STORY. YOU CAN'T JUST KILL PEOPLE TO GARNER SALES. WE AREN'T ANIMALS.
WHAT IN THE GOD DOOMED HELL ARE YOU TALKING ABOUT?
DOES NO ONE LISTEN TO ME?
THE MYSTERY OF HIS DAUGHTER'S KILLER, OF COURSE...THE MONSTER HASN'T BEEN BROUGHT TO--
ENOUGH!
SLAP
YOU'RE NOTHING BUT A CLOWN, ARCADE.
FINISH YOUR "STORY". SHUT HIM DOWN.
OR I WILL.

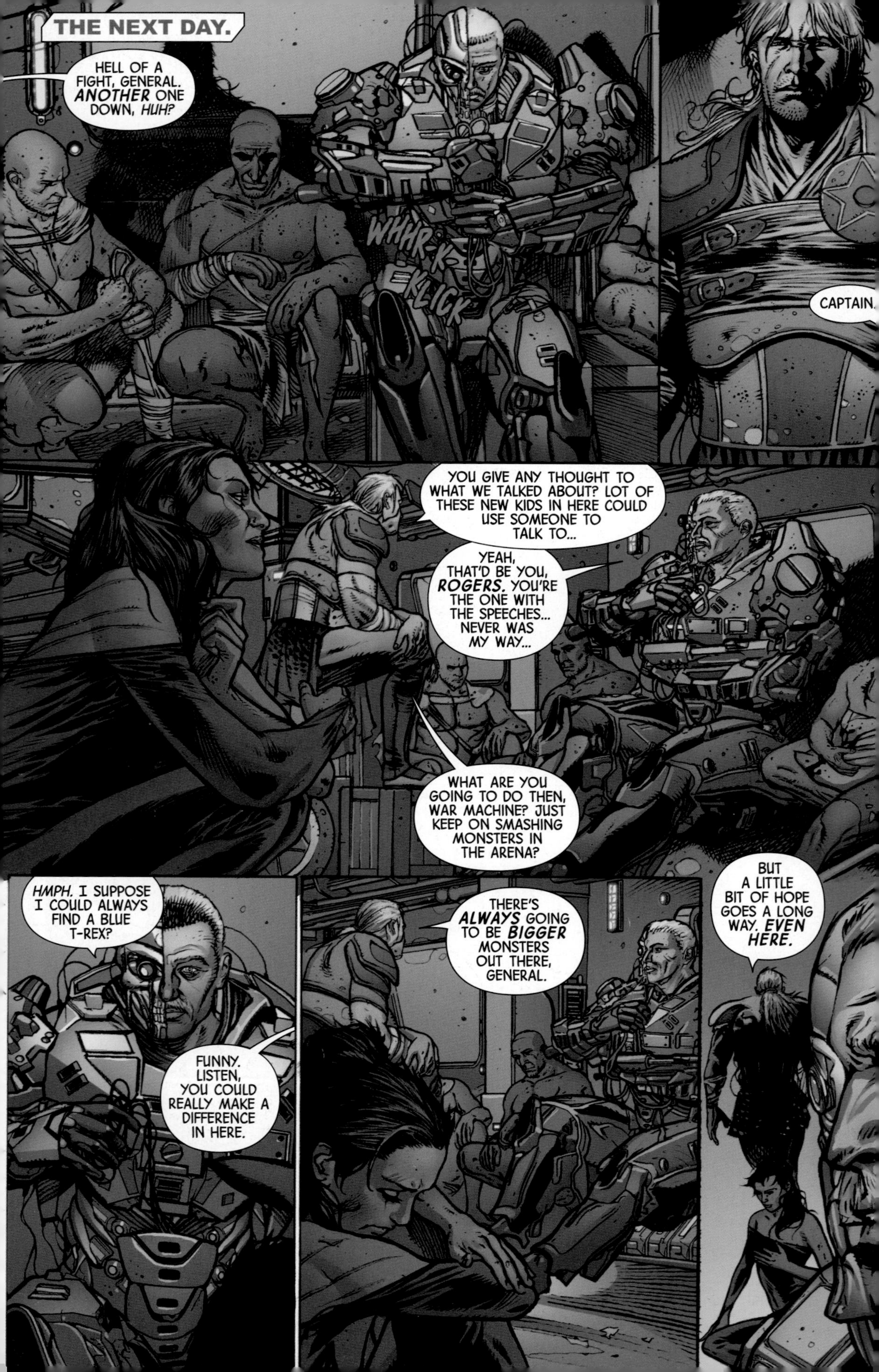
THE NEXT DAY.
HELL OF A FIGHT, GENERAL. ANOTHER ONE DOWN, HUH?
WHHR-K KLICK
CAPTAIN.
YOU GIVE ANY THOUGHT TO WHAT WE TALKED ABOUT? LOT OF THESE NEW KIDS IN HERE COULD USE SOMEONE TO TALK TO...
YEAH, THAT'D BE YOU, ROGERS. YOU'RE THE ONE WITH THE SPEECHES... NEVER WAS MY WAY...
WHAT ARE YOU GOING TO DO THEN, WAR MACHINE? JUST KEEP ON SMASHING MONSTERS IN THE ARENA?
HMPH. I SUPPOSE I COULD ALWAYS FIND A BLUE T-REX?
FUNNY. LISTEN, YOU COULD REALLY MAKE A DIFFERENCE IN HERE.
THERE'S ALWAYS GOING TO BE BIGGER MONSTERS OUT THERE, GENERAL.
BUT A LITTLE BIT OF HOPE GOES A LONG WAY. EVEN HERE.

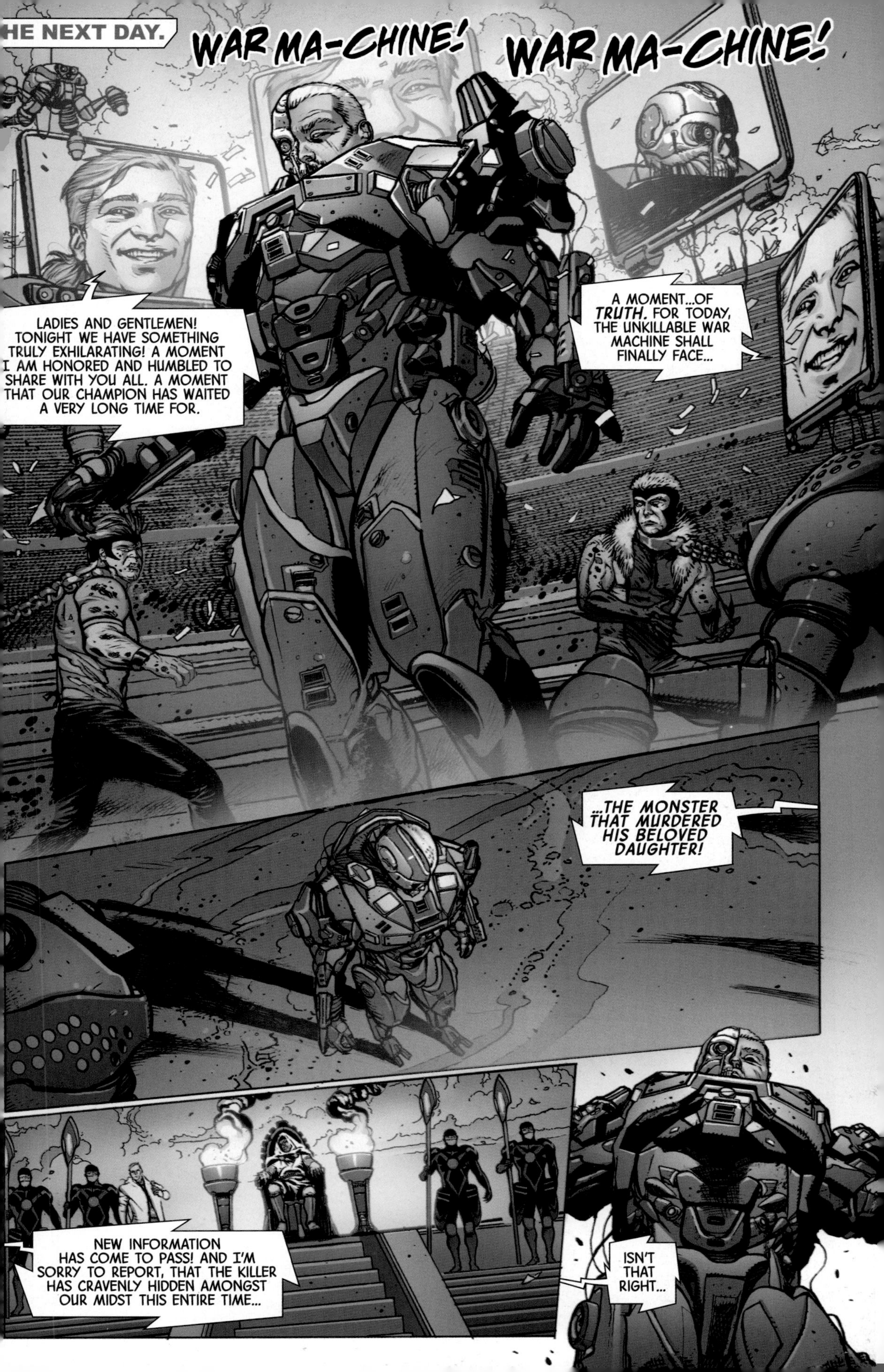
THE NEXT DAY.
WAR MA-CHINE! WAR MA-CHINE!
LADIES AND GENTLEMEN! TONIGHT WE HAVE SOMETHING TRULY EXHILARATING! A MOMENT I AM HONORED AND HUMBLED TO SHARE WITH YOU ALL. A MOMENT THAT OUR CHAMPION HAS WAITED A VERY LONG TIME FOR.
A MOMENT...OF TRUTH. FOR TODAY, THE UNKILLABLE WAR MACHINE SHALL FINALLY FACE...
...THE MONSTER THAT MURDERED HIS BELOVED DAUGHTER!
NEW INFORMATION HAS COME TO PASS! AND I'M SORRY TO REPORT, THAT THE KILLER HAS CRAVENLY HIDDEN AMONGST OUR MIDST THIS ENTIRE TIME...
ISN'T THAT RIGHT...

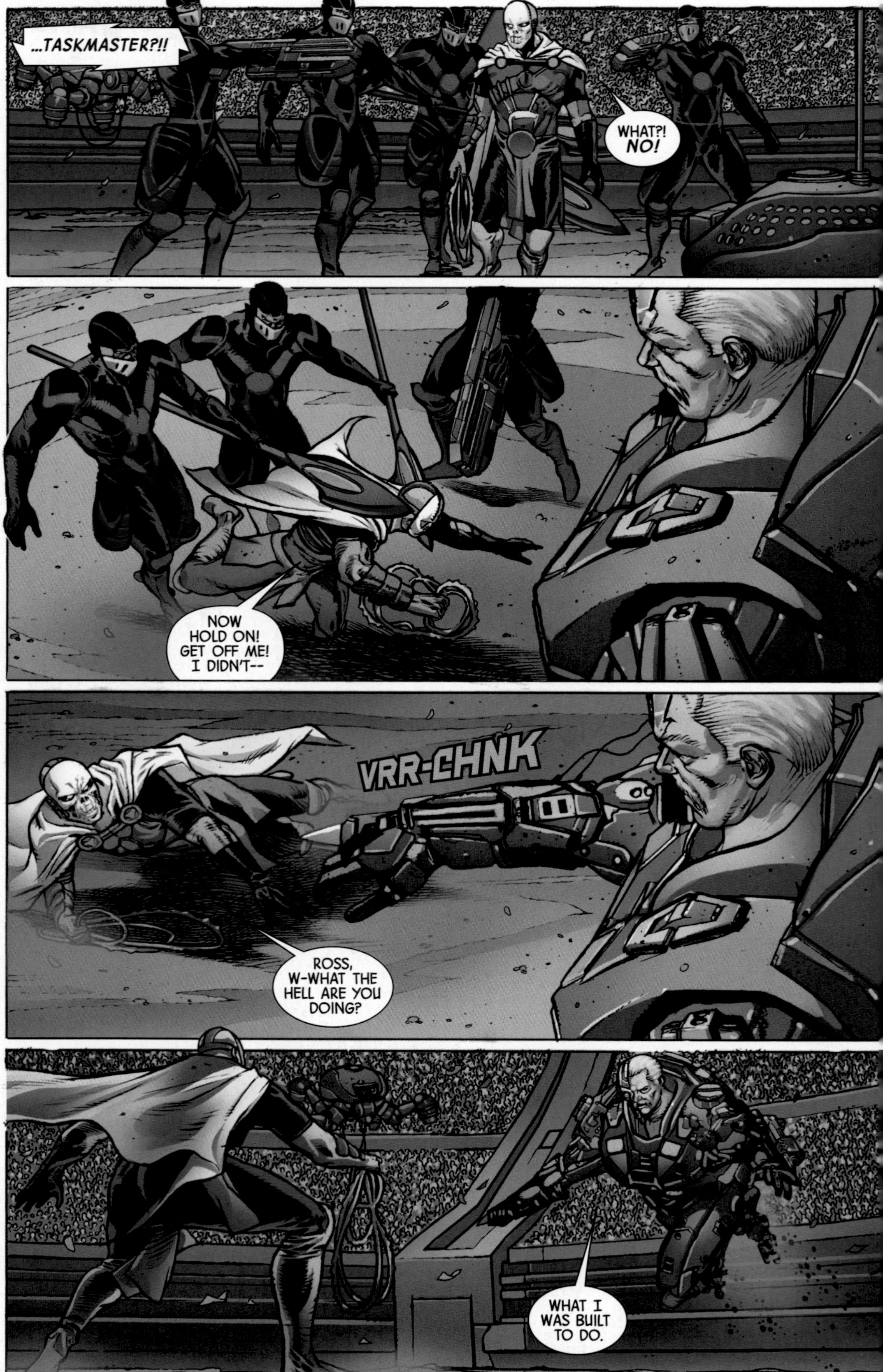
...TASKMASTER?!!
WHAT?! NO!
NOW HOLD ON! GET OFF ME! I DIDN'T--
VRR-CHNK
ROSS, W-WHAT THE HELL ARE YOU DOING?
WHAT I WAS BUILT TO DO.

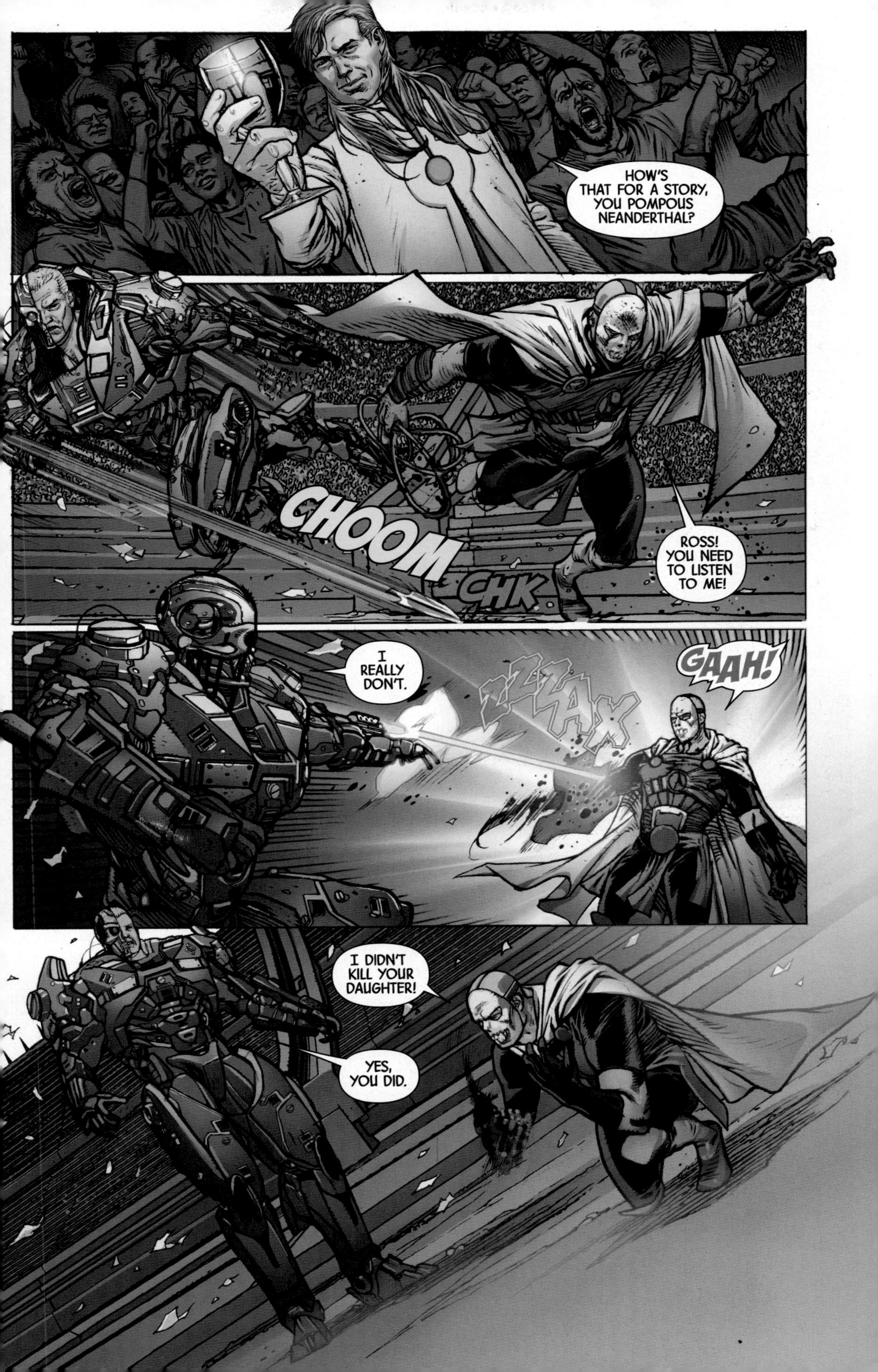
HOW'S THAT FOR A STORY, YOU POMPOUS NEANDERTHAL?
CHOOM
CHK
ROSS! YOU NEED TO LISTEN TO ME!
I REALLY DON'T.
ZZZAX
GAAH!
I DIDN'T KILL YOUR DAUGHTER!
YES, YOU DID.

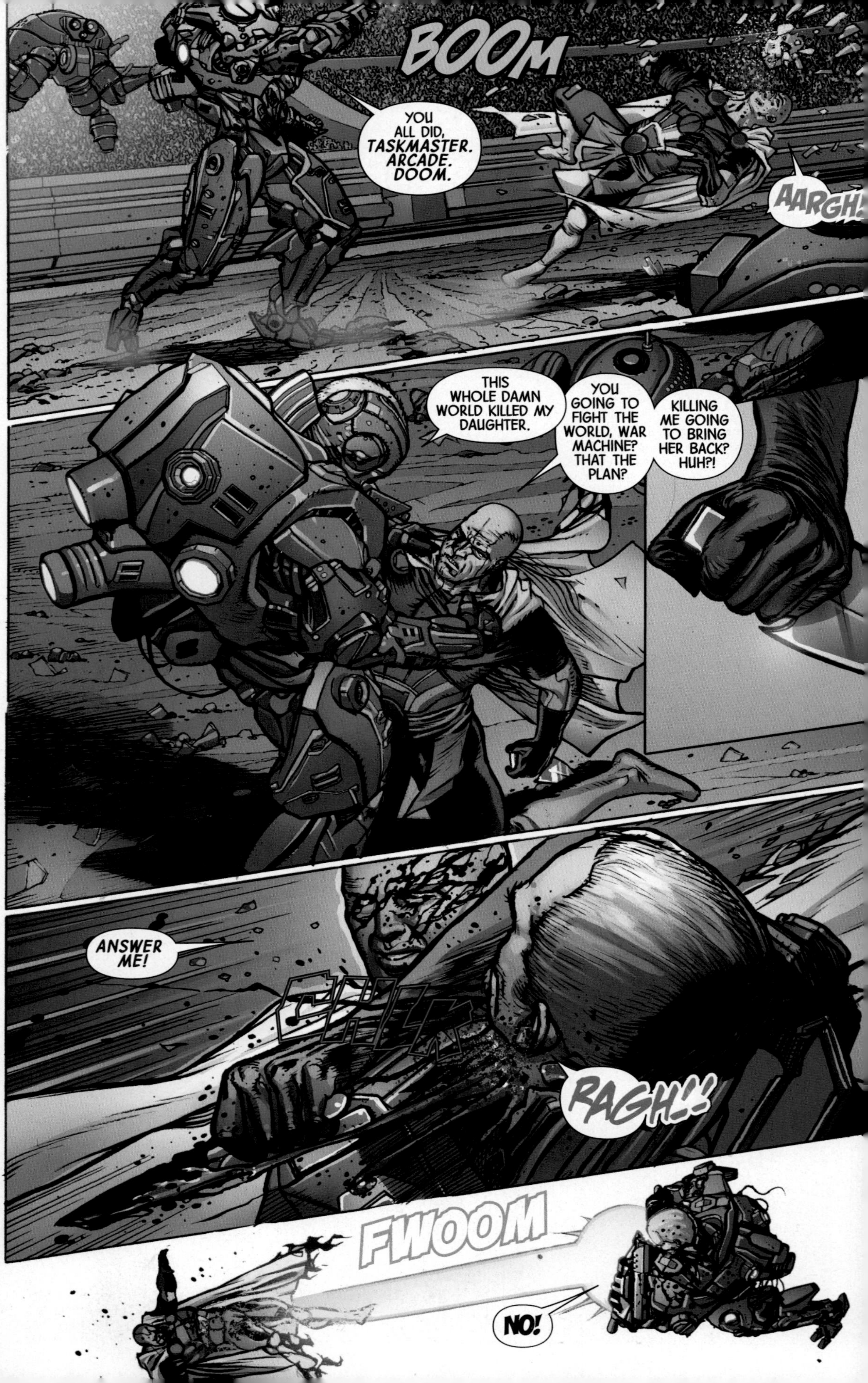
BOOM
YOU ALL DID, TASKMASTER. ARCADE. DOOM.
AARGH!
THIS WHOLE DAMN WORLD KILLED MY DAUGHTER.
YOU GOING TO FIGHT THE WORLD, WAR MACHINE? THAT THE PLAN?
KILLING ME GOING TO BRING HER BACK? HUH?!
ANSWER ME!
RAGH!!
FWOOM
NO!

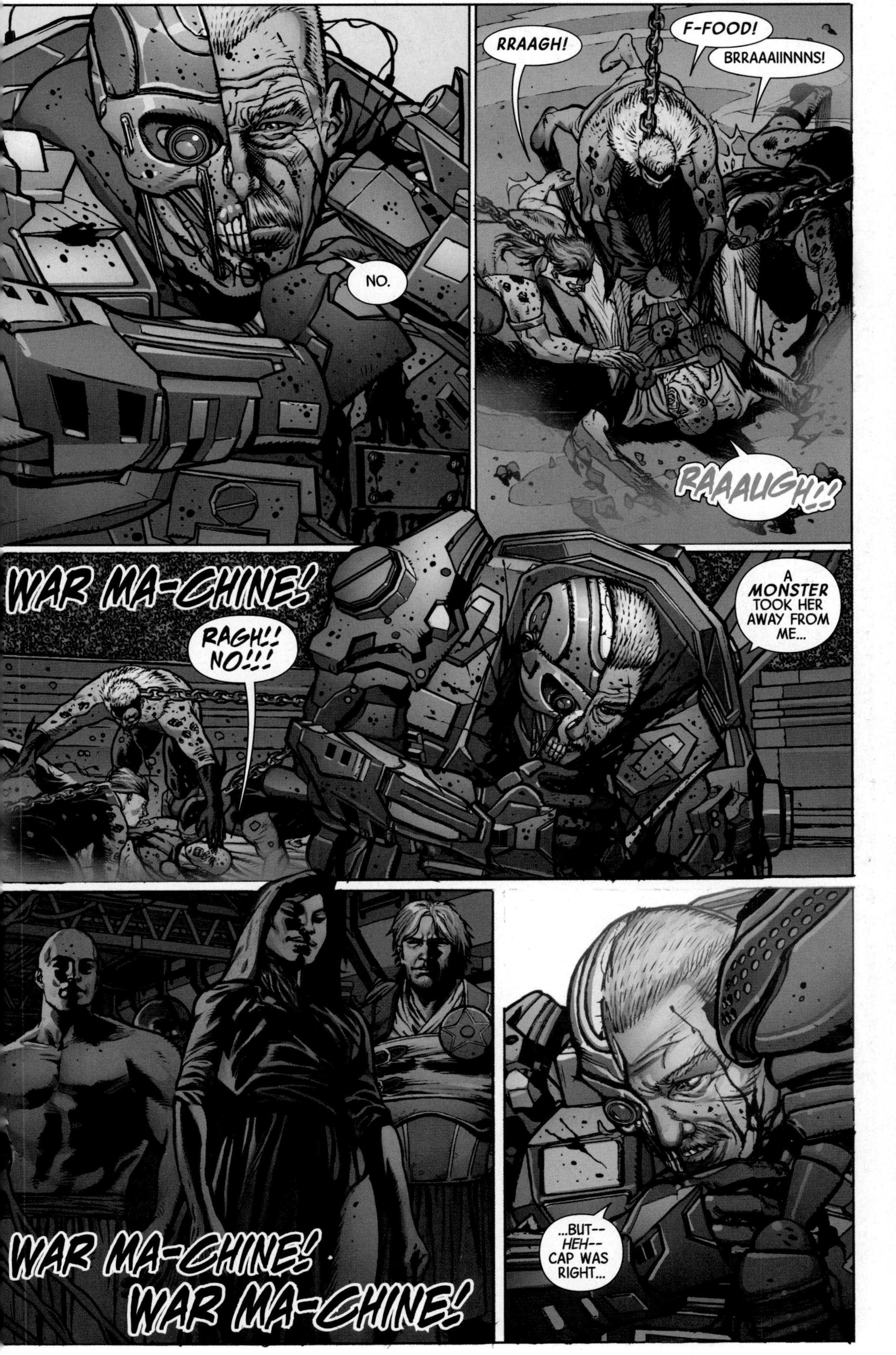
NO.
RRAAGH!
F-FOOD!
BRRAAAIINNNS!
RAAAUGH!!
WAR MA-CHINE!
RAGH!! NO!!!
A MONSTER TOOK HER AWAY FROM ME...
WAR MA-CHINE!
WAR MA-CHINE!
...BUT-- HEH-- CAP WAS RIGHT...

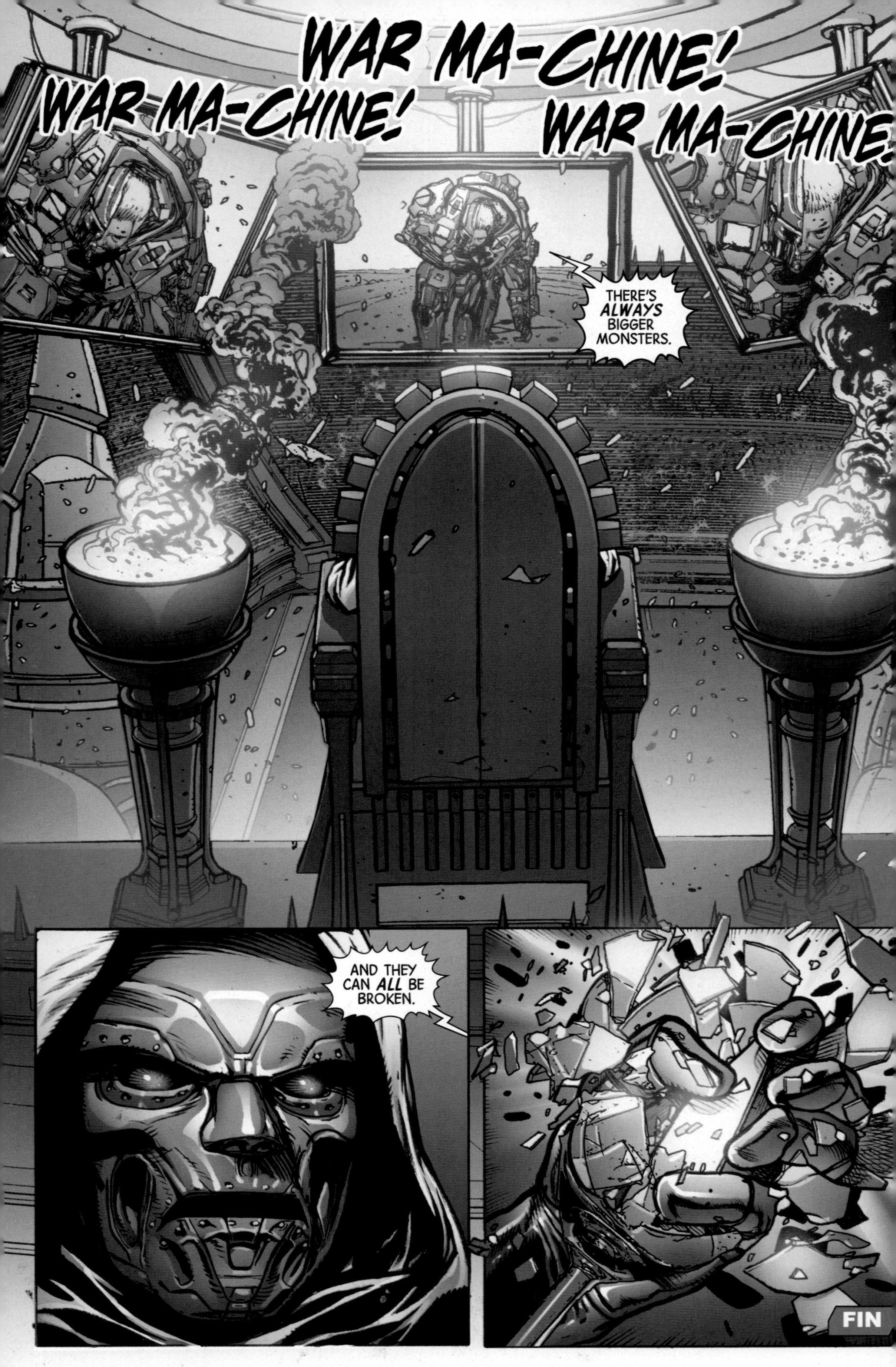
WAR MA-CHINE!
WAR MA-CHINE!
WAR MA-CHINE.
THERE'S ALWAYS BIGGER MONSTERS.
AND THEY CAN ALL BE BROKEN.
FIN

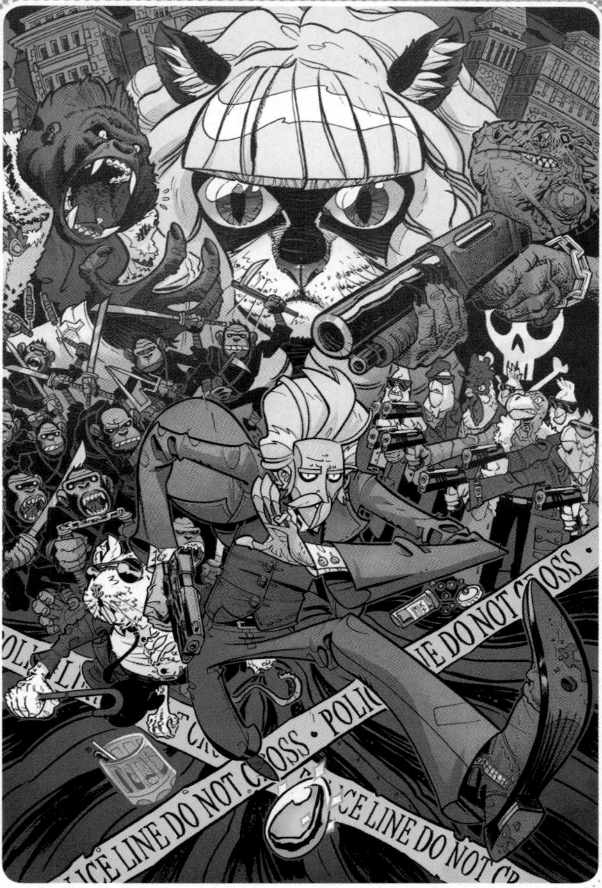
DO NOT CROSS
POLICE
CROSS
CE LINE DO NOT
CE LINE DO NOT

HOWARD THE HUMAN #1 VARIANT
BY AARON CONLEY &
JEAN-FRANCIS BEAULIEU

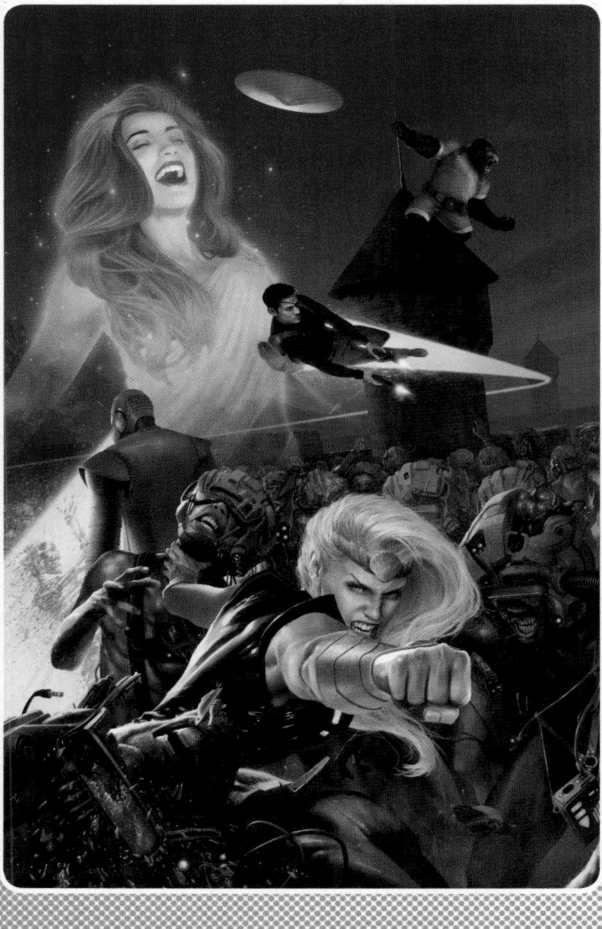

AGENTS OF ATLAS #1 VARIANT
BY SCOTT "RAHZZAH" WILSON

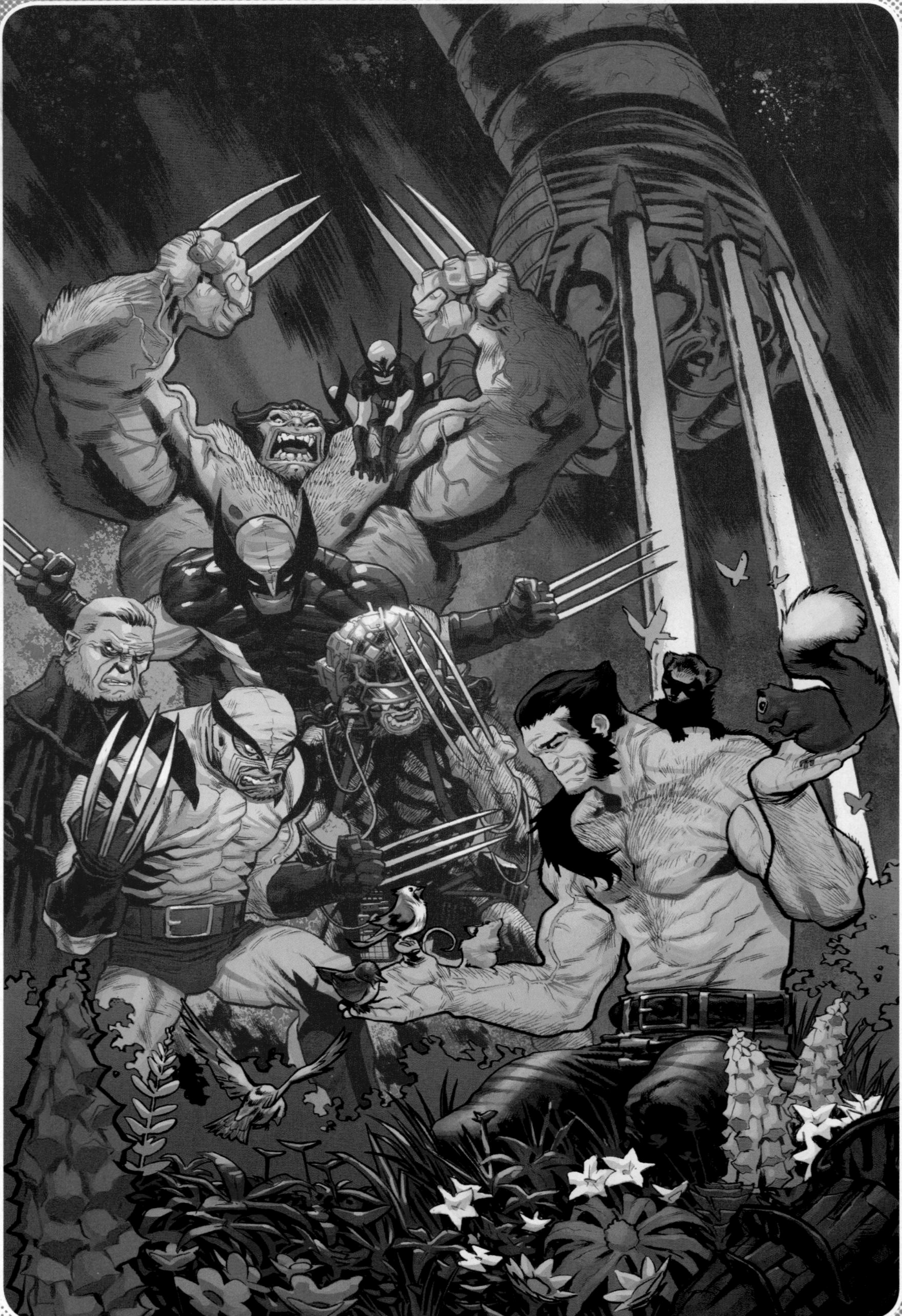

SECRET WARS: BATTLEWORLD #3

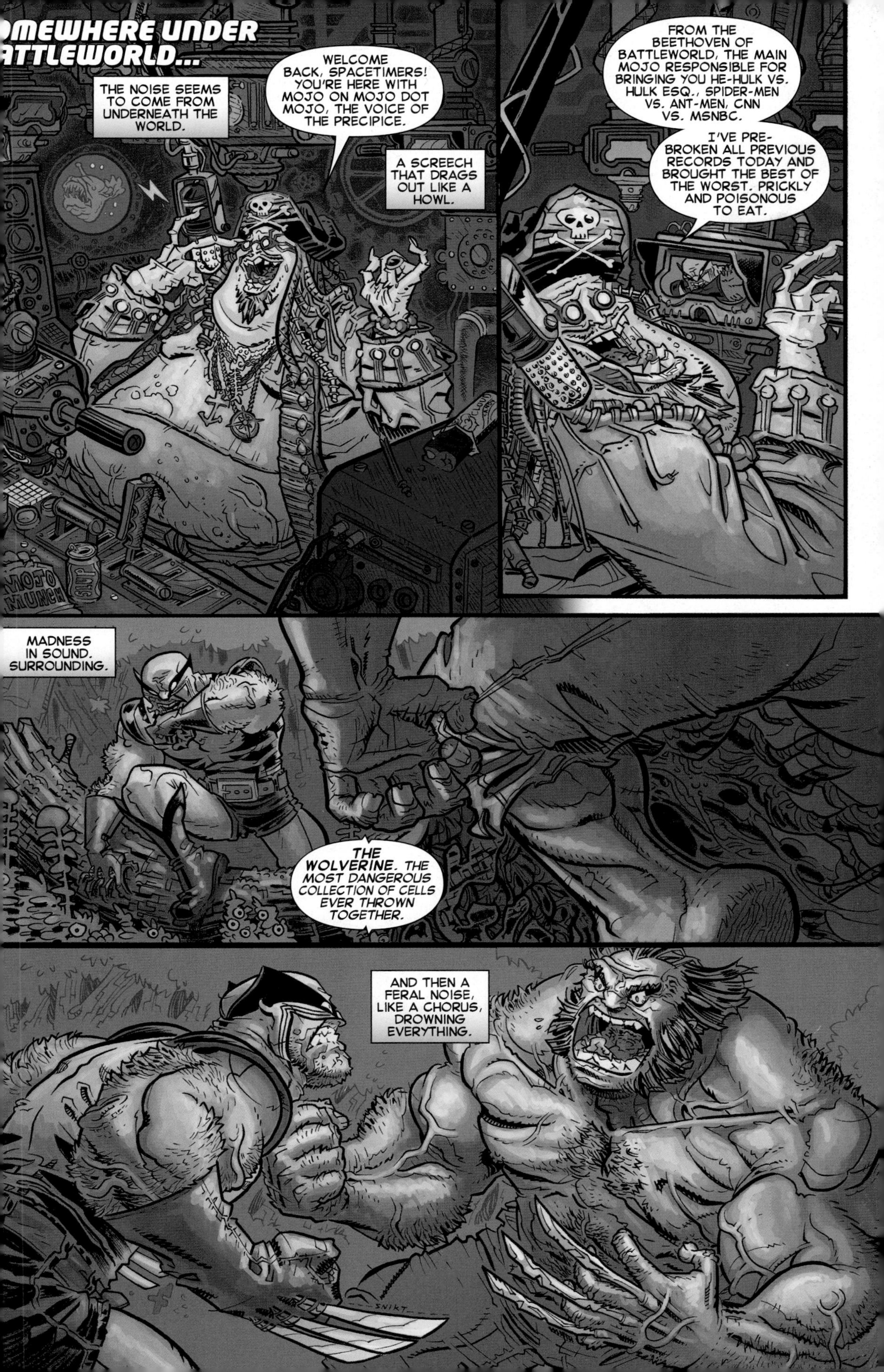
OMEWHERE UNDER
ATTLEWORLD...
THE NOISE SEEMS TO COME FROM UNDERNEATH THE WORLD.
WELCOME BACK, SPACETIMERS! YOU'RE HERE WITH MOJO ON MOJO DOT MOJO, THE VOICE OF THE PRECIPICE.
A SCREECH THAT DRAGS OUT LIKE A HOWL.
MOJO MUNCH
SLUP
FROM THE BEETHOVEN OF BATTLEWORLD, THE MAIN MOJO RESPONSIBLE FOR BRINGING YOU HE-HULK VS. HULK ESQ., SPIDER-MEN VS. ANT-MEN, CNN VS. MSNBC.
I'VE PRE-BROKEN ALL PREVIOUS RECORDS TODAY AND BROUGHT THE BEST OF THE WORST. PRICKLY AND POISONOUS TO EAT.
MADNESS IN SOUND. SURROUNDING.
THE WOLVERINE. THE MOST DANGEROUS COLLECTION OF CELLS EVER THROWN TOGETHER.
AND THEN A FERAL NOISE, LIKE A CHORUS, DROWNING EVERYTHING.
SNIKT

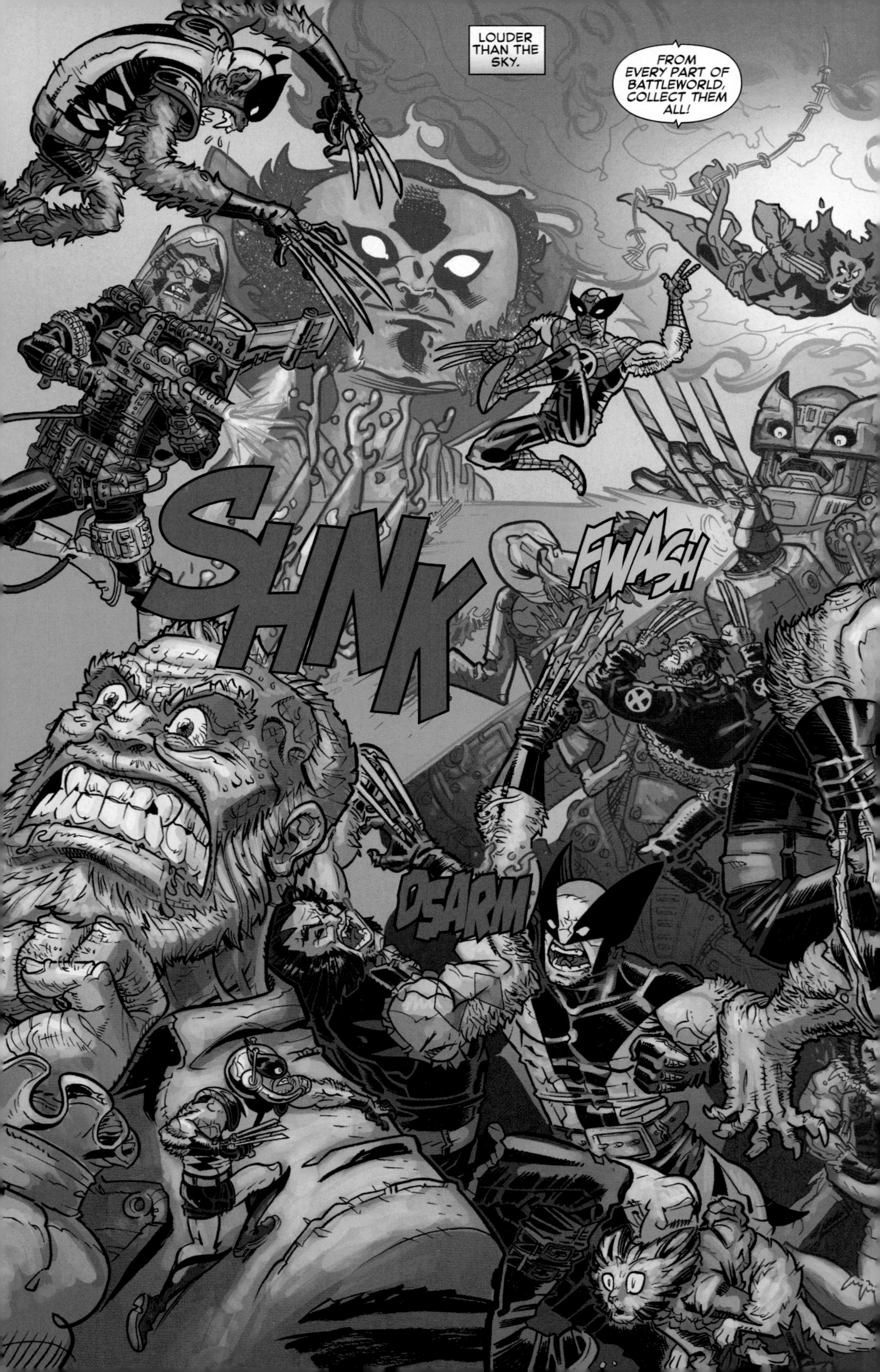
LOUDER THAN THE SKY.
FROM EVERY PART OF BATTLEWORLD, COLLECT THEM ALL!
SHNK
FWASH
DSARM

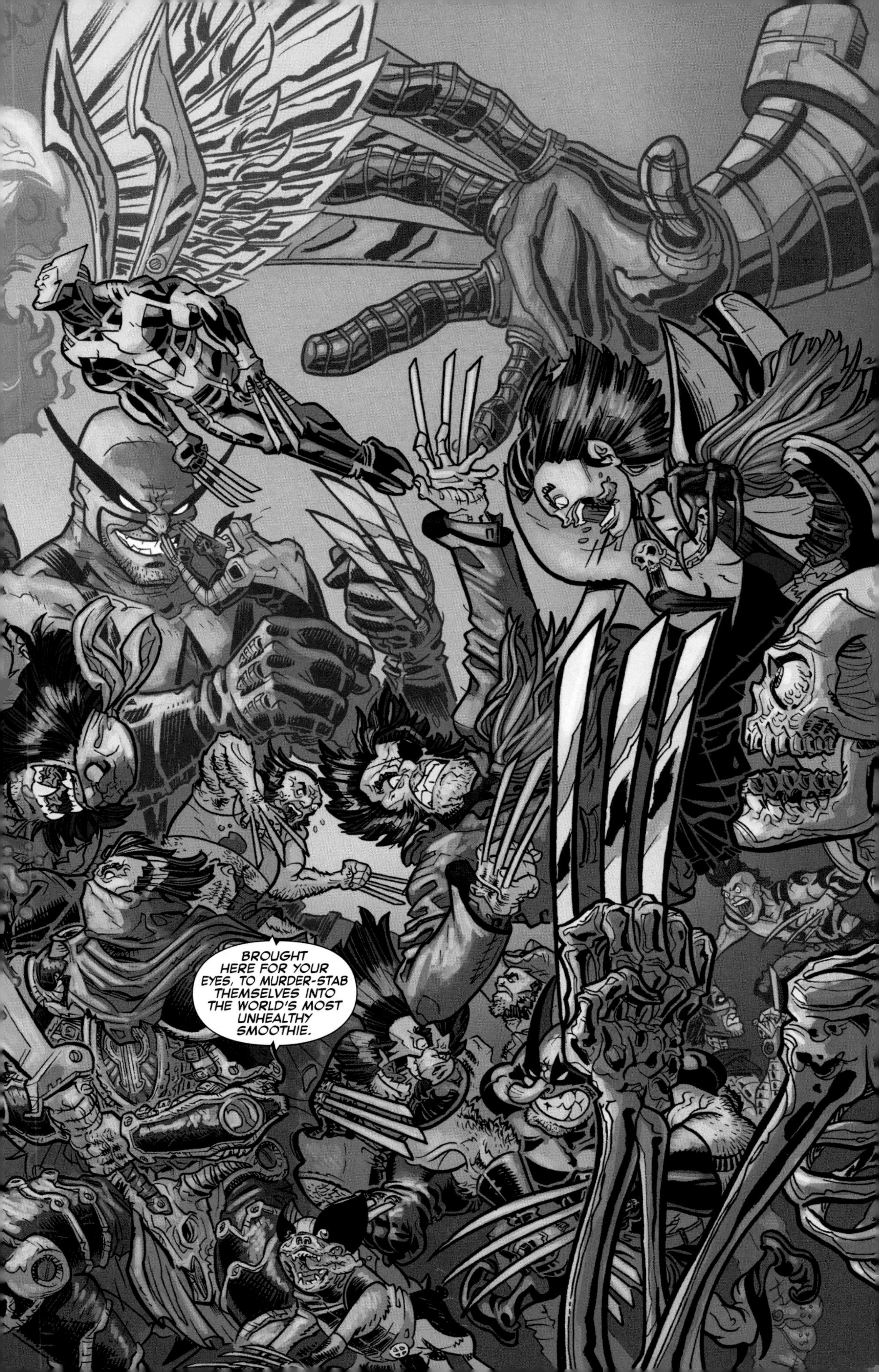
BROUGHT HERE FOR YOUR EYES, TO MURDER-STAB THEMSELVES INTO THE WORLD'S MOST UNHEALTHY SMOOTHIE.

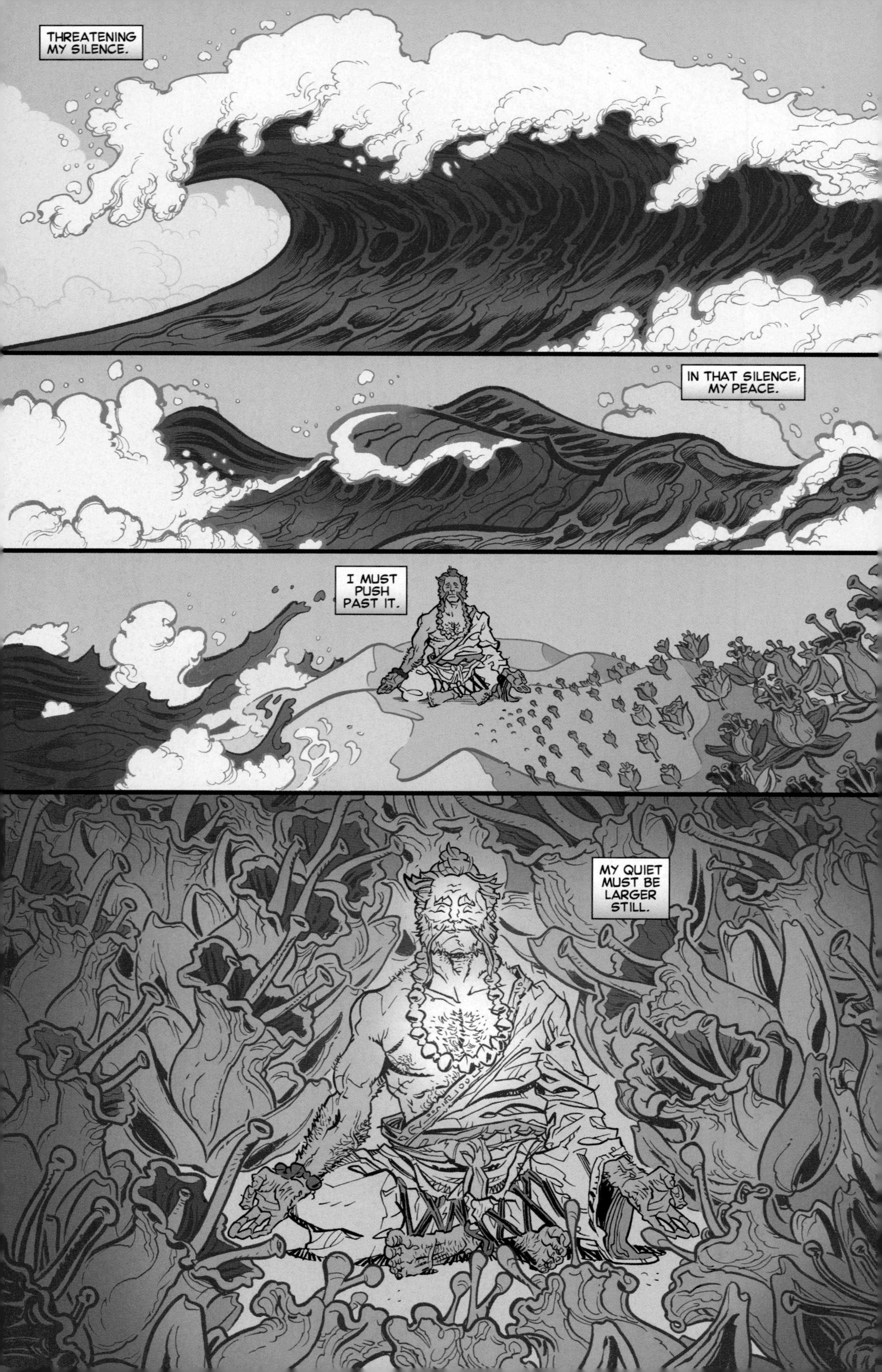
THREATENING MY SILENCE.
IN THAT SILENCE, MY PEACE.
I MUST PUSH PAST IT.
MY QUIET MUST BE LARGER STILL.

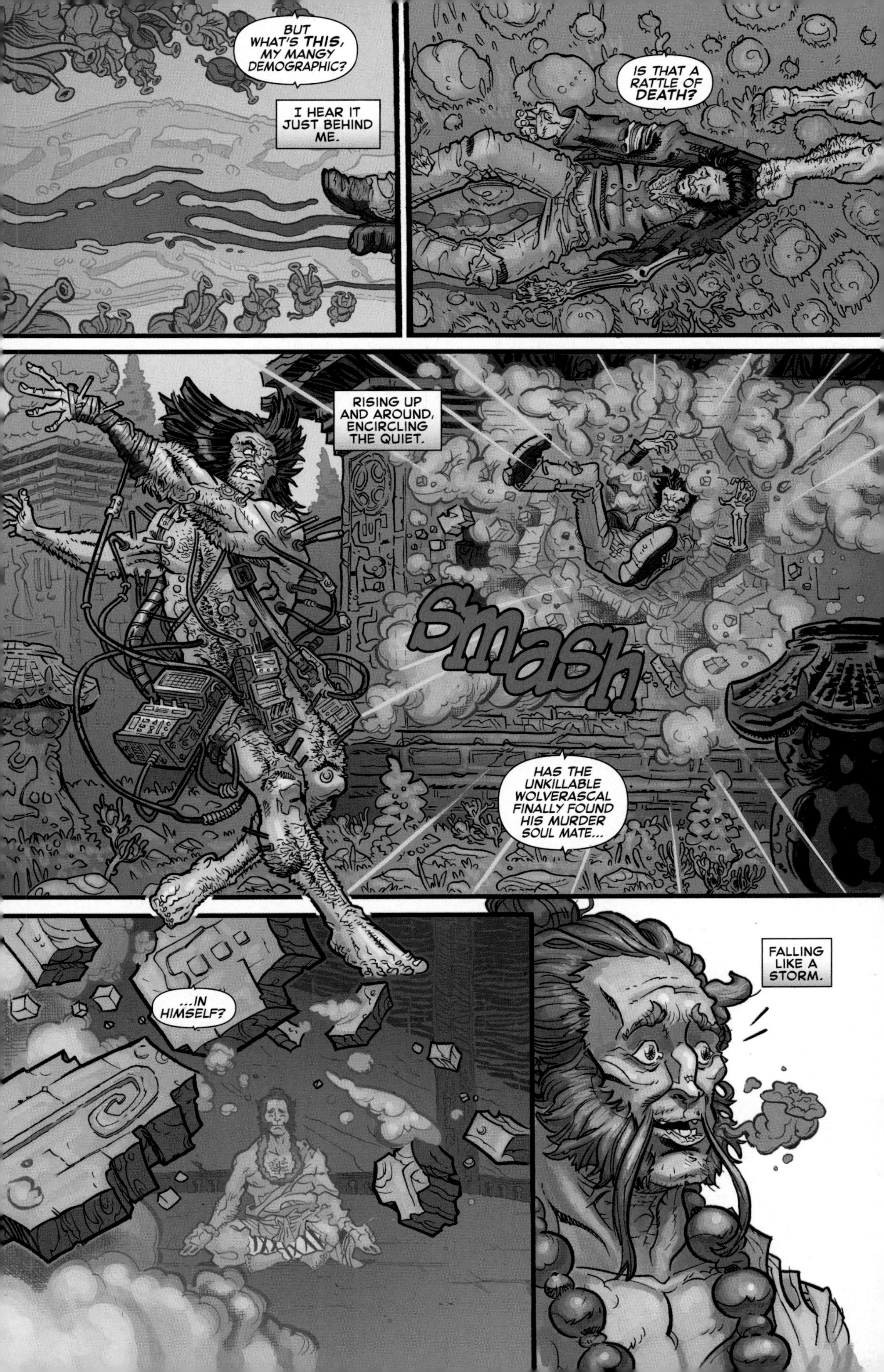
BUT WHAT'S THIS, MY MANGY DEMOGRAPHIC?
I HEAR IT JUST BEHIND ME.
IS THAT A RATTLE OF DEATH?
RISING UP AND AROUND, ENCIRCLING THE QUIET.
SMASH
HAS THE UNKILLABLE WOLVERASCAL FINALLY FOUND HIS MURDER SOUL MATE...
...IN HIMSELF?
FALLING LIKE A STORM.

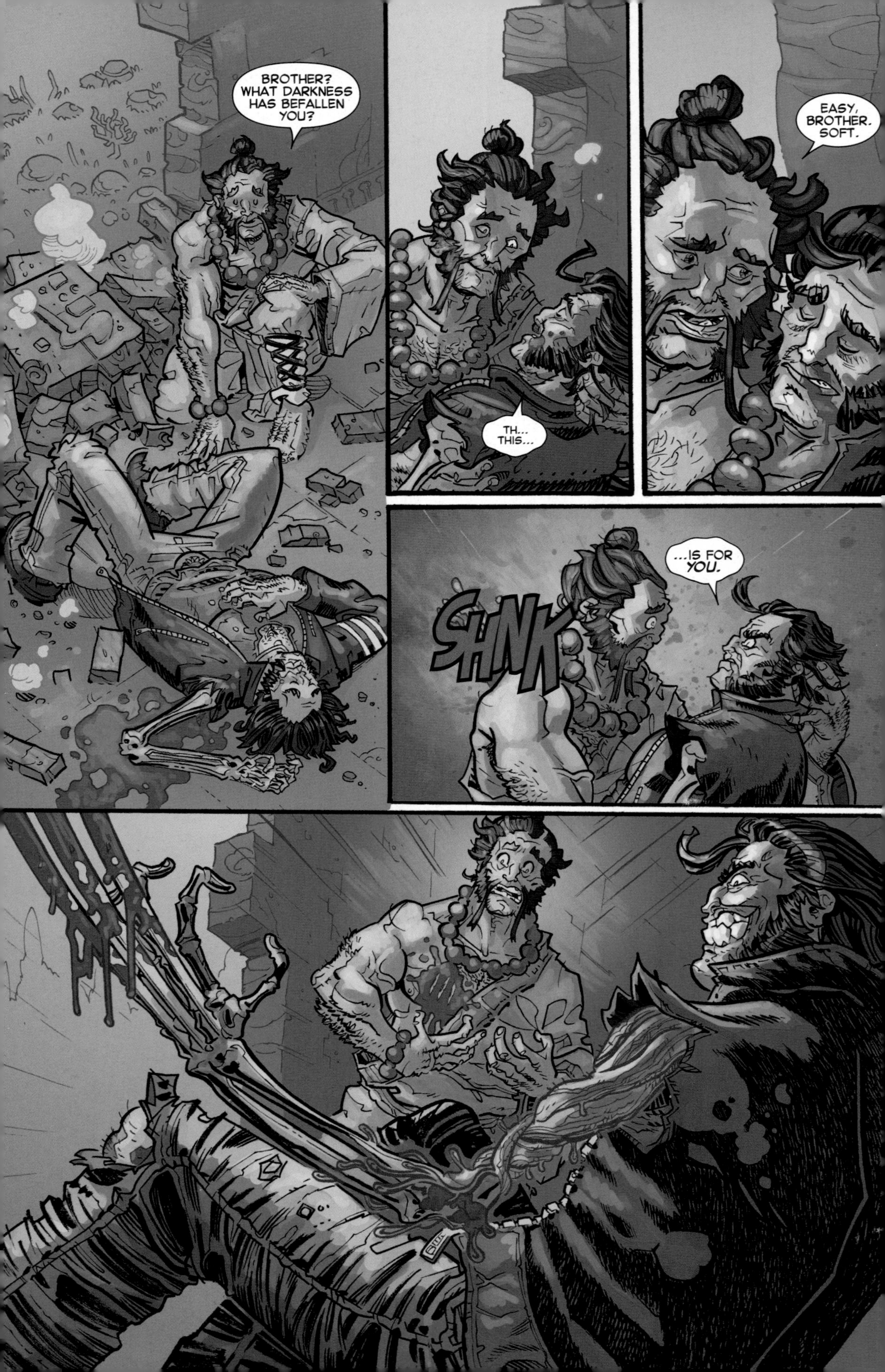
BROTHER? WHAT DARKNESS HAS BEFALLEN YOU?
TH... THIS...
EASY, BROTHER. SOFT.
...IS FOR YOU.
SHNK

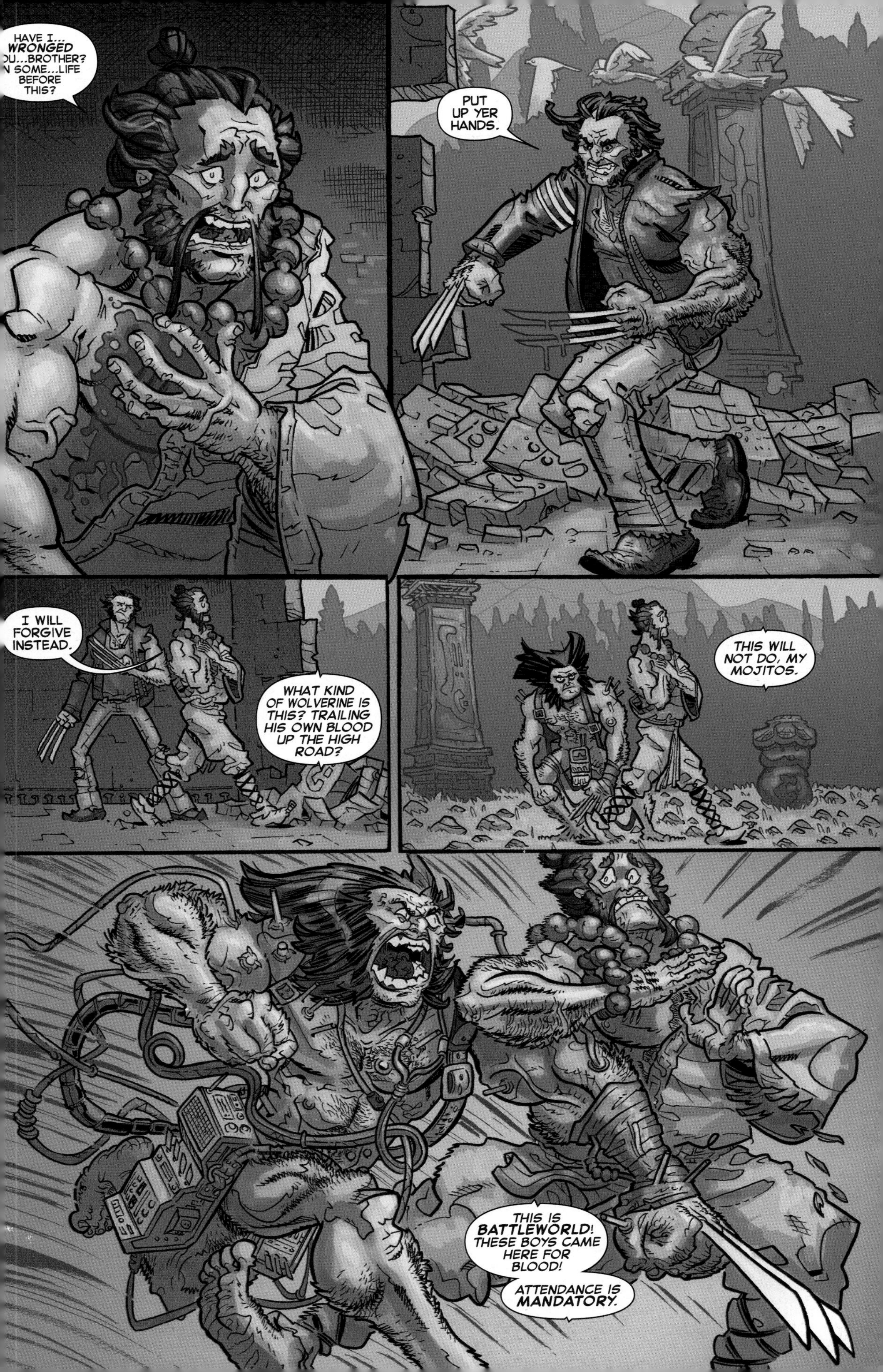

HAVE I... WRONGED OU...BROTHER? N SOME...LIFE BEFORE THIS?
PUT UP YER HANDS.
I WILL FORGIVE INSTEAD.
WHAT KIND OF WOLVERINE IS THIS? TRAILING HIS OWN BLOOD UP THE HIGH ROAD?
THIS WILL NOT DO, MY MOJITOS.
THIS IS BATTLEWORLD! THESE BOYS CAME HERE FOR BLOOD!
ATTENDANCE IS MANDATORY.

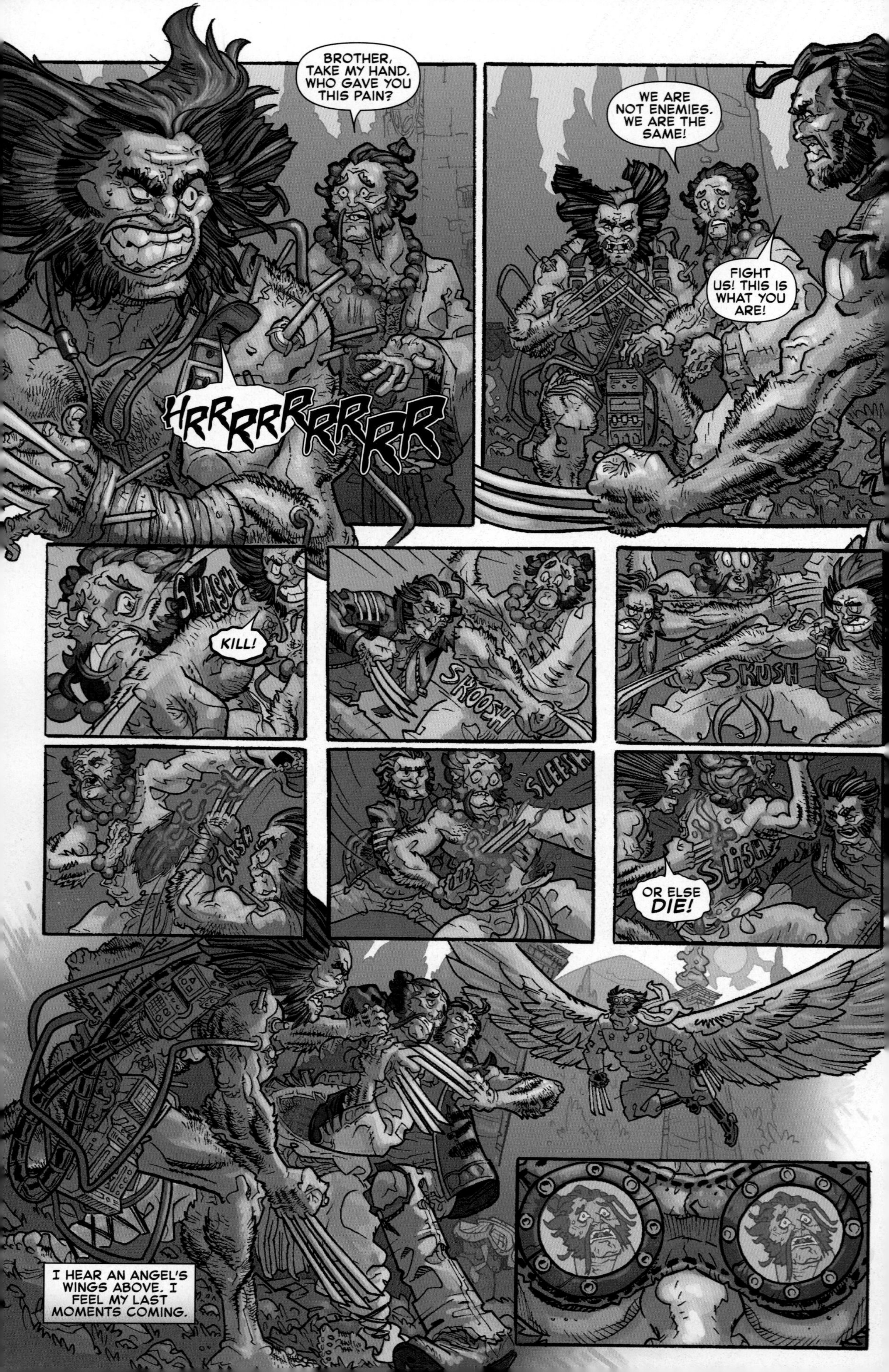

BROTHER, TAKE MY HAND. WHO GAVE YOU THIS PAIN?
HRRRRRRRRRR
WE ARE NOT ENEMIES. WE ARE THE SAME!
FIGHT US! THIS IS WHAT YOU ARE!
SKASCH
KILL!
SKOOSH
SKUSH
SLOSH
SLEESH
OR ELSE DIE!
SLISH
I HEAR AN ANGEL'S WINGS ABOVE. I FEEL MY LAST MOMENTS COMING.

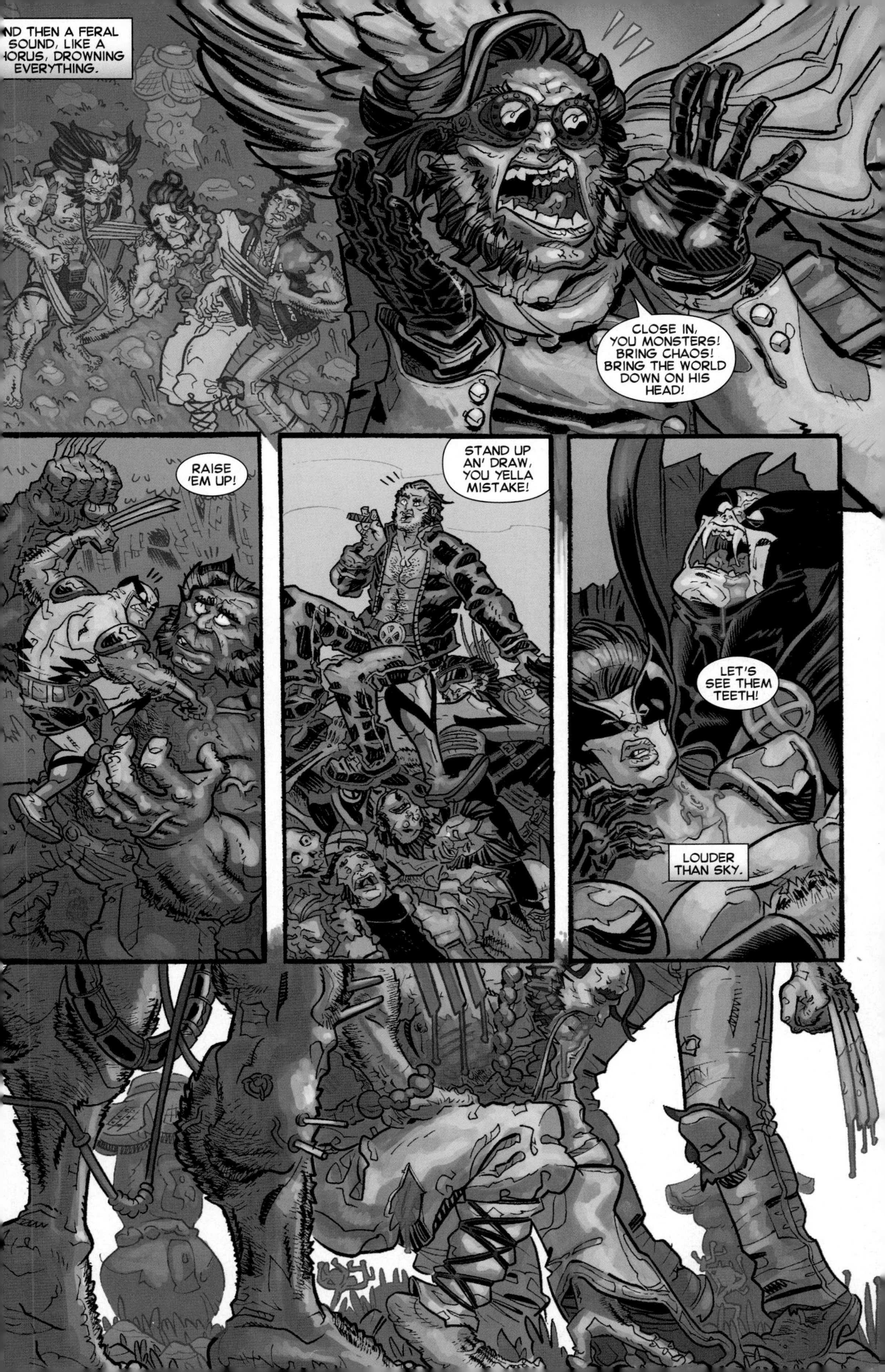
ND THEN A FERAL SOUND, LIKE A HORUS, DROWNING EVERYTHING.
CLOSE IN, YOU MONSTERS! BRING CHAOS! BRING THE WORLD DOWN ON HIS HEAD!
RAISE 'EM UP!
STAND UP AN' DRAW, YOU YELLA MISTAKE!
LET'S SEE THEM TEETH!
LOUDER THAN SKY.

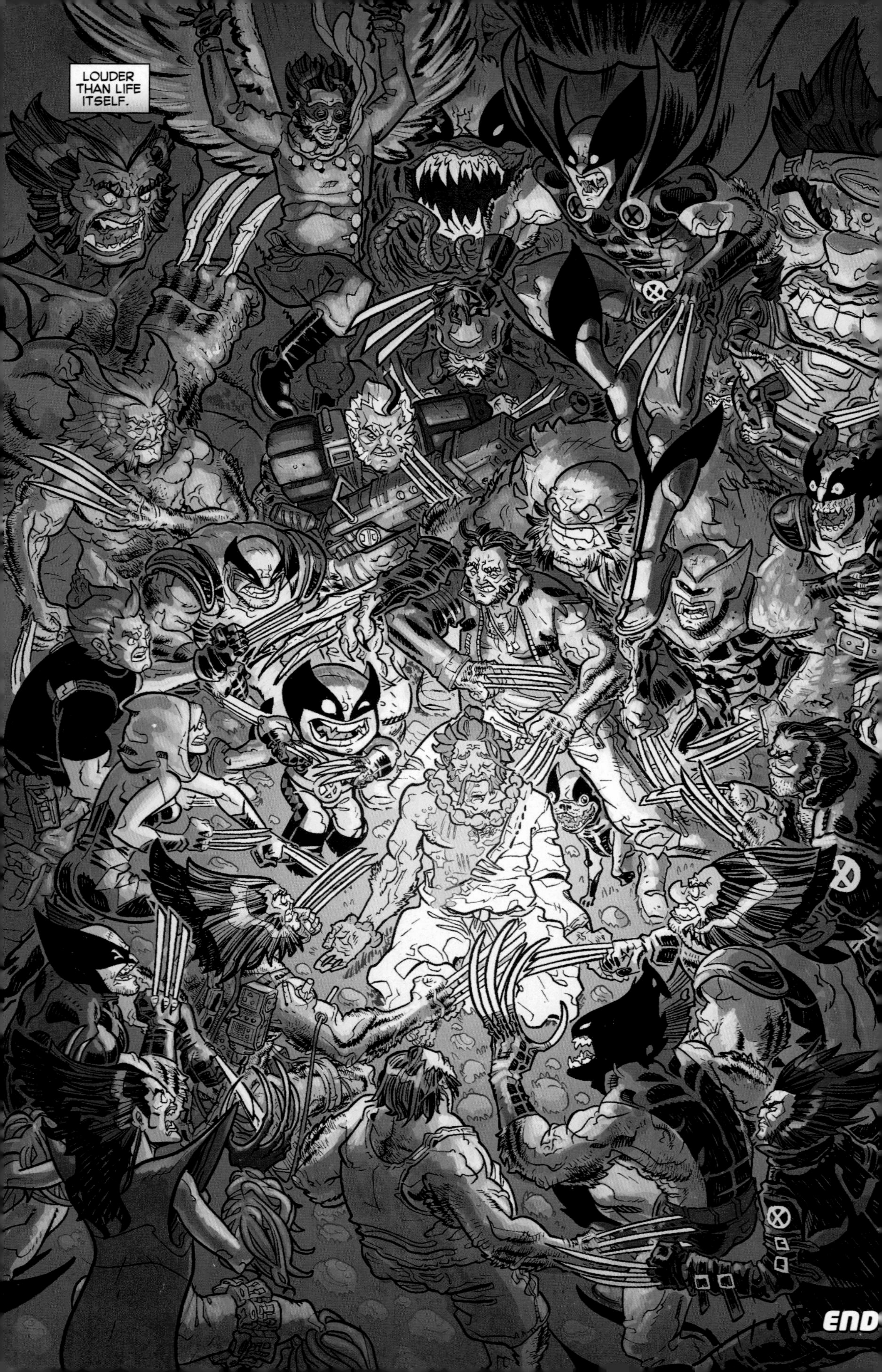
LOUDER THAN LIFE ITSELF.
END

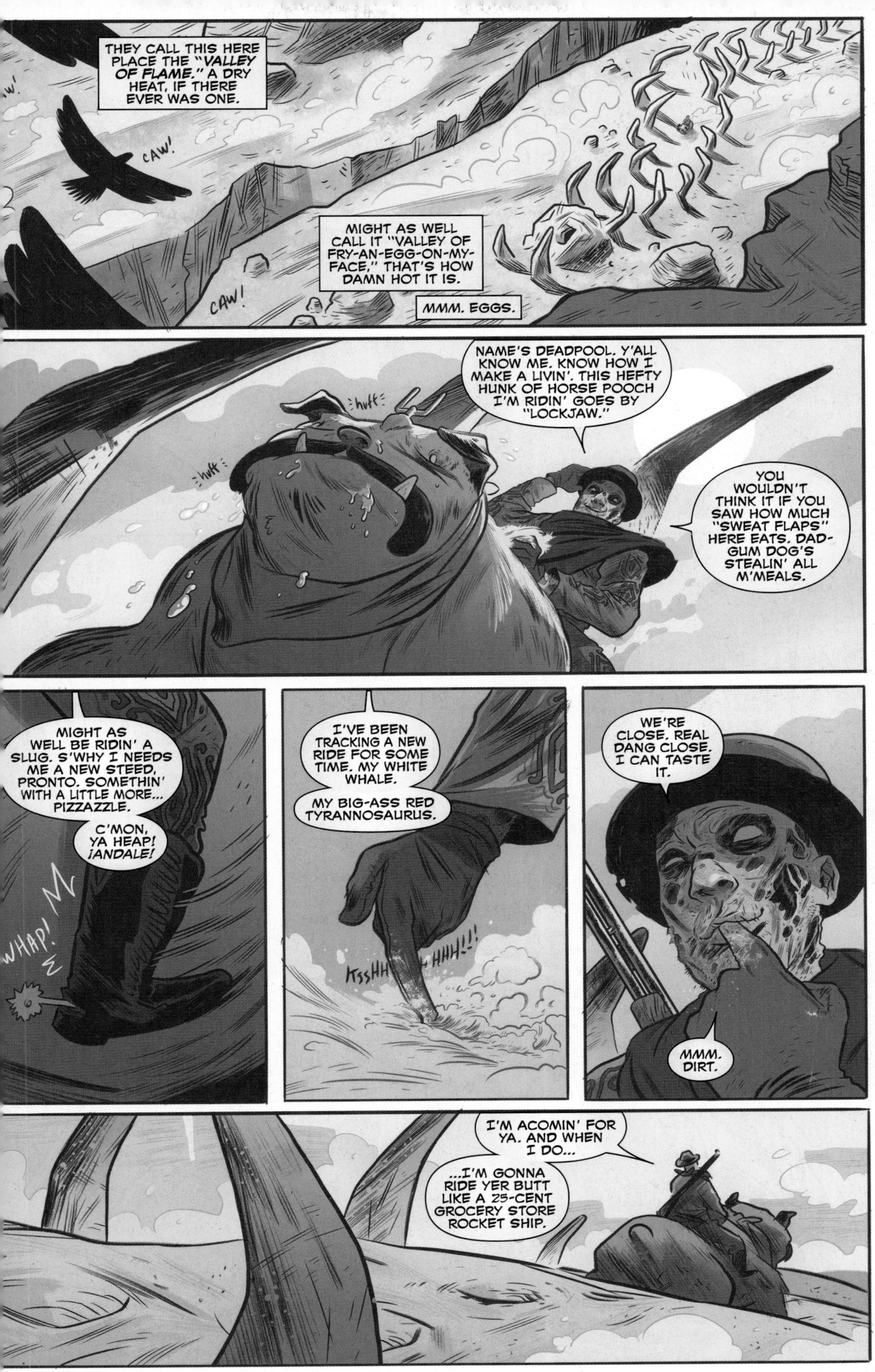
THEY CALL THIS HERE PLACE THE "VALLEY OF FLAME." A DRY HEAT, IF THERE EVER WAS ONE.
CAW!
CAW!
MIGHT AS WELL CALL IT "VALLEY OF FRY-AN-EGG-ON-MY-FACE," THAT'S HOW DAMN HOT IT IS.
MMM. EGGS.
NAME'S DEADPOOL. Y'ALL KNOW ME. KNOW HOW I MAKE A LIVIN'. THIS HEFTY HUNK OF HORSE POOCH I'M RIDIN' GOES BY "LOCKJAW."
huff
huff
YOU WOULDN'T THINK IT IF YOU SAW HOW MUCH "SWEAT FLAPS" HERE EATS. DAD-GUM DOG'S STEALIN' ALL M'MEALS.
MIGHT AS WELL BE RIDIN' A SLUG. S'WHY I NEEDS ME A NEW STEED, PRONTO. SOMETHIN' WITH A LITTLE MORE... PIZZAZZLE.
C'MON, YA HEAP! ¡ANDALE!
WHAP!
I'VE BEEN TRACKING A NEW RIDE FOR SOME TIME. MY WHITE WHALE.
MY BIG-ASS RED TYRANNOSAURUS.
KSSHHHHHH!!!
WE'RE CLOSE. REAL DANG CLOSE. I CAN TASTE IT.
MMM. DIRT.
I'M ACOMIN' FOR YA. AND WHEN I DO...
...I'M GONNA RIDE YER BUTT LIKE A 25-CENT GROCERY STORE ROCKET SHIP.

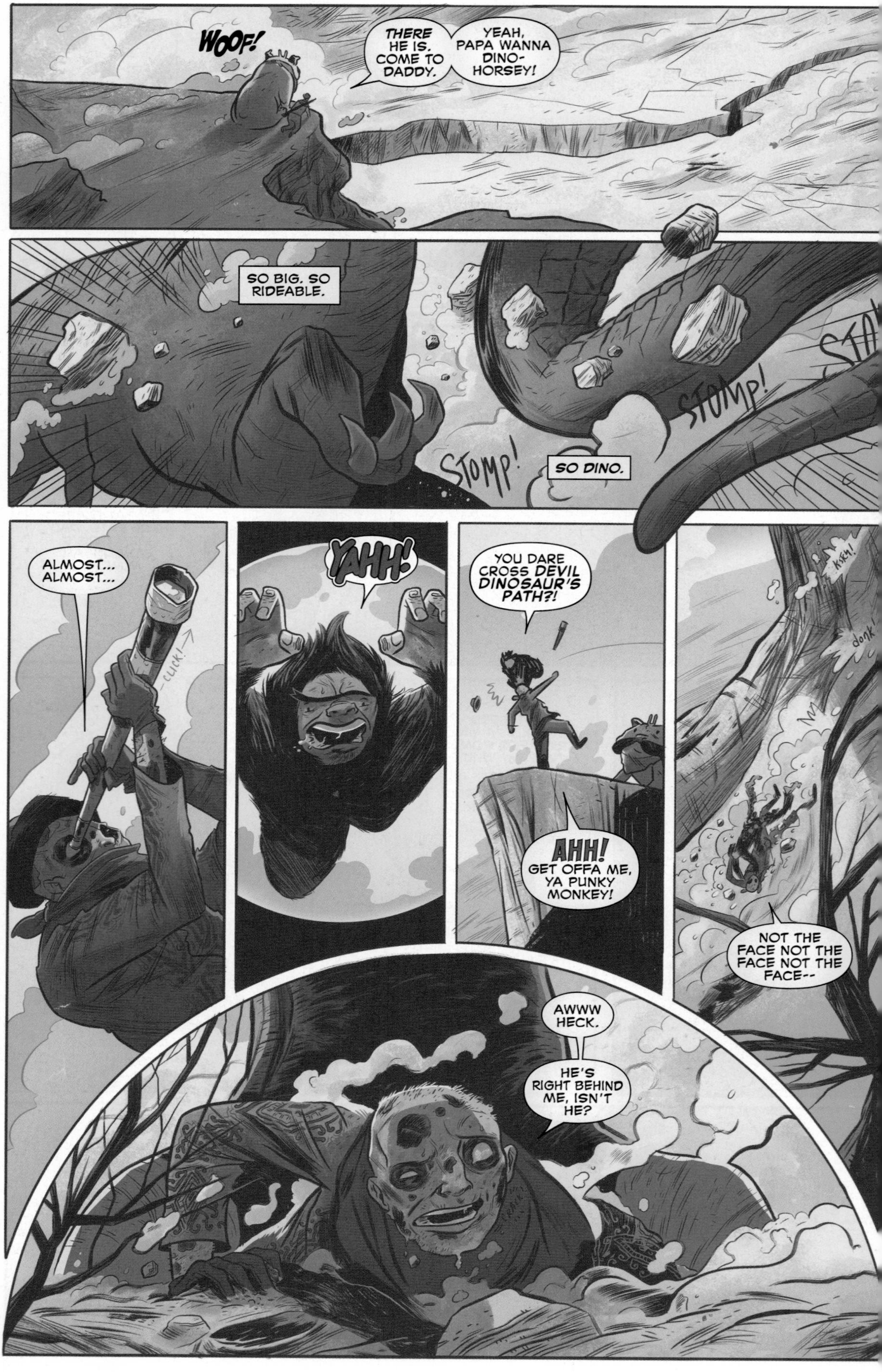
WOOF!
THERE HE IS. COME TO DADDY.
YEAH, PAPA WANNA DINO-HORSEY!
SO BIG. SO RIDEABLE.
STOMP!
STOMP!
SO DINO.
ALMOST... ALMOST...
CLICK!
YAHH!
YOU DARE CROSS DEVIL DINOSAUR'S PATH?!
AHH! GET OFFA ME, YA PUNKY MONKEY!
donk
NOT THE FACE NOT THE FACE NOT THE FACE--
AWWW HECK.
HE'S RIGHT BEHIND ME, ISN'T HE?

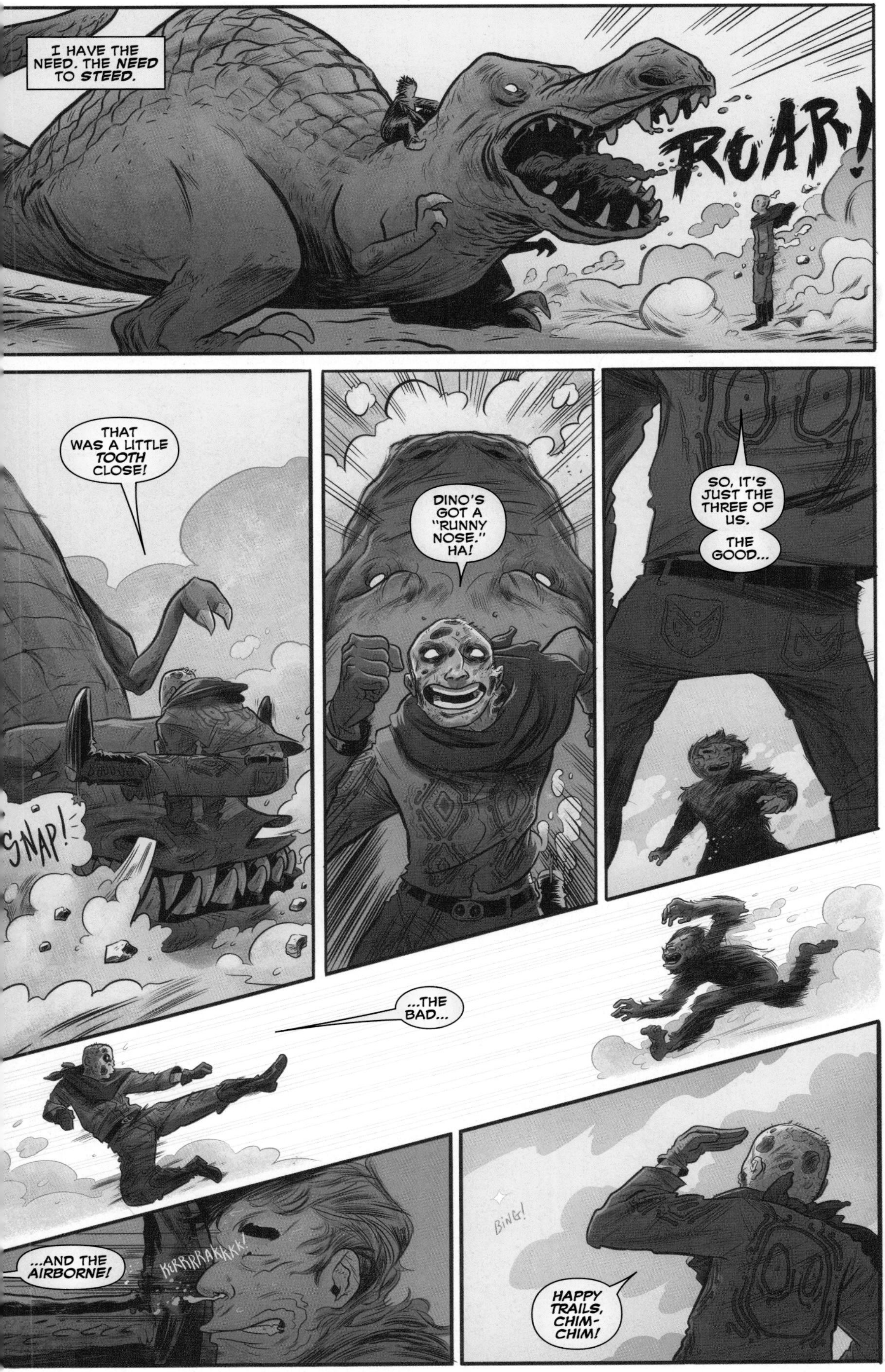
I HAVE THE NEED. THE NEED TO STEED.
ROAR!
THAT WAS A LITTLE TOOTH CLOSE!
SNAP!
DINO'S GOT A "RUNNY NOSE." HA!
SO, IT'S JUST THE THREE OF US.
THE GOOD...
...THE BAD...
...AND THE AIRBORNE!
KERRRRAKKKK!
BING!
HAPPY TRAILS, CHIM-CHIM!

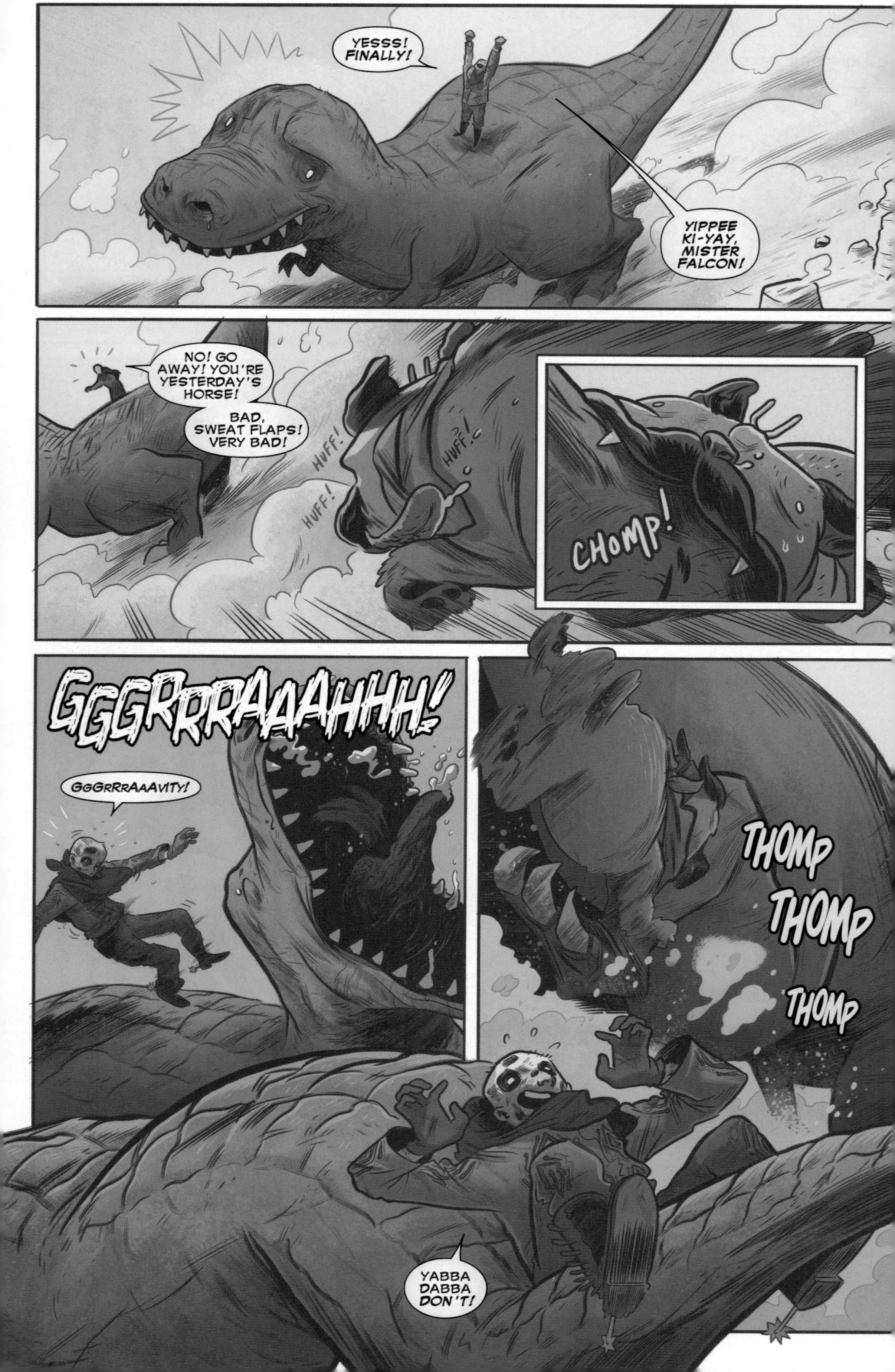
YESSS! FINALLY!
YIPPEE KI-YAY, MISTER FALCON!
NO! GO AWAY! YOU'RE YESTERDAY'S HORSE!
BAD, SWEAT FLAPS! VERY BAD!
HUFF!
HUFF!
HUFF!
CHOMP!
GGGRRRAAAHHH!
GGGRRRAAAVITY!
THOMP
THOMP
THOMP
YABBA DABBA DON'T!

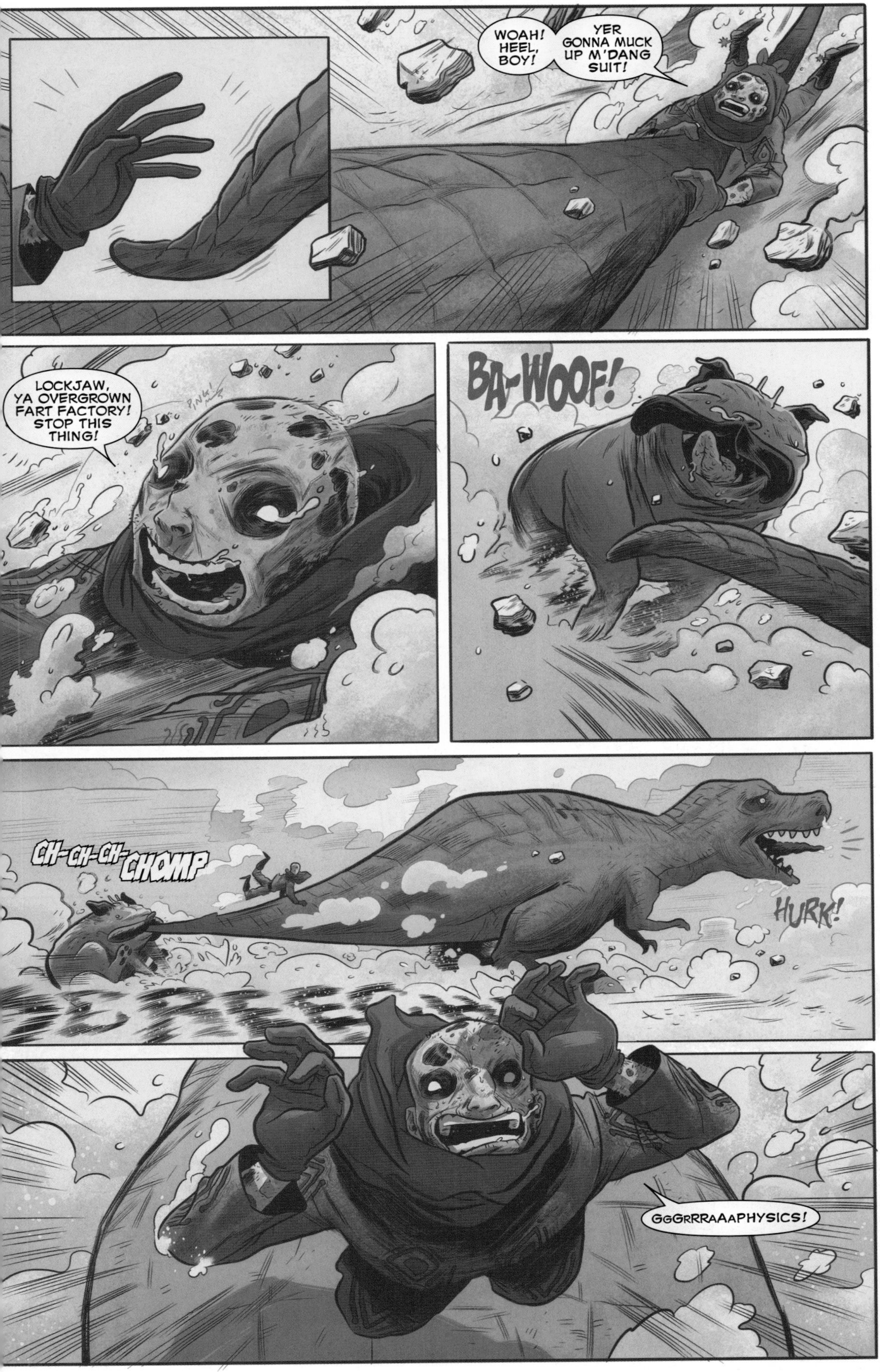
WOAH! HEEL, BOY!
YER GONNA MUCK UP M'DANG SUIT!
LOCKJAW, YA OVERGROWN FART FACTORY! STOP THIS THING!
BA-WOOF!
CH-CH-CH-CHOMP
HURK!
GGGRRRAAAPHYSICS!

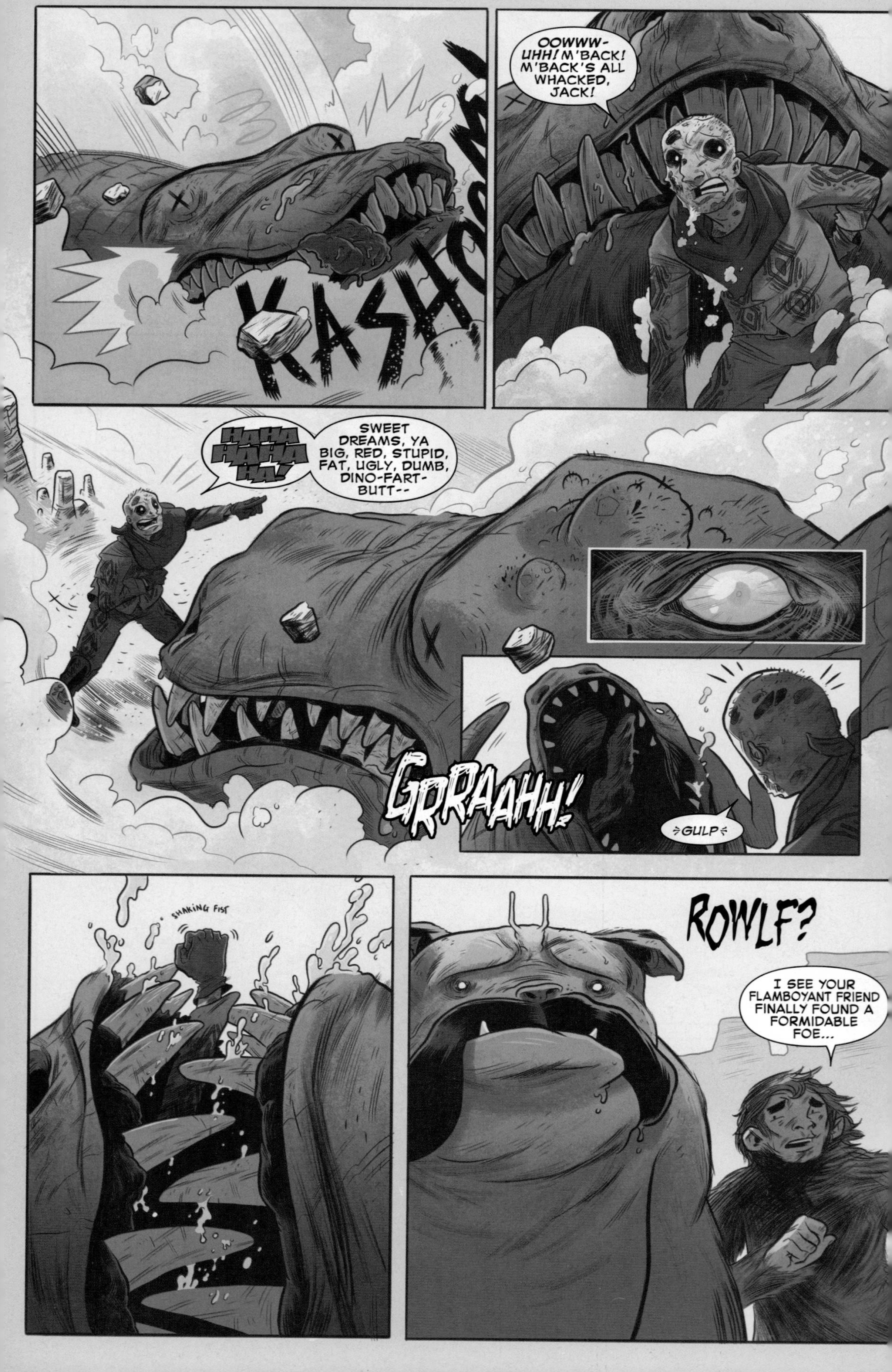
KASHOOM
OOWWW-UHH! M'BACK! M'BACK'S ALL WHACKED, JACK!
HAHA HAHAHA HA!
SWEET DREAMS, YA BIG, RED, STUPID, FAT, UGLY, DUMB, DINO-FART-BUTT--
GRRAAHH!
GULP
SHAKING FIST
ROWLF?
I SEE YOUR FLAMBOYANT FRIEND FINALLY FOUND A FORMIDABLE FOE...

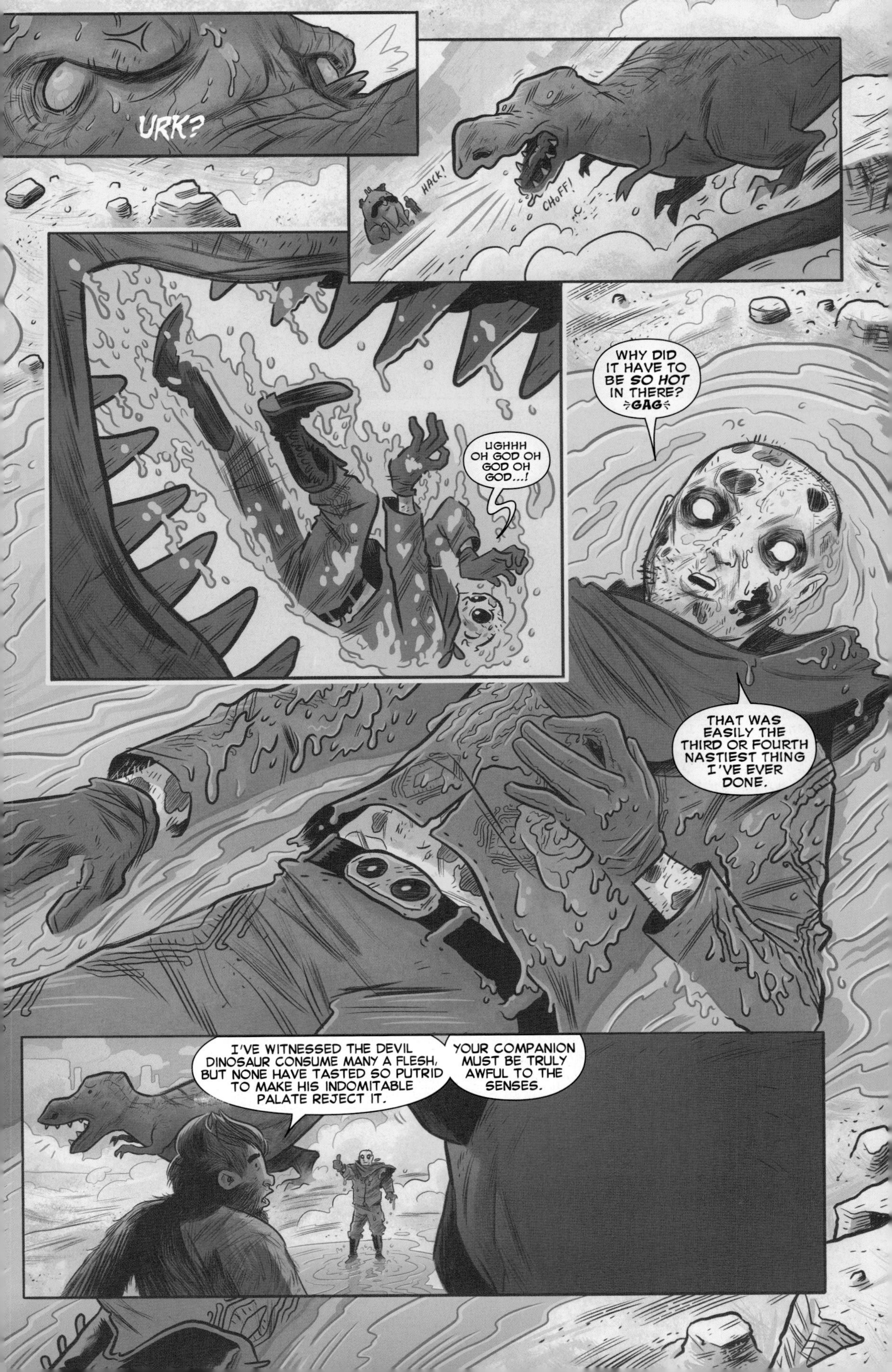
URK?
HACK!
CHOFF!
UGHHH OH GOD OH GOD OH GOD...!
WHY DID IT HAVE TO BE SO HOT IN THERE? GAG
THAT WAS EASILY THE THIRD OR FOURTH NASTIEST THING I'VE EVER DONE.
I'VE WITNESSED THE DEVIL DINOSAUR CONSUME MANY A FLESH, BUT NONE HAVE TASTED SO PUTRID TO MAKE HIS INDOMITABLE PALATE REJECT IT.
YOUR COMPANION MUST BE TRULY AWFUL TO THE SENSES.

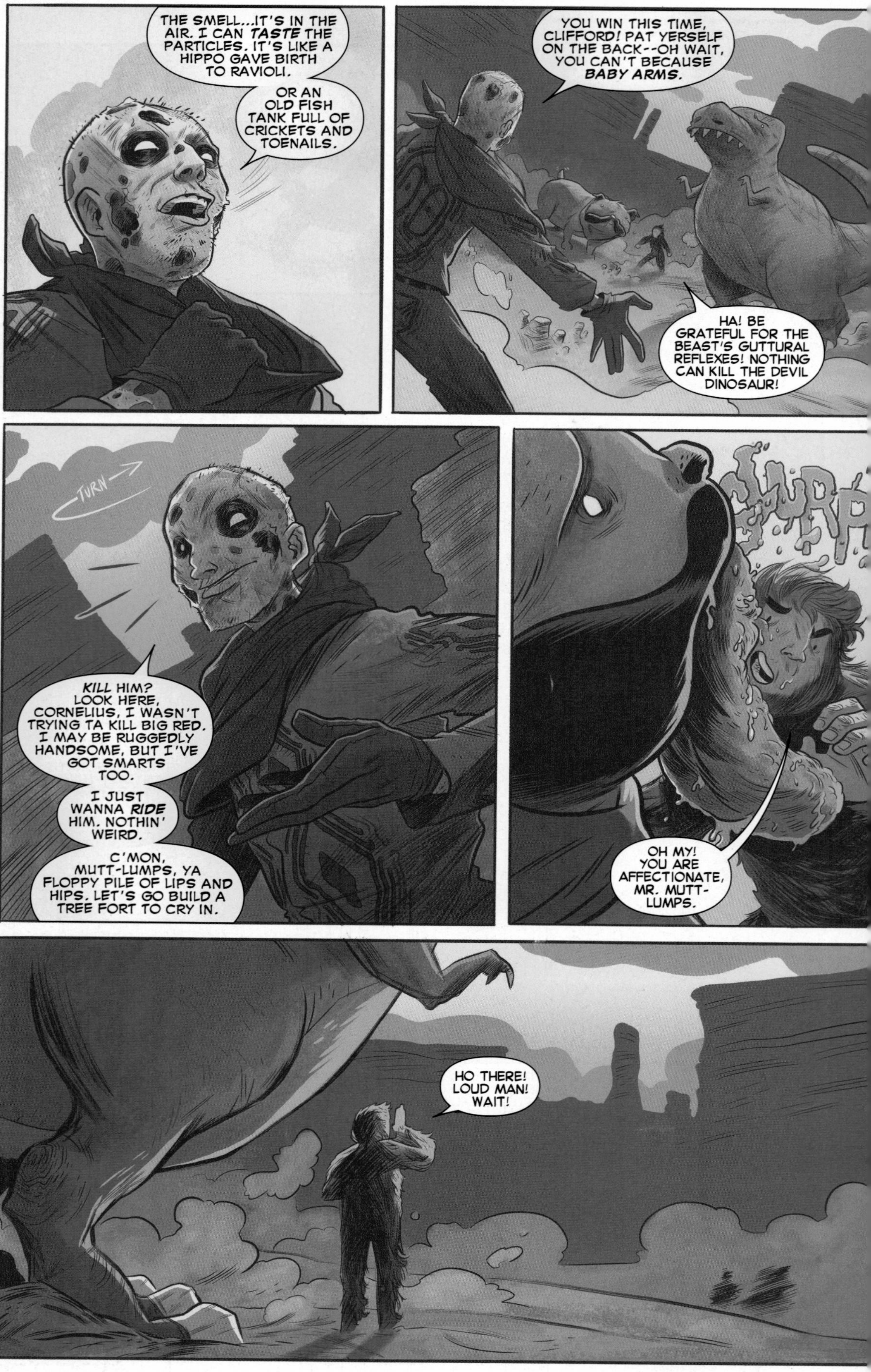
THE SMELL...IT'S IN THE AIR. I CAN TASTE THE PARTICLES. IT'S LIKE A HIPPO GAVE BIRTH TO RAVIOLI.
OR AN OLD FISH TANK FULL OF CRICKETS AND TOENAILS.
YOU WIN THIS TIME, CLIFFORD! PAT YERSELF ON THE BACK--OH WAIT, YOU CAN'T BECAUSE BABY ARMS.
HA! BE GRATEFUL FOR THE BEAST'S GUTTURAL REFLEXES! NOTHING CAN KILL THE DEVIL DINOSAUR!
TURN
KILL HIM? LOOK HERE, CORNELIUS, I WASN'T TRYING TA KILL BIG RED. I MAY BE RUGGEDLY HANDSOME, BUT I'VE GOT SMARTS TOO.
I JUST WANNA RIDE HIM. NOTHIN' WEIRD.
C'MON, MUTT-LUMPS, YA FLOPPY PILE OF LIPS AND HIPS. LET'S GO BUILD A TREE FORT TO CRY IN.
OH MY! YOU ARE AFFECTIONATE, MR. MUTT-LUMPS.
HO THERE! LOUD MAN! WAIT!

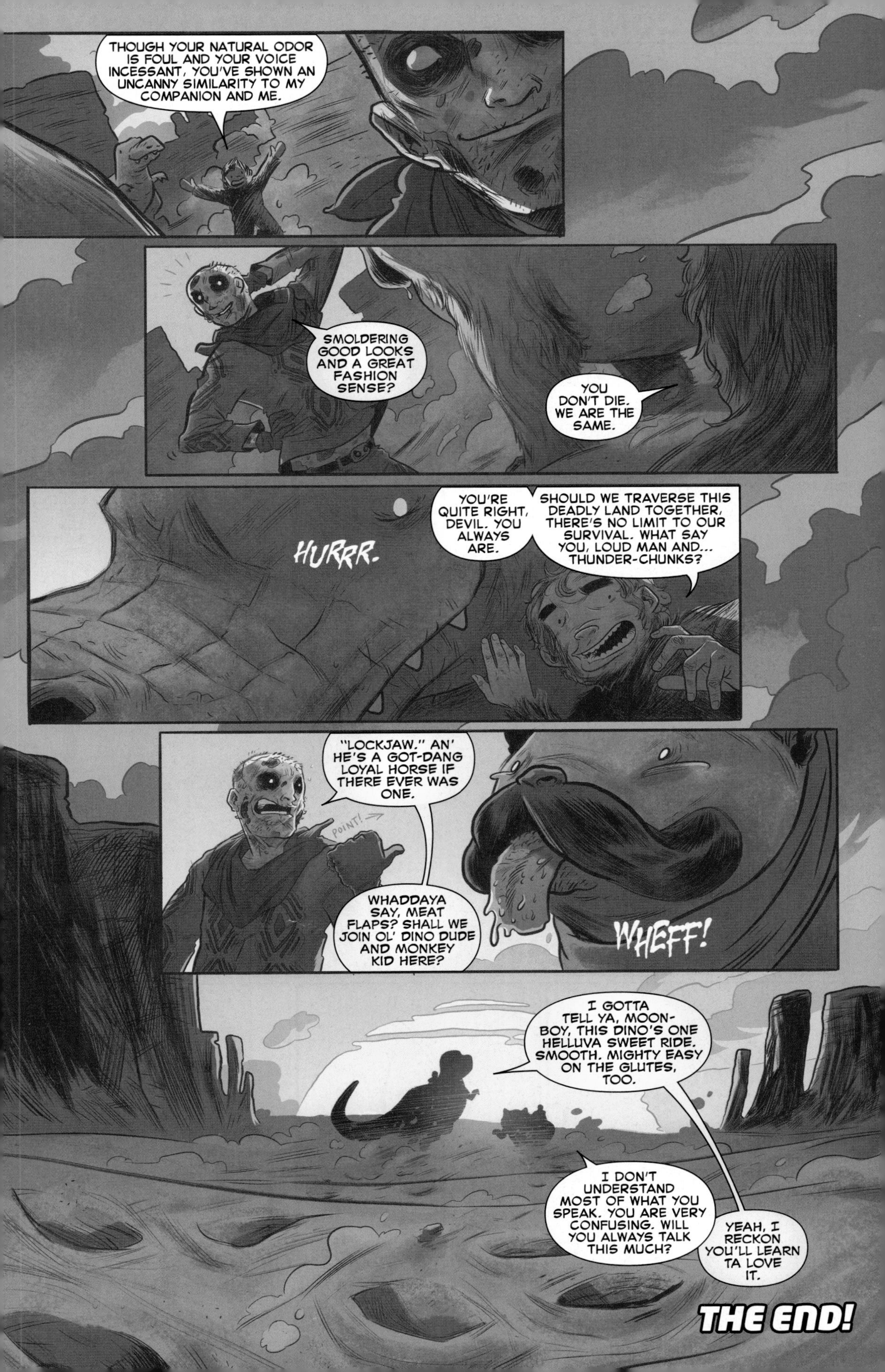
THOUGH YOUR NATURAL ODOR IS FOUL AND YOUR VOICE INCESSANT, YOU'VE SHOWN AN UNCANNY SIMILARITY TO MY COMPANION AND ME.
SMOLDERING GOOD LOOKS AND A GREAT FASHION SENSE?
YOU DON'T DIE. WE ARE THE SAME.
HURRR.
YOU'RE QUITE RIGHT, DEVIL. YOU ALWAYS ARE.
SHOULD WE TRAVERSE THIS DEADLY LAND TOGETHER, THERE'S NO LIMIT TO OUR SURVIVAL. WHAT SAY YOU, LOUD MAN AND... THUNDER-CHUNKS?
"LOCKJAW." AN' HE'S A GOT-DANG LOYAL HORSE IF THERE EVER WAS ONE.
POINT!
WHADDAYA SAY, MEAT FLAPS? SHALL WE JOIN OL' DINO DUDE AND MONKEY KID HERE?
WHEFF!
I GOTTA TELL YA, MOON-BOY, THIS DINO'S ONE HELLUVA SWEET RIDE. SMOOTH. MIGHTY EASY ON THE GLUTES, TOO.
I DON'T UNDERSTAND MOST OF WHAT YOU SPEAK. YOU ARE VERY CONFUSING. WILL YOU ALWAYS TALK THIS MUCH?
YEAH, I RECKON YOU'LL LEARN TA LOVE IT.
THE END!

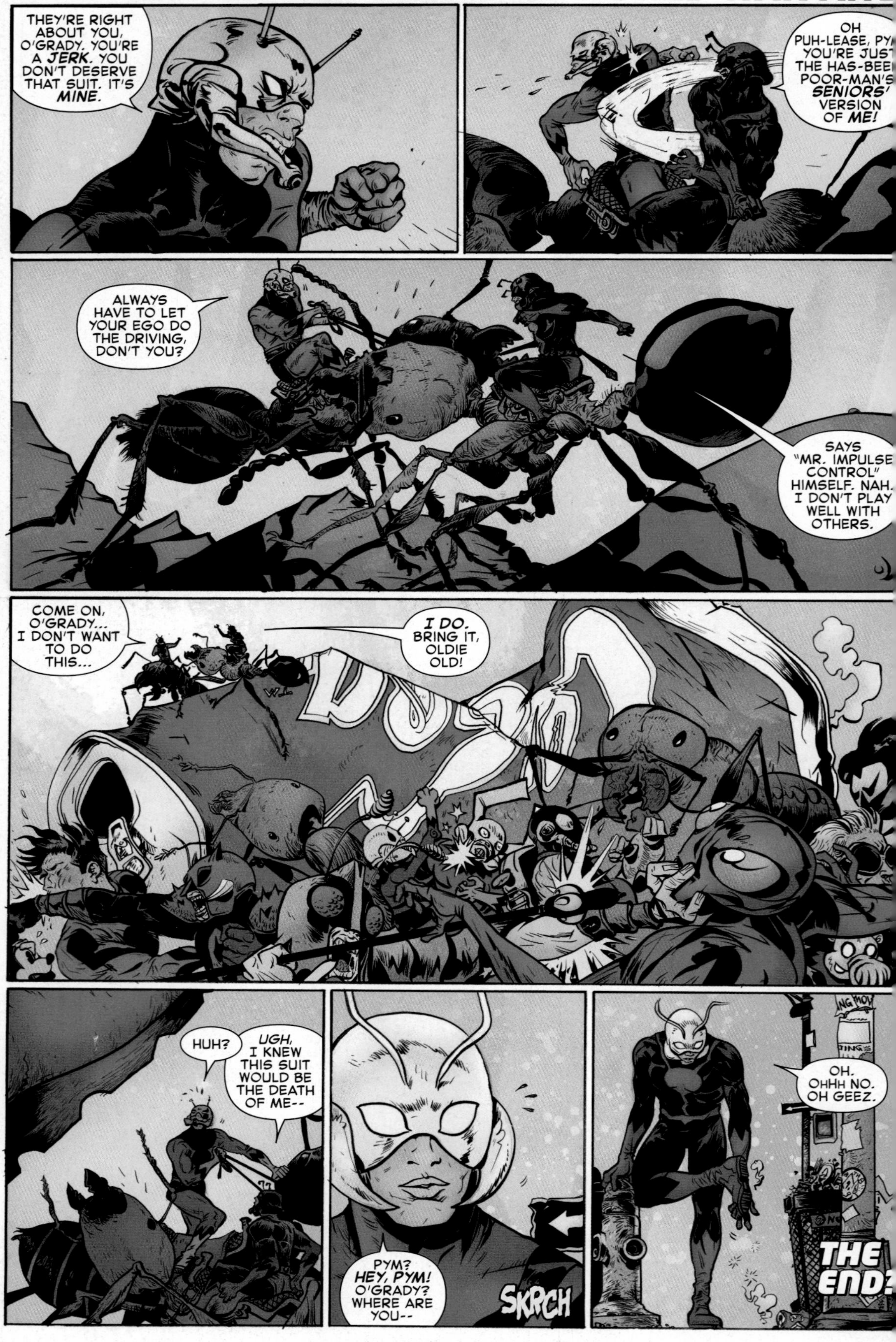
THEY'RE RIGHT ABOUT YOU, O'GRADY. YOU'RE A JERK. YOU DON'T DESERVE THAT SUIT. IT'S MINE.
OH PUH-LEASE, PY YOU'RE JUST THE HAS-BEE POOR-MAN'S SENIORS' VERSION OF ME!
ALWAYS HAVE TO LET YOUR EGO DO THE DRIVING, DON'T YOU?
SAYS "MR. IMPULSE CONTROL" HIMSELF. NAH. I DON'T PLAY WELL WITH OTHERS.
COME ON, O'GRADY... I DON'T WANT TO DO THIS...
I DO. BRING IT, OLDIE OLD!
HUH?
UGH, I KNEW THIS SUIT WOULD BE THE DEATH OF ME--
PYM? HEY, PYM! O'GRADY? WHERE ARE YOU--
SKRCH
OH. OHHH NO. OH GEEZ.
THE END

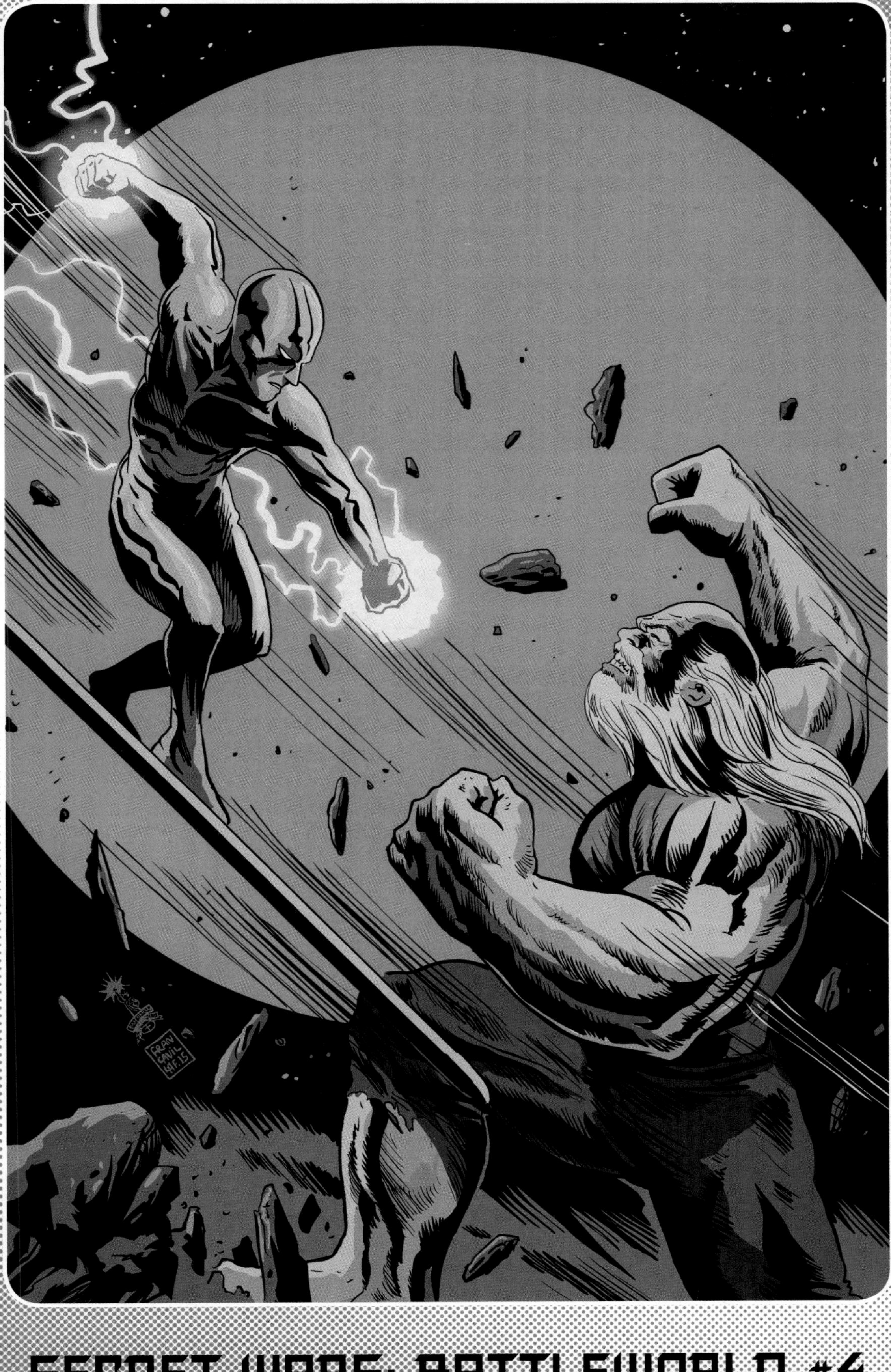

SECRET WARS: BATTLEWORLD #4

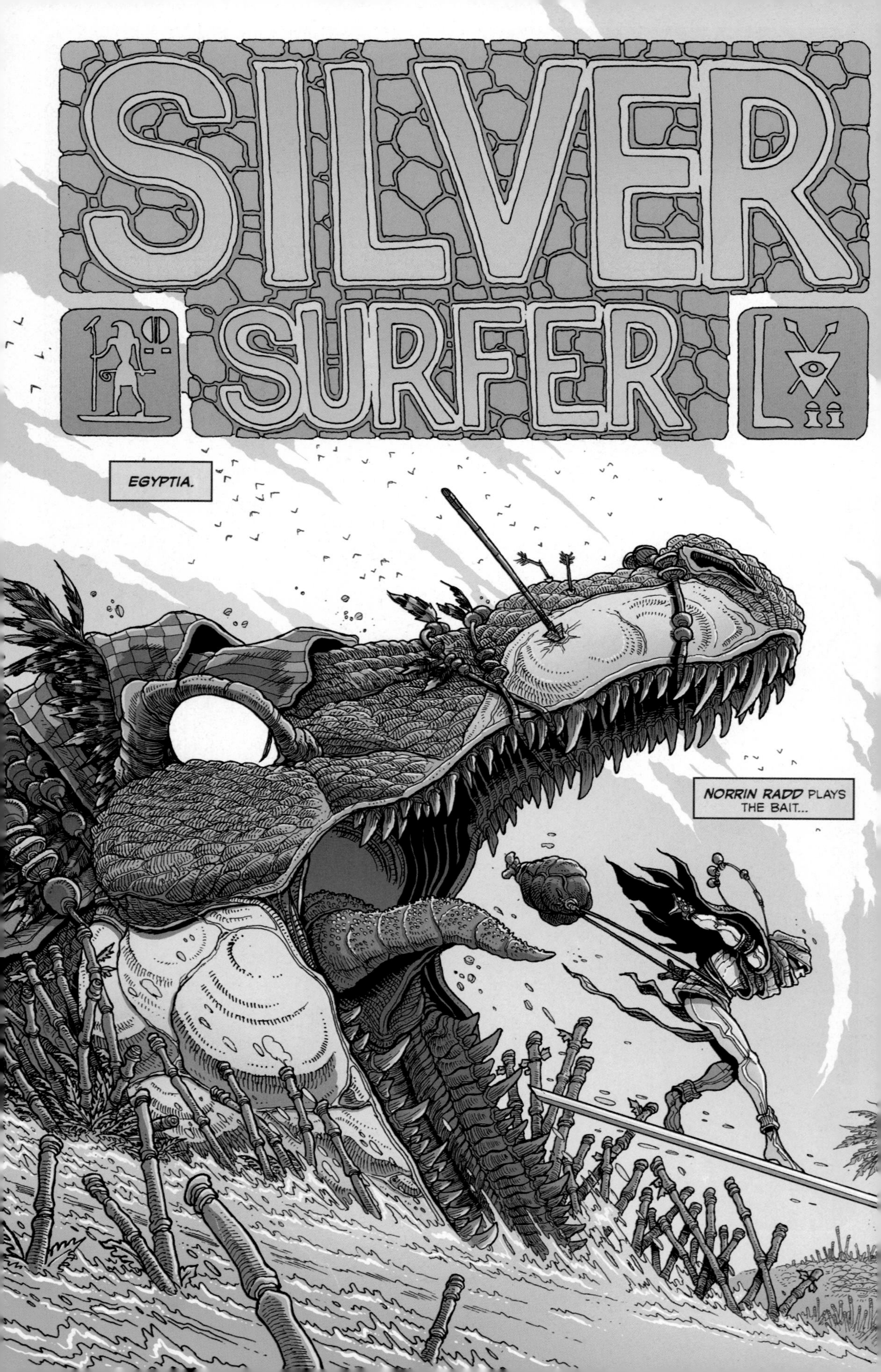
SILVER SURFER
EGYPTIA.
NORRIN RADD PLAYS THE BAIT...

...THE *BEAST* FOLLOWS.

THIS RIVER BANK BELONGS TO THE GREAT *FIN FANG FOOM; EATER-OF-A-THOUSAND.*

THE LOCAL FERRYMEN LEARNED A LONG TIME AGO TO GIVE THIS STRETCH OF THE *NILE* A WIDE BERTH, KNOWING THE TERRIBLE CROC WOULD ALWAYS EXACT ITS TOLL.

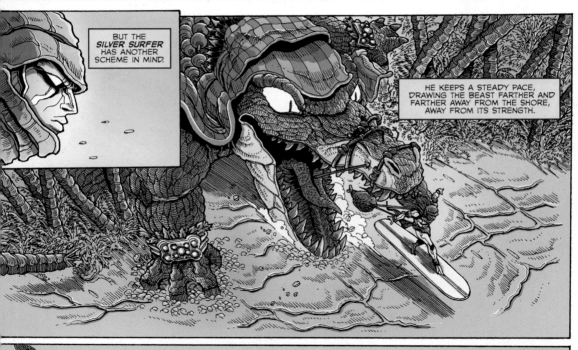

BUT THE *SILVER SURFER* HAS ANOTHER SCHEME IN MIND.

HE KEEPS A STEADY PACE, DRAWING THE BEAST FARTHER AND FARTHER AWAY FROM THE SHORE, AWAY FROM ITS STRENGTH.

THE DEEP SAND SLOWS THE MONSTER, BUT STILL IT CHASES.

THE ALLURE OF THIS STRANGE SILVERED MEAT IS TOO STRONG TO RESIST.

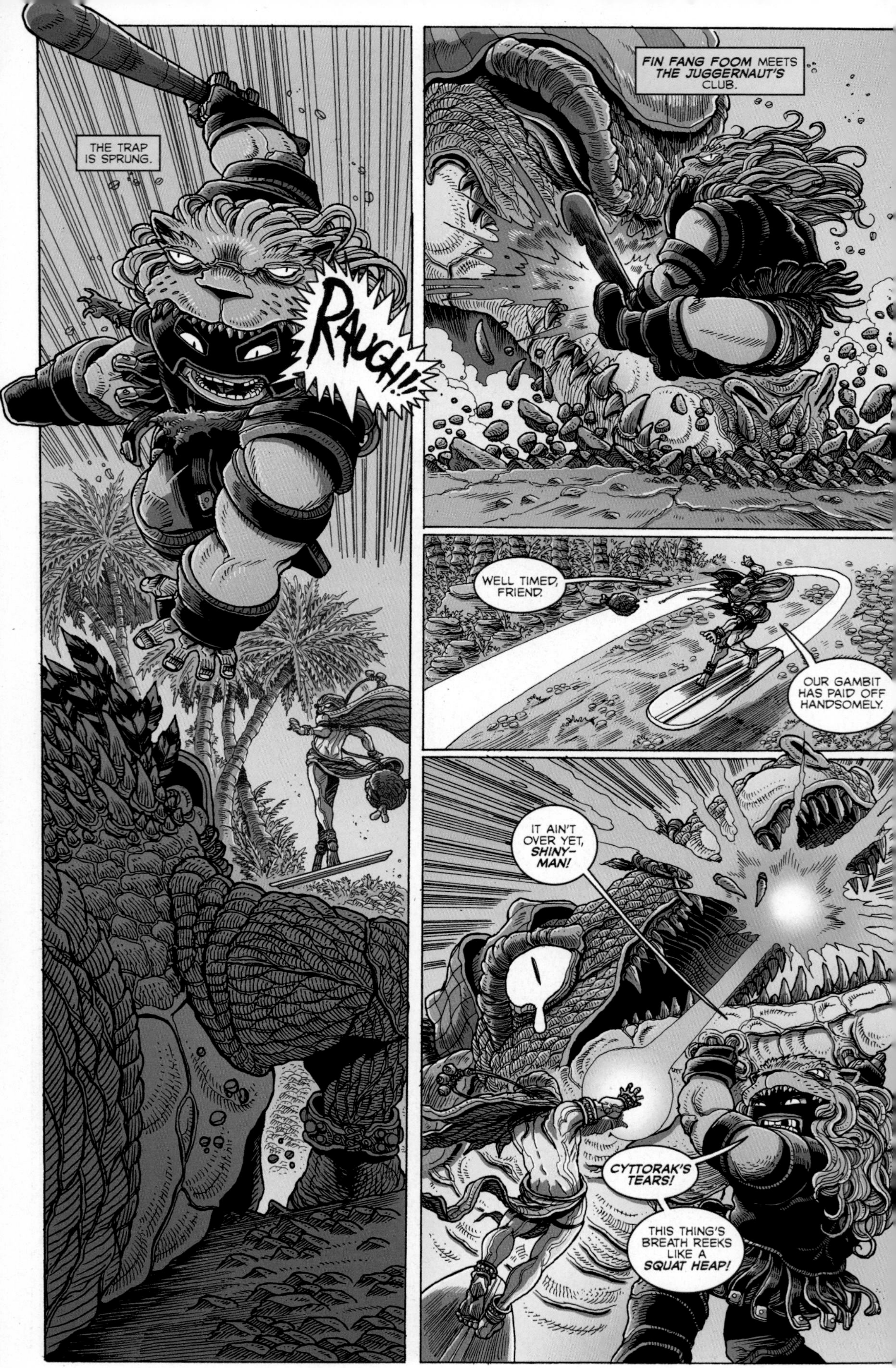
THE TRAP IS SPRUNG.
RAUGH!!!
FIN FANG FOOM MEETS THE JUGGERNAUT'S CLUB.
WELL TIMED, FRIEND.
OUR GAMBIT HAS PAID OFF HANDSOMELY.
IT AIN'T OVER YET, SHINY-MAN!
CYTTORAK'S TEARS!
THIS THING'S BREATH REEKS LIKE A SQUAT HEAP!

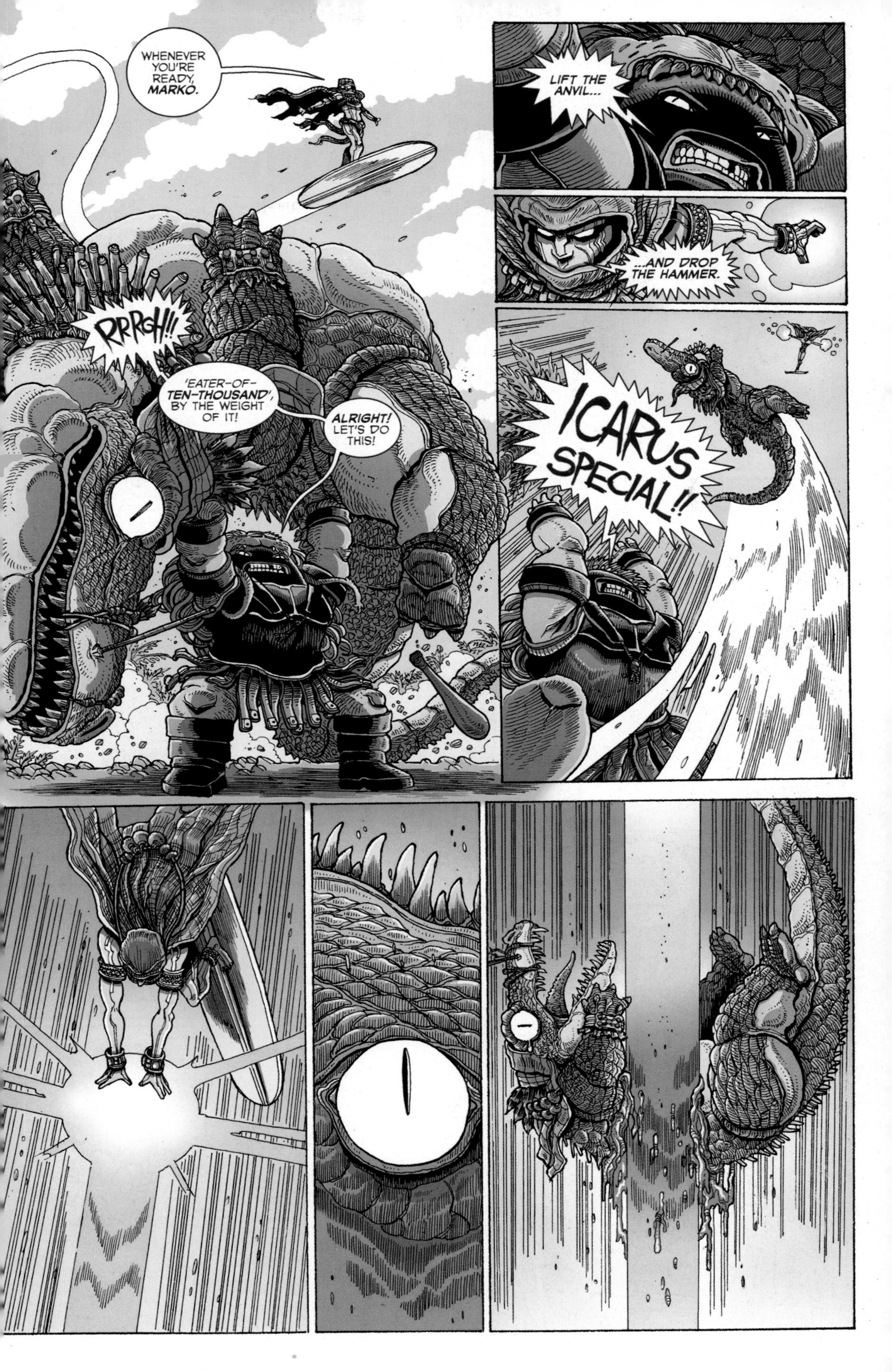
WHENEVER YOU'RE READY, MARKO.
RRRGH!!
'EATER-OF-TEN-THOUSAND', BY THE WEIGHT OF IT!
ALRIGHT! LET'S DO THIS!
LIFT THE ANVIL...
...AND DROP THE HAMMER.
ICARUS SPECIAL!!

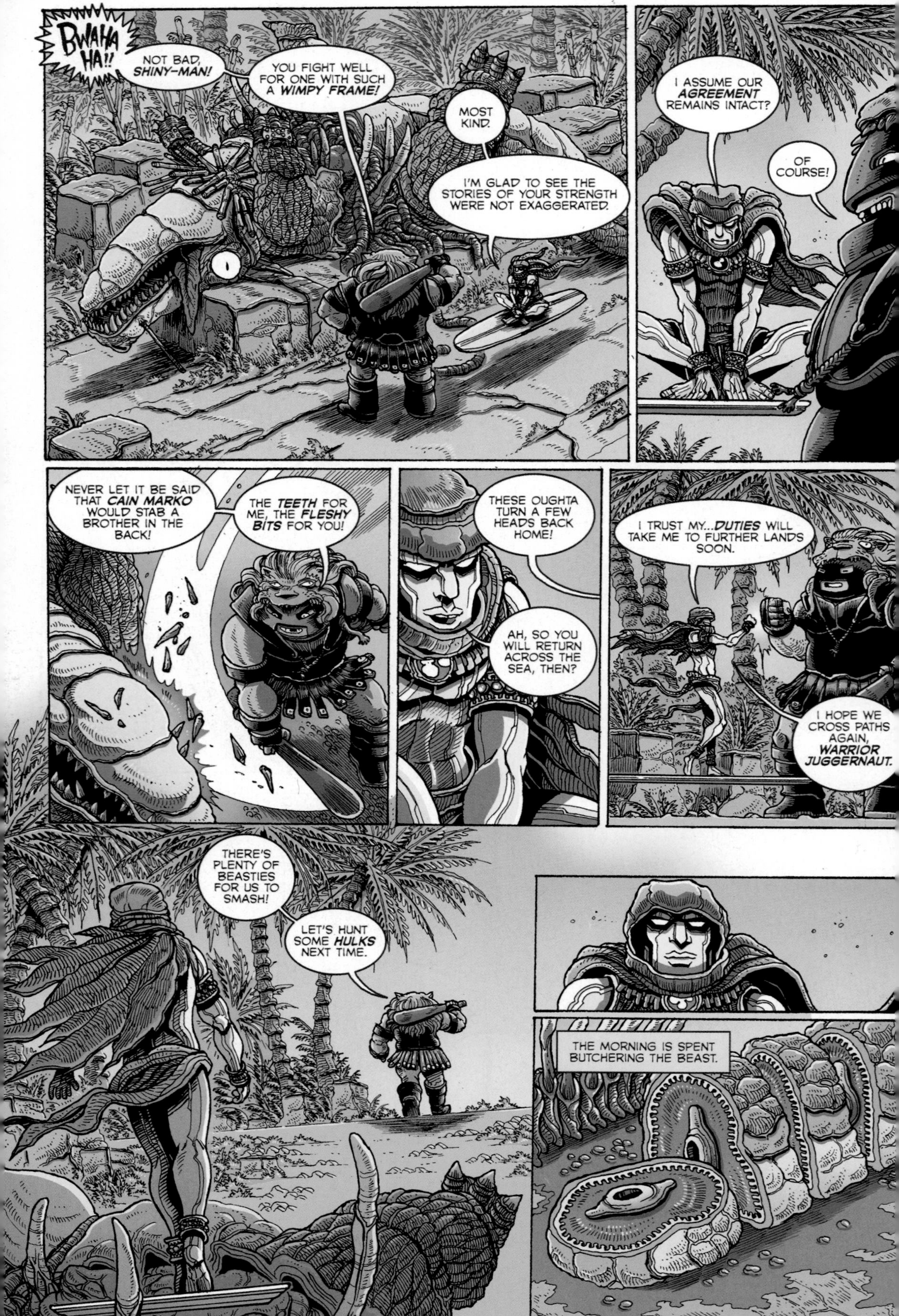

BWAHA HA!!
NOT BAD, SHINY-MAN!
YOU FIGHT WELL FOR ONE WITH SUCH A WIMPY FRAME!
MOST KIND.
I'M GLAD TO SEE THE STORIES OF YOUR STRENGTH WERE NOT EXAGGERATED.
I ASSUME OUR AGREEMENT REMAINS INTACT?
OF COURSE!
NEVER LET IT BE SAID THAT CAIN MARKO WOULD STAB A BROTHER IN THE BACK!
THE TEETH FOR ME, THE FLESHY BITS FOR YOU!
THESE OUGHTA TURN A FEW HEADS BACK HOME!
AH, SO YOU WILL RETURN ACROSS THE SEA, THEN?
I TRUST MY...DUTIES WILL TAKE ME TO FURTHER LANDS SOON.
I HOPE WE CROSS PATHS AGAIN, WARRIOR JUGGERNAUT.
THERE'S PLENTY OF BEASTIES FOR US TO SMASH!
LET'S HUNT SOME HULKS NEXT TIME.
THE MORNING IS SPENT BUTCHERING THE BEAST.

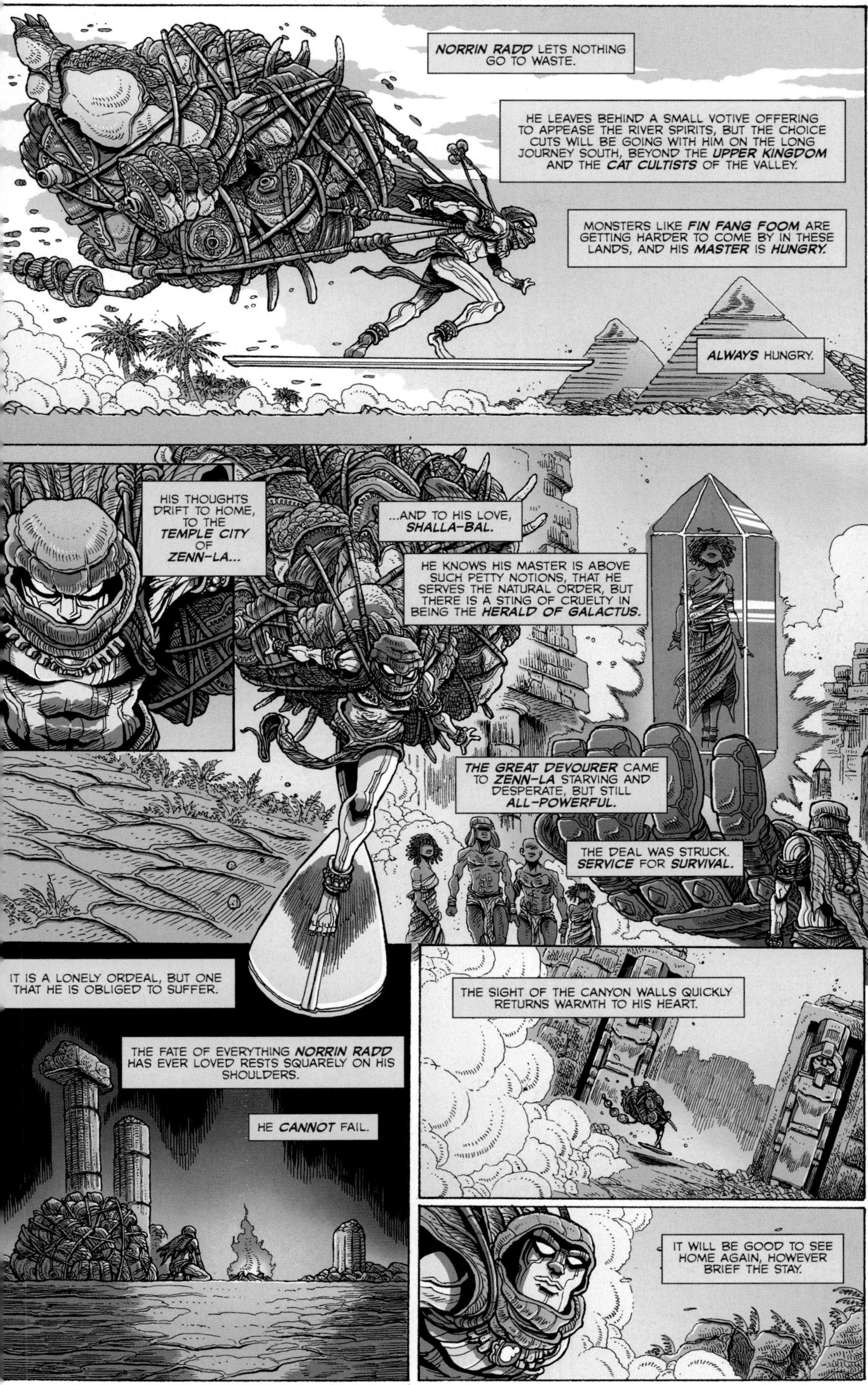
NORRIN RADD LETS NOTHING GO TO WASTE.
HE LEAVES BEHIND A SMALL VOTIVE OFFERING TO APPEASE THE RIVER SPIRITS, BUT THE CHOICE CUTS WILL BE GOING WITH HIM ON THE LONG JOURNEY SOUTH, BEYOND THE UPPER KINGDOM AND THE CAT CULTISTS OF THE VALLEY.
MONSTERS LIKE FIN FANG FOOM ARE GETTING HARDER TO COME BY IN THESE LANDS, AND HIS MASTER IS HUNGRY.
ALWAYS HUNGRY.
HIS THOUGHTS DRIFT TO HOME, TO THE TEMPLE CITY OF ZENN-LA...
...AND TO HIS LOVE, SHALLA-BAL.
HE KNOWS HIS MASTER IS ABOVE SUCH PETTY NOTIONS, THAT HE SERVES THE NATURAL ORDER, BUT THERE IS A STING OF CRUELTY IN BEING THE HERALD OF GALACTUS.
THE GREAT DEVOURER CAME TO ZENN-LA STARVING AND DESPERATE, BUT STILL ALL-POWERFUL.
THE DEAL WAS STRUCK. SERVICE FOR SURVIVAL.
IT IS A LONELY ORDEAL, BUT ONE THAT HE IS OBLIGED TO SUFFER.
THE FATE OF EVERYTHING NORRIN RADD HAS EVER LOVED RESTS SQUARELY ON HIS SHOULDERS.
HE CANNOT FAIL.
THE SIGHT OF THE CANYON WALLS QUICKLY RETURNS WARMTH TO HIS HEART.
IT WILL BE GOOD TO SEE HOME AGAIN, HOWEVER BRIEF THE STAY.

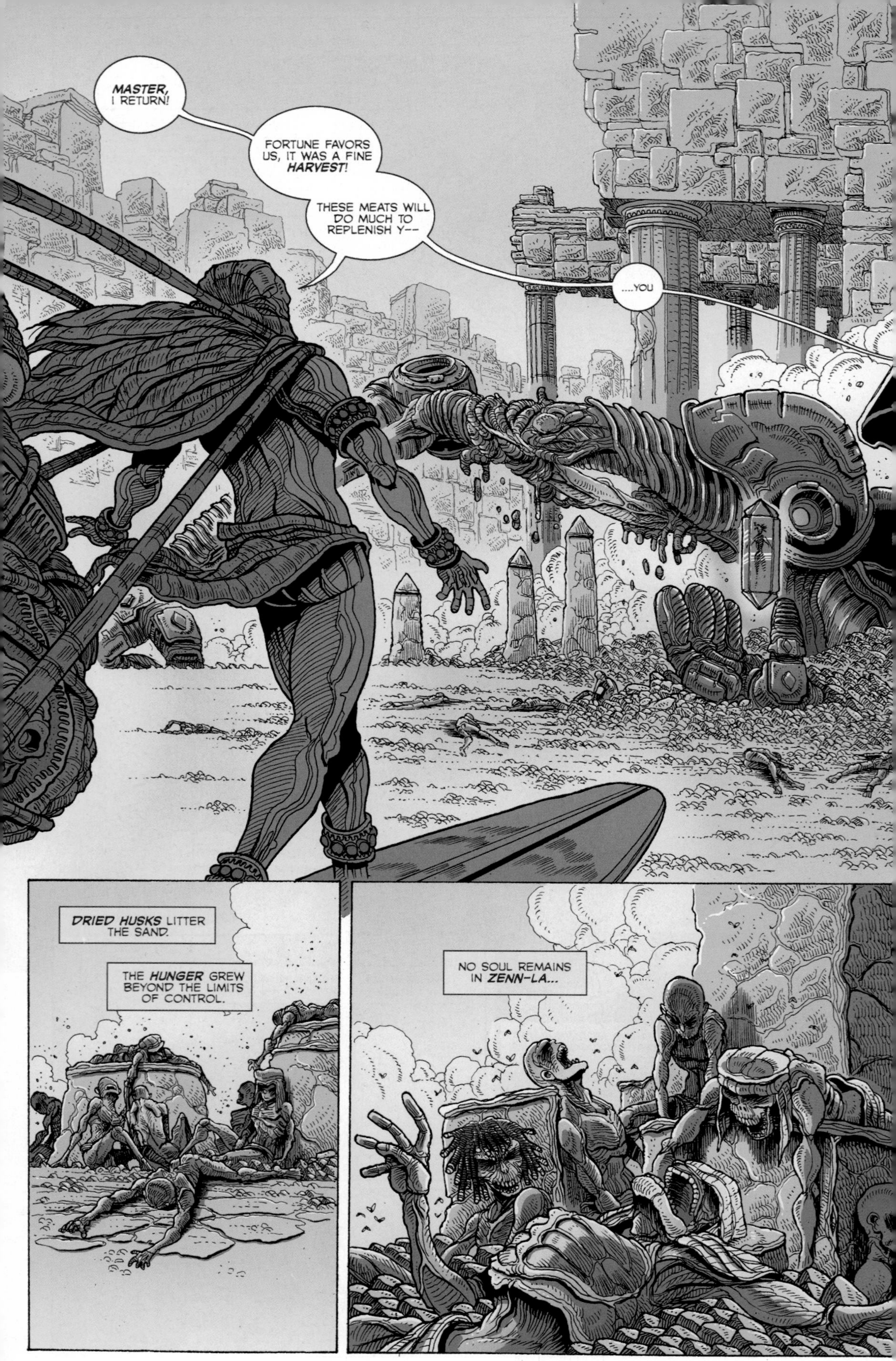
MASTER, I RETURN!
FORTUNE FAVORS US, IT WAS A FINE HARVEST!
THESE MEATS WILL DO MUCH TO REPLENISH Y--
....YOU
DRIED HUSKS LITTER THE SAND.
THE HUNGER GREW BEYOND THE LIMITS OF CONTROL.
NO SOUL REMAINS IN ZENN-LA...

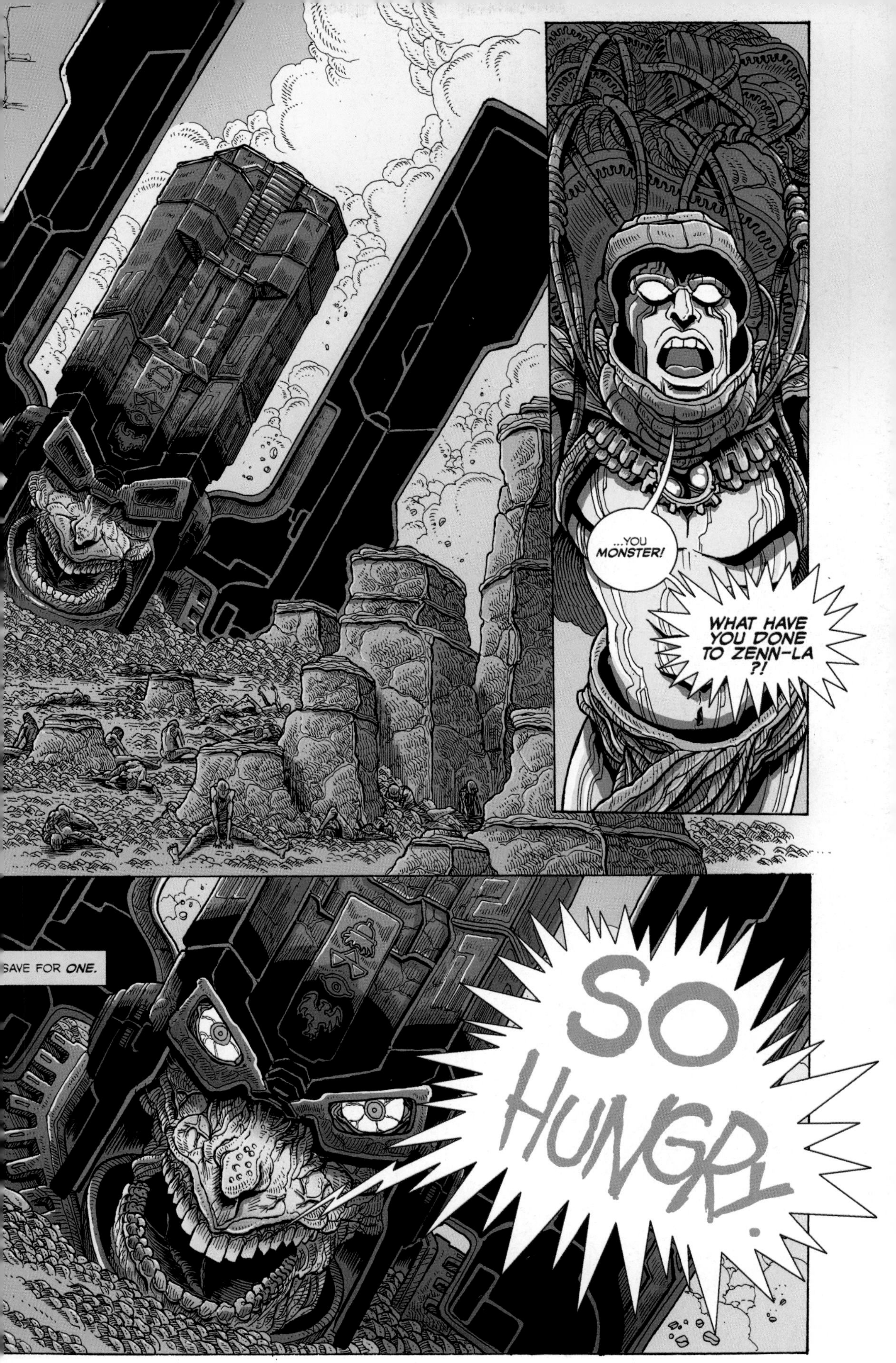
...YOU MONSTER!
WHAT HAVE YOU DONE TO ZENN-LA ?!
SAVE FOR ONE.
SO HUNGRY.

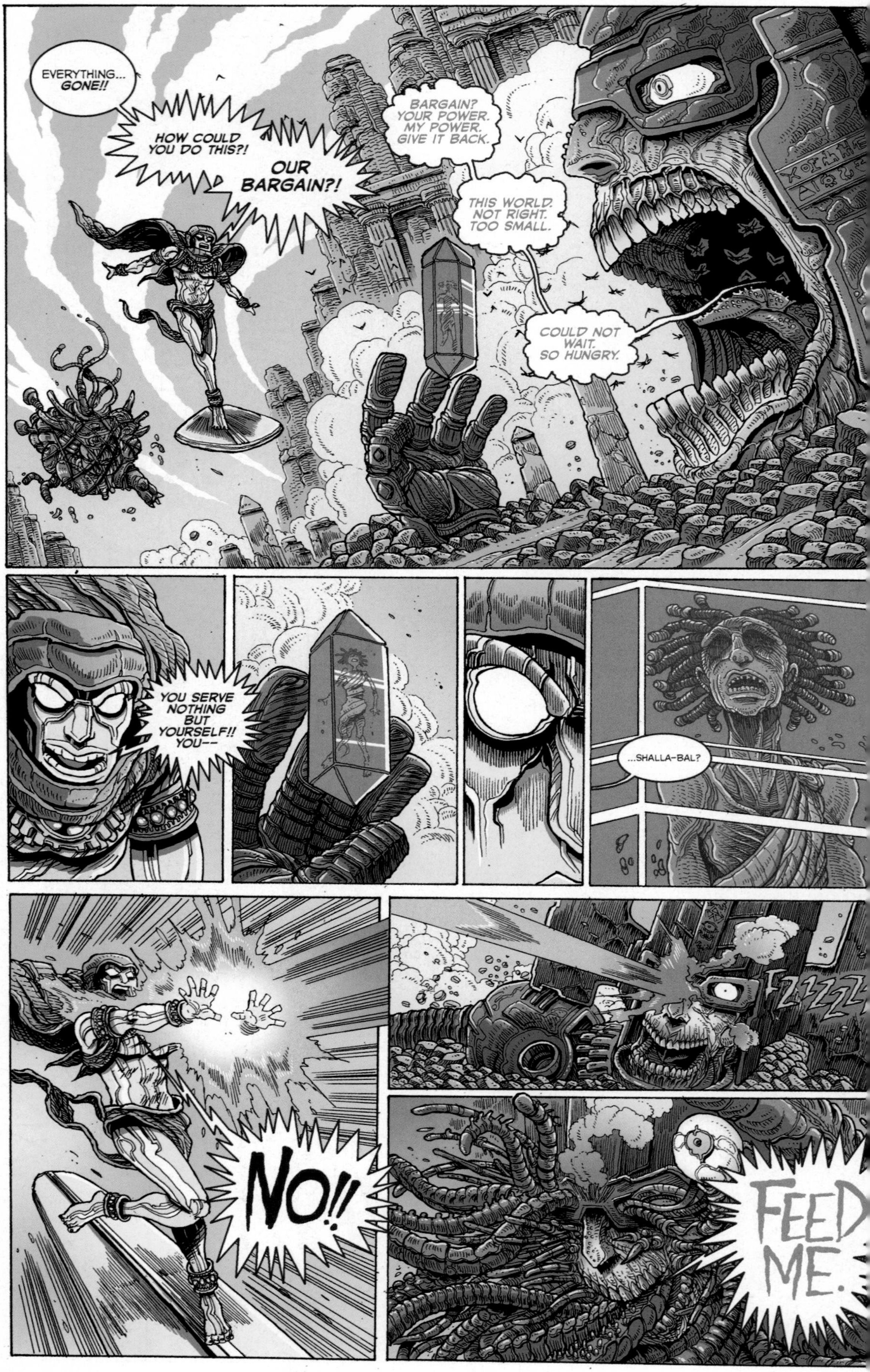
EVERYTHING... GONE!!
HOW COULD YOU DO THIS?!
OUR BARGAIN?!
BARGAIN? YOUR POWER. MY POWER. GIVE IT BACK.
THIS WORLD. NOT RIGHT. TOO SMALL.
COULD NOT WAIT. SO HUNGRY.
YOU SERVE NOTHING BUT YOURSELF!! YOU--
...SHALLA-BAL?
FZZZZZ
NO!!
FEED ME.

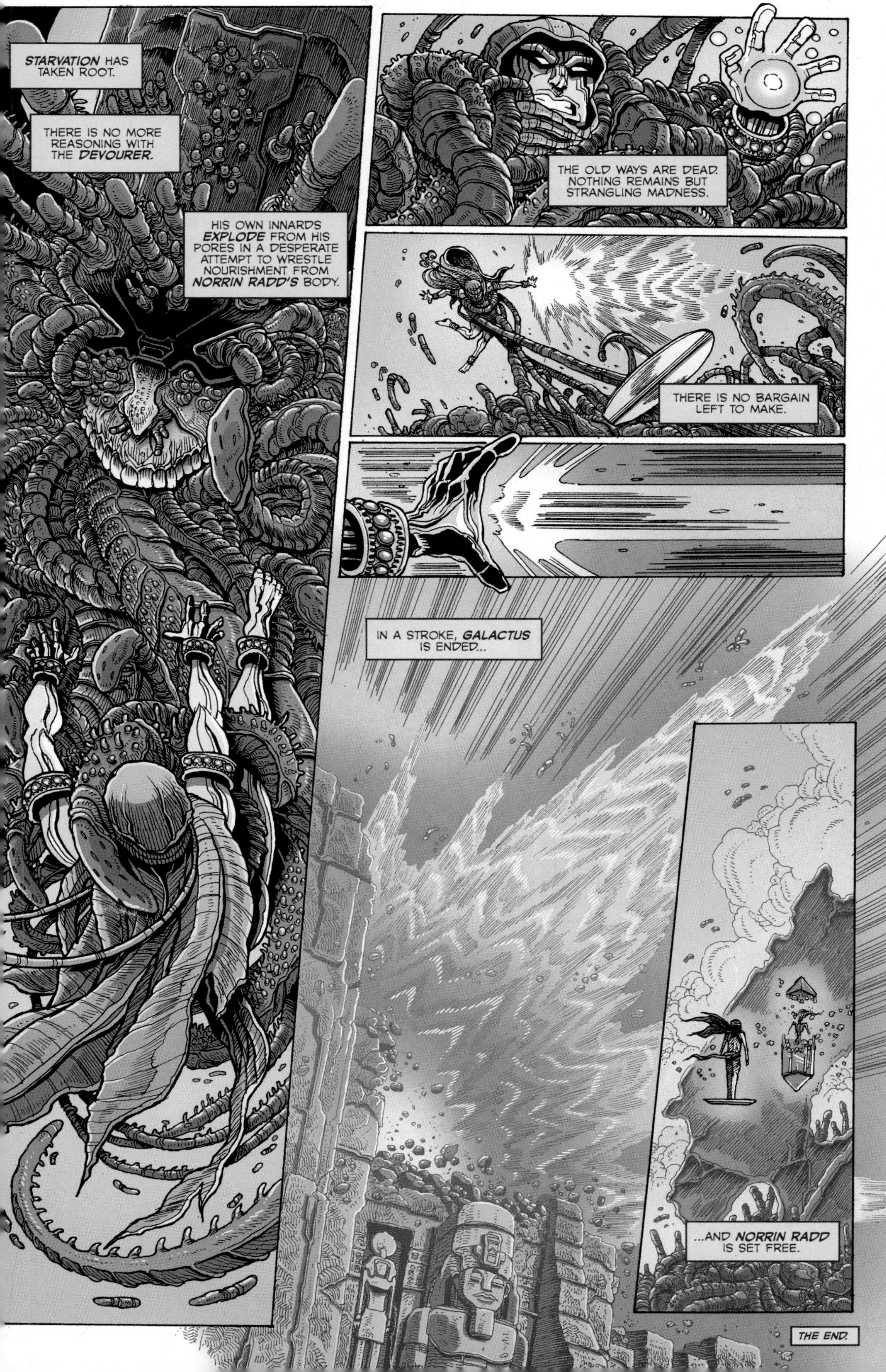
STARVATION HAS TAKEN ROOT.
THERE IS NO MORE REASONING WITH THE DEVOURER.
HIS OWN INNARDS EXPLODE FROM HIS PORES IN A DESPERATE ATTEMPT TO WRESTLE NOURISHMENT FROM NORRIN RADD'S BODY.
THE OLD WAYS ARE DEAD. NOTHING REMAINS BUT STRANGLING MADNESS.
THERE IS NO BARGAIN LEFT TO MAKE.
IN A STROKE, GALACTUS IS ENDED...
...AND NORRIN RADD IS SET FREE.
THE END.

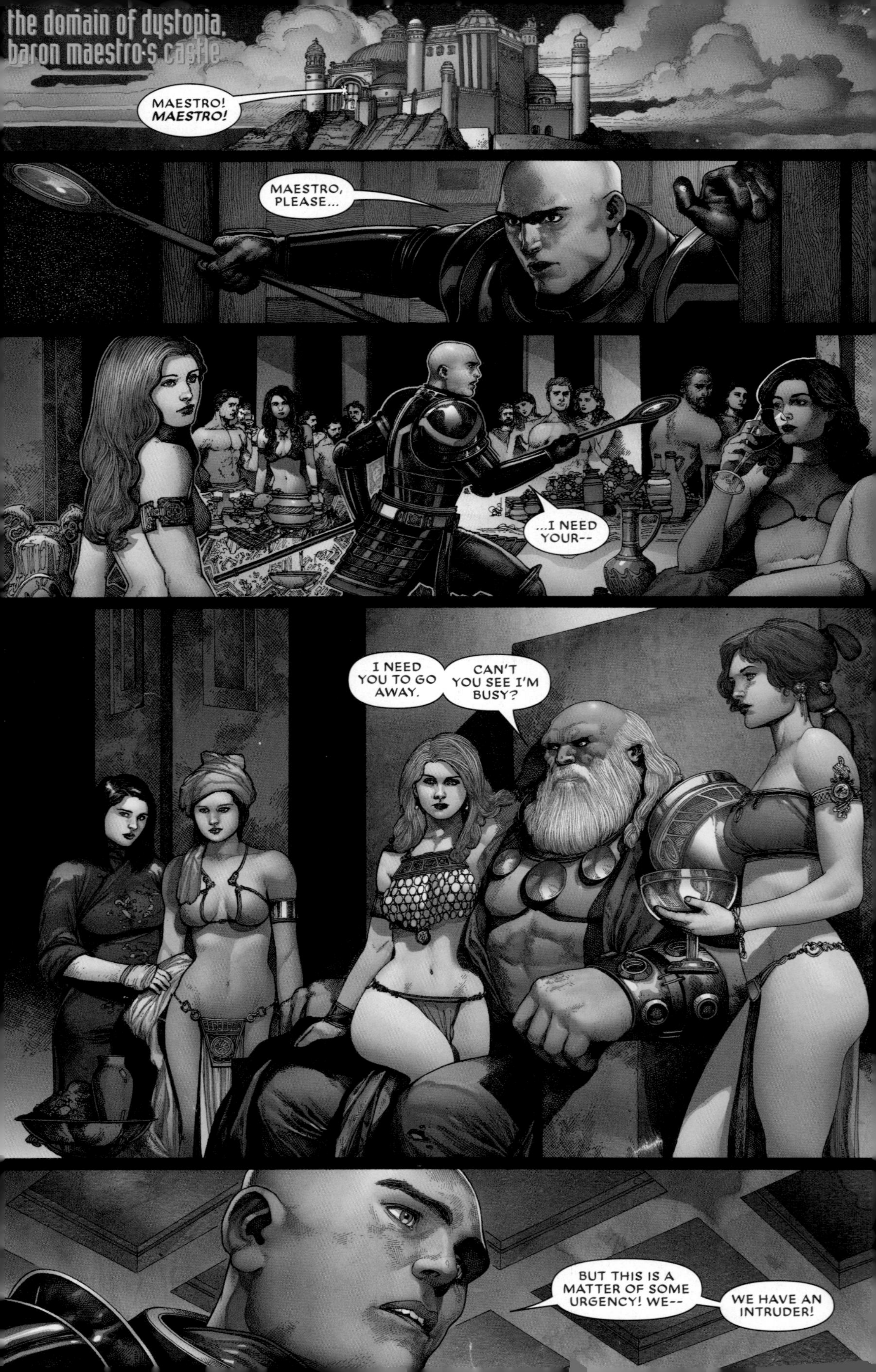
the domain of dystopia, baron maestro's castle
MAESTRO! MAESTRO!
MAESTRO, PLEASE...
...I NEED YOUR--
I NEED YOU TO GO AWAY.
CAN'T YOU SEE I'M BUSY?
BUT THIS IS A MATTER OF SOME URGENCY! WE--
WE HAVE AN INTRUDER!

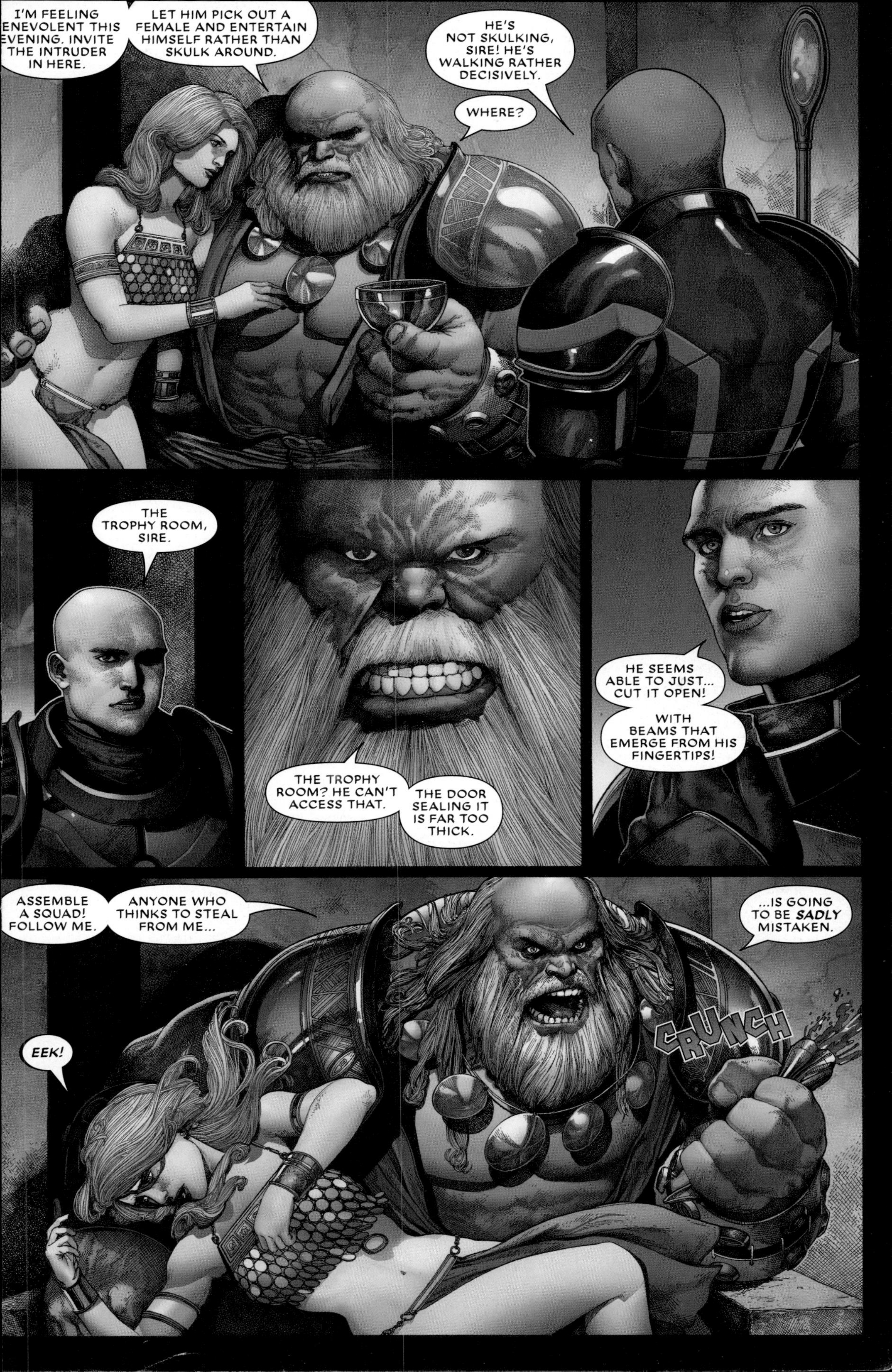
I'M FEELING BENEVOLENT THIS EVENING. INVITE THE INTRUDER IN HERE.
LET HIM PICK OUT A FEMALE AND ENTERTAIN HIMSELF RATHER THAN SKULK AROUND.
HE'S NOT SKULKING, SIRE! HE'S WALKING RATHER DECISIVELY.
WHERE?
THE TROPHY ROOM, SIRE.
THE TROPHY ROOM? HE CAN'T ACCESS THAT.
THE DOOR SEALING IT IS FAR TOO THICK.
HE SEEMS ABLE TO JUST... CUT IT OPEN!
WITH BEAMS THAT EMERGE FROM HIS FINGERTIPS!
ASSEMBLE A SQUAD! FOLLOW ME.
ANYONE WHO THINKS TO STEAL FROM ME...
...IS GOING TO BE SADLY MISTAKEN.
EEK!
CRUNCH

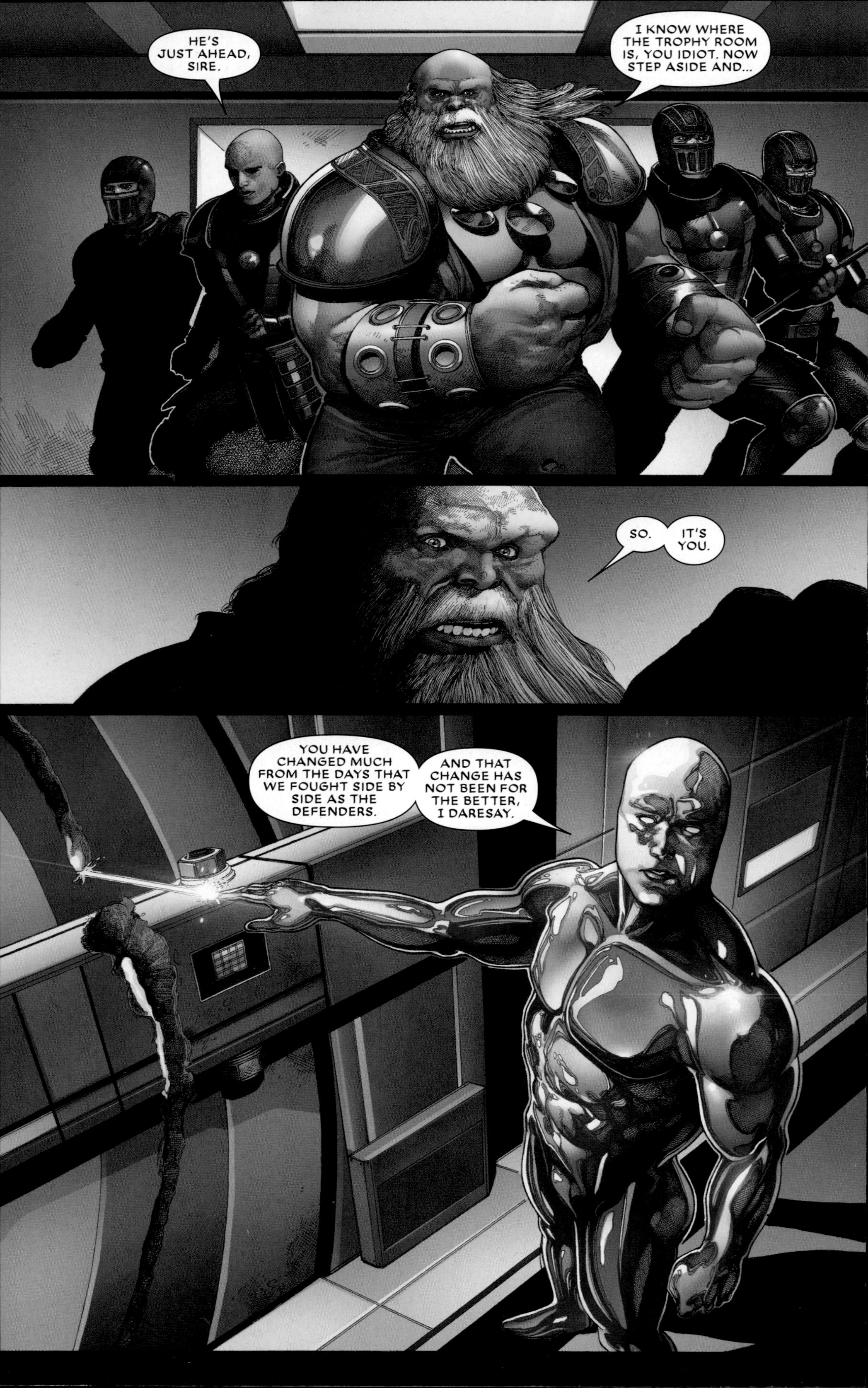
HE'S JUST AHEAD, SIRE.
I KNOW WHERE THE TROPHY ROOM IS, YOU IDIOT. NOW STEP ASIDE AND...
SO.
IT'S YOU.
YOU HAVE CHANGED MUCH FROM THE DAYS THAT WE FOUGHT SIDE BY SIDE AS THE DEFENDERS.
AND THAT CHANGE HAS NOT BEEN FOR THE BETTER, I DARESAY.

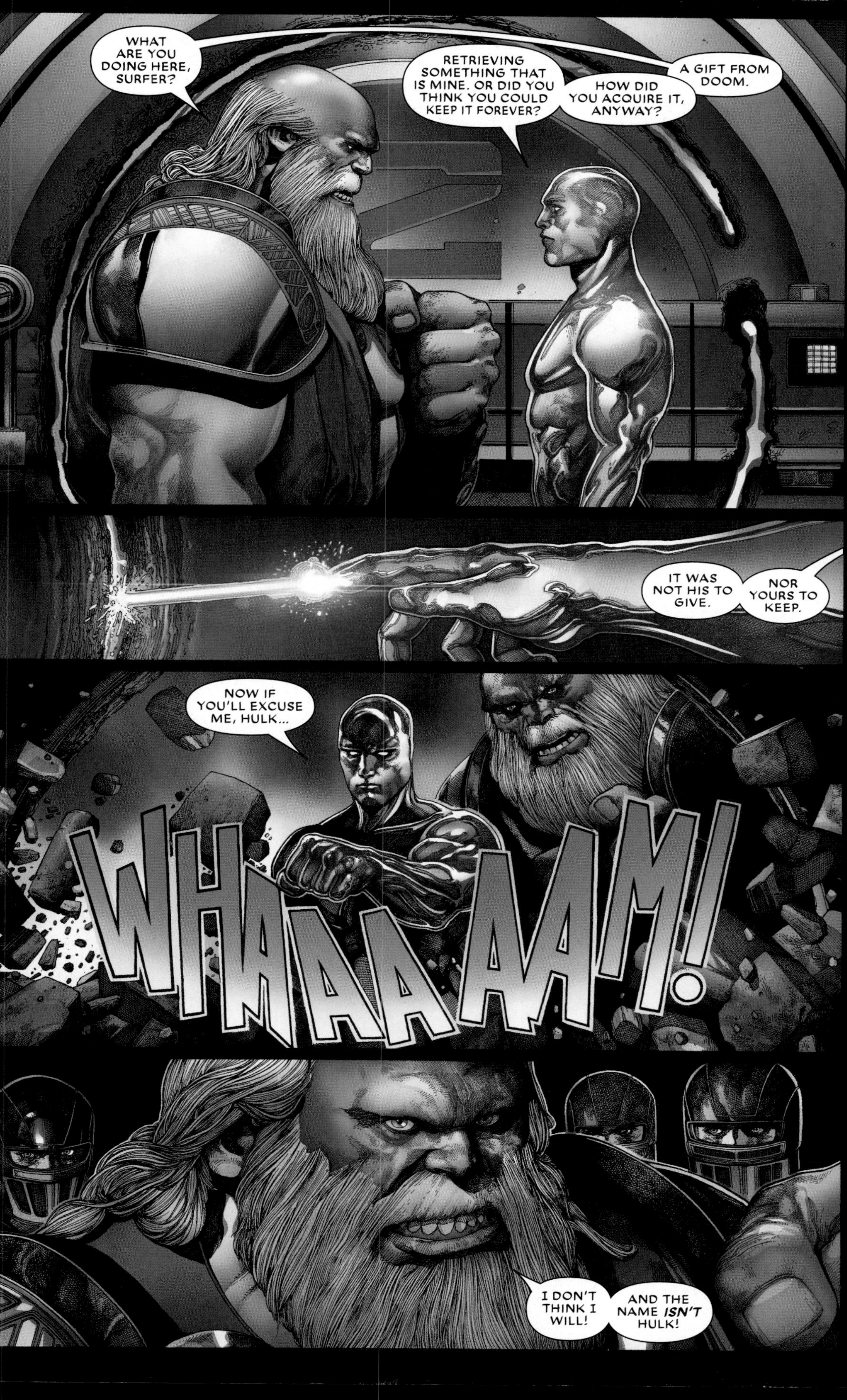
WHAT ARE YOU DOING HERE, SURFER?
RETRIEVING SOMETHING THAT IS MINE. OR DID YOU THINK YOU COULD KEEP IT FOREVER?
HOW DID YOU ACQUIRE IT, ANYWAY?
A GIFT FROM DOOM.
IT WAS NOT HIS TO GIVE.
NOR YOURS TO KEEP.
NOW IF YOU'LL EXCUSE ME, HULK...
WHAAAAAM!
I DON'T THINK I WILL!
AND THE NAME *ISN'T* HULK!

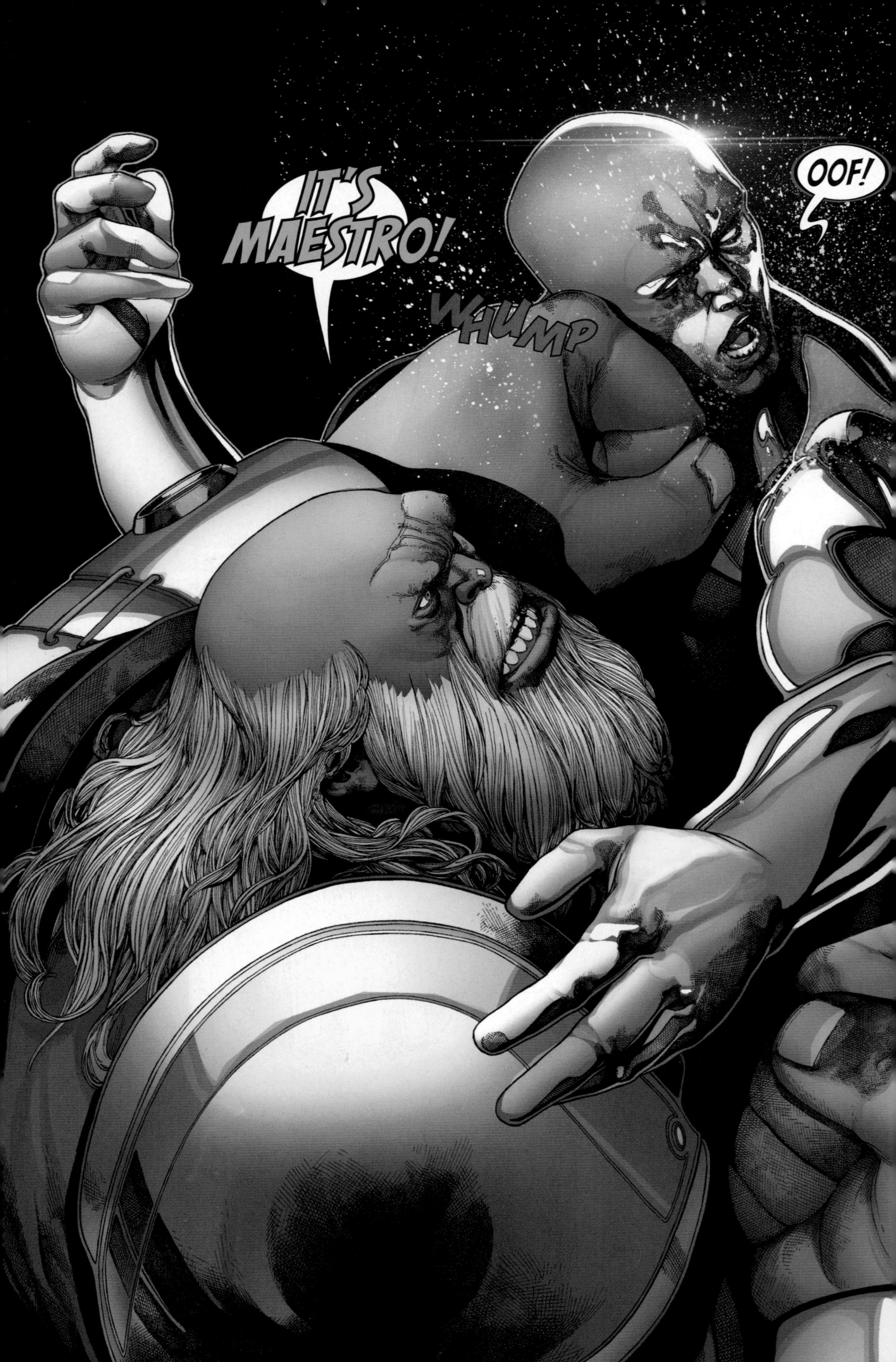
IT'S MAESTRO!
WHUMP
OOF!

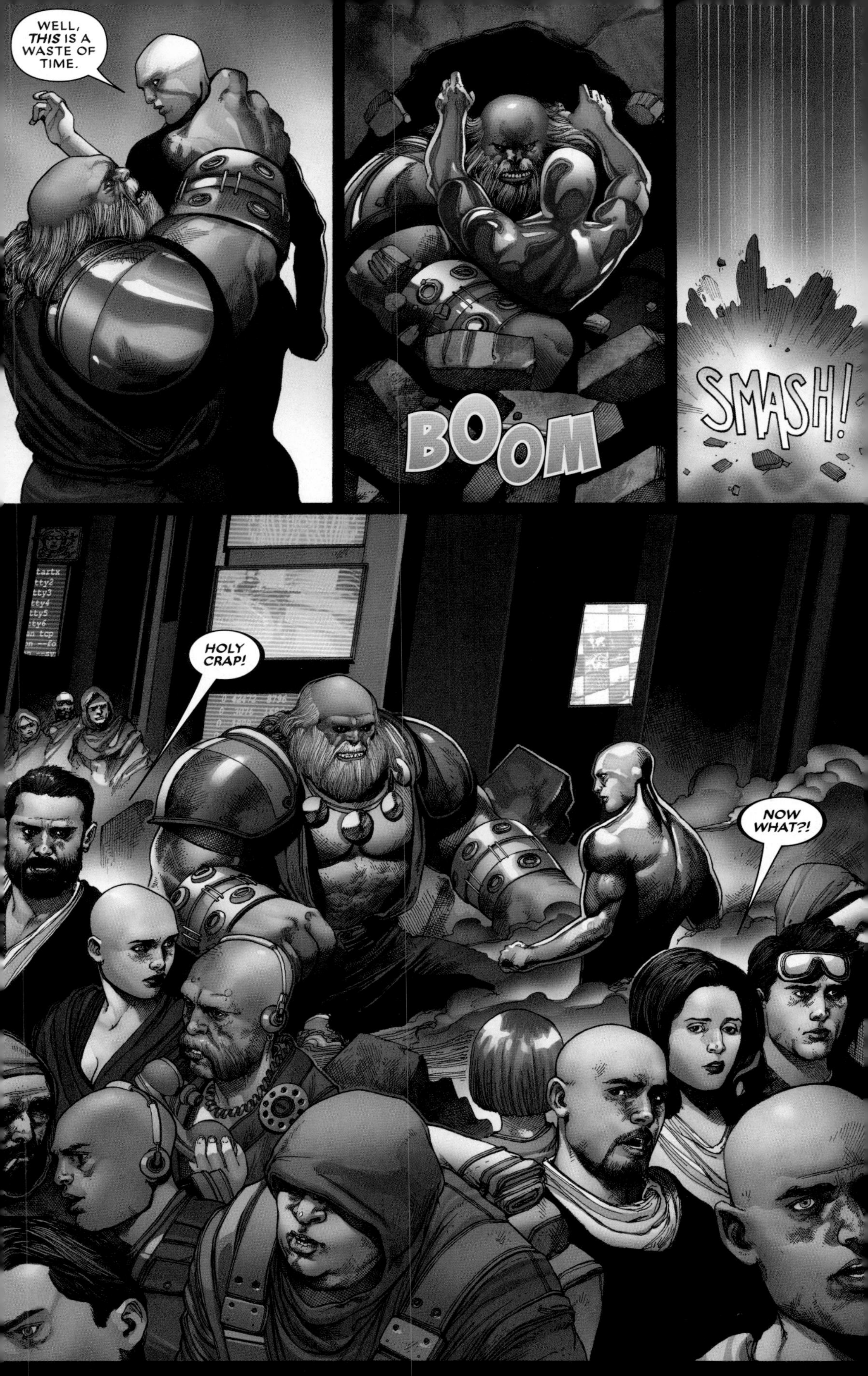
WELL, THIS IS A WASTE OF TIME.
BOOM
SMASH!
HOLY CRAP!
NOW WHAT?!

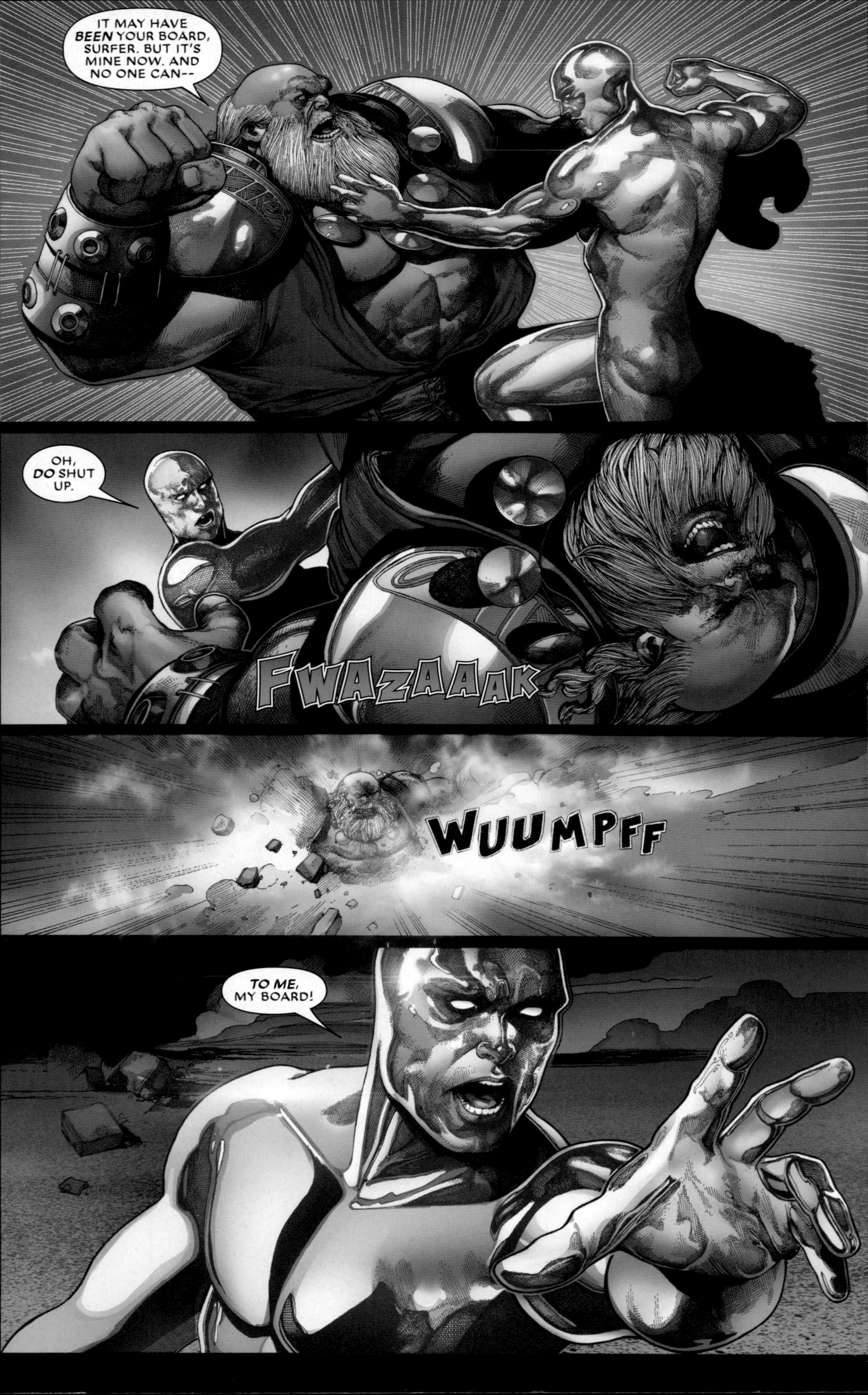
IT MAY HAVE *BEEN* YOUR BOARD, SURFER. BUT IT'S MINE NOW. AND NO ONE CAN--
OH, *DO* SHUT UP.
FWAZAAAK
WUUMPFF
TO ME, MY BOARD!

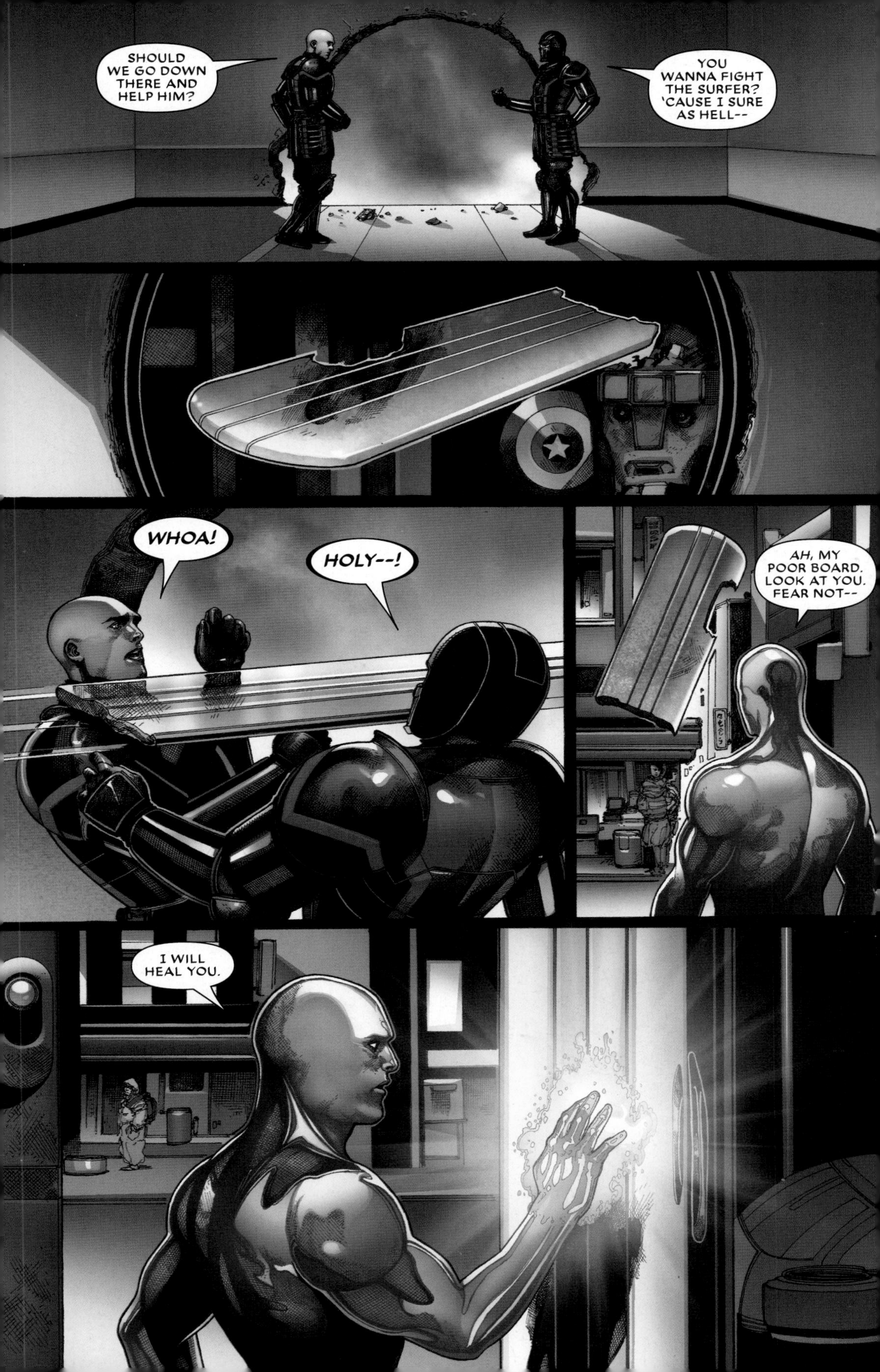
SHOULD WE GO DOWN THERE AND HELP HIM?
YOU WANNA FIGHT THE SURFER? 'CAUSE I SURE AS HELL--
WHOA!
HOLY--!
AH, MY POOR BOARD. LOOK AT YOU. FEAR NOT--
I WILL HEAL YOU.

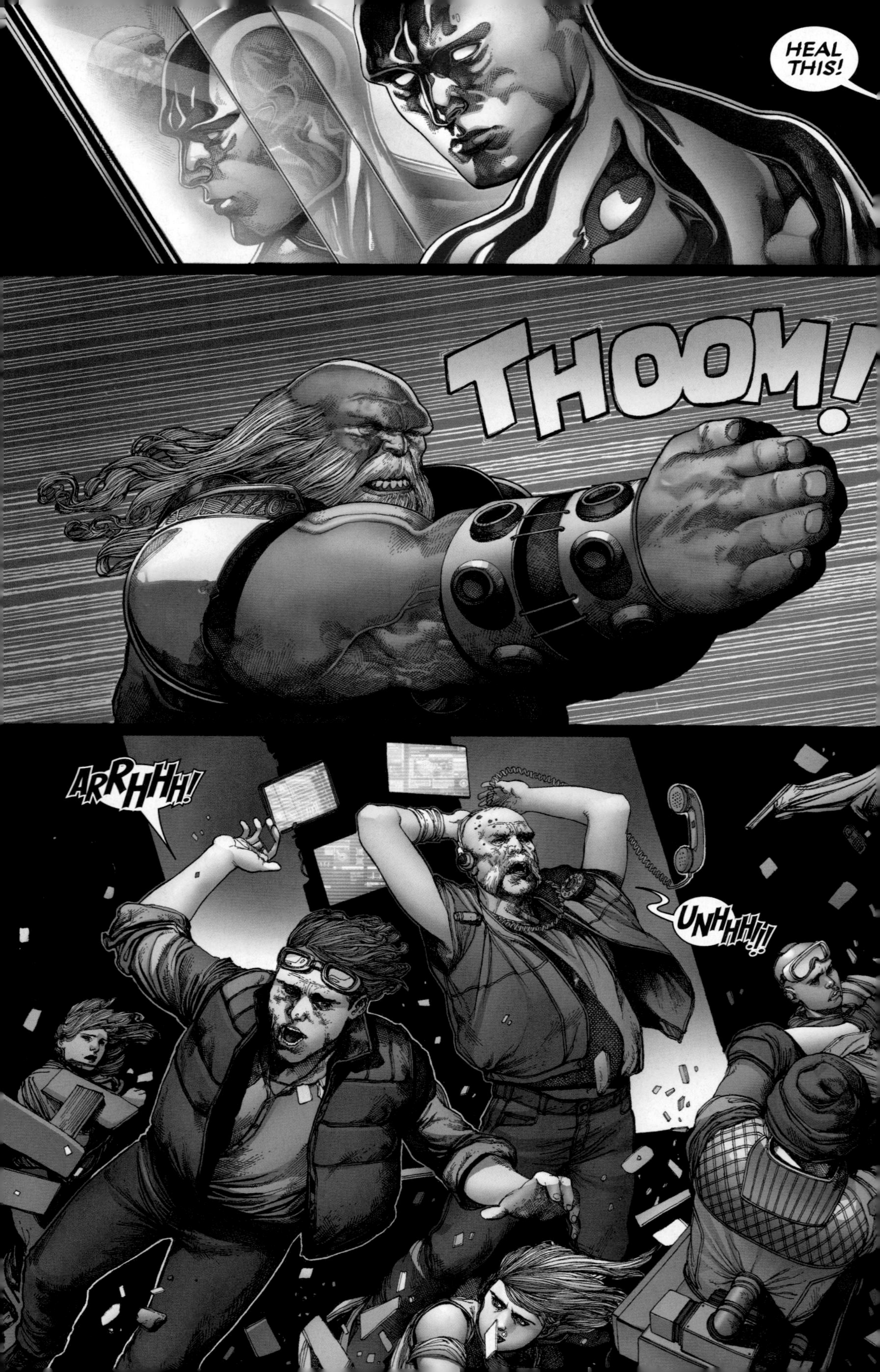
HEAL THIS!
THOOM!
ARRHHH!
UNHHH!!!

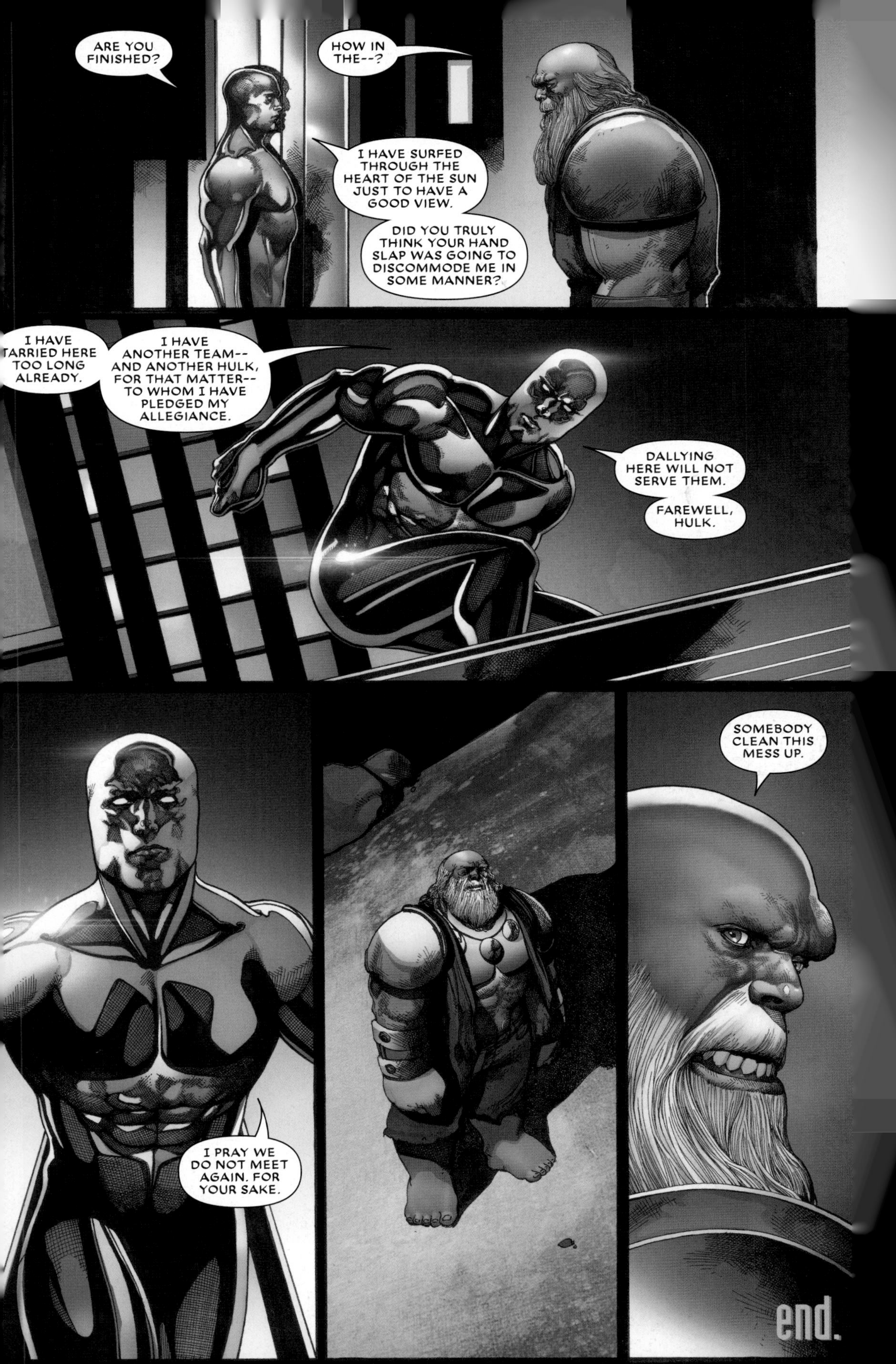
ARE YOU FINISHED?
HOW IN THE--?
I HAVE SURFED THROUGH THE HEART OF THE SUN JUST TO HAVE A GOOD VIEW.
DID YOU TRULY THINK YOUR HAND SLAP WAS GOING TO DISCOMMODE ME IN SOME MANNER?
I HAVE TARRIED HERE TOO LONG ALREADY.
I HAVE ANOTHER TEAM-- AND ANOTHER HULK, FOR THAT MATTER-- TO WHOM I HAVE PLEDGED MY ALLEGIANCE.
DALLYING HERE WILL NOT SERVE THEM.
FAREWELL, HULK.
I PRAY WE DO NOT MEET AGAIN. FOR YOUR SAKE.
SOMEBODY CLEAN THIS MESS UP.
end.

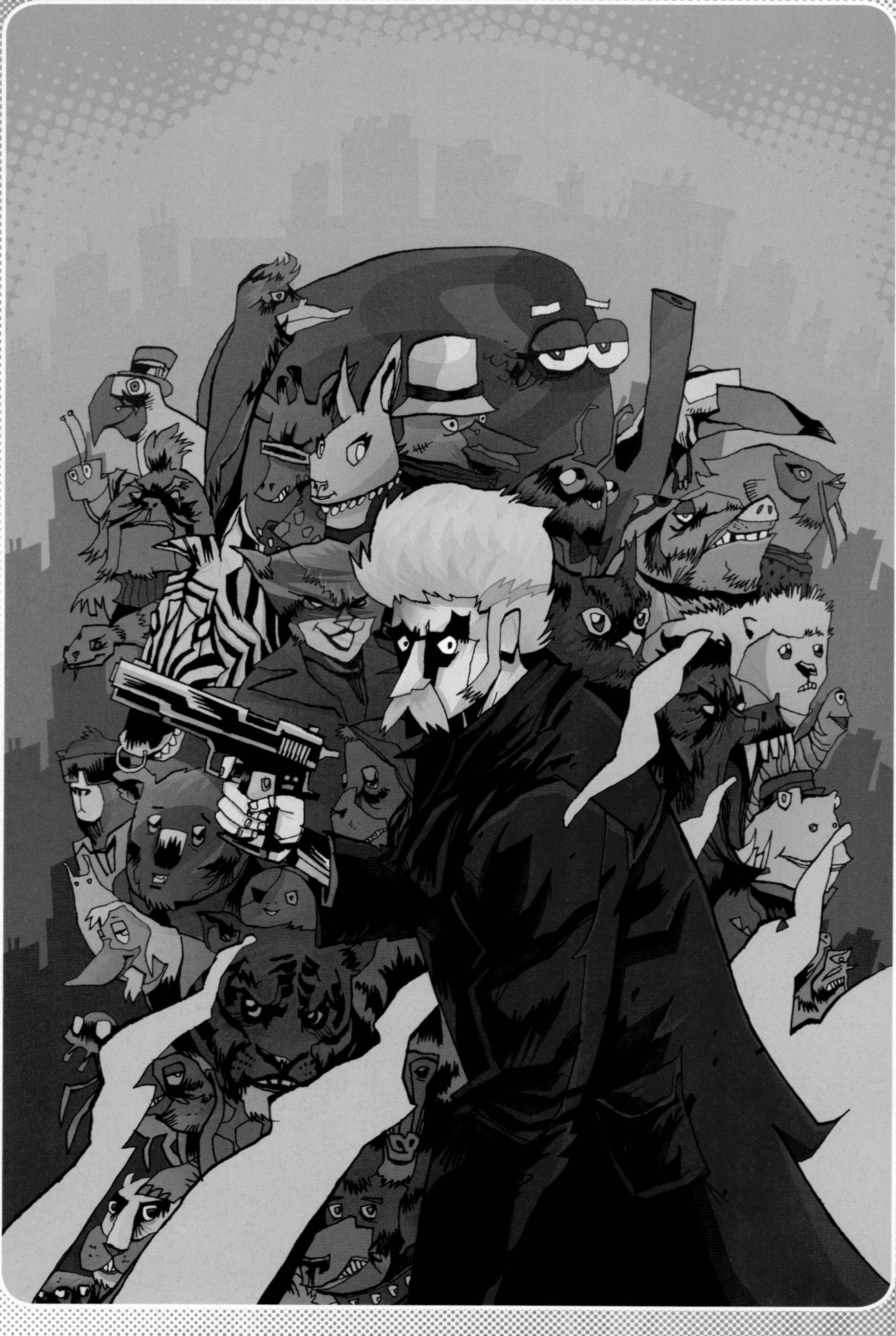

HOWARD THE HUMAN #1

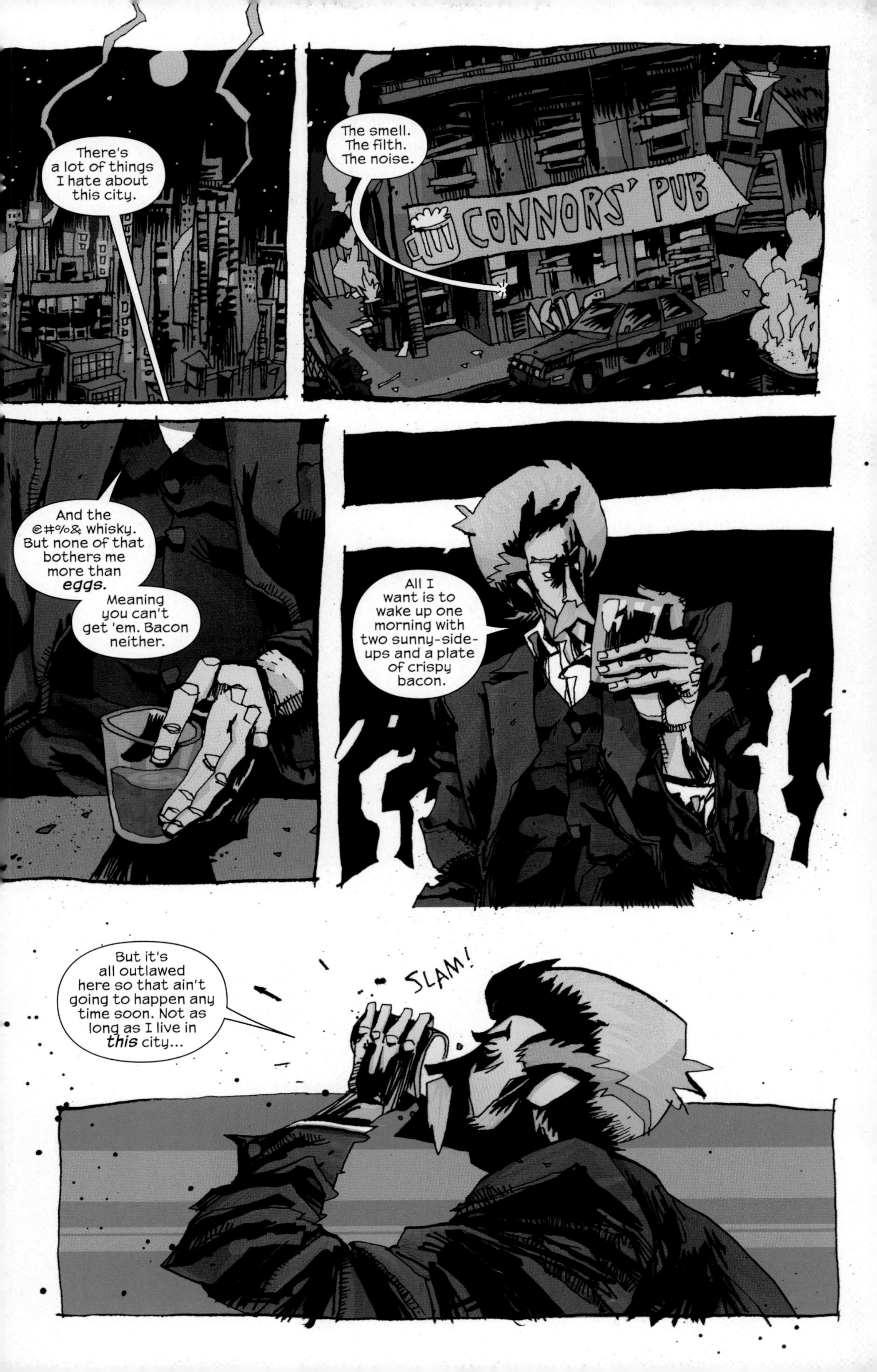
There's a lot of things I hate about this city.
The smell. The filth. The noise.
CONNORS' PUB
And the @#%& whisky. But none of that bothers me more than *eggs.*
Meaning you can't get 'em. Bacon neither.
All I want is to wake up one morning with two sunny-side-ups and a plate of crispy bacon.
But it's all outlawed here so that ain't going to happen any time soon. Not as long as I live in *this* city...
SLAM!

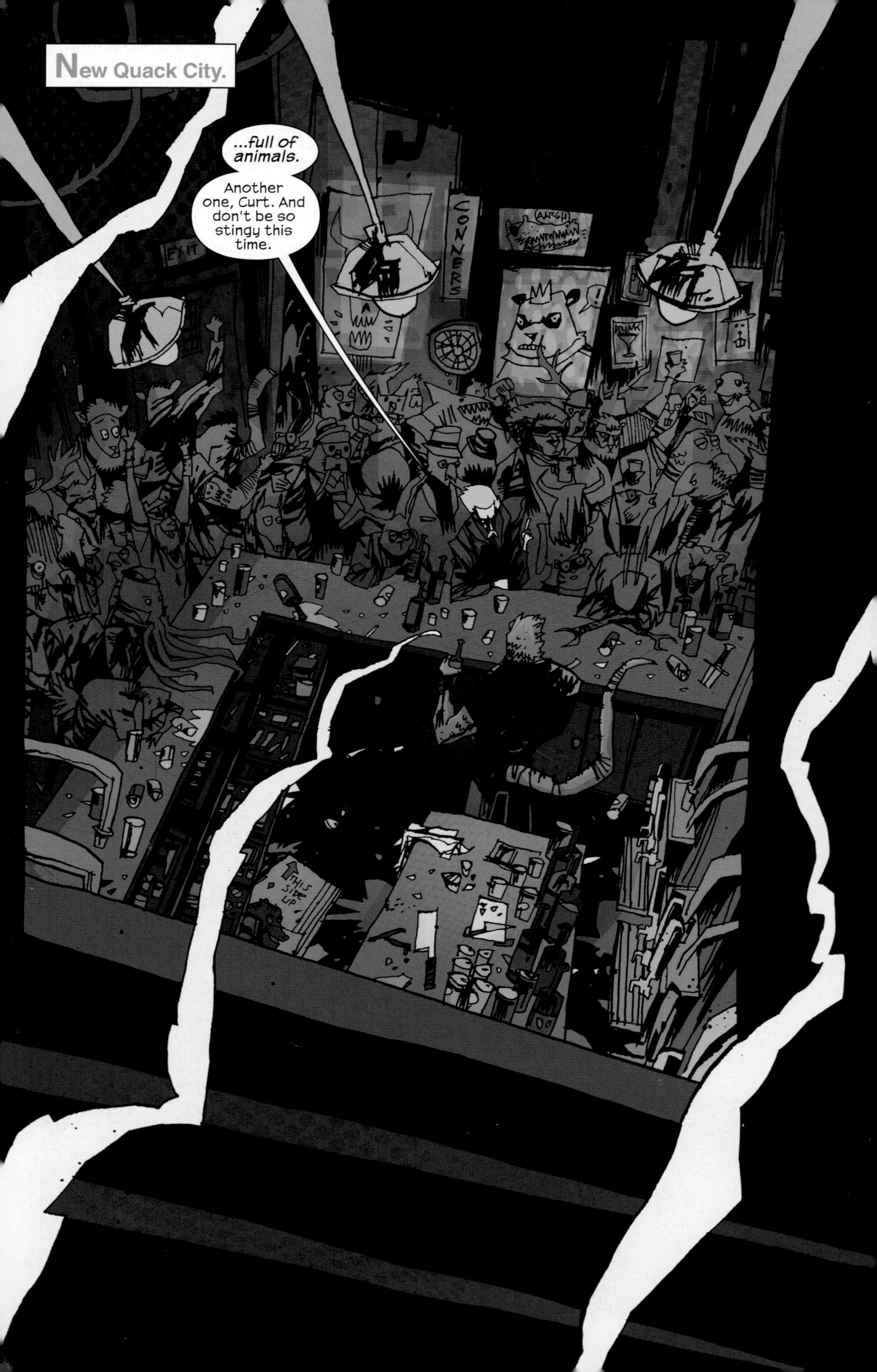
New Quack City.
...full of animals.
Another one, Curt. And don't be so stingy this time.
EXIT
CONNERS
AARGH
DRINK
THIS SIDE UP

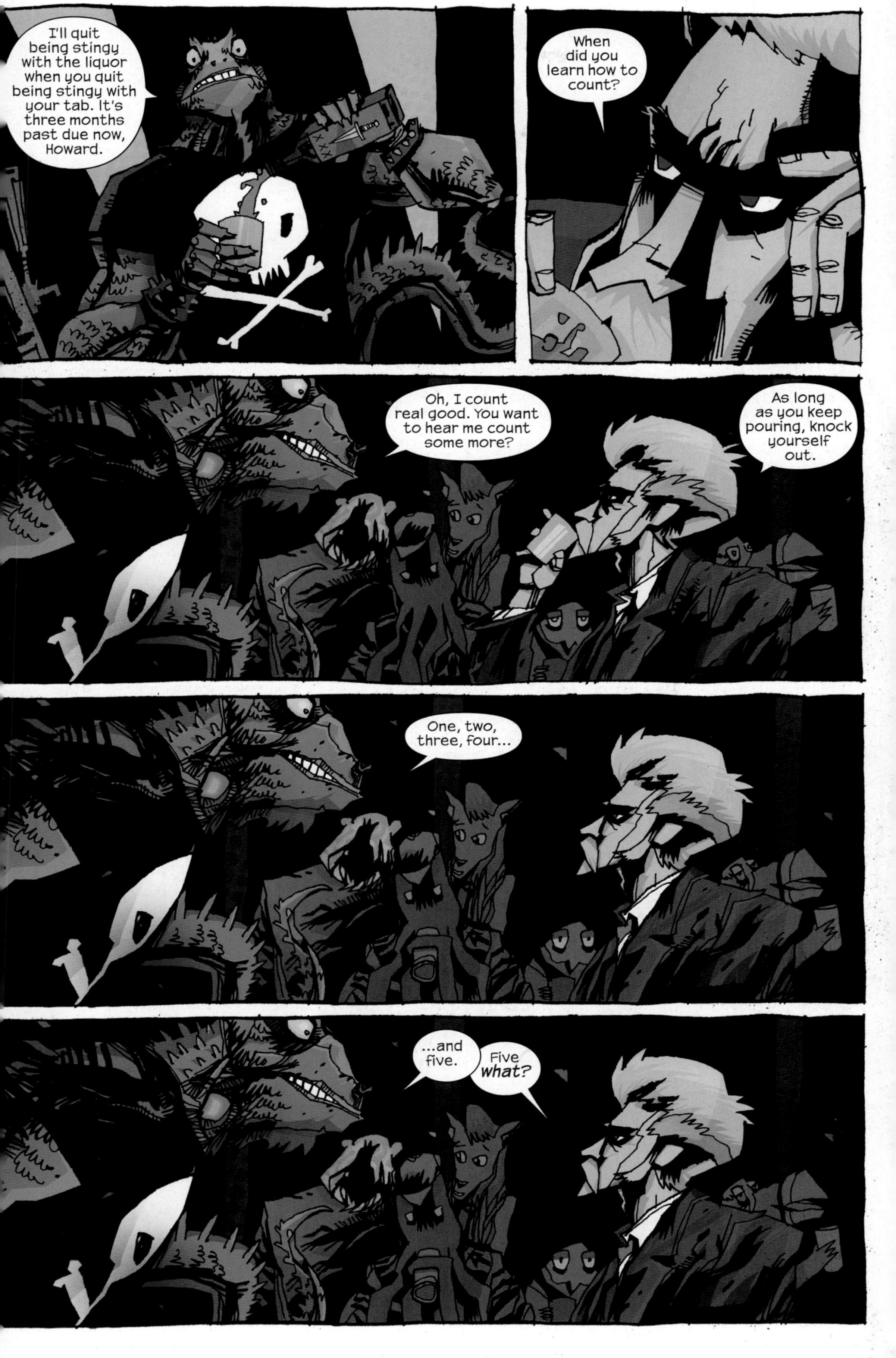
I'll quit being stingy with the liquor when you quit being stingy with your tab. It's three months past due now, Howard.
When did you learn how to count?
Oh, I count real good. You want to hear me count some more?
As long as you keep pouring, knock yourself out.
One, two, three, four...
...and five.
Five *what?*

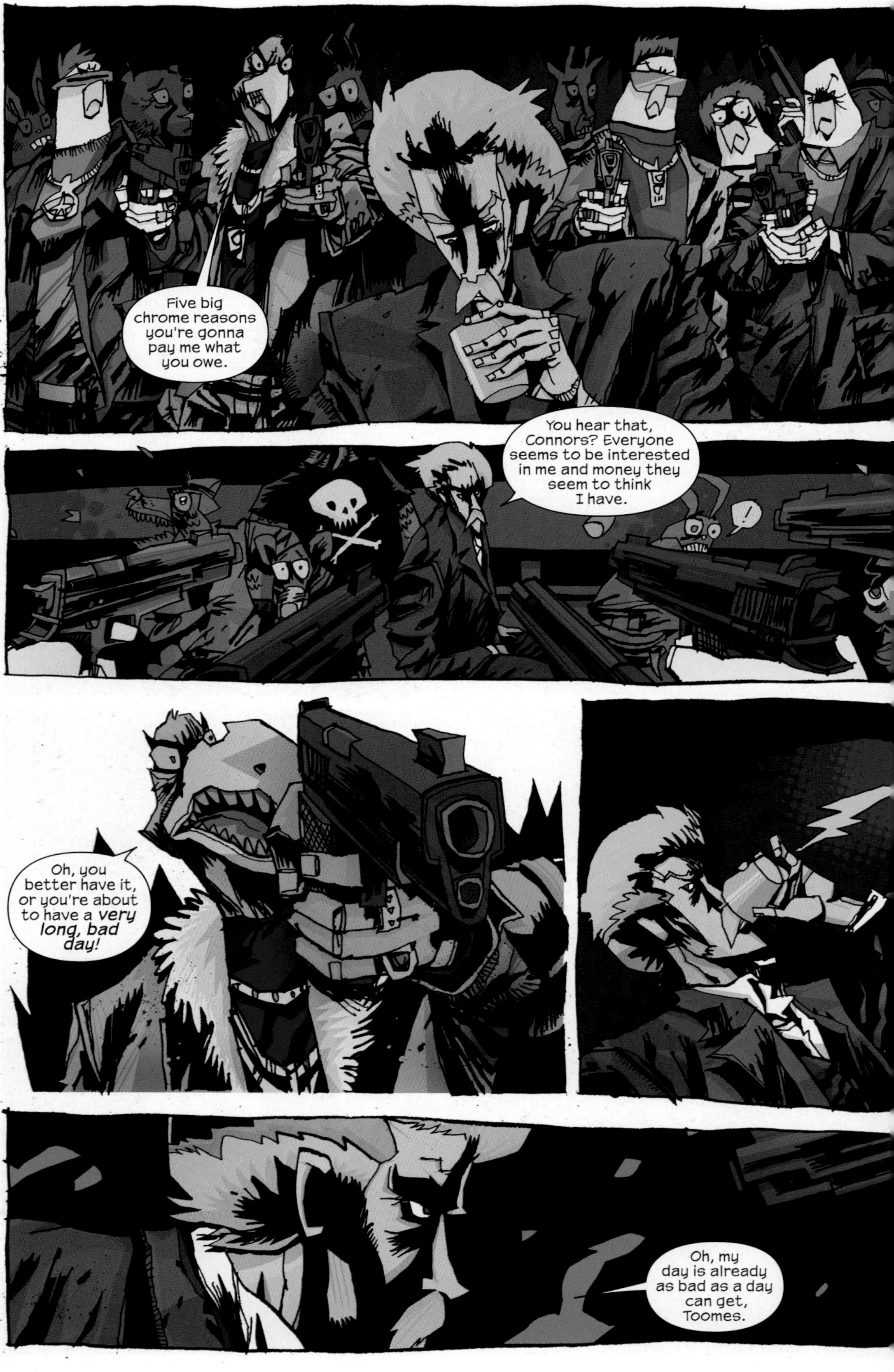
Five big chrome reasons you're gonna pay me what you owe.
You hear that, Connors? Everyone seems to be interested in me and money they seem to think I have.
!
Oh, you better have it, or you're about to have a *very long, bad day!*
Oh, my day is already as bad as a day can get, Toomes.

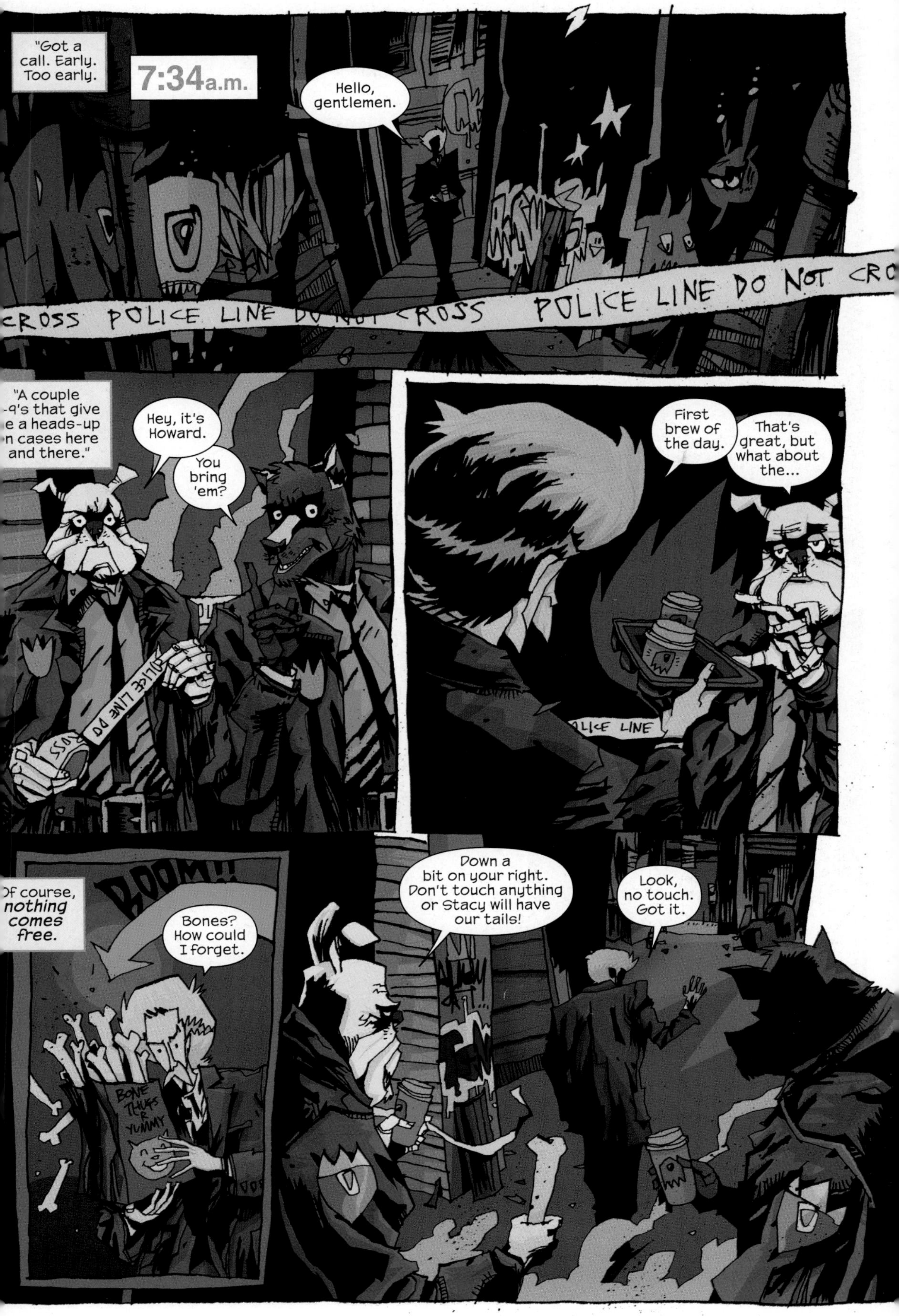
"Got a call. Early. Too early.
7:34a.m.
Hello, gentlemen.
POLICE LINE DO NOT CROSS POLICE LINE DO NOT CROSS POLICE LINE DO NOT CRO
"A couple -9's that give e a heads-up n cases here and there."
Hey, it's Howard.
You bring 'em?
POLICE LINE DO
First brew of the day.
That's great, but what about the...
OLICE LINE
Of course, nothing comes free.
BOOM!!
Bones? How could I forget.
BONE THUGS R YUMMY
Down a bit on your right. Don't touch anything or Stacy will have our tails!
Look, no touch. Got it.

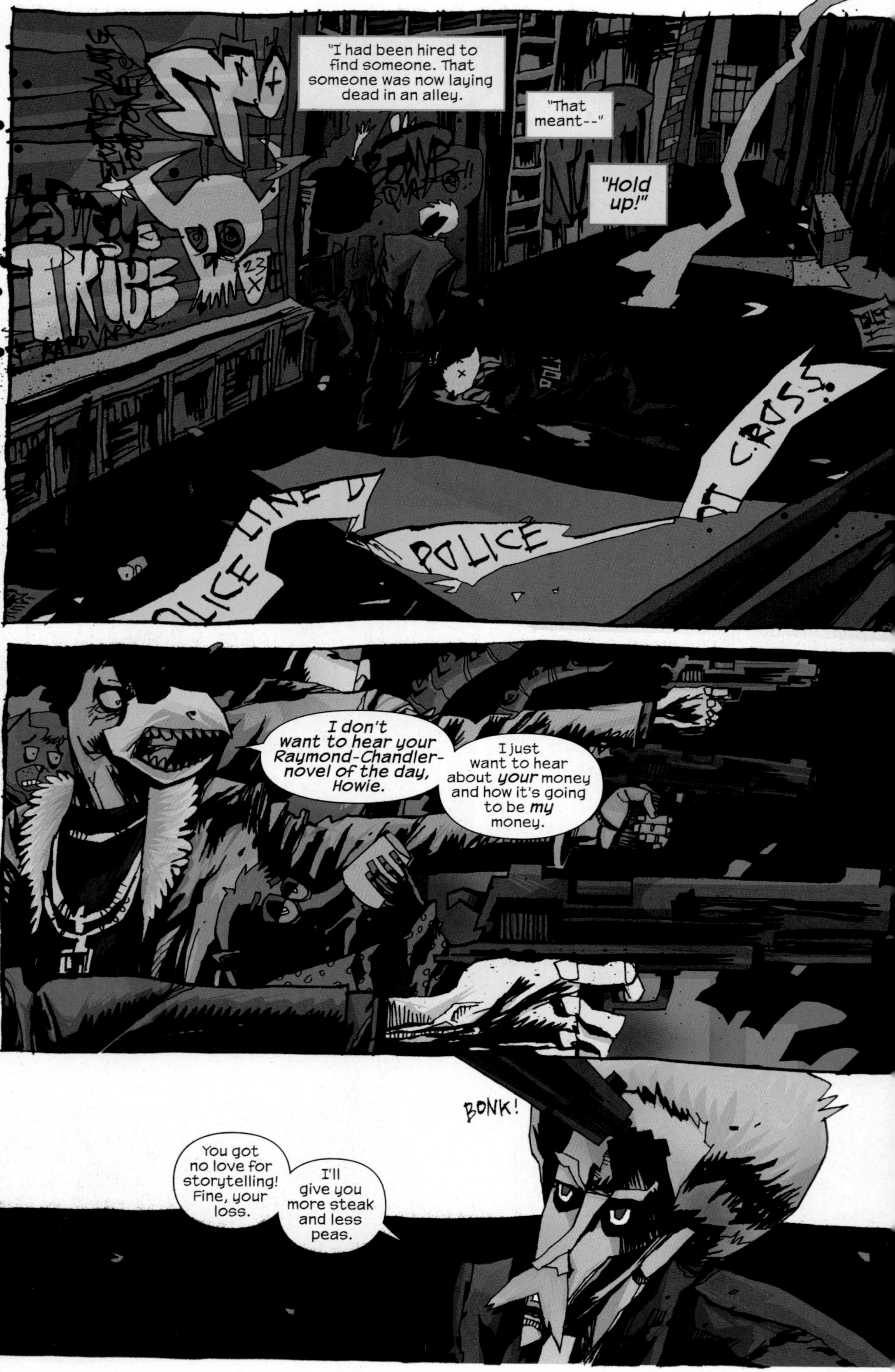
"I had been hired to find someone. That someone was now laying dead in an alley.
"That meant--"
"Hold up!"
POLICE LINE D
POLICE
CROSS
I don't want to hear your Raymond-Chandler-novel of the day, Howie.
I just want to hear about your money and how it's going to be my money.
BONK!
You got no love for storytelling! Fine, your loss.
I'll give you more steak and less peas.

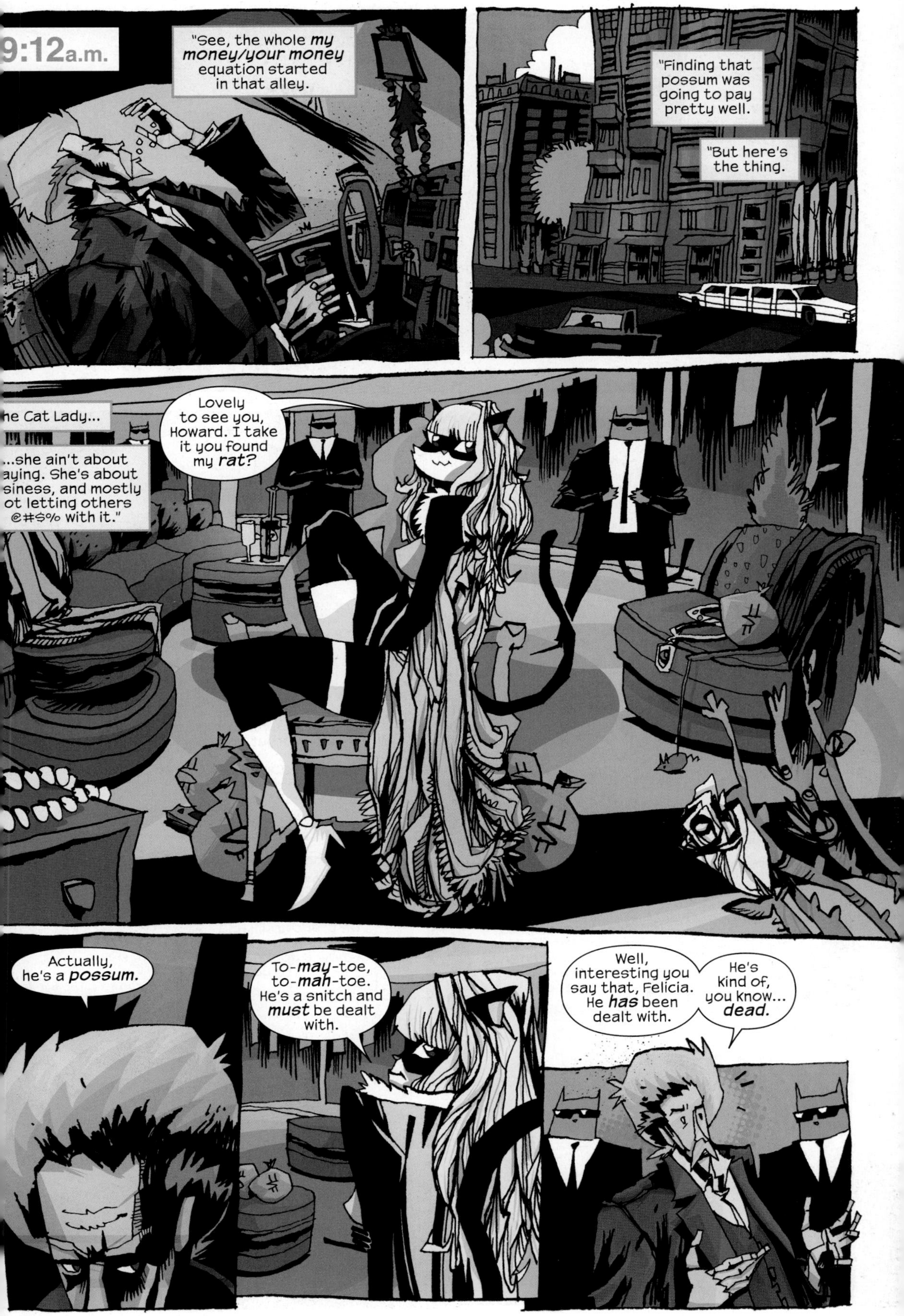
9:12a.m.
"See, the whole *my money/your money* equation started in that alley.
"Finding that possum was going to pay pretty well.
"But here's the thing.
he Cat Lady...
...she ain't about aying. She's about siness, and mostly ot letting others @#$% with it."
Lovely to see you, Howard. I take it you found my *rat?*
Actually, he's a *possum.*
To-*may*-toe, to-*mah*-toe. He's a snitch and *must* be dealt with.
Well, interesting you say that, Felicia. He *has* been dealt with.
He's kind of, you know... *dead.*

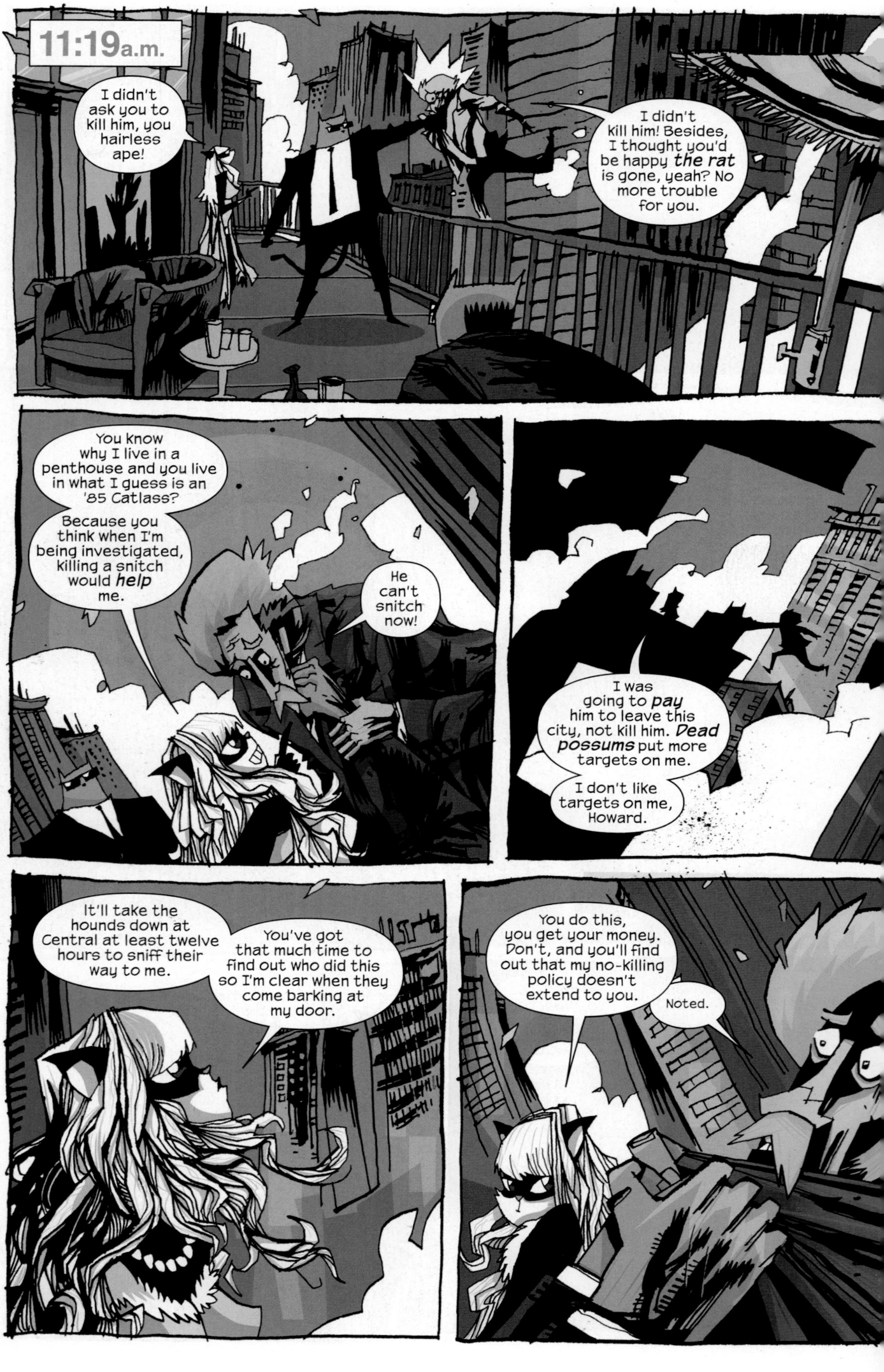
11:19a.m.
I didn't ask you to kill him, you hairless ape!
I didn't kill him! Besides, I thought you'd be happy the rat is gone, yeah? No more trouble for you.
You know why I live in a penthouse and you live in what I guess is an '85 Catlass?
Because you think when I'm being investigated, killing a snitch would help me.
He can't snitch now!
I was going to pay him to leave this city, not kill him. Dead possums put more targets on me.
I don't like targets on me, Howard.
It'll take the hounds down at Central at least twelve hours to sniff their way to me.
You've got that much time to find out who did this so I'm clear when they come barking at my door.
You do this, you get your money. Don't, and you'll find out that my no-killing policy doesn't extend to you.
Noted.

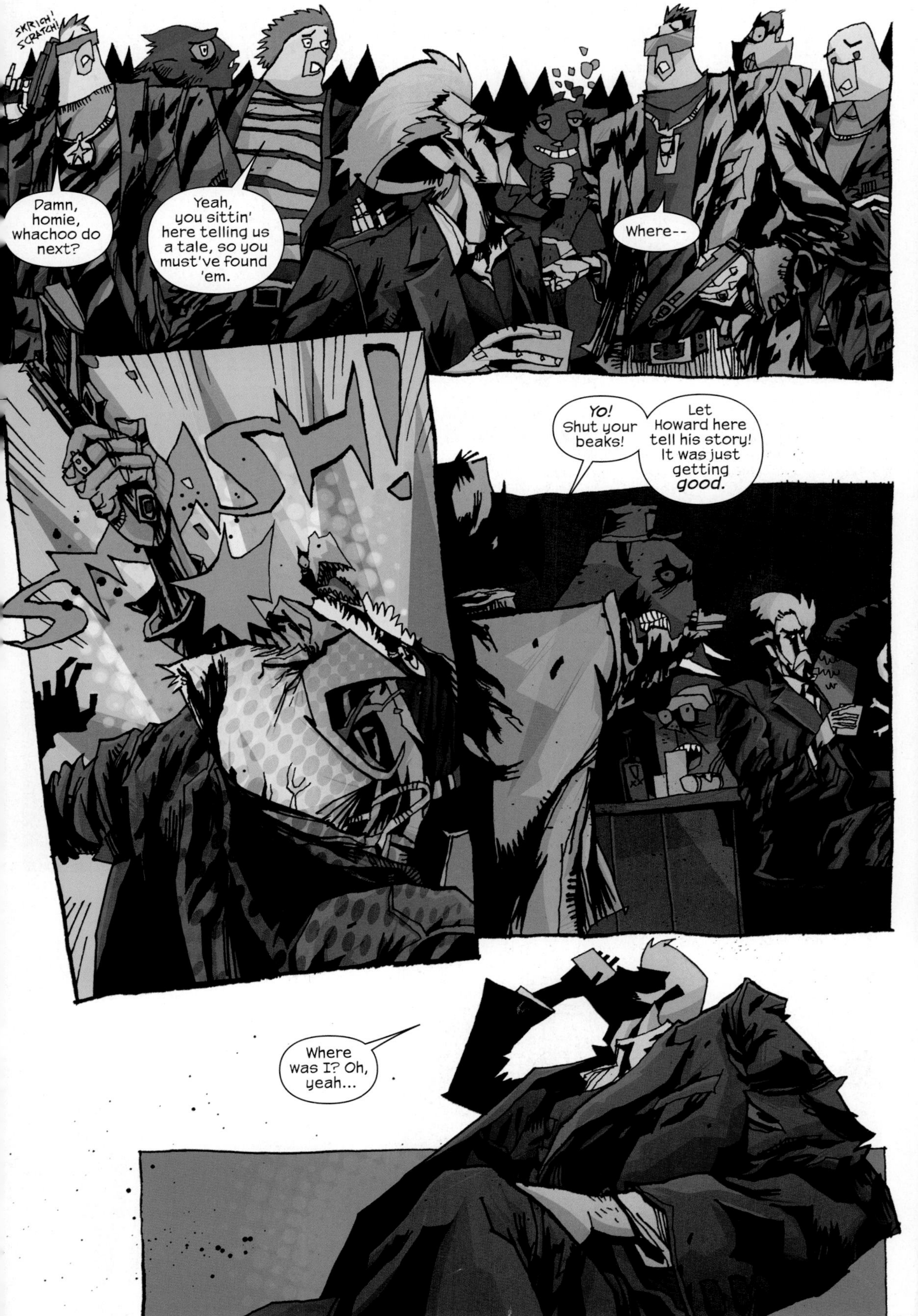
SKRICH! SCRATCH!
Damn, homie, whachoo do next?
Yeah, you sittin' here telling us a tale, so you must've found 'em.
Where--
SMASH!
YO! Shut your beaks!
Let Howard here tell his story! It was just getting good.
Where was I? Oh, yeah...

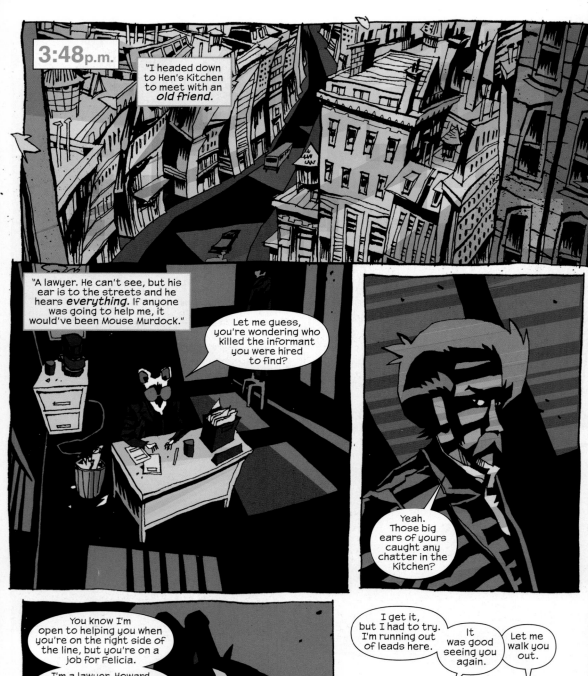

3:48p.m.

"I headed down to Hen's Kitchen to meet with an *old friend.*"

"A lawyer. He can't see, but his ear is to the streets and he hears *everything.* If anyone was going to help me, it would've been Mouse Murdock."

Let me guess, you're wondering who killed the informant you were hired to find?

Yeah. Those big ears of yours caught any chatter in the Kitchen?

You know I'm open to helping you when you're on the right side of the line, but you're on a job for Felicia.

I'm a lawyer, Howard. I can't get caught with the blood of a dead witness on my sleeves. I need to work in this town.

I get it, but I had to try. I'm running out of leads here.

It was good seeing you again.

Let me walk you out.

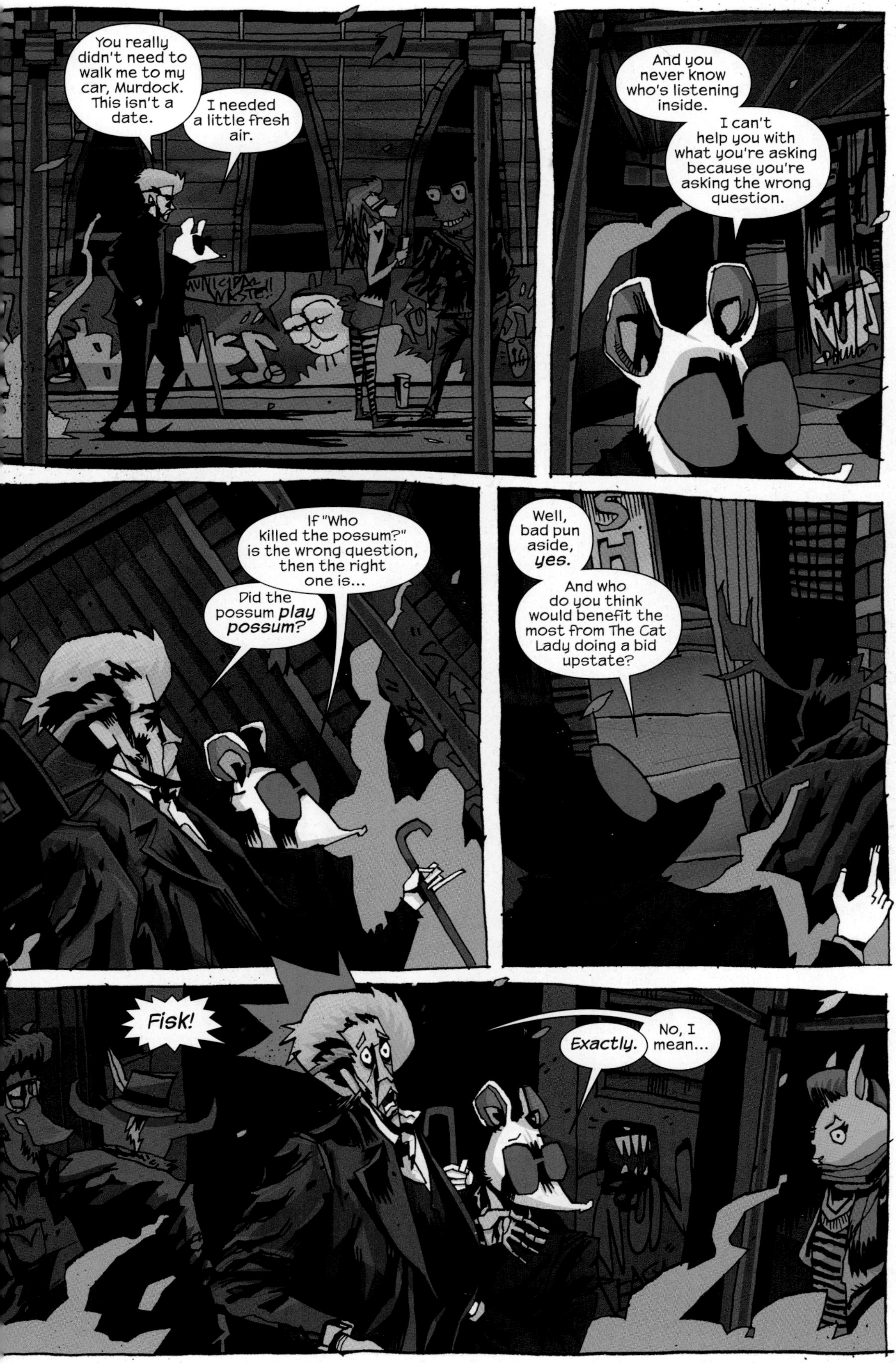
You really didn't need to walk me to my car, Murdock. This isn't a date.
I needed a little fresh air.
MUNICIPAL WASTE!!
And you never know who's listening inside.
I can't help you with what you're asking because you're asking the wrong question.
If "Who killed the possum?" is the wrong question, then the right one is...
Did the possum *play possum?*
Well, bad pun aside, ***yes.***
And who do you think would benefit the most from The Cat Lady doing a bid upstate?
Fisk!
Exactly.
No, I mean...

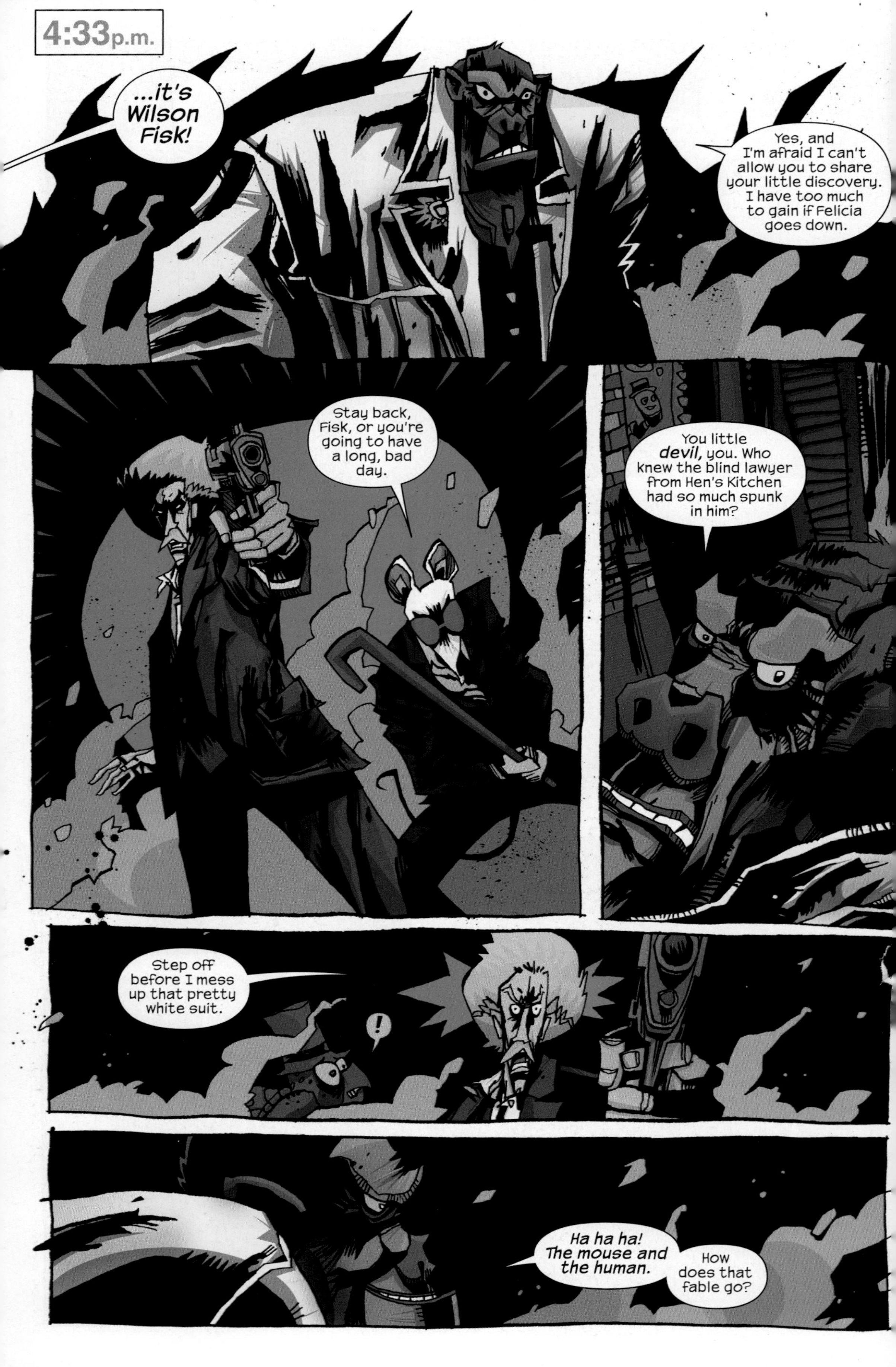
4:33p.m.
...it's Wilson Fisk!
Yes, and I'm afraid I can't allow you to share your little discovery. I have too much to gain if Felicia goes down.
Stay back, Fisk, or you're going to have a long, bad day.
You little devil, you. Who knew the blind lawyer from Hen's Kitchen had so much spunk in him?
Step off before I mess up that pretty white suit.
!
Ha ha ha! The mouse and the human.
How does that fable go?

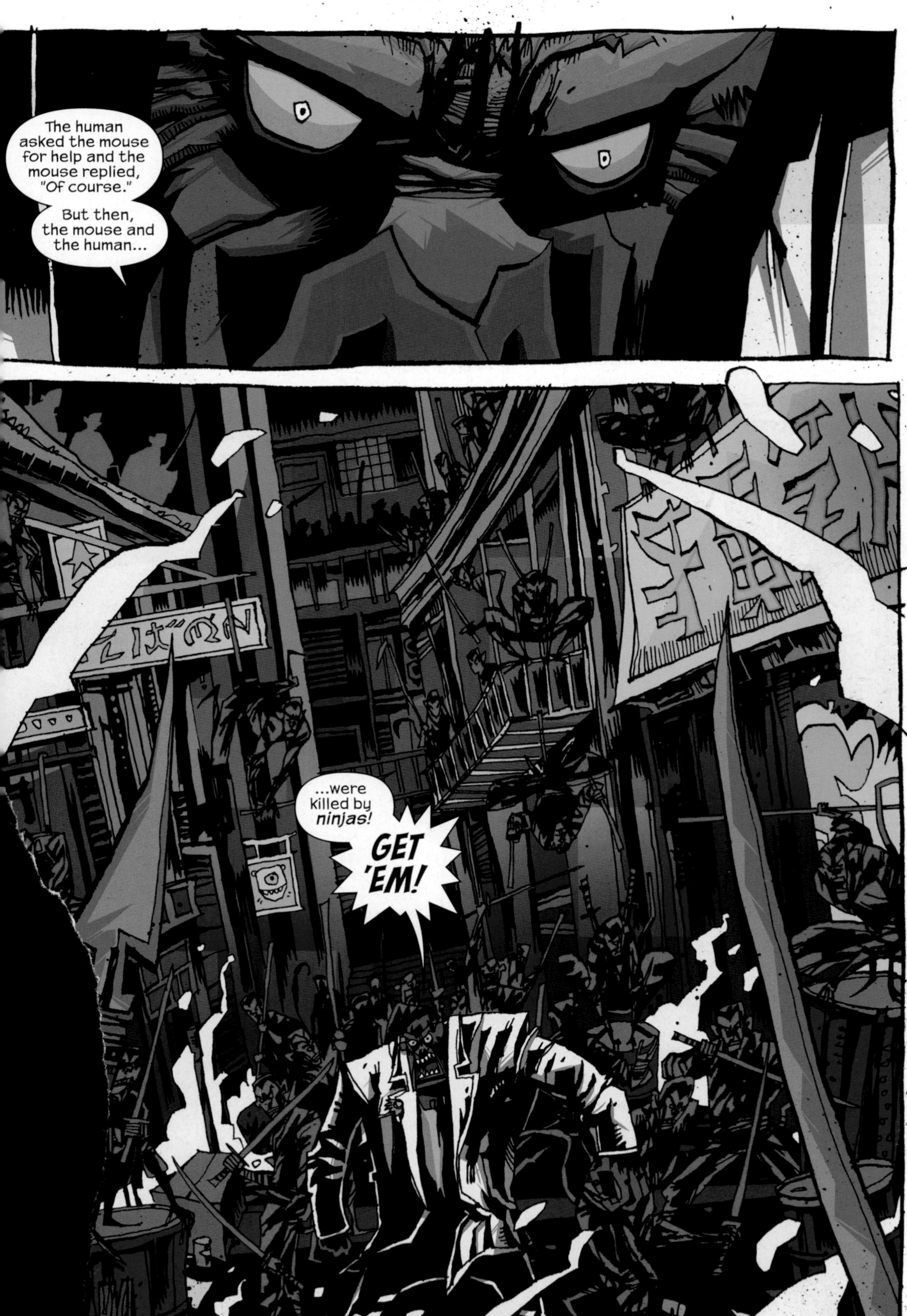

The human asked the mouse for help and the mouse replied, "Of course."
But then, the mouse and the human...
...were killed by ninjas!
GET 'EM!

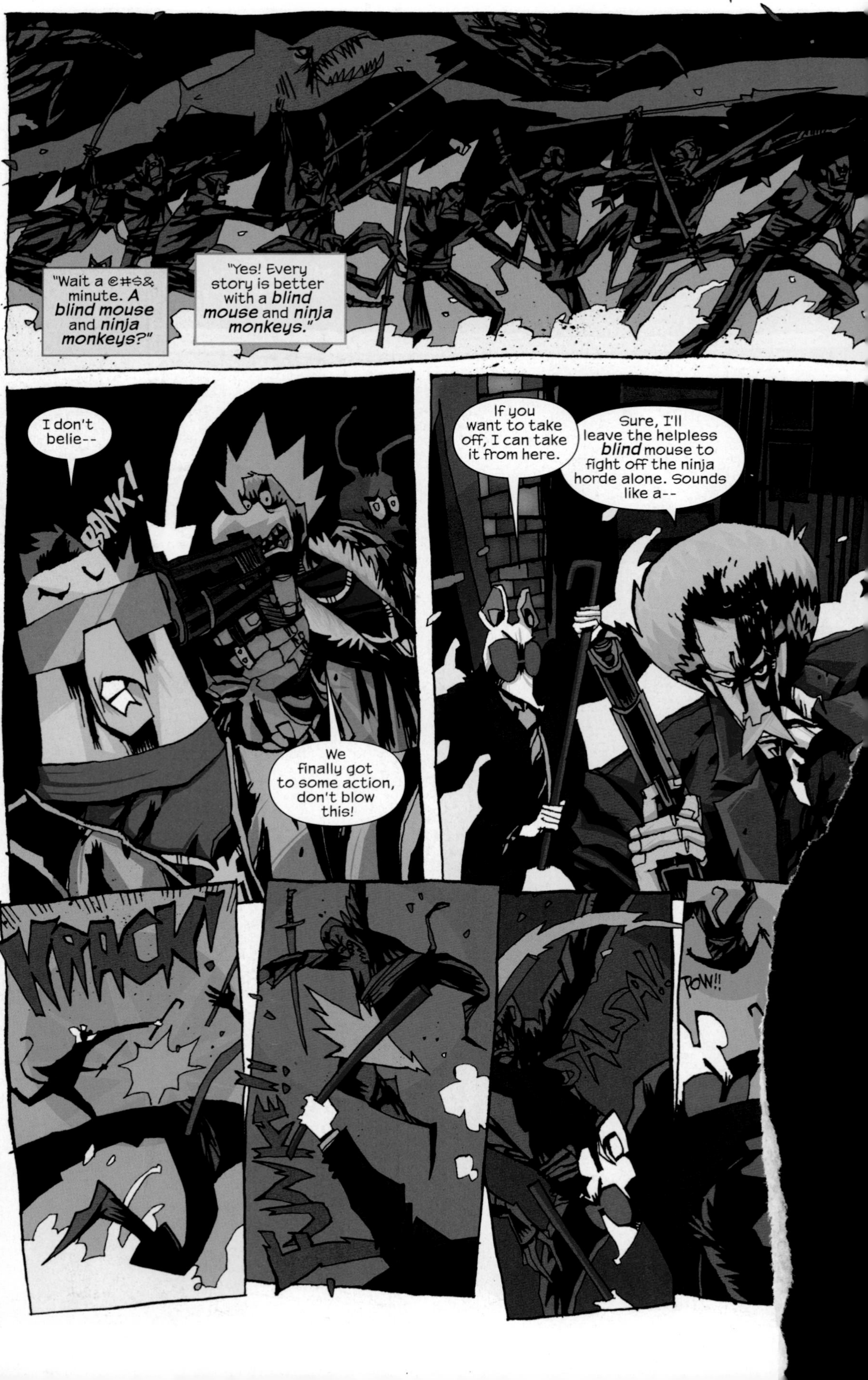
"Wait a @#$& minute. A *blind mouse* and *ninja monkeys?*"
"Yes! Every story is better with a *blind mouse* and *ninja monkeys.*"
I don't belie--
BONK!
We finally got to some action, don't blow this!
If you want to take off, I can take it from here.
Sure, I'll leave the helpless *blind* mouse to fight off the ninja horde alone. Sounds like a--
KRACK!
SALSA!!
POW!!

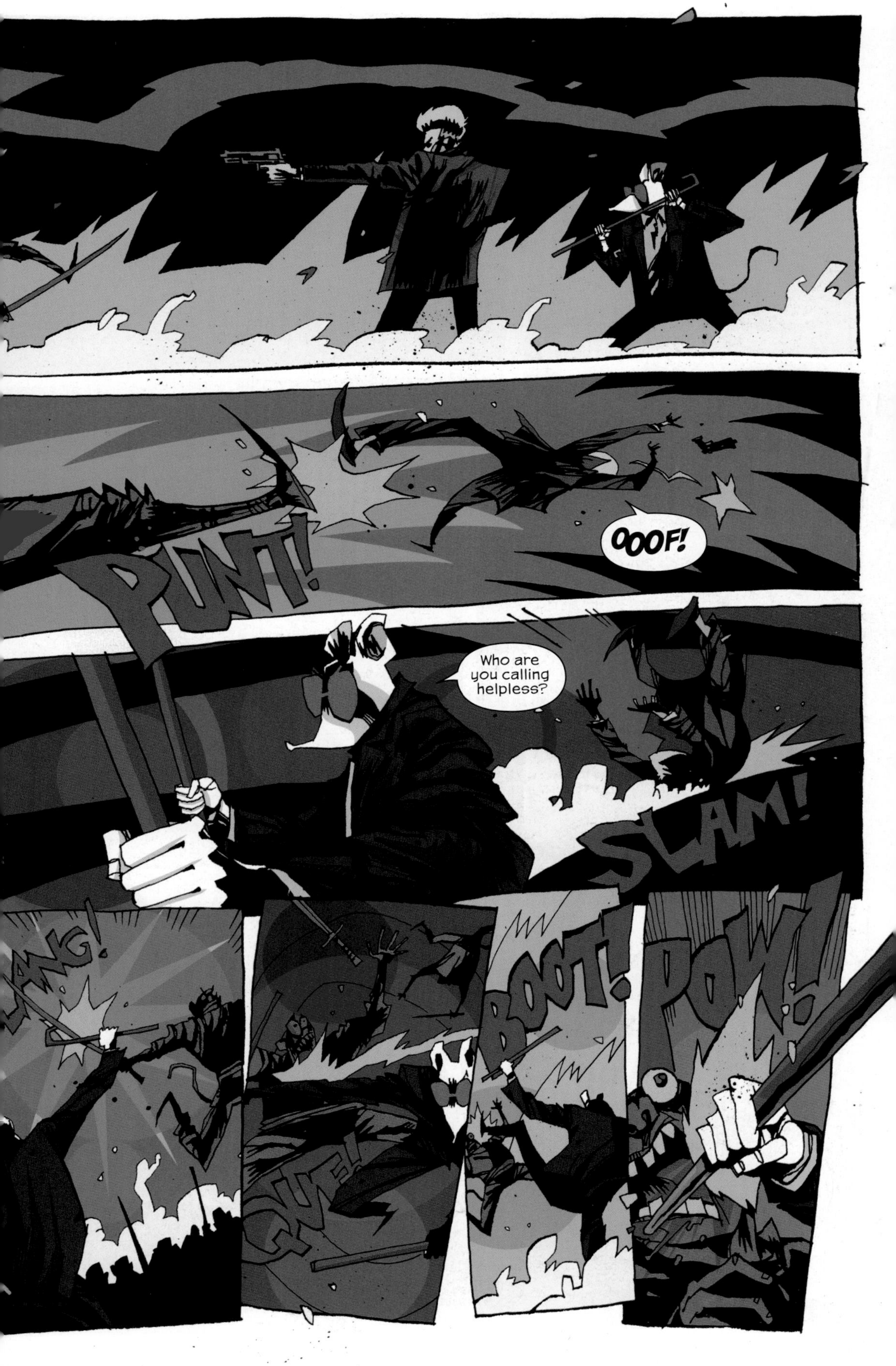
OOOF!
PUNT!
Who are you calling helpless?
SLAM!
ANG!
BOOT!
POW!

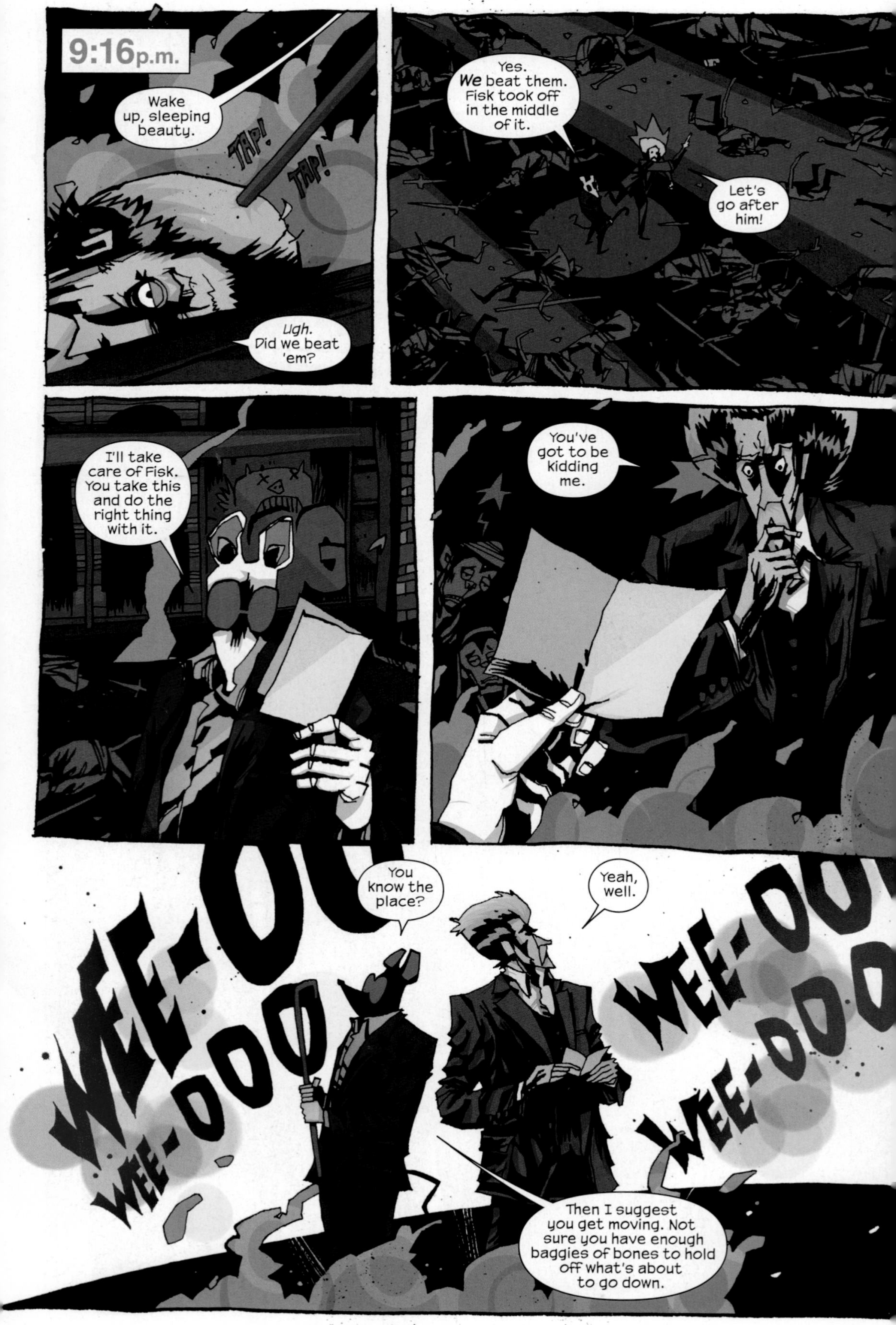
9:16p.m.
Wake up, sleeping beauty.
TAP!
TAP!
Ugh. Did we beat 'em?
Yes. **We** beat them. Fisk took off in the middle of it.
Let's go after him!
I'll take care of Fisk. You take this and do the right thing with it.
You've got to be kidding me.
You know the place?
Yeah, well.
WEE-OO
WEE-OOO
WEE-OOOO
WEE-OOO
WEE-OOOO
Then I suggest you get moving. Not sure you have enough baggies of bones to hold off what's about to go down.

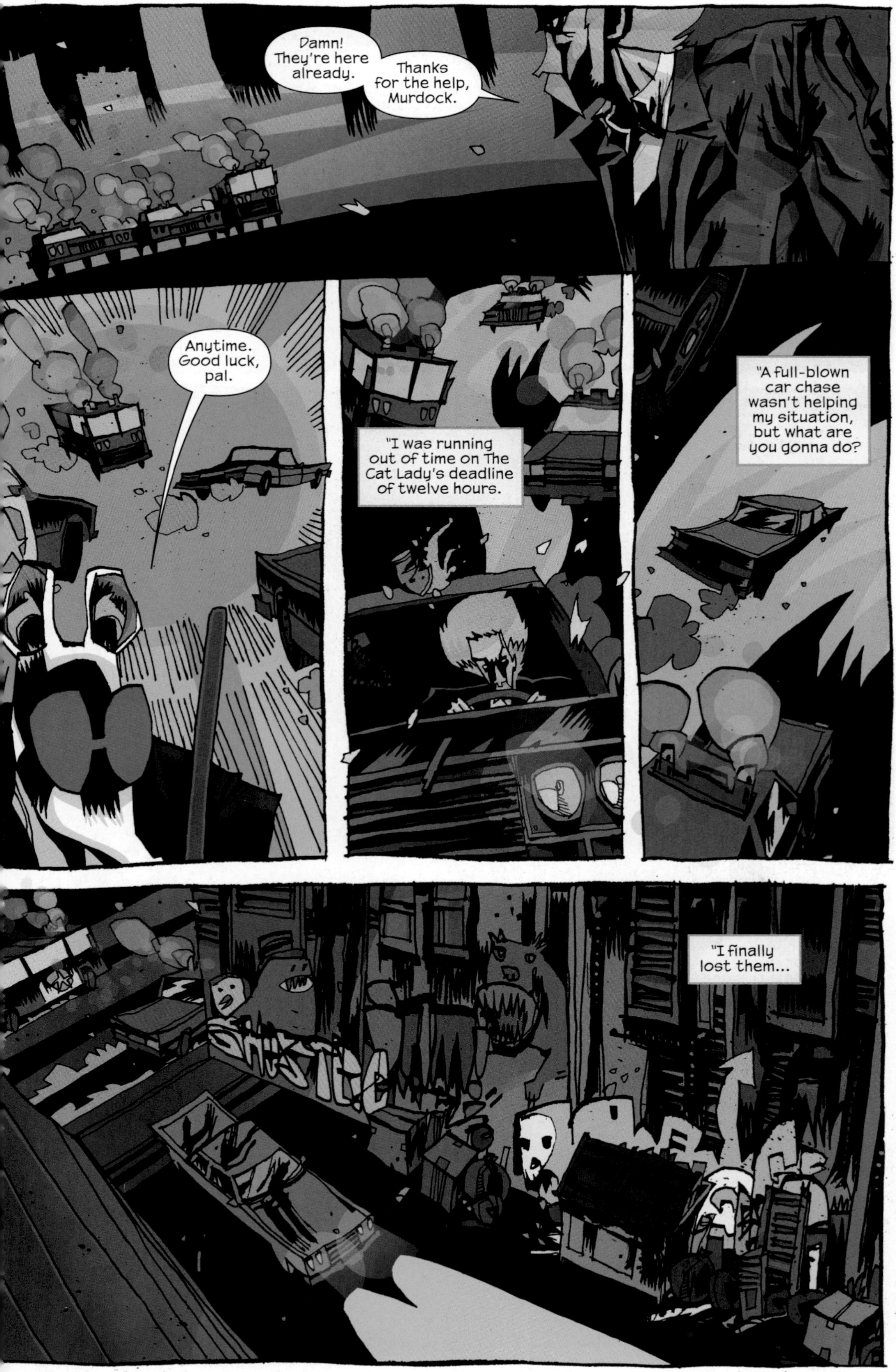
Damn! They're here already.
Thanks for the help, Murdock.
Anytime. Good luck, pal.
"I was running out of time on The Cat Lady's deadline of twelve hours.
"A full-blown car chase wasn't helping my situation, but what are you gonna do?
"I finally lost them...

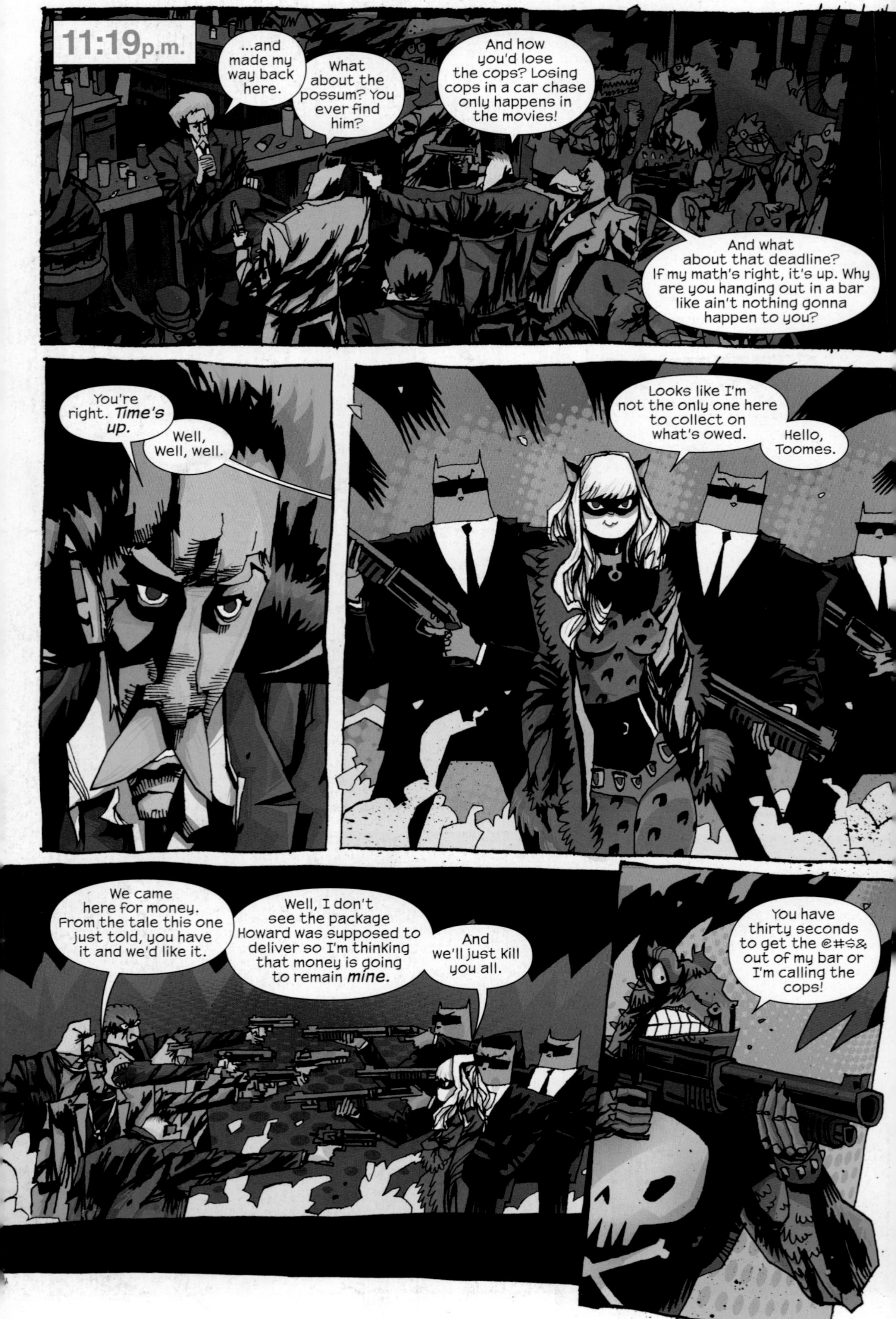
11:19p.m.
...and made my way back here.
What about the possum? You ever find him?
And how you'd lose the cops? Losing cops in a car chase only happens in the movies!
And what about that deadline? If my math's right, it's up. Why are you hanging out in a bar like ain't nothing gonna happen to you?
You're right. Time's up.
Well, Well, well.
Looks like I'm not the only one here to collect on what's owed.
Hello, Toomes.
We came here for money. From the tale this one just told, you have it and we'd like it.
Well, I don't see the package Howard was supposed to deliver so I'm thinking that money is going to remain mine.
And we'll just kill you all.
You have thirty seconds to get the @#$& out of my bar or I'm calling the cops!

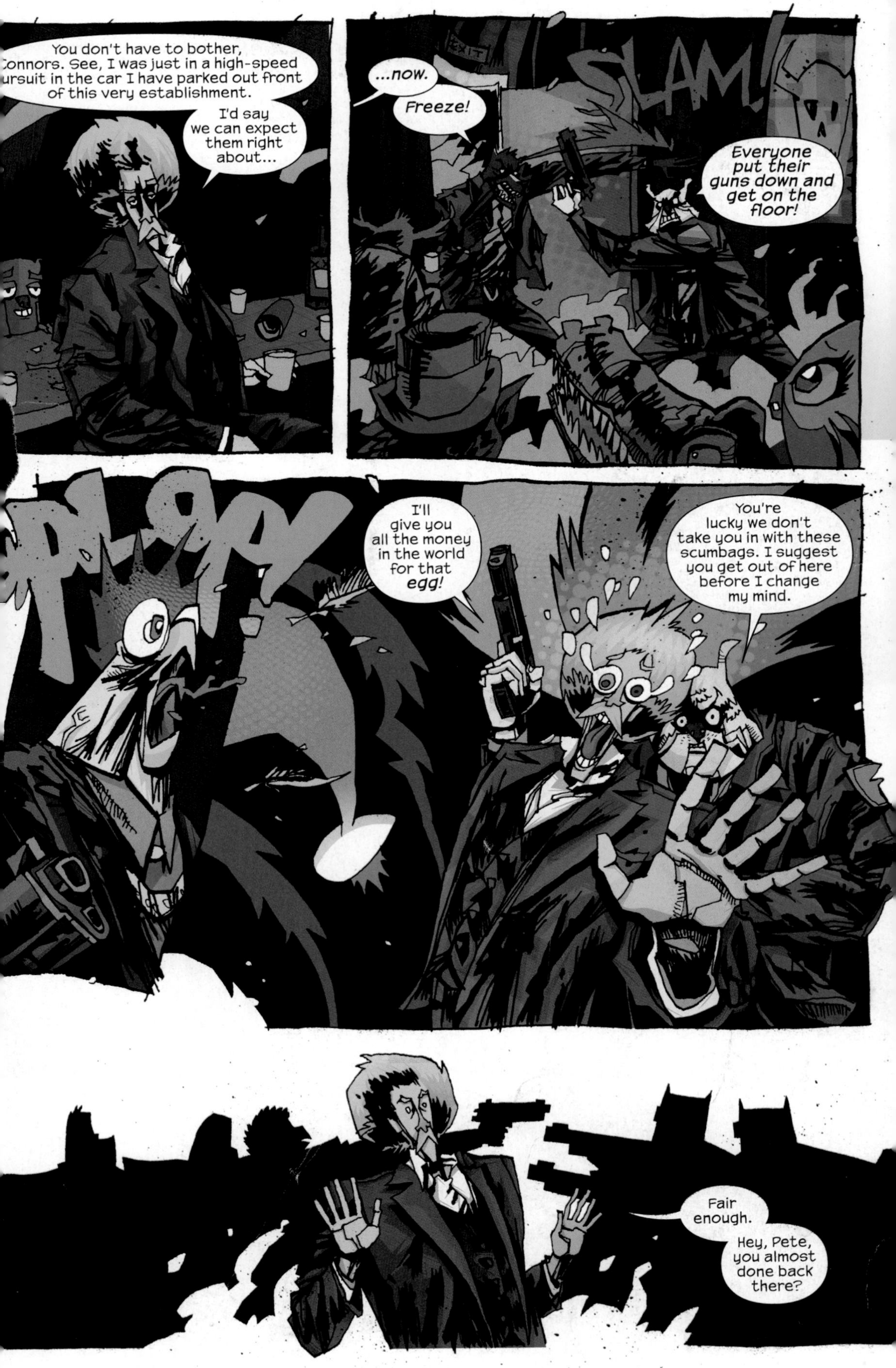
You don't have to bother, Connors. See, I was just in a high-speed pursuit in the car I have parked out front of this very establishment.
I'd say we can expect them right about...
...now.
SLAM!
Freeze!
Everyone put their guns down and get on the floor!
I'll give you all the money in the world for that egg!
You're lucky we don't take you in with these scumbags. I suggest you get out of here before I change my mind.
Fair enough.
Hey, Pete, you almost done back there?

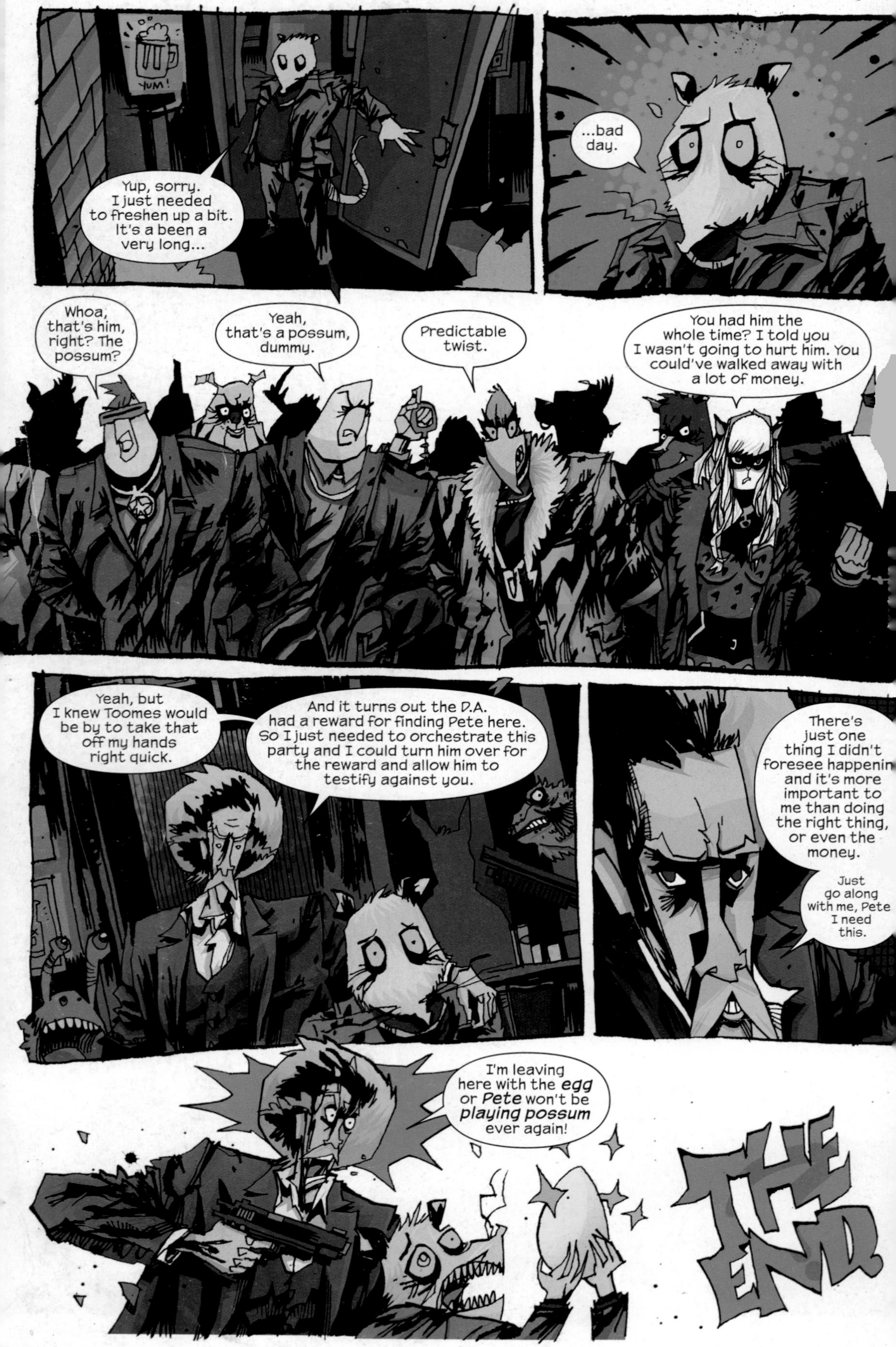

Yup, sorry. I just needed to freshen up a bit. It's a been a very long...
YUM!
...bad day.
Whoa, that's him, right? The possum?
Yeah, that's a possum, dummy.
Predictable twist.
You had him the whole time? I told you I wasn't going to hurt him. You could've walked away with a lot of money.
Yeah, but I knew Toomes would be by to take that off my hands right quick.
And it turns out the D.A. had a reward for finding Pete here. So I just needed to orchestrate this party and I could turn him over for the reward and allow him to testify against you.
There's just one thing I didn't foresee happenin and it's more important to me than doing the right thing, or even the money.
Just go along with me, Pete I need this.
I'm leaving here with the *egg* or *Pete* won't be *playing possum* ever again!
THE END